ENCYCLOPEDIA OF
AMERICAN HISTORY

The Emergence of Modern America
1900 to 1928

VOLUME VII

ENCYCLOPEDIA OF AMERICAN HISTORY

ENCYCLOPEDIA OF AMERICAN HISTORY

The Emergence of Modern America
1900 to 1928

VOLUME VII

Elizabeth Faue, Editor
Gary B. Nash, General Editor

Facts On File, Inc.

Encyclopedia of American History:
The Emergence of Modern America (1900 to 1928)

Editorial Director: Laurie E. Likoff
Editor in Chief: Owen Lancer
Chief Copy Editor: Michael G. Laraque
Associate Editor: Dorothy Cummings
Production Director: Olivia McKean
Production Manager: Rachel L. Berlin
Production Associate: Theresa Montoya
Art Director: Cathy Rincon
Interior Designer: Joan M. Toro
Desktop Designers: Erika K. Arroyo and David C. Strelecky
Maps and Illustrations: Dale E. Williams and Jeremy Eagle

Facts On File, Inc.
132 West 31st Street
New York NY 10001

Library of Congress Cataloging-in-Publication Data

Encyclopedia of American history / Gary B. Nash, general editor.
p.   cm.
Includes bibliographical references and indexes.
Contents: v. 1. Three worlds meet — v. 2. Colonization and settlement —
v. 3. Revolution and new nation — v. 4. Expansion and reform — v. 5. Civil War
and Reconstruction — v. 6. The development of the industrial United States —
v. 7. The emergence of modern America — v. 8. The Great Depression and
World War II — v. 9. Postwar United States — v. 10. Contemporary
United States. — v. 11 Comprehensive index
ISBN 0-8160-4371-X (set)   ISBN 0-8160-4367-1 (v. 7)
1. United States—History—Encyclopedias. I. Nash, Gary B.
E174 .E53 2002
973´.03—dc21   2001051278

Contents

★ ────────────────────────────────────

List of Entries

viii   List of Entries

About the Editors

General Editor: Gary B. Nash received a Ph.D from Princeton University. He is currently director of the National Center for History in the Schools at the University of California, Los Angeles, where he teaches American history of the colonial and Revolutionary era. He is a published author of college and precollegiate history texts. Among his best-selling works is *The American People: Creating a Nation and Society* (Addison Wesley, Longman), now in its fifth edition.

Nash is an elected member of the Society of American Historians, American Academy of Arts and Sciences, and the American Philosophical Society. He has served as past president of the Organization of American Historians, 1994–95, and was a founding member of the National Council for History Education, 1990.

Volume Editor: Elizabeth Faue, Wayne State University, received a Ph.D. from the University of Minnesota. She is the author of *Community of Suffering and Struggle: Women, Men, and the Labor Movement in Minneapolis, 1915–1945* (University of North Carolina Press, 1991) and *Writing the Wrongs: Eva McDonald and the Political Culture of American Labor Reform* (Cornell University Press, 2002).

Foreword

The Encyclopedia of American History series is designed as a handy reference to the most important individuals, events, and topics in U.S. history. In 10 volumes, the encyclopedia covers the period from the 15th century, when European explorers first made their way across the Atlantic Ocean to the Americas, to the present day. The encyclopedia is written for precollegiate as well as college students, for parents of young learners in the schools, and for the general public. The volume editors are distinguished historians of American history. In writing individual entries, each editor has drawn upon the expertise of scores of specialists. This ensures the scholarly quality of the entire series. Articles contributed by the various volume editors are uncredited.

This 10-volume encyclopedia of "American history" is broadly conceived to include the historical experience of the various peoples of North America. Thus, in the first volume, many essays treat the history of a great range of indigenous people before contact with Europeans. In the same vein, readers will find essays in the first several volumes that sketch Spanish, Dutch, and French explorers and colonizers who opened up territories for European settlement that later would become part of the United States. The venues and cast of characters in the American historical drama are thus widened beyond traditional encyclopedias.

In creating the eras of American history that define the chronological limits of each volume, and in addressing major topics in each era, the encyclopedia follows the architecture of *The National Standards for United States History, Revised Edition* (Los Angeles: National Center for History in the Schools, 1996). Mandated by the U.S. Congress, the national standards for U.S. history have been widely used by states and school districts in organizing curricular frameworks and have been followed by many other curriculum-building efforts.

Entries are cross-referenced, when appropriate, with *See also* citations at the end of articles. At the end of most entries, a listing of articles and books allows readers to turn to specialized sources and historical accounts. In each volume, an array of maps provide geographical context, while numerous illustrations help vivify the material covered in the text. A time line is included to provide students with a chronological reference to major events occurring in the given era. The selection of historical documents in the back of each volume gives students experience with the raw documents that historians use when researching history. A comprehensive index to each volume also facilitates the reader's access to particular information.

In each volume, long entries are provided for major categories of American historical experience. These categories may include: African Americans, agriculture, art and architecture, business, economy, education, family life, foreign policy, immigration, labor, Native Americans, politics, population, religion, urbanization, and women. By following these essays from volume to volume, the reader can access what might be called a mini-history of each broad topic, for example, family life, immigration, or religion.

— Gary B. Nash
University of California, Los Angeles

Introduction

The Emergence of Modern America, the seventh volume of the Encyclopedia of American History, covers the period between 1900 and 1928. During these years, the United States experienced economic, political, and social change that was unprecedented in its history. While its population grew at a slower rate than it had in previous decades, it experienced the greatest period of immigration in its history, with more than 1 million immigrants entering the country every year. Internal movements of men and women from rural to urban areas and especially from the rural South to the urban North made the United States a more urban and more racially complex nation. Economically, the nation grew at an astonishing rate, with mass-production industries leading the way. Its role in the world economy changed as it shifted from being a debtor to a creditor nation. Better nutrition and medical care and the spread of technological innovations, from the electric light to the automobile and radio, promised an improved standard of living, one that was reflected in declining mortality rates and an increase in life expectancy over these nearly 30 years.

These changes were reflected in new cultural, social, and political organizations. The federal government that had a small but important role in everyday life began to directly affect economic sectors, local communities, and individual families. In part, it was the economic chaos of the last three decades of the 19th century that brought a new era of government regulation. High unemployment, sporadic but persistent labor protest, social unrest, and individual bad conduct made some long for a more just society and others to seek increased social control. The merger movement among businesses in the early 20th century and the increasingly visible power of corporations in government sparked the interest of journalists and political organizations alike. Women, who had long fought for equal suffrage, were on the verge of winning the vote, and they increasingly participated in the nation's political, economic, and cultural life. Progressivism, the most important political movement of the era, drew upon this discontent to forge a diverse and sometimes internally contradictory agenda for national reform. Presidents during these decades, the vibrant Theodore Roosevelt and scholarly Woodrow Wilson, echoed and helped to shape the reform impulse within government. The high culture of literature and art and the mass culture of pulp magazines and Tin Pan Alley expressed both the despair and the optimism of the day.

World War I presented a turning point for a nation on the brink of world leadership in foreign affairs, economic development, and culture. Unlike the chief combatant nations of France, Germany, and Great Britain, the United States remained outside the conflict for the first three years of the war. Its economy grew in response to the demand for war matériel, food, and clothing. Moreover, its war debt was small in comparison to the enormous indebtedness incurred by both the Allied and Central Powers in the war. Entering the war in 1917, the United States suffered fewer casualties than any other combatant nation and emerged from the war as the leader of the world economy. The war had other costs, however. Internal disputes over the wisdom of intervening in a European war, escalating labor conflict, and racial division sparked government regulation and surveillance. Ethnic and racial conflict added fuel to the fire as the superpatriotic societies and the Ku Klux Klan organized throughout the nation and race riots plagued cities during and after the war. The persistent demand to restrict immigration had its victory in new laws that instituted literacy tests and national quotas. Government agencies repressed labor unions, and socialist political organizations were repressed in the Red Scare of 1919–20; peace organizations found themselves similarly targeted. The federal government, which expanded in the course of the war, quickly dismantled wartime agencies by the 1920s, but the war's impact was not so easily forgotten. The recession of 1921–22 and the agricultural depression of the 1920s had their impact on the nation's attitudes as well.

In the 1920s, while the United States experienced some measure of economic prosperity, there remained questions about the need for greater social justice and more equal distribution of the nation's wealth. Conservative presidential administrations under Warren Harding, Calvin Coolidge, and Herbert Hoover reorganized the executive branch, lowered wartime taxes, and placed the federal government on a conservative fiscal footing, but none of them foresaw what the long-term trends of employment, a farm sector in recession, or the exuberant stock market speculation of the 1920s might do to the American economy. Increased tariffs, the debt crisis in Europe, and heightened international hostilities suggested that the next two decades would bring change as great and traumatic as that experienced by the modern nation that emerged between 1900 and 1930.

ENTRIES
A TO Z

Abbott, Grace (1878–1939)

One of the leading figures in the progressive reform movement, Grace Abbott was best known as the director of the United States CHILDREN'S BUREAU from 1921 to 1934. She had served in a number of other organizations that prepared her for the directorship. Born in Grand Island, Nebraska, Abbott graduated from a local college in 1898 and went to work as a high school teacher. She did graduate work at the University of Nebraska in 1902–03, and in 1906 attended summer school at the University of Chicago. It was at the University of Chicago where she was exposed to the new field of SOCIAL WORK and social reform movements. After returning to teach another year in Nebraska, Abbott moved to Chicago in 1907 in order to take advantage of the opportunities available to women in the fields of social reform. She moved into Hull-House in 1908 and completed her master's degree in political science at the University of Chicago in 1909.

Abbott became director of the Immigrants' Protective League in 1908. In this position she became an expert on IMMIGRATION. She published numerous articles and in 1917 published her first book, *The Immigrant and the Community*. Her work in the Immigrants' Protective League attracted the attention of Julia Lathrop, director of the United States Children's Bureau. In 1917, Abbott joined Lathrop in Washington as director of children's services for the Children's Bureau where she fought for the creation of the first federal CHILD LABOR law, the KEATING-OWEN ACT. After the U.S. Supreme Court ruled the law unconstitutional in *Hammer v. Dagenhart*, Abbott returned to Chicago and reestablished the Immigrants' Protective League. As Julia Lathrop's handpicked successor, Abbott returned to Washington, D.C., as the second director of the Children's Bureau.

As head of the Children's Bureau, Abbott oversaw the implementation of the maternity and infancy protection legislation, known generally as the SHEPPARD-TOWNER ACT. Sheppard-Towner established a federal-state partnership to develop state programs to promote women's and infants' health. The new legislation arose out of the reaction to the large number of babies who died in infancy and to the medical problems that mothers suffered in childbirth. Abbott actively lobbied governors and state legislatures to develop state programs that shared in the federal program. In addition, she reached out to women's organizations in the states, hoping to convince them to lobby their state governments in favor of the programs. Abbott also lobbied on behalf of a child labor amendment to the Constitution. When the Supreme Court overturned a second child labor law in 1922, advocates like Abbott turned their attention to a constitutional amendment that would outlaw child labor. The proposed amendment made it through Congress, but it failed to gain the ratification from the required number of states.

In 1927 Abbott began to face health problems that would plague her until her death. She was forced to take a break from the Children's Bureau in 1927 and again in 1931 to recover from tuberculosis. She resigned as director of the Children's Bureau in 1934 and returned to teach at the University of Chicago. She died from cancer in 1939.

Further reading: Lela B. Costin, *Two Sisters for Social Justice: A Biography of Grace and Edith Abbott.* Urbana: University of Illinois Press, 1983.

— Michael Hartman

Adamson Act (1916)

A key piece of Progressive Era legislation, the Adamson Act in 1916 provided railroad workers with new protections. The turn of the 20th century had witnessed unparalleled expansion in U.S. industrial activity that in turn led to renewed growth of trade unionism. Already by 1904, more than two million workers were trade union members. These new members rallied for expanded rights, and the years between 1905 and 1910 saw the rise of the NEW UNIONISM. Massive strikes, public protests, and political activism brought the labor question into the forefront of political debate. In the 1912 presidential election, the AMERICAN FEDERATION OF LABOR, under the leadership of Samuel Gompers, supported the DEMOCRATIC PARTY. Its demands for a new antitrust act that excluded labor unions, for an eight-hour day for federal employees, and for workmen's compensation laws made their way into the Democratic platform.

Once in office, President WOODROW WILSON was aware that organized labor was a significant part of his constituency. To that end, he tried appealing to them as the "backbone of the nation." At the same time, Wilson was suspicious of large organizations in the American economy, whether business or labor. In creating a Department of Labor (1913), passing the CLAYTON ANTITRUST ACT of 1914, and establishing the INDUSTRIAL RELATIONS COMMISSION to look into recent labor violence, Wilson sought compromises between labor's demands and the open hostility of corporations and small businesses toward recognizing organized labor. Prior to the entry of the United States into WORLD WAR I, labor had attained other victories as well in the areas of CHILD LABOR and workmen's compensation. Working conditions and wages, however, continued to be areas of contention.

Fearing a growing militancy on the railroads and facing the possibility of going to war, the Wilson administration worked to mediate labor disputes on the nation's rails. In 1916, "to protect the pockets of our men," the railway brotherhoods threatened to strike on Labor Day for an eight-hour day. Fearing for both his PREPAREDNESS program and his reelection, Wilson pushed for Congress to pass the Adamson Eight Hour Act, which mandated an eight-hour workday on the nation's railroads. The law limited only the working hours of railroad labor, but its influence spread to other industries as well. After World War I ended, there were setbacks. Despite the defeat suffered in the Railroad Shopmen's strike of 1922, however, the Adamson Act and experiments with federal mediation of railroad labor disputes during the war gave railroad workers a continued and powerful union voice in improving their pay and working conditions.

See also LABOR AND LABOR MOVEMENT; RAILROAD ADMINISTRATION.

Further reading: Joseph McCartin, *Labor's Great War: The Struggle for Industrial Democracy and the Origins of Modern Labor Relations, 1912–1921* (Chapel Hill: University of North Carolina Press, 1997).

— Annamarie Edelen

Addams, Jane (1860–1935)

One of the leading figures in Progressive Era reform, Jane Addams won worldwide recognition for her work in estab-

Jane Addams *(Library of Congress)*

lishing the Hull-House settlement house and as a peace advocate. Throughout her life, she dedicated herself to improving the lives of needy men, women, and children. Born in Cedarville, Illinois, Addams grew up in a politically active household, with a father who served as a state senator for 16 years. She was graduated from Rockford Female Seminary in 1881 and spent the next six years traveling, studying, and contemplating a career. Struggling against the restrictions placed on women at the time, Addams spent these six years searching for a meaningful career that was open to her as a woman. During her travels to London, England, Addams visited a settlement house and discovered her life's ambition. In 1889 she and Ellen Gates Starr leased a home in an underprivileged area of Chicago and established Hull-House with the purpose of providing "a center for higher civic and philanthropic enterprises and to investigate and improve the conditions in the industrial districts of Chicago."

At Hull-House, Addams developed a variety of programs aimed at improving the poor conditions in which working-class immigrants lived. She hoped that the immigrants could learn middle-class social and cultural ways as a means to improving their lives. The programs at Hull-House included kindergarten classes, cooking classes, club meetings, art and English classes. As attendance swelled, Addams expanded into neighboring buildings until Hull-House encompassed a city block. The additions included an art gallery, a public kitchen, a coffee house, a gymnasium, a swimming pool, a bookbindery, an art studio, a circulating library, an employment bureau, and a labor museum.

Under Addams, Hull-House became one of the focal points of American reform. Its influence spread beyond the neighborhood which it served. Many of the key figures in Progressive Era reform, including FLORENCE KELLEY and GRACE ABBOTT, started their careers at Hull-House under Addams's tutelage. In addition, she led investigations into juvenile delinquency, poverty wages, midwifery, narcotics use, milk supplies, sanitary conditions, and working conditions, particularly for women and children. These investigations spurred numerous improvements in the lives of working Americans.

Addams was an ardent opponent of war, a position for which she suffered public criticism during WORLD WAR I. She gave her first speeches against war in 1906, and by 1915 she was chairperson of two peace organizations. Addams publicly opposed America's entrance into the war in 1917, and she was attacked in the press for her position. Despite her opposition to the war, she served in the U.S. government's program to provide relief for European citizens affected by the war. Addams suffered a heart attack in 1926 after which she never fully regained her health. In 1931 she was awarded the Nobel Peace Prize for her lifetime of work helping the unfortunate. She died in 1935 from heart-related ailments and cancer.

See also SOCIAL WORK.

Further reading: Jane Addams, *Twenty Years at Hull-House: With Autobiographical Notes* (New York: Macmillan, 1910); Allen F. Davis, *American Heroine: The Life and Legend of Jane Addams* (New York: Oxford University Press, 1973).

— Michael Hartman

Adkins v. Children's Hospital (1923)

In the Progressive Era, the Supreme Court decision in *Adkins v. Children's Hospital* became part of the crusade to remedy women's poor wages and working conditions. Contemporary studies of working women revealed that the average woman worker was single, between the ages of 16 and 24, and of foreign birth or parentage. Driven by the necessity to earn wages either to support themselves or to contribute to family income, women were forced to accept jobs, many of which paid less than a living wage. Working in mass-production industries or in the new clerical and service industries, women had little bargaining power, often met resistance in organizing unions, and had few political options as women did not yet have the right to vote. The solution, many argued, was a governmentally mandated minimum wage, which would allow working women to earn a respectable income and avert destitution. In the wake of *MULLER V. OREGON*, a Supreme Court decision that confirmed the constitutionality of maximum hour laws to protect women workers on the basis of their future role as mothers, reformers pushed through a wave of state minimum wage laws, many of which were controversial in their regulation of wages, and not working conditions.

The Washington, D.C., minimum wage law for women was contested in *Adkins v. Children's Hospital* on the grounds that it was an infringement of women's right of free contract under the Constitution. The Supreme Court in the case declared that sex-specific minimum wage laws were beyond the powers of government. In part, their justification lay in the recent victory of woman suffrage, which arguably eliminated women's political disabilities. If women had the same political rights as men, including the right to vote, they should no longer be a protected class under the law. The Court also seemed to distinguish law regulating the hours and conditions of labor, which the government had the right to establish to protect the public's interest in motherhood, and minimum wage laws, which were about what a worker received in compensation for labor. The latter, they believed, was a function of the market and not the state.

In subsequent laws and test cases, minimum wage laws for women remained under attack, both on the grounds of limitations on governmental power but also because minimum wage commissions, the device by which most states determined women's wages on an industry basis, were thought to be an inadequate guarantee of an employer's right to due process. Only with the passage of the federal Fair Labor Standards Act in 1938, which created a federal minimum wage for both men and women workers, did the push for women's minimum wage laws start to abate as the Court confirmed the constitutionality of general minimum wage regulation.

Further reading: Judith Baer, *The Chains of Protection: The Judicial Response to Women's Labor Legislation* (Westport, Conn.: Greenwood Press, 1978); Vivian Hart, *Bound by Our Constitution: Women Workers and the Minimum Wage* (Princeton N.J.: Princeton University Press, 1994).

advertising

Advertising as an occupation and an industry gained momentum in the early decades of the 20th century. Advertising began in the field of public relations, as private charities and public agencies found ways to solicit public support and publicize their good works. Acting for these agencies, and later for businesses, advertising agents negotiated for space to advertise the service, product, or organization in newspapers and magazines. By 1900, however, the top two agencies in the United States—N.W. Ayer and Son and J. Walter Thompson—were not only writing advertising copy for their clients but also designing the ads. Local advertising agencies and branches of the larger firms soon cropped up in many cities. Advertising revenues became a major source of profits, both for the new agencies and for the newspapers and magazines that published their copy. Advertising became big business as manufacturers sought new markets for an ever-broadening range of consumer items, from personal toiletries to the automobile. Companies now spent over $100 million a year on advertising, double what they had in 1880. The next 30 years saw the emergence of modern advertising with its new approaches

Advertisement for Sunkist oranges in *The Ladies' Home Journal* (Library of Congress)

to marketing goods and surveying the public, new methods of persuasion, and an advertising creed to match.

The advertising industry began to develop professional standards and organizations. There was the beginning of the movement toward a regular 15 percent commission for advertising as well as the growth of agency services. To promote the industry, the Association of Advertising Clubs of America was formed in 1904. Complaints about unfair and dishonest ads led to new government regulations under the FEDERAL TRADE COMMISSION ACT of 1914. Just a few years later, in 1917, 111 advertising agencies established the American Association of Advertising Agencies to further the industry's growth.

An important figure in developing modern advertising was Albert Lasker. Known as "the Father of Advertising" by his admirers and "the Apostle of the Obvious" by his critics, he started as a floor sweeper with Lord and Thomas, one of the leading advertising firms in Chicago, in 1884. By 1898, he owned the company. Lasker persuaded one client, a hearing aid manufacturer, to increase its advertising budget from $10,000 to $180,000 a year on the basis of his slogans. Master of the "tricky slogan," he attracted big clients to his firm, including Lucky Strike, Pepsodent, Kleenex, RCA, and Frigidaire. By 1921, it was the top-ranked advertising firm in the country. In that year, he left to head the UNITED STATES SHIPPING BOARD and returned to save his failing agency in 1923. His idea of business, he professed, "was to render service and to make money." His ideal of "salesmanship in print" drove up industry competition.

Lasker was only one of a handful of agency heads to push the industry forward in its approach and method. F. Wayland Ayer of N.W. Ayer and Son built his agency by adding branch offices in major cities and creating a new business department. His decision to hire full-time copywriters and artists set the industry standard before 1910, and he pioneered in media research. Having coined the phrase, "It pays to advertise," J. Walter Thompson headed Ayer's major competitor. Thompson was famous for inventing the testimonial ad. In 1921, his agency developed a marketing research department when it hired Harvard psychologist John Watson. In a more direct fashion, advertiser Helen Lansdowne Resor gave advertising a twist of sex appeal with her 1911 ad for Woodbury Facial Soap, "The Skin You Love to Touch." Celebrity advertising also filled up the pages of magazines as advertisers educated the public through "the medium of personalities." These new approaches gave advertising a stronger hold on the imagination of both the public and industry.

By the 1920s, the birth and rapid expansion of public radio programs and a growing number of mass market magazines opened the way for increasing use of advertising. The industry grew rapidly due to the explosion of advertising revenues during WORLD WAR I, when the government sponsored its own "advertising" with the COMMITTEE FOR PUBLIC INFORMATION under George Creel. Advertising whiz Bruce Barton was himself the product of United War Work campaigns that he worked on with later partners Roy Durstine and Alex Osborn. In addition to expanding the domain of advertising, the industry benefited as well from new consumer credit plans. The 1920s saw consumers spend an increasing proportion of their wages on consumer durables such as cars, radios, and household appliances. Ads for consumer products became a staple of the new mass-market magazines and radio broadcasts. By 1923, the first radio series to be sponsored by company advertising, National Carbon Company's *Eveready Hour,* was broadcast. Within a few years, company-sponsored programs such as *The Jack Benny Show* and *General Foods Cooking School* competed for radio time. In an era of expanding markets, advertising budgets climbed from $1.4 billion in 1919 to nearly $3 billion in 1929.

In new consumer-oriented ads, advertisers shifted from focusing on the producer of goods to selling the consumer, from the product to the benefits of its use. New ads focused on the personal and intimate aspects of consumer goods. The consumer, advertisers suggested, was expressing a sense of self in purchasing. There were sexualized images and puns. In an advertisement for an automobile parts maker, "body by Fisher" had a double meaning when the ad model was a stunning woman in an evening dress. At the same time, three of the most successful campaigns of the age—Fleischman's yeast, Listerine, and Kotex—played on consumer's fears of illness and hopes for a successful personal life.

For these reasons, the advertising industry had a powerful pull on the culture of the time. President CALVIN COOLIDGE in 1926 told the American Association of Advertising Agents that they were engaged in "the great work of regeneration and redemption of mankind." "It is," he said, "the most potent influence in adapting and changing the habits and modes of life, affecting what we eat, what we wear, and the work and play of a whole nation." The almost religious zeal of advertising was best illustrated by the life of one of the foremost businessmen of the 1920s, advertising prophet Bruce Barton. Alastair Cooke wrote of Barton that he "came as close as any one will to achieving a philosophy of advertising, because he saw the whole of human history as an exercise in persuasion." Barton's book, *The Man Nobody Knows* (1925), portrayed Jesus as a modern businessman who practiced what Barton called "the creative force" of advertising. He also was known for popularizing the Harvard Classics series and inventing the figure of Betty Crocker. His fame in advertising later led to a political career in Congress.

Advertising reached the end of the 1920s as one of the leading forces in American life. It pervaded thousands of newspapers and magazines and saturated the radio air waves. At the same time, advertising's prosperity depended ultimately on the health of the consumer economy. When, in 1929, the economy began to falter, so too did advertising revenues. From 1929 to 1933, they declined from $3.5 billion to $1.5 billion. Advertising agencies, like other services, suffered from the weakness of the economy as a whole. While it would take more than a decade to restore the economy—and the faith in its self-advertised prosperity—advertising rebounded in the mid-1930s as the New Deal lent great importance to advertising economic recovery.

See also ECONOMY; JOURNALISM; RADIO.

Further reading: Pamela Land, *Advertising Progress: American Business and the Rise of Consumer Marketing* (Baltimore: Johns Hopkins University Press, 1998); Roland Marchand, *Advertising the American Dream: Making Way for Modernity, 1920–1940* (Berkeley: University of California Press, 1985); Daniel Pope, *The Making of Modern Advertising* (New York: Basic Books, 1983); Juliann Sivulka, *Soap, Sex and Cigarettes: A Cultural History of American Advertising* (Belmont, Calif.: Wadsworth, 1998).

Agricultural Marketing Act (1929)

Designed to address the deteriorating farm economy, the Agricultural Marketing Act of 1929 was the most important piece of farm legislation passed under the Hoover administration. Elected in 1928 as the third consecutive Republican president, Herbert Hoover set out to maintain the economic growth much of the nation had witnessed for the past decade. Despite this apparent prosperity, structural problems persisted in the American economy that ultimately contributed to its collapse. In particular, rural residents and farmers were left out of much of the economic prosperity of the twenties. WORLD WAR I had created an expanded market for American agricultural goods; but with the cessation of hostilities in Europe, the market contracted as agricultural production on the continent resumed. With shifting market conditions of the postwar period, agricultural prices in the United States steadily declined. While lower prices for many durable consumer goods such as automobiles resulted in increased demand, most people did not purchase more bread as its price dropped.

Rural residents and farmers accordingly faced economic crisis well before the onset of the Great Depression in late 1929. Some 500,000 individuals lost their farms to bankruptcy during the 1920s. In response, farmers made persistent demands on the federal government for action during the course of the twenties. Hoover, who had served as the wartime food administrator, was aware of the poor economic conditions in rural America at the end of the decade. He had supported agricultural legislation such as the CAPPER-VOLSTEAD ACT as secretary of commerce under WARREN G. HARDING. As president, Hoover pushed bills aimed at stabilizing the agricultural economy through a special session of Congress. For Hoover, glutted markets served as the primary factor undermining the health of agriculture in the United States, and he sought to address that problem.

One of the more favored responses advocated by farm organizations was federal support for cooperative arrangements. If farmers could buy, sell, and process through joint efforts, they could control their profits rather than surrender them to "middlemen" agricultural firms, long seen by farmers as one of the primary threats to their economic well-being. Farm cooperatives remained at a disadvantage in marketing their goods, and it was to this problem that the Hoover administration directed its attention.

The Agricultural Market Act created a revolving loan fund of $500 million to help farm cooperatives market their major commodities and purchase surpluses of these goods off the market to force prices up. While not a solution for all farmers, the act helped to support agricultural cooperatives for the producers of perishable products and items that sold on a national, rather than a world, market. Some of the more successful cooperative arrangements were made in the fruit and dairy sector of agriculture. While many cooperatives began as family farms, they came to include such large cooperatives as Sunkist oranges, Land O'Lakes milk, Diamond walnuts, and Ocean Spray cranberries. The Agricultural Marketing Act stood to benefit a key part of the agricultural economy, but it is unclear how much it would have benefited farm producers after 1929. The act went into effect at the same time that the American economy as a whole collapsed in October 1929, and farm prices slumped and then fell catastrophically.

See also AGRICULTURE; MCNARY HAUGEN FARM BILL.

Further reading: David E. Hamilton, *From New Day to New Deal: American Farm Policy from Hoover to Roosevelt, 1928–1933* (Chapel Hill: University of North Carolina Press, 1991).

— David R. Smith

Agricultural Workers Organization   See Industrial Workers of the World

agriculture
Although farmers had faced a shortage of capital, banking facilities, currency, and credit during the last two decades of the 19th century, the new century brought a wave of prosperity to rural areas of the United States that would last until shortly after the end of WORLD WAR I. Despite experiencing substantial wartime prosperity, the agricultural economy by the 1920s displayed clear signs of the structural weaknesses that would prove ruinous for many farmers. Nevertheless, during the "Golden Age" of agriculture from 1900 to 1920, gross farm incomes doubled and real farm income (gross income adjusted for inflation) increased by some 40 percent. Beyond the yearly increases in income, the real growth in the prosperity of farmers came with steadily increasing land values, holding out the promise of future economic well-being.

The prosperity that farmers experienced during the first two decades of the 20th century largely emanated from increasing demand for their products. While the amount of land under agricultural production more than doubled in the last quarter of the 19th century, only about 12 percent more land was brought into production between 1900 and the early 1920s. Not only had the majority of productive farmland already been brought into production by 1900, but also farmers tended to not increase their landholdings during that time.

An important source of rural prosperity stemmed from foreign markets, where farmers increasingly sold a new, wider range of products between 1900 and the First World War. As farmers steadily pushed into the few remaining productive agriculture lands, in places like Florida and California, the range of agricultural commodities shifted. By 1914, citrus fruits, sugar, oil crops, poultry, and eggs had made steady gains as major agricultural commodities American farmers produced. Despite this shift in the type of products being grown, hay, grains, wool, and meat animals remained key components in the agricultural economy. Technological improvements aided the rapidly growing agricultural economy and led to the introduction of new commodities. Not only mechanization on individual farms, especially the introduction of the internal combustion engine, but also the introduction and expansion of new containers, such as refrigerated railway cars, made the transport of perishable goods easier and more efficient. The citrus fruit industry, for example, expanded as its products could be transported and sold on a national market as opposed to simply within local markets in California and Florida.

Although willing to introduce many modern conveniences to their daily living conditions, many farmers—having witnessed the economic difficulties of the late 19th century—were reluctant to invest in capital improvements. They hesitated to expand landholdings and purchase new equipment to increase farm productivity. As a result, with productivity increasing by only about 1 percent per year, agricultural output could not keep pace with the steady increase (approximately 40 percent) in the nation's population during the first quarter of the 20th century.

Accordingly, the prices of agricultural commodities rose because of an increasing demand that could not be fully met by American farmers. In addition, the world market also became quite friendly to American farmers between 1900 and 1920, which added to their profits. In particular, American agricultural commodities were in high demand across Europe with the outbreak of war in 1914.

Despite the reluctance of farmers to invest in extensive capital improvements, the introduction of mechanical farm equipment had dramatic and long-term consequences on American society, especially in the South. There, even the limited introduction of mechanization resulted in a slowly decreasing demand for African-American laborers, who had made up the bulk of the rural labor force through tenant and sharecropping arrangements. Although cotton remained the least mechanized farm crop through the 1930s, the gradual introduction of mechanical devices helped to loosen some of the economic and political conditions that tied African Americans to the region. In addition to mechanical devices, the infestation of cotton by the boll weevil in the early part of the 20th century meant that for the first time since the end of the Civil War in 1865, a steady number of African Americans managed to migrate to northern cities, especially as the demand for industrial labor increased with the start of the war in Europe.

The war had created an expanded market for American agricultural goods and brought the means to borrow capital for expanding landholdings, but the cessation of hostilities in Europe caused the market to contract. Agricultural endeavors on the continent resumed, and European governments faced a capital shortage as they rebuilt their war-torn nations. With shifting market conditions during the 1920s, agricultural prices in the United States steadily declined. In 1919, wheat sold for $2.19 per bushel, potatoes went for $2.20 per hundredweight, and cotton received $.35 per pound. By the end of the 1920s, however, a bushel of wheat sold for $1.05, potatoes had declined to $1.29, and cotton now received only $.17. While lower prices for many consumer goods resulted in increased demand, most people did not purchase more bread as its price dropped.

Not only did farmers have to contend with declining prices for many of their commodities, but also changing consumer tastes and new federal policies had a profound impact on agriculture. The passage of PROHIBITION in 1919 barred the sale and manufacture of alcoholic beverages and, accordingly, constricted the domestic market for barley and other grains. Similarly, shorter skirt styles and the introduction of such synthetic materials as rayon diminished the demand for cotton and wool. Another major factor that reshaped agriculture was the introduction of tractors to the production process, primarily in harvesting. While mechanization was a response to the shortage of labor, it ultimately meant fewer draft animals were needed by farmers, which further reduced the demand for various field crops traditionally used to feed work animals.

With declining prices and constricting markets, many rural residents and farmers faced an economic downturn well before the onset of the Great Depression in 1929. Some 500,000 individuals lost their farms to bankruptcy during the 1920s. In response, farmers made persistent demands for relief from the federal government during the course of the twenties. Farm advocates had long championed the need for low-interest loans to help promote and make affordable the capital improvements needed to expand individual farms. The FEDERAL FARM LOAN ACT in 1916 created the mechanism to extend low-interest loans for periods of five to 40 years to farmers through a Federal Farm Loan Board, 12 Federal Land Banks that paralleled the Federal Reserve Banks. As part of WOODROW WILSON's NEW FREEDOM initiative, the Farm Loan Act extended capital to farmers through a program that cut out private banks, which farmers viewed as outside institutions that exploited them.

Another mechanism introduced during the early part of the 20th century to address the needs and demands of agriculture was federal support for cooperative arrangements, which actually was one of the more favored responses long advocated by farmers. If farmers could buy, sell, and process through joint efforts, they would be able to better control the profits generated by their products. Cooperative arrangements did not stand to benefit all farmers. Instead, producers of perishable products and of items that sold on a national rather than a world market tended to benefit the most from cooperative arrangements. Some of the more successful cooperative arrangements were made in the fruit and dairy sector of agriculture and included such cooperatives as Sunkist oranges, Land O'Lakes milk, Diamond walnuts, and Ocean Spray cranberries. In 1922, the Farm Bloc in Congress passed the CAPPER-VOLSTEAD ACT, which protected cooperatives from antitrust legislation.

Another major piece of farm legislation was the AGRICULTURAL MARKETING ACT (1929). It created a revolving loan fund of $500 million to help farm cooperatives market their major commodities and to purchase surpluses of goods off the market to force prices up. While this legislation stood to benefit a key part of the agricultural economy, it is unknown what its benefits might have been for producers after 1929. While industrial operations in the United States had benefited from protective tariffs, the prices of agricultural goods could not be pushed by these tariffs, especially as production outdistanced demand on the domestic market. In response to the demands of such groups as the American Farm Bureau, Congress in 1926 passed the MCNARY-HAUGEN FARM BILL in an attempt to create parity for American agricultural goods. While

Congress twice passed the bill, it was unable to override President CALVIN COOLIDGE's vetoes. Despite government efforts to address farmers' needs, the agricultural sector quickly fell into economic crisis with the collapse of the Stock Market in 1929.

See also ECONOMY; TARIFFS.

Further reading: David B. Danbom, *Born in the Country: A History of Rural America* (Baltimore: Johns Hopkins University Press, 1995); Pete Daniels, *Breaking the Land: The Transformation of Cotton, Tobacco, and Rice Cultures since 1880* (Urbana: University of Illinois Press, 1985).

— David R. Smith

Aguinaldo, Emilio (1869–1964)

Emilio Aguinaldo was the Filipino statesman and guerrilla leader who led the nationalist revolt against the American forces during the Filipino Insurrection (1898–1902). The son of the mayor of the town of Kawit, he assumed his father's position after achieving financial success running his family's sugar mill and dealing in cattle. While mayor, he became enamored of the Katipunan, a secret, mystical nationalist organization that combined the rituals of Roman Catholicism and Freemasonry. When the Filipinos rose up against Spanish colonial rule in August 1896, Aguinaldo joined the rebels and quickly distinguished himself as a guerrilla leader. Armed only with the most primitive of weapons, he and his followers managed to control three towns in his native province of Cavite.

Inspiring and resourceful as he was, Aguinaldo eventually was cornered by Spanish forces. With the Spanish unable to muster the resources necessary to storm his camp, and the nationalists unable to break out, the two sides came to a settlement. The Spanish promised reforms, and Aguinaldo agreed to accept 800,000 pesos, sign an oath foreswearing rebellion, and leave the country.

In December 1897, Aguinaldo arrived in Hong Kong, immediately renounced his agreement with Spain, and began to plan a new rebellion. His efforts were given a boost a year later, when Admiral Dewey's fleet was assembling at Hong Kong in preparation for an attack on Manila Bay. Although Dewey asked Aguinaldo to help him defeat the Spanish, the admiral inexplicably sailed to Manila without him. Aguinaldo, who had made alternate travel arrangements, did not arrive until the naval battle was over.

Unable to get a firm answer from Dewey concerning Filipino independence, Aguinaldo declared the Philippines a provisional dictatorship with himself as its head. As his presence in the archipelago became known, Filipinos flocked to his cause. The nationalists soon surrounded Manila, effectively blocking the Spanish from leaving by land while Dewey blocked the routes to the sea.

When American ground forces arrived, they promised the Filipinos several artillery pieces if they would yield a sector of Manila. Aguinaldo agreed, and his troops left their trenches, but the cannons were never delivered. The Americans promptly stormed the city; and in a sham battle, designed to save the Spanish general from court-martial, they captured all of the Spanish troops. As a final insult, Aguinaldo was barred from the surrender ceremony.

Aguinaldo sent his troops to cover as much territory as possible so as to increase his leverage with the Americans. Tensions mounted between Filipino and American troops as they faced each other in the trenches around Manila. Once President William McKinley declared that the United States had sovereignty over the islands, Aguinaldo prepared for war.

Open hostilities began when an American private shot and killed several Filipino soldiers. Fearing that the Filipinos were within American lines, the commander ordered his troops to attack. In the open, pitched battles that followed, the Filipinos were decimated with casualties. Aguinaldo responded by quickly switching over to hit-and-run tactics. His guerrilla war and terrorist activities frustrated U.S. efforts to pacify the islands for the next three years.

The insurrection came to an end in 1902 when, in a daring raid by American troops, Aguinaldo was captured. He signed a document stating that he recognized American sovereignty, and he ceased hostilities. He lived quietly for the remainder of his life, except during World War II when he made pro-Japanese broadcasts. He died in 1964.

Further reading: Stanley Karnouw, *In Our Image: America's Empire in the Philippines* (New York: Random House, 1989).

— Timothy E. Vislocky

Alien Exclusion Act   See Immigration Act of 1917

American Expeditionary Force (AEF)

When the United States entered WORLD WAR I, the U.S. Army numbered only around 128,000 men. The newly appointed commander of the American Expeditionary Force (AEF), General JOHN PERSHING, after touring the battlefields in France, quickly concluded that the United States would need at least 3 million men to be victorious in the war. Eventually over 4 million served. Chosen in April 1917 to lead the American army in Europe, Pershing was one of the few American generals with battle experience.

He had commanded American forces in Mexico in their pursuit of Pancho Villa. Pershing was anxious to keep the American army together as a cohesive unit, rather than dispersing them as the European commanders desired. The need for troops on the European front strengthened Pershing's hand.

The entire initiative of the AEF was extremely important, as this was the first time that the United States sent a large land force outside its borders. Formed in large part by a civilian draft under the SELECTIVE SERVICE ACT of 1917, the AEF as a modern army was trained, equipped, and supplied thanks to the nation's industrial capacity. It was the first of its kind in United States history, an integrated national military, rather than a collection of state militia integrated into regular army divisions as in the past.

The military draft supplied the men, but the soldiers still had to be housed, clothed, armed, equipped, and trained. There were not enough officers, facilities, nor time to train the men. To address housing issues, a Cantonment Division was created, which set to work expanding existing military installations, and 16 tent camps were made for the National Guard in the South and 16 wooden barracks for the national army in the North. Clothing for the men also had to be provided. Almost 132 million pairs of socks were needed at the end of May 1918. Many soldiers had to wait for their full allotment of clothing and equipment. Production of ammunition, radio, and other military equipment fell short as companies sometimes signed contracts they had no hope of fulfilling. The government eventually stepped in, and the Army took control of the manufacturing process in many companies. The WAR INDUSTRIES BOARD set about dictating what it needed to industry and controlling resources.

During the war, a serious shortage of arms also needed to be addressed. Most weapons required lead-time to produce, and there were limits on production. Production on the Springfield service rifle, for example, could be increased to only 1,000 per day. As there were only 600,000 on hand, this was a major problem. It was many months after the United States declared war that it was able to effectively engage in fighting—only because France and Britain supplied weapons, ammunition, transportation, and equipment.

Despite these problems, the American soldiers were fresh compared with the war-weary French and British. With their arrival in Europe, it was clear that a new era had arisen in the West. The American weight was now being heavily felt in the balance. American troops arrived in France in 1918. The first offensive occurred in September. On September 12, 1918, at 1:00 A.M., the Allied artillery opened fire. By September 13, Pershing's First Army controlled the Saint-Mihiel sector at a line from Haudiomont to Vandières. Their victory cost 7,000 casualties.

Enlistment poster for the American Expeditionary Force *(Library of Congress)*

They took 15,000 German prisoners and 450 guns. By the 14th of September, the first units of Pershing's army redeployed to the Argonne sector; 500,000 men of the First Army assembled. On the 26th of September, the American First Army, with the French Fourth, resumed the offensive. Colonel George Patton's tank brigade accompanied them. By October 10, they controlled the forest. On October 12, 1918, Pershing decided that the First Army was too big. He created the Second Army and gave command to General Hunter Liggett.

Although the advancing Americans were eating up their supplies at a rapid rate, victory was close at hand. The Germans were near to conceding as their allies deserted them. The British blockade was causing critical food shortages, and the German armies were reeling. The Germans finally surrendered on November 11, 1918, what came to be called Armistice Day (Veterans Day, after World War II). The American Expeditionary Force saw only 150 days of combat, but in that time it seized 485,000 square miles of enemy held territory and captured 63,000 prisoners, 1,300 artillery pieces, and 10,000 mortars and machine guns.

Further reading: Byron Farwell, *Over There, the United States in the Great War, 1917–1918* (New York: W. W. Norton, 1999); John S. Eisenhower *Yanks: The Epic Story of the American Army in World War I* (New York: Free Press, 2001).

— Annamarie Edelen

American Federation of Labor (AFL)

The American Federation of Labor was the most important labor organization of the Progressive Era. It brought workers together primarily from the skilled trades into a national organization that had as its purpose improving the conditions of labor through collective bargaining. In what was often called "pure and simple trade unionism," the Federation gave priority to economic demands for wages and control over the labor process. The AFL claimed to be the political voice not only of organized labor but also of the working class in the United States. As such, it became increasingly involved in politics in the early 20th century, using its clout to push for state and federal legislation to prohibit child labor, restrict immigration, control the conditions of federal employees, bar labor injunctions, and grant injured workers compensation.

Radical in its origins, the AFL by 1900 had taken on the conservative attitudes and old boy persona of its leaders, President Samuel Gompers, a cigar maker; Adolph Strasser, who belonged to the same trade; and Peter McGuire, the head of the carpenters' union. The AFL's primary constituents were workers in the skilled trades. Unlike the rival Knights of Labor, the AFL's avoided mobilizing workers across industry and occupation, targeting instead craft workers. Moreover, the AFL saw itself as an organization exclusively for workers, and it barred labor reformers, small business allies, and labor scholars from its ranks. There was a logic to the AFL's policy of exclusion. The Knights, many trade unionists believed, had misdirected their energies toward reform. Further, skilled workers such as cigar makers, printers, carpenters, machinists, iron molders, barrel makers, had, by virtue of their knowledge and training, greater control over their work and greater power in negotiating with employers. The length of apprenticeships and the limited pool of skilled labor made it difficult for employers to replace strikers with new workers or to substitute machines for those on strike. Skilled workers also were, due to strict rules and discrimination, primarily male, white, and native-born or naturalized citizens. These characteristics gave their trade unions greater bargaining power and political clout. The AFL's weapon of choice was a small, short, and focused strike against employers. It avoided the lengthy political programs and broad-based community protests that had characterized its predecessors.

At the turn of the century, the AFL was in the midst of an unprecedented expansion. In 1898, it had 278,000 members, and by 1903, its ranks had grown to 1,500,000. Under the influence of the NEW UNIONISM trade unions as well as the new semi-industrial unions like the UNITED MINE WORKERS (UMW), the Amalgamated Clothing Workers, and the INTERNATIONAL LADIES' GARMENT WORKERS UNION (ILGWU), organized those previously outside their domain. Benefiting from massive strikes, AFL unions enrolled growing numbers of skilled workers, especially in the metalworking trades. Indeed, the International Association of Machinists (IAM) was one of the fastest growing unions. Further, as new technologies of power (such as electric lighting) and methods of construction (such as steel-reinforced girders) were created, new groups of workers organized, among them the International Brotherhood of Electrical Workers (IBEW) and the Bridge and Structural Ironworkers. Growth in city streetcar systems also meant growing numbers of drivers and conductors, who organized their own unions. The building trades (carpenters, masons, bricklayers, etc.) were among the chief beneficiaries of urban growth. Their power within the AFL increased proportionately with their numbers. The new organizational strength of labor gave rise to a new wave of labor militancy and an increase in the rate of strike success.

As the labor federation grew, so too did its areas of interest. While it had experimented from time to time with political campaigns, the AFL chose, for the most part, to maintain a non-partisan strategy in politics by rewarding labor's friends and punishing its enemies. In general, the labor movement had been wary of government regulation of the workplace. It preferred to leave the issues of wages, hours, and working conditions to private bargaining and viewed the arena for state intervention as relatively limited. The only legislation it endorsed was concerned with limiting access to the labor market or with specific occupations, such as Chinese exclusion laws and the regulation of child labor.

In the face of growing employer hostility, the AFL began to seek federal relief from court injunctions. Key court decisions such as DANBURY HATTERS and BUCK'S STOVE sharply restricted labor's ability to bargain with employers by penalizing labor for the costs of strikes and even informal boycotts, such as "We Don't Patronize" lists. The AFL now sought legislation to limit the use of labor injunctions and to pass new measures to regulate child labor and institute an eight-hour day for government employees. Under the presidency of WOODROW WILSON, the AFL lobbied for and obtained the passage of the CLAYTON ANTITRUST ACT, which gave labor unions protection from antitrust laws. It witnessed the creation of a Department of Labor and supported new federal legislation for workers' compensation. With the ADAMSON ACT, railroad workers saw the eight-hour day become a reality. When the United States entered WORLD WAR I, the AFL cooperated with the war effort and took part in government efforts to mobilize labor and war industries. It also helped make the first steps toward government intervention in negotiating wages and working conditions during the wartime emergency through the RAILROAD ADMINISTRATION. In many sectors, workers signed no-strike pledges for the duration of the war. The payoff was the new and privileged role the AFL played in the federal government through the NATIONAL WAR LABOR BOARD.

After the war, the massive strikes of 1919, and the political reprisals of the RED SCARE, the labor movement went into shock. Experiments in industrial unionism ended in the losses of the STEEL STRIKE OF 1919 and the postwar strikes in meatpacking and textiles. Labor's defeat in the coal and railroad shopmen's strikes of 1922 signaled a sharp decline in its political clout, as government intervention effectively repressed conflict. In stark contrast to the moderate Wilson administration, WARREN G. HARDING's presidency demonstrated hostility toward labor. Under Harding and his successor, CALVIN COOLIDGE, the chief labor victory was in the area of immigration restriction. Labor's interest in limiting the influx of new workers complemented nativist concerns, and it joined them in endorsing the 1921 QUOTA ACT and the NATIONAL ORIGINS ACT of 1924. By the 1920s, national union leaders rarely touched on issues that concerned the mass of workers politically, such as work accidents, insurance, and relief. State labor federations experienced in politics did try to pass unemployment insurance in such states as Massachusetts, California, and Minnesota. The emphasis on state-level action was a response to the Supreme Court's tendency to declare unconstitutional the extension of federal power to protect the conditions and wages of labor. It also followed from the preference of organized labor for local activism and voluntary association.

With the 1924 death of Samuel Gompers, who had been federation president since 1886, the conservatism of the AFL was set in stone. His successor, William Green, was, if anything, more averse to state intervention in labor relations and demonstrated even greater hostility toward African-American, immigrant, and women workers. Faced with the growing discontent among workers in the late 1920s and the looming unemployment crisis, the AFL tread water. Ambivalent toward mass production industries, it resisted efforts to modernize or to embrace the coming wave of industrial unionism.

Further reading: Julie Greene, *Pure and Simple Politics: The American Federation of Labor, 1881–1917* (Cambridge, U.K.: Cambridge University Press, 1998); Philip Traft, *The AF of L in the Time of Gompers* (New York: Harper, 1957).

American Legion

The American Legion is the largest organization of VETERANS in the United States. Founded in Paris in 1919 by veterans of WORLD WAR I, it held its first convention in St. Louis that same year. The American Legion dedicated itself to fighting for the social and political interests of veterans and promoting Americanism and American interests.

One of several veterans' organizations formed in the aftermath of World War I, the legion's founders hoped to build on the sense of community that troops had shared in the war. The creation of the legion was aided by the makeup of the AMERICAN EXPEDITIONARY FORCE (AEF). Many Americans of impoverished backgrounds failed the physicals required to join the military. Others unrepresented were immigrants who had not become citizens and therefore were not required to register for the draft. The American forces were, therefore, predominately of middle- and lower-middle-class men of northern European ancestry. This dynamic gave the veterans a sense of shared community that they hoped to continue after the war. They also wanted to continue the patriotic crusade for democracy they had began in Europe. The founders of the legion established it for two purposes. The first purpose was to take care of wounded veterans. The second purpose was to promote patriotism at home.

In the 1920s, when LOBBYING AND INTEREST GROUPS were on the rise, the American Legion became the most powerful lobby for veterans' issues, national defense, and anti-radical legislation. Responding to pressure from members, it lobbied the federal government for a payment to World War I veterans. They argued that the veterans had sacrificed earnings by joining the war effort and that the government should pay them for their lost earnings. In 1924 the legion and other veterans' advocates succeeded when Congress passed a bonus bill that granted them future payments. The American Legion also focused on fighting radicalism. Many legionnaires saw communism as a threat to Americanism and fought against radicalism in a variety of ways. In their first years, some legion groups physically attacked people whom they saw as dangerous to America. Although the legion was not clear as to what constituted Americanism, it knew what radicalism was and organized to fight it. Communists, socialists, labor leaders, and the American Civil Liberties Union, for example, all fell into the group of radicals as defined by legion leaders. By the mid-twenties, the legion realized that violence in pursuit of Americanism was counter-productive and turned to legislative lobbying to further its aims. The legion was the most active group fighting radicalism in America.

Members kept watch and publicized their beliefs about what was endangering American society. They also enjoyed access to elected officials who introduced legislation that allowed the legion to shape legislative debates. The legion network of state organizations was used to publicize an issue that it deemed important. In this role, the American Legion became an influential force in American politics.

Further reading: William Pencak, *For God and Country: The American Legion, 1919–1941* (Boston: Northeastern University Press, 1989).

— Michael Hartman

American Plan

After WORLD WAR I, conservative businessmen renewed their opposition to the rights of workers to organize collectively. Faced with massive strikes during and after the war, they turned to new methods to put an end to the work stoppages. At a 1919 meeting on industrial relations, John D. Rockefeller, Jr., newly inspired by Canadian MacKenzie King, suggested a more conciliatory approach to deal with labor. Those attending resisted compromise with the labor movement. Instead, over the next year, organized employers created a plan to roll back the wartime gains of the labor movement. Dubbed the American Plan, prominent industrialists and small business owners encouraged others to refuse to negotiate with labor unions. They launched a public relations campaign to persuade public opinion that closed union shops and labor unions themselves were "un-American."

Recently founded employer organizations in more than 240 cities in some 44 states sponsored the new campaign to promote and maintain the OPEN SHOP. Other aspects of the American Plan called for a comprehensive program of political lobbying, economic campaigns, and efforts to break unions by seeking labor injunctions, blacklisting union employees, and organizing private guard associations. Arguing that American democracy required workers to have freedom of contract, groups such as the National Association of Manufacturers, local chambers of commerce, and employer groups in cities such as Minneapolis, Detroit, Seattle, San Francisco, and Toledo, refused to sign union contracts. They also worked through city and state governments to break local union power. They sponsored political tickets at the local level, bought newspaper ads and even newspapers, denied credit to or boycotted small firms that held union contracts, and lobbied local, state, and federal governments to outlaw certain union practices.

The problem with the American Plan was that both large and small firms faced high labor turnover. Employers needed to maintain a stable labor force and to retain their skilled workers in particular. Under the rubric of WELFARE CAPITALISM, corporate heads put together programs of worker incentives, primarily directed at long-term skilled male employees. The companies provided pensions, stock options, public health nurses, and industrial social work departments. They sponsored company sports teams, picnics, and newsletters as well. Some employee representation programs served as company unions, giving workers a minimal voice in the workplace while forestalling individual grievances and labor trouble. They wanted to bar entirely outside union organizing. Using a "carrot-and-stick" approach, businesses sought to foster company loyalty among workers through a new system of rewards while discouraging them from joining unions through surveillance, blacklisting, and anti-union practices.

Further reading: Irving Bernstein, *The Lean Years: A History of the American Worker, 1920–1933* (Boston: Houghton Mifflin, 1960).

amusement parks   See recreation

Anthracite Coal Strike (1902)

The Anthracite Coal Strike was one of the largest and most significant labor disputes between 1900 and 1930. The strike, which marked the culmination of the UNITED MINE WORKERS OF AMERICA's (UMWA) attempt to organize Pennsylvania coal miners, lasted five and a half months and finally was settled by a special commission appointed by President THEODORE ROOSEVELT. Prior to the strike, there had been numerous attempts to organize the nation's anthracite coal miners. Yet, despite widespread support for organized labor among miners, these early unions proved unable to secure legally binding contracts. In 1890 miners in Pennsylvania formed the UMWA and initially had considerable success organizing the region's bituminous miners. For a variety of reasons, organizing anthracite miners proved more difficult. Anthracite mines had a greater variety of job categories, operated on a larger scale, and had greater ethnic diversity among workers. Their owners were wealthier and more vehemently anti-union.

The UMWA had, without success, tried to organize anthracite miners on several occasions. In 1897, it initiated another organizing effort and quickly succeeded in recruiting new members. Employee opposition, however, remained intense and the organizing drive came to a head. In April and May of 1902, UMWA president JOHN MITCHELL met with mine operators and railroad executives to avoid an industry-wide walkout. When they refused to grant any concessions or recognize the UMWA as a legitimate union, miners voted 57 percent to 43 percent to strike. The strike idled over 140,000 miners. As it lingered on and the nation's supply of coal dwindled, President Roosevelt intervened. He appointed an Anthracite Coal Strike Committee to resolve the differences between the union and financier J. P. Morgan, who was the target of the strike.

Roosevelt, who was establishing a reputation as a foe of business monopolies, and Ohio's Senator Marcus Hanna, who wanted to gain organized labor's support for the Republican Party, saw the 1902 strike as an opportunity to rebuke coal and railroad operators. Roosevelt ordered striking workers back into the mines while the Anthracite Coal Strike Committee gathered information about the dispute. After five months of deliberation, the committee called for a 10 percent pay increase and a reduction in the workday from 10 hours to nine. At the same time, the committee refused to force mine operators to recognize the union and allowed them to maintain an open shop. From a larger perspective, the outcome of the 1902 Anthracite Coal Strike was a break from past practices. Although the committee's ruling was far from a complete victory for the UMWA, the president's refusal to use federal government troops to break the strike or undermine the union marked a change in policy toward organized labor.

See also LABOR AND LABOR MOVEMENT; NATIONAL CIVIC FEDERATION.

Further reading: John M. Laslett, *The United Mine Workers of America: A Model of Industrial Solidarity?* (University Park: Pennsylvania State University Press, 1996).

— Robert Gordon

Antiquities Act (1906)

The Antiquities Act, which granted Congress and the president the power to preserve federal lands for historic and scientific purposes, was part of the Progressive Era effort to conserve national resources for the future. Once president, THEODORE ROOSEVELT had the power to put into practice the CONSERVATIONISM that had changed his worldview. In a comprehensive program, his administration supported the passage of legislation to preserve federal land in national parks, to reclaim land, and conserve, for future use, coal and mineral lands, oil reserves, and forests. Between 1901 and 1909, when he left office, Roosevelt had added to the nation's reserves more than a hundred and fifty million acres, augmenting the 45 million that had already been set aside in the late 19th century. His program, however, dealt with a larger legacy than soil and mineral resources. Roosevelt wanted to protect the nation's geological and historical inheritance as well.

Under his direction, in 1906, Congress passed the Antiquities Act, which granted authority to reserve fed-eral lands for the preservation of historical artifacts and provided for the protection of historic, prehistoric, and scientific sites. The act also granted the president the authority to proclaim public lands as national monuments. Such monuments include geological features, such as Devil's Tower in Wyoming, which President Roosevelt made the first national monument in 1906; archaeological sites revealing Native American cultures, such as the Gila Cliff Dwellings in New Mexico; and places of historical significance, such as Fort Pulaski, Georgia. The Antiquities Act also prohibits excavation or destruction of antiquities without permission of the federal government agency in charge of such lands and authorizes permits for archaeological investigations. In 1908, Roosevelt used the act to proclaim the more than 800,000 acres of the Grand Canyon as a natural monument, which ignored legislative expectations that monuments would be small in area. By 1909, he had created 18 national monuments in addition to the five national parks and 51 wildlife refuges he established while in office. The executive power to create national monuments did not remain uncontested. With the declaration of the Jackson Hole National Monument in Wyoming under Franklin Delano Roosevelt, the act of proclaiming national monuments engendered congressional opposition. Since its inception in 1906, the Antiquities Act has been used more than 120 times to protect the nation's historical and geological heritage in creating or expanding national monuments.

Further reading: William H. Harbaugh, *Power and Responsibility: The Life and Times of Theodore Roosevelt* (New York: Farrar, Straus, and Cudahy, 1961).

anti-Semitism

Anti-Semitism, hostility to or prejudice against Jews, has been a prevalent phenomenon throughout history. The history of the United States is no exception. Prior to the turn of the 19th century, however, American anti-Semitism was relatively mild. One of the principal reasons for its relatively moderate character was the small Jewish population. There were fewer than 3,000 Jews in the colonies on the eve of the American Revolution. The number had grown to just under a quarter of a million by 1877. At that time, Jews represented less than one-half of 1 percent of the American population. Few Americans viewed Jewish immigrants and citizens as threats to their personal or professional aspirations.

Among Jewish immigrants, there were degrees of adaptation and assimilation to American society. While some Americans commended Jews as champions of both hard work and thrift, these qualities caused a great deal of concern. Hard work and thrift often resulted in success.

Success bred a degree of jealousy and distrust. The social and economic mobility of Jewish Americans alienated others who felt threatened not only by them, but also by the modern society that they seemed to accept. For nativist Americans, Jews were not only unfairly successful in the modern environment; they also came to symbolize it. Other industrializing countries similarly viewed Jewish citizens as a symbol of the evil of the modern world.

Significant increases in the number of Jewish immigrants from eastern and southern Europe further threatened many Americans who had, just decades before, migrated from western and northern Europe. From 1880 to 1914, 16.5 million immigrants arrived in the United States. Of these, more than 1.5 million, or slightly over 10 percent, were Jewish immigrants perceived by nativist Americans as a direct threat to their own social and economic prospects. This perception helped to spawn several strands of anti-Semitism that spread across America at the turn of the century.

There were several different waves of anti-Semitism that plagued the United States in the 20th century. The first emerged in the later part of the 19th century and did not dissipate until the end of WORLD WAR I. The primary force behind this strand of anti-Semitism was fear of modernization. Attacks on Jewish immigrants came from two diffuse, yet interrelated sources. The first was from the quasi-agrarian movements of conservative Populists. After the defeat of the Populist Movement in the 1890s, some turned to anti-Semitism and developed an extremely potent attack on the Jewish "money classes." Demagogues claimed that Jews were in control of an immense international financial ring that was responsible for much of the pain and suffering that had afflicted the American farmer. They argued that the Jews had made millions of dollars off the blood and sweat of hard-working Americans, an attack that denied that the new Jewish immigrants could be naturalized as "true Americans." Conservative Populists, however, were not the only group to challenge the Jewish Americans' rights. Members of the self-identified patrician classes also rallied around an anti-Semitic ideology. They excluded Jewish men and women from their communities, schools, and organizations.

As the popular and patrician challenges to the position of Jews in American society began to wane, other rationales emerged to fill the void. During the 1920s, new forces began to drive American anti-Semitism. The KU KLUX KLAN and HENRY FORD each espoused a unique version of hatred toward the Jewish people. When the Klan of the post–Civil War era had dissipated at the end of the 1870s, its ideology, which largely focused on the problem of race in the South, died with it. When it reemerged in the 1920s, it had a new ideological foundation. The new Klan was far less concerned with suppressing southern blacks.

The Klan now championed additional attacks on immigrants, Catholics, and Jews. They viewed both Jewish and Catholic immigrants as antagonistic to traditional American values. The Klan's more inclusive form of hatred allowed it to develop a tremendous following. By the middle of the 1920s, more than 4 million men and women had pledged their allegiance to the Ku Klux Klan.

Even more influential than the Klan in this era was Henry Ford, the automobile maker. For many Americans, Ford represented, with his ingenuity and success, American society. He used this perception to champion a number of causes, especially the crusade against what Ford believed to be an international conspiracy of Jews. Ford published *The International Jew* and a number of other tracts that told of a vast international Jewish conspiracy. He also used his newspaper, *The Dearborn Independent*, to bring down the alleged conspiracy. His attacks were so relentless that Aaron Sapiro, a Jewish-American lawyer, sued Ford for attacks levied through the *Independent*. After a long court battle, the case was settled. Ford apologized for his comments not only about Sapiro but also about the Jewish community in general. As part of the settlement, he had to stop publishing the *Independent*. Ford may have apologized for his indiscretions, but he never fully repudiated his anti-Semitic stance.

Another factor in American anti-Semitism was eugenics. Eugenics was a pseudo-science that was adopted to promote white supremacy. It came to provide a framework for anti-Semitic ideology and practices. No tract was more important in developing the idea of scientific racism than Madison Grant's 1916 work, *The Passing of the Great Race*. Grant was just one of the dozens of authors of the time who argued that white Americans were being destroyed by aliens from within. These racial prophets predicted the decline of American civilization if "mongrelization" was not stopped. For Grant, non-whites were polluting the racial stock of the country. He believed that whites should increase their levels of reproduction while others, whom he believed to be less desirable, should be restricted from immigration. Eugenics attacked all non-white races, but southern and eastern European immigrants, many of them Jews, were especially targeted by these ideas. The fear and loathing of these immigrants was so acute, that immigration from southern and eastern Europe was virtually halted. Anti-immigration legislation such as the QUOTA ACT (1921) and the NATIONAL ORIGINS ACT (1924) helped stem the immigration by using quotas.

Anti-Semitism in the United States began slowly but developed many institutional and political expressions during the Progressive Era. For many Americans, Jews and modernity were synonymous; for others, Jewish immigrants, especially those from eastern and southern Europe, represented backward cultures and social degeneracy as well as greed and avarice. It was not until after World War II that anti-Semitism began to dissipate.

See also IMMIGRATION; IMMIGRATION ACT OF 1917; LEO FRANK CASE; RACE AND RACIAL CONFLICT; RELIGION.

Further reading: Leonard Dinnerstein, *Anti-Semitism in America* (New York: Oxford University Press, 1994); David Gerber, *Anti-Semitism in American History* (Urbana: University of Illinois Press, 1986).

— Steve Freund

anti-suffragists

Once the WOMAN SUFFRAGE cause was reinvigorated in the 1890s, so too was its opposition, the anti-suffragists. While suffragists argued that the vote would allow women to spread their influence and clean up society, their opponents maintained that suffragists endangered society by abandoning the home. Anti-suffrage men and women were persuaded by arguments that, in a culture in which sex roles were defined and separate, the vote threatened femininity and, by extension, society. It would be unnatural, anti-suffragists argued, for women to behave like men by entering politics. Women were believed to be mentally unfit for politics, for they might be corrupted by the rough and tumble masculine world. Other anti-suffragists put forth more overtly self-interested arguments against female suffrage. Political machines and saloon owners, for instance, feared that women's supposed innate moralism would undermine the political, economic, and social status quo just as women's reform efforts jeopardized their livelihoods.

Ironically, some anti-suffragists tried connecting the woman suffrage movement to "un-American" groups, or immigrants, in an attempt to discredit it. Many suffragists, however, made their argument for the vote on the grounds that the votes of middle-class native-born white women would outweigh the votes of "undesirable" elements that already voted. Women would support reform of the corruption and vice associated with urban immigrant life in the eyes of "old stock" Americans. Despite the growing appeal of the suffrage cause, anti-suffragists argued that woman suffrage in the end would have little impact. Pointing to states where women already had the right to vote, they maintained that women did not vote as a bloc and therefore did not bring a distinctive voice to political issues. They also contended that women were not that interested in gaining the vote.

Although anti-suffragist arguments resonated with many voters, anti-suffragism never became as potent a political movement as suffrage. Anti-suffragists, however, did organize to create some effective roadblocks to women's right to vote. In 1911, the National Association Opposed to Woman Suffrage (NAOWS) was founded by

a group of state anti-suffrage organizations. Josephine Dodge was its president. NAOWS helped defeat suffrage referenda in a number of states, including, most notably, Massachusetts. Many NAOWS members were clubwomen who believed that female suffrage diverted women's energies away from women's community-based reform work. Many historians agree that woman suffrage did diminish the single-sex networks and the reform that they spearheaded. NAOWS disbanded after the passage of the Nineteenth Amendment.

Further reading: Susan Marshall, *Splintered Sisterhood: Gender and Class in the Campaign against Woman Suffrage* (Madison: University of Wisconsin Press, 1997).

— Natalie Atkin

architecture

In the first decades of the 20th century, architecture in the United States reacted to changes produced by the industrialization and urbanization of American society. New building materials, modern conceptions of public and private space, and innovative building functions combined to foster a movement away from classical architecture, with its emphasis on rules and reliance on Greek and Roman styles, toward a modern style defined by individualism and a rejection of historical forms. As the period of transition between the two styles, the years between 1900 and 1930 witnessed an eclectic array of architectural styles and forms.

At the turn of the century, in the renaissance of American architecture, architects designed public buildings of America in the classical styles. The embrace of the classical styles was a reaction to the growing size and diversity of the cities. Architects hoped to create an urban environment that countered urban disorder. Their first efforts were on display at the 1893 World Columbian Exposition in Chicago, where the architects designed the buildings in the classical style. They believed that the buildings built for the exposition, although temporary, demonstrated the effect that classical architecture could have in elevating the spirit of the American people by making connections with Greece and Rome, the great republics of the past. Architects manipulated the classical principles in their designs. Classic architecture had, by this time, been codified and published in handbooks. During the building boom at the turn of the century, it was often difficult for architects to spend time designing every facet of a building. They could, however, use the rules set down in classical architecture as a short cut. Coming at a time of great urban growth and an explosion in office buildings, libraries, railroad stations, and government buildings, classical architecture grew to define city public spaces.

Another architectural development to emerge from the 1893 Columbian Exposition was city planning. The streets of the fair had been rationally designed and laid out. Architects designed city plans in an attempt to impose order on the haphazard growth of cities. Most plans relied on radial streets between important nodes of a city such as rail stations, ports, and civic centers. The goal was to create a healthier urban environment by separating the various functions of a city. The city planning movement did not succeed, principally due to the private character of urban growth.

Concurrent with the efforts of some architects to impose classical order on the new urban environment, others embraced new building types and materials in their designs. In the early 20th century, the skyscraper emerged to define the growth and power of American cities. As city populations exploded and land prices skyrocketed, real estate developers wanted to erect ever-taller buildings, but until the 20th century they were constrained by technology. A complex interaction of technological developments made the erection of skyscrapers possible. The first development was steel-frame construction. Prior to steel frames, buildings were constructed entirely of masonry, which limited the height of buildings to 16 stories, because the walls carried the weight of the materials. The new steel-frame construction dispersed the load of the roof and the walls throughout the frame, making it possible to build skyscrapers. The other technological developments that made skyscrapers possible were fireproofing for steel columns, ELECTRICITY, elevators, and telephones. Electric power made it possible for elevators to run farther and more smoothly, making trips to the top of tall buildings practical. The telephone enabled communication between floors.

The first architects to design skyscrapers simply adopted classical principles and applied them to the different heights of the buildings. They remained wedded to the three-part design of the classical style. The first architect who broke from the reliance on classical principles in building design was Louis Sullivan. Sullivan believed that the design of a skyscraper should be based on a building's structural form and its place in modern life. Moreover, he argued that architects should express their individuality more in their designs. Sullivan rose to prominence in the first decade of the 20th century and helped bring a change to American architecture. Architects had first designed skyscrapers with elaborate bases, columns, and cornices, designs that hid the function of the building beneath a classical façade. Sullivan believed that the design of a skyscraper should embrace its function and form. He therefore simplified the design, letting the sheer enormity of the building speak for itself.

The new industrial economy required an enormous number of factories. Because of their functions, factories were designed rationally. One of the key developments in factory design was the use of reinforced concrete. This new material met the fundamental requirements of factory design. It was cheap and standardized. It provided clear lighting, ventilation, and unobstructed, flexible interiors that allowed for changes in production facilities. Albert Kahn was the best-known architect working with reinforced concrete. He worked closely with HENRY FORD in designing the automobile factories that made Ford's assembly lines practical.

Some radical architects reacted strongly to the industrial age. One of the first architectural styles to express this reaction was the Arts and Crafts style. Architects of the Arts and Crafts movement used natural materials in designing houses that fit into their settings. The use of natural material and irregular lines emerged as a critique of both classical architecture and the Industrial Age. Arts and Crafts designs critiqued the rationality and artificiality of industrial construction and idealized the preindustrial order. They also rejected the rules of classical architecture that emphasized order and attempted to rise above a building's location.

The architect credited with doing the most to move architecture from the classical style to the modern was FRANK LLOYD WRIGHT. Wright worked in Sullivan's office until 1893, when he opened his own practice. Influenced by the Arts and Crafts movement, he believed that an architect should design buildings that fit naturally into their space and reflect the individuality of the architect. Where classical designs sought to overcome their setting, Wright's designs embraced the American setting, whether it was a property shaped by the grid of the streets or one defined by streams. His long, horizontal rooflines and open spaces reflected wide-open spaces of the Midwest. Wright also accepted the changes that the machine age had brought to American society and used modern materials in his buildings. In rejecting classical principles in favor of his own designs, Wright was the first American architect to create a truly unique style. Other architects followed him in both his reliance on individuality and in adopting his design principles.

Despite the attempts by architects such as Wright and Sullivan to depart from classical design styles, American architecture never fully rejected classical designs before 1930. In fact, classical architecture enjoyed a resurgence during WORLD WAR I. The growth of the federal government during the war created a demand for large office buildings in Washington, D.C. The war effort required that these buildings be erected quickly. Architects turned, therefore, to the familiar rules of classical architecture.

By 1930, the seeds for the emergence of modern architecture had been planted. In reacting to the industrial age, architects had begun to design buildings that embraced new materials and no longer sought to hide the functions of buildings behind classical facades. In addition, the divergence from classical architecture led to the reliance on individual styles that came to define modern architecture.

Further reading: William J. Curtis, *Modern Architecture since 1900,* 2nd ed. (Englewood Cliffs, N.J.: Prentice Hall, 1987); David P. Handlin, *American Architecture* (London: Thames and Hudson, 1985).

— Michael Hartman

Armory Show (1913)

The International Exhibition of Modern Art, popularly titled the Armory Show, was an enormous art exhibition held in New York City, from February 17 to March 15, 1913. The exhibition, housed in the New York Guards Sixty-ninth Regiment Armory, consisted of an estimated 1,600 works of art. The show was a critical turning point for art, exposing the American public to early modernist art and providing an opportunity for modern works to be purchased by collectors. The Armory Show made an impression on the public and initiated many American collectors, whose support was essential, to modern art. Many of their acquisitions were built out of the Armory Show and became part of many major art museum collections.

The idea for the show itself came from a group of American artists who were frustrated with the restricted exhibitions of the National Academy of Design. They wanted to establish a more open market for exhibitions and create more patronage opportunities. What the Armory Show revealed was the division in American taste. Conservatives disapproved of the show, claiming it as un-American. They associated it with the anxiety many Americans felt at the rapid change of their society under the pressure of immigration.

The Armory Show consisted of American and European-themed sections, exhibiting various mediums of painting, decorative arts, sculpture, watercolors, prints, and drawings. Gallery space was divided into 18 rooms, with the American rooms assigned to the large entry hall and additional rooms flanking each side of the building American artists included John Marin, Childe Hassam, J. Alden Weir, Margaret Hoard, and Edith Dimock. European sections were primarily housed in the central area of the gallery, showing works by Francisco de Goya, Ferdinand Delacroix, Gustave Courbet, the Impressionists, and leading contemporary artists such as Marcel Duchamp and Vassily Kandinsky. It was the European section that generated the most public interest and became the focus of controversy. There was a good deal of criticism and ridicule, particularly directed at Marcel Duchamp's *Nude Descending a Staircase,* but there were also many positive reviews.

In the spring of 1913, the show traveled from New York to Chicago and Boston, creating an enormous impact. It was estimated that over a quarter of a million visitors paid to see it. The Armory Show created a climate more favorable to experimentation and had a profound effect on many young American artists. Important patrons and collectors such as Louise Arensberg, Arthur J. Eddy, and Lillie P. Bliss made their first purchases of modern art from that exhibited at the Armory Show.

The Armory Show was a major event in American art history. It had a tremendous impact on artists, collectors, and the art market. The show balanced American and European standards of reference in progressive art, shaking the rigid structure of the art market. There was an increase in museum attendance, and more art books were published and purchased. Modern art was now publicly accepted with more confidence.

See also ART; ASHCAN SCHOOL; MODERNISM.

Further reading: Milton W. Brown, *The Story of the Armory Show* (New York: Abbeville Press, 1988); Abraham A. Davidson, *Early American Modernist Painting, 1910–1935* (New York: Harper & Row, 1981).

— Marcia M. Farah

art

At the beginning of the 20th century, art was undergoing a process of transformation. Traditionally, art was expected to serve as a civilizing and inspirational force, a carryover from the Victorian ideals of the previous century. A new generation, however, struggled to redefine the role of art. Many artists were impatient with the standardized, approved academic form and struggled to be recognized as American artists, rather than artists in America. These artists worked against cultural norms of the time.

American high culture valued art that exhibited the traditional ideals of discipline and restraint, not artistic individualism and freedom. American neoclassical artists Kenyon Cox and Abbott Handerson Thayer worked within these traditional academic forms. In order to avoid overt personal expression, they used the standard models of art: smooth-painted surfaces, detailed execution, crisp outlines reminiscent of the French-derived neoclassical art. Drawing on images and symbols of the past, Cox and Thayer portrayed order and harmony. They believed in the civilizing power of art, creating work that was academic, mythical, and standard in form. ARCHITECTURE of the time also followed neoclassical standards. Many monuments, sculptures, and murals were executed for public buildings during this period.

Society portraitists used their subject matter to focus on the private experience and personal gesture, rather than the classical imagery and controlled style of neoclassical art. In illustrating the domestic world of refinement, portraitists chose romantic idealism over honesty or duty toward the public world. John Singer Sargent's work embodied the English and German tradition of society portraiture. Other artists such as Cecilia Beaux, John White Alexander, and Charles Hawthorne took their cues from Sargent, composing a world of refined elegance distanced from the harsh reality of contemporary life. As artists, they were "safe" in a technique removed from actual experience. Thomas Eakins, a painter from Philadelphia, along with his pupil Thomas Anshutz, began to illustrate the change from romantic idealism to realistic and more contemporary life portraits. Eakins's portrait, *The Thinker: Portrait of Louis N. Kenton,* combined thoughtful pensiveness with native realism, illustrating the ambivalence of an individual contemplating an uncertain future. In a similar style, Anshutz's portrait, *A Rose,* reflected the upper-class world at the turn of the century. It portrayed a reflective, confident woman, something modern America would confront in the near future. Anshutz's work laid the foundation for the urban realists who would later emerge in New York under the leadership of his pupil Robert Henri.

Henri was a realist painter who observed the activity around him. Unlike his predecessors, his scenes were almost exclusively urban. He also changed the focus and function of art. He believed that art must be a record of daily life with no glossing over its harsher aspects. The academic, mythological scenes of the past had no part in his art. The motion and activity of the urban streets were where Henri's perspective lay.

Exhibition opportunities for American artists were controlled almost exclusively by two New York-based institutions—the Society of American Artists and the National Academy of Design. When the two organizations merged in 1906, the jury's exclusion of works by several of Henri's friends, and two of his own works, provoked a controversy. Henri, a man who believed that art must reflect the spirit of the time and nation, became so frustrated by the lack of artistic vision, that he and his colleague John Sloan arranged for their work to be exhibited at the MacBeth Galleries. In February 1908, "The Eight" opened the Exhibition of Paintings. Known as the ASHCAN SCHOOL of artists, this group had enough experience as journalists to know how to market themselves and promoted their ideas of independence and freedom along with a distinctly American point of view.

In an attempt to address the lack of exhibition opportunities and patronage that artists were facing, Robert Henri and his colleagues organized the 1910 Independents Show. It had only limited success, because of its stipulation that any artists applying to the show were not allowed to submit paintings to the National Academy that year. The group then began discussing the possibility of exhibiting a more ambitious show of American art. In January 1912, a group of 25 artists formed the Association of American Painters and Sculptors. The relatively conservative J. Alden Weir was selected as president. Unable to find an exhibition site after a year and faced with the resignation of Weir as president, the group persuaded Arthur B. Davies to take over. Davies satisfied both conservative and realist factions. He sought to break from the well-established American aesthetic provincialism and successfully pushed for the association to include European art in its exhibition.

The International Exhibition of Modern Art opened its doors on February 17, 1913, at the armory of the New York Guards Sixty-ninth Regiment. Popularly known as the ARMORY SHOW, the exhibition originated out of artists' concerns over the lack of exhibition opportunities and patronage that American artists faced. The impact of the show was incredible, closing the gap between American and European standards of reference. The reaction of the press elevated the show to a position of prominence by labeling its unconventional inclusions MODERNISM. Thus, a foundation for modern art was established, giving it at a stature more equal to that enjoyed by European art.

Other traditional artistic forms of the past were giving way to artistic expression, and they reflected the rapid impact that industrialization had on American culture. Artists began to draw on their experiences and in ways that were seen in the American urban landscape—where the power of American modernity opened up. Artists used the city to express what it meant to be American. Symbols of progress and futurity were the urban architecture of skyscrapers, electric streetcars, automobiles, elevated trains, and subways.

One of the first artists to use this urban landscape style was Alfred Stieglitz, through the medium of photography. Other artists also turned their attention to the urban landscape. Childe Hassam used New York street scenes, skyscrapers, and bridges to achieve the idea of mood and nature, and artists like Jonas Lie responded to the powerful force of American urban life. He painted a scene of industrial steamers at work on the river, their billowing clouds of steam serving as a metaphor for American prosperity and power. John Sloan's painting *Sunday, Women Drying Their Hair* used scenes from the lives of working-class women, revealing his understanding of their freedom. In his painting, they appeared unconfined by the more rigid codes of conduct and behavior expected of middle-class women.

Other urban scenes reflected the growing forces of American social reform, where artists used their art as a tool for social change. Abastenia St. Leger believed artists had a duty to be responsible to others, and her 1913 sculpture of a young woman being auctioned into prostitution was reproduced on the cover of *The Survey* magazine. By the 1920s, artists were engaged with questions concerning issues such as WOMAN SUFFRAGE, BIRTH CONTROL, racism, Freudian analysis, and SOCIALISM.

Forum magazine sponsored the Forum Exhibition of Advanced American Painters in order to advance the public's understanding of abstract art. The realists also sponsored an exhibition at the Grand Central Palace in New York on April 10, 1917, to encourage the country's enthusiasm for American art and the realist agenda. Unfortunately, public attention centered around a dispute over whether or not the organizers would accept Marcel Duchamp's controversial *Fountain* into what was supposed to be an unjuried exhibition. Another reason for the failure of the show was that four days before it was scheduled to open, America declared war on Germany.

The wartime prosperity and the proliferation of new technology and machines allowed Americans to raise industry into a national religion. Communication transformed public life. Domestic machines converted American society into what was thought to be a more efficient, hygienic, mechanized environment. The impact of machines was so pervasive that many people referred to it as the machine age. Businessmen and engineers became the predominant icons of the era.

Technology associated with the United States penetrated the American consciousness in the 1920s. Precisionism was the American version of the "call to order" that swept Europe after the war. Initially labeled cubist, precisionism gave geometric lines to architectural and machinist subjects and expressed stability and permanence. Charles Demuth and Preston Dickinson were two artists who focused on exploring abstract arrangements of flat, uncomplicated shapes without giving up recognition.

The United States became more isolationist in the twenties, reflecting a period of contradiction and excess. Opulence found expression in art through decoration and adornment. The discovery of King Tutankhamen's tomb brought the popularity of Egyptian art to the United States. The carefully organized patterns of Art Deco built upon the popularity of technology and Egyptian art, mixing the ancient with the modern. Artists Florine Stettheimer and Paul Manship expressed the deco movement with their highly ornamented and stylized motifs. This movement drew from earlier, more orderly and tranquil times, while incorporating materials and inventions of the modern world.

Discussions about identifying what was uniquely American became more commonplace, spreading along with the nationalist fervor in the 1920s. Americans wanted to identify what was uniquely American. Stuart Davis was an artist who combined modernism with his vision of contemporary America. He condensed contemporary American culture through collage-like painted images, incorporating themes of jazz, radio, movies, consumer products, and ADVERTISING.

Davis restrained the idea of three-dimensional space and provided visual movement by adding dots, stripes, dashes, and grids. His street scenes also controlled dimension, but they portrayed a particular place. Davis's work illustrated the fascination art had for the visual expressions in advertising.

Themes of art shifted along with American demographics, going from the rural to the urban. American scene painters believed that realism was an attitude toward life and humanity. Edward Hopper's work focused on melancholy and isolation, derived from his sense of a loss of values and an abandoned way of life. He identified with an American past that had been rendered obsolete and transformed it into universal and timeless commentary on the human condition.

The search for American identity also was evident in the HARLEM RENAISSANCE, which began with the migration of a new generation of African-American artists to Harlem. It had as its consequence, an attempt to cultivate racial tolerance by promoting the cultural accomplishments of African Americans. Concentrations of African Americans in cities provided a new sense of self-determination and opportunity. The incorporation of African art

El Capitan in the Yosemite Valley, by Ansel Adams *(Library of Congress)*

and so-called primitive culture integrated modernism with international themes.

American abstract art flourished in the 1920s. Those interested in pursuing art outside the realism genre were encouraged by new galleries and patrons that emerged after the 1913 Armory Show. Alfred Stieglitz ran one of those galleries. In 1925 he opened an exhibition called the "Seven Americans," and nine months later he opened the "Intimate Galleries." His intent was to support the work of American artists committed to the creation of a national culture, and he considered the focal point of that culture to be the land. These artists viewed mechanization as psychologically damaging and saw nature as a means for spiritual wholeness.

Artists such as Arthur Dove, Georgia O'Keeffe, John Marin, and Oscar Bluemner created organic shapes, drawing out nature to its essential quality in order to translate its mystical essence into powerful abstract forms. The transcendental connection is apparent in Dove's work. He had a complex personal style that worked with nature and modern movement in his painting. O'Keeffe's geometrically inspired botanical themes represented expressive, luxuriant visions of nature. Marin saw the architecture in nature very much like the architecture of urban areas, referring to the pushing and pulling of natural forces. Bluemner reduced landscape motifs to bold color planes, seeing color as a "visible creative force."

Artistic debates over which type best represented American national identity continued. But on October 29, 1929, the stock market collapsed, and along with it went the sense of prosperity that Americans had been experiencing. President Franklin Delano Roosevelt's most urgent duty was to find relief and promote recovery of the nation's economy. Art and its institutions continued to change in response to the growing economic crisis and the political message of the New Deal.

Further reading: Abraham A. Davidson, *Early American Modernist Painting, 1910–1935* (New York: Harper and Row, 1981); Henry Geldzahler, *American Painting in the Twentieth Century* (New York: Metropolitan Museum of Art, 1965); Barbara Haskell, *The American Century: Art and Culture, New York, 1900–1930* (New York: Norton, 1999); Barbara Rose, *American Painting: The Twentieth Century* (New York: Rizzoli International Publications, 1986).

— Marcia M. Farah

Ashcan school

The Aschan school is a term that came to define a group of promising young artists in the early 20th century. They chose to paint from what they could see in their world. The bustling life of New York City provided a wealth of subject matter. A critic who did not appreciate their choice of subject—alleys, tenements, and slum dwellings—coined the term Ashcan school. The motivation behind the artistic group was to bring art and life together in an American version of realism and naturalism.

No group of artists better defines the movement than "The Eight" of the Ashcan movement. The original Eight was composed of Robert Henri, the leader, John Sloan, Arthur Davies, Ernest Lawson, Maurice Predergast, Everett Shinn, William Glackens, and George Luks. Other promising artists of the era, such as George Bellows, were considered to be part of the group. Each of the artists had his own take on life in the city. Luks, Sloan, Glackens, and Shinn were newspaper illustrators and cartoonists.

Robert Henri taught at the Art Students League and other schools in New York City. He championed exhibitions, but he did not grade art. Henri promoted the idea that art was in the eye of the beholder. He summed up his personal philosophy and the movement's when he told his art classes to "forget about art and paint pictures of what interests you about life." For these artists, the strain and struggle of urban life was what fascinated them. They were known to create "art for art's sake." They broke from conventional notions that art could be viewed broken down and dissected to determine its worth. The artists of the Ashcan school defined art within the context of life. Henri noted that "the object isn't to make art, it's to be in that wonderful state which makes art inevitable." These artists wanted to experience life; through life, they would be able to produce art.

The Ashcan school began to disintegrate as it gained notoriety. In 1908 the Eight exhibited their work at the Macbeth Gallery. They soon earned a dubious reputation as the apostles of ugliness. The ugliness was not a comment on their abilities as artists; it was an attack on their subject matter. This form of creativity began to attract a sizable following. Within a short time after the showing, the group was incorporated into a larger, more diverse group. Edward Hopper, Glenn Coleman, Eugene Higgins, and Jerome Myers were other prominent members of the emerging Ashcan school. Later on they sponsored the ARMORY SHOW of 1913, which exhibited many new European painters as well.

This Ashcan school helped form the base from which 20th-century American painting developed. In the process, these New Yorkers created an American style of art that would profoundly rebel against the tradition of European artistic interpretations. It was, as Henri had hoped, art for art's sake.

See also ART.

Further reading: Ira Glackens, *William Glackens and The Eight: The Artists Who Freed American Art* (New York: Horizon Books, 1957).

— Steve Freund

automobile industry

The emergence of the automobile industry in the early 20th century had a dramatic impact on American society. Perhaps no other technological invention has so fundamentally altered the way ordinary Americans lived. Important innovations in the production of automobiles took place between 1860 and 1890, but it was the introduction of MASS PRODUCTION and widespread automobile ownership between 1900 and 1930 that had the greatest impact. Prior to 1900, automobiles were handcrafted one by one. These early automobiles were unreliable and very expensive. The early automobile industry was centered in the region around Detroit, Michigan and Toledo, Ohio, in part because that was where the bicycle industry was located. Early automobiles incorporated much of the technology used in the bicycle industry and employed the industry's skilled machinists. By 1900, dozens of small automobile manufacturers were springing up in Detroit. Many of these early manufacturers, including HENRY FORD, built automobiles only after they had received an individual order.

Automobiles began to be mass produced in the first decade of the 20th century. The introduction of precision-made, interchangeable parts and assembly-line labor between 1900 and 1910 allowed manufacturers to increase production. From the beginning, demand for the automobile was widespread. In 1900, Americans owned 2,500 automobiles, and by 1910 the number had jumped to over 450,000. Automobile manufacturers attempted to meet this demand through mass production. First attempted by Ransom E. Olds, it wasn't until Henry Ford introduced the

Row of completed "Tin Lizzies," or Model Ts, come off the Ford assembly line *(Hulton/Archive)*

Model T Ford in 1908 that a reliable automobile became affordable for the average citizen. The no-frills Model T came in only one color (black) and cost a modest $850. Its popularity was phenomenal. Between 1908 and 1927, the Ford Motor Company sold 15 million Model Ts. The key to Ford's success was his ability to automate virtually every aspect of the automobile's construction and to continually find quicker and more efficient methods of production. With the opening of the Highland Park plant in 1910, Ford was able to reduce the time it took to produce an automobile from 728 minutes to 93 minutes. The more cars Ford produced, the cheaper they became, and the more he sold. Ford dominated the auto industry between 1910 and 1920. Sales of Ford automobiles doubled nearly every year, from 13,840 in 1909 to 189,088 by 1913.

Although Ford quickly emerged as the dominant automobile manufacturer, he had many competitors. In 1908, the year Ford introduced the Model T, there were over 50 manufacturers. That same year William C. Durant formed the General Motors Cooperation (GM). Unlike Ford who was obsessed with creating a utilitarian automobile, Durant dreamed of controlling the industry and creating expensive luxury cars. Between 1908 and 1910, he bought out 11 competing automakers, including Cadillac, Buick, Oldsmobile, and Pontiac, but his spending spree left General Motors virtually bankrupt. The fortunes of the company changed when Alfred P. Sloan took control in 1923. Under his direction, General Motors attempted to increase sales and market share by making its automobiles stylish. The company hired artists and designers and sold cars in many different makes, models, and colors. As automobile ownership became more common, consumers placed increased importance on style and design. As competition over sales increased, other innovations took place as well. These included safety features and larger and more powerful engines. Sloan hoped that by constantly changing model styles and colors and introducing new features, consumers would buy new cars more frequently. They would want to buy the latest model and gadget. By 1930, GM was introducing new models every year. Ford, however, steadfastly refused to follow suit. When Ford refused to offer the Model T in any other color than black and resisted other design changes, GM was able to dramatically increase its share of the market. By 1930, it had become the largest automobile manufacturer in the country. GM, Ford, and the Chrysler Corporation (formed in 1925) had become large and powerful enough that they were able to produce higher quality automobiles at lower prices than their competitors. One by one, medium-sized car manufacturers were either forced out of business or bought out by the Big Three automakers.

The emergence of the auto industry had an important impact on labor-management relations. The industry's growth meant that hundreds of thousands of workers were now employed by the auto manufacturers, parts suppliers, repair shops, and other related industries. When Ford's Highland Park plant opened in 1910, it housed more than 3,000 employees under one roof, a staggering number especially considering that in 1903 the company had no more than several dozen employees. By 1917, the Highland Park workforce had increased to 36,000. The pace and nature of autowork changed as well. These changes included the introduction of conveyor belts, the assembly line, and interchangeable parts. Prior to these changes, skilled craftsmen and their assistants typically manufactured one automobile at a time. Using principles of SCIENTIFIC MANAGEMENT, the production process was broken down into isolated stages. Precision machines produced interchangeable parts, which were brought to workers on conveyor belts, where they performed routine tasks of assembly hundreds of times a day. Many skilled machinists who helped the auto industry get off the ground found the new assembly line production repetitive and tedious and began looking for work elsewhere. The turnover rate at Ford in 1914 was more than 300 percent, despite a $5-a-day wage. The pace of assembly line production also changed the nature of work in other industries. Foremen were hired to push the pace of work. The 1917 opening of Ford's River Rouge plant marked the culmination of the changing nature of work in the auto industry. Built on one thousand acres, the Rouge plant was itself a model of the new industrial workplace. The plant had its own railroad and power supply, and it was almost completely self-sufficient. These changes in the nature of work took place over the course of many decades, but the emergence of the auto industry made them widespread and permanent.

The expansion of the auto industry caused other important changes in American society. Prior to 1900, the nation was still predominantly rural and agricultural. In 1920, for the first time, the Census revealed that more than 50 percent of the population lived in urban areas. The large number of workers employed in the auto industry and the mobility created by automobile ownership helped facilitate the growth of urban America. By 1929, there were 26.7 million registered automobiles. In response, federal and state governments built hundreds of new highways. Federal initiatives included the Federal Aid Road Act of 1916 and the Federal Highway Act of 1921. As the ownership of automobiles became more common and thousands of miles of new roads were built, Americans enjoyed a newfound freedom to go places where they had never been and to travel on their own schedule. People used the automobile to get to work, the grocery store, the city, the country, and to visit people and places that would otherwise have been difficult to see. The nation fell in love with its automobiles and would never be the same again.

Further reading: Robert Asher and Ronald Edsford, eds., *Autowork* (Albany, N.Y.: State University of New York Press, 1995).

— Robert Gordon

aviation

Attempts to attain flight date back hundreds of years; but by the turn of the 20th century, the concentrated efforts of inventors both in the United States and worldwide made the first flight only a matter of time. Two American mechanics, Orville and Wilbur Wright, became the first men to put a plane in flight. On December 17, 1903, the WRIGHT BROTHERS managed to send aloft a 120-foot plane for 12 seconds at Kitty Hawk, North Carolina. Before this, people had flown only in balloons and gliders. The first person to fly as a passenger was Leon Delagrange, who rode with a French pilot traveling from a meadow in 1908. The Wrights' passenger, Charles Furnas, was the first American airline passenger at Kitty Hawk. From these beginnings, aviation would come to revolutionize communications and transportation in both the civilian and military sectors, making airmail and air freight regular components of daily life and airline service a principal means of transportation by mid-century.

In the 1910s, aviation struggled along, and the few flights occurring always created news. Most people were afraid to ride. When WORLD WAR I began, however, the military value of aircraft was quickly recognized. The production of airplanes was increased. Elementary planes were first employed for battlefield observation in Europe, and only later were they used for aerial bombardment and air combat. Improvements, especially in the development of more powerful motors, enabled aircraft to reach 130 miles per hour, more than twice the speed of prewar planes. More power made larger aircraft possible. American pilots were among the first Americans involved in the European war and formed the Lafayette Escadrille of the French air service. General WILLIAM MITCHELL was instrumental in expanding the military use of airplanes, and in 1918 he proposed the first airborne assault.

Civilian aviation continued to develop during the war. By 1917, the United States government decided to try the transport of mail by air. The first regular service between Chicago and Cleveland began on May 15, 1919. Airplanes were not able to fly at night, and so they handed off the mail to trains at the end of the day. Regardless of this obstacle, the Post Office was able to save 22 hours off mail delivery from one coast to the other by utilizing planes. In 1921, the army first implemented beacons on the route from Columbus to Dayton, Ohio, which made night flight possible. The system was soon to be expanded.

The decade of the 1920s witnessed the beginning of commercial airline service, airmail, and air freight. In 1925, Congress passed the KELLY AIR MAIL ACT, which established contracts with commercial airlines for the delivery of U.S. mail by air. By the mid-1920s, the Post Office mail fleet was flying 2.5 million miles and delivering 14 million letters annually. The Kelly Air Mail Act was the first step toward the creation of a private U.S. airline industry. Five companies—National Air Transport, Varney Airlines, Western Air Express, Colonial Air Transport, and Robertson Aircraft Corporation—won the first contracts. The Post Office had always used the private sector to move the mail, so it was in keeping with that tradition that private air carriers contracted to deliver mail. Awarding of contracts also spurred the development of several additional airlines. Once the Kelly Air Mail Act was passed, the private carriers who were doing air transport for the United States Post Office expanded into carrying other forms of cargo, and eventually passengers.

The same year Congress passed the Kelly Air Mail Act, President CALVIN COOLIDGE formed a board to recommend a national aviation policy. Dwight Morrow, the future father-in-law of CHARLES LINDBERGH and senior partner of J. P. Morgan, headed the board. The report advised that the government set standards for the air industry and left the military out of the equation.

The Air Commerce Act of 1926 provided for federal regulation of air traffic rules. The legislation authorized the secretary of commerce to designate air routes, develop air navigation systems, license pilots and aircraft, and investigate accidents. Congress also amended the Kelly Air Mail Act by simplifying the payment system. It changed the basis of payment from percentage of postage to weight hauled.

Once airlines addressed flight safety issues, passenger volume increased and new airlines opened up, thereby reducing air fares. This reduction, in turn, increased traffic. Airlines were fully in favor of the passage of the Air Commerce Act of 1926, as with it they had government support in realizing the commercial potential of the air industry.

A landmark event took place in 1927 when airmail pilot Charles Lindbergh flew the first solo transatlantic flight from New York to Paris. Called "the Lone Eagle," he landed his plane, *The Spirit of St Louis,* at Le Bourget after a flight of 33 hours and 30 minutes. As a new national hero, Lindbergh became one of the nation's new experts in aviation.

The expansion of air freight and passenger services increased demand for planes. In 1927, the Ford Motor Company geared up production for aircraft manufacturing. Ford first produced the Ford Trimotor, or Tin Goose. It was one of the first all-metal planes made of duraluminus, a material as light as aluminum but twice as strong. It also was the first plane designed for passenger conveyance. It had 12 seats and room for a stewardess, the first of whom were nurses, to serve meals and assist airsick passengers.

By 1930, there were 43 airlines flying 385,000 passengers a year over routes of 30,000 miles. In 1930, Postmaster General Walter Brown pushed for legislation known as the Watres Act, which allowed the Post Office to enter into long-term contracts for airmail with rates to be based on space or volume rather than weight. Immediately after the bill was passed, Brown held a little-advertised meeting to distribute new contracts. This was called the "Spoils Conference," as only a handful of the larger airlines were invited. Two years later, Brown's actions drew public criticism.

Airlines complaining about the "Spoils Conference" demanded an inquiry into the awarding of contracts. Congressional hearings finally were held in 1934, and the scandal caused President Franklin Delano Roosevelt to turn over the delivery of mail to the army. Chaos ensued as weather turned bad, and pilots, unfamiliar with routes, caused accidents. The plan was quickly overturned as publicity forced Roosevelt's hand. The Air Mail Act of 1934 returned airmail transportation to the private sector, but it added a number of restrictions to increase competition. Aviation continued to develop as a major aspect of communication and transportation in the period.

Further reading: Roger Bilstein, *Flight in America: From the Wrights to the Astronauts*, 2nd ed. (Baltimore: Johns Hopkins University Press, 1994); Tim Brady, ed., *American Aviation Experience: A History* (Carbondale: Southern Illinois University Press, 2000); Tom D. Crouch, *A Dream of Wings: America and the Airplane, 1875–1905* (New York: Norton, 1981).

— Annamarie Edelen

B

Barton, Clara   See Volume V

Baruch, Bernard Mannes (1870–1965)

Presidential adviser and financier Bernard M. Baruch is best known as a proponent of cooperation between business and government. Born August 19, 1870, in Camden, South Carolina, he was the second of four sons of Isabelle Wolfe, the daughter of a plantation owner, and Simon Baruch, a medical doctor who served in the Confederate Army during the Civil War. In 1881, the family moved to New York City. After graduating from the College of the City of New York, Baruch pursued a career at a brokerage house and bought a seat on the New York Stock Exchange. At age 33, Baruch left the brokerage house to invest and quickly made his own fortune. He married Anne Griffen and had three children.

Baruch was active in Democratic Party politics and campaigned for WOODROW WILSON. Baruch became one of Wilson's most trusted advisers. During WORLD WAR I, Baruch accepted an appointment to the advisory commission of the Council on National Defense. In 1918, he became chair of the WAR INDUSTRIES BOARD. Once he joined the wartime government, Baruch sold his holdings and bought millions of dollars in Liberty Bonds to support the war effort. After the war, he accompanied President Wilson at the treaty negotiations at Versailles and framed the economic provisions of the treaty. Baruch also became an adviser to the Harding and Hoover administrations and joined the Brain Trust of Franklin D. Roosevelt's administration. Some of the most innovative creations of the first New Deal, such as the Agricultural Adjustment Administration, were modeled on the private-public cooperation of Baruch's War Industries Board. Foresighted, Baruch anticipated the coming of the Second World War and advised Roosevelt to stockpile essential stores of rubber and tin. As special adviser for the defense effort, Baruch wrote the federal government's report on postwar reconversion of industry in 1943.

After World War II, Baruch continued to advocate United States involvement in the world. President Truman appointed him head of the United Nations Atomic Energy Commission, where Baruch advocated international control of atomic energy. He remained a presidential adviser to the end of his life, although his primary interest in the postwar period was philanthropy. He was a major contributor to Columbia University. He died on June 20, 1965.

Further reading: Jordan A. Schwartz, *The Speculator: Bernard M. Baruch in Washington, 1917–1965* (Chapel Hill: University of North Carolina Press, 1981).

baseball

Baseball in its modern form took shape between the years 1900 and 1930. During this time, baseball became America's most popular sport because it appealed to Americans of all backgrounds and classes. Baseball supporters proclaimed that the baseball player was the model citizen, because as a team member he subordinated his self to the good of the team. As an individual, he had to make instant judgments on the field. During the time of mass emigration from abroad, proponents of baseball held it up as a tool for integrating all American citizens. At the same time, baseball offered the industrial nation a connection to its rural past. Due to its place in the American psyche, baseball gained widespread popularity, not only among spectators watching professional games, but also in the spread of baseball throughout American institutions and geography.

By 1890 professional baseball leagues had formed as a profit-driven business, in place of the amateur gentleman leagues that had defined the sport previously. The National League, the first formed, functioned as a cartel that controlled the expansion of teams into new cities through charters, the movement of players through the reserve clause, and by unofficially suppressing player salaries. Inserted in every player's contract, the reserve clause gave the team the

Babe Ruth (*Library of Congress*)

exclusive rights to a player unless it traded him or sold him to another team. The National League faced a new challenge to its control around the turn of the century. In 1894, a rival league, the Western League, formed; and by 1901 it renamed itself the American League and claimed status as a major league. The two leagues settled in 1903 by establishing a national commission to rule major league baseball. The new league consisted of eight National League teams and four American League teams.

The decades after the settlement creating the National Commission saw the coming of age of professional baseball as an embodiment of the American character. Baseball emerged in this way for a variety of reasons. First, organized baseball undertook an effort to identify baseball as a uniquely American sport. In 1907, the league set up a commission to study the origins of baseball. Ignoring ample evidence that baseball derived from the British game of rounders, the commission found that Abner Doubleday had created baseball in 1839 in Cooperstown, New York. This history gave baseball its mythical standing as a uniquely American game. In addition to the owners' efforts, the players themselves provided the heroes who brought the public into the parks. Players in the Major

Leagues came from every ethnic background, except African American. Fans could thus identify with players of their own ethnic background. The type of play on the field also led to an increase in popularity. In the first two decades of the 20th century, managers and players employed strategies that became known as scientific baseball. Scientific baseball revolved around strategies for scoring one run at a time. Home runs became scarce as hitters rarely took full swings. This new style of play became popular at a time when craft production was declining. At the ball park, fans could go to a game and watch their favorite players plying their craft.

The game's new popularity was evident in the twofold increase in attendance between 1900 and 1910. The owners responded to the new crowds by building new stadiums. Between 1909 and 1923, 15 teams built new concrete and steel ball parks, which attested to the permanency of baseball as an American institution. These ball parks became civic monuments and symbols of a city's standing as a major metropolitan area. The parks also provided retreats from city life for city residents. For the price of a ticket, one could escape the dirt and noise of the city and enter a nonurban setting of green grass that made a connection to the rural past.

Baseball's popularity took a brief slide in the late 1910s as a result of World War I and the 1919 "Black Sox" scandal. Because they had suffered financially during the war, team owners suppressed player salaries after the war, when the major leaguers returned. In the 1919 World Series, eight Chicago White Sox players accepted bribes in return for purposely losing the series to the Cincinnati Reds. The ensuing scandal darkened baseball in the eyes of many of its fans. It also led to the creation of the office of commissioner of baseball, which replaced the old three-person commission that had ruled baseball since 1901. One of the first actions taken by the new commissioner, Judge Kenesaw Mountain Landis, was to ban the eight White Sox, including the legendary player Shoeless Joe Jackson, from baseball for life.

The 1919 scandal caused only a momentary setback in the game's popularity. Its recovery was due to the play of one man, Babe Ruth. Ruth almost singlehandedly ended the scientific baseball era. In his second season as a full-time player, he hit more home runs than all other American League teams combined. Players throughout baseball quickly adapted Ruth's technique of taking a full swing, and run-scoring soared in the 1920s. In addition to his abilities on the field, Ruth became a larger-than-life figure who endorsed countless consumer products. Ruth, who grew up in a Baltimore orphanage and became the most recognizable figure in American sports, appealed to Americans because he represented what many Americans believed to be their own potential.

Americans did not satisfy their appetite for baseball solely as spectators of professional baseball. Baseball teams popped up throughout America. Towns, companies, colleges, military bases, naval ships, Indian schools, and prisons all had baseball teams. In addition, African Americans, who were not allowed on major league teams after 1890, formed their own teams and leagues. After the turn of the century, women also began to form softball teams, both on college campuses and in town and industrial leagues. Baseball was the first sport to spread through college campuses. Employers established baseball teams. They hoped that participation in the healthy leisure activity of baseball would make workers content and less prone to striking. To stock their teams, companies often resorted to hiring workers solely for their baseball ability. Towns of any size also had their own teams. These teams were made up of local players who played teams from other nearby towns. They also often paid a player or two on their roster so that they could win. In fact, some major league baseball players played for local teams on their off-days to earn extra money. By the 1910s, each military base in America had at least one team, and naval captains organized teams and were issued uniforms and equipment as part of their supplies.

The perceived and widely agreed upon beneficial effects of playing baseball led to its use by institutions like federal Indian schools and prisons. Reformers argued that baseball and team sports in general helped build character. The Indian schools aimed at turning their charges into Americans and hoped to use baseball as one of their tools. The rise of baseball coincided with changes in prison organization and baseball became a key component of the new prison reforms that had turned to rehabilitation.

Baseball reflected another part of the American character—racism. Major league baseball barred African Americans beginning in the 1890s. Company teams were segregated by race. African Americans played on some college teams, but those teams often had to cancel games because opponents refused to play against African-American players. African Americans formed their own town teams and semi-pro teams, and many companies formed teams segregated by race. In the 1920s, a group of African-American teams formed the Negro National League, consisting of six teams that played a league schedule and barnstormed to fill out their schedules. The Negro National League teetered on the brink of extinction throughout the 1920s because it relied on the poorest segment of American society for its attendance. It folded in the 1930s.

See also SPORTS.

Further reading: Benjamin G. Rader, *Baseball: A History of America's Game* (Urbana: University of Illinois Press, 1992); Harold Seymour, *Baseball: The Golden Age* (New York: Oxford University Press, 1971); ———. *Baseball: The People's Game* (New York: Oxford University Press, 1991).

— Michael Hartman

Bethune, Mary McLeod   See Volume VIII

Big Stick diplomacy

President THEODORE ROOSEVELT believed it would be necessary for the United States to use its military power to protect American interests, and in 1902 he told Congress that the United States needed to "speak softly and carry a big stick." The president believed that the United States needed an activist foreign policy to serve as a "civilizing" influence for "backward" or "uncivilized" nations, namely: To preserve order and stability in the world, Anglo-Saxon industrial nations had to intervene in the affairs of nonwhite, Latin, or Slavic economically underdeveloped nations. A crucial element for Roosevelt in the new American expansionism was the development of U.S. sea power, which enabled the nation to exert its influence beyond its borders. Under his leadership, the American navy expanded to a size and strength that only Great Britain exceeded. Roosevelt, a "Rough Rider" who had led troops in Cuba in the Spanish-American War of 1898, symbolized the new expansionist role of the United States in the world.

Roosevelt's policies were best illustrated by relations between the United States and Latin America and the Caribbean. According to historian Walter LaFeber, the United States intervened in the Caribbean at least 20 times between 1898 and 1920. In the aftermath of the Spanish-American War, the United States took control of Cuba as a protectorate. In his annual message in 1898, President William McKinley insisted that the American military would control the island until a "stable government" was built. To ensure stability, Congress passed the Platt Amendment, which gave the United States the right to intervene on the island if the Cuban government failed to protect its own independence. The United States granted independence to Cuba only after the new government agreed to U.S. oversight in 1902. When a rebellion threatened the stability of the island in 1906, President Roosevelt sent troops to Cuba; and they stayed there for three years. Between 1912 and 1917, the United States sent Marines to occupy Cuba when American interests were threatened by social unrest.

American military dominance in the Western Hemisphere was symbolized dramatically by the U.S. occupation of the PANAMA CANAL zone. After the United States military backed a revolution in Colombian Panama in 1903, the

A cartoon satirizing President Theodore Roosevelt's foreign policy motto of "Speak softly and carry a big stick."   *(Hulton/Archive)*

new government granted the United States control over the canal zone for 100 years, with an option to renew. The Panama Canal opened in 1914; three years afterward Roosevelt proudly announced, "I took the Canal Zone and let Congress debate!"

In 1909 the administration of WILLIAM HOWARD TAFT sent troops to Nicaragua in support of revolutionaries who were on the verge of toppling the government. The troops seized the customs houses. When peace returned to Nicaragua, the Taft administration lobbied for American bankers to provide substantial loans to the new government, which increased American economic influence over the country.

Under the administration of WOODROW WILSON, the United States set up a military government in the Dominican Republic in 1916 after the Dominicans rejected a treaty that would have made the country a protectorate of the United States. The United States had seized control of the finances of the Dominican Republic in 1905. American troops stayed in the Dominican Republic from 1916 to 1924. In addition, the Wilson administration sent marines to Haiti in 1915 to suppress a revolution. Americans wrote

a new constitution for the country in 1918. United States troops remained in the country until 1934.

The Wilson administration meddled in affairs in Mexico as well. In 1910 Porfirio Díaz, a dictator friendly to American business interests, was overthrown, leading to a series of revolutions. In 1913, a reactionary general, Victoriano Huerta, overthrew the new regime. When Wilson became president in the United States, he refused to recognize Huerta's administration, which he considered a "government of butchers." In 1914 American forces seized the Mexican port of Veracruz. When the troops that Wilson had ordered to land in Veracruz fought the Mexican army, 19 American soldiers died and 126 Mexicans were killed. In turn, the military presence of the United States helped the insurgents led by Venustiano Carranza. When the revolutionaries took over the government, Carranza rejected American proposals for a new government. In 1915, the Wilson administration backed Pancho Villa, who led the opposition to Carranza, but the American administration withdrew its support when it appeared that Villa was a losing cause. In 1915 Wilson gave preliminary recognition to the Carranza government.

In 1916, Villa retaliated by taking 16 Americans from a train in Mexico and shooting them. A few months later his troops crossed into the United States at Columbus, New Mexico, killing 17 Americans. Wilson responded by sending an expeditionary force into Mexico, in what became known as the MEXICAN INVASION, to track down Villa. Rather than finding Villa, the American troops fought with the Carranza army, in which engagements 40 Mexicans and 12 Americans died. On the verge of war, the Wilson administration withdrew the American troops from Mexico. After four years of futile efforts, the United States formally recognized the Carranza government.

The intervention of the United States in Mexico cost quite a few lives but produced few gains for American interests. However, the willingness of the United States to intervene in Latin America signified its increased power and influence in the Western Hemisphere in the early 20th century.

See also FOREIGN POLICY; GREAT WHITE FLEET; MEXICAN REVOLUTION; ROOSEVELT COROLLARY.

Further reading: David Healy, *Drive to Hegemony: The United States in the Caribbean, 1898–1917* (Madison: University of Wisconsin Press, 1988); Lester E. Langley, *The Banana Wars: An Inner History of American Empire, 1900–1934* (Chicago: Dorsey Press, 1985).

— Glen Bessemer

birth control

The years between 1900 and 1930 saw the growth of a social movement to promote birth control. It addressed issues such as censorship laws, lack of public education and knowledge on sexual matters, the ban on the sale, distribution, and advertising of birth control devices such as the condom and diaphragm, and women's health. Under the banner of "voluntary motherhood," birth control advocates had, since the 19th century, advocated the use of abstinence or various folk methods of birth control, including calculating women's monthly cycle in the rhythm method and coitus interruptus, or early withdrawal, as the primary means to prevent pregnancy. They argued that limiting births improved the quality of marriage and family life, extended the time devoted to educating children, and allowed women to become better mothers.

At the turn of the century, a new generation of birth control advocates emerged on the scene. Influenced by European sexual theorists, such as HAVELOCK ELLIS, and the availability of the improved spring-loaded vaginal diaphragm, leaders such as MARGARET SANGER and anarchist EMMA GOLDMAN organized public rallies and campaigns. They sought to educate women about their options for limiting fertility. Arguing that a high birth rate both restricted women's lives and endangered their health, they sought to distribute new information and new means of birth control in their role as community nurses and organizers. The rates of death in childbirth and from illegal abortion and poor maternal health among the working classes presented radical birth control advocates with compelling reasons to make the means of limiting fertility generally available. In this radical phase of the birth control movement, limiting births was linked to the struggle against poverty. Sanger's first publication, embracing both class-based and feminist radicalism, was called *The Woman Rebel.* Being on the radical edge took its toll. With her sister, Ethel Bryne, Sanger opened the first birth control clinic in the United States in Brooklyn, New York, in 1916. They provided advice to nearly 500 women before the police closed its doors 10 days after it opened. For her violation of the New York law forbidding distribution of birth control information, Sanger received a 30-day jail sentence. The decision of the court in her case, however, convinced her that the only way to obtain court endorsement for birth control was to rely on doctor-staffed clinics. In 1917, she founded the more moderate sounding *Birth Control Review* as a forum for her views and made connections with the medical community.

In contrast, feminist sex radicals saw doctors' control, traditional methods of abstinence, and male-controlled means of birth control like condoms as restrictions on women's freedom. Sexual emancipation would come from women's ability to control their own bodies and accept motherhood on a voluntary basis. Double standards of marital and nonmarital sexual behavior too often kept women from achieving individual sexual freedom, which many considered essential to women's equality. Mary Ware Dennett, Sanger's chief rival for the leadership of the birth control movement, founded her own Voluntary Parenthood League. Working for the repeal of federal laws on birth control, Dennett took exception to Sanger's new tendency to give doctors control over access to contraceptives.

A major obstacle to the distribution of birth control pamphlets and devices such as the diaphragm were the regulations prohibiting the circulation of lewd, obscene, or immoral materials through the U.S. mail. Under the Comstock Act of 1873 sex education radicals had been charged with obscenity for such minor infractions as advocating male abstinence. Sanger's *Woman Rebel* was refused mailing privileges, although it contained no specific information about birth control. With the 1914 publication of her pamphlet, *Family Limitation,* Sanger became the target of Comstock prosecution, and she fled the country. Others were arrested and brought to trial under the Comstock laws and local ordinances pertaining to public speeches and published tracts advocating fertility limitation and methods of contraception.

Some conservative groups supported the control of fertility for different reasons and with distinctly different methods. They argued that limiting the fertility of the poor would improve the general character of the population and openly advocated policies to cleanse the population of "degenerate" traits. They preferred medical sterilization to birth control methods. Sterilizing poor women who had too many children or family members who had serious physical or mental health problems (including signs of lower intelligence and the supposedly inherited trait of criminality) became accepted practice in some public hospitals and social work agencies. Linked together with the new science of eugenics, sterilization programs signaled the new willingness of state and local governments to intervene in private lives, especially in PUBLIC HEALTH matters.

The medical profession played a role in distributing birth control and in research on fertility control. Socially conservative and jealous of their professional authority, many doctors opposed the social movement to limit births. Others argued that medical experts should control access to and treatment of patients using birth control. After her public trial, Sanger began to turn toward the medical profession as the only possible way to allow women access to birth control. She compromised on the democratic call for easily available means of birth control in public clinics and agreed, instead, to regulations that gave doctors the power to offer or restrict birth control to women patients. Doctors also began to conduct their own research, and in 1925, Dr. Robert Litou Dickinson founded the Committee on Maternal Health to further fertility research.

The use of contraception increased over the decades of the birth control movement. Women simply had greater access to birth control devices through a proliferating number of organizations and clinics. In 1917, Sanger helped to organize the National Birth Control League, which became the American Birth Control League in 1921. The league established more than 50 clinics in 23 cities by the end of the decade. Access, however, depended on income and region. In a 1925 study, more than 80 percent of middle-class married women, aged 25 to 29, used contraception; only 36 percent of poorer women did. Sanger's Birth Control League became the Planned Parenthood Federation of America in 1942. Under that name, it continued to expand its services until, in 1961, it became an international organization under the name Planned Parenthood–World Population.

Further reading: Linda Gordon, *Women's Body, Women's Right: A Social History of Birth Control* (New York: Grossman, 1976); David Kennedy, *Birth Control in America: The Career of Margaret Sanger* (New Haven: Yale University Press, 1970).

Birth of a Nation

Birth of a Nation was among the first full-length feature films produced in the United States. The movie, released in 1915, was longer and more expensive than any of its American predecessors. Prior to *Birth*'s release, few producers had attempted films of such breadth and depth. American movies were typically short and inexpensive productions. Most were viewed as novelties. Few actually tried to convey stories of substance. In contrast to other early productions, *Birth of a Nation* attempted not only to tell a story but also to convey feelings and emotions. Civil War and Reconstruction, were epic subjects, but DAVID WARK GRIFFITH did more than try to tell a story of the war and its aftermath. He tried to bring out the nationalist feelings of his day.

The movie was more expensive to produce than anything that had come before it. The screenplay, which was only a fraction of the overall expense, cost Griffith $2,500 and 25 percent of the profit. The total cost of production was estimated at approximately $110,000, five times more than had been spent on any previous film. Having run out of money and investors, Griffith borrowed all that he could to bring the production to market. The undertaking was truly monumental compared to other projects of the time. There were six weeks of rehearsals. The shooting that began in July stretched into October. Editing alone took three months in contrast to the six weeks it took for a typical production.

Griffith's gamble paid off. The movie was a tremendously lucrative undertaking. It is estimated that in the first six months of its national run, *Birth of a Nation* drew more people than the performances of all the stage plays in the United States during any five-year period. In the United States the movie ran for 44 consecutive weeks. It grossed an estimated $50 million. Not all of its viewers, however, gave the movie glowing reviews. Audiences in a number of cities were so appalled by its content that they rioted.

The movie was primarily based on Thomas Dixon's book and play, *The Clansman.* Griffith also borrowed from Dixon's *The Leopard's Spots* and a number of other sources. Dixon's racist works, and the movie that followed, offered a slanted perspective on the Civil War, heavily colored by Griffith's own Southern point of view. The film vilified Northerners and blacks. It portrayed Reconstruction as an attempt by Northerners to punish the South by forcing black rule upon it. It idealized the KU KLUX KLAN. It portrayed the Klan as a just and necessary organization instrumental in saving not only the South but also the chastity and sanctity of Southern women. The movie was based on Dixon's favorite premise, that blacks are naturally inferior and that expecting them to govern themselves was cruel and inhumane.

Even before the film was released, Griffith was not oblivious to the controversy that the movie would likely create. Aware of the possible reaction, he cut some of the more offensive scenes from the movie. He removed one scene denouncing the hypocrisy of New England abolitionists, who were portrayed as the descendants of slave traders. He also omitted reference to a letter from Abraham Lincoln to Secretary of War Stanton about Lincoln's belief that blacks were inferior to white people. These compromises proved to be inadequate. Controversy followed the movie.

Controversy was so acute that the film was brought before the United States Senate. The possibility of official action prompted Thomas Dixon to send a cable to James E. Marine, the Democratic senator from New Jersey, warning against the dangers of censorship. Griffith himself was appalled by the response the film provoked. To challenge his critics, he wrote a pamphlet entitled, "The Rise and Fall of Free Speech in America." He defended both the movie and his right to produce movies that were not always popular in all settings.

Birth of a Nation was the first of two great epics produced by Griffith. His next epic stemmed from the criticisms leveled at *Birth.* The movie was called *Intolerance.* Griffith believed that his critics, not he, were intolerant of ideas. He used the movie as a weapon to attack those who were critical of his work. It was based on the premise that things that are good and pure are rarely tolerated. For him, *Birth of a Nation* exemplified something that was good yet soiled by intolerance. To finance *Intolerance,* Griffith spent all of his profits from *Birth of a Nation* and was forced to buy out all of its backers. Unfortunately, *Intolerance* was not a success. With the decline of liberalism, the movie, which championed brotherly love as the solution to many of the world's problems, fell out of fashion. Desperate to recoup his losses, Griffith broke the four-hour-long movie into two shorter films.

Birth of a Nation was a grand achievement in cinema. Not only was it broad in scale and scope, but it also conveyed passion and emotion. However, its message was far less spectacular. It offered a distorted view of history. Whether he knew it or not, Griffith's movie did more than redefine the way movies were made; it displayed the effect that movies could have on the culture.

Further reading: Iris Barry, *D.W. Griffith, American Film Master* (Garden City, N.Y.: Doubleday, 1965); Robert M. Henderson, *D.W. Griffith: His Life and Work* (New York: Oxford University Press, 1972).

— Steve Freund

Blatch, Harriot Eaton Stanton (1856–1940)

One of the most important suffragists of her generation, Harriot Stanton was born in 1856, the daughter of Eliza-beth Cady Stanton, the mother of the women's rights movement in the United States, and Henry B. Stanton, an abolitionist. Harriot Stanton attended Vassar College, where she eventually earned a master's degree in 1894. Throughout her life, Harriot remained close to her mother, whom she aided in the writing of *History of Woman Suffrage.*

In 1882, Harriot Stanton married Harry Blatch, a British citizen, and moved to Britain, where she became active in the suffrage campaign. It was there that Blatch witnessed the militant tactics of British suffrage activists and interacted with prominent British socialists. By the turn of the century, Harriot was dividing her time between Britain and the United States. She returned to the United States full-time in 1902, when she began campaigning for WOMAN SUFFRAGE in New York State. New York was both symbolically and politically important for Blatch and other suffragists. The movement, however, appeared to be stalling under the leadership of the NATIONAL AMERICAN WOMAN SUFFRAGE ASSOCIATION.

Harriot Blatch injected new momentum into the state and national campaigns for female suffrage. As an activist with the NATIONAL WOMEN'S TRADE UNION LEAGUE, she had gained some experience with working-class women. In 1907, she cofounded the Equality League of Self-Supporting Women, an organization dedicated to recruiting working-class women's support for suffrage. The Equality League changed its name to the Women's Political Union and later merged with the Congressional Union, which became the NATIONAL WOMAN'S PARTY in 1916. In addition to broadening the support base for female suffrage, Blatch employed dramatic tactics borrowed from British suffragists. Mass marches, including one down Fifth Avenue, as well as a trolley-car campaign through New York's towns and cities, helped publicize female suffrage and catapult it onto the national political agenda.

When her husband died in 1915, Blatch returned to Britain. She came back to the United States in 1917 and worked for the Food Administration. After the war and the successful suffrage campaign, Blatch remained active in the women's and socialist movements. As an activist with the National Woman's Party, she worked for a federal equal rights amendment. Throughout her career, Blatch wrote several books, including *Mobilizing Woman Power* (1920) and *A Woman's Point of View, Some Roads to Peace* (1920). She died in Connecticut in 1940.

Harriot Stanton Blatch's greatest contributions revolved around her intellectual and tactical innovations for the female suffrage campaigns. Adopting radical methods and broadening the class base of the movement helped raise political awareness among women themselves and among the nation's political elite, eventually leading to the passage of the Nineteenth Amendment for woman suffrage.

In addition, her intellectual work on the history of the women's movement, such as the 1922 volume she published with her brother, *Elizabeth Cady Stanton, as Revealed in Her Letters, Diary and Reminiscences,* set the stage for future women's historians not only to investigate women's history but also to trace women's historiography.

See also WOMEN'S STATUS AND RIGHTS.

Further reading: Ellen Carol DuBois, *Harriot Stanton Blatch and the Winning of Woman Suffrage* (New Haven, Conn.: Yale University Press, 1997).

— Natalie Atkin

blues

The origins of the musical genre of the blues are not well-documented, but its roots can be traced back to the African continent. Much of its foundation is in 16th-century African music. But while its roots can be traced back to Africa, the blues is not an African form of music. Its African origins were augmented by work and gospel songs, folk music, minstrel shows, and other musical forms. These influences combined to create what became a uniquely American style of music. In addition to its musical origins, there were other forces that helped to mold what is now considered the blues from its origins in the post–Civil War South.

Rural blues developed remarkably different identities in different regions. The blues that developed in the southern coastal states differed greatly from the style that developed in Texas. The blues that developed in Texas was very different from that of the Mississippi Delta. Each region had its own flavor. The southern coastal blues was noted most for its steady rhythm and clear enunciation. Blind Boy Fuller was one of the many blues singers who came to represent this unique form of entertainment. Texas blues was characterized by single-string picked arpeggios—not the strummed chords that characterized the blues of other regions. Blind Lemon Jefferson came to symbolize the Texas blues musician. The blues that developed in Mississippi became the most influential of the three forms. The slide, or bottleneck, guitar came to symbolize this blues style. Charley Patton was the earliest blues man to bring the blues style out of the Delta.

WORLD WAR I and the accompanying GREAT MIGRATION transformed the blues. These events caused tremendous demographic shifts that allowed the blues as a musical form to spread to other parts of the country. The rural undertones of the blues artists were adapted by men and women with urban experiences. They revolutionized not only the blues but also American music and culture. Atlanta, St. Louis, Memphis, Detroit, and Chicago all proved to be fertile soil for the growth and development of urban blues. Chicago was by far the most important city in the development of urban blues, and it became synonymous with them. Chicago blues stands apart from other forms in its emotional structure. Paramount Records in Chicago began producing blues recordings in the late 1920s. With a gigantic mail-order business in the South, Paramount was successful in promoting and distributing Chicago blues until it succumbed to the economic hardships of the Great Depression. Even after Paramount had closed its doors, blues musicians continued to develop music in Chicago.

The effect that the blues has had on the development of American music is incalculable. The rhythms, beats, and lyrical styling of blues spread across America and to the rest of the world. The influence that the blues has had on jazz, soul, and rhythm-and-blues is clear. Less evident, but equally true, is the effect that the blues had on rock and roll, rap, and other popular forms of entertainment. It was truly an American art form.

Further reading: Austin J. Sonnier, *A Guide to the Blues: History, Who's Who, Research Sources* (Westport, Conn.: Greenwood Press, 1994); Lawrence Cohn, *Nothing but the Blues: The Music and Musicians* (New York: Abbeville Press, 1993).

— Steve Freund

Boas, Franz Uri (1858–1942)

Anthropologist Franz Boas played a significant role in redefining race in America. He did this by moving the discussion of race away from Social Darwinism and toward an emphasis on individual cultures. By emphasizing the importance of each culture's values, Boas convinced many in the scientific community and in America in general that racial differences were due not to hereditary differences but to culture. Through his path-breaking studies of culture, Boas revolutionized the field of anthropology.

Born in 1858 in Germany, Franz Boas received his doctorate from the University of Kiel in 1881. On a scientific expedition to an island off the coast of Canada, he became interested in the local natives' culture. It sparked his lifelong dedication to the field of anthropology. Boas undertook his first anthropological work in 1886, a study of the Native Americans living in the Pacific Northwest. He later served as the curator of ethnology at the American Museum of Natural History in New York City and in 1899 became Columbia University's first professor of anthropology.

It was in his role as professor of anthropology that Boas created modern anthropology. In the late 19th century, anthropologists rarely made in-depth studies of other cultures, relying instead on theories as to why some cultures differed from European culture. Boas introduced scientific study to the field. He taught his students, among them MARGARET MEAD, Ruth Benedict, and Zora Neale Hurston, to apply scientific rigor and emphasized methodology. He popularized field studies as the chief investigation tool of anthropology. By actually living among the subjects of his studies, Boas came to the conclusion that every culture was dynamic and could change over time, if subjected to new conditions. In his 1911 *Mind of Primitive Man,* Boas deflated the belief that non-Western societies represented a primitive or earlier stage of civilization. The fact that all cultures were not equal meant only that all cultures had not experienced identical historical conditions, Boas argued. Because he believed in the equal worth of all cultures, he attacked social scientists' practice of ranking races based on the perceived superiority of northern European culture. He taught his students and other social scientists to evaluate cultures on their own merits, not to compare other cultures with their own.

Boas applied his findings on cultural differences to critique the prevailing racial attitudes in the United States. His dedication to altering America's views on race arose from a strong liberalism and his commitment to scientific accuracy and purity. Boas stridently argued that people of African ancestry were not naturally inferior to Caucasian people as most white Americans believed. Differences in achievement between the races in the United States could be explained by studying cultural differences and the historical circumstances in which cultures had developed. Boas sought to counteract the prejudices against African Americans by studying and popularizing accounts of the great African civilizations of the past to show that at one time Africans had created greater civilizations than Europeans. African Americans such as ALAIN LOCKE and W. E. B. DU BOIS were influenced by Boas's findings and used them in their struggle for equal rights. The work of Boas and his students helped undermine the grip of scientific racism on American culture and fundamentally altered ideas about race.

Further reading: Vernon J. Williams, *Rethinking Race: Franz Boas and His Contemporaries* (Lexington: University Press of Kentucky, 1996); Marshall Hyatt, *Franz Boas, Social Activist: The Dynamics of Ethnicity* (New York: Greenwood Press, 1990).

— Michael Hartman

Boxer Rebellion (1900)

A popular movement in China that tried to expel foreign powers, the Boxer Rebellion played a key role in the U.S. establishment of the OPEN DOOR POLICY in China. The Boxers were members of a secret organization in China known as the Society of Righteous and Harmonious Fists,

which Westerners nicknamed "shadow boxers," because they practiced martial arts. The Boxers opposed European influence in China. Beginning in the mid 19th century, European powers began to force their way into China. Under a series of treaties, Germany, Great Britain, France, and Russia had gained special economic rights. In these treaties, the Europeans gained benefits such as lower import taxes and the right to build railroads and construct telegraph lines. In return, they helped the Qing dynasty, ruler of China, in its struggles against Chinese who wanted to overthrow their imperial government. All of these treaties were unequal with regard to the rights granted to the Europeans and the benefits gained by China. The Chinese imperial rulers granted economic rights to European countries because the imperial government was weak relative to Europe. The Europeans living in China were not, moreover, subject to Chinese law. The European countries sent missionaries with them who traveled the country seeking converts, which led many Chinese to resent their activities.

The Chinese who took part in the Boxer Rebellion were reacting to the expansion of European influence in rural China. As European economic concerns moved away from the coastal areas, they caused economic problems for the rural Chinese. European steamship companies, for example, put local bargemen out of business. Railroads brought European businesses that undersold local craftsmen. Christianity also posed a threat to the Chinese traditional way of life. Chinese Christians no longer took part in communal celebrations that worshipped ancestors. In the eyes of some Chinese, this made Christians a threat to communal unity. Christianity and the missionaries who spread it were also suspect because they were closely tied to the European colonial powers. They became, therefore, another symbol of the inferior position that China occupied.

The Boxer Rebellion began in the rural areas of northern China. The Boxers were emboldened by their belief that bullets could not hurt them and that they could summon troops of spirit warriors to fight on their side. They targeted any one or thing that symbolized foreign rule. Thousands spread across the countryside, burning churches and killing Chinese Christians. They also tore up railroad tracks and telegraph lines. Initially, the Boxers fought for the expulsion of foreigners and the overthrow of the Qing dynasty. After the imperial government gave support to the Boxers, they changed their goal to expelling foreigners and supporting the Qing dynasty. The support of the imperial government made it possible for the Boxers to attack the foreign residents in the cities. In June 1900, Boxers besieged the foreign quarters in Beijing and Tianjin. They held 600 foreigners, including future president Herbert Hoover, and 4,000 Chinese Christians in the coastal city of Tianjin. In the capital city, Beijing, the rebels blockaded 900 Europeans and Americans in the diplomatic quarter.

The European countries sent an international force to end the sieges and rescue the Europeans. On June 14, 1900, they successfully ended the siege in Tianjin, and on August 14 they regained control of Beijing. By the end of 1900, there were 45,000 foreign troops in northern China. These troops initiated raids against the Boxers and defeated them.

The Boxer Rebellion had significant consequences for Chinese relations with the West. An agreement signed by China's Imperial government and 11 Western powers called for a number of penalties and concessions. For the first time, foreign troops were stationed in Beijing. In addition, the Western countries secured the right to build a series of forts in a line from the coast to Beijing, which would protect their supply and communication lines to the capital city. The agreement also required the Chinese government to pay a large fine. Aside from these consequences, the Boxer Rebellion led the Western powers to change their strategies in dealing with China. Before the rebellion, many Europeans had begun to favor transforming their spheres of influence into formal colonies. The anti-foreign Boxer Rebellion led them to change their minds. It convinced them that they would face tremendous opposition from the Chinese if they attempted to expand their control. The United States played an important role in these developments. In 1900, the UNITED STATES called for an open door policy in China that would give equal opportunity for trade to all nations. The European countries agreed to the U.S. proposal, and the Open Door Policy came to define the relationship between China and the Western powers.

See also FOREIGN POLICY.

Further reading: Arnold Xiangze Jiang, *The United States and China* (Chicago: University of Chicago Press, 1988); Diana Preston, *The Boxer Rebellion* (New York: Walker and Company, 2000).

— Michael Hartman

Brandeis, Louis Dembitz (1856–1941)

One of the most important lawyers and jurists of the Progressive Era, Louis Brandeis is best known for his work on extending the protection of the law to women workers with his brief in MULLER V. OREGON, and for his service on the U.S. Supreme Court. His tenure on the Court began in an age of judicial formalism and ended with the acceptance of expanded federal authority over regulation under the New Deal. Brandeis was born in 1856 in Louisville, Kentucky, the son of a wealthy grain merchant. He completed secondary education in Dresden, Germany, and returned to the United States at age 18 to study law at Harvard University. He graduated in 1877 and practiced law in Boston until 1916. In 1891, Brandeis married Alice Goldmark, the daughter of a wealthy Boston family. The couple had two daughters.

Brandeis began to pursue a career in law that earned him the name "the people's attorney." He worked to secure protective labor laws, block business monopolies, and secure benefits to workers. During this time, he defended small or minority interests against the majority, and he became a prophet of regulation with his books, *Other People's Money* (1914) and *Business: A Profession* (1914). In them, Brandeis supported workers and trade union rights. He also advocated regulation in support of small firms and as a means for maintaining democratic competition in the market. In 1912 he supported WOODROW WILSON's campaign for the presidency as one of the authors of Wilson's New Democracy campaign. Four years later, Wilson appointed Brandeis to the U.S. Supreme Court as an associate justice. He was the first American Jew to be appointed to the high court.

Brandeis's career was directed toward the preservation of individual rights and freedoms and opposition to "bigness" in business as a threat to individual liberty. In this respect, Brandeis straddled the positions of a liberalism that saw the need for legal protections and yet sought to

Louis Brandeis *(Library of Congress)*

restrain the growth of government. As he once wrote, "Experience should teach us to be most on our guard to protect liberty when the government's purposes are beneficent. Men born to freedom are naturally alert to repel invasion of their liberty by evil-minded rulers. The greatest danger to liberty lurks in insidious encroachment by men of zeal, well-meaning but without understanding."

Once on the Court, Brandeis became an ally of OLIVER WENDELL HOLMES in defining civil liberties, and especially First Amendment rights, in a series of landmark dissents from majority Court opinion. The body of this work hinged on the idea that democracy required the individual right to free speech as a necessary ingredient for social change. Without the free circulation of ideas, democracy could not hope to thrive. One of his major court opinions, *Whitney v. California,* engaged Brandeis in defining the role of ideas, education, and government in society.

Brandeis served on the Supreme Court from 1916 to 1939. In his later years, he became a leading court ally of Roosevelt's New Deal initiatives but also opposed such legislation as the National Recovery Act. In the end, however, Brandeis helped build support for the Court revolution of the 1930s. He resigned from the Supreme Court in 1939 and died on October 5, 1941, in Washington, D.C.

Further reading: Phillipa Strum, *Louis D. Brandeis: Justice for the People* (Cambridge, Mass.: Harvard University Press, 1984).

Brownsville Riot (1906)

A glaring example of racial prejudice and military injustice, the Brownsville Riot resulted in the unwarranted dismissal of 167 African-American soldiers. The riot occurred on the night of August 13, 1906, but the tensions that led to the attack had built since the troops had arrived two weeks earlier. At the core of the conflict was the opposition of the Brownsville, Texas, townspeople to the stationing of African-American troops at Fort Brown. The immediate cause was the claim made by a white woman on the night of August 12 that she had been assaulted by one of the African-American soldiers. Tensions were so high that on the night of August 13, the commander of the fort issued a curfew order requiring all soldiers to return to the fort. Later that night, soldiers were awakened by gunfire coming from outside the fort. By the time they could muster, the shooting was over. In the aftermath of the shooting, it was discovered that one man had been killed in the town.

The townspeople immediately claimed that the soldiers in the fort had rampaged through the town, shooting into houses and businesses, and murdering a man. The army convened a commission of officers and townspeople to investigate the incident. It quickly concluded that the

African-American soldiers had done all the shooting. The commission was unable, however, to say which of the soldiers had been guilty. In fact, the commission ignored evidence that the soldiers had not been guilty of the attack. Accepting the commission's report as fact, President THEODORE ROOSEVELT sought to force the innocent soldiers to turn in the guilty ones. To do so, Roosevelt threatened all three companies of soldiers with dismissal if the guilty ones were not found. None of the soldiers ever came forward. Seeing it as a conspiracy by the soldiers to cover for the guilty ones, Roosevelt dishonorably discharged 167 men and barred them from government service for life.

If not for the efforts of Senator Joseph Foraker of Ohio, the incident probably would have ended there. After reading the transcripts of the commission's hearings, Foraker came to the conclusion that the evidence used to convict the soldiers was flimsy and unreliable. Foraker pressured the Senate into holding hearings into the dismissal. In these hearings, it became clear that many of the eyewitnesses who claimed to have seen the African-American soldiers shooting could not have, due to the darkness and their distance from the events. Other evidence used against the soldiers was also disproved. Nonetheless, the Senate voted to uphold the dismissal. The soldiers had their last chance when a Military Court of Inquiry convened in 1909. The court eventually ruled to reinstate 14 of the soldiers who had been dismissed. They never did indicate why those 14 were being reinstated while the other 153 remained discharged. In 1971, after reading John Weaver's book, *The Brownsville Raid,* Representative Augustus Hawkins of California introduced a bill calling for the reinstatement of the men dishonorably discharged. The next year, the Department of Defense recognized the miscarriage of justice by granting honorable discharges to the soldiers.

See also RACE AND RACIAL CONFLICT.

Further reading: John Weaver, *The Brownsville Raid* (College Station: Texas A&M University Press, 1992).
— Michael Hartman

Bryan, William Jennings   See Volume VI

Buck's Stove (1906)

A Supreme Court decision supporting the use of labor injunctions, *Buck's Stove* was one of a series of legal cases in the Progressive Era that worked to restrain the political actions of the labor movement. After the turn of the century, the rising tide of labor militancy had provoked a strong, coordinated response from business and financial interests. They demonstrated their antipathy toward labor and collective bargaining in an array of strategies from employer associations like the NATIONAL ASSOCIATION OF MANUFACTURERS and the American Anti-Boycott Association to strikebreaking with help from local police or state militia. Another tool was to appeal to the judiciary's known conservatism. Using the Sherman Antitrust Act of 1890, large corporations and small businesses alike sought court injunctions against strikes and boycotts as illegal restraint of trade. Courts had enjoined labor unions from carrying on community-level boycotts throughout the late 19th century, but they had not interfered with "We Don't Patronize" lists in union publications. The heightened conflict between Capital and Labor allowed for little room to bargain. In two separate court cases—*Loewe v. Lawlor* (known as DANBURY HATTERS) and BUCK'S STOVE—the United States Supreme Court sided with businesses which that sought relief, first as compensation for financial losses during a boycott and secondly when a national labor organization refused to obey a court injunction.

The *Buck's Stove* case arose when the Iron Molders International Union struck Buck's Stove and Range in St. Louis. In the face of the company's refusal to bargain, the Iron Molders union declared a boycott. As part of the boycott, the AMERICAN FEDERATION OF LABOR (AFL) placed the firm on the "We Don't Patronize List" in its journal, the *American Federationist*. In 1907, the firm's owner, who belonged to an anti-union organization, asked the federal courts to issue an injunction against the AFL, citing its use of the boycott list as an unfair restraint of interstate commerce and a violation of the Sherman Act. The courts found in the firm's favor and ordered the AFL to remove Buck's Stove from the list. Rejecting the court's injunction as a violation of the rights to free speech and a free press, AFL president Samuel Gompers refused. The lower courts held that there was no right to free speech if it involved criminal activity. The federal district court found Gompers and his associates, AFL secretary Frank Morrison and UNITED MINE WORKERS OF AMERICA president JOHN MITCHELL, guilty of violating the Sherman Act and charged them with contempt of court. They fined the union leaders and sentenced them to jail terms. In the appeal, Gompers lost his case before the Supreme Court. By that time, however, the statute of limitations for contempt of court had run out. The Iron Molders Union and the company also had settled the strike. In response, the Supreme Court stayed the lower court sentencing. While union leaders were not forced to pay the fines or endure prison, the *Buck's Stove* case, like *Loewe v. Lawlor,* prompted new caution from union officers in how they used scarce time and resources. Costly court cases, whether fighting injunctions, antitrust suits, or violations of free speech, exhausted the labor movement financially and politically. At the same time, the widespread use of labor injunctions based on anti-

trust law inspired the AFL to return to the political arena. In the elections of 1908 and 1912, labor mobilized its members to vote for the parties and candidates that would address the mounting list of labor's grievances.

Further reading: Daniel Ernst, *Lawyers against Labor: From Individual Rights to Corporate Liberalism* (Urbana: University of Illinois Press, 1995).

Budget and Accounting Act (1921)

The Budget and Accounting Act of 1921 was one of the most significant legislative enactments of the early 20th century. It provided guidelines for the modern budget and a framework for funding an activist state. The act required the president to submit a single, consolidated budget proposal to the Congress each year. It also established the Bureau of the Budget to provide the president with the resources necessary to produce a budget proposal and the General Accounting Office to give Congress the resources to ensure accountability. The Budget Act did more than coordinate the budget. It gave the president greater influence over how federal monies were allocated through the formulation of budget figures and priorities.

The movement toward a budget system in which the executive branch had greater control over federal spending had been building for years. It had its roots in the PROGRESSIVISM of the early 20th century. Progressive reformers sought to rationalize government through the elimination of corruptible interests and political machines. To stem the power of the political machines and challenge government corruption, especially on the municipal level, reformers placed more trust and authority in executive and administrative institutions. In doing so, they promoted the accumulation of power at the executive level.

A number of studies attempted to rationalize the budgetary process, including one conducted by President WILLIAM HOWARD TAFT's Commission on Economy and Efficiency (1910–12). Still, the call for reform of the budgetary process did not stop with investigations. Supported by members of both parties, the creation of a regular budgetary process was a plank for the Republican presidential campaign in 1916 and 1920 and the Democratic campaign in 1920. In 1919, hearings were held in both the House and Senate to research possible changes in budgetary procedure. The legislation made it through both houses of Congress, but President WOODROW WILSON vetoed it because of concern with the constitutionality of the bill. The next president, WARREN G. HARDING, signed the Budget Act in 1921. CHARLES GATES DAWES, who had been in charge of procurement for the American army during WORLD WAR I, took over as the first budget director in that year. Dawes instituted several reforms in how government agencies kept records and accounted for revenue and expenditures. The Budget Act did more than rationalize the budgetary process. It established the foundation for the modern budget and the expansion of presidential power in the 20th century. In doing so, it helped to coordinate the modern state.

Further reading: Robert K. Murray, *The Harding Era: Warren G. Harding and His Administration* (Minneapolis: University of Minnesota Press, 1969).

— Steve Freund

Burke Act (1906)

The Burke Act of 1906, passed by Congress as an amendment to the Dawes Severalty Act of 1887, continued the federal policy of assimilation of Native Americans into white society. The policy of forced assimilation, which began with the Dawes Act, was a reversal of almost 50 years of policies regarding Native Americans. Previously, the federal government had forced indigenous peoples to relocate onto reservations in the United States.

Attempting to assimilate Native Americans, the Bureau of Indian Affairs tried to eliminate the tribal ownership of land and allot plots of land to individual owners. The Dawes Act allotted 160 acres to heads of families and 80 acres to single adults. Congress passed the Burke Act to hasten the transition to individual ownership by eliminating the 25-year trust period required under the Dawes Act. Under the trust system, individuals who were allotted land could not acquire full title to the property for 25 years. The Burke Act amended the allotment law to give the secretary of the interior the power to issue fee-simple titles, which were fees without restrictions on the transfer of ownership. The amendment removed all restrictions on the sale, taxation, and claims on property.

The assimilation policies at the turn of the century had undermined indigenous cultures in two ways. First, Indian children were removed from their families and sent to white-run boarding schools. Second, the policies prevented Indian religious rituals from taking place, and replaced them with Christian ones. But the government ultimately abandoned its assimilation policies, because the white administration of the allotment program was corrupt and inept. However, Native Americans lost much of their land in the process. Native Americans continued to resist assimilation into white society despite government efforts. Attempting to transform traditional, tribal societies into individualist, agrarian ones, Congress had hoped to hasten the forced assimilation of Native Americans with the Burke Act.

Further reading: Frederick E. Hoxie, *A Final Promise: The Campaign to Assimilate the Indians, 1880–1920* (Lin-coln: University of Nebraska Press, 1984); Francis Paul Prucha, ed., *Indian Policy in the United States: Historical Essays* (Lincoln: University of Nebraska Press, 1981).

— Glen Bessemer

business

One of the most far-reaching achievements of the turn-of-the-century United States was the rise of modern business. The reorganization of business transformed virtually every aspect of American life. Due to new forms of organization, American firms became larger and more profitable than anything that had come before them. Their growth led to fundamental changes in the American political and social structure. Americans simultaneously embraced and challenged the encroachment of capitalist enterprises in industry, finance, and transportation.

The concept of incorporation was key to the success of American business. Corporations had several distinct advantages over other forms of organization. The most basic advantage was the ability to pool small quantities of wealth from a large number of people. This allowed corporations to amass wealth that had previously been unimaginable. In addition, corporations offered investors protection against excessive liability. Unlike other forms of partnership, corporations were protected by the doctrine of limited liability. A shareholder in a corporation was committed only to the share invested in the enterprise, and individual investors could not be sued for additional damages. Incorporation made industries of scale not only possible, but also practical. Another advantage of the corporation was its perpetual life. Businesses organized around a mortal person would often fall into disarray when the person passed away. With a corporation, the shares owned by the recently deceased could easily be transferred to one's heirs. Such a transfer would have little if any impact on the life of the corporation. The corporation became so commonplace that the Supreme Court of the United States argued that it had all of the rights and responsibilities of the individual. It was an important legal and social distinction.

The modern corporation relied on new forms of structure and organization. The emergence of both vertical and horizontal methods of integration was crucial to the formation of large international businesses. Vertical integration is based on the practice of developing a corporate structure dedicated to obtaining control of supply, production, and distribution lines. Andrew Carnegie's Carnegie Steel, which later became U.S. Steel, was extremely adept in the art of vertical integration. Through a number of well-planned acquisitions, Carnegie gained control over virtually every aspect of the steel industry. It allowed him to control everything from the raw materials that were needed to produce his steel, to the marketing and distribution of the finished products. Horizontal integration, however, was even more prevalent in the emerging business climate of the late 19th century. It reflected business's pursuit of market monopoly. JOHN D. ROCKEFELLER's STANDARD OIL was especially efficient when it came to horizontal integration. His acquisitions of competitors created such a monopoly that by the turn of the century Standard Oil controlled more than 90 percent of the oil refined in the United States. Carnegie and Rockefeller may have been two of the most successful integrators of their time, but they were by no means the only ones to use these forms of consolidation. Dozens of companies used one form of integration or the other.

The assembly line was another innovation that made the emergence of businesses of scale possible. Meat packer Gustavus Swift not only benefited from the use of vertical and horizontal integration, he also utilized the assembly line that HENRY FORD later perfected. Swift's assembly line was actually more like a disassembly line. He used the mechanized line to slaughter, pack, and ship animals. The development of what became known as "the American System" was crucial in the full utilization of the assembly line process's flexibility and efficiency. Once interchangeable parts were incorporated into the assembly line process, the factory began to replace the artisan's shop. Not long after, skilled workers themselves were either replaced by assembly line workers or incorporated into the process.

In order to manage these large new organizations, new levels of managerial bureaucracy were formed. The deskilling of industrial workers created a need for a new managerial class. No longer would apprentices and skilled workers control the means of production. Professional managers came to replace foremen, skilled workers, and small shop owners in supervising labor. In an ongoing attempt to increase efficiency, managers sought to regulate all facets of the production process. Others practically relegated human workers to the status of machines. FREDERICK WINSLOW TAYLOR provided the intellectual foundation for these attempts at removing human inefficiencies from the production process. He developed and promoted the concept of SCIENTIFIC MANAGEMENT. Taylor's *The Principles of Management* outlined his concept of scientific management. Each task was broken down into its most basic components. Each worker was gauged on his or her ability to complete the basic tasks using the most efficient methods in a prescribed time. Taylor also argued for higher wages and a more rational means of compensating workers. Businesses throughout the country paid homage to Taylor's theories; but for the most part, they were unable to integrate his ideas into their organizational structure. They also resisted paying workers more. These theories did, however, fundamentally alter the way in which both business and labor were perceived.

Equally important to the development of modern businesses were new forms of internal communication. Carbon paper, the typewriter, and the adding machine were only a few of the devices that helped coordinate the internal activities of the increasingly large corporate structures. Without these aids to communication, it would have been virtually impossible for management to effectively organize businesses of scale and scope. New technologies allowed corporations to become bigger and more powerful. Alongside many of the traditional businesses grew other industries that supported business. Insurance, banking, and finance fostered and were fostered by new corporate giants.

New sales and marketing practices were other important factors that allowed for the expansion of American business in the 20th century. Without efficient modes of delivery and distribution, American corporations would have had relatively primitive means for marketing their wares. By the 20th century, the United States went from being a fragmented market, characterized by low volumes, restricted markets, and high prices, to a unified one, characterized by high volumes, a national market, and lower prices. This transformation altered not only the way that manufactures and commodities were marketed and distributed, but also had a profound impact on the life of the average American. New consumer goods made their way into urban and even rural homes. Montgomery Ward, Sears and Roebuck, and other distributors further advanced marketing in the United States by providing national mail order houses for rural customers. Products increasingly became less expensive and more readily available. As products became more readily available, ADVERTISING developed to market them to the growing consumer base. By the middle of the 1920s, the typical American had attained a standard of living that would have been incomprehensible just a half-century before.

Average Americans commercially benefited from the emergence of big business, but they did not all benefit in the same way. The managerial class and new corporate elite received the greatest benefits; as a result, American corporate leaders gained unprecedented power and influence. The ways in which a number of corporations used their influence caused a great deal of alarm. No form of business caused more concern than America's first really large business enterprise—the railroads. A number of politicians and writers voiced their concerns about the negative influence of the railroad. Perhaps no one was more successful in defining the cruelty of the omnipresent railroad than Frank Norris. His novel, *The Octopus* (1901), defined the struggle between a ruthless, all-powerful, malevolent railroad and traditional American life. According to Norris's portrayal, the Octopus, which was a metaphor for the Southern Pacific Railroad, not only destroyed the economic well-being of the typical American community, it would also eventually destroy the moral fiber of the nation if left unchecked. Norris was only one of a generation of authors and journalists, known as MUCKRAKERS, who attacked the emerging political and economic power and control of corporations.

As progressive reformers, muckraking journalists and politicians helped to usher in a political movement to limit the power of the corporation. The public reception of UPTON SINCLAIR's *The Jungle* is an example of this development. While Sinclair's book was a thinly veiled call for a socialist society, it was not received as one. Americans responded to Sinclair's novel by calling for corporate regulation. It led to the passage of the PURE FOOD AND DRUG ACT of 1906. Like the adoption of the Food and Drug Act, the Progressive movement called for new regulations to minimize the negative aspects of business without challenging its supremacy. The Sherman Antitrust Act and the CLAYTON ANTITRUST ACT were other attempts that symbolized the Progressive mission. Under trust-busting efforts such as the Northern Securities case (1904), progressive Presidents ROOSEVELT and TAFT sought to control "bad" trusts, while assisting the development of "good" trusts. In the end, the laws only united the already feeble labor movement of the era.

Regardless of how Americans perceived the rise of business, corporations and corporate power were expanding greatly by the turn of the 20th century. Businesses grew not only in size and in scope, but also became more diverse and powerful. Modern corporations changed the way in which people worked, shopped, and lived. The growth of the American economy allowed for increases in discretionary income and challenged the ways in which people had lived for generations. Business, more than any other force, revolutionized American society.

See also ECONOMY; MASS PRODUCTION; WELFARE CAPITALISM.

Further reading: Alfred D. Chandler, *The Visible Hand: The Managerial Revolution in American Businesses* (Cambridge, Mass.: Belknap Press, 1977); Glen Porter, *The Rise of Big Business, 1860–1920,* 2nd ed. (New York: Thomas Y. Crowell, 1992); Oliver Zunz, *Making America Corporate, 1870–1920* (Chicago: University of Chicago Press, 1990).

— Steve Freund

C

Cable Act (1922)

The Married Women's Independent Citizenship Act (also known as the Cable Act) granted female residents (either native-born or immigrant) who married men of a different nationality the right to U.S. citizenship either by retaining their premarital citizenship or, in the case of foreign-born women, of applying for naturalization separately. Such repatriation restored to women resident in the United States their rights as citizens; female citizens who married foreign nationals and lived abroad continued to be subject to expatriation, or loss of their American citizenship and its rights.

A natural extension of the concerns of the women's rights' movement, the Cable Act was the first step toward establishing equal nationality rights for women. Proponents of the measure included members of the Women's Joint Congressional Committee, the League of Women Voters, and the NATIONAL WOMAN'S PARTY. They argued that the Expatriation Act of 1907, which, for the first time, expatriated women who married immigrant aliens, threatened women's independent citizenship. It denied native-born women the same rights as men to marry whom they chose; it reinforced men's rights to grant citizenship to their spouses and children, while denying American women the same rights; and it allowed for the deportation of women who married non-citizens and, during WORLD WAR I, even subjected them to the loss of property, if their husbands were enemy aliens. Challenging the idea of women's dependent nationality, women's advocates endorsed the legislation authored by Representative John Cable of Ohio that gave back to women the rights of equal citizenship, even as it denied other women the same consideration. As the editors of the *Christian Science Monitor* proclaimed, the Cable Act had "freed a legion of women from an archaic law which took no cognizance of political and moral progress." At the same time, the Cable Act also retracted the right of automatic naturalization to immigrant women who married American men. Racial bars instituted under other immigration legislation had double force in excluding foreign-born women from naturalized citizenship.

While women's organizations championed the law, the Cable Act was shaped as well by campaigns to restrict immigration, which culminated in such laws as the IMMIGRATION ACT OF 1917 (or Alien Exclusion Act) and the NATIONAL ORIGINS ACT of 1924. Anti-immigration sentiment expressed in the DILLINGHAM COMMISSION's reports (1911) and in an executive branch committee on naturalization (1906) sought to restrict access to the rights of citizenship. While foreign-born women who married American men previously were eligible for the benefits and rights of citizenship by the act of marriage, native-born women who gave up their rights to marry the citizen of another country were thought devoid of moral standing. In an era of strident patriotism and Americanization efforts, many thought that women who married foreign nationals should be penalized by losing their citizenship rights. These attitudes, however, were to change. Proponents of women's independent citizenship argued that women deserved the same citizenship rights and privileges as men. Fears of the new immigration also contributed to the change in law. The ratification of the Nineteenth Amendment giving women the right to vote transformed the pro-forma naturalization of foreign-born wives into political privilege. Agitation for married women's independent citizenship, which culminated in the Cable Act, took from immigrant wives these protections. Advocates of immigration restriction argued further that foreign-born women married to American citizens should no longer be eligible for special rights or considerations and had to meet the same requirements for immigration and naturalization as men, a process made more severe by the new immigration quotas.

See also IMMIGRATION; WOMEN'S RIGHTS AND STATUS.

Further reading: Candice Lewis Bredbenner, *A Nationality of Her Own: Women, Marriage and the Law of Citizenship* (Berkeley: University of California Press, 1998).

Cannon, Joseph Gurney (1836–1926)

At the turn of the century, Joseph "Uncle Joe" Cannon was one of the most powerful and influential politicians in the country. He served as the Speaker of the House of Representatives from 1903 until 1911 and exerted almost total control over the chamber. Born in 1836 in New Garden, North Carolina, Cannon attended the Cincinnati Law School and became a member of the Indiana bar in 1858 at the age of 22. A year later, Cannon moved to Illinois and became actively involved in politics. He was elected to the House of Representatives in 1872.

A conservative Republican, Cannon established a reputation as a fiercely partisan politician. As one of the leaders of the "Old Guard" Republicans, he staunchly opposed attempts by Populists and Progressives to enact legislation aimed at limiting the power of corporations or expanding the oversight role of the federal government. Cannon became Speaker of the House in 1903 and utilized arcane congressional rules to control House committees with an iron fist. He steadfastly opposed progressive reformers in both the DEMOCRATIC and REPUBLICAN parties, including THEODORE ROOSEVELT and WOODROW WILSON, and frequently used his power over House committees to block new legislation. Exercising the Speaker's control over the Rules Committee, Cannon controlled the House in this manner between 1903 and 1910.

Cannon's authoritarian leadership led to an important split in the Republican Party that contributed to its loss of the presidency in 1912. Party progressives were frustrated by Cannon's ability to delay or block reform legislation. Under Roosevelt's leadership, important reforms such as the HEPBURN ACT (1906), the PURE FOOD AND DRUG ACT (1906), and the MEAT INSPECTION ACT (1906) were enacted, but many other reforms were defeated. Shortly after his election in 1909, progressives in the party approached President WILLIAM HOWARD TAFT about weakening Cannon's power. Taft rebuffed these overtures and began developing close ties with Cannon and the Old Guard. Frustrated by Taft's refusal to oppose Cannon, a group of moderate and progressive Republicans led by New York reformer George W. Norris joined ranks with Democrats to limit the power of the Speaker. They shifted the power to appoint members to the Rules Committee from the Speaker of the House to the House as a whole. Cannon's defeat was followed by another stinging rebuke when in 1912, after serving nearly 30 years in Congress, he failed to win reelection to his congressional seat. The split in the Republican vote in 1912 brought Democrat Woodrow Wilson to the White House. Republican progressives eventually returned to the party, and Cannon was reelected in 1914. Cannon served another six terms until his retirement in 1923, but he never again wielded the same political clout.

Further reading: Blair Bolles, *Tyrant from Illinois: Uncle Joe Cannon's Experiment with Personal Power* (New York: Norton, 1951); William Rea Gwinn, *Uncle Joe Cannon, Archfoe of Insurgency: A History of the Rise and Fall of Cannonism* (New York: Bookman Associates, 1957).
— Robert Gordon

Capper-Volstead Act (1922)

In response to worsening conditions in the rural economy, Congress passed the Capper-Volstead Act in 1922 to aid agricultural cooperatives. The agricultural depression that followed WORLD WAR I had a devastating impact on American farmers. As farm prices dropped, farm organizations once again sought relief from the economic crisis. For some farmers, nothing short of government price supports for farm commodities would do. Others wanted Congress to maintain and even raise tariffs on agricultural goods. For the American Farm Bureau and its congressional allies, however, the surest way to protect American agriculture was to protect the growing number of farm cooperatives against the power of corporate agribusiness. Specifically, the Farm Bureau wanted to exempt farm cooperatives from the Sherman Antitrust Act of 1890. Agricultural corporations had used the Sherman Act as the legal basis for court challenges to agricultural cooperatives.

In Congress, the politicians who supported farm relief and liberal agricultural subsidies came to be known as the Farm Bloc. Organized by lobbyist Gray Silver of the American Farm Bureau, the Farm Bloc was made up of 25 senators and 100 representatives pledged to aid American farmers. It included such Republican progressives as Senators HIRAM WARREN JOHNSON of California, George Norris of Nebraska, and Arthur Capper of Kansas. Seeking to bolster the farm economy, the Farm Bloc developed legislation to address the problems in agriculture. There was no clear majority for government price supports to return agricultural commodities to parity, or, more specifically, the prices that matched the 1914 economy. Instead, the Bloc opted for more modest means of improving the farmers' lot. They were able to find common ground under the administration of WARREN G. HARDING and worked with the Department of Agriculture on a legislative agenda.

The first result of the Farm Bloc's efforts was the Capper-Volstead Act. According to Senator Arthur Capper, the bill was designed "to give to the farmer the same right to bargain collectively that is already enjoyed by corporations." A solid majority of Congress passed the bill, which exempted farm cooperatives from antitrust laws in order to cooperatively produce, market, handle, and price their products. Earlier, Congress granted general antitrust protection to farm cooperatives and labor unions in the CLAYTON ANTITRUST ACT of 1914. Because the law remained vague, however, the Clayton Act was no more effective in protecting farm cooperatives from antitrust suits than it had been in protecting unions from labor injunctions. The Capper-Volstead Act specifically empowered farm cooperatives by clarifying the activities covered by the antitrust exemption and extending the protection from antitrust laws to a broad class of agricultural cooperatives. While it fell short in addressing the farm crisis, the Capper-Volstead Act signaled the sustained power of farmers' political interests and organizations at a time when the nation was becoming increasingly urban and industrial. It serves today as the major legal protection for agricultural cooperatives from antitrust prosecutions.

Further reading: Robert K. Murray, *The Harding Era: Warren G. Harding and His Administration* (Minneapolis: University of Minnesota Press, 1969); Theodore Saloutos and John Hicks, *Agricultural Discontent in the Middle West, 1900–1930* (Madison: University of Wisconsin Press, 1951).

Carnegie Endowment for International Peace

The Carnegie Endowment for International Peace was one of a group of conservative peace organizations that lobbied the government to abide by international law and build collective security as a way to keep peace and world order. Considered "political internationalists," conservative peace groups included bankers, lawyers, politicians, and academics as their members. The Carnegie Endowment was the largest of these peace organizations. The president of Columbia University, Nicholas Murray Butler, headed the organization, and James T. Shotwell, a Columbia University professor, served as director of the Endowment's Division of Economics and History. Because the Carnegie Endowment included many important leaders in government, business, and higher education, it had a significant influence on disarmament policies in the United States and Europe.

One example of the close links the endowment had to elites in government was when a former law partner of Secretary of State Kellogg left the endowment to serve as assistant secretary of state. In addition, the Carnegie Endowment funded other internationalist organizations such as the League of Nations Non-Partisan Association (LNNPA) and the Foreign Policy Association (FPA). In addition, conservative peace groups with close ties to elites

such as the Carnegie Endowment, the League of Nations Non-Partisan Association, and the National Committee on the Cause and Cure of War (NCCCW), worked for American participation in the World Court.

Overall, the Carnegie Endowment for International Peace preferred the indirect lobbying of political leaders and other elites to the direct pressure tactics used by more radical peace groups. In 1927, to use one important example, Shotwell visited the French foreign minister Aristide Briand to lobby for the United States and France to formally outlaw war. In the end, Briand utilized many of Shotwell's suggestions when he sent a draft of a treaty to Washington on June 20, 1927. When Secretary of State Frank Kellogg hesitated in responding to the Briand proposal, peace groups pressured him to accept the French pact.

Liberal peace organizations such as the National Council for the Prevention of War (NCPW) and the WOMEN'S INTERNATIONAL LEAGUE FOR PEACE AND FREEDOM (WILPF) agreed with more conservative groups about the need for a World Court and for the United States to join the League of Nations. They disagreed politically, however, about militarism and disarmament. Liberal peace groups pushed more actively for disarmament and encouraged reductions in naval appropriations. Meanwhile, the conservative groups such as the Carnegie Endowment advocated U.S. participation in the World Court, but they were less strident about naval disarmament.

The debate over the proposals of Kellogg and Briand illustrated the influence that the Carnegie Endowment for International Peace had on the foreign policies of the United States and the European countries. In the end, many liberal and conservative peace leaders cooperated to promote Briand's draft treaty in Washington. But when Secretary Kellogg proposed an alternative multilateral treaty in the place of Briand's bilateral treaty, the Carnegie Endowment eventually supported it, although reluctantly. The KELLOGG-BRIAND TREATY, which formally outlawed war, was signed by 62 nations in 1928.

Further reading: Richard W. Fanning, *Peace and Disarmament: Naval Rivalry and Arms Control, 1922–1933* (Lexington: University Press of Kentucky, 1995).

— Glen Bessemer

Catt, Carrie Lane Chapman (1859–1947)

Carrie Lane Chapman Catt, a noted woman suffragist, was born in Wisconsin in 1859. After working her way through school and teaching school, she became superintendent of schools in Mason City, Iowa. After the death of her first husband, Leo Chapman, she joined the Iowa Woman Suffrage Association, eventually becoming the organization's state organizer. In 1890, Carrie Chapman married George Catt, who encouraged her to pursue her suffrage activism.

In 1900, Catt assumed the leadership of the NATIONAL AMERICAN WOMAN SUFFRAGE ASSOCIATION (NAWSA). Under her first tenure, which lasted until 1904, she strengthened the national structure, the treasury, and the administration of the organization. In 1904, with her husband dying, she resigned to care for him. After his death, Catt worked on the suffrage campaign in New York State. Catt's suffrage activism was not only a reflection of her ideological commitment to the cause, but also the result of her relationships with progressive men, one of whom, George, willed her enough money to live on while she continued to work on the suffrage issue.

In 1915, NAWSA was in organizational shambles under Anna Howard Shaw's direction. Armed with money that a woman had willed to the cause, Catt returned to lead NAWSA with her own staff. She demanded that the organization become more centralized and hierarchical under her command. Charismatic and well-organized, Catt gained the loyalty of suffrage activists from around the country. As head of NAWSA, Catt proposed her "Winning Plan," which proposed to gain passage of a federal WOMAN SUFFRAGE amendment within six years in conjunction with state campaigns. The plan called for state suffrage associations to lobby their federal representatives to pass and their state legislators to ratify the amendment. It also used the national office to pressure the Democratic and Republican parties to include a suffrage statement in their platforms and keep the suffrage issue alive through publicity campaigns. Even though publicity was the cornerstone of NAWSA's methods, anti-suffragists regularly derided the activists. NAWSA represented the more moderate wing of the suffrage movement, a fact that contributed to its success. In stark contrast to the more radical NATIONAL WOMAN'S PARTY, NAWSA appeared genteel and more acceptable to the men in power, a key constituency that NAWSA was trying to reach.

The breakthrough for Catt and NAWSA came in New York in 1917, when women won the right to vote at the state level. The victory in the East reenergized the struggle at the national level. The House passed the federal suffrage amendment in 1918, but the Senate voted it down, causing Catt to mobilize again. The Senate finally passed the woman suffrage amendment in 1919. In August 1920, the Nineteenth Amendment giving women the right to vote was ratified by 36 states.

Although suffrage certainly preoccupied Catt, she participated in other reform efforts during the suffrage fight. She was active in the Woman's Peace Party, which attempted to pressure the belligerent countries to come to the negotiating table during WORLD WAR I. Somewhat iron-ically, Catt also served on the Women's Committee of National Defense, a government agency that coordinated women's voluntary work.

After the ratification of the Nineteenth Amendment, Catt founded the League of Women Voters and served as its honorary president through the rest of her life. She remained active in peace activism as well. Catt died in 1947 in New Rochelle, New York. Undeniably, Catt's political skills and tenacity, along with the efforts of the foot soldiers of NAWSA and other groups, contributed to the success of the suffrage campaigns at the federal and state levels.

Further reading: Robert Booth Fowler, *Carrie Catt: Feminist Politician* (Boston: Northeastern University Press, 1986).

— Natalie Atkin

Chicago race riot   See race and racial conflict

child labor

Throughout U.S. history children have worked. In pre-industrial America, children worked on family farms, as craft apprentices, and in a variety of other jobs. As large-scale manufacturing increasingly came to characterize the economy, several economic, social, and cultural changes led to the abolition and mitigation of some types of child labor. Child labor was not, however, completely abolished.

According to published statistics 18 percent of children aged 10 to 15 were employed in 1900. These figures undoubtedly understate the number of children working. Children played an important role in America's economy. They could be found working in almost any area of the economy. In the textile industry, for example, 25 percent of the workers were below the age of 15 and the ratio of children to adult workers was the highest of any industry in the United States. In the textile mills, children worked as spinners, constantly walking up and down between the spinning machines, brushing lint from the frames, watching the bobbins for breaks, and making repairs to the threads. The hot humid air that kept the thread from breaking necessitated keeping the windows closed. The atmosphere became filled with lint that the children breathed all day long. Children worked 10 to 12 hour days in such conditions and for low wages.

Children also worked long hours in America's coal mines. Children officially went to work in bituminous coal mines at the age of 12, began work as coal-breakers at age 14, and went underground at 16. These were the legally established ages, but a great many children went to work at earlier ages because enforcement of the laws was lax.

Young boys selling newspapers *(Library of Congress)*

Coal breakers sorted through the coal after it was mined, leaning over the loads of coal, breathing in coal dust all day long. Underground, the children were subject to all the dangers that made coal mining one of the most dangerous occupations. In fact, children suffered accidents at a rate three times that of adults.

Many other child laborers faced similar dangers working in the seafood canning industry, vegetable and fruit canning, the glass industry, and as newsboys, peddlers, and bootblacks. In the seafood canning industry, children as young as five years old helped shuck oysters and peel shrimp. They suffered cuts from the oyster shells and knives. In vegetable and fruit canning, children sometimes worked 80 or 90 hours per week, because the product was perishable and needed to be canned quickly. In addition, the canning industry was not regulated in any state until 1920, because it was classified as agricultural. In the glass industry, child workers were forced to stand or crouch all day, often next to a furnace heated to 2,500 degrees. Cuts

and burns were common, in addition to the dangers posed by the atmosphere filled with fumes and dust. Newsboys have taken on a mythical status in American culture as little businessmen. In reality, they worked long hours in a job that exposed them to the dangers of city streets and could be financially ruinous. The newsboys bought all the papers, so the cost of any that remained unsold at the end of the day came out of their pockets.

A number of factors combined in the early 20th century to abolish or regulate child labor. Some of these factors emerged from the reform movements of the Progressive Era while others were due to changes in the economy and technology. During this time, a new conception of childhood developed. Many reformers feared that the tremendous increases in industrialization, immigration, and urbanization threatened the future of America. Concurrently, they believed that America's children were the future of the nation and needed to be saved from the evils of industrialization.

The reformers pushed through a variety of state laws making education compulsory up to a certain age and restricting the work of children less than 16 years of age in some industries. The coverage of these laws was inconsistent. In 1912, for example, only nine states had laws prohibiting the employment of children under the age of 14 in factories, under 16 in mines, and required the eight-hour workday for children aged 14 to 16. Twenty-two states still permitted children less than 14 years old to work in factories. Thirty allowed boys under 16 years to work in mines, and 31 states permitted children under 16 years of age to work more than eight hours a day. Moreover, many laws were not enforced. In 1912, for example, 23 of the states that had age restrictions for employment required no documented proof of age.

The weakness and inconsistency of the state laws was principally due to opposition on the part of employers and working families. Many working-class families needed the paychecks of their children to survive. They would lie about their children's ages in order to get them into work. Most of the opposition came, however, from employers who claimed that child labor was good and necessary. These opponents, who were most active in states with industries dependent on child labor, resorted to a variety of arguments in opposing the laws. Working children were a blessing for working families in reducing poverty. By working at an early age, opponents of child labor laws argued, children gained valuable skills that they would use later in their work lives. Schooling was a waste for working-class children, because they could learn all they would ever need to know on the job. Child labor laws restricted the child's inherent right to work. Opponents of the child labor laws also argued that child labor was a necessity. Workers over the age of 16 were slow, clumsy, or just too big to accomplish some tasks. It took the nimble fingers of a child to accomplish some tasks. Many industrialists claimed that the very existence of many industries depended on child labor. If child labor were outlawed, manufacturers argued, they would not be able to remain competitive in the world economy and might be forced to move to another state that did not have stringent child labor laws.

The poor enforcement of state child labor laws led reformers to seek a federal child labor law. The first federal child labor bill was introduced in 1906. It sought to impose penalties for transporting across state lines goods produced by children less than 14 years of age. The bill was defeated in the House of Representatives. Opposition to the bill came from two sources. First, lawmakers repeated the arguments listed above. Second, there were congressmen who argued that it was an unlawful extension of the federal government's powers.

Child labor opponents did not rest, and by the mid-1910s, public opinion in most of the country was behind a federal child labor law. In 1915, a bill was introduced in the Congress that would, if passed, outlaw the transport of goods produced by child labor. The bill easily passed the House but never made it to a vote in the Senate, due to the opposition of southern senators whose states relied on child labor. In 1916, opponents of child labor tried again by introducing the KEATING-OWEN ACT, which easily passed both houses of Congress and became law on September 1, 1917. The law banned the employment of children under 14 in factories, workshops, and canneries, and children under 16 in mines and quarries. It also prohibited children under 16 from working more than eight hours a day and between the hours of 7 P.M. and 7 A.M. Numerically, the law barely affected child labor. It freed 150,000 children from work in mines and factories, but 1,850,000 still toiled at home, in fields, and on the streets. Proponents of the new law hoped, however, that it would serve as an example for states to pass their own child labor laws.

The role as a model for local efforts is about all the Keating-Owen Act was ever to accomplish because the Supreme Court ruled it unconstitutional in 1918 in *Hammer v. Daghart.* The case was concocted by the executive committee of the Southern Cotton Manufacturers. A circuit court judge ruled the Keating-Owen Act unconstitutional and granted a permanent injunction against enforcing the law. The Supreme Court ruled, on appeal, that the act was an unwarranted exercise of the federal government's powers and an invasion of states' rights.

Child labor law advocates were again successful in passing federal child labor law legislation in 1918, but the Supreme Court ruled the law unconstitutional in 1922. The final effort at banning child labor came in the 1922 campaign to pass a constitutional amendment outlawing child labor. The amendment passed both the House and the Senate, but it failed to win the required two-thirds majority of the states. It was to be the last effort to federally legislate child labor prior to the 1930s.

Despite the failure of federal child labor laws, the number of children working did decrease during the 1910s and 1920s. Some industries that relied on child workers made technological innovations that replaced child workers with machines. Many states passed or strengthened their child labor laws. In 1904, for example, 17 states set some sort of limit on work by children under 14, and by 1929 all states set some limits and 29 outlawed in entirely. In 1904 two states had outlawed children under 16 working more than eight hours a day. By 1929 36 states had such laws. Thus, the battle against child labor had succeeded to an extent, but it was not until the economic collapse of the Great Depression and the post–World War II affluence that economic considerations minimized the role that child labor plays in the United States economy.

Further reading: Walter Trattner, *Crusade for the Children: A History of the National Child Labor Committee and Child Labor Reform in America* (Chicago: Quadrangle Books, 1970).

— Michael Hartman

Children's Bureau

Created by a 1912 act of Congress, the United States Children's Bureau was charged "to investigate and report . . . upon all matters pertaining to the welfare of children and child life among all classes of our people." The Children's Bureau emerged from concerns of the early 20th century over the health and welfare of America's children. Social reformers feared that future generations were endangered because many children were forced to work at an early age, lived in unsanitary conditions, did not receive an education, and were malnourished. Led by LILLIAN WALD, founder of Henry Street Settlement House in New York City, and FLORENCE KELLEY, head of the National Consumer League, a group of reformers developed the idea of a federal agency that would promote the health and welfare of children. Lillian Wald recounted how, after reading about a government official investigating the damage done by the boll weevil, she wondered why the U.S. government could not have a "bureau to look after the Nation's crop of children?" She and other reformers believed that a federal agency was necessary, because the welfare of children was a nationwide concern and a federal agency could collect data on child welfare throughout the country.

Wald, Kelley, and other reformers undertook a nationwide campaign to mobilize public opinion for the Children's Bureau. In 1909 their cause was boosted significantly when President THEODORE ROOSEVELT came out in support of the idea. Between 1906 and 1912, however, 11 bills failed to make it through Congress, largely due to reservations about expanding the powers of federal government. The challenge of the PROGRESSIVE PARTY at the polls in 1912 compelled lawmakers to pass some progressive measures. The campaign finally succeeded with the passage of the act creating the Children's Bureau in 1912. President WILLIAM HOWARD TAFT signed the bill into law on April 9, 1912. Congress granted the first appropriation of $25,640 later that year. The Children's Bureau was originally in the Department of Commerce and Labor. It was transferred to the newly created Department of Labor in 1913. Julia Lathrop became the first woman to head a federal bureau when she was confirmed by the Senate as chief of the Children's Bureau.

Initially the bureau did not have any administrative power. Its purpose was to research issues that affected children. Among the issues initially suggested for investigation were infant mortality, the birth rate, juvenile delinquency, orphanages, child labor, diseases of children, and sanitation. The Children's Bureau's first big project was to attack the infant mortality problem. It did this by studying the problem and publishing advice pamphlets. The bureau distributed 30,000 copies in six months of its first pamphlet, *Prenatal Care.* Between 1914 and 1921, it distributed nearly a million and a half copies of its second pamphlet on prenatal and infant care. In addition to its efforts with the public, the Children's Bureau also lobbied lawmakers on behalf of issues pertaining to children.

The Children's Bureau assumed new responsibilities in 1921 with the passage of the Maternity and Infancy Act. Popularly known as the SHEPPARD-TOWNER ACT, this act authorized the federal government to allocate $1,200,000 each year to the states to promote health service for children, infants, and pregnant women. The Children's Bureau was made the administrator of these funds. This position established the bureau as the liaison between the states and the federal government, which increased its power over child welfare policy nationwide. Although state organizations were not under any legal control of the Children's Bureau, they acted as its subsidiaries because of its preeminence in the field of child welfare policy. The Children's Bureau's position allowed it to shape the chartering of child welfare programs in the states, including MOTHERS' PENSIONS. The leaders of the Children's Bureau favored public child welfare agencies over private. Women such as Julia Lathrop believed that social reform needed to be professionalized, and she used her position as head of the Children's Bureau to support state agencies that employed professional methods of SOCIAL WORK. Her power came from her control of the Sheppard-Towner funds.

The Children's Bureau's role diminished in the late 1920s due to fighting between it and the Public Health Service, another federal agency concerned with health and welfare issues. Congress allowed the Maternity and Infancy Act to lapse in 1929 and transferred the health and medical functions of the Children's Bureau to the Public Health Service. The Children's Bureau remained a strong advocate for children after 1930, but it never again enjoyed the power that it had in the 1920s.

See also EDUCATION; YOUTH.

Further reading: Kristie Lindenmeyer, *"A Right to Childhood": The United States Children's Bureau and Child Welfare, 1912–1946* (Urbana: University of Illinois Press, 1997).

— Michael Hartman

cities and urban life

During the early decades of the 20th century, cities came to dominate the economic, social, and cultural landscape of the United States. For the first time, in 1920, more Americans lived in urban places than rural. By 1930, 56.3 percent of Americans lived in urban places. These numbers do not, however, tell the complete story of the city's place in America. The industrial expansion of the U.S. economy took place in its cities. The cities became the site for America's cultural development and the symbol of America's progress as a great power. To migrants from rural America and abroad, the city was a beacon that offered opportunities unavailable in the communities from which they migrated. These and a variety of other factors led the explosion of cities into the mainstream of American thought and life.

The first indication of the rising importance of cities during this period was the increase in urban population. In 1900, 39.7 percent of Americans lived in urban places. By 1930, 56.3 percent of Americans called a city home. From 1900 to 1930, the U.S. population increased 61.6 percent while the urban population increased 128.8 percent. In 1900 there were 38 cities with populations over 100,000. By 1930 there were more than 75.

New York City street crowded with pedestrians (Hulton/Archive)

This explosion in population came from several sources. First, the United States experienced a rise in the birth rate and a decline in the death rate. Thus, some of the population growth in cities was due to natural increase in the population. Most of the population growth came, however, from migrating individuals. Rural birth rates were increasing at a time when the demand for farm labor was falling. Mechanization decreased the need for farm workers, and economically tough times for farmers led to a decrease in the number of farms. Many young rural Americans chose therefore to migrate to the cities. New city residents also came from the migration of African Americans from the South, especially during the GREAT MIGRATION. An unprecedented number of foreign immigrants also sought their fortunes in American cities. Between 1900 and 1920, an estimated 8,778,000 immigrants came to America to stay. The vast majority of them remained in America's cities.

The people flocked to the cities primarily because of the job opportunities. The American economy underwent incredible change at the end of the 19th century as a wave of consolidation altered American industry. Driving this consolidation was the rise of the business corporation. Corporations brought a managerial and organizational revolution to American industry that allowed a tremendous increase in the size of manufacturing plants. Huge factories employing thousands of workers became common in cities all over America. The General Electric plant in Schenectady, New York, employed 15,000 workers in 1910. The Pullman Car Company, International Harvester, Goodyear Tire and Rubber, and U.S. Steel all employed over 15,000 workers at their main plants by the middle of the 1910s. The Ford Motor Company also employed 15,000 workers by the mid-teens, and by 1924 it employed 68,000 workers at its new River Rouge plant in Detroit.

The exploding population required cities to expand. In an unprecedented building boom, houses, apartment buildings, factories, stores, and office buildings all sprang up. Skyscrapers reached ever-greater heights and came to define the city. Cities also expanded outward by annexing neighboring towns.

As cities expanded, several factors combined to reshape their spatial arrangements. Some of these factors encouraged movement to the outer fringes of a city, while others concentrated activity in the city center. Technological and social factors helped spur the move by some residents out of the city center. Before transportation improvements made expansion possible, city residents lived in mixed neighborhoods that included residents of all classes. Most neighborhoods formed around a common ethnicity. As the size of the factories located in the center city grew, and the number of new immigrants from southern and eastern Europe increased,

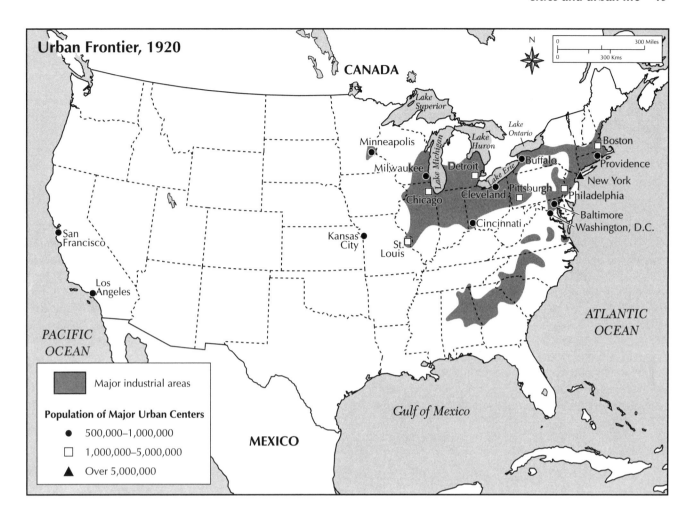

many wealthy and middle-class residents wanted to escape from the center city. The move of individuals to the outer fringes of the city was made possible by the development of transportation technologies, namely the electric streetcar and the automobile. The spatial arrangement of people and businesses had always been determined by the time it took a person to get to work. During the period before the creation of URBAN TRANSPORTATION systems, American cities were packed around the core, because residents had to walk to all activities. By the mid-19th century, horse-drawn streetcars appeared, making it possible for residents to live outside the city center. In the late 19th century, the invention of electric streetcars revolutionized urban transportation. The new streetcars were capable of traveling at much greater speeds, which made it possible for city residents to live farther away from their jobs than in the past. Electric streetcars caught on quickly, and by 1902, 97 percent of urban transit mileage had been electrified.

City growth contributed to the social differentiation and separation among city residents. The streetcars made it

possible for the wealthy and middle class to move out of the city center while the working class stayed. This rearrangement of people altered the social landscape of cities as residents sorted themselves out based on economic class and race, instead of ethnicity. The wealthy and middle class followed the streetcar lines and settled in the outer sections or in suburbs. The working-class residents were left behind where they lived in the older housing stock that had been abandoned by the wealthy.

Social differentiation also took the form of segregating African Americans into urban ghettos. Before World War I, African Americans lived in small enclaves in America's cities. As African Americans migrated to the cities in large numbers during the Great Migration, they pressed against the established racial boundaries, which often led to a violent backlash from white city residents. Opposition forced the now larger African-American population to live in the same area as the smaller group had previously. The African-American sections of cities became the most densely crowded sections, as residents were forced to divide and redivide apartments and older homes to make living spaces.

These ghettos were some of the most expensive places to live, because landlords knew that the African Americans had no other place to go due to segregation.

At the same time that many city residents were moving out of the city center, a building boom was taking place in the city center as American industry sought to centralize financial, industrial, commercial, government, and entertainment functions. The skyscraper became the visible symbol of this centralization. Made possible by new technologies, the skyscraper offered building developers a way to counter the high cost of land in central business districts and helped businesses operate more efficiently by placing all the necessary inputs closely together.

This physical expansion, both up and out, required improvements in public services. New roads had to be built and old roads paved, streetcar lines extended, electric and telephone lines strung, and sanitation facilities built. Because these were seen as essential for cities' health, they were done either by the cities or by private companies regulated by the city. City services were not, however, always equally distributed. Politically well-connected developers could, for example, convince city governments to extend water service to a neighborhood they were developing, aiding in the development of such a neighborhood.

The physical expansion of cities altered human relationships within them. In the older, more compact cities, residents interacted on a face-to-face level. The modern city became characterized by more impersonal relationships, due to the sheer size of the cities and the number of people with whom an individual interacted daily. This impersonal nature led many Americans to see the cities as dangerous places. Authors such as Theodore Dreiser wrote best-selling novels in which young female migrants came to the city and fell victim to its dangers. In these stories, unsavory men who sought to exploit innocent young females for immoral purposes lured their victims into a life of sin. To counter the perceived evil nature of the city, concerned social reform organizations such as the YOUNG MEN'S CHRISTIAN ASSOCIATION (YMCA) AND YOUNG WOMEN'S CHRISTIAN ASSOCIATION (YWCA), founded programs and institutions to help young city residents find their way.

At the same time that many Americans viewed the city as dangerous, the city also took center place in American culture. Young migrants were attracted to the options for POPULAR CULTURE and RECREATION in the city. The electrification of the city streets opened new public spaces by making it safe to venture out at night. A vibrant nightlife emerged from which residents could choose an ever-increasing variety of activities ranging from attending motion pictures to going to an amusement park. The cities also drove cultural change. The mass population in the cities provided a market for entertainment, making it profitable for producers. Jazz musicians, for example, relied on the African-American populations in northern cities to buy their recordings and attend their shows.

The power that cities exerted over all parts of American society made America an urban country both in its demographics and its culture. Whether one celebrated them or feared them, the city became the center of American economic, cultural, and social life during the urban explosion of the early 20th century.

See also ARCHITECTURE; SUBURBS; URBAN REFORM.

Further reading: Raymond Mohl, *The New City: Urban America in the Industrial Age, 1860–1920* (Arlington Heights, Ill.: Harlan Davidson, 1985); Eric Monkkonen, *America Becomes Urban: The Development of U.S. Cities and Towns, 1780–1980* (Berkeley: University of California Press, 1988); Oliver Zunz, *The Changing Face of Inequality: Urbanization, Industrial Development, and Immigrants in Detroit, 1880–1920* (Chicago: University of Chicago Press, 1982).

— Michael Hartman

Clark Memorandum

In 1928 Under-Secretary of State J. Reuben Clark issued a report that repudiated the ROOSEVELT COROLLARY, a policy that had extended the reach of the Monroe Doctrine by stating that the United States not only would protect the Western Hemisphere from interference by the major powers of Europe, but also promised to intervene in the domestic affairs of Latin American countries if they failed to protect American interests. The Clark Memorandum rejected this position, stating that the Monroe Doctrine could not be used to justify American intervention in the region. The doctrine had referred only to European interference, not to the right of the United States to intervene in Latin American nations.

Between 1929 and 1933, President Herbert Hoover followed policies outlined in the Clark Memorandum. He made a 10-week goodwill tour in Latin America before he was inaugurated into office. His administration moved to withdraw troops from Haiti. The president announced that the United States would recognize any new government that came to power in the region, regardless of whether or not the United States favored it. In addition, he refused to allow American intervention when several Latin American nations defaulted on their debts during the world economic crisis in 1931.

Even though the Clark Memorandum rejected the Monroe Doctrine as the rationale for intervention, it did not preclude entirely the U.S. right to interfere in Latin America. In practice the memorandum meant that the

United States simply found other explanations for intervention in the region.

The Clark Memorandum set a precedent for the Good Neighbor Policy of President Franklin Delano Roosevelt. In 1933, Roosevelt declared the policy of good neighbors, which was intended to express mutual respect for the rights of all countries in the Western Hemisphere. The Good Neighbor Policy represented a shift in the means the United States used to ensure its power in the region. Rather than use military intervention, American administrations utilized economic or diplomatic leverage to sustain a foothold in Latin America.

Further reading: Thomas O'Brien, *The Century of U.S. Capitalism in Latin America* (Albuquerque: University of New Mexico Press, 1999).

— Glen Bessemer

Clayton Antitrust Act (1914)

The Clayton Antitrust Act of 1914 was an effort to clarify the Sherman Antitrust Act of 1890 and protect labor unions from antitrust rulings. The need to change the Sherman Act grew more apparent between 1896 and 1914 as labor unions faced a barrage of antitrust actions. When workers from many different industries joined labor unions in increasing numbers after 1900, the chief beneficiary proved to be the conservative AMERICAN FEDERATION OF LABOR (AFL). Led by Samuel Gompers, the AFL focused its efforts on organizing skilled, white male workers. While some business leaders, such as those in the NATIONAL CIVIC FEDERATION, viewed the AFL as a safe alternative to more radical unions like the INDUSTRIAL WORKERS OF THE WORLD (IWW), the majority of corporations resisted all organizing efforts. The courts proved to be their first line of defense.

Between the 1890s and 1914, corporations, judges, and politicians opposed to unionization used the Sherman Antitrust Act to break strikes either through intimidation or injunctions against strikes and boycotts. The Sherman Act originally was enacted to prevent monopolies, ensure competition, and check the growing power of corporations. In actual practice, however, antitrust legislation was used primarily to prevent the spread of organized labor, with conservative, anti-union judges ruling that unions and strikes interfered with interstate commerce and free trade.

The AFL concluded that federal antitrust legislation constituted the greatest impediment to further organizing. When the labor federation changed its position on political non-partisanship and helped secure the election of Democratic presidential candidate WOODROW WILSON in 1912, AFL president Samuel Gompers used his influence to pressure the new president and the DEMOCRATIC PARTY to overhaul federal antitrust legislation. When finally enacted, the Clayton Antitrust Act established that workers had the right to organize and that strikes were not illegal. It further restricted federal injunctions against unions and legal strikes.

Gompers insisted that the Clayton Act was "the greatest measure of humanitarian legislation in the world's history" and would be remembered as labor's "Magna Carta." However, President Wilson was reluctant to enact "class legislation" and allowed powerful congressmen to insert loopholes in the law. The changes ensured that employers would continue to benefit from judicial intervention in labor disputes. Over the long term, the Clayton Act proved largely ineffective, prompting critics from both the left and the right to question Gompers's tactics. Corporations opposed to organized labor were still able to rely upon judicial relief, as anti-union judges largely ignored the legislation and continued to issue restrictive injunctions.

Further reading: Melvin Dubofsky, *The State and Labor in Modern America* (Chapel Hill: University of North Carolina Press, 1994).

— Robert Gordon

Committee for Public Information (Creel Committee)

President WOODROW WILSON formed the Creel Committee on April 14, 1917, to mobilize public support for American entry into WORLD WAR I. Prior to the war, there was widespread support for the nation to maintain its NEUTRALITY in international conflicts. Although many prominent public figures supported American intervention, others vocally championed pacifism. Among both radical and progressive organizations were voices that urged that the war raging in Europe was nothing more than a fight between competing capitalist factions and that the United States should isolate itself from the conflict. Isolationist and pacifist sentiment was strong enough that, in seeking reelection in 1916, President Wilson ran on the slogan "He kept us out of war."

In order to mobilize public support for American involvement, the Wilson administration launched an all-out propaganda campaign headed by the Committee on Public Information, or the Creel Committee. Headed by journalist George Creel, the committee was created on April 14, 1917. Although Wilson had run on the promise of keeping the country out of the war, the administration had sided with the British and French from the outset. As a result, part of the mission of the Creel Committee was to persuade the public that Germany was responsible for the war. The pro-war, anti-German efforts of the Creel Committee neglected few venues for propaganda, including renaming sauerkraut "liberty cabbage" and German measles "liberty measles." It encouraged public high schools to drop the instruction of the German language and supported banning German books and music.

Run almost single-handedly by Creel, the Committee for Public Information hit upon the idea of the Four-Minute Men to spread its message. The Four-Minute Men addressed movie audiences to underscore the importance of registering for the draft, buying war bonds, and rationing food and war-related materials. Eventually, the Four-Minute Men spoke to public gatherings throughout country. Creel also enlisted the support of the entertainment industry. He got some of the nation's biggest stars, including Douglas Fairbanks, Mary Pickford, George M. Cohan, Charlie Chaplin, and others, to create patriotic movies and songs. The committee produced pro-war movie shorts and distributed thousands of pamphlets exhorting the need for vigilance against German aggression at home as well as abroad. In many overt and subtle ways, the Creel Committee fueled anti-German sentiment. Such national prejudice frequently spilled over into discrimination or even hostility toward German Americans.

The Creel Committee had the additional objective of undermining the legitimacy of those who opposed the war. It did so by churning out propaganda that portrayed the war as a "Crusade for Democracy." In order to combat radical organizations that opposed the war, the efforts of the Creel Committee were reenforced by the ESPIONAGE ACT of 1917 and the SEDITION ACT of 1918. The Espionage Act prohibited the distribution of leftist anti-war material and imposed a $10,000 fine and/or prison term of up to 20 years for those who violated the law. Although controversial, the law was upheld by the Supreme Court in *SCHENK V. UNITED STATES* (1919). Similarly, the Sedition Act made it a crime to "willfully utter, print, write or publish any disloyal, profane, scurrilous, or abusive language" about the government or to "willfully urge, incite, or advocate any curtailment of production necessary or essential to the prosecution of the war. . . ."

The Creel Committee was largely successful at mobilizing support for the war. Within months, more than 10 million men had signed up for the military draft; and defense production and liberty bond sales skyrocketed during the war. The committee effectively silenced critics of the war with its campaigns. Between 1917 and 1919, it spent more than $2 million and helped create a rising tide of pro-war patriotism. Many foreign-born workers came to believe that the war was one for democracy at home as well as abroad, and they carried the spirit of industrial democracy into postwar labor struggles, such as the STEEL STRIKE OF 1919. In contrast, conservative politicians and business leaders, many of whom viewed strikes as threats to democ-

racy, tapped into this wave of patriotism once the war had ended. They argued that Bolshevik sympathizers and supporters of the RUSSIAN REVOLUTION inflamed worker discontent and incited political demonstrations. By the end of the war, under the influence of such propaganda, many had come to believe that all dissent was "un-American." The conservative backlash was largely effective in its support for the RED SCARE and other postwar labor repression. By 1921, political radicals, liberals, progressives, and labor unions were all in retreat.

Further reading: George Creel, *How We Advertised America* (New York: Arno Press, 1920, 1972); Paul L. Murphy, *World War I and the Origins of Civil Liberties in the United States* (New York: Norton, 1979).

— Robert Gordon

Communist Party

In the aftermath of the RUSSIAN REVOLUTION of 1917, American radicals and socialists formed several competing communist parties in 1919. In March 1919, the Third Communist International announced that it would actively support and work toward the spread of communism throughout the world. American socialists who supported the Russian Revolution met in September 1919 to form an American Communist Party. Disagreements over the pace at which revolution should be spread resulted in the formation of two parties—the Communist Labor Party and the American Communist Party. JOHN REED, who had been one of the few Americans to witness the Russian Revolution firsthand, was among those who formed the smaller Communist Labor Party. The American Communist Party was the party officially recognized by the Soviet Comintern, which was responsible for overseeing the spread of communism.

While many American socialists supported the goals of the Russian Revolution, rival parties kept the Left relatively weak. It soon fell under attack. The strike wave of 1919 resulted in a conservative backlash against American radicals. In April 1919, 36 government officials, including Attorney General A. MITCHELL PALMER and Supreme Court Chief Justice OLIVER WENDELL HOLMES, received "May Day" bombs. Palmer and the federal government responded between November 1919 and January 1920 by launching a series of raids against radicals and suspected radicals, especially those of foreign ancestry. The RED SCARE of 1919–20 severely undermined the effectiveness of communist parties at all levels.

In 1924, under orders from the Soviet Comintern, the two communist parties agreed to merge. The new party went through several different names before settling on the Communist Party of the United States of America (CPUSA) in 1929. When the two factions joined in 1924, the party launched its weekly newspaper, the *Daily Worker,* which at its peak had a circulation of 35,000. Throughout much of the 1920s, the Communist Party had a small, but extremely dedicated following. In 1929, for example party officials claimed to have 7,000 members. The party's highest vote total in any presidential election came in 1932 when William Z. Foster received 102,000 votes. The Socialist Party of America remained free of any hint of foreign control and consistently had a much larger following, with its perennial presidential candidate, EUGENE VICTOR DEBS, garnering close to a million votes in 1912 and again in 1920. Still, the postwar split among factions had denied the more moderate Socialist Party of support.

Despite this small following, the Communist Party had a significant impact on political and social developments throughout the 1920s. Led by Foster and James P. Cannon, the Communist Party defended the rights of workers, opposed the KU KLUX KLAN and capital, and it advocated equality for African Americans and immigrants. In 1925, the Communist Party formed the International Labor Defense Fund (ILDF) to defend workers and others it viewed as under attack from the "ruling class."

One of the driving forces behind the ILDF was the SACCO AND VANZETTI case. The two Italian immigrants had been tried, convicted, and sentenced to death for armed robbery and murder. The case became a cause célèbre for many on the political left who were convinced of Sacco and Vanzetti's innocence. Although the ILDF's defense of Sacco and Vanzetti ultimately proved ineffective, it earned the Communist Party a reputation for defending those who opposed American capitalism. The Communist Party also attempted to recruit African Americans throughout the 1920s. The Sixth World Congress of the Communist International in 1928 declared African Americans an oppressed people. Party leaders were instructed to increase their efforts on behalf of African-American workers. The party made important inroads with African Americans in pockets throughout the South and in large urban centers, such as Harlem and Chicago. Despite these efforts, the Communist Party remained weak and largely ineffective until the Great Depression in the 1930s.

Further reading: Albert Fried, *Communism in America: A History in Documents* (New York: Columbia University Press, 1997); Philip Jaffe, *The Rise and Fall of American Communism* (New York: Horizon Press, 1975).

— Robert Gordon

Congress

For most of the 19th century, the dominant branch of the federal government was the Congress. Major political conflicts and initiatives for reform arose primarily from the Senate and the House. Its leaders became household names, and its failure to contain political conflict, from the sectional debate over slavery that led to the Civil War to arguments about immigration, had significant consequences for the nation. Between 1900 and 1930, however, the Congress lost power while the presidency gained in stature. As the United States emerged as a world power, the presidency took on a new role in governing the nation. Compared to most of the 19th-century presidents, THEODORE ROOSEVELT and WOODROW WILSON had significantly greater power to initiate legislation, create new agencies and bureaus, appoint and oversee government employees, set aside national lands and resources, and allocate funds. While Congress continued to play a vital role, the expanding powers of the Executive Branch and greater public skepticism about Congress diminished its prestige and authority.

In these decades, the REPUBLICAN PARTY dominated the U.S. Congress, much as it did the presidency. Between 1900 and 1911 and from 1919 until 1932, Republicans ruled the House of Representatives; and from 1900 to 1913 and 1919 to 1932, they also controlled the Senate. It was not simply that the Republicans held an edge over the Democratic Party in number of seats. During most of the period, the Republicans had a substantial majority that made it possible to dominate the legislative agenda. These majorities also reinforced the power of the leaders of the House and Senate, as long as party discipline was in force. In particular, the Speaker of the House, JOSEPH GURNEY CANNON of Illinois, had an iron grip on the House legislative agenda. His power derived from the House custom of giving to the Speaker of the House the power to appoint committee chairs. Under Cannon's term as Speaker (from 1903 to 1911), the control of such appointments was refined to an art. His Old Guard Republicans simply kept legislation from the floor of Congress. These rules not only concentrated power in the hands of the Speaker and the majority party, they also became the chief obstacle to passing reforms.

Rebelling against "Cannonism," the Congress instituted fundamental changes in how it governed itself. As PROGRESSIVISM swept through the Midwest and western states, newly elected Republicans displayed a growing discontent about the power of Cannon and the "Old Guard." Under the administration of President WILLIAM HOWARD TAFT, Cannon continued to block any legislation that threatened to change the status quo. Most galling was the fight over the tariff. Long a supporter of high protective tariffs, Cannon undermined the effort to revise duties downward in the PAYNE-ALDRICH TARIFF and persuaded Taft to sign a bill that raised some rates. The new alliance between Taft and Cannon suggested that it was time to challenge the speaker's authority. Senators ROBERT LA

FOLLETTE of Wisconsin, HIRAM WARREN JOHNSON of California, and Representative George Norris of New York formed the National Progressive Republican League for that purpose. By 1911, they had dismantled Cannon's regime in the House by working with other congressional Republicans and reform Democrats to change the rules by which the House was governed. Committee chairs were now determined by seniority, not appointed by the Speaker of the House.

Ironically, the new system of seniority, in which committee chairmanships were determined by the years that a senator or representative served, gave even greater weight to conservative politics. It shifted regional power to the South, where incumbents were elected for consecutive terms and thus could gain and hold on to positions in critical committees, like committees on Ways and Means and Rules in the House and Finance and Foreign Relations in the Senate.

Further reading: Joel H Silbey, ed. *The United States Congress in a Nation Transformed, 1896–1963,* 3 vols. (Brooklyn, N.Y.: Carlson, 1991).

Congressional Union   See Paul, Alice

conscription

The United States entered WORLD WAR I on April 6, 1917. Its ground forces at the time numbered only 128,000 men with only one infantry division. General JOHN JOSEPH PERSHING, newly appointed commander of the AMERICAN EXPEDITIONARY FORCE, called for a force of three million men that, in his assessment, was needed to claim victory in the war. President WOODROW WILSON's administration was faced with a dilemma as to how best to fill the gap between these two figures. The president turned to a military draft, or conscription, as the means to build an army.

Since its inception, the United States had a tradition of voluntary military service. Only during the Civil War, in fact, had a draft been relied upon to provide soldiers for wartime. Even during that crisis, the imposition of a draft had caused anti-draft riots in the anthracite region of Pennsylvania and in New York City. For that reason, President Wilson had hoped to rely on a call to public service. Conscription, however, was the only way to raise a huge army in a short time.

Initially, Wilson opposed a military draft, but he later supported and defended it as a "disagreeable but necessary evil." There was, at the time, some public opposition to the "European war" and to conscription specifically. It was a long six weeks between the time Congress declared war and the passage of the SELECTIVE SERVICE ACT of 1917,

which implemented the military draft. Wilson appointed General Enoch Crowder to head the new Selective Service System. All men between the ages of 18 and 45 were required to register. No exemptions, outside of those in vital wartime industries, were allowed. No one was allowed to hire a substitute, as was the case during the Civil War. Crowder set up local draft boards staffed by community volunteers, who decided who would be sent into, or deferred from, military service. The use of community volunteers, in addition to government propaganda promoting patriotic service, prevented "the streets from running red with blood" on registration day, as many had feared.

The COMMITTEE FOR PUBLIC INFORMATION (CPI), created by President Wilson shortly after America joined the war in 1917, raised public support for the war effort through propaganda. War posters urged Americans to join the army. Movie stars, marching bands, and billboards celebrated those who "did their duty." Fighting to keep the world "safe for democracy" was a potent recruiting slogan. Speakers from the CPI gave speeches in schools, camps, and public gatherings of all kinds. They were highly effective in inspiring patriotic fervor and stirring anti-German feeling.

Registration day, for those who did voluntarily register, was a day for patriotism. Twenty-four million men responded to the call and registered, and in only a few months, the United States Army grew to over four million soldiers. For the first time in the history of the United States, women also were allowed to join as volunteers. Twenty-one thousand women served in the Army and Navy Nurse Corps, and another 13,000 worked as clerks for the U.S. Navy and Marine Corps. Their service came less as a response to compulsory military service than as an expression of patriotism or a desire for adventure.

To maintain the peace and ensure the success of the draft, Congress and the Wilson administration instituted a number of measures. Congress passed the ESPIONAGE ACT of 1917 and the SEDITION ACT of 1918 as well as the TRADING WITH THE ENEMY ACT, all to suppress popular opposition to the conscription in speech, writing, or public protest. The Justice Department prosecuted anti-war socialists and members of the radical INDUSTRIAL WORKERS OF THE WORLD (IWW) under these acts. Government officials also prompted support for military service by playing on public fears of violent radicals and German spies who, they said, were active throughout the United States. CPI posters encouraged citizens to report anyone who they thought might have pro-German sympathies. In fact, approximately 337,000 men refused to answer the draft call. Called "slackers" in the jargon of the day, many of these men were hunted down by civilian agents of the Justice Department. Under the name of the American Protective League, they organized raids in New York City. In addition, some 65,000 men objected to war and became conscientious objectors, due to their religious beliefs. Many of these were also imprisoned. By World War II, the idea of a compulsory military draft in the United States was no longer foreign. Conscription became the major means by which the ARMED FORCES raised troops for foreign wars until the 1970s.

Further reading: John Whiteclay Chambers, *To Raise an Army: The Draft Comes to America* (New York: Free Press, 1987).

— Annamarie Edelen

conservationism

The nation's industrial development and westward expansion accelerated dramatically between 1900 and 1930. As they did, there was a corresponding concern about the impact economic growth was having on the environment and the nation's natural resources. A small but vocal group of naturalists, artists, and outdoorsmen directed their attention to the ways in which natural resources were being squandered. They formed the core of an emerging conservation movement. At the same time, an even smaller group of environmentalists began calling for the complete preservation of wilderness areas.

Concern about the conservation of natural resources dates back to as early as the 1830s and 1840s and the transcendentalist writings of Ralph Waldo Emerson and Henry David Thoreau. They, along with later naturalists John Muir, John James Audubon, and George Perkins Marsh, warned that the nation's natural heritage was being unnecessarily squandered. The conservation movement began to emerge in earnest when wealthy landowners began to consolidate and exploit western land and water rights. Many viewed the lush forests and rugged beauty of the West as a national treasure and feared that unless something was done the West would be stripped of its abundant resources. Several pieces of federal legislation were enacted between 1870 and 1900, all of which aimed at ensuring the efficient utilization of resources. These included the Timber Culture Act (1873), the creation of the U.S. Forest Service (1876) and the U.S. Geological Survey (1879), and the Forest Reserve Act (1891).

John Muir was the most influential of the early conservationists. Inspired by the near loss of his eyesight, Muir became a world-renowned botanist and used his influence to lobby for the creation of Yellowstone National Park (1872) and Yosemite National Park (1890). He founded the Sierra Club, which today remains the nation's most important conservation organization, in 1892. From the outset, the conservationist ranks were extremely diverse. They included sportsmen and hunters like THEODORE ROO-

SEVELT, naturalists such as Muir and Audubon, scientists, and land use proponents, such as GIFFORD PINCHOT. By 1900, two distinct camps had emerged—conservationists and preservationists. The conservation camp, which would be led by Secretary of the Interior Gifford Pinchot, emphasized the rational and efficient use of resources in order to conserve them for future economic expansion. Preservationists, led by Muir among others, while not opposed to the efficient use of resources, argued that some regions, because of their intrinsic aesthetic beauty, ought to be preserved and unspoiled by human use. Both Muir and Pinchot vied for the ear of Roosevelt and attempted to influence federal policy. Muir urged Roosevelt to establish more federal wilderness areas, even if it meant that some resources would be permanently off-limits to development, while Pinchot insisted only that resources be utilized efficiently. Permanently preserving natural resources, Pinchot argued, would serve only to curtail the nation's growth and development.

The conflict between Muir and Pinchot and between preservationists and conservationists came to a head in 1912 with the creation of the Hetch Hetchy dam. When California public utilities introduced a plan to dam and flood the Hetch Hetchy valley, Muir and other preservationists urged the president to block the dam's construction. The dam, which would provide freshwater to residents of San Francisco, was precisely the type of efficient use of resources called for by Pinchot and other conservationists. For Muir and the preservationists, the damage caused by the flooding of the scenic Hetch Hetchy valley would be catastrophic and far outweighed any short-term economic benefit the dam might bring. Of the proposed dam Muir stated, "These temple destroyers, devotees of ravaging commercialism, seem to have perfect contempt for Nature. Instead of lifting their eyes to the God of the Mountains, they lift them to the Almighty Dollar." Conversely, Pinchot concluded, "I am fully persuaded that by substituting a lake for the present swampy floor of the valley, the injury is altogether unimportant compared to the benefits to be derived from its uses as a reservoir." Pinchot, the conservationists, and those favoring economic development persuaded the government that the dam's utility far outweighed the damage to the valley, and the dam was built in 1913.

The influence of preservationists dwindled in the aftermath of the Hetch Hetchy debate. The conservationist sentiment dominated federal policy toward natural resources and the environment until after the end of World War II. The end result was that, while there was substantial concern about how natural resources were utilized, the conservation movement placed little emphasis on preserving natural resources or wilderness areas between 1900 and 1930.

See also ANTIQUITIES ACT; NATIONAL PARK SERVICE; NATIONAL RECLAMATION ACT.

Further reading: Char Miller and Hal Rothman, eds. *Out of the Woods: Essays in Environmental History* (Pittsburgh: University of Pittsburgh Press, 1997); Henry Edward Clepper, *Leaders of American Conservation* (New York: Ronald Press, 1971).

— Robert Gordon

Coolidge, Calvin John (1872–1933)

A staunch conservative and supporter of business, Calvin Coolidge became the 30th president of the United States when he assumed office following the death of WARREN GAMALIEL HARDING. Born in 1872 in Plymouth, Vermont, Coolidge was raised by his father after his mother's death. Active in politics, his father held several jobs, including farmer and storekeeper. He taught young Calvin to be honest, hardworking, fair, religious, and conservative. Coolidge was the first in his family to attend college, graduating from Amherst College in Massachusetts in 1895. He then stud-

Calvin Coolidge poses with his two sons, 1924 *(Library of Congress)*

ied law privately and passed the bar in 1897. In 1905, he married Grace Anna Goodhue, who was a teacher at the Clark Institute for Deaf Children.

A lifelong Republican, Coolidge entered politics at an early age. He first ran for public office in 1898, winning a seat on the city council of Northampton, Massachusetts. Over the next decade, Coolidge held numerous elected offices in Northampton, finally becoming mayor in 1908. Though reserved, Coolidge developed into a capable public speaker and earned a reputation for honesty, fairness, compassion, party loyalty, and fiscal conservatism. He proved willing to support efforts to improve the lives of those less fortunate, so long as it didn't cost too much money. Elected to the Massachusetts Senate in 1911, Coolidge became the lieutenant governor in 1915. In 1918 he was elected governor of Massachusetts. As governor, Coolidge supported the ratification of the Nineteenth Amendment giving women the right to vote, efforts to reduce the workweek for women and children, and other progressive reforms. He was not, however, aligned with Republican progressives who had supported THEODORE ROOSEVELT, and his support for progressive legislation had limits.

Coolidge first entered the national spotlight in 1919. For several years, police officers in Boston had struggled to improve their pay and working conditions without success. Frustrated by the lack of response from city officials, officers formed the Boston Social Club and applied to the AMERICAN FEDERATION OF LABOR (AFL) for union recognition. Boston city officials refused to recognize the union or meet its demands for pay increases. On September 9, 1919, three-quarters of the city's police force went out on strike. The move infuriated local government officials, who appealed to Coolidge and President WOODROW WILSON for help. The 1919 police strike occurred at the height of a wave of postwar strikes and radicalism, which included the STEEL STRIKE OF 1919 and the SEATTLE GENERAL STRIKE. Led by Attorney General A. MITCHELL PALMER, the federal government responded by cracking down on organized labor, progressive reformers, radicals, and anyone who seemed to threaten the social order. Initially, Coolidge appeared reluctant to act; but when rioting broke out in Boston, he responded swiftly and dramatically. Stating that, "There is no right to strike against the public safety by anybody, anywhere, any time," Coolidge called out the state militia and permitted the Boston police commissioner to fire any striking officers. New recruits replaced the striking officers who were not given their jobs back when the strike ended.

The swift and aggressive manner in which Coolidge dealt with the strike earned him high praise from conservatives throughout the country and catapulted him into the 1920 race for the Republican presidential nomination.

The Republican convention nominated Warren G. Harding as its presidential nominee and selected Coolidge to be the party's vice presidential candidate. Harding and Coolidge aligned themselves with the party's Old Guard and in opposition to party progressives. Promising to return the country to prosperity and "normalcy," Harding and Coolidge defeated their Democratic rivals, James Cox and Franklin D. Roosevelt, in a landslide. The electoral vote was 404 to 127. Between taking office in 1921 and 1923, Coolidge played a barely visible role in the Harding administration and received little national attention. By 1922, when President Harding found himself besieged by scandal and corruption, his health took a turn for the worse. He died of a heart attack on August 2, 1923, and Coolidge took the oath of office at 2:47 A.M. the next day.

When Coolidge assumed office, he was immediately confronted by rampant rumors of scandal and corruption among Harding's cabinet officers. Many of the charges of corruption aimed at the Harding administration centered on Attorney General Harry Daugherty. Initially reluctant to fire one of Harding's closest confidants, Coolidge finally asked Daugherty to resign in 1924. That same year, an even larger scandal, known as the TEAPOT DOME scandal, became public. Public confidence in the presidency was at an all-time low. Coolidge confronted these scandals head-on and quickly removed from office anyone involved. In office, he continued to be reserved, earning him the nickname "Silent Cal." Efficient, productive, and honest, Coolidge convinced the nation that the government was in the hands of someone they could trust. He easily won the Republican presidential nomination in 1924. With running mate CHARLES GATES DAWES, Coolidge handily defeated challenges from John W. Davis, the DEMOCRATIC PARTY nominee, and ROBERT LA FOLLETTE, the candidate of the reformed Progressive Party. Coolidge won the electoral vote 382 to 136 for Davis and 13 for La Follette.

Elected in his own right, Coolidge presided over the country during a time of general economic prosperity. Between 1922 and 1927, the economy grew 7 percent annually. Although the economic prosperity primarily benefited corporations and the wealthy, the general public benefited as well. Coolidge and his secretary of commerce, Herbert Hoover, believed that the best way to perpetuate this economic boom was for the federal government to give whatever assistance was necessary to the private sector. As Coolidge put it in 1925, "the business of America is business." Under his secretary of the treasury, ANDREW WILLIAM MELLON, one of the administration's primary objectives was to reduce federal taxes. Arguing that a large tax cut was the best way to ensure continued prosperity, Coolidge proposed a series of reductions that would benefit all taxpayers and eliminate income taxes for the poorest citizens. These cuts were passed in 1926.

Foreign policy issues also shaped Coolidge's presidency. Anti-Japanese sentiment had been growing, especially in the West, as more Japanese immigrants came to the United States. Congress passed legislation that prohibited Japanese from entering the country and set strict quotas for other Asian immigrants. Following upon the QUOTA ACT of 1921, the new act sharply reduced the quota for immigrants entering the United States from southern and eastern Europe. Though Coolidge personally opposed the legislation and attempted to block it, he agreed to sign the NATIONAL ORIGINS ACT of 1924. When in 1919 Congress had refused to join the LEAGUE OF NATIONS following the end of WORLD WAR I, the nation's role in world affairs became unclear. Not wanting to antagonize isolationists in the REPUBLICAN PARTY, Coolidge was still convinced that the nation ought to be more active internationally. In 1924, he secured the passage of the DAWES PLAN, which reduced German reparation payments and secured American loans to stabilize the German economy. His administration also convinced the Senate to pass the KELLOGG-BRIAND TREATY outlawing war. Although it lacked an effective enforcement mechanism and quickly proved unrealistic, the pact captured the optimistic mood of the 1920s. In the final analysis, however, the Coolidge administration had no great vision or overarching agenda other than perpetuating the economic boom that had begun in 1922. To this extent, Coolidge could claim success; but by 1929 it was clear that the boom of the Roaring Twenties had been built on excess consumer spending and overproduction. Not only were real wages stagnant and unemployment figures on the rise, but also certain sectors such as AGRICULTURE, textiles, and coal had never recovered from the postwar recession of 1921–22. When the inevitable slowdown came, the hands-off approach established by Coolidge and continued by his successor, President Herbert Hoover, resulted in a complete economic collapse and the Great Depression. Coolidge died in 1933, only a few years after he left office.

Further reading: Robert K. Murray, *The Politics of Normalcy: Governmental Theory and Practice in the Harding-Coolidge Era* (New York: Norton, 1973); John E. Haynes, ed., *Calvin Coolidge and the Coolidge Era: Essays on the History of the 1920s* (Hanover, N.H.: University Press of New England, 1998).

— Robert Gordon

cosmetics and beauty industry

Prior to the 1920s, cosmetics were part of the prostitute's dress. In Victorian America, women who used cosmetics contradicted expectations for women to be pious and selfless. Women should not, after all, draw attention to their appearance. As the United States entered the modern era after WORLD WAR I, advertisers and marketers sought to define what made women "modern." Their definition rested on consumption of cosmetics and other beauty products.

Partially the result of publicity techniques developed during the war, the ADVERTISING industry took off in the 1920s. From the perspective of advertisers, Americans had to be taught how to shed their puritanical notions of thrift and how to consume. While earlier economic growth periods had relied on manufacturing, it was the consumer economy that generated growth in the 1920s. The cosmetics industry was an important part of that development. The war also provided better-paying jobs and greater economic and social independence for women. With more disposable income, women chose to purchase cosmetics. The proliferation of chain stores and dime stores in cities further expanded the availability and attraction of new beauty products.

Hollywood contributed significantly to the appeal of cosmetics. Colored eyes and lips, powder, and rouge were tools that Hollywood make-up artists like Max Factor and Helena Rubinstein used to adorn female actresses. As Hollywood increasingly set the cultural trends for the rest of the country, cosmetics became more acceptable for women to wear. They were encouraged to shed their selfless images for pretty faces that required powder and rouge. Advertisers emphasized that women needed to attract men through their appearance and their smell. To do so, women needed lipstick, mouthwash, and perfume. Attracting men was one goal that advertisers promised women would achieve with cosmetics; happiness was another. It could be attained through material acquisition and more self-indulgent behavior. Hair and clothing styles changed alongside the emergence of cosmetics. Beauty parlors proliferated, which was another venue for cosmetics sales. In 1927, chemical inventions allowed women to "perm," or permanently wave, their hair.

The emphasis on physical attraction reflected changing attitudes about gender relations. Increasingly, women and men engaged in sexual relations before marriage, often with the person they intended to marry. This trend counteracted behavior during much of the Victorian era, when men often engaged in premarital sex with prostitutes while women were encouraged to be chaste.

Cosmetics were disproportionately associated with younger women who wished to be defined as modern. Younger women's use of cosmetics sometimes resulted in the ire of Americans who were a generation older. Cosmetics also defined part of the youth culture that wished to distance itself from parents by smoking, consuming alcohol, dancing, and listening to JAZZ.

Much of the cosmetics industry focused on changing the attitudes of the white middle-class in order to accept images of women that differed from the selflessness of an earlier time. However, what came to be labeled as "modern" was already being practiced by single working-class women who challenged social mores about women's proper behavior long before middle-class youth embraced cosmetics and aesthetic definitions of beauty. African-American women also invested in the cultivation of beauty, defining their own race-specific standards. Indeed, Madam C. J. Walker and Annie Turnbo Malone made their fortunes selling cosmetic products to black consumers. Cosmetics became and remained a major industry in these years.

See also DRESS; SEXUALITY; YOUTH.

Further reading: Kathy Lee Peiss, *Hope in a Jar: The Making of America's Beauty Culture* (New York: Metropolitan Books, 1998).

— Natalie Atkin

Creel, George See Committee for Public Information

criminal justice

The criminal justice system in the United States underwent dramatic changes in the late 19th and early 20th centuries. At the turn of the century, police departments across the country attempted to professionalize their workforce. There was an effort to lift the standards of police work by training men and establishing a merit system for hiring and promotion. August Vollmer, police chief of Berkeley, California, was a leader in the movement to upgrade the standards of the police force. In 1916, Vollmer developed the first academic law-enforcement program at the University of California at Berkeley. By 1915, 122 out of the nation's 204 largest police departments were regulated under civil service systems.

Despite efforts to modernize policing across the country, police departments still faced the problems of discipline, graft, corruption, and police brutality. In the early 20th century, "nightstick" justice was still common. For example, a policeman new to the New York City police force was told that his job was to "protect the good people and treat the crooks rough." His role was to protect law-abiding citizens. At the same time, the police who walked the city streets presumed that people with past criminal records were guilty and needed to be intimidated through brute force.

In addition to the police force, widespread reforms during the Progressive Era permanently altered the criminal justice system. Between 1900 and 1920, progressives initiated many reforms in the treatment and punishment of offenders. Reformers set out to establish individualized programs for rehabilitation. In state after state, a broad coalition of judges, district attorneys, wardens, superintendents, citizens, settlement house workers, criminologists, social workers, psychologists, and psychiatrists helped to pass probation, parole, and indeterminate sentencing laws for adult offenders, and created juvenile courts for delinquents.

In the early 20th century, probation became a common alternative to incarceration for adult offenders. Probation was the immediate release of a criminal into the community after conviction. Limitations were placed on the freedom of offenders, and they remained under supervision by authorities. In 1900, six states had probation systems; by 1920, 33 states provided for probation. Another alternative to traditional incarceration was indeterminate sentencing, when the offender was sent to prison for an indefinite term until the criminal was "cured." Before 1900, judges set the specific term of sentencing for adult offenders. After 1900, judges set minimum and maximum terms. Meanwhile, parole boards held discretionary power and decided the precise time of release within the limits set by the judge. The parole system spread across the country as rapidly as other innovations in criminal justice. In 1900, only a handful of states allowed for paroles. By 1923, over half of all offenders in the nation were released by parole.

Between 1900 and 1920, reformers created a new juvenile justice system. Progressives thought that it was inhumane to lock up juveniles in the same institutions as habitual criminals. Under these circumstances, reformers argued, the prison system of the 19th century served as schools in which troubled youths learned the ways of vice. Consequently, in the late 19th century, many states had set up separate reform schools for boys and girls as an alternative to prison. Expanding on the idea, progressives created special criminal courts to administer juvenile justice. The juvenile courts gave the criminal justice system broad discretionary authority in dealing with delinquents, troubled youths, and neglected and abused children. The juvenile courts originated from a movement of "child savers," led by settlement house workers such as JANE ADDAMS at Hull-House in Chicago, Illinois. In 1899, a groundbreaking law in Illinois set up a juvenile court for Cook County, which included the city of Chicago and its suburbs. Although the Illinois law separated juveniles from adult offenders, it continued to place delinquents in the same institutions as children who had not broken the law but were abandoned, abused, or neglected.

The juvenile courts extended state control over poor children and imposed middle-class, Protestant values on them and on working-class families who were, more often than not, Catholic or Jewish immigrants. Many officials who served on juvenile courts considered delinquency not an illegal act but a "state, condition, or environment into which the child enters." Thus, they intervened to prevent

troubled children from becoming criminals, rather than institutionalizing children after they had already broken the law. On the other hand, parents were not wholly victims of the juvenile justice system. Instead, working-class and immigrant parents used the courts as a tool of last resort to control their rebellious children. More often than not, parents, not social workers or policemen, brought troubled children into court.

Early in the 20th century, the movement against vice and immorality reached its peak, climaxing during the PROHIBITION era. In many cases, vices were made illegal by new legislation in the 20th century, but the public and authorities still either tolerated the activities or looked the other way. For example, gambling was an illegal vice, and many cities cracked down on gambling establishments periodically. But after a wave of arrests, gambling tended to bounce back.

The campaign against sexual immorality met with more success. In 1910, Congress passed the MANN ACT, or "White Slave Traffic Act." Intended to prevent women who lived in cities from falling prey to a life of immorality and prostitution, the Mann Act prohibited harboring women across state lines for the purposes of commercialized vice. The Red-Light Abatement Movement, the effort to close down vice districts where houses of prostitution were concentrated, also peaked in the early 20th century. Between 1910 and 1917, at least 43 cities created vice commissions that investigated the underworld of vice and prostitution. A wave of crackdowns on red-light districts took place across the country. But after the police shut down houses of prostitution and arrested prostitutes in cleanup campaigns, vice seemed to resurface. Vice also gave rise to opportunities for police corruption.

In the 1920s and 1930s, crime prevention increasingly became a national issue. Before the 20th century, the criminal justice system operated mostly at the state level. The number of prisoners in federal institutions slowly gained ground compared to the number housed in state prisons. In 1910, there were 66,831 prisoners in the state system, compared to 1,904 in federal institutions. By 1940, there were 146,325 in state prisons and 19,260 in the federal system.

In 1919, the adoption of the Prohibition Amendment (the Eighteenth Amendment), which made the liquor trade illegal, contributed to the increasing power of the federal government in the criminal justice system. In the same year, the enforcement mechanism to the Prohibition Amendment, the Volstead Act, also was passed. Violating the Volstead Act was a federal crime. As a result, the law put thousands of people in jail across the nation.

With enormous profits to be made in bootlegging and blind pigs (illegal after-hour drinking establishments), organized crime flourished during the Prohibition era. Bootlegging, gambling, and prostitution were part of the underworld culture of organized crime. After 1925 Al Capone, the boss of organized crime in Chicago, ruthlessly murdered his rivals until he went to jail for tax evasion. Ultimately, criminalizing the liquor trade proved to be a failure, and the Prohibition laws were repealed in 1933. Prohibition was unenforceable in a nation that was "dry" in public, but "wet" behind closed doors.

In 1929, crime symbolically became a national issue when President Herbert Hoover stated in his inaugural address, "Crime is increasing." He proposed a federal commission to study the problem. The result was the National Commission on Law Observance and Enforcement, chaired by George W. Wickersham, a former attorney general in the administration of WILLIAM HOWARD TAFT. In 1931, the Wickersham Commission published 14 reports, studying police behavior, penal institutions, and the causes of crime. It accused the criminal justice system of brutality, corruption, and inefficiency. In the end, the commission's recommendations collected dust on the shelf, but the commission brought crime to the public's attention as a national issue. As a member of the Wickersham Commission, Morris Ploscowe had asked whether the state of the criminal justice system suggested that something was wrong in "the very heart of . . . government and social policy in America." According to legal historian Lawrence Friedman, the role of the federal government in responding to crime increased when the New Deal "sucked power" from the states to deal with the economic crisis of the Great Depression.

See also PROGRESSIVISM.

Further reading: Lawrence M. Friedman, *Crime and Punishment in American History* (New York: Basic Books, 1993); Nicole Hahn Rafter, *Partial Justice: Women, Prisons, and Social Control,* 2nd ed. (New Brunswick, N.J.: Transaction Publishers, 1997); David J. Rothman, *Conscience and Convenience: The Asylum and Its Alternatives in Progressive America* (Boston: Little, Brown, 1980).

— Glen Bessemer

Currency Act (1900)

The Currency, or Gold Standard, Act of 1900 placed the United States firmly on the gold standard. What may seem to be a trivial event, however, was the result of one of the most turbulent battles in U.S. history. Disputes over currency raged during the final decades of the 19th century. For nearly a hundred years, the United States had used two metals, gold and silver, for coining legal currency. In 1873 this practice changed. Due primarily to the high price of silver, the United States passed a law that made gold the basis of its currency. At first this act drew scant attention. Soon after, however, due to major ore discoveries, silver became more plentiful and less expensive. As a result, American farmers and silver miners called for the coinage of silver. They referred to the Act of 1873 as the "Crime of 1873." In 1878, this pressure led to the issuance of silver certificates, and silver dollars. Many farmers believed that these measures were not sufficient to carry out the business of the country. This argument was especially prevalent in the southern and western states. As borrowers, farmers also were concerned with deflation of the economy and falling agricultural prices. To increase the flow of currency and spur on inflation, they rallied around the call for the free coinage of silver, "Free Silver."

Their pleas were finally recognized when William Jennings Bryan became the presidential nominee for the DEMOCRATIC PARTY in 1896. In Bryan's famous "Cross of Gold" speech, he stated that "you shall not press down upon the brow of labor this crown of thorns; you shall not crucify mankind upon a cross of gold." His opponent, Republican candidate William McKinley promised to pass a law that would settle the question once and for all. McKinley's supporters believed that gold was the only stable basis for currency, and that the United States position in the world economy required that it base its currency on gold. If he were elected, the United States would officially convert to the gold standard.

The sides were clearly drawn, and the election was heated. Bryan was at a significant disadvantage. Businessmen, fearful of many of his policies, foremost of which was his stance on currency, donated unprecedented amounts to the REPUBLICAN PARTY. McKinley spent as much as $7 million on the election. Bryan had only $300,000 to spend. The election was a landslide victory for McKinley. He received 271 electoral votes. Bryan received only 176.

As promised, the McKinley administration sponsored the Currency Act of 1900. Its advocates claimed that prosperity followed closely behind the passage of the act, but it had little to do with the new prosperity. New discoveries of gold increased the flow of currency. Gold became even more plentiful than McKinley and his supports had hoped. Regardless of the policy's merits, gold standard advocates won the battle. As a result, gold remained the standard until the 1970s.

— Steve Freund

D

Danbury Hatters *(Loewe v. Lawlor)* (1908)

In the Danbury Hatters case, the United States Supreme Court ruled that a 1902 boycott launched by the United Hatters Union in Danbury, Connecticut, violated the Sherman Antitrust Act of 1890. The labor movement had been gaining strength throughout the 1890s and into the first decade of the 20th century. Union membership grew at a rapid pace, from 447,000 in 1897 to 2 million in 1904. Many employers vigorously resisted this expansion of organized labor. Anti-union employers often went to great lengths to keep their employees unorganized and found numerous allies in courts and legislatures, both at the state and national level.

As the Danbury Hatters case indicates, anti-union employers were frequently able to turn pro-labor legislation against workers and unions. The Sherman Antitrust Act had been enacted in response to growing concerns about the power of large corporations that monopolized entire industries. Employers immediately turned the Sherman Act against workers and unions. They did so by convincing courts and legislatures that unions, strikes, picketing, and boycotts interfered with free trade and prevented competition. Until the CLAYTON ANTITRUST ACT replaced it in 1914, the Sherman Act was invoked frequently to break strikes and undermine the power of labor unions.

When unions found their ability to conduct strikes limited by court injunctions, they increasingly turned to boycotts. Because boycotts were not limited to employees in a specific workplace, they frequently proved more effective than strikes. Confronted by a boycott by all union members in a community, employers often agreed to meet union demands. As the strength of organized labor increased, so too did the opposition of anti-union employers. The NATIONAL ASSOCIATION OF MANUFACTURERS (NAM) helped coordinate the counterattack by hiring strikebreakers, providing spies, keeping lists of labor activists, and financing legal challenges. A related organization, the American Anti-Boycott Association (AABA), pursued similar goals in court challenges to union boycotts.

When the United Hatters' Union launched its boycott against a company owned by E. W. Loewe, Loewe, with support from the AABA and NAM, took the union to court. The Supreme Court heard the case in 1908 and ruled that boycotts did in fact constitute a violation of the Sherman Act. The ruling required that the union compensate Loewe with triple any damages the boycott may have caused. The ruling, along with other anti-union decisions such as BUCK'S STOVE, severely undermined the ability of unions to put pressure on employers, secure union contracts, and organize new union members.

See also LABOR AND LABOR MOVEMENT.

Further reading: Melvin Dubofsky, *The State and Labor in Modern America* (Chapel Hill, N.C.: University of North Carolina Press, 1994).

— Robert Gordon

Darrow, Clarence Seward (1857–1938)

For more than a generation, Clarence Darrow earned a reputation as a champion of organized labor, political radicalism, and progressive reform. A fierce opponent of the death penalty and a supporter of civil liberties, he was the nation's most famous defense attorney between 1905 and 1930. The son of a furniture maker, Darrow was born in Kinsman, Ohio, in 1857. Outspoken, ambitious, and nonconformist, he was profoundly influenced by the political and economic changes that convulsed the country between 1860 and 1880. Darrow studied law at the University of Michigan and passed the Ohio bar in 1878. He spent the next nine years practicing law in Kinsman, Andover, and Ashtabula, Ohio; but the ambitious lawyer was determined to play a larger role.

In 1887 Darrow moved to the bustling metropolis of Chicago. His early activities in the city reflect his determination to establish himself as an influential attorney. Almost immediately upon his arrival, he became involved in efforts to defend anarchists implicated in the Haymarket bombing of 1886. Defending anarchists, however, did not pay well, and Darrow developed close ties with judge and future Illinois governor John Peter Altgeld, who helped him secure a lucrative job as a lawyer for the Chicago and North Western Railway in 1890.

A few years later Darrow quit his job defending the Chicago and North Western Railway to defend EUGENE VICTOR DEBS, the head of the American Railway Union, who had been arrested and convicted on a charge of contempt of court for his part in the Pullman strike in 1894. Though the Supreme Court upheld Debs' conviction, Darrow became famous as an ally of organized labor and a determined defense attorney. He solidified his reputation by defending miners arrested in connection with the 1902 ANTHRACITE COAL STRIKE and Western Federation of Miners leader WILLIAM "BIG BILL" HAYWOOD.

Haywood had been accused of masterminding the 1905 murder of Idaho's Governor Frank Steunenberg. Amidst the chronic violence between western miners and mine operators, the trial received national attention. Some described the case as "the greatest trial of modern time." Idaho's Senator William E. Borah led the prosecution. Each side blatantly attempted to rig the jury, bribe or coerce witnesses, and otherwise influence the outcome of the trial. Darrow's moving 11-hour summation was widely credited for Haywood's surprising acquittal.

Darrow secured his reputation as the great defender with the case of LEOPOLD AND LOEB and the SCOPES TRIAL. In 1924, he agreed to defend Nathan Leopold, the 19-year-old son of a millionaire box manufacturer, and Richard Loeb, the 18-year-old son of a former vice president of Sears Roebuck. The two had been accused of murdering 14-year-old Bobby Franks. Faced with overwhelming evidence, Darrow convinced the pair to plead guilty so that he would be able to argue against their execution in front of a judge instead of a jury. The trial has often been called the first modern trial as both sides relied heavily upon psychiatrists and attempted to explain the motivation for the murder. Darrow's 12-hour summation, which is considered a classic legal oration, was filled with poetry and a scathing critique of the death penalty. It convinced Judge John R. Caverly to spare the pair's lives.

In 1925, at the age of 70, Darrow, a long-time member of the American Civil Liberties Union (ACLU), agreed to be the lead defense in the SCOPES TRIAL. John Scopes, a high school biology teacher, was accused of violating a Tennessee law barring the teaching of evolution. The trial highlighted divisions that had developed between religious and cultural modernists and religious fundamentalists. By the time of the trial, those who viewed the theories of Charles Darwin as apostasy had succeeded in getting anti-evolution statutes passed in 15 states. With William Jennings Bryan, a three-time presidential candidate, as the chief attorney for the prosecution and Darrow the lead attorney for the defense, the stage was set for a titanic clash of egos, values, and ideas. The climax of the trial came when he ruthlessly questioned Bryan, who consented to take the witness stand as a biblical scholar, on the literal truth of the Bible. Darrow, who effectively undermined Bryan's credibility and won the public relations battle, convinced the jury to find Scopes guilty, so that the law could be appealed before the Tennessee Supreme Court. While the jury found Scopes guilty and fined him $100, the ruling was overturned on a technicality.

In a time before radio and television, public speeches and debates were an essential form of communication and a primary means of shaping and influencing public opinion. Through his oratory, Clarence Darrow became a popular hero. His eloquent closing statements were often broad critiques of big business, injustice, the death penalty, and American society in general. From a legal and political perspective, Darrow was extremely effective. In his long career, he never lost a death penalty case; and his closing statements formed a body of political discourse that influenced policy and were closely followed by a captivated public. Darrow was a master attorney and had few equals.

Further reading: Anthony J. Lukas, *Big Trouble: A Murder in a Small Western Town Sets off a Struggle for the Soul of America* (New York: Simon & Schuster, 1997); Arthur Weinberg and Lila Weinberg, *Clarence Darrow, a Sentimental Rebel* (New York: Putnam, 1980).

—Robert Gordon

Dawes, Charles Gates (1865–1951)

Born in Marietta, Ohio, in 1865, Charles Gates Dawes established a number of major accomplishments both in the private and public sectors during the course of his life. After completing a bachelor's degree from Marietta College in 1884 at the age of 19, he studied law for two years at the University of Cincinnati. Having been admitted to the bar in his early twenties, he subsequently relocated to Lincoln, Nebraska. Dawes had decided to move to Lincoln not only to practice law, but also to take advantage of its growing economic opportunities.

While in Lincoln, Dawes began to amass a small fortune that he used to purchase, starting in 1894, some 28 gas and electric plants across the United States. Having further expanded his economic well-being with these gas and electric plants, he founded the Central Trust Company of Illinois—often referred to as the "Dawes Bank"—in 1902.

Dawes served as president of this financial operation until 1917 when he enlisted in the United States Army. During his 26 months of active duty, Charles Dawes went from the rank of major to brigadier general. His primary responsibility as a member of General Pershing's central staff during WORLD WAR I was to devise and implement an effective supply procurement and distribution system. During congressional hearings following the war, Dawes earned the nickname of "Hell and Maria" for his blunt response to allegations that the army had been charged excessive prices in France for draft animals to move supplies to the front. Accordingly, Dawes exclaimed,"Helen Maria, I'd have paid horse prices for sheep if the sheep could have pulled artillery to the front!"

Despite facing stiff opposition from fellow members of the Republican Party, Charles Dawes supported President WOODROW WILSON's efforts to secure congressional approval of the TREATY OF VERSAILLES and U.S. membership in the newly formed LEAGUE OF NATIONS. Despite his support for Wilson's treaty, Harding appointed Dawes director of the newly created Office of the Budget.

Using the principles of efficiency that he had honed while serving as the chief officer for procurement and distribution of supplies to the AMERICAN EXPEDITIONARY FORCE during World War I, Charles Dawes committed himself to the task of reforming budgetary procedures for the government of the United States during the early 1920s. Under his leadership, each department of the federal government now had to prepare a true budget that projected future expenditures and was expected to stay within those budget projections. It is estimated that the budget reform implemented by Dawes saved the U.S. government some $2 billion annually during the early part of the 1920s. Dawes's growing reputation for efficiency and fiscal management ultimately led the League of Nations in 1923 to appoint him chair of an international committee to deal with the question of German war reparations, which Germany no longer could afford to pay, creating much instability in the international economy. The final report issued by the Dawes commission provided facts on Germany's budget and resources, outlined measures needed to stabilize the currency, and suggested a new schedule for meeting the payments due the international community as reparations for the war.

Because of his work on the German reparations issue, Charles Gates Dawes was named the co-recipient of the 1925 Nobel Peace Prize. Dawes donated the prize money to Johns Hopkins University to establish the Walter Hines Page School of International Relations. Charles Gates Dawes reached the pinnacle of his public life in 1924 when he was elected vice president of the United States. He served in this capacity during Calvin Coolidge's administration from 1925 to 1929.

Further reading: Bascom N. Timmons, *Portrait of an American: Charles G. Dawes* (New York: Holt, 1953).
— David R. Smith

Dawes Plan (1924)

Because the U.S. ability to trade with Europe was compromised with the outbreak of war in 1914, the restoration of international trade became a major focus of recovery efforts following the cessation of hostilities in 1918. Prior to the onset of WORLD WAR I, the United States imported more goods from Europe than it had exported to the European continent. The destructive nature of the war severely crippled the European economy—both in terms of infrastructure and the availability of labor. Before the war U.S. citizens owed some $3 billion to Europeans. After the war, European citizens owed private Americans $3 billion and their governments owed another $10 billion. Wartime loans from the United States to Europe constituted the primary source of this capital imbalance.

Complicating the ability of European nations to repay these loans to the United States was the reparations that Germany owed to the international community as a result of the TREATY OF VERSAILLES in 1918. Ravaged by war, the French wanted to cripple Germany at the Peace Conference. Accordingly, the French along with the British included in the final treaty a "war guilt clause" that held Germany directly responsible for damages caused by the war. To determine the amount of reparations, the Versailles Treaty established a commission to make a specific dollar amount recommendation. In 1921, the Reparations Commission concluded that the German nation, which also had been ravaged by the war, owed the international community $33 billion.

The repercussions of this extensive bill undermined international economic relations for more than a decade. The international trade system depended on the flow of capital between nations to maintain at least a semblance of equitable trade relations between nations. European nations, which owed the United States some $13 billion, relied on U.S. investments and the sale of goods to raise the capital for repayment of these loans. In addition, the reparation payments from Germany served as a critical source of capital for loan repayments.

Given the extensive payments by the Reparations Commission forced on Germany in 1921, the German government soon found itself increasingly unable to make the necessary payments to the international community. By 1922–23, Germany defaulted on its payments. As reparations further eroded the German economy, other European nations were left without the necessary infusion of capital to meet their loan repayments to the United States. As a result, Great Britain began calling upon the United

States to cancel the debts that they owed the American government and private banks. Great Britain argued that the United States should write off these loans and consider them part of their contribution to the Allied victory over Germany.

With the international economy in jeopardy, the U.S. government reevaluated the issue of German reparations. Accordingly, in 1924, under the auspices of the U.S. Department of State, CHARLES GATES DAWES was sent to Germany to discuss their economy and to devise a means for the government better to meet its international obligations under the Treaty of Versailles. The resulting Dawes Plan sharply reduced German reparations from $542 million to $250 million annually and renegotiated the schedule for the payment of these monies. Dawes also devised a systematic program to promote direct capital investment in the German economy by such leading U.S. financial institutions as the J. P. Morgan Company. Despite the revised schedule of payments, the Dawes Plan proved to be a superficial solution. The European economy could not bear the heavy weight of both loan repayments and reparations. Similarly, the U.S. economy could not provide enough capital to keep the European economy afloat. Reparations and debt issues contributed to the structural weaknesses in the world economy that led to the economic crash of the 1930s.

Further reading: Stephen A. Schuker, *The End of French Predominance in Europe: The Financial Crisis of 1924 and the Adoption of the Dawes Plan* (Chapel Hill: University of North Carolina Press, 1976).

— David R. Smith

Caricature of Eugene Debs, pictured wearing a crown labeled "Deb's American railway union." *(Library of Congress)*

Debs, Eugene Victor (1855–1926)

Eugene V. Debs was one of the most prominent and effective socialist politicians and labor organizers of the late 19th and early 20th centuries. Born in Terre Haute, Indiana, in 1855, Debs left home at an early age and took a job at a local railroad as a locomotive fireman and quickly joined the Brotherhood of Locomotive Firemen. By 1880, Debs had become the secretary-treasurer of the national brotherhood. From this early involvement with organized labor, Debs became convinced that American capitalism and industry exploited workers, created a wealthy elite, and threatened to undermine traditional midwestern values.

Initially, Debs attempted to work within the political system to push for reform. In the early 1880s, he joined the DEMOCRATIC PARTY, winning election to the Indiana state legislature in 1884. Despite this brief foray into mainstream party politics, Debs continued to focus his efforts on organizing railroad workers. In 1893 he became president of the nation's largest union, the American Railway Union (ARU). Debs was immediately thrust into the national

spotlight as he led the ARU in several railroad strikes between 1894 and 1895. In 1894 the ARU conducted a successful strike against the Great Northern Railroad and launched a similar strike against the Pullman Palace Car Company in May 1894. The Pullman Company had reduced wages by 25 percent in reaction to the Panic of 1893 and in the spring of 1894 refused to negotiate with the ARU. When the company refused to agree to arbitration, the Chicago ARU local voted to walk off the job.

Debs called for a national boycott of the Pullman Company, and sympathy strikes spread to 27 states, but he also rebuffed those in the ARU and the larger labor movement who advocated a general strike that would bring Chicago to a standstill. When violence broke out in Chicago and elsewhere, George Pullman called on Illinois's progressive governor, John Peter Altgeld, to employ the state militia to restore order and break the strike. When Altgeld refused, President Grover Cleveland and Attorney General Richard Olney ordered 2,500 federal troops to take control of the situation and charged Debs with violation of the Sherman Antitrust Act (1890). The intervention of federal troops not only ended the strike, but also led to the destruction of the ARU when in 1895 Debs was sentenced to a six-month prison sentence for contempt of court.

Federal intervention and the final outcome of the Pullman strike convinced Debs that those who had advocated expanding labor politics into a larger class struggle had been correct and that Progressive and Democratic Party calls for gradual reform were doomed to failure. While in prison, Debs spent considerable time reading the works of Karl Marx and shortly after joined the recently formed Social Democratic Party (SDP). Debs assumed the post of secretary-treasurer of the SDP and attempted to reconcile differences between the SDP and the Socialist Labor Party, playing an instrumental role in merging the two factions into the Socialist Party of America (SPA). Debs also played a leading role in mobilizing the left wing of the labor movement between 1900 and 1920, helping to form the INDUSTRIAL WORKERS OF THE WORLD in 1905. As head of the Socialist Party, Debs ran for the presidency in 1900, 1904, 1908, 1912, and 1920. Although he received only 96,000 votes in 1900, by 1904 the SPA had become the largest third party in the country. That year Debs received more than 400,000 votes and tallied 897,000 votes in 1912.

When war broke out in Europe in 1914, Debs and the SPA opposed American intervention and warned the public against American involvement. When Congress and President Woodrow Wilson declared war against the Central Powers on April 6, 1917, Debs reiterated his opposition to the war. Wartime legislation, specifically the ESPIONAGE ACT of 1917 and the SEDITION ACT of 1918, made it illegal to criticize the American government and its involvement in the war. Debs, however, continued to criticize Wilson and the war effort. Following a speech in Canton, Ohio, Debs was arrested and charged with sedition. After a short trial, he was convicted, sentenced to a 10-year prison term. His prison term did not diminish his popularity among socialist voters. When Debs ran for the presidency in 1920 from his cell in the Atlanta Federal Penitentiary, he received almost 1 million votes. Nevertheless, the SPA and the socialist movement in general lost ground during the Red Scare of 1919–21. Debs was released from prison in 1921 and died five years later in 1926.

See also RADICALISM; SOCIALISM.

Further reading: Marguerite Young, *Harpsong for a Radical: The Life and Times of Eugene Victor Debs* (New York: Alfred Knopf, 1999); Nick Salvatore, *Eugene V. Debs: Citizen and Socialist* (Champaign: University of Illinois Press, 1982).

— Harold W. Aurand and Robert Gordon

Democratic Party

One of the two national political parties between 1900 and 1930, the Democratic Party frequently found itself the minority party. It won the presidency only twice in the first three decades of the 20th century. The party had even less success in Congress, controlling the House of Representatives from 1911 to 1919 and the Senate only from 1913 to 1919. The primary reason that the Democratic Party failed to achieve greater political success was that for much of this period the party was deeply divided and lacked an effective national agenda. In the decades after the American Civil War, the Democratic Party had most of its support located in the rural Midwest, South, and West. It opposed strong central government and state intervention in the economy and local matters, like education. It distrusted the eastern financial and business elites. As the nation became increasingly urban and ethnically diverse, the Democratic Party made important inroads with urban immigrants and Catholics. In the 1890s, the Democratic Party achieved political success by attracting the support of struggling farmers and radical reformers, who had given rise to the Populists, and by addressing the concerns of urban immigrants. These agendas were not, however, compatible.

The Panic of 1893 and the ensuing depression marked an important turning point in the party's fortunes. As more and more rural farmers found themselves facing bankruptcy, radical agrarian organizations gained strength. The Democratic Party responded to the challenge from the Populists by reiterating its opposition to the business elite, resisting protective trade tariffs, and supporting cheap money policies. These themes culminated in the presidential election of 1896 and helped ensure that the party remained out of national power until 1912. In that election, William Jennings Bryan won the Democratic presidential nomination with his moving "cross of gold" speech, in which he blamed the depression of 1893 and the economic difficulties of ordinary workers and farmers on bankers and industrialists. Wherever Bryan went on the campaign trail, he drew large and enthusiastic audiences. Under the direction of McKinley and party leader Mark Hanna, the REPUBLICAN PARTY secured the support of business and financial leaders and raised and spent much more money than did the Democrats. The Democratic Party was also divided over Bryan's monetary policy and his attitude toward organized labor. These divisions in the party and Bryan's focus on agrarian issues dampened enthusiasm among urban immigrants and industrial workers and led to McKinley's narrow victory.

At the national level, Bryan maintained his control over the party until the election of 1912. He was the party's presidential candidate in 1900 and again in 1908, suffering decisive defeats each time. The presence of Bryan at the head of the national ticket alienated many of the party's urban immigrants and Catholics, who were growing in numbers and influence. In many large cities in the East and Midwest, the Democratic Party had established a dominant presence. Party leaders rewarded loyal party supporters with jobs or city contracts. In return, party leaders demanded political loyalty. Long-standing political machines controlled the party and its patronage jobs in New York, Chicago, Boston, Detroit, and elsewhere.

Success at the state and local level did not translate into success at the national level until 1912. In 1911 Democrats, capitalizing on the unpopularity of Republican president WILLIAM HOWARD TAFT, took control of the House of Representatives for the first time since 1895. Taft had alienated important elements in his own party and was viewed as indecisive and ineffective. The Democratic nominee was little-known New Jersey governor WOODROW WILSON. When progressive Republicans, led by ROBERT LA FOLLETTE and THEODORE ROOSEVELT, broke ranks with Taft and formed the PROGRESSIVE PARTY, the Democratic party took advantage. Wilson won the election easily.

Strong leadership and the passage of a number of progressive reforms marked Wilson's first term in office. Progressives in both parties had been attempting to pass reform legislation for more than a decade only to have it blocked by the conservative Speaker of the House, JOSEPH GURNEY CANNON. With progressive Democrats in control of both the presidency and Congress, the Wilson administration addressed the concerns of organized labor with the CLAYTON ANTITRUST ACT (1914), the ADAMSON ACT (1915), and the child labor, KEATING-OWEN ACT (1916). Between 1912 and American entry into WORLD WAR I in 1917, the Wilson administration developed a cordial relationship with the AMERICAN FEDERATION OF LABOR (AFL). Democrats also created a FEDERAL INCOME TAX, passed the FEDERAL RESERVE ACT (1913) to oversee the nation's banking industry and the FEDERAL TRADE COMMISSION ACT (1914) to oversee business practices.

The outbreak of World War I presented Wilson and the Democratic Party with important questions and challenges. The country had a long-standing tradition of NEUTRALITY. Wilson, who strongly supported England and France, publicly insisted that the United States would remain neutral in the conflict while he privately worked to ensure the defeat of Germany. During the election of 1916, Wilson promised to keep the country out of war and narrowly defeated Republican nominee CHARLES EVANS HUGHES. When German submarines resumed attacking American ships carrying supplies to Great Britain, however, Congress declared war on April 6, 1917.

At war's end, Wilson hoped to use the power of the United States to ensure a lasting peace. In January 1918, he announced a "fourteen point" peace plan. He was determined to bring about a workable peace agreement that would not be excessively harsh on Germany. In order to do so, he decided to attend the Paris Peace Conference personally and spent seven months in exhausting negotiations. The British, French, and Italians all had committed and lost significant resources in the conduct of the war and insisted that Germany make financial and territorial reparations. Wilson finally relented and the final peace agreement, known as the TREATY OF VERSAILLES, was signed in June 1919. Wilson hoped that the creation of the LEAGUE OF NATIONS would counterbalance punitive measures of the treaty. Once back in the United States, the exhausted Wilson submitted the treaty to Congress for approval. Congressional Republicans, led by Senator HENRY CABOT LODGE, worried that American involvement in the League of Nations would entangle the country in foreign affairs. Wilson embarked on a cross-country tour to promote the treaty, but the effort proved too exhausting; on October 2, 1919, he suffered a massive stroke. While recovering, Wilson refused to compromise with Lodge and other Republicans, and the treaty was defeated when it failed to get the necessary two-thirds support.

By 1919, the Democratic Party was losing strength. The Republicans had taken back the House and the Senate in the elections of 1918, and Wilson's lingering disability meant a lack of leadership at the head of the party. Following the end of the war, the economy went into a tailspin. A strike wave broke as workers, frustrated by rising inflation and liberated from wartime pledges not to strike, demanded pay increases. Wilson's attorney general, A. MITCHELL PALMER, had become convinced that labor unions and political radicals posed a serious threat and met their resistance with his own counterattack, a series of raids in which labor militants and radicals were arrested and held without bail. Later, they were either released or deported. The RED SCARE alienated labor support from the Democratic Party.

The defeat of the Versailles Treaty and the Red Scare of 1919–21 enabled the Republican Party to regain the presidency in 1920 with the election of WARREN GAMALIEL HARDING, who promised to return the nation to normalcy. In the elections of 1920 and 1924, the Democratic Party revealed that the cultural and social issues that had begun to divide it in the early 20th century had come to a head. In both elections, the issues of PROHIBITION, evolution, the legacy of the Wilson administration, and the KU KLUX KLAN split the convention votes over platform and candidate. Unenthusiastically, the party nominated nondescript businessmen to run against similarly bland Republicans. Throughout the 1920s, the Republican Party relied upon close ties with business leaders, conservative economic policies, and a prolonged economic boom to dominate the national political scene. In 1928, the candidacy of ALFRED E. SMITH signaled a sea change in Democratic

Party fortunes. While he lost the presidency, the party showed surprising strength among ethnic voters in northern urban strongholds. The new Democratic base, drawing on the support of labor, ethnic voters, Catholics, and the new middle class, grew as the economy worsened in the late 1920s. While it retained much of its southern rural constituency, a new factor was the growing number of African-American voters who began to shift their loyalties to the Democratic Party after being disaffected by Republican policies. Despite these trends, the Democratic Party controlled neither the presidency nor the Congress until its return to power when Franklin Delano Roosevelt was elected in 1932.

Further reading: David Burner, *The Politics of Provincialism: The Democratic Party in Transition, 1918–1932* (New York: Knopf, 1968); Douglas B. Craig, *After Wilson: The Struggle for Control in the Democratic Party, 1920–1934* (Chapel Hill: University of North Carolina Press, 1992); Ralph Morris Goldman, *The Democratic Party in American Politics* (New York: Macmillan, 1966).
— Robert Gordon

Dempsey, William Harrison "Jack" (1895–1983)

Jack Dempsey, one of the most dominant and charismatic boxers in American history, held the heavyweight championship between 1919 and 1926. Dempsey emerged on the boxing scene just as the sport was reaching the peak of its popularity. One of 11 children, Dempsey was born in Manassa, Colorado, in June 1895. He got involved in boxing at an early age. Absolutely ruthless in the ring, he generated great strength from his legs and packed an incredibly powerful punch. As a result, Dempsey was the most feared and successful boxer of his generation, compiling a record of 60 wins, 50 by knockout, with only six losses.

By the 1920s the United States was still convulsed with economic fluctuations, labor disputes, and the Red Scare. Many yearned for nonpolitical distractions, and sports—professional boxing in particular—fit the bill. Because boxing was still developing as a sport and few fighters had professional managers, Dempsey had a difficult time finding boxers who were willing to take him on. He bounced around from one mining community to another, fighting as often as he could. Dempsey's professional career finally took off when he met Jack "Doc" Kearns, who became his manager. Dempsey and Kearns decided it was time to hit the big time, and the pair moved to New York, where Dempsey handily defeated all the top heavyweight title contenders.

Dempsey finally got a shot at the heavyweight title in 1919 in a bout with reigning champ Jess Willard. Willard, near the end of his career, was not in top shape. When he saw the "Manassa Mauler," he told his wife he was afraid he would not survive the fight. Dempsey showed Willard no mercy, knocking him down seven times in the first round and fracturing his jaw. As heavyweight champ, Dempsey found few opponents willing to challenge him. He had no title fights in 1924 or 1925. Dempsey finally lost his title belt in 1926 when challenger Gene Tunney defeated him. The following year, Tunney agreed to a rematch. Before a huge crowd, Tunney was again defeating the challenger on points when Dempsey knocked him to the canvas. Instead of beginning the 10-count right away, the referee waited until Dempsey had retreated to a neutral corner, giving the champ an extra four to five seconds. "The long count," as it became known, allowed Tunney time enough to recover, and he went on to win the controversial bout on points.

Although others have had a longer reign as heavyweight champion, Dempsey's impact is hard to exaggerate. Dempsey realized the importance of self-promotion. His boxing exploits were captured on film and shown to audiences across the country, giving him the kind of exposure no other fighter had ever enjoyed. Part of Dempsey's popularity was due to the desire of many white boxing fans for a great white champion. Jess Willard's victory over African-American heavyweight champion JACK JOHNSON had remained controversial. When the untainted, handsome, rugged, and gregarious Dempsey arrived on the scene, he was, for many white boxing fans, the right kind of champion.

As champion, Dempsey helped popularize the sport. Prior to the 1920s, professional prizefights had a small but loyal following. With his arrival, the sport's popularity expanded to the point that a crowd of 105,000 saw Dempsey's 1927 rematch with Gene Tunney, and the fight generated a purse of $2.6 million. Dempsey's popularity continued well after the end of his boxing career, and he was not bashful about exploiting it for political purposes. During the 1930s, Dempsey was an ardent New Dealer and made numerous campaign appearances on behalf of Franklin Delano Roosevelt and other Democrats.

See also SPORTS.

Further reading: Roger Kahn, *A Flame of Pure Fire: Jack Dempsey and the Roaring '20s* (New York: Harvest Books, 2000); Randy Roberts, *Jack Dempsey, the Manassa Mauler* (Baton Rouge: Louisiana State University Press, 1979).
— Robert Gordon

Dewey, John (1859–1952)

An educator and philosopher, John Dewey was best known as America's preeminent philosopher of education and founder of pragmatic philosophy. He placed his greatest efforts into convincing Americans that ethics could be directly applied to life in the new industrial world. Dewey argued that the survival of democracy depended on the application of philosophical ethics to everyday life. It was in his attempts to relate his philosophy to education that he made his greatest impact.

Dewey was born and raised in Burlington, Vermont. He graduated from the University of Vermont in 1879 and afterward worked as a teacher for two years. He then enrolled in graduate school at Johns Hopkins University in Baltimore to study philosophy. After earning his doctorate in 1884, Dewey went to teach at the University of Michigan, where he remained until 1894. It was during his time in Michigan that he developed his interest in using philosophy to solve social problems. There he also met his wife, Alice Chipman, whom he married in 1886. In 1894, Dewey took a job at the University of Chicago. It was there that he developed his belief that philosophy should be empirically based and socially concerned. This pragmatic philosophy attempted to connect philosophy to everyday issues.

Dewey came to believe that the consequences of his philosophy would best be revealed in education. To test his theories, Dewey established a school called the Laboratory School. He also published his first book on education, *The School and Society,* in which he laid out his philosophy of what role education should play in a democratic society. He wrote that each school should function as a community that reflects the larger society and trains children into membership in that society. Once the schools accomplished that by instilling students with a "spirit of service and providing him with the instruments of effective self-direction, we shall have the deepest and best guarantee of a larger society that is worthy, lovely, and harmonious."

In 1904, Dewey joined the faculty at Columbia University, where he remained for the rest of his career. During his years at Columbia, he became publicly known. He wrote several books elaborating his philosophical argument that ethics was not a separate domain from everyday life, but should be manifest in social, political, and economic issues. In 1916, he published *Democracy and Education,* in which he laid out his conception that democracy was not just a political system but also a form of social life that required educated citizens. His conception of education differed from other educational philosophers. Education was a social process, Dewey argued, that nurtured the social, intellectual, and aesthetic growth of individuals, which then led to the renewal of society. Because of the importance that education held for their futures, democratic societies required an education that would nurture in individuals social relationships and control, while fostering social change without disorder.

On a practical level, Dewey urged educators to create schools that taught schoolchildren how to be individual actors in a democracy. Because a democracy required that each individual make decisions, education should, argued Dewey, train students in scientific inquiry. An important component of his proposed curriculum was the education of the whole individual through instruction in both intellectual and manual subjects. The purpose of this was to give all students, regardless of their future occupation, an appreciation of the skills on which the new industrial society depended. Dewey argued that this type of education would flow naturally with children's natural curiosity and sense of wonder. In order for students to have the opportunity to develop decision-making abilities, he argued that the schools must be reformed as democratic communities in which students are allowed to make decisions on their own and create their own knowledge. Students would do this by engaging in ongoing communication, experimentation, and self-criticism, which they would undertake in student-centered instruction through small-group work and project activities.

Dewey's educational plans formed the basis of many of the educational reforms that emerged during the Progressive Era. Many of his reforms were not implemented as he had intended. Proponents of vocational education, for example, used his call for training in both manual and intellectual subjects to justify educating some students solely in vocational subjects. In addition, many teachers used small-group work as an addition to their regular teaching as rather than making it the core. Whether his philosophy was accepted whole-cloth, partially, or rejected all together, Dewey shaped the debate in American education that continues today.

See also EDUCATION; YOUTH.

Further reading: Robert B. Westbrook, *John Dewey and American Democracy* (Ithaca, N.Y.: Cornell University Press, 1991).

— Michael Hartman

Dillingham Commission

In the Progressive Era, increasing immigration and fear of foreign nationals led Congress to create the Dillingham Commission to investigate current trends and recommend changes in immigration law. Through much of the 19th century, the United States had an "open door" immigration policy that allowed individuals and families from Europe to enter the country with relatively few restrictions. As the economy of the United States became more concentrated in urban areas and focused on industrial production, the volume of migrants to America steadily increased. The growing congregation of immigrants in urban centers quickly became an issue of much concern. As a result, it gave raise to a vocal anti-immigrant movement by the end of the 19th century. Although Congress enacted legislation that restricted the ability of Chinese immigrants to enter the United States in 1882, immigrants from areas other than China and Asia faced few restrictions in migrating to the United States before the outbreak of the European war in 1914. With a liberal immigration policy and steady improvements in transatlantic transportation, European migrants were able to reach the United States in ever-increasing numbers and from a wider range of areas between the 1880s and the war. In 1882 some 788,922 immigrants entered the United States, and 1,285,349 in 1907. The countries of origin dramatically shifted as well. Although there was little immigration from eastern and southern Europe in the 19th century, by 1907 these countries combined sent nearly 75 percent of the immigrants who arrived in the United States.

As the United States witnessed major economic changes during the last quarter of the century, immigrants often became the scapegoat for the rapid changes taking place in American society. The vocal anti-immigrant sentiments of this time period ultimately pushed Congress to appoint the so-called Dillingham Commission to investigate immigration-related issues. Headed by Senator William P. Dillingham of Vermont, a moderate restrictionist, the committee ultimately issued a 42-volume report that played on the fears held by the growing anti-immigrant faction in the United States. Despite drawing alarming conclusions about the effects of immigration on American society, the evidence amassed by immigration officials across the United States did not support the arguments of Senator Dillingham and his fellow committee members about the need for immigration restrictions. The committee argued in its report that the so-called new immigrants were racially inferior to the old immigrants from northern and western Europe. Manipulating statistical data on these "new" immigrants, the Dillingham Commission provided a "scientific" argument calling for legislation to restrict their entry to the United States. In essence, the Commission's contention that the "new" immigrants from southern and eastern Europe were incapable of becoming Americans found a welcome audience in the United States, especially as hostilities in Europe broke out and calls for "Americanization" of immigrants reemerged. The passage of the IMMIGRATION ACT OF 1917 was only the first in a series of increasingly restrictive immigration policies, culminating in the 1924 Immigration Act, which Congress adopted in response to the Dillingham Commission's recommendation to close the immigration door, especially for immigrants from Asia, Africa, and southern and eastern Europe.

Further reading: U.S. Immigration Commission, *Reports of the Immigration Commission,* 41 vols. (Washington, D.C.: Government Printing Office, 1907–10).

— David R. Smith

direct election of senators (Seventeenth Amendment) (1913)

Reform movements in the late 19th and early 20th centuries had as a primary goal the expansion of democracy in the political system. Shifting the power to elect senators from state legislatures to the voting population was one of the most important means of democratizing the system. In an era of concentrated wealth and political power, money played a large role in determining both who was elected to political office and in how the government acted. For many progressives, the symbol of the corrupting influence of money in government was the United States Senate. Indeed, they pointed to the Senate's loss of public esteem as a result of how the Senate seemed to operate both as a "rich man's club" and as an obstacle to political reform. In 1906, David Graham Phillips, a muckraking journalist, published a series of essays in *The Treason of the Senate,* which exposed corruption and bribery in the Senate chambers. Between 1900 and 1910, three senators were indicted for accepting bribes, and 12 more faced charges of corruption. The reform press saw the Senate increasingly as an "obstructive, spoils-seeking, courtesy-bound, corporation-fed" group.

The chief problem, reformers argued, was that the Constitution had given the authority to select senators to state legislatures, where Senate seats were, some said, "a matter of purchase." In 1907, Senator Simon Guggenheim admitted that he had received his Senate seat by contributing to the political campaigns of Republican members of the Colorado legislature. There was a groundswell of popular support for the passage of an amendment for the direct election of senators. By 1912, the House of Representatives had already considered an amendment five times, but each time the Senate blocked the amendment. In 1912, when the issue was raised again in the wake of the Senate expulsion of William Lorimer, a Chicago political boss, for vote-buying, 29 states already had moved to elect senators by popular vote. WOODROW WILSON, then governor of New Jersey, had earned public respect for blocking the appointment of a political boss to the Senate, and Franklin Delano Roosevelt gained political visibility when he lead insurgents against the appointment of a Tammany candidate to the Senate. Faced with this new political climate, the Senate passed the resolution for what would become the Seventeenth Amendment, for the direct election of senators. The required number of states ratified the amendment in 1913, and it became law in the 1914 election year.

The struggle to pass an amendment for the popular election of senators was only one of a series of political reforms central to PROGRESSIVISM. In seeking greater political access for ordinary people, progressive reformers and politicians sought to expand the franchise in a rational manner (the extension of the vote to women) and to grant to ordinary citizens the powers of initiative and referendum, which enabled direct legislation; recall, to make representatives and judges more responsive to popular opinion; and the direct primary, a means of dismantling the power of party bosses in the electoral process. These later reforms, unlike woman suffrage and popular Senate elections, were not adopted into the Constitution. They remained in the province of progressive state politicians. By 1914, 12 states, all of them west of the Mississippi, had adopted some form of direct democracy. None of the democratic reforms, however, changed the way in which the Senate or politicians fundamentally did business. The Senate has remained for most of the 20th century a governmental body with a disproportionate number of wealthy members, and direct primaries did not stop political party bosses from working the backrooms of conventions to ensure their candidates' success.

See also CONGRESS; ELECTIONS; POLITICS.

Further reading: George Mowry, *The Era of Theodore Roosevelt, 1900–1912* (New York: Harper, 1958).

dollar diplomacy

In what was later called Dollar Diplomacy, the U.S. government attempted to control the finances of nations in Latin America and Asia to protect U.S. business interests. Under dollar diplomacy, American administrations applied economic intervention in order to prevent military intervention. As proponents of policy in the WILLIAM HOWARD TAFT administration said, it used dollars instead of bullets.

President Taft was not as interested in international relations as his predecessor, THEODORE ROOSEVELT. Taft's secretary of state, Philander C. Knox, worked hard, however, to promote the economic interests of the United States overseas. Although the previous administration had made an agreement with Japan in 1905 to limit its involvement in Manchuria, the Taft administration aggressively sought to increase American economic interests in the region. Knox worked to include the United States in a group of Western powers attempting to build railroads in China. When the European powers agreed to the consortium, the United States tried to exclude the Japanese from the construction of railroads in Manchuria. The railroad building project then collapsed when Japan formed an alliance with Russia.

The Taft-Knox foreign policy in the Caribbean was a continuation of Roosevelt's policy in the region. The Taft administration sought to keep the European powers out of the region at the same time that it expanded American influence. Under the policies of dollar diplomacy, the Taft administration attempted to replace European investments with investments from the United States.

Taft and Knox were not unwilling to turn to military intervention when financial backing was not enough. The Taft administration sent troops to Nicaragua to support the insurgents when a revolution broke out in 1909. The U.S. troops seized the customs houses until peace was restored. Then Knox increased the economic influence of the United States in the country by encouraging American bankers to provide loans to the insurgent government. Taft sent troops to Nicaragua again two years later when an insurrection broke out. This time, they stayed for over a decade.

See also FOREIGN POLICY.

Further reading: Walter V. Scholes and Marie V. Scholes, *The Foreign Policies of the Taft Administration* (Columbia: University of Missouri Press, 1970); Thomas O'Brien, *The Century of U.S. Capitalism in Latin America* (Albuquerque: University of New Mexico Press, 1999).

— Glen Bessemer

dress

In the early decades of the 20th century, American society attached great significance to the clothes people wore. As new fashions and styles of clothing emerged, debate over their effect on the social and moral order also arose. Americans believed that morality was communal; therefore, what one wore was a public expression bound up with the moral order of the community. Changes in clothing styles could be seen as a threat to the moral order. Debates over dress occupied a significant place in American society because styles were changing tremendously throughout the first three decades of the century.

Before the turn of the century, only wealthy women had the ability to purchase new clothes often enough to make changing styles possible. Most Americans either made their own clothes, bought rough, ready-made clothing, or had their clothes made by a tailor. Ordinary people tried to make each item of clothing last as long as possible. In the late 19th and early 20th centuries, the availability of better-styled ready-to-wear clothing changed this practice. Ready-to-wear refers to clothing made in large quantities in different sizes, just as it does today. The economies of scale realized in making large numbers of women's shirtwaists, for example, allowed the manufacturers to sell them at a price that women could afford. It became possible, therefore, for women of all social backgrounds to wear new styles of clothing.

The opportunity to wear the latest fashions meant a great deal to many men and women, especially immigrants. Many immigrants used their clothing to express their identity as Americans. They were no longer forced to maintain the dress of their native land, but they could instead dress like any other American. Some critics argued that the availability of ready-to-wear clothing convinced the lower classes to buy clothes for the purpose of appearing above their station in life. Despite lower prices, many working-class men and women could not afford the new styles, and their desire to own new clothes had a negative effect on their economic situation.

The most significant shifts in clothing were twofold. First, the women's ready-made clothing industry developed the shirtwaist, a tailored blouse tucked into a skirt. The shirtwaist allowed women to change their dress more frequently and to vary the color and style of their blouses. It also gave to a new generation of working women a professional look. The parallel development for men was the soft collar shirt. In the 19th century, detachable starched cloth and paper collars gave businessmen a formal look, while working men were more often seen in a working man's blouse or shirt with a soft collar. Better fabric and a soft collar democratized men's clothing.

Some of the most strident debates occurred over women's clothing. Changes in women's clothing styles actually began as a health crusade at the end of the 19th century. Dress reformers argued that dresses that reached the ground gathered all sorts of dirt and germs as they swept along city streets. Women's dresses also contained numerous creases and folds of heavy material that trapped dirt and disease. Reformers also demonstrated that the weight of women's clothing made it difficult for women to carry out many everyday activities. Partially in an attempt to improve health, clothing designers began to raise the hemlines of women's dresses and use less material. The changes caused considerable debate. Critics argued that the new styles symbolized a moral collapse as women's ankles became visible and fashion became overly important to many American women. Shorter hemlines also touched off a debate about femininity, as many argued that rising hemlines threatened women's special place as the moral center of society.

By the mid-1920s, fashion had emerged as a powerful force in opposition to community morality. Hemlines that had risen to the knee in the early 1920s came back down, but not because of moral outrage. Hemlines were simply following fashion. Americans had not yet accepted that fashion should be used to express their individuality, but the groundwork was laid for the role that fashion would come to play in American culture.

Further reading: Jenna Weissman Joselit, *A Perfect Fit: Clothes, Character, and the Promise of America* (New York: Henry Holt, 2001).

— Michael Hartman

Du Bois, William Edward Burghardt (1868–1963)
A writer and sociologist, Du Bois was a leader in the African-American struggle for racial equality and social justice.

Although his political and social views evolved over time, Du Bois consistently struggled to win access to America's economic riches and political rights for African Americans. He is perhaps best known for his dispute with Booker T. Washington over the proper strategy for winning civil rights. In this dispute, Du Bois rejected Washington's conservative policies and argued that confrontational strategies were needed. The height of his influence came in the years stretching from 1909 to 1934 when he used his position as editor of the *Crisis,* the journal of the NATIONAL ASSOCIATION FOR THE ADVANCEMENT OF COLORED PEOPLE, to further the African-American civil rights struggle.

Du Bois was born in Great Barrington, Massachusetts. He graduated from Fisk University and went on to do graduate work at Harvard and the University of Berlin. In 1895 he became the first African American to earn his doctorate from Harvard and wrote his doctoral dissertation, which was later published as *Suppression of the African Slave Trade in the United States, 1638–1870* (1896). After teaching at Wilberforce College and the University of Pennsylvania he became professor of history and economics at Atlanta University, where he conducted many important sociological studies of African-American life. In 1899, he published his influential *The Philadelphia Negro,* and a series of studies thereafter.

Du Bois's political and social ideals evolved throughout his life. He initially accepted Booker T. Washington's conservative strategies, agreeing with Washington that African Americans could embrace self-help and community development and temporarily temper their demands for political and civil rights. During his early career Du Bois also argued that African Americans were distinct from white Americans and therefore should seek the development of separate identities and cultures within the same society. However, as southern states enacted Jim Crow laws and disenfranchised black voters, Du Bois began to distance himself from the philosophy of Washington. In his 1903 work, *The Souls of Black Folk,* Du Bois attacked Washington over his strategy in regard to education, suffrage, civil rights, and the African-American relationship with the South.

By this time, Du Bois had decided that African Americans needed "a talented tenth" to lead the struggle for civil rights. Washington's brand of industrial education, Du Bois argued, would never produce an educated leadership. He also argued, in repudiation of Washington, that African Americans should fight for immediate political and civil rights. Only through immediate and militant action could African Americans force white Americans to change. In adopting this position, Du Bois rejected Washington's belief that the future of African Americans lay in the South. Du Bois argued that the Jim Crow South was not changing, and therefore African Americans should move, if necessary, in their struggle for equal rights. In making these arguments, Du Bois distanced himself both from Washington and from his earlier thought. He firmly rejected SEGREGATION and the development of separate cultures that he had earlier embraced.

In 1905 Du Bois helped create a practical outlet for his philosophy by helping to found the NIAGARA MOVEMENT. In opposition to the more moderate course of Booker T. Washington, the Niagara Movement espoused direct protests and demanded immediate civil and political rights. Washington used the influence he had built up through the Tuskegee Institute and his connections with white philanthropists to oppose the new direction of civil rights activism. By 1911 the Niagara Movement had failed. However, many of its leaders, including Du Bois, became founding members of the NAACP.

During his time in the NAACP, Du Bois had his greatest influence on American racial issues and politics. In 1909, he quit his job at Atlanta University and moved to New York City to work full-time for the new civil rights organization. The NAACP succeeded where the Niagara Movement had failed. Largely due to its biracial composition, it was immune to Washington's ability to restrict the flow of funds from white donors to African-American organizations. Du Bois founded *The Crisis,* the NAACP's monthly journal, and used it to espouse his ideas on the issues of the day. From 1910 until he resigned as editor in 1934, Du Bois used *The Crisis* to push a militant civil rights agenda focused on political agitation. Although he was often at odds with more conservative members of the NAACP, he managed to keep control of the content of *The Crisis* throughout most of his tenure.

During his time as editor, Du Bois's political and social ideals continued to evolve. He often found himself in opposition to other African-American leaders in the 1920s. On the one hand, he drew fire from more conservative NAACP leaders who did not support his militant ideals. On the other hand, he faced opposition from other African-American

leaders who did not believe he was militant enough. By the early 1920s, Du Bois had come to believe that socialism offered a political choice for African Americans. However, because he embraced a moderate evolutionary socialism, he came under attack from African-American leaders who believed that a more radical brand of socialism or communism offered African Americans more. Du Bois also became interested in Pan-Africanism, a movement that sought to unify Africans and people of African descent worldwide, but he faced opposition from MARCUS GARVEY and his UNIVERSAL NEGRO IMPROVEMENT ASSOCIATION.

By the end of the 1920s, Du Bois had embraced Marxism as the answer to the African-American struggle. Because racism was based in maintaining the African Americans as a permanent lower class, Du Bois argued, the answer to their plight was the overthrow of the capitalist economic system and all classes. Surprisingly, his interest in Pan-Africanism led him back to supporting segregation as a strategy for improving the lives of African Americans. Du Bois argued that segregated schools and hospitals were better than no schools and hospitals. This rejection of the NAACP's ideal of integration and his turn to radical politics alienated him even further from the NAACP leadership; in 1934 he resigned from the organization he had helped create. For the rest of his life, he continued to write and struggle for the rights of African Americans, but he never again achieved the prominence he enjoyed during his years with the NAACP. Du Bois died in self-imposed exile in Ghana after joining the Communist Party and renouncing his U.S. citizenship.

Further reading: David Levering Lewis, *W. E. B. DuBois: Biography of a Race* (New York: Henry Holt, 1993); ———, *W. E. B. DuBois: The Fight for Equality and the American Century, 1919–1963* (New York: Henry Holt, 2000).

— Michael Hartman and Howard Smead

E

economy

The years from 1900 to 1930 witnessed the maturing of the United States as an industrial and financial power. The growth of BUSINESS at home and abroad, the merger movement of the early 20th century, and banking and financial reform, as shown in the CURRENCY ACT of 1900 and the passage of the FEDERAL RESERVE ACT (1913), contributed to the ascendancy of American economic power. During these decades, the United States changed from a debtor nation, which imported and borrowed more from nations than it exported, to a creditor nation, to which many European nations owed both war debts and peace loans. The United States took the lead in the production of steel, oil, and automobiles, which rapidly supplanted the older industries of iron, coal, and rail as the leading sectors of the world economy.

Foreign trade and foreign investment grew substantially through these years, as the United States expanded into new markets. Latin America, Mexico, and the Caribbean long had been the destination of American agricultural commodities and manufactured goods. After the turn of the century, tentative steps toward developing a market in Asia and the expansion of trade with Canada and Europe shifted the balance of trade in America's favor, especially after WORLD WAR I. This also stabilized the U.S. dollar. Protective tariffs continued to play a role in fostering American industry and protecting its agriculture. The restrictive trade policy of the United States and its high tariffs, however, undermined the health of the world economy as a whole.

For most of its history, the well-being of the United States has hinged on the state of its farm economy. The turn of the century witnessed the "golden age" of AGRICULTURE, as farm producers grew and sold a large share of the world's agricultural exports, especially in wheat, cattle, and cotton. From 1900 to 1920, the value of cultivated land and agricultural crops increased by nearly 400 percent, as prices soared to 300 percent of their 1900 value. Trends toward more intensive farming and use of scientific farming methods, however, slowed the growth of improved land. As part of a trend toward more scientific methods, new agricultural colleges sprung up, which taught young farmers to keep books, count costs, and calculate profit and loss. Farm agents in newly developed Agricultural Extension services pushed farmers toward scientific livestock raising, the use of alfalfa, rust-resistant wheat, and expanded egg and poultry, milk, sugar, and citrus fruit production. The gas engine tractor also replaced earlier equipment. These changes increased the value of crops and livestock produced from $4,717,000,000 in 1899 to $19,331,000,000 in 1917. The agricultural labor force remained about the same size, or 11 million laborers, despite expanded production.

By the 20th century, manufacturing dominated the nation's economy and surpassed in value the agricultural sector. A slight decline in food exports between 1900 and 1913 was more than compensated for by iron and steel manufacture, which was surpassed only by raw cotton in the value of its exports. Refined copper and copper products, refined mineral oils, lumber, timber, and wood products, cars and carriages, cotton goods, and agricultural implements topped the list of goods exported. After 1897, there was a great increase in foreign trade, despite the prohibitively large tariffs instituted in the late 19th century (especially the Dingley Tariff of 1894). After 1889, the United States achieved a positive trade balance, as both agricultural and manufacturing goods came to represent a larger proportion of the nation's economy. Industry led the way. By 1913, manufactured goods constituted 48.8 percent of all exports, in contrast to 35.3 percent of trade in 1900. Europe declined as a destination for American-made goods. In 1900, Europe received 75 percent of all U.S. exports. By 1917, this had declined, despite the need for war materiel, to two-thirds. In 1919, after the war had ended, Europe received only 40 percent of all American exports, while U.S. exports to Canada and Asia doubled.

73

The war in Europe intensified these trends. Arms and munitions, chemicals, and transport vehicles, as well as cotton and wool textiles, oil and coal, and foodstuffs were exported to Europe in ever-growing quantities as the conflict wore on. Unable to continue domestic food production and in desperate need of war material, combatant nations considered natural allies of the United States—Britain, France, and Italy—increased their demand for such goods, driving up domestic prices, wages, and profits. A British blockade did obstruct trade with Germany, Austria, and their allies, but these had never been major markets for American goods. With the U.S. declaration of war in April 1917, the need for the production of arms, munitions, and other war materiel further increased. For the first time, the United States produced its own high-grade textiles and chemicals, two products that had a profound effect on the postwar domestic economy. Finally, the war forced the United States to build its own merchant marine and import directly from source countries, rather than using European brokers.

The United States emerged from World War I as the only major power with a stable economy. War and its consequences weakened European economies at the same time it strengthened the industries and finances of the United States. New markets were opened to American agricultural and financial goods, and more importantly, American businesses capitalized on strengths they had developed over decades. Corporate managers reorganized and merged businesses. New technology, hiring policies, and improved management led to greater efficiency and growth in worker productivity. The prosperity of the postwar years was rooted in the boom in industrial production. The Gross National Product (GNP) rose from $85.1 billion in 1923 to $103 billion in 1929. Income from such sources as payrolls, pensions, dividends, and profits grew from $74.2 billion in 1923 to $89 billion in 1928. Corporate income increased nearly 25 percent, from $8 to $10 billion. Savings, building and loan assets, insurance assets, and stock holdings all increased, as did total wages.

The cornerstone of this prosperity was the AUTOMOBILE INDUSTRY, which was growing in size, influence, and wealth. The most famous of the manufacturers, and the one whose name became synonymous with MASS PRODUCTION and the assembly line, was HENRY FORD. His efforts to "get prices down to buying power" transformed the auto industry as he streamlined car production, and his "Five Dollar Day," which boosted the wages of skilled workers in his employ, gave Ford much of the publicity he needed to maintain a stable labor force. His sales and profits soared, as they did among all automobile companies.

Originally a highly competitive industry with a wide range of producers, the auto industry in the 1920s featured some of the most dramatic mergers. William C. Durant, a carriage manufacturer, took over the Buick Motor Car Company in 1905. By 1908, with loans from the Dupont Company, Durant had combined a number of small companies into General Motors (GM), soon "the greatest industrial corporation in the world." By 1920, when he was forced out as company president, Durant had managed to take over 40 percent of the domestic automobile market. In 1923, Walter P. Chrysler, head of production at GM, resigned to buy and reorganize the Maxwell Motor Company, renamed the Chrysler Corporation. By 1928, Chrysler bought Dodge Brothers and formed a corporation to rival Ford and GM. Within a year, the "Big Three" automakers were producing 83 percent of all automobiles.

The automobile and the assembly line were only two outward symbols of industrial expansion and prosperity. The making of automobiles required other industrial products: steel, glass, leather, chemical paints, and textiles in car manufacture; rubber for tires; oil refining for gasoline; and the construction of new roads. In the 1920s alone, more than a billion dollars was spent on highway construction and nearly half a billion on city streets. In the wake of the automobile boom, the number of car sales agents, filling stations, garages, motor homes, tourist motels, restaurants, and attractions also grew rapidly. With the widespread use of the automobile came the further expansion of cities and a boom in building construction. Apartment buildings, houses, factory and commercial construction, new schools, churches, and hospitals were the product of the suburbanization encouraged by the automobile. Innovations in electrical manufacturing and communications triggered a remarkable increase in domestic goods. These industries (radio, electric light, phonograph, telephone, and furniture, among others) expanded domestic markets and turned over high rates of profit in the prosperous years of the 1920s.

The key to much of the success in corporate profits was the growth of productivity. Since the turn of the century, corporations had used the ideas of FREDERICK WINSLOW TAYLOR to streamline work processes. Managers used time-and-motion study to simplify human action in the workplace for greater efficiency. They centralized decision making about production, personnel, and distribution. In addition, INVENTION AND TECHNOLOGY had a tremendous impact. By 1928, the Committee on Economic Trends reported that the nation's per capita productivity had increased in eight years by 35 percent.

Increased productivity and profits, expanding markets, and the use of consumer credit made possible new corporate consolidations and mergers. Following the pattern of the automobile industry, almost every sector of the economy witnessed this phenomenon. Over the course of the 1920s, over 8,000 businesses disappeared, captured by corporate takeovers. Banks, utility companies, and retail stores led the way. In banking, merger mania and the development of branch, or chain, banks, aided industry concentration. In 1920, there were 1,280 branch banks; a decade later, there were over 3,500. In 1919 alone there were 80 bank mergers; in 1927, there were 259. From 1919 to 1924, utility companies consolidated into huge regional conglomerates. More than 3,700 local companies vanished as 10 holding companies controlled 72 percent of all power. What was true in manufacturing and power was equally true of wholesale and retail businesses. Chain stores, like chain banks, sprang up all over the nation, forcing out smaller family-owned grocery markets and ethnic food stores. Large chains such as Atlantic and Pacific Tea (A&P) soon dominated the retail food market, growing from 400 stores in 1912 to over 15,000 in 1932. In 1918, there were 29,000 chain retail stores; by 1929, they had increased to 160,000, including drugstores, grocery stores, and clothing stores.

Through the course of the First World War, the United States moved from being a debtor to a creditor nation. Both the U.S. government and private investors lent combatant nations more than $10 billion for the war effort and reconstruction. In addition, private lending and postwar trade imbalances shifted from a nearly $3 billion deficit to a more than $3 billion surplus. The response to this shift, however, was not to lower tariff barriers and encourage trade but to resurrect the higher customs duties and protect American goods. In 1922, under the influence of business and farm LOBBYING AND INTEREST GROUPS, Congress passed the FORDNEY-MCCUMBER TARIFF, which restored prewar taxes on imports.

Trade and economic ties with other countries spurred economic growth at home and internationally. The war had already increased the U.S. presence abroad. In the years that followed, the United States increased its dominance of the world economy as it took its products, branch businesses, and investment capital abroad. American products, such as wheat, corn, steel, and automobiles, found new foreign markets. In mass communications too, American motion pictures, cable, radio, news services, and advertising dominated the market. As some observed, America's "economic miracle" in the 1920s was based on access to consumer goods, mass production, and easy credit at home and abroad.

Trade was further supported by American finance and investment abroad. The Federal Reserve Act of 1913 provided the legal basis for branch banks in other countries. The demand for capital was so strong that by 1920 there were over 180 foreign branches and affiliates of American banks. Capital followed, as businesses increased their stake from an estimated $3.8 billion in 1919 to $7.5 billion in 1929. Market-oriented Ford, General Motors, and International Business Machines increased their investments in foreign countries. There was new emphasis as well on developing raw materials. Before the war, the United States had primarily exported resources from its domestic stores. During the 1920s, American corporations developed a global strategy in acquiring raw materials and mineral sources in other countries. Oil corporations expanded into Mexico, Venezuela, and Colombia. Rubber companies turned Liberia into an American protectorate. American mining corporations like the Anaconda Company, Union Carbide, and the Guggenheim Brothers exploited deposits of copper, zinc, manganese, chrome, nitrates, and other minerals in Latin America.

Another area of U.S. involvement was the increasing availability of loans to stimulate development abroad. To aid in postwar reconstruction under the DAWES PLAN of 1924, the United States arranged to lend $100 million to Germany and scaled down war reparations to ease its financial burden. From 1924 to 1929, German banks and corporations borrowed from 50 to 80 percent of their capital loans from American banks. At the same time, British and French war debts limited their ability to seek credit from the United States, a cycle that figured prominently in the world economic crisis of the 1930s.

The 1920s is often characterized as a decade of economic rebirth and widespread prosperity. But higher productivity and national income did not help certain industries and regions, which suffered severe economic depression. By 1920, the wartime prosperity in agriculture had evaporated in the postwar international economy. During the war, farmers took on new debt in response to an expanding market both at home and abroad. European nations had been hungry for American wheat, corn, and cotton. Farmers mortgaged property to expand their acreage, equipment, and production. As battlefields were returned to peacetime agriculture, the international market collapsed. American farm products had to compete with Argentinian and Canadian wheat and beef, Egyptian cotton, and European foodstuffs.

The decline in the farm economy was precipitous and severe. Farm income dropped over 50 percent from 1919 to 1921. Over 13 million acres were abandoned in the first decrease in land tilled in American history. Farm bankruptcies skyrocketed. In 1905, farm bankruptcies were only 1.5 per 10,000 farmers; in 1920, that figure had soared to 20 per 10,000. The total number of bankrupt farms amounted to 453,000 over the course of the decade. Agricultural commodity prices were to blame. In 1920, the price of the leading 10 crops declined by 57 percent; in 1921, they were one-third of the prices in the previous year. The loss of family farms due to debt and bankruptcy reinforced the trend toward corporate farming.

In their experience of the 1920s as a decade of decline, farmers were not alone. As one historian wrote, "Hundreds of thousands of workers did improve their standard of living in the 1920s, but inequality grew." Real wages stagnated over the course of the decade, and there was a great disparity of income among workers as new industries like automobile and electrical manufacturing benefited and older industries like coal and textiles experienced declining wages and unemployment. These factors contributed to the economic crisis of the 1930s.

See also OIL INDUSTRY; STEEL INDUSTRY.

Further reading: Harold Faulkner, *The Decline of Laissez-Faire Economy, 1897–1917* (New York: Rinehart, 1951); Morton Keller, *Regulating a New Economy: Public Policy and Economic Change, 1900–1930* (Cambridge, Mass.: Harvard University Press, 1990); George Soule, *Prosperity Decade: From War to Depression, 1917–1929* (New York: Holt, Rinehart, Winston, 1962).

education

The modern educational system in the United States took shape during the period from 1900 to 1930. As part of the Progressive reaction to the growth of cities, the effects of industrial society, and the new immigration, educators reformed school curricula from kindergarten to universities. They created the modern school system, in which the state mandates schooling to a certain age and education beyond elementary schools is tracked according to assumptions about a student's future occupation. The ideas of JOHN DEWEY, which emphasized learning through practical application, were influential in the emerging education reform. Most importantly, American universities became the site for the production of knowledge and training of experts.

The educators who reformed the schools during the first three decades of the 20th century were reacting to social, economic, and cultural changes in American society. In the eyes of many reformers, American society had begun to disintegrate due to the pressures brought to bear by modern industry, mass immigration, and rapid urbanization. In response, reformers embraced the doctrine of efficiency as the means for saving American society. Social efficiency was the belief that all the different parts of society could be formed into an efficient functioning whole. Educators believed that they could use the schools to prepare each student for his or her place in society, thus making America socially efficient and ending the threat to the social order. These beliefs steered educators as they modernized schools during the early part of the century.

Although school systems chose to modernize in different ways, the educational changes across the country shared certain characteristics. First, educators extended schooling to include a much larger proportion of children. Second, schools expanded and differentiated their curricula. Third, educators sought to use the schools to solve social and economic problems. Fourth, schools sought to individualize the school program. Educational institutions from grade school to the university based their modernization efforts on these principles.

During this period, the most significant change in American schools was the tremendous increase in the number of students attending school, particularly high school. Between 1900 and 1930, the proportion of 14-to 17-year-olds enrolled in high school grew from 10.6 percent to 54.9 percent. Total enrollment increased almost 700 percent. In comparison, the total population of 14-to 17-year-olds increased by just over 50 percent. The increase in high school enrollment far outstripped the growth of the high school-aged population. The percentage of 17-year-olds who graduated from high school increased from 6.4 percent in 1900 to 32.1 percent in 1930. A variety of factors contributed to these increases. The most significant were compulsory education laws and the fact that high school education had become more valuable.

State legislatures across the United States passed compulsory education laws in reaction to changes occurring in the economy. By the 20th century, the apprentice system for learning a trade was all but nonexistent. In addition, many of the jobs in large factories that dominated American industry did not offer opportunities for advancement. Educators feared that the young men and women entering factory work faced a life of toil without the hope of advancing to better-paid positions. Educators also feared that the immigrants streaming into the United States would not adopt American ways and values if they did not receive an education. To counteract these threats, educators undertook efforts to bring more children into school. Compulsory education laws were favorite tools in their efforts. Most states passed compulsory education laws in the late 19th century and expanded the targeted ages early in the 20th century. By the end of the first decade, many states had passed laws that mandated education up to at least 14 years of age. Many of these laws exempted youths aged 15 and 16 only if they proved that they could read and write at a satisfactory level

High school also became more valuable as a path to a career. Many large manufacturers began to require a high school education for new employees. High schools also began to offer practical courses that prepared students for jobs immediately upon graduation. These changes helped increase the high school enrollments throughout the country by making high school beneficial for a larger number of teenagers.

The growth in the number of high school students changed the methodology of education. Prior to the 20th century, schools focused on teaching basic literacy and arithmetic at the grade school level. High schools offered

Four African-American women participate in a cooking class *(Library of Congress)*

courses of study targeted toward preparing students for college. Students who did not fit the system stayed out of school. Any child who completed elementary school and was not interested in college would drop out. Children who were unable to complete the regular courses in the elementary schools because of physical or mental handicaps did not attend schools. Educators thought that children leaving school early was a threat to society. Because they had placed themselves at the center of a healthy social order, educators moved to expand their offerings to attract more students. They did this by differentiating the curriculum to appeal to the widest range of students.

In all grade levels, educators created programs for students unable to complete the regular course of study, including students who were deaf, blind, developmentally disabled, delinquent, gifted, anemic, and suffering from tuberculosis. In the high schools, educators first differenti-

ated the curriculum in their effort to meet the needs of students who attended school only because they were required to attend. At the turn of the century, America's high school students could choose from two to five courses of study, in which most of the classes were required. Educators felt that the influx of a group of students who were not interested in the courses of study offered would disrupt regular classes. They were compelled, however, to offer all students an education. Schools, therefore, set up special classes. The problem arose of what to teach in these classes. Teachers eventually settled on a course of manual training, in which the schools would teach the students basic manual skills that might help them once they left school. As compulsory education laws forced more students into high school, educators expanded these programs.

From its beginning, manual training developed into vocational education. Initially, schools expanded manual training to make education more practical for all students. At the same time, educators realized that many youths were leaving public school to enter private business schools, which taught skills such as stenography and bookkeeping. To attract these students, schools began to teach business skills. Educators soon applied the same model to appeal to students who left school as soon as legally possible to work in industry. Manual training courses evolved into vocational education. Schools began to offer courses in trades such as bricklaying, painting, dressmaking, and automobile mechanics.

Educators' belief in vocational education led them to differentiate the curriculum by sex. Because female students faced restrictions in the labor force, educators saw it as socially wasteful to offer them training in all fields. Thus, educators introduced vocational courses in dressmaking, millinery, retail selling, and domestic science. Restricting students to specific courses was a change from the 19th-century system in which all students could select their course of study. The differentiation by sex in vocational education spread to other areas of the curriculum, leading to further discrimination against female students.

From these beginnings, vocational education came to define the American high school as general education, while college preparation curricula also assumed students' vocational paths. Many vocational education proponents, however, began to discern a problem with the educational system. School systems realized that many students were so far below grade level that they never reached high school before they turned 16, at which time they could legally leave school. The danger in this, according to school officials, was that these were the students most in need of vocational training. Schools reacted in two ways. They created junior high schools and instituted INTELLIGENCE TESTS.

The idea behind junior high schools was that the oldest grades of elementary schools would be separated and provided with the same type of differentiated curriculum offered at the high schools. Students who planned on continuing through high school took academic courses while those students who never intended to go to high school studied vocational subjects. School officials believed that this served the needs of all students equally.

Intelligence testing also worked to keep students at the grade level deemed appropriate for their age. The tests were first extensively used by the U.S. Army in WORLD WAR I. America's schools adopted them immediately after the war. By the mid-1920s, the school systems of 37 out of the 40 largest cities used intelligence testing to place students in instructional tracks. Many school systems gave students intelligence tests as early as first grade and assigned them to instructional tracks based on the results. Instruction was then differentiated between the tracks. Students who received the lowest scores were taught basic literacy and

vocational skills while those who scored the highest were offered an education that prepared them for high school. By matching instruction to the perceived intelligence of the students, the schools hoped that all students could pass to the next grade level each year. However, there were problems built into the tests. Intelligence testing was in its infancy, and tests were biased in favor of native English-speaking students. Thus, across the country, foreign-born students were placed in the lower instructional tracks in a much greater proportion than their percentage in the population as a whole. Fortunately, most schools realized these problems; and by the 1930s they decreased their reliance on intelligence tests.

The separation of students into tracks remained an integral part of the schools. Coupled with the continued belief in social efficiency, tracking led to the abandonment of a broad, meaningful education for large numbers of American students by the late 1920s, as schools struggled to offer education to an ever-increasing student body. They discovered that, beyond a certain point, education ceased to offer vocational value for students who planned to work in factories. The schools' goals for these students became simply to pass them from grade to grade without expecting much from them. The General Track, as it was known in many school systems, failed to challenge students. It offered grade promotion in return for good behavior in school. Students were not expected to demonstrate mastery of any subject beyond the basics.

America's colleges and universities went through changes similar to those of its secondary schools. In seeking to modernize, colleges first sought to make themselves the center for the production and dissemination of knowledge. Second, they promoted the use of scientific knowledge to improve agriculture and industry and to address economic and social problems in collaboration with government and business interests. Third, colleges expanded their programs in an effort to spread knowledge to as many people as possible.

Much in the same way as high schools, colleges in the 19th century had offered limited courses of study. As society and the economy became more complex, college presidents began to see a need for a more complex curriculum. They realized that the experts needed in the industrial economy would need to be trained at the universities. Professionals such as chemists, physicists, social workers, engineers, and lawyers required training. America's colleges and universities developed specialized curricula to meet these needs. In order to teach these new subjects, university faculty members had to become experts themselves. Faculty thus began to undertake research as part of their roles as educators. It was the beginning of the university as an important site for scientific, economic, and social research.

Many other professions were beginning to require education past high school, but not four years at a university. Outside of the university, new post-secondary educational institutions emerged. Normal schools for teacher training, business schools, and nursing schools arose to meet the needs of newly specialized professions. In addition to the training offered to students pursuing a definite occupation, colleges began to offer classes to students not necessarily interested in a degree. Many college presidents believed that the knowledge being discovered by university faculty should be spread. Colleges developed classes and lecture tours that reached out to interested citizens not enrolled in a university.

The knowledge gained through research was not used solely for instructing new students. University faculty began to work with government and private organizations to help solve problems. Agricultural colleges developed new crops, fertilizers, and farming techniques to help farmers, and also extension programs. University social work programs undertook studies on which government and private agencies based their policies. Finally, new professional schools of education emerged to reinforce progressive reforms and to further modernize school systems. Collaboration between universities and other agencies became an important component of the modern educational system.

See also IMMIGRATION; YOUTH.

Further reading: Lawrence A. Cremin, *American Education: The Metropolitan Experience, 1876–1980* (New York: Harper and Row, 1988); David Tyack and Larry Cuban, *Tinkering Toward Utopia: A Century of School Reform* (Cambridge, Mass.: Harvard University Press, 1995); David Tyack, *The One Best System A History of American Urban Education* (Cambridge, Mass.: Harvard University Press, 1974).

— Michael Hartman

Eighteenth Amendment   See Prohibition

elections

The political culture of the late 19th century gave a central place to the ritual of election campaigns. Torchlight parades and party picnics were the occasion for fiery partisan oratory, and elections took on the aura of great battles between the Grand Old Party (Republicans) and the Dinner Pail Brigade (Democrats). By 1920, however, POLITICS had been transformed. A critical realignment in 1896 made the REPUBLICAN PARTY the majority party in both the White House and Congress, and the competitiveness that characterized elections evaporated. High levels of voter participation declined, as the old battleground

states of Ohio, Indiana, New York, Connecticut, and, to a lesser extent, New Jersey and Pennsylvania became rocksolid Republican. As the minority, the DEMOCRATIC PARTY relied on its strength in the South and the rural Midwest. There were other changes as well. The ratification of the Nineteenth Amendment (1920) for WOMAN SUFFRAGE gave the vote to women. In many respects, however, voting and electoral politics were of declining significance. The initiative for legislation came increasingly from LOBBYING AND INTEREST GROUPS, and the center of political gravity shifted from local party politics to mass democracy. At the same time, elections—at least national presidential elections—remained the central drama of American political life.

After 1900, several political reforms—new voting regulations, early registration, residency requirements, and stricter enforcement of voting laws—changed who was defined as a citizen and a voter. More independent voters and declining party loyalty increased such practices as split-ticket voting (where individuals voted for candidates of more than one party) and the use of pasters (stickers with independent candidates' names). Initiative, referendum, and recall and the direct primary changed how politicians and party officials did business, as did the increasing levels of campaign funding required by improvements in communication and in how party campaigns were conducted. Fear of the power of immigrant political machines encouraged an URBAN REFORM movement, which worked to shift power away from ward organizations to central government. The introduction of citywide elections and the shift toward city commissions undermined ward-level politics. By the 1920s, the spate of laws restricting immigration also diminished the importance of the immigrant and ethnic vote.

The expansion of the right to vote to women ironically helped to lower voter participation rates. In 1920, for example, the rate had fallen to 53 percent. Following declines in party identification, fewer voters voted. What was more, newly enfranchised women were not voting in the same proportion as men. Women did not vote as a bloc as many opponents of suffrage had feared. Rather, women seemed to have as many political opinions and as varied political interests as men. Their presence as voters—and later as candidates for political office—was deemed negligible. The changing composition of the American electorate, from the new women voters to the naturalized citizens and second-generation ethnic children, eventually caused a realignment in the two major political parties that brought about Democratic dominance of the federal government in the 1930s.

Before 1930, however, the mainstream political parties had little to distinguish them in terms of issues. For the Republicans, monetary policy, especially establishing the Gold Standard for the dollar and support for high protective tariffs, dominated their platform. Democrats stood against the enhancement of federal power and for a greater voice for the people in politics. Both parties endorsed the sanctity of property rights and the virtues of democracy. The sameness in their platforms sparked dissent in the creation of third-party candidacies. Throughout the period from 1900 to 1930, third-party activity on the local and state levels allowed the election of socialist and farmer-labor aldermen, mayors, state representatives, and members of Congress. In successive elections of 1912, 1916, and 1920, socialist EUGENE VICTOR DEBS received increasing support from voters disenchanted with the business-oriented politics of the Republican and Democratic Parties. The Progressive Republicans' revolt against the "Old Guard" gave rise to the PROGRESSIVE PARTY campaigns of 1912 and 1924. Throughout the period, the Prohibition Party also ran national campaigns dedicated to building a consensus for state control of alcohol and eventual passage of the Eighteenth Amendment, which instituted national PROHIBITION.

In 1900, the election of William McKinley to a second term in office was a confirmation of fundamental shifts in party loyalty in the late 19th century. The previous election had been a critical one, in which party support shifted and the Republicans became the majority party in Congress and the White House. The Democratic Party, which was divided between a solid South and uneven support in the rural Midwest, lost critical ground by nominating Bryan again. His support for Free Silver (inflation through monetary policy) alienated urban voters from both the working class and the middle class. The Republicans had for their platform a consistent emphasis on the Gold Standard for money and a high protective tariff. Besting for a second time Democrat William Jennings Bryan, McKinley benefited from a large campaign fund and a well-orchestrated political campaign under Republican businessman Mark Hanna. McKinley won the election by a margin of 7,218,491 to Bryan's 6,356,734.

With the assassination of McKinley in 1901, THEODORE ROOSEVELT assumed office. When he campaigned for office in his own right in 1904, his popularity among voters buoyed him against his opponent, the Democratic candidate, corporate lawyer Alton B. Parker. Not only was Roosevelt better known and liked, but also he was the incumbent. His boisterous campaign to regulate trusts and his support for healthy government-business relations gave him an edge with both sides of the class divide. Roosevelt won the election 7,628,461 votes to Parker's 5,084,223. The electoral vote was even more decisive, with Roosevelt winning 336 to Parker's 140.

Custom prevented Roosevelt from running for his second full term, since he had already served nearly eight years in the White House. The Republican Party still con-

trolled crucial states, and it continued to have majority strength, so eventually Roosevelt gave the go-ahead to WILLIAM HOWARD TAFT, his handpicked successor, to run for the presidency on the Republican Party ticket. In that campaign year, 1908, Bryan once again stood as Democratic candidate for the White House. His conservative populism played well in the rural South and Midwest, but it did not convince the majority of voters. Taft, running a low-key and conservative campaign, won the election handily, 7,675,320 votes to Bryan's 6,412,294. Socialist Debs, on this third campaign for the presidency, won over 420,000 votes.

In 1912, tensions within the Republican Party, and the renewed ambition of former president Theodore Roosevelt, helped spark the creation of the Progressive (or Bull Moose) Party. By this time, there were clear divisions among Republicans. Opposition to Taft and to the Old Guard in Congress under JOSEPH GURNEY CANNON prompted the creation of a National Progressive Republican League under ROBERT LA FOLLETTE. In the election campaign, there was a strong contrast between reform politics aimed at bolstering the federal government power, idealized under the rubric of Roosevelt's NEW NATIONALISM, and the more competition-centered, small business language of the NEW FREEDOM under WOODROW WILSON. Running as the incumbent, Taft spent most of his attention and fire on the Progressive Party. While Roosevelt continued to have a grasp on the public's loyalty and imagination and outpolled Taft, Woodrow Wilson won the election. The split between Progressive voters and Republican stalwarts opened the door for the Democrats to take the White House for the first time since the election of 1892.

Woodrow Wilson's presidency confirmed that a Democratic Congress had overcome the obstacles to reform. In the first four years of his presidency, Wilson used Democratic majorities in the House and Senate to pass several important pieces of legislation, including the child labor KEATING-OWEN ACT, the ADAMSON ACT, the FEDERAL RESERVE ACT, and the UNDERWOOD-SIMMONS TARIFF, which finally lowered the high protective tariff rates of Republican administrations. In 1916, running against Wilson, Republican CHARLES EVANS HUGHES tried to mobilize the discontent with the reforms from both Republicans and Democrats. As incumbent, however, Wilson held the edge, and the Republican Party still suffered from its earlier split. Wilson narrowly defeated Hughes, riding on his pledge to keep the country out of WORLD WAR I. With a margin of 9,127,695 votes to Hughes' 8,533,507, Wilson was reelected.

Changes in the electorate were not at first noticed during the Republican ascendancy of the 1920s. Republican politicians followed the call of their presidential candidate,

Senator WARREN GAMALIEL HARDING of Ohio, for a "politics of normalcy." As the "best available man," he became the party's candidate in preference to other reforming politicians. His opponent, Ohio politician James Cox, similarly won the Democratic Party nomination by defeating the politics of reform within the party. Such Wilson administration stalwarts as Attorney General A. MITCHELL PALMER and William McAdoo, the president's son-in-law, lost out in the struggle to find a consensus candidate. Winning the election by a nearly two to one margin in popular votes (16,143,407 votes to 9,130,328), Harding became president not so much because voters rejected reform in general as because they refused to endorse the particular reforms that had dominated American politics since Wilson's election in 1912.

Harding's death and the subsequent presidency of CALVIN COOLIDGE distanced the Republican Party from charges of corruption and graft, and in 1924, he ran for president in his own right against an opposition split between a new farmer-labor alliance and a Democratic Party with a divided constituency. Ever since the election of 1896, the Democrats had kept a balance between urban immigrant voters and their larger national base among rural and southern voters. By 1924, the strain of trying to keep together the party was beginning to show. Democratic voters and politicians were divided over the KU KLUX KLAN, Prohibition, and FOREIGN POLICY. The Klan, which had become powerful in local and state governments across the nation, was the object of an anti-Klan resolution in the party convention. For every state, which, like New York and Minnesota, had passed anti-Klan laws, however, there were other states where Klan members held major political offices. The chief contestants for the Democratic nomination were on opposite sides of the issue. William McAdoo, a politician with strong rural and southern ties, an advocate of Prohibition and supporter of the Klan, ran for the nomination against ALFRED E. SMITH, governor of New York, allied with Tammany Hall, and an opponent of both the Klan and Prohibition. More than 100 ballots were needed to decide the Democratic candidate for president—John W. Davis, a conservative Wall Street lawyer. Davis had neither strong ties to the Wilson administration nor did he represent the urban/rural divide within the party.

Discontent over politics as usual helped spark a third-party political campaign in 1924. A coalition of socialists, trade unionists, farm advocates, and progressives created a Progressive Party ticket. Robert La Follette, whose achievements as a reforming senator gave him national fame, agreed to be the party's presidential candidate. Burton Wheeler, who had gained notoriety as the chief investigator of the Harding administration, became the vice presidential candidate. The controversial role of the Communist League

in the party and divisions among progressive voters weakened the party's chances in the election. Calvin Coolidge was elected president, winning 15.7 million votes to 8.4 million for Democrat John Davis. Third-party candidate La Follette received 4.8 million votes.

The elections of Harding, Coolidge, and later Herbert Hoover were in many ways emblematic of a political system at a standstill. Republican Party politics went no further than arguing for, in Harding's words, "Less government in business and more business in government." The positive legacy of the Harding administration was a reorganized and streamlined federal bureaucracy. Coolidge, Harding's successor, had a similar eye toward the limited scope of government. Unaddressed problems of race, poverty, and the relation between government and the economy lay beneath the surface of the politics of normalcy.

By 1928, the strains of the political system began to show. Coolidge, who had support for a second term, withdrew from the race early, leaving the Republicans to nominate stalwart Herbert Hoover for the presidency. Hoover had served in both Democratic and Republican administrations, but most notably as secretary of commerce under Harding and Coolidge. A former engineer, Hoover was committed to the same principles of rational and efficient government. Like many Republicans, however, he believed that the country should rely on the market to stabilize the economy and address inequality.

For urban voters, an increasingly important segment of the voting population, the candidacy of Herbert Hoover, a staid midwesterner associated with business interests, was just more of the same. Instead, they found their interests represented in the candidacy of Democrat Alfred E. Smith. A Catholic, urban politician, and a "wet" (anti-Prohibitionist) to boot, Smith garnered the votes of urban working-class and white voters. A realignment of northern cities away from the Republican and into the Democratic Party column was a sign of a different politics in the making. But during an election year characterized by anti-Catholicism and a strong Prohibitionist vote, Smith could not make headway against Hoover. Hoover won the election by a landslide of 21 million votes to Smith's 15 million (444 electoral votes to Smith's 87). The election of Hoover was the last stand for the politics of normalcy. The onset of the Great Depression brought with it realignment in party politics and a permanent shift in how elections would be conducted in the future.

Further reading: David Burner, *The Politics of Provincialism: The Democratic Party in Transition, 1918–1932* (New York: Knopf, 1968); John D. Hicks, *The Republican Ascendancy, 1921–1933* (New York: Harper and Row, 1960); John Reynolds, *Testing Democracy: Electoral Behavior and Progressive Reform in New Jersey,*

1880–1920 (Chapel Hill: University of North Carolina Press, 1988).

electricity

Electricity, long an object of curiosity and wonder, became a major source of power and technological innovation in the late 19th and early 20th centuries. Daily life in the home, in the streets, and in shops and factories was directly affected by the new inventions of URBAN TRANSPORTATION, lighting, heating, and mechanization, all fueled by electricity, a source of power that was largely more efficient, cheaper, safer, and more versatile than the technologies it replaced. At the same time, the creation and utilization of electricity also could have negative effects on the environments of city and countryside. Hydroelectric power was relatively clean; and coal-generated electricity removed coal from the direct environment of home and factory, but it still polluted urban air and poisoned water and land in mining districts. Electrical mechanization of factories made workers more productive but also contributed to technological unemployment, and electric appliances lessened some forms of domestic work on the one hand and raised expectations for cleanliness on the other.

Electrification of urban transport was one of the earliest changes in the 20th-century United States. Substituting electrified wire or track for oil- and coal-driven engines, streetcar companies were able to realize profits from greater speed in transit, fewer repairs, and greater efficiency as well as the sale of surplus energy to private utility companies. The electric trolley transformed cities by making suburban areas more accessible, and many streetcar companies were able to cash in on the sale of real estate along its lines and operation of amusement

Charging the battery of a Detroit electric automobile *(Library of Congress)*

parks at the end of its lines. Public lighting also changed the urban landscape.

The perfecting of an efficient alternating current (a.c.) motor in 1910 had made possible the creation of a range of electrically powered industrial machinery and domestic appliances. First to take advantage of the cheap cost, broad applicability, and increased availability of electrical power were manufacturers, who turned toward the electrification of machinery in most major consumer industries. Electrical machines that helped produce canned goods and meat products, cigarettes, wheat flour, and milk were all introduced in the period. On the whole, it was the versatility of electric engines that enabled their use in industry to expand that rapidly. Electric motors could drive a full range of small motors and large ones, link machines through belts and wires, and regulate the process through gauges and meters. For that reason, electric motors replaced coal- and oil-driven engines and thus increased speed and efficiency and lowered production costs. In 1905, motors powered by electricity accounted for less than 10 percent of industrial production. By 1930, they accounted for 80 percent of all manufacturing output. American consumption of electrical power increased as dramatically as its uses. Between 1899 and 1919, the use of electric power increased from 1.8 percent of industrial production in 1899 to 31.7 percent.

Within private households, electricity worked a revolution in domestic work. First, the proportion of residential homes wired for electricity increased dramatically in the first three decades of the century. In 1907, only 8 percent of households were electrified. By 1920, this figure had increased to 34.7 percent. By 1930, nearly 70 percent of all households were wired for electricity. Following on these developments, the invention and adoption of such appliances as electric fans, refrigerators, sewing machines, washing machines, toasters, mixers, and vacuums reshaped the labor of women who worked within the home and increased the amount of time spent on laundry, cooking, and cleaning. The availability of electricity also allowed for the wider adoption of RADIO for entertainment and news. Once limited to crystal sets, new radios ran on the same electricity as other household appliances. Standardization of wiring and equipment meant that electricity also was cheap.

The electrical industry grew over the course of the 1920s. Utility companies, which were increasingly subject to government regulation, continued to grow in revenue and assets, as they provided one of the most important sources of power in cities. While rural areas remained outside the power grid, rural electrification was only a decade away. The manufacture of electrical appliances, in particular, electric motors, lights, radios, and phonographs, became a major industrial sector in the 1920s, and its work-

ers were among the better paid industrial workers. While still a mass production industry, the increased demand for new electrical goods guaranteed employment for its work force, at least while the economy remained relatively prosperous. Even with the advent of the Great Depression in 1929, electrical manufacturing and the electrification of the home and workplace continued, almost uninterrupted, at the pace of the 1920s.

See also ECONOMY; MASS PRODUCTION; WORK, HOUSEHOLD.

Further reading: David E. Nye, *Electrifying America: Social Meanings of a New Technology, 1880–1940* (Cambridge, Mass.: MIT Press, 1990); Ronald Schatz, *The Electrical Workers: A History of Labor at General Electric and Westinghouse* (Urbana: University of Illinois Press, 1983).

Elkins Act (1903)

The Elkins Act was one of two important Progressive Era laws that provided for the federal regulation of railroads. Antitrust reformers lobbied the government to rein in what they saw as unfair rate-fixing practices by railroad companies. When THEODORE ROOSEVELT became president after William McKinley was assassinated in 1901, he did not have as a priority a reform agenda opposing monopoly. Initially, Roosevelt was more concerned about appeasing the conservative leadership of the Republican Party to win reelection in 1904. Changes in corporate structure and a new spirit of reform pushed Roosevelt in a new direction, toward "trust-busting."

In the late 19th century, merchants and shippers in the Midwest had sought to have the federal government regulate what they saw as the monopolistic practices of the railroad companies. Midwestern companies and small farmers sought to reduce what they perceived as the unfair advantages in railroad shipping rates held by rival companies in the East and Far West. In 1887 Congress had passed the Interstate Commerce Act, which created the Interstate Commerce Commission (ICC) to regulate rate-setting by the railroad companies. The courts limited the powers of the commission over the years, and railroad regulation remained largely unenforceable, much like the Sherman Antitrust Act of 1890.

Substantial support for Roosevelt's antitrust policies surfaced in the congressional elections of 1902. Soon after the elections, Congress passed the ELKINS ACT of 1903 to prohibit discriminatory railroad rebates. The act strengthened the ICC's ability to regulate railroads by making both receiving and granting rebates a crime and holding railroad officials personally liable if rebating occurred. In addition, it forbade railroad companies from setting rates different from their published rates.

During the 1904 presidential campaign, Roosevelt called for a Square Deal, promising ordinary Americans fairness on the free market by controlling the abuses of corporate power. After his reelection, he pushed further for railroad regulation, but the conservative Republican bloc in Congress adamantly opposed any government rate setting. After two years of debate, Congress passed the HEPBURN ACT of 1906, which gave the ICC the power to set maximum rates once a shipper filed a complaint. In addition, the act dictated using uniform methods of bookkeeping and authorized the ICC to inspect the financial records of railroad companies. The courts preserved the power over the ICC to review its rate decisions.

As a result of Roosevelt's active efforts to regulate monopolies, the president became known as a trustbuster. Roosevelt believed that corporate monopolies presented the most serious problem of the time and that unregulated competition was ultimately destructive to American capitalism. At the same time, he viewed big companies as part of "modern progress." He wanted to reduce the misuse of corporate power, not to eliminate big corporations altogether.

See also MANN-ELKINS ACT; NORTHERN SECURITIES CASE.

Further reading: Lewis J. Gould, *Reform and Regulation: American Politics from Roosevelt to Wilson*, 2nd ed. (New York: Alfred A. Knopf, 1986); Albro Martin, *Enterprise Denied: Origins of the Decline of American Railroads, 1897–1917* (New York: Columbia University Press, 1971).
— Glen Bessemer

Ellis, Henry Havelock (1859–1939)

One of the earliest and most successful popularizers of SIGMUND FREUD's theories of sexuality and a prolific author and translator, Ellis was born in Croydon Surrey, England, in 1859, to Edward Peppin and Susannah Wheatley Ellis. Havelock Ellis's father was a merchant sea captain, and his mother assumed primary responsibility for raising Havelock and his four sisters. He later argued that his childhood shaped his own unconventional sexual identity. Ellis was educated in a boarding school, where he focused on literature, language, and philosophy. At age 16, he joined his father's ship crew as a cabin boy, but left the ship to take a teaching position when it reached Australia. He returned to England in 1879.

Soon after he returned, Ellis took up the study of medicine at St. Thomas Hospital in London. He read broadly in the fields of science, philosophy, and sociology. Greatly influenced by Freud, Ellis became a physician but spent most of his career in the scientific study of sexuality. *Sexual Inversion*, the first of his *Studies in the Psychology of Sex*, was published in 1897 and banned on grounds of obscenity. The series, published in seven volumes between 1897 and 1928, made a major contribution to the knowledge of human sexuality. In particular, it helped to open the door to understanding homosexual identity and experience. Throughout his life, Ellis continued to publish on the subject, authoring such studies as *The Dance of Life* (1923).

A member of the socialist Fabian Society in Great Britain, Ellis had wide influence internationally and especially in the United States. For MARGARET SANGER and other American sexual radicals, he became the voice of sexual liberation. His repudiation of Victorian repression and celebration of sexual freedom informed Sanger's thought, and their friendship aided her in her crusade for BIRTH CONTROL. Their correspondence lasted over 25 years with little interruption, and Sanger later assisted Ellis financially in paying a salary to his companion and giving him money for a small house. The challenge Ellis presented to both puritanical sexual codes and even the institution of marriage meant that his work suffered from the censorship laws that dogged Sanger's early career. Her support of his work gave him access to an American audience he might otherwise not have reached. His writings made him more popular than Freud in the early 20th century.

In his twenties, Ellis met and corresponded with South African novelist Olive Schreiner, and the two had an affair. He later married Edith Lees in 1891. The marriage lasted until her death in 1916. Ellis wrote at length about this marriage in his autobiography, *My Life* (1940), as one of both companionship and convenience, as Lees was an acknowledged lesbian. Ellis later became involved with his assistant, teacher and translator Francoise Lafitte Cyon. Havelock Ellis died in 1939 at age 80.

Further reading: P. Grosskurth, *Havelock Ellis: A Biography* (New York: Knopf, 1980); Paul Robinson, *The Modernization of Sex: Havelock Ellis, Alfred Kinsey, William Masters, and Virginia Johnson* (New York: Harper and Row, 1976).

entertainment, popular

The years between 1900 and 1930 saw a growth in the forms and availability of popular entertainment. From open air concerts and VAUDEVILLE shows to nickelodeons, big-screen films, and radios, people from all walks of life spent an increasing amount of time and money to be entertained. The chief trends were toward a consolidation of the entertainment industry, from the creation of theater syndicates and moving picture chains to the growing dominance of major labels in the recording industry and national networks in radio. While musicians and dancers continued to perform on the streets, in parks, on porches and in small theaters, in saloons and juke joints, popular entertainment was on its way to becoming mass entertainment, controlled by large corporations that had superior technology, distribution, and production.

Popular theater, including melodrama, musical theater, burlesque, and legitimate drama had long held a place in American society. What was different was that the range of theatrical entertainment and its venues broadened considerably. The turn of the century witnessed the emergence of the Broadway theater district in New York City and the creation of major theater syndicates to fund Broadway productions and touring shows. By 1910, there were over 40 legitimate theaters in the district, and it bristled with activity from the production of operettas, musicals and musical revues, and repertory theater. That decade saw many new operettas, including Victor Herbert's *Babes in Toyland* (1903) and *Naughty Marietta* (1910), and Franz Lehár's *The Merry Widow* (1907). Soon, however, operettas lost out in competition with new musical shows and legitimate theater. Repertory theater under such lights as Eva Le Gallienne emerged to take its place in the district. The rapid rise of playwright Eugene O'Neill also gave new importance to the Broadway stage. Having begun in Provincetown, Massachusetts, as part of the GREENWICH VILLAGE crowd, O'Neill dominated Broadway drama in the 1920s, and his plays such as *Beyond the Horizon* (1920), *The Emperor Jones* (1920), *Desire Under the Elms* (1925), and *Strange Interlude* (1928) earned him both appreciative audiences and three Pulitzers.

The most popular form of entertainment was the vaudeville show. Modern forms of movies and broadcast television owe much to the early years of the century when vaudeville dominated the entertainment industry. Vaudeville had many influences—minstrel shows, ethnic humor, and music from TIN PAN ALLEY, which was in itself a mixture of musical styles. The bill of any vaudeville production brought to its audience jugglers, musicians, tap dancers, women singers, muscle men, slapstick routines, and standup comedians such as W. C. Fields, Jack Benny, George Burns, and Mae West, who later found fame in RADIO and movies. Vaudeville entrepreneurs were inventive enough to showcase boxer JACK JOHNSON, and they even offered a contract to anarchist EMMA GOLDMAN to speak to popular audiences.

At the high end of vaudeville stood the musical revue. *The Follies* was among the most famous and most opulent. Beginning in 1907, Florenz Ziegfeld launched a series of 20 annual musical revues that captured the popular imagination. Gorgeous costumes highlighted the American Girls in the chorus, and music and comic sketches made up the balance of the show. By the 1920s, Ziegfeld had hired away from vaudeville such legendary performers as Fanny Brice, Bill "Bojangles" Robinson, and Eddie Cantor. For those in musical theater, Ziegfeld's productions were a hard act to

follow; but the period after 1900 saw the proliferation of Broadway musicals written by such giants as George M. Cohan and Jerome Kern. Cohan's shows were much in the vein of musical revues. strung along less by a plot line than a song list. Musicals like *Little Johnny Jones* (1905) and *Forty-Five Minutes from Broadway* (1906) produced such hits as "I'm a Yankee Doodle Boy," "Give My Regards to Broadway," and "Mary, It's a Grand Old Name." In 1920, Noble Sissle and Eubie Blake produced *Shuffle Along*, which was the first major show by African Americans and signaled the increasing presence of black actors and writers in theater. Among other musicals, GEORGE GERSHWIN's *O, Kay!* (1926) and Kern's *No, No, Nanette* (1925) and *Show Boat* (1927) continued to build Broadway's reputation.

Increasingly, though, the Broadway musical was oriented toward a narrative, often of love lost and regained, in which the songs helped to move the story along. *Show Boat* was the pioneer in this development. At the same time, touring companies helped to spread the word of what was happening in New York with performances in theaters around the country, and the musicals and plays, like vaudeville shows, made much of their money on the road. Touring companies had another effect, however, in helping to suppress much local ethnic and working-class theater. Public halls and theaters became the venues of big ticket shows, and smaller independent theaters often closed or converted to movie theaters to survive the change.

Early movies appeared about the turn of the century as filmmakers moved to take over a novelty item and turn it into a popular art form. Edwin Stratton Porter was one of the pioneers in the MOVIE INDUSTRY. In late 1902 or early 1903, he created the *Life of an American Fireman*, his first motion picture. The following year, he made his classic, *The Great Train Robbery*, the first of a long line of Western movies. Porter's studio also first employed DAVID WARK GRIFFITH, who began his film career as an actor. By 1908, he began experimenting with his own films, and in 1915 he produced what was considered his masterpiece, BIRTH OF A NATION. Mack Sennett's studio produced a series of Keystone Kops movies, and it helped to foster the career of Charlie Chaplin as well. In these early years, there was great movement from one studio to the next and in the types of film produced.

The first silent films were relatively cheap to make and could be distributed through informal networks nationwide. In this era, immigrant neighborhoods had their own small theaters, above or in community buildings and neighborhood stores. They showed foreign-language movies produced independently or dubbed from studio films. Middle-class theaters were larger and more palatial, but they too had access to a large range of independent and studio-made films. One way to view the new films was the nickelodeon, an individual viewing machine. John P.

Actress Clara Bow, Hollywood's "It" girl *(Library of Congress)*

Harris and Harry Davis opened the first nickelodeon arcade in Pittsburgh in 1905. Patrons could view a movie for five cents. It was well within the means of working-class viewers. As a result, the industry spread rapidly. By 1908, the number of nickelodeons in American had reached an astounding 10,000.

Music also found a mass audience in the creation of the phonograph. Originally a luxury item, phonograph recordings became popular in the years before and after WORLD WAR I. In 1901, the Victor Talking Machine Company was mass-producing phonographs to play recorded music on cylinders of celluloid or wax or on discs made of laminated shellac. By 1906, the Victrola model gramophone, which stood upright and had an enclosed tapered horn, became the industry standard. Victor spent over $50 million on print advertising for its new product. The flat disc triumphed over the cylinder, and new technology made for mass production of music. In 1919, though electrical recording was still experimental, the first recording to become a million seller hit the market. Paul Whiteman and his orchestra recorded "Japanese Sandman" and "Whispering" and set off a music craze. JAZZ, BLUES, bluegrass and country music, classical music, and patriotic songs all saw their first recordings from 1917 on. Gennett Record Com-

pany, one of the largest labels, issued some of the earliest jazz recordings by Jelly Roll Morton. Record sales reached a decade high of $106 million in sales in 1921. Bessie Smith recorded "Downhearted Blues" in 1923, and Fiddlin' John Carson made "Little Old Log Cabin in the Lane," the first country hit. That year, however, the growing popularity of radio and the increasing availability of music programming started to erode the market for records. Only a few years later, in 1925, electric recording became standard, which tended to displace smaller record companies. At the end of the decade, in 1928, the Radio Corporation of American bought the Victor Talking Machine Company and became RCA Victor. All of these moves consolidated power in the recording industry into the hands of a few companies—RCA Victor, Columbia, and Edison. None of these corporate moves, however, discouraged popular audiences from listening to and even, on occasion, purchasing recordings.

The spread of RADIO technology and broadcasting altered popular entertainment, including the recording industry. In 1920, station KDKA in East Pittsburgh made the first commercial broadcast. By 1922, there were over 3 million homes with radios. By 1930, 40 percent of all homes had radios. Over the decade, there were more than $60 million a year in radio sales. By 1929, more than $850 million in radios had been sold. In addition, by 1930, more than 150 stations filled the airways with music, news, and entertainment.

Locally sponsored shows broadcast folk songs, down-home blues and gospel, and hillbilly music, political party and labor union news, and church hours. New musical forms from jazz to country-western emerged as local musicians moved from juke joints to the radio dial. Urban ethnic and minority communities could lay claim to their own radio shows, which mixed community news with news from the nation and abroad. But the spread of radio narrowed the audience for records, even as it advertised musicians.

Such breadth in radio was a function of the low cost of early radio facilities. As technology improved, demanding more power from transmitters and a larger investment, there was a corresponding loss of diversity in programming. Further, new government regulation of the radio industry raised licensing fees and shifted more stations into the new radio networks—the National Broadcasting Company (NBC) established in 1927 and Columbia Broadcasting Company in 1928. Much of the local flavor was lost when networks set local programming from national radio networks in New York.

The transformation of the movie industry followed the same path as radio, although the consolidation of the industry began earlier. When the studios began to merge and create theater chains, the choices and content of films narrowed. Independent films became harder to make, both because new technology made filmmaking more expensive and because the chain theaters refused to book independents. By 1927, with the advent of sound pictures in *The Jazz Singer,* the cost of making films increased and edged independents out from the national market completely. Further, sound movies, which featured stars from the silent era as well as new stage actors, were available largely through the chains. As a result thousands of small movie theaters failed. The major movie studios soon began to refuse to assign women directors, producers, and screenwriters work, which in turn marginalized women in the industry. At the same time, the popularity of the movies increased the number of large theaters. By 1930, there were over 22,000 movie theaters nationwide.

The 1920s movie audience was drawn toward nostalgic views of the past—as in the popularity of *westerns*—and toward movies that explored modern life and morals, from the sexual ambiguity of Rudolph Valentino and Douglas Fairbanks (*The Sheik* [1921] and *The Thief of Bagdad* [1924]) to a fascination with airplanes, trains, and automobiles in adventure films and the "dancing daughters" of the silver screen. Comedies starring Charlie Chaplin, Harold Lloyd, and Buster Keaton continued to draw audiences, but an increasing number of younger viewers opted for feature films that echoed changing sexual mores. As a bookish matron in *Why Change Your Wife?* (1920), Gloria Swanson adopted a "sleeveless, backless, transparent, indecent wardrobe" and transformed herself into the object of her former husband's attentions. In *It* (1927), Clara Bow revealed her "good old-fashioned sex appeal" as a "slam-bang kid" with "spirited bravado." For a devoted youth audience, the movies had become "a liberal education in the art of making love." Further, surveys suggested that movie stars had replaced politicians, military leaders, and cultural figures as the principal role models of young men and women.

Entertainment industries continued to expand their products and profits throughout the 1920s and into the depression decade of the 1930s. For most entertainers, the growth offered an opportunity to expand their audience and showcase their talents. Still, the corporate look and feel of popular entertainment could also undermine talent. Local theaters, music halls, and radio stations had to compete with the national product, and small ethnic or rural enterprises often lost out to the emerging national culture.

See also POPULAR CULTURE; MUSIC; SPORTS.

Further reading: Lee Davis, *Scandals and Follies: The Rise and Fall of the Great Broadway Revue* (New York: Limelight Books, 2000); Larry May, *Screening Out the Past: The Birth of Mass Culture and the Motion Picture Industry* (New York: Oxford University Press, 1980); Ethan Mordden, *Make Believe: The Broadway Musical in the 1920s* (New York: Oxford University Press, 1997); Robert

W. Snyder, *The Voice of the City: Vaudeville and Popular Culture in New York* (New York: Oxford University Press, 1989).

Equal Rights Amendment (ERA)

Called the "Alice Paul Amendment," this constitutional amendment was first introduced into both houses of the U.S. Congress in 1923. The Equal Rights Amendment (ERA) proposed to add the simple language that "Men and women shall have equal rights in the United States and every place subject to its jurisdiction" to the Constitution. Its author, ALICE PAUL, was the motive force behind militant suffrage tactics in the Congressional Union and the NATIONAL WOMAN'S PARTY (NWP). After the Nineteenth Amendment granting women the right to vote was ratified in 1920, the NWP turned away from conservative approaches to women's rights in order to launch massive lobbying efforts in favor of equal rights for women at the national and state levels. The key to their campaigns was the case for women's absolute equality under the law. Arguing against those who treated women as a protected class, the NWP urged that women should have the same rights that men had. For Alice Paul and her followers, no sexual difference between men and women justified unequal pay, restrictions on women's labor, or women's lack of political rights. Women's loss of citizenship when they married foreign nationals, for example, discriminated against women, since men suffered no such loss. While women could fight for legal changes on an issue-by-issue basis, as they did with the CABLE ACT, a blanket constitutional amendment was preferable. Despite these arguments, the Paul amendment did not receive support for passage in the 1920s. Similar bills were proposed and failed in several states, including Minnesota and Wisconsin.

The Equal Rights Amendment sparked a debate among feminists on the appropriate strategy to ensure women's equality in public life. Women activists divided into two camps: one advocated women's rights on an equal basis with men, the other was more concerned with granting women legal protection based on their differences from men. The latter group believed that women's role as mothers required legal protections that were more important than formal legal equality. Further, those who fought for protective wage and hour legislation for women workers, including labor unions such as the INTERNATIONAL LADIES' GARMENT WORKERS UNION, thought that the passage of an equal rights amendment would jeopardize these laws. When the Supreme Court declared a District of Columbia minimum wage law for women unconstitutional in *ADKINS V. CHILDREN'S HOSPITAL* in 1923, the fears of the protectionists seemed to be confirmed. Arguments about women's equality continued to block efforts to introduce and pass state and national equal rights legislation.

Divisions among women on the various merits of sexual difference and sexual equality were only one barrier to the passage of the ERA. Women's political weakness in the decades between World War I and World War II, and the failure of women to demonstrate unity at the polls, kept legislation for women, whether equal rights acts or social welfare provisions, such as the continuation of the SHEPPARD-TOWNER ACT for maternal and infant health care, from passing Congress or state legislatures. It would not be until 1946 that the ERA was shown any serious consideration from Congress, in response to women's contributions to the war effort. And it was not until the 1970s, with the revival of the feminist movement, that the ERA was finally reconsidered and passed through Congress. It remains unratified today.

See also WOMAN SUFFRAGE; WOMEN'S STATUS AND RIGHTS.

Further reading: Susan Becker, *The Origins of the Equal Rights Amendment: American Feminism between the Wars* (Westport, Conn.: Greenwood, 1981); Christine Lunardini, *From Equal Suffrage to Equal Rights: Alice Paul and the National Woman's Party, 1910–1928* (New York: New York University Press, 1986).

Espionage Act (1917)

Enacted as a guard against domestic subversion of the U.S. effort in WORLD WAR I, the Espionage Act of 1917 was a controversial law that threatened domestic civil liberties. As the efforts at progressive reform in the early 20th century gave way to a focus on the war in Europe, the Wilson administration grappled to find ways to bolster support for American intervention. Public opinion was sharply divided about the conflict and how the United States should respond. Given the large influx of immigrants to the United States since the 1880s, new ethnic and national groups contributed to the social and political conflict over the war. German immigrants still formed the largest foreign-born group, 2.3 million, in the population. In addition, there were more than two million immigrants from the various parts of the Austro-Hungarian Empire, another major combatant.

Throughout his first term as president, WOODROW WILSON and others expressed concern about the large immigrant population in the United States and frequently referred to the need for national loyalty. Running for reelection in 1916, President Wilson made Americanism a dominant theme of his campaign. Along with Wilson's desire to build a sense of national unity, the war led his administration to secure legislation to dampen dissent and

opposition and to further promote the cause of national unity in the United States. As Wilson moved toward a pro-intervention policy in the European conflict, he saw this as an opportunity to publicize and export American democratic ideals.

Fearing that opposition would undermine his ability to bring the United States directly into the conflict, Wilson favored policy initiatives that fostered and promoted patriotism. In this vein, the COMMITTEE FOR PUBLIC INFORMATION was created in 1917 to publicize and popularize the war and the reasons for American involvement in this conflict. A major outcome of this drive for national unity was to actually create more division within the United States. In particular, what originated as an anti-German campaign resulted in an anti-immigrant crusade, which culminated in the first in a series of restrictive immigration laws passed by Congress between 1917 and the mid-1920s.

During the controversial debate about national identity, the Wilson administration called upon Congress to pass legislation that would silence dissent and encourage support for the United States in World War I, which the country officially entered in April 1917. As Wilson called upon Congress to declare war on Germany and its allies, Representative Edwin Webb of North Carolina and Senator Charles Culberson of Texas began to craft legislation that would give the president the ability to impose "stern repression" to ensure unity behind the nation's emerging war effort. The Espionage Act, as it was known when enacted in early June 1917, furnished the government with ample power for the suppression of those who opposed the war. The act imposed stiff fines of between $5,000 and $10,000 and jail sentences of up to 20 years for individuals convicted under this law. The law went far beyond simply attempting to prevent spying for the enemy. Instead its main objective was to make it illegal to write or utter any statement that could be construed as profaning the flag, criticizing the Constitution, or opposing the military draft.

The extreme nature of this legislation constituted the most drastic restriction of free speech since the enactment of the Alien and Sedition Acts of 1798. The Socialist Party and the INDUSTRIAL WORKERS OF THE WORLD (IWW) had emerged by 1917 as the most vocal and organized forces to oppose America's involvement in the war in Europe. Accordingly, they quickly became among the first groups to feel the strong arm of the American legal system after the passage of the Espionage Act. The head of the Socialist Party, EUGENE VICTOR DEBS, received a 10-year jail term for making an anti-war speech in Canton, Ohio, in 1918. In that same year, some 2,000 members of the IWW were arrested under the authority of the Espionage Act. The Espionage Act helped fuel a movement to protect civil liberties in the postwar era.

See also SEDITION ACT.

Further reading: Paul Murphy, *World War I and the Origin of Civil Liberties in the Untied States* (New York: Norton, 1979).

— David R. Smith

ethnic organizations

In the wake of the mass immigration of the early 20th century, ethnic organizations flourished in the United States between 1900 and 1930. The first 14 years of the century brought a peak in total arrivals for the long and massive wave of immigration that had lasted from 1830 to 1914. During this 80-year period, more than 22 million immigrants arrived in the United States, with some 6 million alone arriving at the shores of the United States between 1900 and 1910. On the whole, the American economy expanded sharply during these decades. Despite this widespread expansion, large numbers of the immigrants arriving in the United States were not in a position to be primary beneficiaries of economic growth. Instead, most found work as industrial laborers in the rapidly expanding industrial economy.

Arriving in urban industrial centers, immigrants after 1900 often had little choice but to find employment as unskilled workers in the factories that characterized the American economy. The size of the industrial workforce grew dramatically from 957,000 in 1849 to 4,252,000 in 1889 and 7,036,000 by the eve of WORLD WAR I. Finding work in the nation's industrial economy did not necessarily bring with it the prosperity and economic gain that many immigrants sought. The economy faced several episodes of crisis. Having no recourse to government programs for relief, many immigrants faced desperate economic straits with each turn of the business cycle.

To help soften the economic conditions that many immigrants faced in the United States, many ethnic groups organized fraternal societies that provided assistance during difficult times. Not only did immigrant workers face periodic bouts of unemployment, but also family illnesses, unexpected deaths, or housing problems created trying times for newly arrived individuals and their families. Given the sometimes hostile response that many immi-

grants faced, they became suspicious of some forms of public assistance. Most philanthropic organizations attached conditions to their assistance and often had difficulty understanding and communicating with immigrants. These factors contributed to the emphasis placed on self-help organizations in immigrant communities. Ethnics tried to care for their own. Such organizations as the Bohemian Charitable Association, the Polish Welfare Association, and the Jewish Home for the Aged were formed in the early part of the century with the express purpose of assisting their members. Within their ethnic communities, most immigrants could expect to be assisted not only by formal ethnic organizations, but also by their neighbors and fellow immigrants. Everything from bread to haircuts and donations of money was extended to neighbors in trouble.

The onset of war in Europe in 1914 evoked renewed efforts by ethnic communities and organizations as they sought to help refugees displaced by the conflict. After the war, many small ethnic organizations moved toward consolidating their efforts into large umbrella groups. In Chicago, for example, the Associated Jewish Charities and the Associated Catholic Charities emerged from several smaller community-level groups. The attempt to provide economic relief to immigrant workers in the United States through ethnic organizations survived through the 1920s. The onset of the Great Depression and the enactment of various pieces of social legislation resulted in many ethnic organizations being displaced by the federal agencies and services created by President Franklin D. Roosevelt's New Deal.

See also IMMIGRATION; SOCIAL WORK.

Further reading: John Bodnar, *The Transplanted: A History of Immigrants in Urban America* (Bloomington: Indiana University Press, 1985); Roger Daniels, *Coming to America: A History of Immigration and Ethnicity in American Life* (New York: Harper & Row, 1991).

— David R. Smith

evolution   See Scopes Trial

F

Farmer-Labor Party

With roots in the Populist Movement of the 1890s and midwestern PROGRESSIVISM in the early 1900s, the Farmer-Labor Party formed as a third-party alternative in American electoral politics. The Farmer-Labor Party and its predecessor, the NON-PARTISAN LEAGUE (NPL), grew out of farmer discontent over deteriorating conditions in agriculture in the early 20th century. Increased agricultural production in the 1910s had resulted not in a better standard of living for farmers, but in overproduction and a sharp drop in farmers income. Falling into debt, many farmers were forced into tenancy, or they left agriculture altogether.

In 1915, wheat farmers in North Dakota formed the NPL on a platform of state-run enterprises. Independent politics spread throughout the West after the NPL had successes in the 1916 elections. In Minnesota, farmer-laborites established the Minnesota Farmer-Labor Party after they failed at the nonpartisan strategy in the Republican primary of 1918.

When employers went on the offensive after WORLD WAR I to establish the OPEN SHOP in many mass production industries, trade unions shifted their efforts to political action. With participation from the NPL, the Socialist Party, local farmer and labor parties, and labor unions set up the Conference for Progressive Political Action (CPPA) in 1922. Independent CPPA candidates were quite successful in the 1922 elections. Twelve out of 16 CPPA gubernatorial candidates won. The Minnesota Farmer-Labor Party took control of the state legislature and won half Minnesota's seats in Congress. Farmer-Labor candidates were elected to one Senate seat in 1922 and won the other Senate seat in 1923.

In 1924, the CPPA ran and independent ticket in the national elections, with Wisconsin Progressive ROBERT M. LA FOLLETTE and Montana Democrat Burton K. Wheeler as presidential and vice presidential candidates. The La Follette ticket did surprisingly well in the 1924 elections, winning nearly 17 percent of the popular vote. La Follette won in Wisconsin and came in second in nine western states. Along with Wisconsin, the states of California and Minnesota had significant industrial populations.

Although the Farmer-Labor Party had many state-level successes, the third-party movement ultimately failed at the national level. Immediately after its formidable challenge to the national two-party system in 1924, the third-party movement collapsed. The obstacles to waging a national effort proved to be insurmountable. The major labor leaders ultimately maintained their ties to the Democratic and Republican Parties. Meanwhile, the farmer-labor coalition suffered from persistent internal divisions that undermined its successes. In addition, its supporters faced other setbacks: the decline of organized labor on the national level as well as an increasingly conservative political climate in the 1920s. Only in Minnesota did the farmer-labor efforts remain strong through the 1930s.

Since the Populist era, American radicals had attempted to forge farmer-labor unity, seeing both groups as producers exploited by the capitalist system. In the 1924 presidential elections, the loose coalition of farmer-laborites came closer than at any other time in mounting a third-party challenge in the electoral system. However, the Farmer-Labor Party and other progressive movements of the era were unable to translate their state successes into a long-term national alternative to the two-party system.

Further reading: Millard L. Gieske, *Minnesota Farmer-Laborism: The Third-Party Alternative* (Minneapolis: University of Minnesota Press, 1979); Richard M. Valelly, *Radicalism in the States: The Minnesota Farmer-Labor Party and the American Political Economy* (Chicago: University of Chicago Press, 1989).

— Glen Bessemer

Federal Farm Loan Act (1916)

A primary goal of farm organizations in the United States in the early 20th century was to create a government program for farm credit. Passed in 1916, the Federal Farm Loan Act opened the door to federal government support with a program of low-interest loans. Having been elected president in 1912 on the platform of the NEW FREEDOM, WOODROW WILSON sought to preserve political and economic liberty in the United States through various legislative and executive initiatives. In particular, Wilson opposed the consolidation and abuse of economic power that had increasingly occurred since the turn of the century. One of the main emphases of his administration was to prevent the further consolidation of economic power that curbed free competition and to increase the ability of individual producers and small businesses to compete.

Despite his focus on slowing the growth of economic power, Wilson remained fairly unreceptive to the demands of labor and of farm organizations during his first term. Both these groups had sought to protect the power of individuals against the consolidation of economic power by corporations. Despite his initial reluctance to directly aid unions and farmers, he relented on his opposition to pro-farm and pro-labor legislative initiatives as the 1916 election approached. Accordingly, President Wilson approved the Federal Farm Loan Act in 1916, which provided agriculture with the low-interest rural credit system long advocated by farmers and rural residents.

Although farmers had faced a shortage of capital, banking facilities, currency, and credit during the last two decades of the 19th century, the new century brought a wave of prosperity to rural areas of America that would last until shortly after the end of WORLD WAR I. During this "Golden Age" of agriculture, farmers tended to spend their newfound prosperity on consumer goods to improve their standard of living. However, many farmers, having witnessed the economic difficulties of the late 19th century, were hesitant to invest in capital improvements, whether in expanding their landholdings or in purchasing new technologies. The farm advocates long had championed the need for low-interest loans to help promote and make affordable the capital improvements needed to expand individual farms.

The Federal Farm Loan Act created the mechanism to extend low-interest loans for periods of five to 40 years to farmers through the control of a Federal Farm Loan Board. The board was comprised of 12 Federal Land Banks that paralleled the Federal Reserve Banks. As part of Wilson's New Freedom initiative, the Federal Farm Loan Act extended capital to farmers through a program that cut out private banks, which long had been viewed by farmers as outside institutions that easily exploited vulnerable farmers.

Further reading: David B. Danborn, *Born in the Country: A History of Rural America* (Baltimore: Johns Hopkins University Press, 1995).

— David R. Smith

federal income tax (1913)

The United States has had a long history of local and state income taxes. The majority of the states in the Union experimented with one form of income tax or another long before the first federal income tax was levied. By 1910, 20 states had income tax laws on their books. Income taxation at the federal level, however, was a more hotly contested issue. During the War of 1812, the Congress considered the idea of a federal income tax. Due to the relatively short duration of the war, it did not act upon this. During the Civil War, however, the financial needs of the Union were so acute that a federal income tax provision was adopted as an emergency war measure. This first federal income tax, adopted in 1862, was a moderate tax levied on a small portion of the population. The temporary nature of the measure became apparent in 1872 when it was repealed. The repeal of the statute did not mark the end of the debate. It marked the beginning of a half-century-long struggle over the readoption of a suitable federal income tax.

During nearly every session of Congress in the post–Civil War era, representatives from the South and West proposed new federal income tax bills. During the depression of 1893, southern and western Democrats finally succeeded in passing the Wilson-Gorman Tariff. It marked the first national, nonwartime, direct tax on the incomes of American citizens and corporations. The Supreme Court voided portions of the act the following year by declaring that aspects of the federal tax were unconstitutional. In 1894, the Supreme Court expanded its position on the constitutionality of a direct income tax when it declared in *Pollock v. Farmers' Loan and Trust Company* that a direct income tax was a breach of the constitutional provision that direct taxes must be apportioned among the states according to population. Leaders in the DEMOCRATIC PARTY claimed that the Supreme Court's decision was judicial usurpation aimed at protecting those with wealth and privilege. This criticism provided southern and western Democrats with a means not only of attacking the Supreme Court, but also for challenging the REPUBLICAN PARTY, which controlled the other two branches of government.

As a result of this partisan struggle, the idea of a federal income tax become a plank in the Democratic Party's 1896 election platform. The tax began as a political maneuver used by the Democrats to challenge the Republican Party's dominance. The Democrats, supported by opponents of the tax who believed that they could derail the tax with its own momentum, helped to put forward the bill as an amendment to the constitution. The opponents who signed onto the bill miscalculated. Both the Senate and the House of Representatives passed the law in 1909, which allowed for the taxation of citizens in accordance to their income.

After four years, the amendment was ratified by the states and became law. The Federal Income Tax became the Sixteenth Amendment to the Constitution of the United States. The amendment, which began as a partisan struggle, took on a life of its own. The Democrats who supported it championed the bill as a means of achieving social justice. The revenue that the government would collect from the tax was viewed by many of its supporters as an afterthought. The law, however, became extremely important during WORLD WAR I. The ratification of the amendment provided the government with needed revenue to finance the war effort. It also created a model for financing government activities for generations to come.

In addition to the political maneuvering that was required in making the amendment a reality, there were a number of challenges to making the income tax practical. The first challenge was how to define what exactly would be taxed under the law as income. The next step was to determine how much each individual would be taxed. The creators had to weigh advantages and disadvantages to individuals as well as the economic well-being of the country in general. They decided upon a progressive income tax that would tax those with a higher income at higher rates. Politically, it satisfied all but the most zealous Democrats. These radical Democrats wanted to use the tax to aid in restructuring a classless society. Economically, it won the support of the most prominent economists of the time.

The Sixteenth Amendment for a federal income tax proved to be much more than a political victory for the minority party trying to establish its supremacy. It established the means necessary for the U.S. government to take a much more active role in the development of American life and commerce.

Further reading: John D. Buenker, *The Income Tax and the Progressive Era* (New York: Garland Publishing, 1985); Jerold Walterman, *Political Origins of the U.S. Income Tax* (Jackson: University Press of Mississippi, 1985).

— Steve Freund

Federal Reserve Act (1913)

After a century of political struggle over the government's role in banking and currency, the Federal Reserve Act of 1913 settled the question by establishing a national network of banks in aid of the monetary system. Despite much acrimonious debate about the supply of money in the economy throughout the late 19th century, the CONGRESS had not instituted any large-scale reforms to change the banking and financial structure of the nation since the time of the Civil War. The crisis over the supply of money and its relationship to the nation's economic well-being was once again highlighted by the Panic of 1907. Banking reform became one of the major issues addressed by progressive reformers and politicians.

As one of the principal concerns of WOODROW WILSON during his first term as president, banking reform had strong support from both aisles of Congress. Unlike many other areas of reform that divided Democrats and Republicans, both parties favored the need for greater federal regulation of banking and the supply of currency as a key to preventing future economic panics or depressions. As national debate turned to restructuring and regulating banking, much concern was voiced about whether public or private concerns should have the leading influence in any new agencies created by federal legislation.

In 1913, Wilson assumed leadership over this issue and pushed through Congress the Federal Reserve Act, perhaps the most significant piece of legislation signed by Wilson during his first administration. The principal aim of this legislation was to control the supply of money in circulation by creating a federal agency charged with regulating interest rates. With its ability to determine the rate at which private banks could borrow money from the government, the Federal Reserve was able, by this legislation, to either expand or deflate the availability of money in the nation's economy. To control this process, the Federal Reserve Act established 12 regional banks. All private banks in the United States were required under this legislation to deposit an average 6 percent of their assets in their regional Federal Reserve Bank. These deposited funds were then used to make loans to member banks and to issue paper currency, or Federal Reserve notes, that facilitated financial transactions. When market conditions shifted in one region, regional banks were empowered to raise or lower interest rates in order to provide a quick response to sudden changes in credit demand.

To respond to public pressure that banking reform reflect the needs and concerns of the public and not just that of private bankers, the Federal Reserve Act charged the president with appointing a Federal Reserve Board that was responsible to the public, not the banking industry. The board set policy and administered the activities of the 12 regional banks. Although the Federal Reserve Act stands as a major achievement of the Wilson administration, it reflected the philosophical shift in Wilson's thinking from the time of the 1912 presidential campaign to the policy initiatives of his first administration. During the campaign, Wilson had pledged to use the federal government to break up the power held by large industries. Within the Federal Reserve System, he in effect consolidated bank power.

While the Federal Reserve Act did a great deal to strengthen the financial health of the American economy, it did precious little to break the concentration of banking that had emerged in the late 19th century. With the collapse of the U.S. (and world) economy in 1929, the Reserve fell under attack for failing to prevent the onset of economic crisis. In general, Wilson had crafted the Federal Reserve system in a way that worked with large banks, rather than attempting to break them up. Much of the thinking and impetus behind this legislation had been to create a mechanism that could stave off economic crisis. Although during the 1990s, the Federal Reserve skillfully oversaw the largest expansion of the American economy, in the 1920s it was not as successful. Accordingly, the legislation seemed more in line with the thinking of Theodore Roosevelt's NEW NATIONALISM that Wilson had campaigned against in 1912.

Further reading: James Livingston, *Origins of the Federal Reserve System: Money Class and Corporate Capitalism, 1890–1913* (Ithaca, N.Y.: Cornell University Press, 1986).

— David R. Smith

Federal Trade Commission Act (1914)

The Federal Trade Commission Act of 1914 laid the foundations of government regulation of trade and commerce by creating a commission to collect information on prices, competition, and trade. In response to the consolidation of economic power among corporations, monopoly and unfair trade practices became central issues of progressive reform. They also became major points of conflict in the presidential election of 1912. Of the four major candidates in 1912, three advocated progressive reforms to address the growing power of corporations. The socialist candidate, EUGENE V. DEBS, argued that the federal government should assume ownership of the trusts. For the other primary candidates, THEODORE ROOSEVELT, WILLIAM HOWARD TAFT, and WOODROW WILSON, this solution was unacceptable. Despite their unity in rejecting socialist ideas, Wilson and Roosevelt clashed during the 1912 campaign over their respective plans to address the trust issue in the American economy. Running on the PROGRESSIVE PARTY ticket, former president Theodore Roosevelt advocated a NEW NATIONALISM that would strengthen the federal government. The reinvented government would create powerful government agencies that regulated and, when necessary, limited the power of trusts.

In contrast, the Democratic candidate, Woodrow Wilson, found the proposal to strengthen the federal government to be a threat to state governments. Accordingly, his proposal did not call for stringent regulation, but rather for the government to actually break up the trusts. Wilson contended that the monopolies created by various trusts undermined the competition and commerce that had been responsible for much of the economic prosperity of the nation since the last century. While the federal government would be empowered and, accordingly, strengthened to dismantle the trusts, it would be only a temporary arrangement, ending the concentration of economic power in the hands of the few. Once this objective was achieved, Wilson insisted that the federal government would relinquish these new powers. Wilson presented these ideas to the American public during the 1912 campaign as the NEW FREEDOM that would restore economic opportunity to the people.

Despite making the pledge to break up the trusts during the 1912 campaign, Woodrow Wilson ultimately deviated from that position after assuming the office of the president in 1913. Two initiatives—banking and antitrust—became the core of his progressive reform agenda during his first term in office. In 1914, Congress passed the Federal Trade Commission Act, which created the federal agency by that name. The Federal Trade Commission (FTC) was empowered to collect information on corporate pricing procedures and competition between companies. Wilson eagerly signed the Federal Trade Commission Act into law, declaring that the break-up of large-scale industry was no longer practical for the American economy. Instead, he now fully embraced Theodore Roosevelt's position that large industry was an inescapable aspect of 20th-century America and that the proper role for government would be to regulate industry through government agencies. Despite wide powers of investigation, the FTC was left without any significant enforcement mechanism as Congress stripped its companion legislation, the CLAYTON ANTITRUST ACT, of the power to break up trusts. The Federal Trade Commission, like other Progressive Era reforms, only partly addressed economic consolidation issues of the period.

Further reading: Marc Allen Eisner, *Antitrust and the Triumph of Economics: Institutions, Expertise, and Policy Change* (Chapel Hill: University of North Carolina Press, 1991).

— David R. Smith

Flynn, Elizabeth Gurley (1890–1964)

During the Progressive Era, the growing power of the NEW UNIONISM in the workplace and the sustained influence of SOCIALISM in the labor movement created a new context for working-class activism. An important part of that activism involved working women in mass production industries and the new turn in the WOMAN SUFFRAGE movement, which dedicated itself to recruiting women workers and to improving their working conditions. Into this context emerged a new generation of women labor activists who captured the imagination of both the mainstream and the RADICAL PRESS. One such figure was Elizabeth Gurley Flynn.

Born in 1890, Flynn was the daughter of Thomas and Annie Gurley Flynn, Irish-American socialists. In her early adolescence, Elizabeth Flynn's father took her to rallies to hear speakers and learn socialist principles. In 1906, she gave her first public speech and thereafter became a frequent speaker for socialist and labor causes. In 1907, she met John Archibald Jones, an organizer from the Mesabi Iron Range, and married him the next year. Flynn gave birth to her second and only surviving child, Fred, in 1910. Flynn's desire to remain active led to her separation from Jones, and he divorced her in 1920.

Active as a speaker and organizer for the INDUSTRIAL WORKERS OF THE WORLD, Flynn engaged in several important labor struggles of the day. She participated in free speech fights in Missoula, Montana, and in Spokane, Washington. In 1912, Flynn helped to coordinate the LAWRENCE STRIKE with IWW's "BIG BILL" HAYWOOD, Arturo Giovannitti, and Joe Ettor. During the strike, Flynn, along with MARGARET SANGER, organized families to send their children to supportive families in New York. The violent response of the police to the children's exodus built public sympathy for the strike. Flynn reacted strongly and publicly to the poverty, illness, and deprivation of workers in an age when industry was largely unregulated. She knew that labor violence did not stop at the factory door or even the picket line. Her courage in these early battles earned the admiration of IWW songster Joe Hill, who wrote a song in her honor. As Hill's "Rebel Girl," Flynn carried the banner of women's emancipation within the IWW, and she spoke out in support of BIRTH CONTROL. Throughout her life, she worked for the dual causes of labor and the equality of women.

Flynn's personal life was rocky. Once separated from her husband, she became involved with mercurial IWW organizer Carlo Tresca. They lived together in New York for 10 years. She left him in 1925. After joining the COMMUNIST PARTY (CP) in 1926, Flynn took ill. A physician, Marie Equi, took care of Flynn, and the two women lived together in Portland, Oregon, for 10 years. She returned to New York in 1936 to become active once again, this time in national communist politics. In the 1950s, she was put on trial under the Smith Act and convicted. She served two years in Alderson Prison.

For the rest of her life, she fought for the working class under the communist banner. As one of the few well-known women in the party, Flynn became a member of the national committee and helped to set party policy. Despite its residual sexism, the CP offered women the opportunity to be politically active and committed itself, at least on paper, to discussing the Woman Question. For Flynn, however, the issues of gender equality came second to the class struggle. Through her life, she would give priority to the agenda and issues of the Communist Party

Elizabeth Gurley Flynn *(Library of Congress)*

and only secondarily to the women in that party. She died in 1964.

Further reading: Rosalyn Fraad Baxandall, ed., *Words on Fire: The Life and Writing of Elizabeth Gurley Flynn* (New Brunswick, N.J.: Rutgers University Press, 1987).

Ford, Henry (1863–1947)

Henry Ford's introduction of the Model T Ford automobile and his innovations in assembly line production fundamentally transformed American society. Born in Dearborn, Michigan, in 1863, Ford displayed a genius for mechanical innovation at an early age. Ford moved to Detroit when he turned 16 and began working as an apprentice in a machine shop. In the 1890s, while working for the chief engineer for the Detroit Edison Company, Ford began experimenting with an internal combustion engine. He built his first automobile in 1896 and sold it to raise money to build more. In 1899, he secured enough financial backing to create the Detroit Automobile Company, which later became the Henry Ford Company. During these early years, Ford frustrated many of his backers when he insisted that his automobile was not yet ready for sale to the public. Frustrated by these disputes, he left the company, which later became the Cadillac Motor Car Company. In 1903, he created the Ford Motor Company.

Ford's first automobile, the Model A Ford, was well-built, relatively inexpensive (at $850 it was among the least expensive automobiles on the market), and sold exceptionally well. By 1904, Ford had sold 1,700 of the Model As and had established himself as one of the leading manufacturers in the city. Ford's rise to prominence, however, was almost derailed before it began. His reluctance to push his early models into production had alienated many of Detroit's wealthiest financiers and manufacturers. When Ford introduced the Model A, Ford was taken to court because he was not a licensed manufacturer. Other licensed automakers charged that Ford had violated the 1895 patent given to George Baldwin Selden, an early innovator. Ford finally won the suit on an appeal in 1911. Ford's commitment to manufacturing good quality, inexpensive automobiles, along with his decision to fight wealthy manufacturers in Detroit and their financial backers, made him a popular figure with many ordinary citizens.

Not content to have only a minority share of the automobile market, Ford announced in 1908 that he was going to build a durable, inexpensive car that would enable ordinary citizen to enjoy the benefits of automobile transportation. Although critics scoffed at the idea that automobiles could be mass-produced, the Model T Ford was released in March 1908 and became an instant success. The Model T featured top-of-the-line engineering and construction but no frills. Priced at $850, Ford boasted that no car offered more for less, and the American public agreed. Between its introduction in 1908 and its discontinuation in 1927, Ford sold 15 million Model Ts.

The early success of the Model T convinced Ford that he could in fact sell an automobile to every family in the country. In order to do so, he had to make them even cheaper and faster. Ford concluded that MASS PRODUCTION would be the key. The more Model Ts he produced, the cheaper he could sell them. Building on the SCIENTIFIC MANAGEMENT ideas introduced by FREDERICK WINSLOW TAYLOR, Ford created an intricate assembly line for the production of the Model T and set about to integrate every aspect of the car's production. Ford realized that his current facility was not capable of housing a fully integrated assembly line, and so in 1910 the company moved its operation to the newly designed Highland Park plant. Built by architect Albert Kahn, the plant was a massive complex, complete with state-of-the-art machinery. With the opening of the Highland Park Factory, Ford created a revolutionary process, in which every step of the Model T's production had been automated. The Model T's production time dropped from 728 minutes to a remarkable 93 minutes. The result was that Ford was able to mass-produce the Model T, further reduce the car's cost (in 1927, only $290), and maximize profits. By 1921, Ford controlled 55 percent of the automobile industry and had a net annual income of $78 million.

In 1914, Ford was in the national spotlight when he announced that all Ford employees would be paid the incredible amount of $5 a day for an eight-hour work day. At the time, industrial employees were averaging only $11 a week, and they often worked more than nine hours a day. Praised by some and denounced by others, Ford insisted that keeping skilled and loyal employees was essential to maintaining his rigorous production schedule. Knowing the value of their skills, craft workers were frequently late for work or simply moved from job to job. Ford's decision to pay his employees such a handsome wage was not motivated by a commitment to humanitarianism, but rather by a desire to homogenize and discipline his employees. He provided many of his employees with affordable housing but also insisted that they learn how to speak English,

Henry Ford *(Library of Congress)*

refrain from consuming alcohol, and become upstanding American citizens. Ford created a Sociological Department to investigate how his employees lived. The company also withheld part of a worker's $5 a day wage if he was late or did not fill her production quota. Part of the withheld money could be retrieved if workers agreed to meet the demands of the Sociological Department. Ford's personal beliefs also were highly controversial. In 1918, he purchased the *Dearborn Independent* and published a series of articles attacking Jews. Finally, Ford regularly employed company police and spies to intimidate employees; and until the 1940s, his company vigorously opposed attempts by employees to form a union.

The innovations introduced by Ford helped transform the country, while throughout the world Ford's achievements with the new assembly-line production methods became identified as "Fordism." Widespread ownership of the automobile helped spread the construction of goods roads and the expansion of cities. Over the next several decades, the automobile changed virtually everything about American society. In addition, the introduction of mass production, the assembly line, scientific management, and corporate paternalism changed the very nature of American industry.

Further reading: Robert Lacey, *Ford: The Man and the Machine* (Boston: Little, Brown, 1986).

— Robert Gordon

Fordney-McCumber Tariff (1922)

With the return of Republican control to the White House in 1921, President WARREN G. HARDING's administration set about to restore many traditional Republican policies, such as tax cuts and higher protective tariffs. President Harding's secretary of the treasury, ANDREW W. MELLON, strongly advocated that both these policies be adopted shortly after the new administration entered office. In particular, WORLD WAR I had allowed the chemical and metal industries to develop a number of innovative technologies. Industry leaders, along with Mellon, argued for a higher protective tariff to allow them further time to develop these advantages. The Fordney-McCumber Tariff of 1922 increased tariff rates on chemical and metal products as a safeguard against the revival of German industries, which had dominated these sectors of the international economy prior to the outbreak of hostilities in Europe in 1914.

The imposition of a new protective tariff in the United States had far-reaching consequences previously unimagined by the federal government. In particular, while the United States had been a debtor nation prior to the war, it emerged from the war as a creditor nation. As a result, the international economy increasingly depended upon U.S.

capital for its economic development. European nations and their citizens owed some $13 billion to the United States at the end of the world war. Moreover, the United States steadily made additional foreign loans and investments in the postwar period. The need to make loan repayments in U.S. dollars meant that the international community had a real need to be able to export its products to the United States in order to receive an influx of dollars that could be used to make the necessary payments on their loans. The Harding administration was adamant that European nations needed to repay all of their debts from the war. Consequently, the need for an open trade system became more and more apparent.

The return of a protective tariff to the United States often priced foreign goods out of the American economy. Although not the only factor, the protective tariff imposed by the United States in 1922 contributed to the extremely difficult economic conditions that Europe faced as a result of shifting economic power in the international community and the heavy reparations that constructed the German economy. Clearly, the First World War had altered the position of the United States in the international economy, and its economic policies would no longer affect only domestic conditions, but would also have implications that extended well beyond its own borders. The Fordney-McCumber Tariff, like the Hawley-Smoot Tariff that followed in 1930, contributed to world economic crisis in the 1930s.

Further reading: Edward S. Kaplan, *Prelude to Trade Wars: American Tariff Policy, 1890–1922* (Westport, Conn.: Greenwood, 1994).

— David R. Smith

foreign policy

The victory of the United States in the war with Spain in 1898 was a turning point in American foreign policy. Until 1898, American officials thought that their government should stay out of foreign entanglements, and they restricted expansion to territories on the North American continent. By the late 19th century, however, American presidents argued that the country needed to expand into foreign territories to search for new markets. At the turn of the century, the United States reorganized its military system and built up its naval power to ensure access to foreign markets and to meet the needs of the expansion of American capitalism and culture. Although 80 percent of American exports went to Europe and Canada in the late 19th century, the United States competed with the great industrial powers for markets in Asia and Latin America.

Leaders in the United States used two reasons to justify the expansion of American capitalism and culture

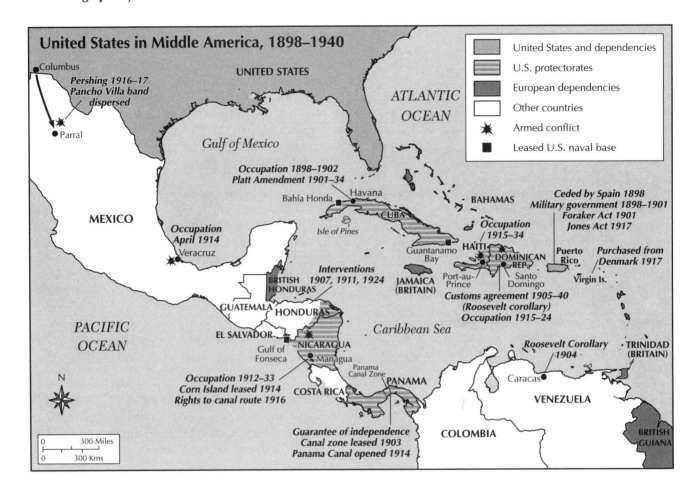

United States in Middle America, 1898–1940

Legend:
- United States and dependencies
- U.S. protectorates
- European dependencies
- Other countries
- ✴ Armed conflict
- ■ Leased U.S. naval base

Columbus

Pershing 1916–17 Pancho Villa band dispersed

Parral

UNITED STATES

Gulf of Mexico

ATLANTIC OCEAN

MEXICO

Occupation April 1914
Veracruz

Occupation 1898–1902 Platt Amendment 1901–34

Bahía Honda   Havana

Isle of Pines

CUBA

BAHAMAS

Ceded by Spain 1898 Military government 1898–1901 Foraker Act 1901 Jones Act 1917

Guantanamo Bay

Occupation 1915–34

HAITI

DOMINICAN REP.

Puerto Rico

Purchased from Denmark 1917

PACIFIC OCEAN

BRITISH HONDURAS

Interventions 1907, 1911, 1924

GUATEMALA   HONDURAS

JAMAICA (BRITAIN)

Port-au-Prince

Santo Domingo

Virgin Is.

Customs agreement 1905–40 (Roosevelt corollary) Occupation 1915–24

Caribbean Sea

EL SALVADOR

Gulf of Fonseca

NICARAGUA

Managua

Panama Canal Zone

PANAMA

Caracas

Roosevelt Corollary 1904

TRINIDAD (BRITAIN)

VENEZUELA

N

Occupation 1912–33 Corn Island leased 1914 Rights to canal route 1916

COSTA RICA

Guarantee of independence Canal zone leased 1903 Panama Canal opened 1914

COLOMBIA

BRITISH GUIANA

0   300 Miles

0   300 Kms

---

around the world. First, the American business community had reached a consensus that, by expanding into foreign markets, the country could solve its economic, social, and political problems that stemmed from the Industrial Revolution. Second, American leaders increasingly believed that the country needed strategic naval bases to compete with European countries in Asia and Latin America. Alfred Thayer Mahan's *The Influence of Sea Power upon History* (1890) had a significant influence on American elites. Mahan had argued that the United States would need naval supremacy and control of the seas to maintain its national power. His theories inspired the GREAT WHITE FLEET as a policy tool under THEODORE ROOSEVELT.

The Spanish-American War of 1898, which began as an intervention for humanitarian reasons in a civil war in Spanish Cuba, became a contest for colonial expansion. After the United States took possession of the Philippines in the war with Spain, a revolt broke out against the new colonial power under EMILIO AGUINALDO. Although Americans saw themselves differently than the previous European imperial rulers, the United States found that subjugating other people required military force and bru-

tality. After four years of fighting, 4,300 Americans had died and about 50,000 Filipinos were killed in the Philippine War. By 1902, American troops under JOHN PERSHING finally suppressed the Philippine insurrection.

The American presence in Asia increased with the acquisition of the Philippines. In particular, the U.S. administration sought to expand trade with China. At the turn of the century, the major European and Asian powers had begun to carve up China in a rapid imperialist expansion. Wanting to protect American interests in China, President William McKinley stated in 1898 that, although the United States sought no special advantages, he encouraged the European and Asian powers to maintain an "open door" in China. Secretary of State John Hay translated McKinley's message into the Open Door notes, addressing it to England, Germany, Russia, France, Japan, and Italy. The major powers ignored the OPEN DOOR POLICY until the United States participated in an international expeditionary force that suppressed the nationalist BOXER REBELLION in China. England and Germany agreed to abide by the Open Door policy after the rebellion was crushed in 1900.

Although the United States won the war with Spain and acquired Cuba, Puerto Rico, and the Philippines, the war illustrated obvious inadequacies in the American ARMED FORCES. President McKinley appointed Elihu Root, a corporate lawyer from New York, as secretary of war to reorganize the entire military system. Between 1900 and 1903, Root transformed the military system into a modern one. The reforms enlarged the regular army, established federal army standards for the National Guard, created officer training schools, and organized a central planning agency to coordinate military operations.

The United States assumed a more active role in international affairs between 1901 and 1917. Theodore Roosevelt became president after McKinley was assassinated in 1901. Roosevelt brought stability to Asia and won the Nobel Peace Prize in 1906 for his efforts at negotiating the Treaty of Portsmouth, which ended the RUSSO-JAPANESE WAR of 1904–05. He also agreed to the Japanese presence and territorial status quo in the Pacific under the ROOT-TAKAHIRA AGREEMENT of 1908.

Despite his work as a peacekeeper, Roosevelt extended American military power and dominance in the Western Hemisphere. In 1904 the president added the ROOSEVELT COROLLARY to the Monroe Doctrine. He claimed the right to intervene in the domestic affairs of Latin American countries if they were not able to maintain order themselves. This policy expanded on the right under the Monroe Doctrine of the United States to oppose European intervention in the region. Using the Roosevelt corollary, the United States intervened in the Dominican Republic when the country was unable to make payments on its $22 million debt. In 1905, the United States took control of the nation's finances for three decades.

The United States intervened in other Caribbean countries as well. In exchange for granting Cuba independence, the United States required that the country put the Platt Amendment of 1901 in its constitution, which maintained the right of the United States to intervene in Cuba to prevent a foreign power from having undue influence there. In 1903 Roosevelt prevented the Colombian government from suppressing a revolution in its province of Panama. Immediately after Roosevelt recognized the independent nation, the Panamanian government agreed to a PANAMA CANAL treaty. In 1911, three years before construction of the canal was completed, Roosevelt had claimed, "I took the Canal Zone and let Congress debate."

Roosevelt's successor, WILLIAM HOWARD TAFT, attempted to preserve the economic interests of the United States in the world. Using policies termed as DOLLAR DIPLOMACY, Taft's secretary of state, Philander C. Knox, worked to extend American investments throughout the world. The value of American exports increased from $800 million in 1895 to $2.3 billion in 1914, an increase of close

to 240 percent. Taft resorted to military force when economic influence proved insufficient. In 1909, when revolution broke out in Nicaragua, the Taft administration sent troops to support the government's opponents and to seize the country's customs houses. Two years later, Taft sent troops to Nicaragua again to protect the pro-American government. The American troops occupied the country for over a decade.

When WOODROW WILSON entered the White House in 1913, he continued the interventionist policies of earlier presidents. Although Wilson opposed dollar diplomacy, which he thought forced weaker countries into inequitable financial relationships, he agreed with the importance of promoting economic development overseas. In addition, he sought to conduct a foreign policy that followed democratic principles. In particular, he wanted to extend constitutional liberty to the country's neighbors in Latin America. Having taken control of the Dominican Republic's finances in 1905, the United States set up a military government there in 1916. Wilson sent the U.S. Marines to Haiti in 1915 to crush a revolution, and American troops occupied that country until 1934.

In 1914 Wilson sent troops to the Gulf of Mexico port of Veracruz after the Mexican army had arrested American sailors who had gone ashore in Tampico. Wilson expected to establish a pro-American government in a bloodless intervention, but the two countries came to the brink of war. Nineteen Americans and 126 Mexicans were killed in skirmishes, and the Wilson administration backed off. When the military intervention helped to strengthen the position of Venustiano Carranza, the United States decided to back the opposition led by Pancho Villa. However, when Villa appeared to be losing the power struggle, the United States abandoned him and granted preliminary recognition to the Carranza government. To retaliate, Villa killed 16 Americans on a train in northern Mexico; later his forces crossed the border into Columbus, New Mexico, killing 17 more Americans. Wilson then ordered an expeditionary force into Mexico to find Villa. Although the U.S. troops never found Villa, the two countries engaged in battles that killed 40 more Mexicans and 12 Americans. The United States finally withdrew its troops and formally recognized the Carranza government in 1917.

In the 1920s the U.S. government encouraged economic expansion in Latin America. Between 1924 and 1929, U.S. investments more than doubled in Latin America as the U.S. military maintained a presence in several countries there. At the same time that the United States intervened in the affairs of Latin American countries, public opinion wanted to sustain American NEUTRALITY in the European conflict.

When WORLD WAR I broke out in Europe, the United States attempted to stay neutral. However, as British and

German warfare gradually restricted American trade and freedom of the seas, President Wilson became involved in the conflict. When the British imposed a naval blockade on Germany, the United States was able to withstand an interruption of its trade with the Central Powers (Germany, the Austro-Hungarian Empire, and the Ottoman Empire); but abiding by any embargo of the Allies (Britain, France, Italy, and Russia) would harm the U.S. domestic economy, especially when war orders increased dramatically from Britain and France after 1914. Defense production helped to bring about one of the most expansive economic booms in American history.

By 1915, the United States had sided with the Allies by supplying them with war materials. Meanwhile, the Germans resorted to a new tactic, submarine warfare, to cut off the flow of supplies to England. A German submarine sank the British passenger liner, LUSITANIA, on May 7, 1915, killing 1,198 people, 128 of whom were Americans. After the incident, the Germans agreed to Wilson's demands that the Central Powers affirm their commitment to neutral rights and promise not to launch more attacks.

By 1917, the Germans had decided that the advantages of unrestricted submarine warfare outweighed the risk of American entry into the war. By then, Wilson had concluded that, if provoked to enter the war, the United States could use the war as a means of creating a new democratic world order. In a speech to the Congress in January 1917, Wilson presented a plan for a postwar order and "peace without victory." The United States would help to maintain peace through a LEAGUE OF NATIONS, a world organization of nations that would arbitrate conflicts and ensure the self-determination of nations.

Meanwhile, a number of events made American entry into the war nearly inevitable. In February, the British gave Wilson an intercepted telegram from the German foreign minister to the Mexican government. In the ZIMMERMANN TELEGRAM, the foreign minister proposed that the Mexicans ally with the Germans if the United States joined the war. In exchange, when the war was over, Mexico would reacquire Texas and much of the American southwest. Publication of the telegram helped to create popular support in the United States for entry into the war.

In the following month, a republican government replaced the czarist regime in the RUSSIAN REVOLUTION. When the Bolsheviks took control in the October Revolution of 1917, Wilson refused to recognize their new government. Diplomatic relations between the two countries were not restored until 1933. The possibility—and eventual reality—of Russia withdrawing from the war put additional pressure on the Wilson administration to join the Allied war effort.

In April 1917, the United States entered the war as an ally of Britain. Within months of the arrival in 1918 of American troops in Europe, Germany agreed to an armistice. By the time war had come to a close, the European population and economy were decimated. In contrast, the United States emerged from the war relatively unscathed and as a global power; and the nation's economy experienced an industrial boom that stretched into the 1920s.

The TREATY OF VERSAILLES, which formally ended the war, differed significantly from what Wilson had hoped for. He was unable to win approval for most of his proposals, such as freedom of the seas, free trade, and the principle that the negotiations should result in "open covenants openly arrived at." The Paris agreements were negotiated in secret. Rather than gaining support for the "impartial mediation" of colonial claims, Wilson had to accept a transfer of German colonies in the Pacific to Japan, which Britain had promised in exchange for Japanese help in the war. In addition, the economic and strategic demands of the Allies undermined his promise of "national self-determination" for all peoples.

The major difference between the American and Allied agendas for peace was the demand that the Central Powers pay reparations to the Allied governments to compensate for their losses. Wilson opposed the idea. When the Allies refused to compromise, he reluctantly accepted the principle of reparations. A commission in 1921 determined that Germany had to repay $56 billion to the Allies. Germany eventually paid only $9 billion, but the amount was still far more than the decimated economy of Germany could afford.

Although the treaty was far from Wilson's hopes for peace based on the principles of justice and democracy, it provided for a League of Nations, which Wilson believed would create a new international order. Even though Wilson lobbied passionately for the passage of the treaty, the Senate refused to ratify it. Its defeat at the hands of Senator HENRY CABOT LODGE and other Republicans signaled an end to Wilsonian internationalism.

Having rejected Wilsonian diplomacy and its promises of a new world order, the United States retreated from European affairs for two decades after World War I. In a policy of what historian Joan Hoff Wilson has called "independent internationalism," American policymakers in the 1920s hoped to create protective measures against future wars without restricting the nation's freedom of action in the world. When WARREN G. HARDING took office, Secretary of State CHARLES EVANS HUGHES secured a series of agreements at the WASHINGTON CONFERENCE ON NAVAL DISARMAMENT of 1921–22 from the major European and Asian powers to curb the destabilizing naval arms race. In 1927, the major powers attempted unsuccessfully to extend the disarmament measures of the Naval Disarmament conference in Geneva. In 1928, 62 nations signed onto the

KELLOGG-BRIAND TREATY, which outlawed war. Unfortunately, these peace and disarmament measures contained loopholes and lacked enforcement measures so that they became meaningless.

Although the Kellogg-Briand Treaty was unenforceable, it was seen as a victory for the peace movement, which had come together as a loosely organized coalition. The most active groups included the World Peace Foundation, the Foreign Policy Association, the Woodrow Wilson Foundation, the Council on Foreign Relations, the League of Nations Non-Partisan Association, the CARNEGIE ENDOWMENT FOR INTERNATIONAL PEACE, the Social Science Research Council, and the Institute of Pacific Relations. Having a significant influence on foreign policy, the members of these organizations included mostly American elites who shared a vision of Wilsonian internationalism, a liberal new world order, and collective security. In fact, James T. Shotwell, a professor at Columbia University who headed the Carnegie Endowment, had helped to develop the Kellogg-Briand Treaty of 1928. Meanwhile, other groups that lobbied for the outlawry of war but emphasized pacifism rather than collective security, included the WOMEN'S INTERNATIONAL LEAGUE FOR PEACE AND FREEDOM (WILPF) and the Fellowship for Christian Social Order. While the members of the pacifist groups were skeptical of the potential for peace, most of them supported a Christian pacifism.

Even though the United States retreated from the Wilsonian vision of a new world order in the 1920s, American policymakers sought to ensure the economic redevelopment and stability of Europe, a continent devastated by World War I. The Allies had to repay $11 billion in loans to the United States. In addition, the reparations Germany was required to pay the Allies under the terms of the Treaty of Versailles weighed down the German economy. In 1924, CHARLES GATES DAWES, an American banker and diplomat, negotiated an agreement among France, Britain, Germany, and the United States. American banks provided loans to Germany so that it could pay the reparations and invest in its economy. Meanwhile, Britain and France agreed to reduce the amounts of the reparations if the Germans made their payments. Debt repayment fueled American economic expansion in Europe until the international financial system broke down after 1929. However, the DAWES PLAN did not solve the economic troubles in Europe. In fact, the circular flow of debt repayments helped to destabilize international finance, one of several factors that brought on a world economic depression in the 1930s.

The political chaos around the world sparked by the Great Depression, and the rise of fascist governments and military regimes in Europe and Asia intent on territorial expansion, severely undermined the fragile international system created after World War I. These powerful international forces gradually pushed the United States to greater involvement in international affairs.

In 1929 President Herbert Hoover faced a looming international economic and political crisis. He attempted to protect American farmers from international competition by raising agricultural tariffs with the Hawley-Smoot Tariff of 1930. Rather than helping farmers in the United States, the tariffs, at the highest level in American history, only exacerbated the international economic crisis. Other governments retaliated by enacting their own trade restrictions, thus shrinking the market for agricultural goods from the United States.

By the time that Hoover left office in 1933 the international system had collapsed. The system of the 1920s that failed had been based on voluntary cooperation among nations and a refusal by the United States to restrict its freedom of action by establishing international obligations. Continued investment and intervention in Latin America and the Caribbean were not seen as contradictory solutions but rather as protecting America's sphere of interest. Under the administration of Franklin Delano Roosevelt, the United States gradually moved from a position of isolationism to intervention in the European and Asian conflicts that culminated in World War II.

See also CLARK MEMORANDUM.

Further reading: Michael J. Hogan, *Ambiguous Legacy: U.S. Foreign Relations in the "American Century"* (Cambridge, U.K.: Cambridge University Press, 1999), Gordon Martel, ed., *American Foreign Relations Reconsidered, 1890–1993* (London: Routledge, 1994); Emily S. Rosenberg, *Spreading the American Dream: American Economic and Cultural Expansion, 1890–1945* (New York: Hill and Wang, 1982); William Appleman Williams, *The Tragedy of American Diplomacy*, new ed. (New York: Norton, 1988).

— Glen Bessemer

Fourteen Points See Versailles, Treaty of

Freud, Sigmund (1856–1939)
The Viennese doctor Sigmund Freud was one of the most influential thinkers of the 20th century. The founder of the new science of psychoanalysis, Freud developed a therapeutic method for treating disorders that had their origins in the unconscious. Freud's psychological theories, which put new emphasis on early psychosexual development, became increasingly influential in the United States after 1910. They shaped the sexual revolution of the 1920s.

After Freud began his career as a research scientist in anatomy, he began studying the irrational, or "unconscious," thinking that it could be studied with the same scientific rigor as anatomy. In 1886, he opened a medical office in Vienna to treat patients with nervous disorders. Freud coined the term "psychoanalysis" in 1896, claiming that dreams were the expression of unconscious conflicts of the mind. He encouraged his patients to free associate, unlocking painful memories that had been repressed since childhood. The basis of Freud's theory of the unconscious was sexuality and the repression of sexual urges. His theory of human development established the irrational as a driving force of the human mind. Early critics of Freud's theory of the unconscious were threatened by the theory's potential for individual self-discovery, which could undermine the traditional moral codes of church and state.

Freud had been introduced to the American psychiatric community when he visited Clark University in 1909. Even though Freud's theories were referred to in discussions and publications of the American psychiatric community by the early 1910s, only a few professional psychiatrists used psychoanalysis in private practices. In general, Freud gained influence when psychiatrists achieved professional dominance over psychologists in the 1920s. While psychiatrists had gained an institutional foothold in diagnostic and treatment programs in the United States, psychologists had been relegated to the role of "mere" intelligence testers.

By the 1920s, mainstream psychiatry in the United States had become accustomed to psychoanalysis and had refashioned it into a peculiarly American form. Finding Freud's theories to be too deterministic, many in the field of dynamic psychiatry, or adjustment psychiatry, rejected them. American psychiatrists in psychopathic hospitals retained part of Freud's methods that linked with the theory of the unconscious, namely the psychiatric analysis of a patient's confession of disclosure of intensely private information.

Psychiatrists adjusted their theories to the sexual revolution that had reached the working and middle classes in the United States. For example, sexologist HAVELOCK ELLIS popularized a new standard of sexual morality in his book, *Psychology of Sex*, which recorded and classified forms of human sexual desire. Under the new sexual mores, women who had been labeled "hypersexual" before the 1920s became normal, as long as their sexual behavior was confined to heterosexual marriage. Psychiatrists diverted their attention from hypersexual working-class women to sexual psychopaths, who were most often male homosexuals, who were labeled as rapists, child molesters, on sex offenders.

Significant differences distinguished European psychiatry and psychology from the American traditions. Freud had blurred the distinction between the normal and abnormal, which was a stark separation that had characterized much of the thinking about human beings in the 19th century. In contrast, American psychiatrists lacked skepticism, often promoting presumptions about what was normal for humans, especially when it came to sexuality.

Freud had a significant influence on the psychiatric profession, bringing the new science of psychoanalysis to the United States. Although Freudian psychoanalysis merged with the modern treatment models of psychiatry, significant differences between the European and American professions remained.

Further reading: Nathan G. Hale, Jr., *Freud and the Americans: The Beginnings of Psychoanalysis in the United States, 1876–1917* (New York: Oxford University Press, 1971).

— Glen Bessemer

Fuel Administration

The Lever Food and Fuel Act of August 10, 1917, established the Fuel Administration as an agency to coordinate the production, supply, and distribution of vital resources of gasoline and oil. Once the United States had entered WORLD WAR I in April of that year, President WOODROW WILSON's administration began its preparations. Ensuring a sufficient supply of goods and resources was essential. The administration created the COMMITTEE FOR PUBLIC INFORMATION in April 1917 to begin preparing the public for the sacrifices they would be asked to make. The administration created the WAR INDUSTRIES BOARD and the NATIONAL WAR LABOR BOARD to oversee war production and labor disputes, and it secured passage of the ESPIONAGE ACT and the SEDITION ACT to ensure public support for the war. In addition, consumers were encouraged to ration food and conserve the products they used.

One of the products increasing in public demand was oil and its by-products, particularly gasoline. The growth of both consumer and defense industries, along with the expansion of automobile ownership, meant oil, coal, and gasoline were in high demand. Waging a modern war meant the supervision and, if need arose, rationing of fuel. Wilson created the Fuel Administration in August 1917 and appointed Harry A. Garfield to oversee its operation. The Fuel Administration asked the public to voluntarily conserve coal and oil by driving less, using less coal to heat their homes, and restricting nonessential consumption. It fixed the price of coal higher to bring less efficient coal mines into operation and increased coal production by 50 percent. It also had the power to ration supplies of coal and oil.

In the winter of 1917–18, heavy demands on the fuel supply led to a coal shortage across the United States. Coal trains were stopped en route, and towns appropriated coal supplies. Police had to safeguard coal stockpiles, and industries vital to defense, including armaments and ship-building, ground to a halt. Fuel administrator Garfield shut down factories east of the Mississippi for four days in order to ensure coal deliveries to ships headed for France. After January, however, the shortage began to ease. There were few problems for the rest of the war.

Labor problems, though, loomed on the horizon. The UNITED MINE WORKERS (UMW) had signed a no-strike pledge, known as the Washington Agreement, with the Fuel Administration. Bituminous coal miners received no raise under the agreement, and wartime inflation eroded the pur-chasing power of their wages. The agreement, which did not expire at war's end in November 1918, held the miners in check for nearly a year, but by September of 1919, the UMW actively sought increases from mine operators. The mine owners refused to budge, and the UMW set a strike deadline of November 1, 1919. When Attorney General A. MITCHELL PALMER advised the UMW of the consequences of disregarding the Washington Agreement, the union pres-ident backed down. The miners did not go back until a few days later, when they received a 12 percent wage increase. A subsequent mining commission found that real wages for miners had lagged behind inflation, and they granted a 27 percent wage hike for all miners. By the time of the settle-ment, the wartime Fuel Administration had already been disbanded, having closed its doors in June 1919.

Further reading: David M. Kennedy, *Over Here: The First World War and American Society* (New York: Oxford University Press, 1980).

— Robert Gordon

★

Garvey, Marcus (1887–1940)

The leader of the first black nationalist movement in the United States, Marcus Garvey tried to establish a separate black-governed country in Africa. He ultimately failed, but his efforts to create a black-run economy in the United States and his appeals to black pride made him one of the most important African-American leaders of the early 20th century.

Born in 1887 in Jamaica, Garvey founded the UNIVERSAL NEGRO IMPROVEMENT ASSOCIATION in 1914. The initial platform for the UNIA called for caring for the needy of the race, civilizing backward African people, and developing schools and colleges for African and African-American youths that would teach a commitment to racial brotherhood around the globe. In addition, it called for the establishment of agencies around the world to protect the rights of blacks and for the creation of commercial and industrial trade between blacks. Garvey was not very successful in his first two years. The organization had only 200 members in 1916. In March of that year, Garvey toured the United States to raise funds for UNIA. During his tour, he was impressed by the condition of African Americans in relation to those faced by Africans in Jamaica. He hoped that the relative wealth of the African-American community in America and the existence of black leadership would help his organization. He decided to move UNIA's headquarters to Harlem in New York City.

UNIA enjoyed a measure of success in the years following its move to the United States. Answering Garvey's own call for the establishment of black-owned businesses, UNIA bought its own building in Harlem, opened a restaurant, began a newspaper, the *Negro World,* and established a steamship line, the Black Star Line. The Black Star Line was the most visible manifestation of Garvey's philosophy. The black-owned and operated Black Star Line would not only carry black immigrants to Africa but would also foster trade among blacks in the United States, the Caribbean, and Africa. According to Garvey, this trade would form the basis of the worldwide black economy of the future. UNIA raised the money needed to buy steamships by selling stock in the Black Star Line. African Americans embraced the idea, and UNIA had no trouble selling the stock.

Garvey reached the peak of his power in 1920, when UNIA held its first international convention in Madison Square Garden. For one month, 25,000 delegates met to establish it as an international organization. The convention elected Garvey as the provisional president of Africa and approved a 54-article *Declaration of Negro Rights,*

Marcus Garvey *(Library of Congress)*

which called for equal rights for Africans throughout the world. It named injustices suffered and demanded equal treatment before the law, access to economic opportunity for blacks, an end to colonialism, the return of Africa to African rule, and also adopted an African national anthem.

Garvey's power and influence began to decline soon after the convention. In 1920–21, the United States suffered through an economic recession. As unemployment rose among African Americans, sales of Black Star Line stock plummeted. In addition to its financial troubles, Garvey faced harsh criticism from established African-American leaders, including A. Philip Randolph and W. E. B. DUBOIS. Critics questioned his financing of the Black Star Line. They charged that he was selling more stock than he legally could. In 1922, Garvey provided further fuel to the fire when he met with the second-in-command of the KU KLUX KLAN. His critics charged that he had made a deal with the Klan to remove African Americans from the United States, leaving it as the white man's country that Garvey had always claimed it was. Garvey responded to these charges by purging his critics from UNIA's leadership, but he did not last long enough to take advantage of this situation. He was convicted of mail fraud in a federal court in New York City in June of 1923. The court sentenced Garvey to five years in prison and a $1,000 fine. After losing his appeal, he began to serve his sentence in 1925. In 1927, President Calvin Coolidge commuted his sentence, and Garvey was deported to Jamaica. Garvey attempted to re-create UNIA in Jamaica; but by the mid-1930s, both UNIA and Garvey had fallen into obscurity. He died in obscurity in 1940.

Further reading: Cary D. Wintz, ed., *African-American Political Thought, 1890–1930: Washington, DuBois, Garvey, and Randolph* (New York: M.E. Sharpe, 1996).

— Michael Hartman

Gastonia Strike (1929)

In the spring of 1929, 3,500 textile operators at the Loray Mill in Gastonia, North Carolina, went on strike against the company. Under the leadership of Fred Beale, the National Textile Workers Union, a union allied with the Communist Party, had been organizing in Gastonia for months. Low wages, the stretch-out system of assigning looms to workers, and long hours were among the workers' chief grievances. On April 1, workers from both shifts walked out, demanding employers meet their demands and give the union recognition. They were met with a well-organized resistance. Local employers formed a Committee of One Hundred to break the strike, and the governor of the state sent in the National Guard to keep the mill open.

Within weeks of the walkout, thousands of workers in the Piedmont South joined the Gastonia workers in massive strikes in protest against employer decisions to increase their workload and lower wages. Impoverished not simply by a low-wage economy but also by a decade of recession in the textile industry, mill workers had been silent when employers speeded up the machines at which they worked. By 1929, however, the industry was showing some signs of revival. With that upturn, workers organized throughout the Piedmont region in North Carolina, South Carolina, and Georgia. While the campaign benefited from outside funding and leadership, some of its most visible labor activists were long-term employees with roots in local communities.

In Gastonia, labor violence escalated. Police and National Guardsmen harassed those walking the picket line, and a local crowd destroyed the union office. Employers then ordered the workers evicted from company housing. In an exchange of gunfire one night, the local chief of police was killed. Sixteen strikers and leaders, including Beale, were charged with the murder. Seven were eventually convicted of second-degree murder. They fled to the Soviet Union while out on bail. Locally, one worker, Ella Mae Wiggins, had caught the attention of the press with her songs written from her mill experience, such as the "Mill Mother's Lament." Wiggins became another victim of the violence. She was killed on September 14, when the car she was riding in was ambushed on the way to a strike meeting. Although five Loray Mill employees were charged, no one was convicted of her murder.

The fierceness of conflict between local workers and local police caught the attention of labor reformers nationwide. Reporters from labor and radical newspapers and organizers, some of whom belonged to the Communist Party, went south to support the strike. Newspaper reporters told the powerful story of how textile workers, long viewed as passive, stood up to employers. The strike also made it into radical literature as the subject of six novels, including Mary Heaton Vorse's *Strike!* (1930) and Fielding Burke's *Call Home the Heart* (1932). Still, the workers fought an uphill battle. Evictions from mill housing and lack of resources made it difficult for strikers to sustain the conflict. Although the conflict lasted throughout the summer, in Gastonia, as throughout the region, the strike was lost.

Further reading: Jacquelyn Dowd Hall, et al., *Like a Family: The Making of the Southern Cotton Textile Mill World* (Chapel Hill: University of North Carolina Press, 1987); John Salmond, *Gastonia, 1929* (Chapel Hill: University of North Carolina Press, 1995).

General Electric (GE)

Created in 1892, the General Electric Company (GE) invented and produced numerous products that changed the way ordinary Americans lived their lives. GE's formation in 1892 was an attempt to manufacture and distribute many of the new electrical products that had been invented by Thomas Alva Edison and others. Edison had formed his own corporation, the Edison Electrical Light Company, in 1878, which then became the Edison General Electric Company. Engineered by financier J. P. Morgan, General Electric merged the competing manufacturers, Edison General and the Thomson-Houston Electric Company.

In 1900, GE created a research lab in Schenectady, New York, with the hope that it would be able to duplicate the kind of creative environment Edison had established at his famed Menlo Park. GE president Edwin Rice set out to hire leading scientists from around the world. According to Rice, "It has been deemed wise during the past year to establish a laboratory devoted exclusively to original research. It is hoped by this means that many profitable fields may be discovered." The idea of committing a large amount of money to research and development, with no guarantee that anything profitable or marketable would come from it, revolutionized American industry. Prior to the development of industrial research labs, innovations were the domain of individual scientists and inventors. Corporations emerged only after new products or new ideas were developed. GE spared no expense in building the labs, developed close ties with university science departments, and hired some of the leading scientists of the day, including Charles Steinmetz, William Coolidge, Irving Langmuir (who won the Nobel Prize in chemistry in 1932), and Willis Whitney. Whitney, who had been a chemistry professor at MIT prior to joining GE, served as head of the company's research lab between 1900 and 1928.

From the very beginning, the work of GE's research laboratory was extremely productive and profitable. Early triumphs included innovations in the incandescent light bulb, vacuum tubes, and an X-ray machine. Improvements in lighting allowed GE to play an important role in the emerging electrification and lighting industry as communities and individuals brought electricity and electric lighting into their towns and homes. By 1930, GE had become one of the most prominent and profitable companies in the country; and its products, including radios, refrigerators, and stoves, began appearing in every household.

See also ELECTRICITY; INVENTION AND TECHNOLOGY.

Further reading: Leonard S. Reich, *The Making of American Industrial Research: Science and Business at GE and Bell, 1876–1926* (New York: Cambridge University Press, 1985); Ronald Schatz, *The Electrical Workers: A History of Labor at General Electric and Westinghouse, 1923–1968* (Urbana: University of Illinois Press, 1983).

— Robert Gordon

Gentlemen's Agreement (1907)

Following on decades of racial hostility toward Asians, the Gentlemen's Agreement of 1907 was an informal pact between the United States and Japan to slow emigration from Japan. Between the 1880s and the onset of WORLD WAR I, there was a steady increase in the number of immigrants to the United States. In 1907, at its height, some 1,285,349 immigrants entered the country. Asian immigration was a specific area of concern. By 1882, the federal government responded to the demands of white workers in California and enacted legislation that prohibited the entry of emigrants from China, in the Chinese Exclusion Act. While this legislation effectively halted the major source of Asian immigrants, it did not close the door to Asians. In 1885, the emperor of Japan lifted that country's prohibition on emigration, and a steady flow of Japanese laborers entered the United States. Their primary destination was the sovereign island kingdom Hawaii, where Japanese immigrants found employment on American sugar cane plantations. With the subsequent annexation of Hawaii by the United States in 1898, Japanese migrants were free to move to the continental United States. In the early part of the 20th century, Japanese immigrants entered the country at a rate of about 10,000 per year.

Although the number of immigrants reaching the United States from Japan and other Asiatic countries remained relatively small, opposition to Chinese, Japanese, and other Asian immigrants steadily mounted in places like California. In 1906, opposition to Japanese immigrants in California had reached a point where the San Francisco school board ordered the segregation of Japanese and other Asian schoolchildren. The school board and many white residents of San Francisco did not hide racist attitudes toward the Japanese. They argued for the segregation of the schools in order to prevent the "contamination" of white children. In addition to segregation, anti-Asian riots erupted in several California cities during 1906, including San Francisco and Los Angeles. California's anti-Asian prejudices were encouraged and fed by hysterical stories in the press about the "Yellow Peril" of Asian immigration. This so-called Yellow Peril caused outrage in Japan, and pro-military elements within the Tokyo government began calling for a war with the United States.

To calm tensions between the two countries and quiet public sentiment, President THEODORE ROOSEVELT sought to work out a solution with the Japanese government. The Gentlemen's Agreement with Japan in 1907 resolved the mounting tension between the two nations. In exchange for

Japan agreeing to refuse passports to unskilled laborers seeking to immigrate to the United States, Roosevelt promised to have the San Francisco school board rescind its segregation order. While the agreement halted most migration between Japan and the United States, it did not bar Japanese residents already in the country from sending for their wives. Accordingly, thousands of Japanese women continued to enter the United States. Many of these immigrants were actually so-called picture brides who had been married by proxy in Japan in order to gain entry into the United States. Fearing that he would be attacked for being soft with the Japanese, President Roosevelt subsequently ordered the GREAT WHITE FLEET on its world tour late in 1907.

Further reading: Roger Daniels, *The Politics of Prejudice, the Anti-Japanese Movement in California, and the Struggle for Japanese Exclusion* (Berkeley: University of California Press, 1962).

— David R. Smith

Gershwin, George (1898–1937)

An important American composer, George Gershwin is remembered for his musical comedies, popular songs, orchestral works, and an opera, *Porgy and Bess.* Combining jazz and classical composition, Gershwin had many successes that crossed the line between classical and popular MUSIC, including *Rhapsody in Blue,* among the most frequently played pieces of American classical music.

George Gershwin (Jacob Gershovitz) was born in Brooklyn, New York, on September 26, 1898, the son of immigrant Russian Jewish parents. At the age of 12, he began to study the piano, and at age 15 wrote his first compositions. Gershwin studied with American composers Rubin Goldmark, Henry Cowell, and Wallingford Riegger and the Russian-born composer Joseph Schillinger. An accomplished pianist, Gershwin began his career in 1918 as a musician and song promoter for Jerome Remick Company, a TIN PAN ALLEY music publisher. In his songs, Gershwin drew upon the idioms and rhythms of JAZZ and BLUES music, as revealed in his first popular success, "Swanee."

By the 1920s, Tin Pan Alley was declining in musical influence as sheet music gradually lost its popularity. It had fostered much new talent, including Gershwin and composer Irving Berlin, but Broadway theater companies slowly took its place as venues for introducing and distributing popular music. Both in New York and on tour, Broadway plays and reviews publicized new songs and composers. Starting off as a rehearsal pianist, Gershwin began composing for Broadway shows. In 1920, he wrote the entire score for the review *George White's Scandals,* which introduced him to theater audiences. Gershwin

followed with a string of hit shows, including *Lady, Be Good* (1924), *Tip-Toes* (1925), *Oh, Kay!* (1926), *Funny Face* (1927), and *Girl Crazy* (1930). Working with his brother Ira, George produced such classic anthems as "'S Wonderful," "Someone to Watch Over Me," and "I Got Rhythm." Like Cole Porter, another great popular composer of the time, Gershwin benefited from the use of his tunes in movie musicals of the 1930s, most memorably those starring dance duo Fred Astaire and Ginger Rogers. Such exposure led to national recognition. In the 1930s, Gershwin moved into political satire and spoofs with such comedies such as *Strike Up the Band* (1930) and George S. Kaufman's *Of Thee I Sing* (1931), which won the Pulitzer Prize.

Along with popular music, Gershwin began experimenting with classical symphonic works in the 1920s. At the request of band leader Paul Whiteman, in 1924 he wrote his now-famous *Rhapsody in Blue,* a piece for piano and jazz band, scored by American composer Ferde Grofé. Gershwin composed a longer piece, *Concerto in F,* for piano and orchestra in 1925. His symphonic poem, *An American in Paris,* written in 1928, was rhythmically and harmonically challenging. In 1935, Gershwin completed

George Gershwin *(Library of Congress)*

Porgy and Bess, an opera based on DuBose Heyward's book about life on Catfish Row in Charleston, South Carolina. Using African-American themes and jazz and blues rhythms in classical forms, the opera reached popular audiences with its evocative and haunting music, especially the memorable song, "Summertime." On July 11, 1937, at the age of 39, Gershwin died in Beverly Hills, California. His music remains a vital part of the popular music repertoire in the United States and internationally.

Further reading: Rodney Greenberg, *George Gershwin,* (London: Phaidon, 1998); Deena Rosenberg, *Fascinating Rhythm: The Collaboration of George and Ira Gershwin* (New York: Dutton, 1991).

Gilman, Charlotte Perkins (1860–1935)

One of the most creative social thinkers of the Progressive Era, socialist feminist Charlotte Perkins Gilman wrote extensively in journals and magazines and authored several important books, including her first major work, *Women and Economics* (1898). Born into a well-known family in Providence, Rhode Island, Gilman's childhood abruptly changed after her mother and father separated. She grew up in genteel poverty. She attended Rhode Island School of Design for a few years and then worked as a teacher and commercial artist. After she married artist Charles Stetson, she grew increasingly unhappy. Her depression only increased after the birth of a daughter, Katherine. After undergoing unsuccessful psychological treatment, an episode she later dramatized in the short story, "The Yellow Wallpaper," Gilman divorced her husband and sent her daughter to live with him. She chose to live independently, supporting herself with journalism, fiction, and public speaking. In 1900, at age 40, she married George Houghton Gilman, a cousin who was more accepting of her public career. They remained married until his death in 1934.

Gilman's career took off with the publication of *Women and Economics* in 1898. Heavily influenced by sociologist Lester Frank Ward, the study took on the challenge of analyzing women's status and work in society. In it, Gilman argued that women had been socially and emotionally disabled by their isolation in the home. Their absence from the public world of work devalued them in an increasingly materialist society. As a remedy, Gilman advocated that women enter the workforce and the professions. In subsequent books, she argued for revolutionary new arrangements for domestic life, including the creation of day nurseries and shared household work. *Women and Economics* was published and later translated in several editions in the United States and abroad. Less well known were her books *Concerning Children* (1900) and *The Home*

(1903), which further explored collective housekeeping and childcare. *Human Work* (1904) offered a social Darwinist perspective on the social division of labor.

From 1909 to 1916, Gilman published the independent socialist journal, *The Forerunner.* In *The Forerunner,* she serialized a number of novels, including *Herland.* The utopian novel, which is now widely read as a socialist feminist work, imagined an isolated society organized along maternal lines. Three earnest young men, one a sociologist and the other two adventurers, discover a secluded mountain community of women. There, motherhood is the highest good, and all efforts are bent toward developing moral and cultural values in children and adults. As a satire, the novel targeted the relationship between the sexes of the day, in particular its disregard of women's productive and creative powers. Such neglect, Gilman suggested, rendered women helpless victims of men's egotism. For all its touting of female and maternal values and critique of masculine and patriarchal power, the novel implied that cooperation and the absence of "male" values had made Herland's society stagnant. The end of the novel foresaw a progressive integration of masculine and feminine values.

With the end of WORLD WAR I and the RED SCARE, feminism and socialism fell into disrepute. Old-fashioned women's rights advocates like Gilman fell out of favor. The growing popularity of SIGMUND FREUD's sexual theories changed socialism, but Gilman stayed her own course to the end and continued to advocate social evolutionary ideas. Her autobiography, *The Living of Charlotte Perkins Gilman* (1935), gave testimony to the importance of women's individual emancipation within the framework of progressive social reform. Gilman died in 1935, having contracted breast cancer and taken her own life.

Further reading: Ann Lane, *To Herland and Beyond: The Life and Work of Charlotte Perkins Gilman* (New York: Pantheon Books, 1990).

Goldman, Emma (1869–1940)

One of the most famous radicals of the 20th century, anarchist Emma Goldman promoted the causes of labor, free love, free speech, and revolution throughout her life. She was born on June 27, 1869, in Russian Kovno (now Kaunas, Lithuania), to Abraham and Taube Bienowitch Goldman. Financial difficulties prompted the family to move to Königsberg in Prussia, where Emma attended school for three and a half years. In 1881, the family moved to Saint Petersburg, Russia.

The political repression following the assassination of Czar Alexander II outraged Goldman, who was already sensitized to injustice by Russian anti-Semitism and the brutality of her own father. Participation in underground

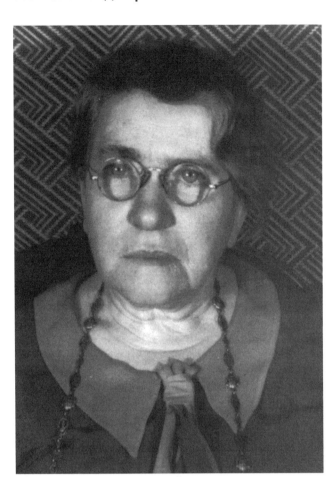

Emma Goldman, 1934 *(Library of Congress)*

discussion groups exposed her to radical literature, which she eagerly absorbed. Her political activities and sexual adventures, however, increased turmoil at home, which she escaped by migrating to America with her half-sister, Helena, in 1885.

The events surrounding the Haymarket Riot in 1886 rekindled her interest in radical literature. She soon became an avid reader of *Die Freiheit*, an anarchist newspaper published by Johann Most. She was intrigued by his support of violence and his emphasis on the individual, rather than the state. In 1889 she moved to New York, where she met Most. He quickly became her mentor and lover. Under his direction, she embarked on a lecture tour, speaking in Yiddish to immigrant audiences.

As Goldman's relationship with Most cooled, she became involved with Alexander Berkman, another anarchist. Berkman, incensed by the Homestead Strike, decided to assassinate Henry C. Frick. Goldman endorsed the plan and helped raise money to purchase a revolver and a new suit so her lover could gain access to Frick's office. Berkman only wounded Frick, but he received a 20-year

prison sentence. Her role in the plot undiscovered, Goldman publicly defended her lover, declaring that the use of violence is justified when one is pushed to extremes by injustice. Her argument enraged most people. Indeed, public harassment was so great that, for a time, she could find lodging only in a brothel.

Although neither she nor Berkman acknowledged her role in the assassination plot, she was a target for police surveillance. At a speech to the unemployed, she was arrested for inciting to riot, found guilty, and sentenced to one year in prison. While in jail she served as an assistant to the prison's physician and became fluent in English.

Upon her release, she worked for a while as a practical nurse and midwife in the slums of New York, an experience that convinced her of the necessity for birth control. In 1895 she traveled to Europe where she took the nursing course at the Allgemeines Krankhaus in Vienna, Austria. While there she attended lectures by Sigmund Freud that clarified her ideas on sexuality. She then returned to the United States, where she became notorious for expounding such radical ideas as anarchy, free love, and BIRTH CONTROL.

Goldman was best known for her activism after 1910. On her lecture tours, she spoke on topics that ranged from modern drama, anarchist philosophy, free love, and women's emancipation to the evils of capitalism. From 1906 to 1917, she published a monthly journal, *Mother Earth,* which incorporated a similar mix of culture and anarchist thought. During WORLD WAR I, both Goldman and Berkman were arrested for counseling young men to resist the draft. After serving in prison for two years, they were both deported as radicals to Soviet Russia during the RED SCARE. Critical of the Bolshevik government, Goldman left the Soviet Union to spend the last 20 years of her life in exile from the United States, which she had long regarded as her home. She published her two-volume auto-biography, *Living My Life,* in 1931 and died in Toronto in 1940. She is buried in Waldheim Cemetery in Chicago.

Further reading: Alice Wexler, *Emma Goldman: An Intimate Life* (New York: Pantheon Books, 1984).
— Harold W. Aurand

Goldmark, Josephine Clara (1877–1950)

Known for her social investigations into industrial hygiene, fatigue, child labor, and education, Josephine Goldmark was born on October 13, 1877, the daughter of Joseph and Regina Goldmark. Born in Poland, her father went to school in Hungary and pursued his medical education at the University of Vienna, where he became involved in the political ferment of 1848. Immigrating to the United States, Joseph Goldmark became a doctor. Doing chemical research in explosives, he took out patents on safety caps and cartridges. The Union Army in the Civil War used his inventions extensively. He died in 1881, when Josephine was three. Josephine grew up in a political household. Her older sister Helen married Felix Adler, of the Society for Ethical Culture, who acted as surrogate father for Josephine. Her sister Alice married LOUIS D. BRANDEIS, who eventually became a Supreme Court justice.

Josephine went to private school and then Bryn Mawr College. Graduating in 1898, she undertook graduate work at Barnard. She was working there as a tutor in 1903 when she met FLORENCE KELLEY of the National Consumers League (NCL). The NCL was a national organization that served as a watchdog on working conditions in the United States. It lobbied for protective labor legislation, including maximum hour and minimum wage laws, and for state and federal laws prohibiting or regulating child labor. It also gave its resources to defend protective labor laws against court challenges.

Hired as Kelley's assistant at the league, Goldmark wrote several publications, including *Child Labor Legislation Handbook* (1907). Her most important work for the league, however, was to compile the massive social data her brother-in-law Louis Brandeis used in several of his most important cases, including *MULLER V. OREGON* (1908). In that landmark case, the Supreme Court decided in favor of Brandeis. Arguing for the rights of states to limit women's working hours because of the state's interest in protecting the health of mothers and children, Brandeis had argued that long hours and fatigue endangered women's health and, what was more, eroded their efficiency as workers. Goldmark later compiled her research on work in the book, *Fatigue and Efficiency: A Study in Industry* (1912). The product of five years of research, the study made an eloquent case for progressive social legislation. Goldmark used social statistics from American and European health officers and factory inspectors, labor bureaus and investigative commissions, to demonstrate that long hours not only eroded workers' health but also undermined their productivity. On the strength of her growing reputation, Goldmark was appointed to serve on the committee investigating the TRIANGLE SHIRTWAIST FIRE (1911).

Later in her career, Goldmark become involved in surveying and improving nursing education. Serving on the Rockefeller Foundation's Committee for the Study of Nursing Education, Goldmark contributed to its 1923 report, *Nursing and Nursing Education in the United States*. The committee's recommendations for higher standards in nursing education and more academic training led to the founding of nursing schools at Yale, Vanderbilt, and Case Western Reserve. Nursing schools also developed new university affiliations. Goldmark pursued her interests in public health and hygiene through the rest of her career. She died in 1950.

Further reading: Phillipa Strum, *Louis D. Brandeis: Justice for the People.* Cambridge, Mass.: Harvard University Press, 1984).

Gompers, Samuel   See Volume VI

Great Depression   See Volume VIII

Great Migration

From WORLD WAR I through the 1920s, over a million African Americans migrated from the South to northern industrial cities. Known as the Great Migration, their movement marked a crucial transition in the history of African Americans, cities, and the working class. The causes of the migration were complex and involved factors that pushed the migrants out of the South and others that attracted them to the North. It is important to remember, however, that at the base of the migration were millions of individual African Americans who decided that their hopes for full citizenship lay in the northern cities.

African Americans had been migrating since the end of the Civil War in their search for independence. Traditionally they sought freedom from white control through land ownership, moving anywhere that whites did not restrict their actions and rights. By the 20th century, with the enactment of SEGREGATION laws throughout the South and efforts by whites to control African-American labor, dreams of independence through land ownership were fleeting. Many farmers who did own their own land were at the mercy of white-owned banks and businesses to which they owed money. When hard times hit, African-American farmers who were already living on the edge of subsistence found it increasingly difficult to make ends meet. Many were forced to sell their farms at discounted prices in order to pay off their debts. The African-American farmers were hit particularly hard when the cotton crops were destroyed by the boll weevil in the first decade of the century.

Farmers forced off the land had few choices about where to work. They could join other African Americans who already farmed as sharecroppers and tenant farmers, or they could move to southern cities. Sharecropping and tenant farming were uncertain ways of making a living from farming. In both, African-American farmers rented land from white landowners. In sharecropping they paid their rent with a share of the crop produced, while in tenant farming they paid their rent through cash payments. In the case of many small farmers, the value of their crops never exceeded their rent, so every year they fell further and further into debt. The process forced them to remain on the same farm because local laws made it illegal to move if one owed a debt. Those African Americans who lived in southern cities faced similar restrictions on their actions. Only the jobs lowest on the occupational hierarchy were available to them.

In addition to their economic plight, African Americans living in the South suffered from legal, physical, and social exploitation. The denial of voting rights was at the center of the efforts by southern whites to exert control over African Americans. After Reconstruction ended,

white-controlled state legislatures disenfranchised African-American voters throughout the South. Whites also created a segregated social order determined by a strict set of racial protocols. Separate facilities for whites and African Americans were created. Individual relationships were determined by these racial customs based on the subservience of African Americans to whites at all times. If African Americans overstepped social boundaries, they often faced a violent backlash. Whites used

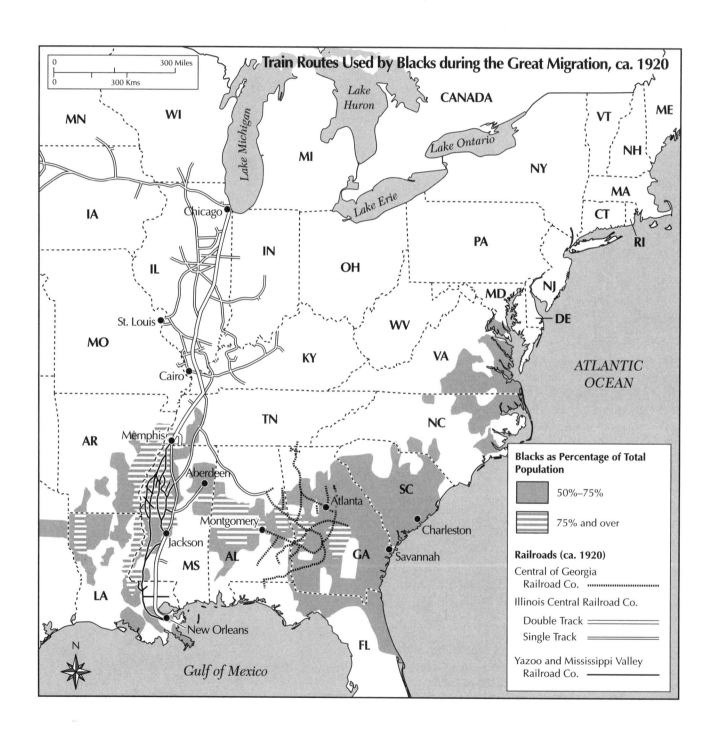

lynching to punish African Americans who overstepped racial bounds.

It was not until changes occurred in the industrial North that large numbers of African Americans seized the opportunity to migrate. Blacks in the North had experienced many of the same restrictions on their occupational choices prior to World War I. They were relegated to domestic services or to work as laborers. Higher paying industrial jobs were closed to them. This changed during the war. Immigration from Europe, one of the major sources of industrial labor, slowed to a trickle. Whereas a few years earlier approximately one million immigrants annually entered the United States, the flow slowed to around 100,000 each year during the war. In addition, when America entered the war, many white workers left their jobs to join the Armed Forces. Without a labor supply from abroad, American industrial corporations began to hire African Americans for the first time. These new economic opportunities were integral to the decisions of many African Americans to migrate North.

Many southern African Americans learned of the new opportunities from friends, relatives, and neighbors who had traveled north. Some migrants remember their communities being struck with migration fever, as they called it. As more people migrated, the news spread, which served to attract more migrants. Pullman car porters and other African-American railroad workers made up another network communicating the news. Many of these men lived in Chicago, and spread the news as they traveled from town to town. They also played another significant role by distributing African-American newspapers, such as the Chicago *Defender*. The papers served as militant voices for black aspirations. Many migrants drew their images of life in the urban North from the pages of these newspapers.

Despite reports of migrant fever, most African Americans undertook the migration with a great deal of planning. They sought out information about their destinations, and many patiently waited for their chance by saving up enough money to make the trip. Many of those living in the Deep South made the migration in steps, moving first to a nearby city and then city by city until they reached their final destination. This way they earned enough money at each step to continue to the next one.

Upon reaching their destination, migrants found an environment that provided them with new possibilities but fell far short of full citizenship and personal independence. The jobs in Chicago's meat-packing houses and Pittsburgh's steel mills that had lured many North paid two to three times what African Americans could earn in the South. There was little chance, however, for promotion beyond entry-level positions. Schools were almost incomparably better than those provided for African Americans in the South, but even with a high school education, many gradu-

ates faced difficulty finding a job that afforded them a chance to use their skills. Migrants soon realized that the right to vote did not automatically give them political power. They also found that they faced discrimination in housing. African Americans were forced to live in segregated areas of the cities. This segregation was imposed in many ways. Realtors and landowners refused to rent or sell property to African Americans in certain sections of cities. In addition, whites often physically attacked African Americans who moved outside the prescribed boundaries. With their choices restricted, African Americans were forced to live in areas that became defined by overcrowding and high rents. African Americans also faced racial violence in northern cities. In East St. Louis in 1917 and Chicago in 1919, to name two examples, race riots occurred that left 39 African Americans dead in St. Louis and 23 in Chicago.

Despite all these restrictions, African Americans managed to create vibrant urban communities that played significant roles in America's cultural history. Without the migration to the North, for example, BLUES music would never have made the contribution that it has. Only by gaining access to urban audiences and the RADIO could blues musicians popularize their work. Other contributions in literature, art, and music such as the HARLEM RENAISSANCE grew directly out of the urban communities created by the Great Migration.

The Great Migration thus marked a crucial transition in the history of America. For African Americans, it marked the end of their reliance on agricultural independence as the means for gaining full citizenship and shifted the center of African-American population to the northern cities. The African-American communities became the driving force in the freedom struggles. The migration also reshaped the political, social, economic, and demographic landscapes of America's cities. Finally, the migration reshaped the history of the American working class as African Americans entered the industrial workforce in large numbers for the first time.

See also CITIES AND URBAN LIFE; LABOR AND LABOR MOVEMENT; RACE AND RACIAL CONFLICT.

Further reading: James R. Grossman, *Land of Hope: Chicago, Black Southerners, and the Great Migration* (Chicago: University of Chicago Press, 1989); Joe William Trotter, Jr., ed., *The Great Migration in Historical Perspective: New Dimensions of Race, Class, and Gender* (Bloomington: Indiana University Press, 1991).

— Michael Hartman

Great White Fleet (1907–1909)
President THEODORE ROOSEVELT often said that the United States needed to "Speak softly and carry a big stick."

While Roosevelt on several occasions used the American military to directly intervene in Caribbean and Latin American nations, he approached foreign policy issues in a very different way when it came to Asia. Competing with European nations in that sphere, his policy was more nuanced. Indeed, in 1907 Roosevelt ordered the main part of the U.S. Navy's fleet, the so-called Great White Fleet, which included 16 battleships, to embark on a 45,000-mile world tour. He hoped that the show, rather than the use, of American seapower would preserve American interests in Asia.

In Asia, Roosevelt's main foreign policy objective was to maintain the OPEN DOOR POLICY in China. He also was concerned about maintaining the balance of power that existed in East Asia. The chief threats to the balance of power in the region came from Russia and Japan, both of which wanted to control a greater share of China. In 1904, these two nations—Russia and Japan—had gone to war with each other as they were attempting to build a stronger sphere of influence in Asia. For the most part, President Roosevelt supported Japan's efforts to obtain world-power status, which he recognized could not be prevented. He thought, however, that such status could be obtained through peaceful means, rather than war and conflict.

Accordingly, with the outbreak of the RUSSO-JAPANESE WAR, President Roosevelt initiated secret negotiations to arrange a peace. These efforts to negotiate an end to this conflict resulted in Roosevelt's winning of the Nobel Prize for Peace in 1906, the first American to earn that award. Roosevelt's goal in supporting the Japanese was to allow them to secure a sphere of influence in East Asia (similar to what Roosevelt had done in Central America, the Caribbean, and Latin America), and second, to secure a tighter link between Japan and the United States. While Roosevelt sought to build a lasting relationship with Japan, his efforts were frustrated by the anti-Asian nativism rampant in the United States in the early part of the 20th century. This controversy was particularly played out in California where the state legislature debated laws to bar further Japanese immigration and local school boards ordered the segregation of Asian schoolchildren so that they would not "contaminate" white children. The so-called Yellow Peril caused outrage in Japan, and pro-military elements within the Tokyo government began calling for a possible war with the United States. To calm this growing sentiment, President Roosevelt put aside his own racist tendencies to find a solution to this growing controversy. Roosevelt's GENTLEMEN'S AGREEMENT with Japan in 1907 resolved the mounting tension between the two nations as Japan agreed to halt immigration to the United States and the San Francisco school board agreed to rescind its segregation order.

Fearing that he would be attacked for appeasing the Japanese, President Roosevelt subsequently ordered the Great White Fleet on its world tour late in the year. The fleet would make many stops across the globe, but perhaps most significantly, it made an appearance in Tokyo Bay. While many in the United States, including members of Congress, feared that this show of American military strength might rekindle the militarist sentiment in Japan, Japan instead responded in a calm fashion that emphasized its recognition of American military strength. President Roosevelt demonstrated skill in his dealings with Japan. His policies are credited with staving off direct conflict with Japan while at the same time preserving a strong United States presence in East Asia.

Further reading: Kenneth Wimmel, *Theodore Roosevelt and the Great White Fleet: American Seapower Comes of Age* (Washington, D.C.: Brassey's, 1998).

— David R. Smith

Greenwich Village

Greenwich Village is a neighborhood on the lower west side of Manhattan. Bounded on the east by Washington Square and Fifth Avenue, it is marked on the west by the Hudson River, and on the south and north by Houston Street and Tenth Street. At the turn of the century, the Village, as insiders know it, was home to both working-class immigrants and young middle-class professionals, who were looking for inexpensive housing in New York City. Soon, however, Greenwich Village became nationally known for its bohemian atmosphere and modern ways. Artists, actors, journalists, writers, labor organizers, and radicals patronized its cafés and participated in its street life. Anarchists and suffragists were found drinking coffee and arguing about the revolution. A center of modernist art and culture, the Village became the place where young talent migrated and flourished. Surrounded by the cosmopolitan influences of European immigrant radicals and intellectuals, a new generation of writers and activists challenged the relations between the sexes, class inequality, and the cultural establishment. Through their art and politics, they sought to re-fashion American identity in the modern mode.

During this period, the core group of intellectuals and artists identified with Greenwich Village were those associated with the journal, *The Masses*. Edited by Max Eastman, *The Masses* published work from radical thinkers and writers such as JOHN REED, Floyd Dell, and Mary Heaton Vorse. Its sheer range dazzled readers, for in any issue could be found articles on the class struggle, art criticism, feminism, and birth control. Having broken with the narrow legacy of the Left, *The Masses* writers connected sexual equality with the class struggle, art with politics. These same writers crossed class lines to support the LAWRENCE

STRIKE of 1912 and the PATERSON STRIKE of 1913 and allied themselves with the INDUSTRIAL WORKERS OF THE WORLD. From this group as well came support for MODERNISM in ART. John Sloan, one of the primary figures in the ASHCAN SCHOOL and a contributor to the ARMORY SHOW of 1913, also engaged in strike support. His wife, Dolly, helped organize the children's exodus during the Lawrence Strike. Among those in the Village were the core of the Provincetown Players, an experimental theater group that fostered the talents of playwrights Susan Glaspell and Eugene O'Neill. Writers Hutchins Hapgood, Neith Boyce, Mary Heaton Vorse, Jack Reed, and Louise Bryant participated in the Provincetown plays.

For the Greenwich Village intellectuals as well as for the labor movement, the central issue of the day was free speech. The crisis of culture at the turn of the century put civil liberties and, indirectly, the role of the state into relief. The Comstock Laws, passed in 1873 to outlaw the mailing of printed matter judged obscene, including information on contraception, silenced the press and kept many literary works under wraps. Vigilante violence and civil ordinances prohibiting political meetings, used against unions in many locales, called into question the role of the state in suppressing dissent. When the Wilson administration during WORLD WAR I further regulated newspapers, books, and speeches under the TRADING WITH THE ENEMY and ESPIONAGE ACT government interference became an immediate threat. Greenwich Village was the center of this maelstrom, as many of its residents—including anarchist EMMA GOLDMAN, birth control advocate MARGARET SANGER, and Margaret Anderson, editor of the *Little Review,* and *The Masses* group itself—were subjected to arrest under various censorship laws.

The influence of Greenwich Village went far beyond the bounds of New York. While modernist artists and writers could be found in artist colonies in San Francisco, Chicago, and Taos, New Mexico, Greenwich Village became the national center of modern culture. It also became a Mecca for independent book publishers and radical literary magazines and political journals. Along with *The Masses,* the *Little Review, Seven Arts,* Sanger's *Woman Rebel* and Goldman's *Mother Earth* had their editorial offices in Greenwich Village. With an eclectic range and respect for diverse cultures and ideas, the Village helped to foster modern American art and LITERATURE. Yet the Village's reputation for bohemianism remained one of its lasting legacies. By the 1920s, it had become a stop for both city newcomers and tourists curious to see the place where modern art flourished, the NEW WOMAN walked, radicals spoke on street corners, and free love reigned.

Further reading: Leslie Fishbein, *Rebels in Bohemia: The Radicals of the Masses, 1911–1917* (Chapel Hill: University of North Carolina Press, 1982); Christine Stansell, *American Moderns: Bohemian New York and the Creation of a New Century* (New York: Metropolitan Books, 2000).

Griffith, David Wark (1875–1948)

D. W. Griffith, the celebrated director and producer, was born in 1875 in Kentucky. Being born in the South during the Reconstruction era had a profound impact on his life and art. Equally influential was Griffith's father. Best known as Colonel "Roaring Jake" Griffith, he had been a Confederate cavalry officer during the Civil War. His vision of American society had a profound influence on his son. This influence would appear in a number of D. W. Griffith's productions.

Griffith was first introduced to the motion picture industry in 1907 when he played the hero's father in Edwin S. Porter's *Rescued from an Eagle Nest.* Griffith had no intention of embarking upon a career as an actor. He envisioned himself as a playwright. To save his name for the stage, he acted under the alias Lawrence Griffith. His dreams of a career as a playwright proved illusive. He produced only one play, and it was a flop. Success in the emerging motion picture industry came much easier. Griffith's career as an actor soon provided him with the opportunity to write and direct. He learned that, while he could earn only $5 a day as an actor, he could receive $10 to $15 for story ideas. In 1908 he directed his first film, *The Adventures of Dollie.*

Griffith's most important insight was that the shot, and not the scene, was the basic unit of film language. He moved the camera up close to gain a level of intimacy that was previously unknown. He integrated the close-up with the medium shot and the distant scene to tell a more complete and intimate story. He also challenged the idea that motion pictures needed to be short. In 1913 he completed *Judith of Bethulia.* The four reel-long film was twice as long as any picture he had previously released. He wanted to produce even longer films, but his employer, the American Biograph Company, was hesitant to finance the production of larger film projects. As a result, Griffith left the firm.

After joining a small independent company called Mutual, Griffith directed a number of routine productions. At that point, he produced his classic film, THE BIRTH OF A NATION. *Birth of a Nation* transformed the motion picture industry. It was longer and more costly than any project previously attempted in the United States. In 1915 it opened as *The Clansman* in Los Angeles and later as *Birth of a Nation* in New York. The change of name was suggested by Thomas Dixon, author of the racist novel on which the movie was based, who wanted the film to symbolize not only the rise of the KU KLUX KLAN but also the development of America.

Birth attempted to tell a story of the Civil War and Reconstruction. The scale and scope of the movie were enough to make the release a noteworthy event, but *Birth of a Nation* was far more than just the first full-length American feature film. It was a cultural event of tremendous proportion. The movie defined American history in such a way that it caused celebration in some cities and rioting in others. Aware of the impact that the film would likely have, Griffith took out a number of the more objectionable scenes. The film's premise, that the Reconstruction era was a time of fraud and revenge, was based upon the assumption that blacks were inferior. It also portrayed the Ku Klux Klan as a just organization, dedicated to saving the South.

The reception that *Birth of a Nation* received was unprecedented. The movie's message was even brought before the Senate. In an attempt to challenge those who had attacked his work, Griffith published the pamphlet, "The Rise and Fall of Free Speech in America." He thought that attacks upon him and his movie should be viewed as assaults on freedom of speech and expression. He believed that it was his obligation to defend not only himself, but the right of free speech. His next work, *Intolerance*, was an attempt to launch this crusade

After *Birth* was completed, Griffith produced *The Mother and the Law*. Its opening sequences were based on an incident of conflict and violence in the American labor movement. The movie was a sound piece of work; but in the shadow of *Birth*, it was a disappointment. Griffith decided to make the movie into something more ambitious. To do so, he added three other stories to *The Mother and the Law* to make one grand movie, *Intolerance*. The film presented Griffith's vision of a historical battle against ignorance and intolerance. To finance the undertaking Griffith spent all of the proceeds form *Birth* and was even forced to buy out his fellow backers. The picture cost $1.9 million. The movie ran for nearly four hours. After being released in Los Angeles and New York to disappointing audiences, Griffith began a long series of edits. Even after the edits, the film was not well received. Desperate for money, Griffith divided the work into two films, *The Mother and the Law* and *The Fall of Babylon*.

After *Intolerance*, Griffith directed a number of other movies. In 1919 he released *Broken Blossoms,* the next year he made *Way Down East,* and two years later he released *Orphans of the Storm*. All were of considerable skill and charm, but they paled in comparison to his two great epics. Griffith will be known best for his production of *Birth of a Nation*.

Further reading: Iris Barry, *D. W. Griffith: American Filmmaster* (Garden City, N.Y.: Doubleday, 1965); Robert M. Henderson, *D. W. Griffith: His Life and Work* (New York: Oxford University Press, 1972).

— Steve Freund

H

Harding, Warren Gamaliel (1865–1923)

Born in 1865, in Blooming Grove, Ohio, Warren Harding was the son of George and Phoebe Dickerson Harding. Warren attended school and then Ohio Central College. In 1882, the family moved to Marion, Ohio, where Warren studied law and sold insurance. He also taught school. After working a stint for the Caledonia *Argus,* he took a job as a printer and reporter for the Marion *Democratic Mirror.* He seized an opportunity in 1884 to buy out a small local newspaper, the Marion *Star.* In 1891, Harding married Florence Kling De Wolfe, a widow. Harding invested her money in the weekly *Star* and made it a success.

As his newspaper flourished, Harding developed a strong interest in public affairs. He joined the state Republican Party and served in the *Ohio State Senate* from 1898 to 1902. In 1903, with the help of his friend, lawyer Harry Daugherty, Harding was elected lieutenant governor. After a brief retreat from public life, Harding ran for the U.S. Senate in 1914. He won the election by a large margin. In the Senate, he supported a high protective tariff, supported the U.S. entry into WORLD WAR I, opposed high taxes, and voted against American participation in the LEAGUE OF NATIONS. Having served only one term in the Senate, Harding won the Republican nomination for president. Unlike more recent presidential candidates, he maintained his distance from newspaper reporters throughout the campaign.

Protected by the media's acceptance of public officials' right to privacy, Harding had a tumultuous personal life. Not only had he married Florence De Wolfe, a woman who had been divorced and bore a child out of wedlock, but Harding also was known in the language of the time as a "womanizer." Long-term affairs with a family friend and a younger woman surfaced after his death, as did reports of other liaisons. At the same time, Harding's public persona was almost that of a grandfather figure. His white mane and patrician good looks seemed assurance of his moral standing and personal responsibility.

During the 1920 campaign, Harding ran on a platform of a return to "normalcy." Normalcy signified, in the words of editor William Allen White, that Americans were "tired of the issues, sick at heart of ideals, and weary of being noble." Throughout the campaign, Harding played the role of an elder statesman. He had, in fact, an undistinguished

Warren G. Harding *(Facts On File)*

senatorial career. Yet his profile was likened to that of a Roman senator, and he enjoyed posing for reporters. Harding barely left his hometown during the presidential campaign. Instead, he spoke from his front porch, allowing his ornate speech to carry the day. His language revealed that he was a consummate politician of the old school. Writer H. L. MENCKEN said that Harding's political speech was like "a string of wet sponges. . . . It is rumble and bumble. It is flap and doodle. It is balder and dash. . . . It is so bad that a kind of grandeur creeps into it." In one famous speech, Harding proclaimed that, "America's present need is not heroics but healing. . . . not agitation, but adjustment. . . . not the dramatic, but the dispassionate. . . . not submergence in internationality, but sustainment in triumphant nationality." The speech captured the core of the campaign. Voters were asked to abandon the reforming impulse of PROGRESSIVISM and attend to business.

Defeating DEMOCRATIC PARTY candidate James Cox by an overwhelming margin of 16 million votes to 9 million, Harding became the 29th president of the United States. For those in the Republican administration, Harding's election expressed a public desire for normalcy. The majority of voters believed that the government should cut back and limit its functions but also wanted it to address the social and economic disorder of the war years. The foremost example of this impulse was the passage of the BUDGET AND ACCOUNTING ACT (1921) in Harding's first year as president. It set up the structure for the federal budget system by creating the Budget Bureau in the executive branch. Before its passage, government allocations were haphazard, divided among different pieces of legislation, with no overall plan or intended balance. With the creation of the Budget Office under its original head, CHARLES GATES DAWES, the U.S. government was to develop an overall budget plan that limited deficits such as those accumulated during World War I and began to pay off federal debts. Over the course of the 1920s, even with new expenditures to enlarge the Commerce Department and the VETERANS BUREAU and the loss of revenue from tax cuts, the national debt declined from $25.5 billion in 1919 to $16.9 billion in 1929.

Harding's administration was committed to other programs that would return the country to normalcy. Seeking to disentangle the United States from foreign involvement, Harding encouraged arms reduction negotiations that culminated in the WASHINGTON CONFERENCE ON NAVAL DISARMAMENT in 1921–22. He also signed peace treaties with Germany, Austria, and Turkey. In agriculture, his administration supported moderate measures to address the farm crisis through the CAPPER-VOLSTEAD ACT. And in the area of labor relations, Harding pushed for and held an unemployment conference. At the same time, many workers held his administration personally responsible for the loss of the

Railroad Shopmen's Strike of 1922 and the blows dealt to labor as employers filed repeated strike injunctions.

Despite the trend toward more rational government, Harding's administration revealed a talent for habits of patronage and corruption. In the first year of Harding's term, post office positions, which had been given over to civil service, were reclaimed as political appointments. Harding also appointed a number of his old political cronies from "the Ohio gang" to major cabinet offices. Dependent on the advice and aid of his political network, Harding found many of his political appointees entangled in massive graft, bribery, and corruption. His selection of Harry Daugherty as attorney general, Charles Forbes as director of the VETERANS BUREAU, and Albert Fall as secretary of the interior opened the door to major scandals in government. Daugherty's appointments to the Prohibition Bureau led to widespread corruption among its agents, and he was implicated in other scandals. Forbes was convicted of having stolen more than $33 million from the Veterans Bureau in fraudulent land deals and purchasing schemes. As secretary of the interior, Albert Fall was responsible for the illegal leasing of naval oil reserves to oil industry magnates Harry Sinclair and Edward Doheny in what became known as TEAPOT DOME. Investigations of the Veterans Bureau and Teapot Dome were just underway in 1923, but they led to the indictment and conviction of some of the major officers of Harding's administration.

On a trip to Alaska and California in 1923, Warren G. Harding died suddenly as a result of poor medical treatment and a heart attack. He was buried quickly and without an autopsy, a fact that engaged the public imagination for years. Harding's administration, then under investigation, was in chaos. As his chief defender, his widow Florence Harding saw to it that many of his papers were burned. That act cast permanent doubt about Harding's culpability in the scandals and about the cause of his death. CALVIN COOLIDGE, nicknamed "Silent Cal," succeeded to the presidency after Harding's death, but his distance from Harding's administration saved the REPUBLICAN PARTY from repercussions of the scandals.

The legacy of the Harding administration is hard to assess. His unexpected death in 1923 shortened his term in office and kept him from fulfilling his ambitious program of conservative retrenchment. Harding's successor, Coolidge, became even more committed to a business-oriented government. He was, as journalist Walter Lippmann wrote, "a frugal little man who in his personal life is the very antithesis of the flamboyant ideal that everybody is frantically pursuing." Although he had a much quieter presence than Harding, Coolidge followed up on many of his political promises. Peace and prosperity, the two bywords of the Harding era, were the hallmark of Coolidge's presidency as well.

Further reading: Robert K. Murray, *The Harding Era: Warren G. Harding and His Administration* (Minneapolis: University of Minnesota Press, 1969); A. C. Sferrazza, *Florence Harding: The First Lady, the Jazz Age, and the Death of America's Most Scandalous President* (New York: William Morrow, 1998).

Harlem Renaissance

One of the most important cultural movements of the 20th century, the Harlem Renaissance was a movement in LITERATURE, MUSIC, ART, and performance that celebrated the African-American heritage and revitalized American arts through its incorporation of African traditions and themes. Reaching its peak in the years between 1923 and 1929, the movement fostered an emerging generation of African-American writers, musicians, and composers and formed the center of a more general cultural revival centered in New York City. National in scope, this explosion of creativity was not so much a rebirth of African-American cultural expression as its integration into modern literature and art. For most of the 19th century, African-American music and literature had been excluded from mainstream culture. Beginning in the 1920s, audiences across the racial divide were given new access to the mythology, language, and musical traditions of African Americans.

The Harlem Renaissance was the product of the social movement of African Americans from the rural South to northern cities in the GREAT MIGRATION. Southern migrants brought with them musical forms derived from gospel and secular songs and helped to create new genres of JAZZ and urban BLUES. New migration from the West Indies to New York in particular introduced new African and West Indian elements into the mix. The growth of Harlem set the stage for a cultural revival among African Americans and the diffusion of their ideas to a national stage.

Revitalized political organizations also furthered the cultural revival. First, the creation of the NATIONAL ASSOCIATION FOR THE ADVANCEMENT OF COLORED PEOPLE (NAACP) brought African Americans and white supporters into a coalition to protest discrimination and open the door for expanded civil rights. Their political coalition became a cultural one, as white patrons of African-American education and art supported new cultural institutions and individual careers. Second, the NAACP, the Urban League, and the UNIVERSAL NEGRO IMPROVEMENT ASSOCIATION (UNIA) under leader MARCUS GARVEY fueled social and cultural activism in African-American communities. The UNIA also contributed to the spread of race pride and fostering of African-American traditions. Finally, the publication of new journals, including the NAACP's *Crisis,* the Urban League's *Opportunity,* and the Brotherhood of

Zora Neale Hurston *(Library of Congress)*

Sleeping Car Porters' *Messenger,* opened up new venues of publication for literature, criticism, and communication. Literary editor Jessie Fauset of the *Crisis* played a significant role in sponsoring new authors.

African-American novels, plays, and art proliferated with the spread of black journals and newspapers and a growing white audience and white patronage for African-American artists. ALAIN LOCKE captured this ferment in his 1925 book, *The New Negro.* Among the writers associated with this cultural flowering were Langston Hughes, Jean Toomer, Countee Cullen, Claude McKay, Nella Larsen, and Zora Neale Hurston. Hughes in particular became the voice of the black community, moving from cultural modernism in the 1920s to sharper social and political critique in his later work. All of the writers shared the concern of defining African-American identity as dualistic, a product of both African and American experience. They came to explore the dimensions of racial life and consciousness in Toomer's *Cane* (1923), Alain Locke's *The New Negro* (1925), Larsen's *Passing* (1929), and Hughes's *Weary Blues* (1925) and *Not Without Laughter* (1930).

Visual artists were an important part of the Renaissance. For the first time, numbers of African-American artists attended art schools, often with the support of white patrons. Painters Aaron Douglas, Palmer Hayden, Malven Johnson, William H. Johnson, and sculptor August Savage developed artistic styles that incorporated African elements with European techniques. Musicians and composers of blues and jazz similarly developed styles that incorporated the diverse elements of African-American and popular American culture into a music of growing popularity. In recordings that crossed race lines, African-American music reached white audiences as well as African-American ones. Their influence was seen in the work of white composers, songwriters, and musicians who adopted elements of jazz into their work.

Unlike the white counterparts of the LOST GENERATION to whom they might be compared, African-American writers and artists of the Harlem Renaissance neither repudiated religion as a formative and critical force in their culture, nor embraced a postwar pessimism about the future. Ironically, WORLD WAR I, which had been followed by severe racial conflicts, also opened the doors for African-American participation in American life in economic, cultural, and political terms. Rather than a lost generation, the Harlem Renaissance writers were a "found" one, newly discovered or recovered by the white cultural establishment. The influence of the Harlem Renaissance continued through the decade of the Great Depression.

See also RACE AND RACIAL CONFLICT.

Further reading: Ann Douglass, *Terrible Honesty: Mongrel Manhattan in the 1920s* (New York: Farrar, Straus, and Giroux, 1995); Nathan Huggins, *Harlem Renaissance* (New York: Oxford University Press, 1971); David Levering Lewis, *When Harlem Was in Vogue* (New York: Knopf, 1981).

Haywood, William Dudley (1869–1928)

One of the major labor leaders of the early 20th century, Haywood was associated with the upsurge in labor militancy, first in the Western Federation of Miners (WFM) and later in the INDUSTRIAL WORKERS OF THE WORLD (IWW). An advocate of industrial unionism, he organized workers by industry and not by specific trade or occupation. Haywood was born in Salt Lake City, Utah, on February 4, 1869, as the son of a one-time Pony Express rider who died when Bill Haywood was three. He began work in the mines at 15, then married Nevada Jane Minor, the daughter of a rancher, and filed for and then lost a homestead claim. After returning to the mines, Haywood joined the WFM. His organizing skills brought him to the forefront of labor struggles in Idaho and Colorado, especially the violent Cripple Creek strike of 1904. In 1905, he was accused of conspiracy in the murder of Frank Steunenberg, former governor of Idaho. Ably defended by CLARENCE DARROW, Haywood was tried and acquitted in a showcase trial. In 1905, he helped to organize the IWW at its founding convention in Chicago.

Having left the WFM and the Socialist Party, Haywood became an organizer at large for the IWW and participated in some of the major strikes of his era. In the LAWRENCE STRIKE of 1912 and the PATERSON STRIKE of 1913, his persuasive oratory and personal skills helped to maintain worker unity and drew public support for the beleaguered strikers. For his role in these strikes, he earned the admiration of a new generation of intellectuals and radicals centered in GREENWICH VILLAGE, and the hostility of employers and government officials alike.

During WORLD WAR I, while Haywood cautioned against violating the ESPIONAGE ACT, he argued against the U.S. entry into the war. He advocated resistance to the military draft. For these reasons, he was arrested and jailed during the war. Despite the lack of evidence, Haywood was convicted and received a 20-year prison sentence. Awaiting a new trial, he fled the country on bail and went to the recently formed Soviet Union. He died there on May 18, 1928, and he is buried in the Kremlin Wall, alongside American communist JOHN REED.

Haywood was renowned as a speaker at labor rallies. As he once told Elizabeth Gurley Flynn, words were tools and not every one had access to a full tool chest. He was, therefore, always straightforward in address and spoke at the level of his audience. A proponent of a particular kind of pragmatic unionism, he often counseled workers to use the leverage they had at the workplace, rather than to seek political power through the ballot box. Labeled a dangerous agitator, Haywood knew that the workers' chief power was in limiting or stopping production. He repeatedly counseled against violence, despite his reputation as an advocate of worker sabotage. Calling for a broad-based unionism that went beyond skilled trade unions and brought in workers in every industry, he understood the importance of worker unity and the cost of divisions between workers, whether by ethnicity, race, skill, or gender.

Further reading: William Haywood, *Bill Haywood's Book* (Westport, Conn.: Greenwood Press, 1983); J. Anthony Lukas, *Big Trouble; A Murder in a Small Western Town Sets off a Struggle for the Soul of America* (New York: Simon & Schuster, 1997).

Hearst, William Randolph (1863–1951)

William Randolph Hearst created the first American media empire by using family money to purchase newspapers and magazines and to found syndicates and movie newsreel companies throughout the United States. Born in San Francisco, California, on April 29, 1863, to millionaire parents who had amassed a fortune in mining properties, Hearst had the best of everything in life, including education. Two years after being expelled from Harvard, he wrote his father, George, "I want the San Francisco *Examiner*," a newspaper that his politician father had taken for payment of a gambling debt. Granted his request, Hearst returned to California in 1887 and began a decades-long career in newspapers during which he both embraced and furthered the "new journalism" of scandalous stories, gossip, and exposés. Critics questioned Hearst's brand of reporting on prurient stories and labeled most of his "news" fakery. With the San Francisco *Examiner* as his springboard, he began to build an empire of 42 newspapers.

In 1895, after his father's death, Hearst moved his headquarters to New York City. He used some of the $7.5 million his mother, philanthropist Phoebe Apperson Hearst, gave him to purchase the New York *Morning Journal*. Again, he boosted circulation with society gossip, tales of sex and scandal, and sensational stories. The *Journal*'s coverage of atrocities in Cuba aroused the public and helped spark support for the Spanish-American War. He also lowered the price of the paper. In so doing, he began a newspaper war with Joseph Pulitzer's New York *World*, especially for Sunday circulation. Hearst hired away the *World*'s entire Sunday staff, including Richard Outcault, who drew the popular comic strip "The Yellow Kid." Pulitzer hired the artist, George Luks, to continue the comic in the *World*, and both publishers advertised the strip widely, leading to the term "yellow journalism" as shorthand for the sensationalism spawned by newspaper rivalry.

Having made a splash in San Francisco and New York, Hearst moved on. Continuing to acquire major newspapers, he purchased the Chicago *American* in 1900, the Chicago *Examiner* in 1902, the Boston *American* in 1904, and the Los Angeles *Examiner* that same year. Hearst also founded King Features Syndicate and published and acquired magazines, including *Good Housekeeping, Cosmopolitan,* and *Harper's Bazaar.* A true multi-media maven of his day, Hearst also made a foray into movie newsreels.

Hearst was a maverick, and his papers took controversial positions. A progressive in his early years, he supported labor unions and the eight-hour work day, attacked monopolies, favored public ownership of utilities, and a progressive income tax. Although he thought of the Spanish American War as the *Journal*'s war and of himself as a flag-waving patriot, Hearst was an isolationist prior to both world wars. Not an ideologue, but an undiscriminating, impulsive admirer of men of action, he at first welcomed the Bolshevik Revolution in Russia, admired Benito Mus-

solini, initially supported Franklin Roosevelt's New Deal, and published columns by Nazis. He later attacked communism and Roosevelt. Upon meeting Adolph Hitler in 1934, Hearst tried to move him away from anti-Semitism.

Hearst owned gold and silver mines, and at one time he was one of the leading real estate owners in New York City, California, and Mexico. Politically active like his father, who had been a senator, Hearst served two terms in the U.S. House of Representatives from New York City (1903–07) and ran unsuccessfully for mayor of New York City (1905) and governor of New York State (1906). He moved permanently to his 200,000-acre ranch in San Simeon, California, in 1927, where he amassed art and archaeological treasures. As a result of reckless spending in acquiring newspapers, real estate, and art, and investing millions in the movies of his mistress, actress Marion Davies, Hearst's empire came crashing down in 1937. The corporation owning his media conglomerates was $126 million in debt. Hearst managed to stave off bankruptcy by selling off art, real estate, and 25

William Randolph Hearst *(Library of Congress)*

newspapers. In 1940 he still had a publishing empire that included 17 newspapers. He died at San Simeon on August 14, 1951, at the age of 88.

Further reading: David Nasaw, *The Chief: The Life of William Randolph Hearst* (Boston: Houghton Mifflin, 2000), W. A. Swanberg, *Citizen Hearst: A Biography of William Randolph Hearst* (New York: Charles Scribner's Sons, 1961).

— Ellen Tashie Frisina

Hepburn Act (1906)

The Hepburn Act of 1906 responded to the growing corporate concentration of the early 20th century by strengthening the regulatory powers of the Interstate Commerce Commission (ICC). The progressive movement, which had emerged from local-and state-level reform efforts in the late 19th century, had begun looking to make more sweeping policy changes to the ways in which Americans lived. The consolidation of economic and political power in the hands of a few, corruption and inefficiency in government, and the cost of industrialization were among the main concerns of reformers. With the opening of the century, and the succession of THEODORE ROOSEVELT to the presidency, the progressive movement had a new and powerful voice in the administration.

One of Roosevelt's first initiatives as president was an attempt to regulate the trusts or monopoly enterprises that had come to dominate American industry. He did not believe in breaking up all, or even most, large corporations. Instead, he firmly believed that industrial concentration brought the United States wealth, productivity, and a rising standard of living. Accordingly, President Roosevelt advocated that government should be used to regulate these corporate consolidations and mergers, punish those that used their power improperly, and protect individual citizens from the power of industrial giants. He sought to expand government powers to allow for the oversight of economic development. In particular, he wanted to prosecute industries that attempted to monopolize the market, and to negotiate conflicts between capital and labor. The way to address the concentration of economic power, he argued, was not to break up these corporations and return to a simpler economy, but to regulate industry through the good offices of an enlarged and strengthened federal government.

Prior to Theodore Roosevelt's first term in office, the major piece of legislation that regulated industry in the United States was the 1887 Interstate Commerce Act, which created the Interstate Commerce Commission. This commission specifically had been designed to review and regulate shipping rates on American railways in order to

protect the interests of individuals against the increasing power of railroads in the late 19th century. The ICC actually was rendered virtually powerless by a combination of weak enforcement powers and a judicial branch that often ruled against the ICC and its regulatory decisions. By the 20th century, there existed little legislation that could be used to effectively regulate any industry, including railroads. Roosevelt responded to this lack by recommending that the ICC be given broader powers to enforce its rulings. In 1906, on Roosevelt's initiative, Congress passed the Hepburn Act. As signed into law, the act gave the ICC specific powers of enforcement. Beyond giving the ICC greater power, the Hepburn Act set a precedent for future federal legislation aimed at regulating various aspects of the American economy.

Further reading: Marc Allen Eisner, *Antitrust and the Triumph of Economics: Institutions, Expertise, and Policy Change* (Chapel Hill: University of North Carolina Press, 1991).

— David R. Smith

Holmes, Oliver Wendell (1841–1935)

One of the American jurists most responsible for the retreat from legal formalism, Oliver Wendell Holmes served on the U.S. Supreme Court for over 30 years. In his career on the bench, Holmes contributed to a growing body of civil liberties and policy law that expanded the role of the federal government. At the same time, he argued for the protection of individuals' rights to free speech, free assembly, and free press. Most of Holmes's influence, ironically, came from his articulate dissents from majority opinion. At a time when judges at both the state and the federal level continued to be enamored of natural law and highly protective of property rights, Holmes ventured into a legal philosophy that saw law and the courts not as a natural and inevitable development but as a response to the needs of society. Arguing for judicial restraint, Holmes envisioned a judiciary that would not heedlessly reject the democratic will. He developed his arguments for flexible and pragmatic application of the law in conversation with a younger generation of legal theorists, including LOUIS D. BRANDEIS and Roscoe Pound. His influence lingered on the Supreme Court with the appointment of Brandeis and later Felix Frankfurter to the bench.

Few of Holmes's achievements could have been predicted from his family background. His father, Oliver Wendell Holmes, Senior, was a doctor and a poet, whose poem on "Old Ironsides" kept the USS *Constitution* from being scrapped. The younger Holmes was born on March 8, 1841, in Boston, Massachusetts. After graduating from Harvard University, he joined the Union Army and served for three years during the Civil War, seeing action in the Union Debacle at Ball's Bluff, at Antietam, where he was left for dead, and at Fredericksburg. He was wounded three times before requesting and receiving a staff job. He left the army with the rank of captain. In 1867, Holmes was admitted to the bar and began to practice law. Holmes married Fanny Bowditch Dixwell in 1872. From 1870 to 1873, he edited the *American Law Review* and publicly lectured on common law. In 1882, while in his first term as law professor at Harvard, Holmes received an appointment to the Massachusetts State Supreme Court. He served on the court for 20 years, the last three as chief justice. In 1902, THEODORE ROOSEVELT appointed Holmes to the U.S. Supreme Court as an associate justice. In that role, he wrote some of his most significant judicial opinions. In a series of cases after WORLD WAR I, Holmes essentially created the modern theory of civil liberties. Although in the first of these, *SCHENK V. UNITED STATES,* he argued a more conservative point of view that freedom of speech was not unlimited, his later dissents in *Abrams v. United States* and other cases redefined the First Amendment. Holmes wrote that it was the "theory of our Constitution" that "the ultimate good desired is better reached by the free trade in ideas—that the best test of truth is the power of the thought to get itself accepted in the competition of the market." Democracy, he proclaimed, required us to be "eternally vigilant against attempts to check the expression of opinions that we loathe." Holmes served on the Court until he retired in 1932 at age 91.

Further reading: Albert W. Altschuler, *Law without Values: The Life, Work and Legacy of Oliver Wendell Holmes* (Chicago: University of Chicago Press, 2000), G. Edward White, *Justice Oliver Wendell Holmes: Law and the Inner Self* (New York: Oxford University Press, 1993).

Hoover, Herbert C.   See Volume VIII

Houdini, Harry (1874–1926)

One of the most renowned magicians of the 20th century, Harry Houdini was born Erik Weisz on March 24, 1874, in Budapest, Hungary. His father brought the Weisz family to Appleton, Wisconsin, when Erik was still a baby. As a young man, he began to go by the name Ehrich. He later called himself Erie and finally settled on Harry. As a teenager, he worked as a cutter in a necktie factory. Working as a cutter proved to be too restrictive. He decided to escape the constraints of his work by becoming a magician.

Houdini's career progressed slowly at first. For many years he lived on the brink of poverty. He soon created a niche for himself. He began to captivate audiences with

Harry Houdini *(Library of Congress)*

his own unique form of magic—the dramatic escape. His ability to escape from seemingly inescapable situations earned him a reputation that spread throughout the country and eventually the world. Houdini's exploits allowed him not only to build a successful career as an escape artist, but also to redefine the art of illusion in the process. He amazed audiences by escaping from ropes, handcuffs, and locked containers in countless settings. In one show he was suspended, head down, 75 feet in the air. In the next he was submerged under water. Regardless of the setting, he played on the audience's fears and emotions. He was careful not to escape too early or too easily, in order to build excitement and anticipation. By the turn of the century, the act had begun to earn Houdini international acclaim. He performed in front of audiences of thousands. As the new medium of motion pictures developed, Houdini's notoriety spread even further.

Long before Houdini had found professional success, he had fallen in love with a young woman named Wilhelmina Rahner. In 1894 they were married. Thereafter, Houdini's young wife went by the name Beatrice, or Bess, Houdini. She worked as his stage assistant. Together they captivated millions. Harry Houdini took his stage name from the great French magician Jean-Eugène Robert-Houdin. He did not, however, follow in his predecessor's footsteps. In 1908 Harry challenged the abilities of his namesake in his book, *The Unmasking of Robert-Houdin* as a way of declaring his independence not only from his predecessor but also from others in his profession. Unlike other magicians of his time, Harry claimed no supernatural intervention. His animosity for those who boasted of supernatural powers led him to launch a full-scale campaign against mind-readers, mediums, and others who claimed to have divine or supernatural powers. He wrote *Miracle Mongers and Their Methods* in 1920 and *A Magician Among the Spirits* in 1924. Through these works, Houdini tried to expose men and women whom he believed were charlatans using tricks to fool gullible audiences. He argued that astrology and fortune-telling had no scientific basis. But even as Harry Houdini attacked those who claimed to have supernatural abilities, self-proclaimed spiritualists like Arthur Conan Doyle steadfastly maintained that Houdini himself used supernatural abilities to perform his miraculous feats.

On Halloween night in 1926, Houdini died of peritonitis that stemmed from a stomach injury. Years before his death, in an attempt to expose myths about the afterlife, he and his wife Beatrice made a pact. The first to die would do everything in his or her power to contact the survivor. Before her death in 1943, Beatrice declared the experiment a failure.

Further reading: Christopher Milbourne, *Houdini: The Untold Story* (New York: Thomas Y. Crowell, 1969).

— Steve Freund

Hughes, Charles Evans (1862–1948)

Charles Evans Hughes had a long and prolific political career in which he served as governor of New York, secretary of state, ran as Republican presidential nominee in 1916, and twice served as a justice on the Supreme Court, the second time as chief justice in the 1930s. Hughes was born in Glens Falls, New York, in April 1862. After completing his undergraduate education, Hughes took a law degree at Columbia University Law School. He began practicing law in New York City.

In 1905, after teaching law for many years at Columbia, New York University, and Cornell, Hughes gained regional notoriety following his appointment by the New York legislature to investigate state utilities and insurance companies. Capitalizing on this exposure, Hughes decided to run for the New York governorship in 1906, at the urging of President THEODORE ROOSEVELT. He handily defeated newspaper magnate WILLIAM RANDOLPH HEARST. Hughes was reelected in 1908. In 1910, Republican president WILLIAM HOWARD TAFT appointed him to the Supreme Court, where he gained a reputation for being a liberal justice. Hughes's first stint on the court was short-lived. In 1916, he resigned and reluctantly accepted the presidential nomination of both the Republican and Progressive parties. Running against incumbent president WOODROW WILSON, Hughes ran a very effective campaign only to lose by fewer than 500,000 votes. Wilson received 277 electoral votes to Hughes' 254.

Hughes's political career was far from over. In 1921 President WARREN G. HARDING appointed Hughes to run the State Department. As secretary of state, he advocated enforcing the OPEN DOOR POLICY in China, negotiated a peace agreement with Germany after the Senate refused to ratify the TREATY OF VERSAILLES, and supported attempts to ensure American entry into the LEAGUE OF NATIONS. Hughes served from 1921 to 1929, first under Harding and then under President CALVIN COOLIDGE. Hughes was rewarded for his long tenure in office when President Herbert Hoover reappointed him to the Supreme Court, this time as chief justice.

As chief justice, Hughes clashed frequently and often publicly with President Franklin Delano Roosevelt (FDR). Hughes attempted to limit some of the more progressive and radical aspects of the New Deal, leading the Court in its rulings against the National Recovery Administration, the Agricultural Adjustment Act, and other New Deal initiatives. Hughes's conflict with FDR came to a head in 1937 when he led the charge against Roosevelt's attempt to "pack" the Court by expanding the number of justices from nine to 15. In order to protect the integrity of the Court, Hughes effectively marshaled public support against the plan. Behind the scenes, he proved willing to compromise and was the decisive vote in support of the National Labor Relations Act and the Social Security Act. Hughes retired from the Supreme Court in 1941. Harlan Stone replaced Hughes as chief justice, by which time FDR had appointed several other pro-New Deal justices. Hughes died in 1948.

Further reading: Dexter Perkins, *Charles Evans Hughes and American Democratic Statesmanship* (Boston: Little, Brown, 1956); Robert F. Wesser, *Charles Evans Hughes: Politics and Reform in New York, 1905–1910* (Ithaca, N.Y.: Cornell University Press, 1967).

— Robert Gordon

immigration

In terms of immigration, the period from 1900 to 1930 witnessed at least three noticeable trends. The first 14 years of the century brought with them the highest levels of arrival in the long wave of immigration that lasted approximately from 1830 to 1914. During this 80-year period, more than 22 million immigrants arrived in the United States, with some six million alone arriving during the decade from 1900 to 1910. Along with this steady increase in the volume of immigration to the United States between 1900 and 1914 came a dramatic and noticeable shift in the origins of immigrants. The third significant factor in immigration between 1900 and 1930 was that in the two decades after 1910 there was a sharp decline in the total number of immigrants arriving. The ending of the open door for immigration can be attributed first to the onset of WORLD WAR I and, secondly, to the passage of restrictive immigration legislation in the early 1920s. Combined, these two factors effectively closed the door to immigration and brought migration worldwide to a virtual standstill.

The steady stream of immigrants to the United States at the turn of the century were often the victims of nativist attacks, especially during the world war. Despite the common image of immigrants flooding the country, immigrants did not account for the sharp rise in the nation's population by 1930. Instead, natural increase (the excess of births over deaths) represented the main factor contributing to the population gains. From the Civil War to the First World War, only about 13 to 15 percent of the U.S. population were foreign-born. Although the number of newcomers accounted for about 40 percent of the nation's total population growth, the American-born children of immigrants were a major factor in the total population growth. Thus as the United States witnessed major economic changes with the advent of industrialization and urbanization, immigrants, especially given their different origins after 1890, often became the scapegoat for social problems in the growing nation. Without a doubt, immigrants played a central role in the industrialization of the American economy. The availability of industrial work furthered the attraction of the United States to migrants from across the globe. Arriving in urban industrial centers, immigrants often had few other choices but to find

A family of immigrants looks out to the Statue of Liberty from Ellis Island *(Library of Congress)*

125

Distribution of Foreign Born in the United States, 1910

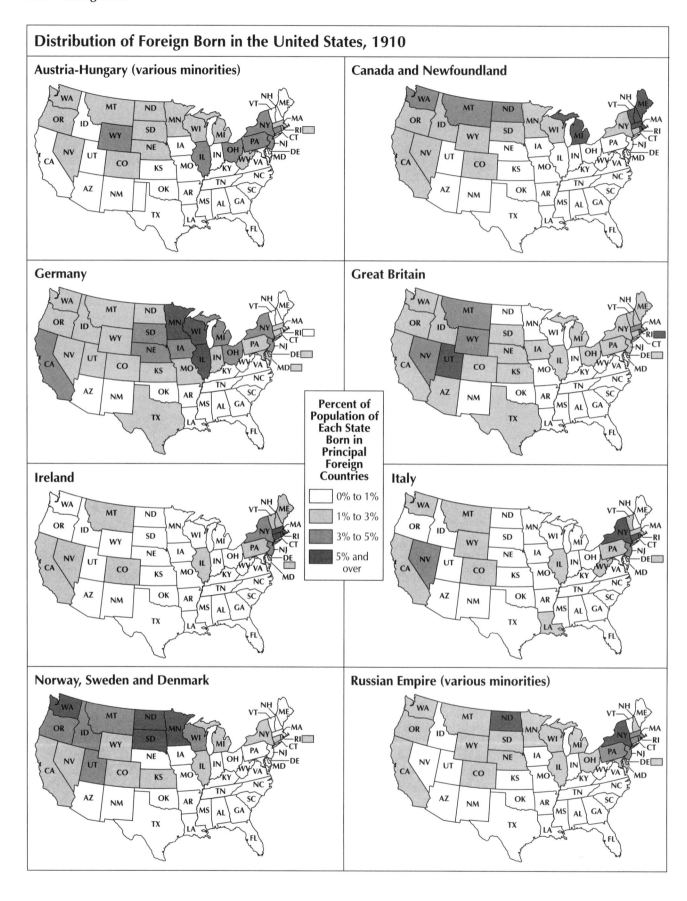

employment as unskilled factory workers. The size of the industrial workforce grew dramatically from 4,252,000 in 1889 to 7,036,000 by the eve of World War I.

Mass production industry brought significant changes to Europe as well. Accordingly, new and more efficient forms of transportation reached further into Europe, allowing eastern and southern Europeans to more easily migrate. In 1854, of the 427,000 immigrants entering the United States, more than 400,000 originated in Northwest Europe (e.g., Germany, Great Britain, and Ireland). By 1907, when some 1.2 million immigrants came to the United States, more than 900,000 were from Russia, Italy, Austria-Hungary, and the Balkans. While overall the percentage of foreign-born individuals in the total population remained virtually unchanged between 1860 and 1914, the percentage of immigrants and their American-born children throughout the Northeast and Midwest often exceeded 70 percent in cities like Chicago, New York, Milwaukee, and Detroit.

The new immigration faced hostility from nativist organizations like the Immigration Restriction League in 1894. Under its influence, members of Congress proposed various grounds for excluding immigrants, ranging from radical political views (e.g., anarchists) to illiteracy. Arguing that "the coming of Chinese laborers to this country endangers the good order of certain localities," Congress in 1902 indefinitely extended the Chinese Exclusion Act's ban on Chinese immigration. Other laws soon followed that established new grounds, ranging from radical political views (implemented in the so-called anarchist law of 1903) to marriage, on which to restrict entry and even rescind citizenship rights. The Expatriation Act of 1907, for example, stripped citizenship status from women, whether they were native-born or naturalized, if they married foreign nationals. An Asiatic Barred Zone, which cemented into place bars to immigration from all Asian countries except Japan and the Philippines, then an American protectorate, was declared in 1917. With this legislation, the federal government set the precedent of using race, as determined by nationality, as the basis for denying entry to the United States.

The vocal anti-immigrant sentiments of this time period ultimately pushed Congress in 1907 to appoint a commission to investigate issues related to immigration. Headed by Senator William P. Dillingham of Vermont, a moderate restrictionist, the committee ultimately issued a 42-volume report. Playing on growing anti-immigrant sentiment, the report's conclusions were not supported by the evidence amassed by immigration officials across the United States. The commission argued that the so-called new immigrants were racially inferior to the old immigrants from northern and western Europe. Manipulating statistical data, it provided a "scientific" argument calling for legislation to restrict entry to the United States. In essence, the commission's contention that the "new" immigrants from southern and eastern Europe were incapable of becoming Americans found a welcome audience, especially as hostilities in Europe broke out in 1914. The IMMIGRATION ACT OF 1917, passed during World War I, was the first in a series of increasingly restrictive immigration policies that the Congress ultimately adopted in response to the Dillingham Commission. The 1921 QUOTA ACT and the 1924 NATIONAL ORIGINS ACT, with their use of restrictive quotas, cemented the commission's recommendations into national policy.

Although the main focus of immigration policy after 1900 was on restricting entry from Europe and Asia, countries within the Western Hemisphere also contributed significant numbers of newcomers. Because the borders between Canada, Mexico, and the United States remained open, they allowed for the relatively easy movement of migrants among the nations. Only with the passage of the 1924 National Origins Act did the federal government create an agency (the Border Patrol) specifically charged with the policing of the land borders between the United States and its northern and southern neighbors. Although today the border between Mexico and the United States receives far more attention, between 1900 and 1930 more immigrants entered the United States from Canada than from Mexico. Nonetheless, both nations became more important as sources of immigration after the passage of the 1924 National Origins Act, which excluded them from its restrictions.

MAJOR SOURCES OF IMMIGRANTS TO THE UNITED STATES, 1901–1930 (THOUSANDS BY DECADE)

	Great Britain	Germany	Austria-Hungary	Italy	Canada	Mexico
1901–10	526	341	2,145	2,046	179	50
1911–20	341	144	896	1,110	742	219
1921–30	330	198	64	455	925	459

Source: U.S. Bureau of the Census, Historical Statistics of the United States: Colonial Times to 1970 (Washington, D.C.: GPO, 1975).

Further reading: John Bodnar, *The Transplanted: A History of Immigrants in Urban America* (Bloomington: Indiana University Press, 1985); Roger Daniels, *Coming to America: A History of Immigration and Ethnicity in American Life* (New York: Harper and Row, 1991); Lucy Salyer, *Laws Harsh as Tigers: Chinese Immigration and the Shaping of Modern Immigration Law* (Chapel Hill: University of North Carolina Press, 1993).

— David R. Smith

Immigration Act of 1917

The Immigration Act of 1917 was the first immigration law to employ a literacy test. Passed in reaction to the high tide of immigration between the 1880s and the onset of World War I, it sought to limit the number of immigrants, particularly those from southern and eastern Europe. The number of immigrants was 788,922 in 1882 and reached 1,285,349 in 1907. Not only did the number of immigrants steadily increase, but the countries of origin for immigrants dramatically shifted as well. Although emigrants from Austria-Hungary, Italy, Russia, and the Balkans were nonexistent in the 19th century, combined these countries sent nearly 75 percent of the immigrants who arrived in the United States in 1907. By this time, vocal opposition already challenged earlier "open door" immigration policies, but the nativist movement in the United States failed to enact any major pieces of legislation affecting the migration of individuals into the country.

The context for immigration policy changed with the entry of the United States into WORLD WAR I. Patriotic and national unity efforts, and fears of immigrant subversion, culminated in increasing and systematic efforts at the "Americanization" of immigrants. The champions of immigrant restriction reached their first significant victory in 1917 with the passage of the Immigration Act, also known as the Alien Exclusion Act. It was the first in a series of restrictive immigration laws based on the findings of the DILLINGHAM COMMISSION. The cornerstone of the 1917 act was a literacy test. All immigrants over 16 years of age who could not pass were denied entry to the United States. The Immigration Act also banned the immigration of laborers from India, Indochina, Afghanistan, Arabia, the East Indies, and several other countries within an Asiatic Barred Zone. The act did not explicitly prohibit the entry of emigrants from China and Japan, because other laws already restricted emigration from these two countries. The 1917 legislation was the first step in establishing restrictive federal immigration policies based on a rank order of eligible immigrants that favored national groups thought to be most assimilable—primarily emigrants from northwest Europe. When President Wilson received the legislation, he declared the act was a violation of American ideals and tra-

ditional open door immigration and vetoed the law. Congress overrode his veto. The Immigration Act of 1917 would stand as the major piece of federal policy governing immigration to the United States until more restrictive policies were enacted in the 1920s.

Further reading: John Higham, *Strangers in the Land: Patterns of American Nativism, 1860–1925,* 2nd ed. (New Brunswick, N.J.: Rutgers University Press, 1988).

— David R. Smith

Industrial Relations Commission (USCIR)

Congress created the Industrial Relations Commission in 1912 to study the rise in labor violence. As the labor movement grew steadily between 1900 and 1910, some unions adopted more aggressive methods for gaining recognition and concessions. Many employers met the new growth and militancy of the labor movement with rigid opposition. They were willing to adopt more aggressive means for defeating strikes and keeping unions out of the workplace. Their methods included industrial spying, private security forces, and using local police forces and state militias to physically remove striking employees. When employers launched a counteroffensive against the labor movement, violent confrontations escalated. The incident that prompted Congress to take action was the October 1, 1910, bombing of the antiunion newspaper, the *Los Angeles Times.* The commission was created as one of the last actions of WILLIAM HOWARD TAFT's presidency.

The new president, WOODROW WILSON, had developed ties with the AMERICAN FEDERATION OF LABOR (AFL). In 1912, he was the first U.S. president elected with the backing of organized labor. Looking to strengthen government's labor ties and concerned that the spread of labor violence would spill over into a larger class conflict, Wilson named labor progressive Frank Walsh to head the Commission on Industrial Relations. As chair of the commission, Walsh had strong ideas about the plight of American workers.

Under Walsh's direction, the Industrial Relations Commission went beyond its original mandate of uncovering the reasons behind the recent rise in labor violence. In its report, the commission laid most of the blame at the feet of employers and the growth of economic inequality. The final report of the commission argued that workers found it increasingly difficult to organize unions and conduct successful strikes. Employers fired suspected union sympathizers, secured court injunctions against strikes and boycotts, hired replacement workers to break strikes, created company controlled unions, and forced employees to sign yellow-dog contracts agreeing not to join an independent union. Workers and unions felt frustrated at every turn. This situation was exacerbated, the commission concluded, by the use of spies, private security forces, and state and federal troops, which intimidated, harassed, and even killed union members. The commission also pointed out that the turn-of-the-century boom in industrial production had created tremendous poverty and suffering.

Although the commission covered numerous labor disputes, it spent much of its time examining the causes of the LUDLOW MASSACRE of 1914. During a routine mining strike, private security forces and local National Guard troops fired upon striking miners and their families, resulting in 32 deaths. In investigating the causes of the violence, the commission called dozens of witnesses, including mine owner John D. Rockefeller, Jr. The commission's final report was extremely critical of Rockefeller's handling of the strike and held him personally responsible for the miners' deaths. Released in the summer of 1915, the report was a scathing indictment of Rockefeller in particular and antiunion employers in general. It set off a political firestorm. Antiunion employers and conservative politicians were outraged. Arguing that Walsh was in the pocket of the labor movement, they maintained that the report should be ignored. Conversely, the generally divided and contentious labor movement greeted the Industrial Relations Commission's findings with universal support and enthusiasm. Many in the labor movement agreed with commission chair Walsh when he concluded that the only viable way to prevent future labor violence was for employers, the courts, and government to adopt a policy of industrial democracy. Workers should be allowed to form unions, he argued, free from employer interference and company violence. Under such a system, wealth would be distributed more equitably and social peace would reign. In the long run, both politicians and industrialists ignored the commission's recommendations, and violent clashes between workers and employers continued to occur.

See also NEW UNIONISM.

Further reading: Joseph McCartin, *Labor's Great War: The Struggle for Industrial Democracy and the Origins of Modern Labor Relations, 1912–1921* (Chapel Hill: University of North Carolina Press, 1997).

— Robert Gordon

Industrial Workers of the World (IWW)

The Industrial Workers of the World (IWW) was a union movement that surfaced in the first decade of the 20th century as a more radical alternative to the AMERICAN FEDERATION OF LABOR (AFL). Also known as the Wobblies, the IWW emerged in response to changing social, economic, and political circumstances. The post–Civil War industrial revolution and the growth of trusts and giant national corporations resulted in tremendous social inequality. The new industrial working class that emerged in these years was much more ethnically and racially diverse than ever before, as millions of eastern and southern European immigrants entered the country and found employment in urban factories.

The industrial working class was expanding at the same time that the nature of work was changing. Building on the principles of SCIENTIFIC MANAGEMENT introduced by FREDERICK WINSLOW TAYLOR and others, corporations began to break down the production process into specialized tasks. Each separate motion was studied and analyzed, so it could be performed with maximum speed and minimum training. The new machine operators were not the kind of workers that the AFL had helped organize in the past. Between 1880 and 1900, the labor federation had been successful in organizing white craft workers. Because they often shared similar ethnic and regional backgrounds and, moreover, had specialized knowledge that employers could not easily replace, skilled workers were easier to organize. The decision of employers to de-skill and diversify the industrial workforce was directed at undermining the power of skilled workers and preventing them from forming unions.

Under the leadership of Samuel Gompers, the AFL had built a solid base of support among skilled white workers. Adhering to "pure and simple" unionism, the AFL avoided mass organizing tactics and did not seek control over employers' profits. Between 1880 and 1900, the labor federation did little to oppose these efforts in mass production industry. In exchange, the AFL often secured guaranteed contracts, pay increases, and shorter workdays for its trade union members. This cautious strategy led to important gains for skilled white workers, but it did little for dislocated farm laborers and unskilled African-American and foreign-born workingmen and women.

The IWW attempted to fill the void left by the AFL. Officially organized in 1905, it traced its origins to the labor organizations of silver, copper, and gold miners in the West. By 1890, mine workers were engaging in frequent conflicts with mine owners determined to maximize their profits. Disgruntled and militant miners formed the Western Federation of Miners (WFM) in 1892 and began demanding better pay and working conditions. Between 1894 and 1905, conflicts between the WFM and mine owners grew increasingly common and violent. Often strikes were defeated when mining companies convinced state and federal officials to use military troops to arrest strikers and keep the mines open. When the state militia brutally put down a 1904 strike in Cripple Creek, Colorado, leaders of the WFM concluded that a national movement of industrial workers, miners, and migratory farm laborers was nec-

Cartoon lampooning the Industrial Workers of the World
(*Library of Congress*)

essary to challenge the dominance of antiunion employers, state legislators, and federal officials.

In 1905, the WFM joined with over 40 labor organizations to form the IWW. Some of its leaders included WILLIAM "Big Bill" HAYWOOD, EUGENE V. DEBS, ELIZABETH GURLEY FLYNN, Mary Harris "Mother" Jones, Joe Hill, William Z. Foster, Lucy Parsons, and Daniel De Leon. Highly critical of the conservative AFL, the IWW committed itself to organizing semi-skilled and unskilled workers, regardless of their race, ethnicity, or gender. In contrast to the AFL's cooperative approach, the IWW advocated socialism and syndicalism. Reluctant to sign union contracts, it preferred to pursue goals through work stoppages, general strikes, boycotts, strikes and other forms of direct action.

Championing the slogan "One Big Union," the Wobblies had limited success organizing western miners, semi-skilled and unskilled factory workers, lumber workers, farmers, and western shipyard workers between 1905 and the outbreak of WORLD WAR I in 1914. Internally, the IWW was racked by conflicting ideological viewpoints. One faction, led by De Leon and Debs, advocated political action and close ties with the Socialist Party of America. Led by Big Bill Haywood, the rival faction championed syndical-

ism, or the theory of industrial organization. As syndicalists, they advocated the use of strikes, boycotts, general strikes, and even industrial sabotage to improve workers' conditions. These internal divisions came to a head in 1908 when the more radical syndicalists gained control of the IWW, and Debs, De Leon, and other socialists left the organization.

Under Haywood's leadership, the IWW aggressively pursued direct action against anti-union employers. In 1912, textile workers in Lawrence, Massachusetts, the majority of whom were women and underaged children, walked off the job when managers at the American Woolen Company announced a plan to reduce wages. Company officials had intentionally hired an ethnically diverse workforce, believing that ethnic animosity would prevent workers from forming a union or conducting an effective strike. The IWW's commitment to organizing all workers bridged the ethnic divide in the workforce and created a unified front. Several striking workers were killed before public pressure persuaded the company to agree to the IWW's demands. A year later, the IWW backed a strike by silk workers in Paterson, New Jersey. Almost immediately, the strike turned violent. Private security forces hired by the company killed several strikers, and local police arrested over 3,000 workers. The Paterson strike ended in defeat when the union was unable to provide pay or food for striking workers.

The IWW was most successful in organizing miners and migrant farm and timber workers in the West and Northwest, many of them through the Agricultural Workers Organization. Although the organization never achieved the level of success of the AFL or seriously challenged corporate power, the IWW remained an anathema to many employers and politicians. With the outbreak of World War I, the IWW came into greater national prominence when it publicly opposed American entry into the war. Many Wobblies were jailed under state criminal syndicalism laws. Haywood and 165 other IWW leaders were arrested and convicted under the ESPIONAGE ACT of 1917 for hindering the war effort. Haywood received the harshest sentence, a 20-year prison term. He fled the country when released pending an appeal of the sentence. Between 1917 and 1920, the IWW was the target of coordinated attacks led by the federal government. In May 1918, IWW offices in Centralia, Washington, were raided by a local mob led by prominent political and business leaders. In November of the following year, a mob once again attempted to raid the IWW's offices in Centralia only to be met by armed resistance. When the fighting was over, five people had been killed, including the IWW's Wesley Everest, who had been castrated and lynched by the mob. Similar repression took place throughout the Northwest where the IWW had been strongest. By the end of the year, the union was in total disarray, and it ceased to be an effective force in the labor movement. As an organization committed to organizing workers regardless of their skill level, gender, race, or ethnicity, the IWW represented a radical alternative to the conservative trade unionism of the AFL.

See also LABOR AND LABOR MOVEMENT; NEW UNIONISM; SOCIALISM.

Further reading: Melvin Dubofsky, *We Shall Be All: A History of the Industrial Workers of the World* (Chicago: Quadrangle Books, 1969), Howard Kimeldorf, *Battling for American Labor: Wobblies, Craft Workers, and the Making of the Union Movement* (Berkeley: University of California Press, 1999).

— Robert Gordon

intelligence tests

Intelligence tests emerged in the Progressive Era as a means for evaluating individual abilities, channeling individuals into particular lines of education and work, and restricting immigration. Battles over the nature of intelligence, however, had been waged for centuries. In the middle of the 19th century, two prominent scientists formally structured the terms of the debate. John Stuart Mill and Francis Galton promoted two diametrically opposed theses regarding the development of behavior and intelligence. Where Galton saw nature, Mill saw nurture. Galton was convinced that genetics were the predominant force in the development of intelligence. Mill, on the other hand, championed the idea that social conditioning was the prevailing force. Galton used his idea of the supremacy of nature to develop the first intelligence tests, which were hindered by his preconceptions. He saw a direct correlation between intelligence and motor functions. Thus, his tests assessed motor skills and not intelligence.

Dozens of scientists followed in Galton's footsteps. It was not until Alfred Binet (1857–1911) developed his theories, based on assumptions closer to Mill than to Galton, that real progress was made at charting human intelligence. Binet pioneered the method of analysis that is still prevalent in many intelligence tests today. When Binet's theories were fully developed, the resulting tests were far superior to anything that Galton or his followers had offered. Tests that followed Binet's fundamental assumptions attempted, and to a degree succeeded, in ascertaining some of the roots of intelligence.

As variations of the Binet intelligence tests became the norm in the early 20th century, they were used to distinguish differences. The first major distinction made was based on sex. Men and women scored differently on the test. As a result, assumptions were made regarding the relative intelligence of men and women. The tests also were used in an attempt to determine who was more likely to commit a crime, and it was discovered that prisons were filled with men and women who tested low on the Binet Scale. The term "feebleminded" was used to describe adults who tested at a level below that of a 13-year-old child. Both of these theories were challenged soon after they were presented. Despite advancements in testing methods, the test was culturally biased in its measurements.

During WORLD WAR I the U.S. Army used the best available test, the Stanford-Binet intelligence test, to determine the mental competency of soldiers. The tests, like those before them, relied on assumptions that those tested would have a firm understanding of American history as well as social and cultural norms. As a result, testees without the requisite background were deemed less intelligent. The army dropped the tests in 1919, but alternative intelligence tests were soon developed and implemented to measure intelligence both in and out of the Armed Forces.

During the 1920s, intelligence testing became closely associated with ethnic, racial, and class-based stereotypes. During that decade of ethnic and racial division, intelligence tests were used to support limits on the rights and liberties of ethnic and racial minorities. They provided support for legal restrictions on immigration. While ethnic and racial minorities were the primary targets, these were not the only stereotypes to be reinforced through intelligence testing. It became an effective tool in reinforcing the political, social, and economic systems. Simply put, intelligence tests provided the rationale for social inequality. But when wealthy rural Americans scored poorly on the tests, the idea that the rich were naturally smarter than the poor was undermined.

Intelligence tests presented more new questions than they answered. The nature of intelligence, whether determined by nature or nurture, was not solved by the tests. In fact, IQ tests provided ammunition for proponents of both schools. Those who supported the idea that intelligence was rooted in heredity could use the scores as proof. Those who championed nurture over nature also employed them as evidence of the importance of environment in cultivating intelligence.

See also IMMIGRATION; RACE AND RACIAL CONFLICT.

Further reading: Raymond Fancher, *The Intelligence Men: Makers of the IQ Controversy* (New York: Norton, 1985); Carl Degler, *In Search of Human Nature: The Decline and Revival of Darwinism in American Social Thought* (New York: Oxford University Press, 1991).

— Steve Freund

International Ladies' Garment Workers Union (ILGWU)

A semi-industrial union of workers in the women's and children's clothing industry, the ILGWU was formed in

New York in 1901. Influenced heavily by Jewish radicals, it combined conservative craft unionism with industrial organization in an industry that was predominantly female. Primarily a union of skilled workers such as cutters and pressers, the ILGWU expanded its membership in a series of dramatic strikes in 1909–10 and later in 1913–15 in the clothing industry. The chief of these strikes, the SHIRT-WAIST MAKERS STRIKE, or Uprising of the 20,000, involved garment operatives in sweatshops in the New York shirtwaist trade. Begun by skilled male workers, the strike came to involve tens of thousands of young women garment workers. The industry's labor force, mostly Eastern European Jews and Italians, with a small contingent of native-born American women, went on strike when garment manufacturers refused to sign union contracts. While many smaller garment shops negotiated with the union, the majority of large garment companies simply waited out the protest. That same year, the Cloak Makers' Strike of 50,000 successfully concluded with the Protocols of Peace, an agreement that provided for increased wages and a 50-hour week. It also promised to end strikes in the industry, in exchange for concessions from employers. A year later, in 1911, the tragedy of the TRIANGLE SHIRTWAIST FIRE brought thousands to join the union in protest of the conditions that had led to the fire, namely locked doors, flimsy fire escapes, and hazardous working conditions. From 1913 to 1915, the ILGWU once again led strikes that made it the dominant union in the garment trade and a major player in union politics in the 1920s.

In the 1920s, factional fighting between socialists and communists weakened the union. The socialist leadership, under president Benjamin Schlesinger, later suspended ILGWU members who belonged to the communist Trade Union Education League. The loss of union negotiating power was largely attributable, however, to the ability of clothing shops to leave union strongholds for other areas. Runaway shops were almost impossible to organize, as they were easily moved and had little capital invested. Finally, fundamental differences between the older men who ran the union and the women who constituted the majority of the workforce contributed to the ILGWU's declining membership. The union's predominantly male leadership paid little attention to the more than 75 percent of the membership that was female. It preferred to negotiate contracts without reference to women workers whom it believed were temporary sojourners in the garment trade. Male union leaders saw their work as a route to political influence and upward mobility and excluded all but a few women from their ranks.

During the 1920s, the union spent much of its time and resources building a range of benefits and institutions to retain members' loyalty. The ILGWU had a strong workers' educational program. It trained workers in union leadership and in basic cultural and citizenship skills. It supported special programs for workers' health and Unity House, a summer retreat for workers. It also had its own newspaper, called the *Ladies' Garment Worker*. These resources and programs helped the union survive the decline in its membership and aided the union in its rebirth in the 1930s.

Further reading: Lewis Lorwin, *The Women's Garment Workers: A History of the ILGWU* (New York: Huebsch, 1924).

invention and technology

Technology—things human beings invent, discover, manufacture, and use—has been part of humanity as long as humanity itself. We may think of ourselves as living in a technological age, but machines and systems, tools and artifacts, have affected Americans in profound ways. The 20th century is often referred to as "the American Century," largely because the growth of big business, sophisticated industrialized systems, and a powerful military complex made the United States a leading superpower. Technological change and advance were central to America's maturity.

Inventions introduced during the early 1900s have now become hallmarks of American culture. Individual examples include crayons, the ice cream cone, Life Savers® candy, and liquid paper. African-American inventor Garrett Morgan invented the traffic light in 1920; and in 1930, Ruth Wakefield introduced Toll House Cookies. But the technological vitality of the United States in the first three decades of the 20th century is demonstrated less by particular inventions than by new technological systems that were embraced and reshaped American society.

Although there were many important advances in science and technology prior to the 20th century, the development of complex technological systems after 1900 changed the nature of humankind's relationship with machines. Advances in technology coincided with the rise of an industrial economy at the turn of the century, as Americans witnessed a technological explosion unprecedented in recorded history. Improvements on an earlier "American System" of manufacturing standardized, interchangeable parts culminated in a system of MASS PRODUCTION in the early 1900s. It opened the way for technology to play a central role in the modern consumer economy. The application of ELECTRICITY to such areas as public lighting and urban streetcars spread into the domestic sphere to include the powering of household appliances by public utilities, a change that shaped people's lives perhaps more than any other technology. Electrodynamic principles applied within the communications industry also resulted in major advances such as wireless telegraphy, the amplification of sound, and broadcasting. Between 1900 and 1930, technological development increasingly became the domain of corporations competing for patent rights and control of the market, resulting in a shift of emphasis in American invention from machine shop to industrial laboratory. Early 20th-century advances in transportation and industrial manufacturing, the rise of "big SCIENCE," and advances in communications constitute some of the most crucial examples of systems building in American history.

Achievements in transportation included the introduction of powered flight and the mass production of gas-powered automobiles during the first decades after 1900. The WRIGHT BROTHERS, Wilbur and Orville, are probably the most famous of aerodynamic designers to achieve controlled, powered flight in the United States. On December 17, 1903, the Wright Brothers demonstrated their success with their *Flyer I* in North Carolina, and by 1908 they took their airplane across the Atlantic to give demonstrations in Europe. WORLD WAR I was a powerful impetus for all industrialized nations to pursue technological improvements on airplanes. By 1920, the National Advisory Committee on Aeronautics convinced Congress to establish facilities for developing aircraft in the United States, integrating civilian and military aircraft manufacture into a major industry.

While the automobile was not a uniquely American invention, development of a moving assembly line to mass-produce affordable cars was pioneered by entrepreneur HENRY FORD. Ford revolutionized automobiles and industrial manufacturing with the production of his Model T. Designed in 1908, the Model T first was produced on an assembly line in Highland Park, Michigan, in 1913. By 1923, production of the Ford Model T had risen to nearly 2,000,000 a year. The simplified design of the car, the decision to freeze the design and stick with one model, and the use of specialized machines allowed Ford to build an enterprise that forever changed American industrial manufacturing.

Ford's application of the moving assembly line to the production of his motorcars integrated the principles of the American System of Manufactures, a 19th-century technology, with the modern principles of SCIENTIFIC MANAGEMENT, championed in the 20th century by American engineer FREDERICK WINSLOW TAYLOR. Scientific management rationalized the entire system of manufacturing as a whole and sought to eliminate wasted movement through the use of single-purpose machines and automated assembly lines. The drive for efficiency reduced labor to the bare minimum, as single-purpose machines created single-movement jobs for unskilled workers, resulting in a reorganization of shop culture. One of Ford's major innovations was his decision to shift the production layout to a sequen-

tial arrangement, so that parts and machines could be set up in the order they were assembled. His introduction of a system of vertical integration at his River Rouge plant in the 1920s allowed scientific management and mass production to reach their logical extremes. It set a precedent for modern industrial ARCHITECTURE and manufacturing in the United States.

Scientific management and a drive for order, efficiency, and control within a free-market economy influenced the rise of scientific industrial research laboratories within large corporations. Whereas independent inventors operating in small machine shops created the bulk of new technology, economic growth and expansion changed the nature of invention, speeding the transformation from small-scale, isolated experimentation to large research industries. The stipulations and time limits imposed by the American patent system, coupled with strict enforcement of antitrust laws, fostered competition among corporations who sought to control new technologies and the market. Corporations such as GENERAL ELECTRIC, Du Pont, Westinghouse, and Dow Chemical developed model industrial research labs between 1900 and 1930. These companies invested large

New technology such as the electric fan helped cool down the hot summer months *(Library of Congress)*

budgets on high salaries and almost unlimited resources for the best minds to collaborate and apply scientific techniques to technological problems. Despite the heroic myth of the lone inventor, technological development in the 20th century has largely resulted from the collaborative efforts of engineers, scientists, and entrepreneurs working in industries sponsored by business and government. While the independent inventor did not disappear, the first three decades of the 20th century laid the foundation for the development of a military-academic-industrial complex. Military and wartime strategies have largely influenced collaborative technological development since World War I.

Research and development was driven by efforts to increase productivity and profits. Largely successful, it resulted in a new type of technological partnership between private industry, universities, and the federal government. Government technological leadership included the establishment of the National Bureau of Standards in 1901, introduced with the mission of "working with industry to develop and apply technology, measurements, and standards in the national interest."

Attempts to standardize tools and processes within the context of "big science" have no doubt altered industrial and social organization. But even as experimentation led to new improvements in old products and processes, the market ultimately controlled the development and spread of new technologies. Advances in chemistry, electric power, and electronic communications have been the result of a race to make new technologies better through a combination of scientific theory and application.

The rise of big science—collaboration between corporations, universities, and the military—was significantly shaped by the race to control technological development in the area of communications. Photography had already become a familiar technique by the end of the 19th century, but the 1900s witnessed the introduction of George Eastman's portable, handheld camera. Cinematography also evolved into a popular medium during this period. But the race to control the communications industry really involved research and development in electronics. Major advances in wireless communications between 1900 and 1930 included Italian-American inventor Guglielmo Marconi's successful achievements in wireless telegraphy; achievements in the transmission of real sounds, pioneered by Americans Lee De Forest and Edwin Armstrong; progress in wireless RADIO broadcasting, sponsored by corporations such as RCA, GE, Westinghouse, and AT&T; and Philo Farnsworth and Vladimir Zworykin's experiments with cathode-ray tubes, which led to the development of television. Control of these new mechanisms and systems was sought through the buying and selling of patent rights, and legislative regulations such as the Radio Acts of 1912 and 1927, which established the Federal Communications

Commission. Once the American Navy, in particular, became increasingly dependent upon wireless communications and had a vested interest in the development of vacuum tube technology, military research and development demanded federal regulation.

Throughout the 20th century, no one individual or institution has been able to control the market for electronic technologies. Isolated amateur inventors outside the military-academic-industrial complex, the federal government's strict regulations against monopolies, and the competitive nature of the American free market have ensured rapid changes in communication technologies.

The most profound American technological developments from this period involved the creation of complex systems that have produced useful products, but also created an interconnected technological society, thereby truly transforming the United States into a modern industrial society. The unintended consequences of the implementation of these developments are crucial to assessing American technology's far-reaching impact.

See also EDUCATION.

Further reading: Ruth Schwartz Cowan, *A Social History of American Technology* (New York: Oxford University Press, 1997); Thomas P. Hughes, *American Genesis: A Century of Invention and Technological Enthusiasm, 1870–1970* (New York: Viking, 1989); Patricia Carter Ives, *Creativity and Inventions: The Genius of Afro-Americans and Women in the United States and Their Patents* (Arlington, Va: Research Unlimited, 1987); Anne L. McDonald, *Feminine Ingenuity: How Women Inventors Changed America* (New York: Ballantine Books, 1992); Zvi Griliches, ed. *R&D, Patents, and Productivity* (Chicago: University of Chicago Press, 1984).

— Lauren Kata

investments, foreign

The international movement of capital has played a critical role in the economic development of the United States. Prior to the early 1890s, American investors' sustained capital investment abroad was minuscule. Between 1890 and 1914, however, the United States became a major exporter of foreign capital, particularly to Canada, Latin America, and Europe. Well into the 1930s, U.S. investments in countries of the Western Hemisphere accounted for an estimated 65 percent of all American investments abroad.

Prior to the 1890s, Great Britain long had been the chief source of foreign capital investments, even in the Western Hemisphere. As the manufacturing base of the United States matured in the 1890s, American investors had additional capital available for export. Great Britain's dominant form of capital investment had been loans to governments and to railway companies. In contrast, the dominant way that the United States exported capital was in the form of direct investments abroad.

Although the United States did loan capital to foreign governments, especially during WORLD WAR I, the creation of branch plants that manufactured goods for foreign markets characterized most of its economic expansion abroad. While the United States and Great Britain competed with one another at the turn of the century, the onset of the war in Europe brought a dramatic shift to the international capital market. Because Great Britain had to expend much of its surplus capital on the war effort the United States had new opportunities to further expand its industrial production and thus had additional surplus capital for investment abroad.

Prior to the onset of war in 1914, the United States imported more goods from Europe than it had exported to the European continent. The destructive war severely crippled the European economy, both in terms of its factories and cities and the availability of labor. The United States benefited both by exporting more goods to Europe and by changing the balance of trade and investment. After the war, European citizens owed private Americans $3 billion, and their governments owed another $10 billion. Wartime loans from the United States to Europe constituted the primary source of this capital imbalance. The increasing level of American capital invested abroad reflected the changing position of the United States in the international economy between 1900 and 1914. Between 1897 and 1914, American direct investments abroad more than quadrupled, increasing from an estimated $634 million to $2.6 billion. Although investments abroad took many different forms, investing directly in manufacturing operations in Europe and Canada tended to be the major form. By contrast, American investments in Latin America tended to be in transportation and raw materials.

During the early part of the 20th century, promoters of American economic expansion abroad contended that this activity promoted development and not economic dependence. President THEODORE ROOSEVELT's secretary of state, Elihu Root, argued, "Our surplus energy is beginning to look beyond our own borders, throughout the world, to find opportunity for the profitable use of our surplus capital." Along with investors, the federal government played an active role in promoting the export of American capital. In particular, such agencies as the U.S. Consular Service, an office of the State Department, provided manufacturers and merchants with regular information about investment and market opportunities in locations across the globe. The monthly reports submitted by the Consular Service were published in the State Department's *Monthly Consular and Trade Reports*. They were further disseminated as numerous newspapers and

trade journals reprinted various parts in their own publications. To further assist manufacturers with their plans for economic expansion, the Departments of State and Commerce often requested specific information from various consulates. For example, they would ask that consulates provide information on the condition of a particular industry or presence of a commodity in various markets around the world.

While foreign capital investments found much support in the United States, they had a profound effect on the development of the nations that received much of this capital. In particular, American manufacturers owned some 60 percent of Canada's industries by 1919. This meant that the Canadian standard of living was indirectly set by the United States. American-owned companies determined wages, output, and investment strategies for a significant segment of the Canadian economy.

The investment in manufacturing enterprises abroad was made in various ways, ranging from the transfer of patent rights to the investment of actual dollars in the company. In 1904, Gordon MacGregor founded the Ford Motor Company of Canada, not with a direct capital investment from Ford in the United States, but rather by granting the latter 51 percent equity in the new company in exchange for all Ford rights and processes in Canada, New Zealand, Australia, India, South Africa, and British Malaya. Often the impetus to set up manufacturing in another country was motivated by high tariffs in that country. In Canada, a high tariff had prevented many American companies from exporting to the Dominion, so investing in branch plants that manufactured for the Canadian market provided a means to bypass the high tariff wall constructed by the Canadian government.

Because the United States had emerged from World War I as the dominant nation, its economic expansion would have far-reaching ramifications. The international economy had increasingly become integrated, and the United States relied heavily on foreign trade and foreign investments. In particular, given that European nations owed substantial amounts to the United States, there was a vested interest in the open movement of capital and goods through the international economy. The collapse of the stock market in 1929 would, accordingly, have profound effects not only on the American economy but also on the world.

Further reading: Lance E. Davis and Robert J. Cull, *International Capital Markets and American Economic Growth, 1820–1914* (Cambridge: Cambridge University Press, 1994), Cleona Lewis, *America's Stake in International Investments* (Washington, D.C.: Brookings Institute, 1948).

— David R. Smith

J

James, William   See Volume VI

jazz

A uniquely American genre of music, jazz had its origins in New Orleans and in the urban North, where musicians and more recent migrants brought together diverse elements of African-American and European music into a new form. In music clubs, musicians drew upon their cultural traditions of down-home blues, minstrelsy, and brass band music, while others brought in elements from their formal European musical training. Jazz was and remains an amorphous music that is both rhythmically driven and at the same time open to the freedom of individual improvisation and interpretation. Syncopation, blue or indeterminate notes, rough vocal style, and improvisation form the boundaries of the genre. Within these lines, there is a multitude of styles. GEORGE GERSHWIN, whose music was a hybrid of TIN PAN ALLEY and jazz influences along with classical technique, wrote, "It is difficult to determine just what enduring values, aesthetically, jazz has contributed, because 'jazz' is a word which has been used for at least five or six different types of music." Expatriate musician Sidney Bechet, a native of New Orleans, claimed that jazz was "a name the white people have given to the music."

Whatever jazz was, it drew from a range of cultural influences. In New Orleans, diverse musical traditions first began to reshape musical idiom into what became recognizable as jazz. By the 1890s, ragtime, a syncopated jazz music, emerged and became popular with African-American listeners and increasingly with white audiences. By 1906, Jelly Roll Morton started touring nationally with his new jazz piano compositions. Dixieland jazz, ragtime's first heir, first made its appearance in recording in 1917. Other innovators, such as Chicago's Joe "King" Oliver, New Orleans' Sidney Bechet, and New York's Fletcher Henderson began to work out arrangements that combined blue notes with ragtime rhythm for a "hot" sound. In 1923, King Oliver's band recruited New Orleans jazz trumpeter Louis Armstrong to make recordings for a broader audience. Armstrong moved on to make his own mark with the classic Hot Five and Hot Seven recordings (1925–28) that featured jazz solo improvisations. In New York, jazz music became, with African-American literature, one of the lasting elements of the cultural rebirth known as the HARLEM RENAISSANCE and greatly contributed to the emergent culture of the 1930s. Jazz music, early defined as an African-American musical style, attracted growing numbers of white patrons and musicians by the late 1920s. Further, while Fletcher Henderson created the first jazz dance band in 1923, the demand for hot jazz dance music fueled the careers of Edward "Duke" Ellington and others. Innovative white musicians such as Bix Beiderbecke, Hoagy Carmichael, Benny Goodman, and Artie Shaw adopted these jazz styles and organized their own bands in the 1930s, when swing music began to take hold of the popular imagination.

Further reading: Burton Peretti, *The Creation of Jazz; Music, Race and Culture in Urban America* (Urbana: University of Illinois Press, 1992); Gunther Schuller, *History of Jazz*, vol. 1 (New York: Oxford University Press, 1968); Geoffrey C. Ward, *Jazz; A History of America's Music* (New York: Knopf, 2000).

Johnson, Hiram Warren (1866–1945)

The Progressive Era was a time of political realignment, in which political parties were divided in sentiment and program and regional party loyalties were at stake. The career of Hiram W. Johnson reflected these tides of change. As a western progressive, Johnson fought for and achieved democratic reforms in his home state of California. He also struggled against the dominance of business in local and national politics and urged the adoption of labor laws and farm relief. In foreign affairs, Johnson was an isolationist and, toward the end of his career, an opponent of the New Deal. He fought internationalism and spent the last 28 years of his life in the U.S. Senate seeking to keep his country out of foreign entanglements.

The son of Lawrence Grove Johnson and Anne Williamson de Montfredy Johnson, Hiram was born on September 2, 1866, in Sacramento, California, as the third of five children. His father Grove was a lawyer who served for short periods of time in the California state senate and later in its house of representatives. Grove Johnson's reforming instincts brought him to the Republican Party, where he supported such causes as temperance, free textbooks, compulsory education, and women's rights. Hiram Johnson graduated from high school in 1882 at age 16 as class valedictorian and entered the University of California at Berkeley two years later. He left the university early to marry Minnie McNeal, the daughter of a carpenter and contractor. The couple had two sons, Hiram, Jr., and Archibald. Hiram Sr., read law in his father's office and joined the family firm.

Although Johnson revealed little inclination for following his father into politics, he became Sacramento city attorney in 1900. In 1902, he moved to San Francisco to practice law with his brother Albert; and two years later, he joined the team prosecuting former political boss Abraham Ruef and other city officials for bribery and graft. With this record, he arrived at the forefront of state reform politics, and he ran for the governorship as a Republican in 1910. Johnson won the election and served for six years, becoming the first governor in state history to be reelected. As governor, he supported a series of progressive reforms including railroad regulation, a workers' compensation law, and the popular election of senators, and helped frame constitutional amendments for woman suffrage. In 1913, in an act reflecting the racial hostility of his day, he signed a bill denying Japanese immigrants the right to own agricultural land in California. In 1911 Johnson helped to form the National Progressive Republican League; and in 1912, he was nominated on the PROGRESSIVE PARTY ticket as THEODORE ROOSEVELT's vice presidential running mate.

In 1916 Johnson ran for the U.S. Senate on the Republican ticket. Reelected to that office four more times, he served a total of 28 years in Congress. The spring he began serving in the Senate, the United States declared war on Germany. Informally, Johnson was opposed to the war, and he objected when his own son volunteered for the army. At the same time, as senator, Johnson publicly supported the nation's war effort. After the war, he became an outspoken critic of the LEAGUE OF NATIONS and became one of the "irreconcilables" who opposed ratifying the TREATY OF VERSAILLES. An isolationist by inclination, Johnson fought against U.S. participation in the World Court, worked to stave off American intervention in the growing

crisis in Europe in the 1930s, and voted against the United States joining the United Nations at the end of his long career. Johnson also worked for farm legislation, supporting the MCNARY-HAUGEN FARM BILL and sponsored the act in Congress that created Hoover Dam on the Colorado River.

Further reading: Richard Cole Lower, *The Bloc of One: The Political Career of Hiram W. Johnson* (Stanford, Calif.: Stanford University Press, 1993).

Johnson, Jack (1878–1946)
Born in Galveston, Texas, in 1878, Jack Johnson was the first African-American heavyweight boxing champion in U.S. history. He is still considered by many to be among the most gifted heavyweights ever to enter the ring. Johnson took up boxing relatively late, but he quickly gained a reputation as a fearless fighter. In excellent physical condition, he turned professional in 1897. Remarkably quick for a heavyweight, Johnson had great strength inside the ring. By 1903 he was considered to be among the top fighters in the country; but many in the profession, including the two most dominant heavyweights, John L. Sullivan and Jim Jeffries, refused to give the African-American boxer a shot at the heavyweight title. While he waited for a chance at the heavyweight crown, Johnson defeated another top-ranked African-American fighter, Sam McVey, in 1904 in what many called the "Black Heavyweight Championship." Johnson was forced to wait five years for the opportunity to fight for the heavyweight crown. Finally in 1908 the reigning champion, Canadian Tommy Burns, agreed to fight Johnson in Sydney, Australia. Johnson won the fight handily and remained heavyweight champion until 1915.

The period during which Johnson was the reigning heavyweight champion was one of rampant racism in America. Jim Crow laws and social custom had established racial SEGREGATION as common practice in both North and South, and African Americans faced systematic discrimination, loss of the right to vote, and racial violence. In the face of widely accepted beliefs of African-American inferiority, Jack Johnson proudly asserted not only his equality but also his dominance over his white peers. His arrogance infuriated many white Americans. Refusing to retreat from the public spotlight, Johnson was highly visible and in many ways larger than life. He relished his role as hero in the African-American community. In response, many white boxing fans, managers, promoters, and reporters were desperate for someone to "put Johnson back in his place." Author Jack London put out a call for a "Great White Hope" to defeat Johnson. In 1910 London and others convinced former heavyweight champion Jim Jeffries to come out of retirement for a July 4 fight for a record prize of $100,000. Johnson, who was at the peak of his career, put

Jack Johnson and James Jeffries in the World Championship battle, July 4, 1910 *(Library of Congress)*

on a brilliant boxing display and knocked Jeffries out in the 15th round. News of Johnson's victory was greeted with enthusiastic celebrations in African-American communities throughout the country.

As champion, and for the rest of his life, Johnson disregarded the social conventions of his day. Bold, outspoken, and proud, he infuriated white America by his two marriages to white women. In 1912, Johnson was charged and convicted of violating the MANN ACT, which prohibited an individual from transporting a woman across state lines for "immoral purposes." The crime Johnson committed was that he and his future wife, Lucille Cameron, traveled across state lines together. In order to avoid imprisonment, Johnson fled the country and moved to Paris. While in Paris, the Champ successfully defended his title three times. He eventually lost the heavyweight title to Jess Willard in a controversial bout in Havana, Cuba, in 1915. At the time and ever since, Johnson and many of his supporters claimed that he threw the fight in an attempt to have his prison sentence overturned. Whether or not John-

son intentionally lost the fight, the charges were not dropped. Johnson returned to the United States in 1920 and served a one-year prison sentence in Leavenworth, Kansas. Even after his retirement from boxing in the early 1920s, he remained a prominent figure, appearing in VAUDEVILLE acts and operating several businesses until he died in a car accident in 1946.

Further reading: Randy Roberts, *Papa Jack: Jack Johnson and the Era of White Hopes* (New York: Free Press, 1983); Jeff Wells, *Boxing Day: The Fight That Changed the World* (New York: Harper Collins, 1999).

— Robert Gordon

Johnson, Tom Loftin (1854–1911)

Early in the 20th century, large cities faced the need for reform. Garbage wasn't picked up on time; streetcar companies refused to improve lines; prostitution and crime seemed out of control; and bribery and graft were the only way to make the wheels turn. Journalist LINCOLN STEF-FENS spoke to these problems in his book, *The Shame of the Cities;* another response was the URBAN REFORM movement led by a group of exceptional mayors, including Hazen Pingree of Detroit, Samuel "Golden Rule" Jones of Cincinnati, and Tom Johnson of Cleveland.

Tom Loftin Johnson was born in Blue Spring, Kentucky, on July 18, 1854. The son of Helen Loftin and Albert W. Johnson, a failed planter-turned-businessman, Tom Johnson had little formal schooling. He began working at an early age. When he turned 15, wealthy relatives purchased the smallest of three streetcar lines in Louisville and hired him as office clerk and, four years later, superintendent of the line. In 1874, Johnson married his cousin, Maggie J. Johnson. The couple had two children—Loftin and Elizabeth.

With good mechanical aptitude and a knack for invention, Johnson became an engineer-entrepreneur in the booming streetcar business. He began to invest in streetcar lines himself, buying his first line in Indianapolis in 1876. Although the line had snarled finances, Johnson helped turn the company around and sold his shares for $800,000 a few years later. While he bought shares in streetcar lines in other cities, he made his largest investment in Cleveland, where his company eventually controlled 60 percent of the streetcar lines in the city.

Johnson's fascination with the working of streetcar lines led to his invention of mechanical improvements for streetcars and their lines. He invented and began to manufacture a streetcar pay box and the girder groove rail, which was a metal electric streetcar rail. In addition, he improved upon designs for, or invented, curved tracks, crossovers, frogs, and special track devices. To manufacture the steel streetcar rails, Johnson founded the Johnson Company in 1883 in Johnstown, Pennsylvania. He also established the Johnson Electric Company in Cleveland to repair steel motors. In the 1880s and early 1890s, newcomers were able to enter and quickly dominate the business of parts and motor manufacture and to buy streetcar franchises. By the late 1890s, however, competition in steel manufacturing and urban transport began to crowd out entrepreneurs like Johnson. He eventually sold his shares in both of his companies to devote himself to reform.

Having become a member of an elite business class, Tom Johnson discovered the problems of poverty, taxes, and cities through the writings of Henry George. George's *Progress and Poverty* influenced reformers for a generation. In George's thinking, it was speculation on undeveloped land, and the concentration of land in the hands of the few, that was at the root of social ills in the United States. Using his wealth to further the cause, Johnson supported George's political campaigns and a number of single-tax journals.

George's ideas about tax reform helped inspire Johnson into running for elective office. He ran for Congress and served two terms (1891–95) in the House of Representatives, where he was known for his single-tax oratory. In his next move, he ran for and won election as mayor of Cleveland, where he served as mayor from 1901 to 1910. Johnson called for tax reform in scientific tax assessments and equitable property taxes. He also campaigned and fought for centralized city government, municipal ownership of streetcars and utilities, lower streetcar fares, city beautification, and local prison reform. Johnson was bankrupt by 1908; under a flurry of charges of corruption, he lost the mayoral election in 1909. He died in 1911 at age 57.

See also CITIES AND URBAN LIFE; URBAN TRANSPORTATION.

Further reading: Eugene C. Murdock, *Tom Johnson of Cleveland* (Dayton, Ohio: Wright State University Press, 1994).

Joplin, Scott (1868–1917)

Called "the King of Ragtime," Scott Joplin composed many of the most popular as well as artistically realized piano rags. He was born in Texarkana, Texas, on November 24, 1868. His father, Giles Joplin, was a former slave, and his mother, Florence Givens, had been free from birth. At an early age, Joplin showed unusual ability at the piano. By the time he was 11, he had come to the attention of a local, German music teacher, who offered him lessons free of charge. This teacher taught Joplin to read music, and the elements of music theory, and introduced him to the works of the great European composers.

At about age 14, Joplin began what was probably the most significant part of his music education. He became an itinerant pianist employed in the honky-tonk and red light districts of towns and cities of the Mississippi Valley. In the course of the next three years, he met many musicians, both black and white, and became exposed to the evolving ragtime style of music popular in such establishments. This was a pivotal era in American musical history, as it was the first time black and white musicians were meeting as musical equals. The emerging style borrowed its form and harmonic structure from white European culture, but the essential polyrhythms came from black African culture.

In 1885, Joplin arrived in St. Louis, which served as his base for the next 10 years. He formed a small orchestra that played in Chicago during the World's Columbian Exposition in 1893. After-hours, he was able to hear and play for some of the country's best ragtime pianists. He settled in Sedalia, Missouri, around 1895, and in 1895 and 1896 published his first music. In 1897, Joplin enrolled in the

George R. Smith College for Negroes in Sedalia, where he studied harmony and composition.

In 1899, John Stark published "The Maple Leaf Rag," the composition that was to earn Joplin the nickname "King of Ragtime." Stark, the white owner of a local music store in Sedalia, purchased it for $50 with an arrangement for continuing royalties to Joplin. This arrangement, unusually fair for the time, soon provided Joplin with financial stability, as "The Maple Leaf Rag" was a national hit within six months. Joplin was now able to concentrate on composition. His first large-scale composition, *The Ragtime Dance,* was completed and performed in Sedalia in 1899. This work consisted of choreographed dance numbers with sung narration. Although published by Stark in 1902, the score is now lost.

With his publishing business flourishing, Stark moved it to St. Louis in 1900, and Joplin, recently married to Belle Hayden, soon followed. The next six years saw Stark's publication of many Joplin rags, including "The Entertainer," "Elite Syncopations," and "The Cascades." Joplin also concentrated on his first ragtime opera, *A Guest of Honor.* This work (now lost) was completed and presumably performed in St. Louis around 1903.

In 1904 Stark moved his publishing business to New York, and Joplin, after separating from his wife, also settled in New York in 1907. In 1909 he married his second wife, Lottie Stokes. Joplin continued composing rags and teaching, but he put most of his energy into the composition of his second opera, *Treemonisha,* a work that consumed him for the rest of his life. *Treemonisha* is scored for 11 voices and chorus with piano accompaniment. The story has the character of a fable, and the music draws from African-American folk tradition as well as ragtime. Joplin and Stark parted ways, leaving Joplin to publish the score of *Treemonisha* in 1911 at his own expense. In the hope of attracting backers for a full production, he put together a performance in a hall in Harlem in 1915. The performance was a failure, and Joplin was devastated. The final years of his life were marked by depression and illness. In 1916, Joplin was committed to Manhattan State Hospital on Ward's Island, and on April 1, 1917, he died there.

Joplin's music enjoyed a revival in the early 1970s. *Treemonisha* received its first performance in Atlanta in 1972 and its first full-scale production by the Houston Grand Opera in 1975. His piano rags have found a secure place in the modern repertoire, equally at home in movie soundtracks and on the concert stage.

Further reading: Edward A. Berlin, *King of Ragtime: Scott Joplin and His Era* (New York: Oxford University Press, 1994); Rudi Blesh and Harriet Janis, *They All Played Ragtime,* rev ed. (New York: Grove Press, 1971).

— William Peek

journalism

The most important trend in journalism in the period between 1900 and 1930 was the maturing of what was called "the new journalism" or, more critically, "yellow journalism." At a time when newspapers became large businesses, owners and editors sought new ways to attract the reading public and to capture subscribers from their competitors. They sought the profits not only from increased subscriptions but also from ADVERTISING revenues based on circulation. City newspapers like the *New York World* and the *San Francisco Chronicle* used innovative newspaper formats that relied on larger headlines, more graphics, and comic strips with colored ink to attract readers. Sensationalist reporting on murders, scandals, and campaigns drew new groups of subscribers. Working-class men and women, especially immigrants with limited English, became devoted followers of the major city dailies, which used bold print, plentiful illustration, and clear language to convey the news.

The Progressive Era was the Age of the Reporter. Previously newspapers had published largely unsigned articles; even editorial matters were often the anonymous voice of the owner/editor or that of a columnist using a pen name. During the 1890s, the journalistic wars between newspaper giants Joseph Pulitzer and WILLIAM RANDOLPH HEARST gave new weight to the personality of the star reporter. One new practice was that of stunt reporting. Posing as mental patients, workers, and band members, stunt reporters investigated government offices, factories, asylums, and prisons. Hundreds of newspapers around the country followed this lead and employed reporters to investigate conditions in their cities. Stunt journalism helped to emphasize the individual reporter at work while routine reporting required a team effort. Writing up a single murder investigation could take up to eight writers and editors, each of whom specialized in their work.

In contrast to sensational news stories were the new standards of objectivity, with which *New York Times* editor Adolph Ochs was associated. Directing his paper at an educated middle-class audience, he defined journalism differently from his mass circulation rivals, the *New York World* and the *New York Journal.* "Facts" rather than "stories" were the key. Ochs also altered the newspaper's appearance and expanded wireless service. Reinvestment of profits into new buildings, state-of-the-art presses, and professional staff placed the *Times* at the forefront of newspaper journalism. From 1896, when Ochs took over the newspaper, to 1921, when he retired, the circulation of the *New York Times* increased from 100,000 to 330,000 daily and 500,000 Sunday readers.

The demand for investigative reporting to bolster newspaper circulation gave rise to another development. In the context of PROGRESSIVISM, mass circulation newspapers began conducting their own investigations of private and public misdeeds. In 1905, seeking to launch yet another challenge against its rivals, the *New York World* began to investigate the Equitable Life Insurance Society. The ensuing public furor over the ways in which insurance companies "gambled" with their shareholders' funds spiraled into a major state investigation and then state regulation of the industry. Not to be outdone, Hearst's *Journal American* directed its attention to a new domestic agenda. Charging that "criminal trusts" were undermining democracy, Hearst's editorial page showed its colors in attacking big business and urging the adoption of a graduated income tax, public ownership of utilities, DIRECT ELECTION OF SENATORS, and improvement of the public schools. At the same time, Hearst expanded his empire with the acquisition of newspapers in major cities. By 1930, his claim to be the "people's champion" echoed in 26 daily newspapers and 17 Sunday newspapers in 28 cities.

The investigative efforts of big city dailies also inspired a new generation of journalists. Called MUCKRAKERS, the reporters took on a range of social and political problems as the target for investigation. The central themes of their work were the growing concentration of corporate wealth, political corruption, and the deplorable conditions of poverty and disease in the new industrial society—leitmotifs for both the new journalism and progressive reform as a whole. Investigative reporting soon spread to mass-market magazines like *McClure's, Cosmopolitan,* and *Collier's,* which already had expanded their circulation in the 1890s. By 1900, their expanded subscriber base ensured that the "literature of exposure" had a wide audience. Even the stalwart *Ladies' Home Journal* got in on the act by attacking the patent medicine trade. Talented muckraking writers such as Lincoln Steffens, IDA TARBELL, Ray Stannard Baker, and UPTON SINCLAIR became household names. Investigating big city bosses, conditions in meat-packing plants, and corporate monopolies, the muckrakers built support for progressive reform. At the same time, the magazines for which they wrote saw subscriptions increase substantially.

The new environment of newspaper and magazine publishing opened the door for qualitative changes. Newspapers became big business in the period, and their profits encouraged the founding of many new city and country newspapers. In the decade between 1900 and 1910, the number of dailies in the United States increased from, 1,967 to 2,600. There were 14,000 general circulation weeklies. The new business of advertising stimulated the expansion of newspapers across the country. Between 1915 and 1929, advertising revenues nearly tripled from $275 million to $800 million annually. Revenues often were reinvested in the industry as newspapers and journals acquired high-speed and color presses, typesetting machines, and engraving plants, all of which required new infusions of capital. Competitive pressure from city dailies and standardization of news through services like the United Press Association, the Newspaper Enterprise Association, United Features, and Science Service Syndicate cost many country weeklies their subscriber base.

In smaller industrial cities, Edward W. Scripps founded a new chain of low-priced afternoon newspapers designed for the mass of readers. Beginning with the *St. Louis Chronicle,* Scripps invested small sums of capital to acquire local newspapers such as the *Detroit News, Cleveland Press,* and *Cincinnati Post,* extending the chain to 14 papers by 1911. The newspapers were, for the most part, well written in simple but direct prose. Small in size, they printed short news and human interest stories and local reform crusades. Dependent on circulation revenue and thus on general reader support, Scripps embraced a progressive agenda of support for public ownership of utilities and urban reform; he also backed labor unions. By the 1920s, the Scripps-Howard chain had become one of the largest in the country.

The advent of WORLD WAR I had a tremendous impact on journalism in the United States and abroad. Not surprisingly, the war became a primary focus for newspaper coverage even before the United States entered the war. Wartime government censorship, paper rationing, and taxes fundamentally changed the political economy of newspaper and journal publishing. First, major newspapers such as the *Chicago Daily News,* the *New York Times,* and the *New York Sun* created news services and established European bureaus to cover the war. At the front line, reporters were confronted with severe restrictions on their access to military information, which often was released only as official communiqués from government offices. They were largely restricted to feature stories from the frontlines, and even those stories, sent by either wireless or mail, faced government censors. Further, the WAR REVENUE ACT of 1917 and the TRADING WITH THE ENEMY ACT of the same year adversely affected newspapers and journals by introducing new costs and restrictions. The War Revenue Act raised postal rates every year for four years beginning in July 1918. The consequence of raising the rates was to undermine the financial base of small newspapers and to shift delivery and distribution of news out of the postal service. The Trading with the Enemy Act was somewhat more insidious. It required all foreign-language periodicals to translate their materials and submit them to a censor before publication. Hundreds of journals went out of print as a result. The same act allowed the postal inspector to refuse mailing permits to journals that voiced opposition to American intervention in the war or otherwise published radical sentiments. Finally, wartime inflation and escalating prices on paper, ink, linotype metal, and machinery put many publications out of business. The cost of paper alone tripled in the years between 1916 and 1921.

The economic pressures of the war and the suppression of foreign language newspapers furthered the movement toward consolidation of newspapers in the 1920s. The number of newspapers had begun to decline from its peak of 2,600 in 1910 to 2,042 in 1920 and 1,942 in 1930, a net loss of 258 newspapers. In the four years after World War I, more than 100 dailies were lost. At the same time, however, newspapers flourished in the more than 70 percent of cities and 80 percent of small towns that had a single newspaper. Circulation grew from 27.5 million in 1910 to 40 million in 1930.

In the arena of magazine publishing, there were similar stories. By 1900, there were over 3,500 magazines read by 65 million readers. The real growth in magazine readership, however, was still to come. In the 1920s, new mass-market magazines captured the readership of older dime novels. These magazines focused on real-life stories and confessional articles such as "What I Told My Daughter the Night before Her Marriage," "Indolent Kisses," and "The Confessions of a Chorus Girl." The increasing popularity of the movies encouraged star journals as well. *True Confessions, Western Stories,* and *Detective Story* drew a huge readership. *True Story,* which Bernarr Macfadden began publishing in 1919, had over 300,000 readers by 1923. In 1924, the number rose to 828,000 and to almost two million in 1926. Other magazines in such new areas as muscle-building (Macfadden's *Physical Culture* and *Health and Body*) opened the door for ever greater specialization. There was a corresponding move for magazine consolidation as well.

Magazine publishers also helped introduce tabloid journalism to New York City. Modeled on the *London Daily Mirror,* newspapers such as Macfadden's *Daily Graphic,* the *Daily Mirror,* and the *New York Daily News* began in 1920 to compete with older, more established newspapers. Their small size made them easier to read on crowded streetcars, but it was their news content that had a mass appeal. Instigating a new wave of sensationalist reporting called both "jazz" and "gutter" journalism, the *Daily Graphic* tapped such society scandals as the Fatty Arbuckle murder trial and the Kip Rhinelander interracial divorce case. Their graphic coverage of sex and crime scandals provoked the wrath of the Society for the Suppression of Vice, which brought Macfadden and his editor, Emile Gauveau, into court. Tabloids also directed new attention to Hollywood and sports celebrities, such as Babe Ruth and Knute Rockne. Circulation increased from 400,000 in 1922 to nearly a million readers in 1925. At the same time, how-

ever, the failure of the tabloids to attract sufficient advertising revenue caused the *Mirror* and the *Graphic* to go out of print in the 1930s; only the *Daily News* survived.

The emergence of RADIO brought journalism to a new medium. Although radio stations were still small and had a limited audience, radio introduced amateur news coverage of elections as early as 1916. In 1920, stations KDKA in East Pittsburgh and WWJ in Detroit broadcast the national election returns. Regular news coverage was introduced in New York on stations WNYC and WEAF. Large city newspapers invested in the new medium and acquired stations to broadcast coverage derived from their print reports. Despite initial protest, the Associated Press and the United Press formalized the use of news services on radio by creating two daily broadcast reports in 1928. This development coincided with the creation of national radio networks to distribute news and sports coverage. NBC emerged in 1926, and CBS in 1928. Throughout the period, there was at least the urge to distinguish radio news, which presumed equal access and neutrality, from the partisanship of newspaper reporting. The Radio Act of 1927, however, brought little regulation to news programs, and news stories continued to focus on political reporting that narrowly covered the two major political parties at their party conventions and national political addresses.

Despite the growth of radio news, mass-circulation newspapers reached new heights in 1930. The Hearst newspaper chain, which had begun modestly with two major city dailies, now included 26 dailies and 17 Sunday newspapers in 28 cities. The advent of radio broadcast news, however, suggested that there was a qualitatively different future ahead. Broadcast journalism on the radio and, within a few decades, on television began to supplement and then dominate how average citizens learned the news of their community, country, and world. The medium of broadcasting altered fundamentally the subject and approach of journalism and the definition of what was newsworthy.

See also LITERATURE; RADICAL PRESS.

Further reading: Gerald Baldasty, *E. W. Scripps and the Business of Newspapers* (Urbana: University of Illinois Press, 1999); Douglas B. Craig, *Fireside Politics: Radio and Political Culture in the United States, 1920–1940* (Baltimore: Johns Hopkins University Press, 2000); Thomas Leonard, *The Power of the Press; The Birth of American Political Reporting* (New York: Oxford University Press, 1986); Frank L. Mott, *American Journalism; A History, 1690–1960* (New York: Macmillan, 1962).

K

Keating-Owen Act (1916)

A federal statute that outlawed the transportation of goods produced by CHILD LABOR, the Keating-Owen Act was the culmination of a Progressive Era movement to outlaw child labor. The act passed Congress on September 1, 1916, and went into effect on September 1, 1917. Before it could have much of an effect, however, it was challenged in federal court and ruled unconstitutional by the U.S. Supreme Court in June 1918.

Progressive reformers believed that child labor was the greatest evil threatening America's children and thus the future of America. In 1900, 18 percent of children aged 10 to 15 worked, many of them in factories, mines, and mills. The millions of children working in dangerous conditions attracted the efforts of numerous reformers. Opponents of child labor initially sought to legislate against it in the states, but they realized that many states were unwilling to pass laws because their industries were dependent on the labor of children. Child labor law advocates therefore decided that federal legislation was necessary. The federal government did not, however, have the explicit constitutional power to prohibit child labor. Still, proponents of child labor laws believed that the federal government had the right to restrict interstate transport of goods produced by child laborers. By restricting the transport of these goods, the Keating-Owen Act effectively set national guidelines for child labor. It outlawed the labor of children under 14 years of age in factories, mills, and canneries, and under 16 years in mines and quarries. It also prohibited workers under 16 from working more than eight hours a day.

Opposition to the bill in Congress came from the states that employed more children than all others combined, the southern textile-producing states and Pennsylvania. Congressmen from these states argued that child labor was good for all involved. There were not enough schools, employers claimed, to handle all the children who would be thrown out of work by child labor laws. Work was therefore important in preventing delinquency by keeping children off the streets. It was also important for children to learn work skills early in life that would prepare them for careers as factory operatives. Opponents also claimed that workers over the age of 16 were too slow and clumsy and that only the nimble fingers of a child could handle some jobs. Prohibiting child labor would rob widow mothers of their sole means of support and restrict the children's inherent right to work. These arguments were ineffective, and the Keating-Owen Act passed by a vote of 343 to 46 in the House of Representatives and in the Senate by 52 to 12, with 32 abstentions.

Almost immediately upon passage, the Keating-Owen Act was challenged in the federal courts. In a case brought by the executive committee of the Southern Textile Manufacturers, a federal judge ruled the act unconstitutional. The case was then appealed to the U.S. Supreme Court. In *Hammer v. Dagenhart*, the Supreme Court judges ruled five to four that the law was unconstitutional. They argued that it was an unwarranted exercise of the federal government power to regulate commerce and an invasion of state's rights. In the nine months in which it was in effect, the Keating-Owen Act freed 150,000 children from work in mines, factories, and mills. More importantly, it acted as a model for state legislation against child labor and helped spur efforts in many states to limit the labor of children under the age of 16.

Further reading: Walter Trattner, *Crusade for the Children: A History of the National Child Labor Committee and Child Labor Reform in America* (Chicago: Quadrangle Books, 1970).

— Michael Hartman

Kelley, Florence (1859–1932)

One of the leading figures in Progressive Era reform, Florence Kelley dedicated her life to improving the lives of working men, women, and children. Born near Philadelphia, Pennsylvania, Kelley graduated from Cornell University in 1882. After the University of Pennsylvania refused to admit her to graduate study because she was a woman, Kelley began her career in reform. She joined the Philadelphia Woman's Club and established and taught at an evening school for working women and children. On an 1883 European trip, Kelley discovered that the University of Zurich allowed women to earn graduate degrees, and she enrolled. While in Zurich, she became a socialist and translated several works of Karl Marx and Frederick Engels into English. She also met her future husband, a Russian medical student, Lazare Wischnewtzky. The two married in 1884 and in 1886 moved to New York City. In 1891, in response to her husband's physical abuse, Kelley took their three children and moved to Illinois. She moved there both because of Illinois' lenient divorce laws and Chicago's reputation for social reform.

Upon coming to Chicago, Kelley joined JANE ADDAMS at Hull-House and took up residence in 1891. She took charge of the Hull-House Women's Labor Bureau and convinced the Illinois Bureau of Labor Statistics to hire her to investigate the conditions in Chicago's sweatshops. Her work led to further appointments as an investigator for the federal commissioner of labor to study Chicago's slums. Kelley uncovered the appalling conditions under which workers lived, and her findings spurred a movement to pass labor laws in Illinois. As a result of her investigation, the state of Illinois passed laws restricting CHILD LABOR, limiting the working hours of women, and regulating the conditions in sweatshops. In 1893, Kelley became Illinois' first chief factory inspector. In 1897 the governor of Illinois replaced her with a patronage appointment, putting her out of work.

Kelley became the executive secretary of the National Consumers League, a position she held until her death. As league secretary, she lobbied on behalf of protective labor legislation for women and children. She helped establish 64 consumers' leagues throughout the United States and traveled promoting policies agreed upon by the national board. Working with the Oregon consumers' league, Kelley helped successfully defend the state's 10-hour working-day legislation for women in the 1908 *MULLER V. OREGON* case. Under her leadership, the National Consumers League became the most effective lobbying group for protective labor legislation for women and children. She also continued to campaign against child labor in a number of ways. A founder of the National Child Labor Committee in 1904, Kelley made the creation of the CHILDREN'S BUREAU one of her top priorities. The effort was successful in 1912. Kelley was also instrumental in 1921 in the passage of the SHEPPARD-TOWNER ACT. She died in 1932.

Further reading: Kathryn Kish Sklar, *Florence Kelley and the Nation's Work: The Rise of Women's Political Culture, 1830–1900* (New Haven, Conn.: Yale University Press, 1995); Kathryn Kish Sklar, ed., *Florence Kelley, Notes of Sixty Years: The Autobiography of Florence Kelley* (Chicago: Charles H. Kerr, 1986).

— Michael Hartman

Kellogg-Briand Treaty (Kellogg-Briand Pact; Pact of Paris) (1928)

A product of the interwar peace movement, the Kellogg-Briand Pact was a 1928 agreement among several nations to seek to stop war. In 1927 James T. Shotwell, a Columbia University professor and trustee of the CARNEGIE ENDOWMENT FOR INTERNATIONAL PEACE, visited French foreign minister Aristide Briand to lobby for a formal repudiation of war by the United States and France. When the French refused to attend the Geneva Naval Conference, Briand attempted to mollify American concerns that the French might be engaging in an arms race by sending a draft of a treaty to Washington on June 20, 1927, along the lines that Shotwell had suggested. Worried about the revival of German militarism, the French hoped to forge an alliance with the United States as a security measure against their historic enemy.

America's secretary of state Frank Kellogg proposed an alternative to Briand's alliance, a multilateral treaty that outlawed war. Eventually 62 nations signed the treaty in Paris in 1928. The nations agreed to "condemn recourse to war for the solution of international controversies, and renounce it as an instrument of national policy." The signatories, however, watered down the treaty by attaching amendments refusing to outlaw, for example, wars of self-defense. The U.S. Senate attached an amendment to the pact that allowed for the use of force to uphold the Monroe Doctrine as well as to protect national interest or honor. Perhaps more troubling was the fact that the U.S. Congress passed legislation to increase its navy at the same time that it formally renounced war in the Kellogg-Briand Treaty. On the same day that the Senate approved the treaty 85–1, it appropriated funds for 15 new cruisers.

Furthermore, the Kellogg-Briand Treaty had no mechanism for enforcement. Instead, according to Kellogg, it relied on "moral force." The treaty was in fact only a statement of principle that required no sacrifices or responsibilities. It did not provide a sense of security to its signatories, nor did many peace advocates believe that the treaty guaranteed a peaceful world. American statesmen and peace advocates who supported the pact saw it as only a first step in a longer process toward a peaceful world. It was viewed more or less as a tool to educate the public about the costs of war. However, it proved useful after World War II, when the treaty was revived by the Allies to punish German leaders for war crimes at the Nuremberg Trials.

See also FOREIGN POLICY.

Further reading: Lewis Ethan Ellis, *Frank B. Kellogg and American Foreign Relations, 1925–1929* (New Brunswick, N.J.: Rutgers University Press, 1961); Richard W. Fanning, *Peace and Disarmament: Naval Rivalry and Arms Control, 1922–1933* (Lexington: University Press of Kentucky, 1995).

— Glen Bessemer

Kelly Air Mail Act (1925)

Also known as the Contract Air Mail Act, the Kelly Air Mail Act established a competitive bidding system for private airlines to provide mail transport for the U.S. Post Office in 1925. It was the first major step toward the creation of a private U.S. airline industry, and was named after its chief sponsor, Representative Clyde Kelly of Pennsylvania. Winners of the five initial contracts were National Air Transport (Curtiss Aeroplane Company), Varney Airlines, Western Air Express, Colonial Air Transport, and Robertson Aircraft Corporation. Various air transport holding companies soon appeared, including American Airways, which later transformed into American Airlines, and United Aircraft, which later became United Airlines. By the mid-1920s, the Post Office mail fleet was flying 2.5 million miles and delivering 14 million letters annually. The formation of a mail transport system by the Post Office Department further spurred the development of the air transportation industry. Once the Kelly Air Mail Act was passed, the private carriers who provided air transport for the Post Office expanded into carrying other forms of cargo, and eventually passengers.

The same year Congress passed the Kelly Air Mail Act, President CALVIN COOLIDGE formed a board to recommend a national aviation policy. Dwight Morrow, the future father-in-law of CHARLES LINDBERGH, was named chairman. The report advised that the government set standards for the air transport industry. It argued that the military should not be involved. The Air Commerce Act of 1926 provided for federal regulation of air traffic rules. The legislation authorized the secretary of commerce to designate air routes, develop air navigation systems, license pilots and aircraft, and investigate accidents. Congress amended the Kelly Act by simplifying the payment system. Pilots would get paid by the weight of the mail, not as a percentage of postage paid.

As the industry grew, the Post Office increasingly had influence over the airline industry and limited the number of carriers that were granted the coveted mail transport contracts. These practices were ruled anti-competitive, and the industry once again opened up to a competitive bidding system, until 1938, when the Civil Aeronautics Authority was developed.

See also AVIATION.

Further reading: Roger Bilstein, *Flight in America: From the Wrights to the Astronauts,* 2nd ed. (Baltimore: Johns Hopkins University Press, 1994).

— Annamarie Edelen

Ku Klux Klan

The original Ku Klux Klan emerged in the wake of the Civil War. The primary emphasis of the organization was to reassert the racial caste system that its followers believed was in jeopardy with the end of slavery. Attempting to "redeem" the South, southerners formed paramilitary groups dedicated to suppressing southern African Americans. Organized in 1866, the original incarnation of the Klan was led by former Confederate general Nathan Bedford Forrest. Forrest and other leaders of this quasi-secret organization devised elaborate rituals in order to unify its members and create an aura of mystique and passion. The hoods and robes were central to the organization's identity, but even more important were the midnight rides. These rides became the defining element of the organization. They not only spread fear and terror throughout the South, but also helped to unite the Klansmen. When Reconstruction ended, however, the midnight rides lost their functionality. Soon after, the perceived need for the Klan declined. Within five years, the Klan ceased to exist as a coherent organization.

The Klan lay dormant for nearly a half-century before it reemerged in a position of even greater influence than before. What began as a small meeting of white supremacists on Stone Mountain in Georgia in 1915 provided the nucleus for the resurgence of the organization. The new Klan grew slowly at first, but soon it became the most influential organization in the South. The premiere of D. W. GRIFFITH's film, BIRTH OF A NATION, was a seminal event in the Klan's reemergence. Adapted from Thomas Dixon's racist novel, *The Clansman,* the film portrayed the Klan as a chivalrous organization of the post–Civil War era that was both necessary and just. Its purpose was supposedly to save southern society and southern institutions from the ignorance and greed of blacks and northerners. *Birth of a Nation,* which opened in Atlanta not far from Stone Mountain, provided a base for the revived Klan. The movie's immense popularity helped to give legitimacy to the organization's past.

The new Klan attained a level of acceptance that the previous Klan had coveted. With acceptance came numbers. By the middle of the 1920s, nearly 4 million men and women were members of the revitalized organization. In the beginning, the new Klan was merely a new version of the old organization. Its primary goal was to subordinate southern blacks. But due to social changes brought by new immigration and technology, the Klan adopted a broader vision. Klan members claimed to be against anything and everything that was contrary to "America" and directed their venom toward Catholics, Jews, and recent immigrants. Klansmen viewed these minority groups as serious threats to the health and sanctity of the nation. While the promotion of racial hegemony remained central to the Klan's image and philosophy throughout its second incarnation, race was soon subordinated to culture. Members of the Klan championed themselves as defenders not of a racial or caste system but of traditional values. This vision allowed the Klan to win the support of people who would not normally have supported it. New recruits saw modernization, not necessarily racial minorities, as a threat to their traditional ways of life. They flocked to the organization that they believed would defend their value system.

The new Klan expanded not only in membership and ideology but also geographically. For the first time since its inception, it was no longer a predominantly southern organization. By the early 1920s, local Klan chapters were popping up throughout the United States. In Chicago alone,

the Klan had several thousand members. Men and women from all parts of the country, from New York to California, flocked to the organization. A chapter was even established at Harvard University. The more cosmopolitan nature of the organization can be seen by its membership. During this era, the Klan attracted more members in Indianapolis than it did in Mississippi. Like its southern predecessor, moreover, the new Klan was a powerful political force. It controlled key branches of local government throughout the country. In Anaheim, California, for example, the Klan controlled the police, the city council, and other public offices.

The Klan reached its peak in the middle of the 1920s. It then declined as fast as it had emerged. After 1925, due to a series of power struggles and scandals, the Klan began to lose its following. Many of its members left the organization because they believed it was more concerned with making profits than defending their way of life. Still others believed that inefficient leadership was corrupting the Klan. The biggest blow to the organization, however, came from David Stephenson, head of the Indiana Klan. He kidnapped his secretary and raped her. When she poisoned herself, he left her to die. This act challenged much of what the new Klan was claiming to be. It was difficult to tout

Parade of the Ku Klux Klan through counties in Virginia *(Library of Congress)*

the organization's position as a defender of traditional Christian morality when its leaders had such an appalling disrespect for these ideals. The organization faded into obscurity where it remained until its next incarnation.

See also ANTI-SEMITISM; IMMIGRATION; RACE AND RACIAL CONFLICT.

Further reading: Kenneth Jackson, *The Ku Klux Klan in the City, 1915–1930* (New York: Oxford University Press, 1967); Leonard Moore, *Citizen Klansman: The Ku Klux Klan in Indiana, 1921–1928* (Chapel Hill: University of North Carolina Press, 1991); Richard Tucker, *The Dragon and the Cross: The Rise and Fall of the Ku Klux Klan in Middle America* (Hamden, Conn.: Archon Books, 1991).

— Steve Freund

L

labor and labor movement

The nature of work, and the way in which workers responded to the challenges work presented, changed dramatically between 1900 and 1930. Prior to 1900, most American workers spent their days engaged in work that varied little from the time when the country had been founded. Farming, skilled craft work, domestic service, mining, and fishing typified the way in which most wage earners secured their livelihood. To be sure, some important changes had begun to change the nature of work. The post–Civil War industrial revolution and the influx of millions of immigrants increased the number and ethnic diversity of laborers and wage earners. Small- and large-scale factory production altered entire industries, such as tailoring. Where skilled craft workers had once produced hand-sewn, high-quality goods, by the 1880s skilled tailors had been replaced by semi-skilled factory workers who were mass-producing inexpensive garments.

While few industries had been as thoroughly transformed as the tailoring industry, these changes had spread throughout much of the economy by 1900. Business innovators, such as JOHN D. ROCKEFELLER in oil, J. P. Morgan in banking, and Andrew Carnegie in steel, were determined to rationalize and control every aspect of their industries. Key features of this attempt to rationalize and modernize American industry included mass-producing goods, vertical and horizontal integration of production, scientific management, hiring an ethnically and racially diverse workforce, and efforts to replace skilled craft workers with unskilled or semi-skilled workers. Employer motivation was to monopolize control over an entire industry and maximize profits by mass-producing inexpensive goods and keeping labor costs as low as possible. Industrial corporations were joined in their efforts by small business owners. Together, employers large and small formed organizations such as the NATIONAL ASSOCIATION OF MANUFACTURERS, the American Anti-Boycott Association, and local chambers of commerce. Their ultimate goal was to structure their businesses and American industry to be more efficient, scientific, productive, and profitable.

Attempts to modernize American industry resulted in significant changes in the nature of work. Employers routinized the production process by mass-producing goods and introducing SCIENTIFIC MANAGEMENT to ensure greater productivity and control over the workforce. New management techniques included a specialized division of labor, employee training, creating sales and distribution departments, and more sophisticated methods of accounting and record keeping. One important consequence was the proliferation of middle managers, secretaries, college-educated professionals, and other white-collar occupations. Gradually, white-collar occupations became specialized and divided along gender lines. Middle-level managers, accountants, sales representatives, and technical experts were predominately male employees, while clerks, receptionists, secretaries, typists, and company nurses were typically female.

Working-class Americans responded to these changes in a number of ways. First, there was significant growth in the number of labor unions. Workers sought to gain greater control over their working conditions and improve their lives by forming unions for most of the 19th century. Their efforts met with mixed results; but by the end of the century, few American workers belonged to labor unions. In 1897, union membership in the United States stood at a paltry 447,000. Union membership remained low for a variety of reasons. Many employers, citing moral, philosophical, and financial objections, vigorously resisted labor unions. Employers opposed to unions hired ethnically and racially diverse workforces and then exploited divisions among workers to prevent them from forming unions. When strikes did occur, some employers hired replacement workers from other ethnic and racial communities. Employers also embarked on a prolonged attempt to replace relatively well-paid skilled workers with poorly paid unskilled or semi-skilled workers. In other industries, such

Workforce, 1910, 1920, 1930

as textiles and tailoring, women and children were hired to replace more highly paid male workers. Employers relied upon the nation's conservative legal and political environment to prevent workers from forming unions. Strikes, boycotts, and other forms of labor pressure were frequently undermined by court injunctions and decisions. For example, in 1908, the U.S. Supreme Court ruled in the DANBURY HATTERS case that the union's consumer boycott violated the Sherman Antitrust Act of 1890.

Prior to 1900, some union efforts had been successful. Although the 1890s witnessed several stunning defeats, such as the 1892 Homestead Strike and 1894 Pullman Strike, there was also substantial growth in union membership. Led by JOHN MITCHELL, the UNITED MINE WORKERS OF AMERICA (UMWA) formed in 1890 and grew steadily throughout the decade. Similarly, the much larger AMERICAN FEDERATION OF LABOR (AFL), led by Samuel Gompers, experienced steady gains in membership. As the largest labor union in the country, the conservative AFL built a solid foundation by focusing its efforts on recruiting skilled white craft workers. While the efforts of the AFL helped these skilled workers fend off attempts to lower their wages, it left the vast majority of American workers poorly paid and unorganized.

By 1900, proponents of NEW UNIONISM attempted to fill the void left by the AFL. Where the AFL had restricted its efforts to organizing only highly skilled workers, many of the new unions attempted to organize workers throughout entire industries. One of the early examples was the UMWA. The UMWA attempted to

organize mine workers regardless of their job classification within the industry. Other unions, such as the INDUSTRIAL WORKERS OF THE WORLD (IWW), went even further and attempted to organize workers throughout the entire country, regardless of their gender, race, ethnicity, or occupation.

These new semi-industrial unions, such as the UMWA, the INTERNATIONAL LADIES' GARMENT WORKERS UNION, and the Amalgamated Clothing Workers differed from the AFL in that they attempted to organize workers both along craft lines and throughout entire industries. They were progressive and even radical in their politics and more willing to confront employers with direct action to gain recognition or secure their demands. In 1902, when the UMWA encountered resistance to its attempts to organize the nation's anthracite miners, 140,000 miners walked off the job in one of the nation's largest strikes. Led by WILLIAM "Big Bill" HAYWOOD and others, the IWW pursued its goals through work stoppages, general strikes, boycotts, strikes, and other forms of direct action.

One result of the rise of new unionism was that the labor movement grew in size and strength between 1900 and 1920. Union membership increased from 2 million in 1904 to 5 million in 1920. Throughout the country, workers were organizing unions and demanding pay increases, shorter workdays, and improved working conditions. The growth in union membership was sharpest among skilled white male workers, but it also included a rise in the number of women, immigrants, and workers of color who belonged to unions.

The burgeoning labor movement began flexing its political muscle at both the state and federal level. In several states, labor-friendly Democratic or Socialist candidates were able to gain control of important political offices and helped secure the passage of pro-labor legislation, including child labor laws, workmen's compensation legislation, and maximum hour laws. At the national level, the labor movement was able to secure the passage of the CLAYTON ANTITRUST ACT (1914). Through the INDUSTRIAL RELATIONS COMMISSION, it played an active role in shaping federal policy on labor relations. The AFL was the chief beneficiary of the increased power of the labor movement. It supported with some success Democratic Party candidates in 1906, 1908, and 1912; and Gompers and other AFL leaders worked closely with the administration of Woodrow Wilson and supported the war effort.

Cooperation between the AFL and the Democratic Party reached its zenith in 1918 with the formation of the NATIONAL WAR LABOR BOARD. The AFL agreed to a no-strike pledge and the maintenance of OPEN SHOP workplaces, where employers had the ability to pressure employees not to join the union. In exchange, business leaders agreed to pay union wages and refrain from the most egregious forms of anti-labor behavior that had been typical in the years before WORLD WAR I.

The end of the war, however, brought an end to the National War Labor Board and cooperation between the labor movement, employers, and the federal government. Across the country, workers frustrated by no-strike pledges, low wage increases during the war, and rampant postwar inflation, walked off the job in one of the largest waves of strikes in the country's history. The STEEL STRIKE OF 1919, which began on September 22, 1919, and lasted until January 8, 1920, involved 365,000 steelworkers and marked the end of the uneasy labor accord reached during the war. The backlash against the labor movement was swift and widespread. Many employers had only reluctantly tolerated the AFL's presence on the National War Labor Board. With the war's end, conservative employers and anti-union business organizations launched a movement for the Open Shop.

U.S. Attorney General A. MITCHELL PALMER was convinced that many of the new unionists were supporters of the Bolshevik Revolution in Russia and were plotting to overthrow their own federal government. With the backing of the AFL and many employers, Palmer launched a series of raids against suspected radicals, the chief target of which was the IWW. During the war, many IWW leaders were arrested and convicted under the ESPIONAGE ACT (1917) for opposing the war. Now, widespread repression took place throughout the Northwest where the IWW had been strongest. In states where the IWW and socialists had become influential, local laws were passed making socialism and syndicalism illegal. By the end of 1920, the organization was in total disarray and ceased to be an effective force in the American labor movement.

The demise of new unionism undermined the strength of the labor movement and ensured that it remained in a weakened state throughout the 1920s. The new unions had brought thousands of previously unorganized workers into the labor movement, and challenged the supremacy of employers and conservative state and federal policies toward organized labor. The massive post–World War I strike wave indicated the extent to which new ideas and a willingness to take direct action had taken root among

Young women protesting unfair labor conditions *(Library of Congress)*

American workers, but the divisions between the new and more radical unions, such as the IWW and the older, more conservative AFL, undermined the effect of the strike wave and helped ensure the demise of the new unionism. Additional setbacks occurred in 1921 when the Supreme Court, led by Chief Justice WILLIAM HOWARD TAFT, undermined the effectiveness of the Clayton Antitrust Act, and in 1922, when national coal and railway strikes were defeated.

Despite the gains made between 1900 and 1920, the labor movement proved unable to resist the postwar reaction. The gains made under the Wilson administration and during the war were the product of an administration that needed the support of the labor movement to pass legislation and ensure reelection. Employers tolerated the formation of the Industrial Relations Commission and the National War Labor Board to ensure labor peace during the war, but only after the AFL and other unions agreed not to strike during the war.

When the war came to an end, Gompers and the AFL mistakenly hoped that cooperative relations would continue. Most employers, however, were determined to preserve the open shop and hold the line against postwar wage increases. The strike wave of 1919 convinced them of the need to respond aggressively. The labor movement was unable to respond to this challenge effectively largely because the vast majority of workers remained unorganized. Despite attempts to organize recent immigrants, African Americans, and women into unions, most workers continued to toil in difficult, poor-paying, non-union jobs. The nation's largest and most influential union, the AFL, did little to address the plight of these workers.

Although the 1920s has typically been characterized as a decade of economic growth, few American workers shared in this general prosperity. Part of this economic malaise can be attributed to an overall weakness in heavily unionized industries such as textiles and coal. The weakness of the labor movement and the increasing conservatism of the AFL played an important role in the inability of many working-class Americans to enjoy the prosperity of the decade. From the early 1920s to the Great Depression, wages and overall standards of living declined steadily for many workers. Unable to fend off the anti-union backlash of the postwar period, the AFL and the labor movement in general failed to deliver on such bread-and-butter issues as wage increases, job security, and an improved standard of living.

Frustrated by stagnant real wages and by the ineffectiveness of the AFL, some workers began considering more radical alternatives. These included the Socialist Party and the small, but well-organized Communist Party with its labor organization, the Trade Union Education League. When the economy collapsed in 1929, American workers turned to more radical alternatives. Millions of workers, particularly those who found themselves unemployed or underemployed, became radicalized, pressured the AFL to become more active and progressive, and—when that failed—formed the Congress of Industrial Unions (CIO).

Further reading: Irving Bernstein, *The Lean Years: A History of the American Worker, 1920–1933* (New York: Da Capo Paperbacks, 1960); Melvin Dubofsky, *The State and Labor in Modern America* (Chapel Hill: University of North Carolina Press, 1994); Joseph McCartin, *Labor's Great War: The Struggle for Industrial Democracy and the Origins of Modern Labor Relations, 1912–1921* (Chapel Hill: University of North Carolina Press, 1997); David Montgomery, *The Fall of the House of Labor: The Workplace, the State, and American Labor Activism, 1865–1925* (New York: Cambridge University Press, 1987).

— Robert Gordon

La Follette, Robert (1855–1925)

Born in Primrose, Wisconsin, on June 14, 1855, Robert La Follette was one of the key figures in the formation of the Progressive Party. The son of a farmer, La Follette attended the University of Wisconsin, where he graduated in 1879. After graduation, La Follette began a successful legal practice in Madison at a time when midwestern farmers were finding it almost impossible to remain in business. Falling food prices due to mechanization and competition from large-scale farms meant that many independent farmers were caught in a vicious cycle of planting ever more crops, taking out ever larger loans, getting ever lower prices at harvest time, and falling ever deeper into debt. Resentment toward large-scale, urban food manufacturers and eastern banking elites led many small farmers to call for progressive reforms.

La Follette tapped this progressive sentiment for reform in his bid for the governorship of Wisconsin in 1900, promising to tax wealthy corporations, regulate the state's railroads, create a merit-based civil service, and increase state spending on public education. La Follette won the contest, and he was reelected in 1902 and 1904. Over the course of his political career, he consistently supported progressive reforms in an attempt to limit or prevent corporate exploitation of the state's farmers and workers. Prior to assuming the governorship, La Follette had been a mainstream Republican who briefly held a seat in the House of Representatives. In his legal practice, he had represented the state's railroads and other wealthy clients on numerous occasions. However, in 1891, shortly after La Follette lost his House seat, Senator Philetus Sawyer (R–Wisc,) attempted to bribe him to influence a pending case. When the story became public, La Follette became an outcast among the state's Republicans and business elite, forcing him to build a popular base of support. Drawing on his base, La Follette championed the "Wisconsin Ideal" and enacted many of the progressive reforms he had championed in 1900.

In 1906 La Follette was elected to the U.S. Senate, where he continued to push for progressive reforms, including legislation for greater federal oversight of the railroads and regulation of industries. He also pushed successfully for a constitutional amendment establishing the DIRECT ELECTION OF SENATORS and eventually developed presidential aspirations. In order to further his political ambitions, La Follette founded *La Follette's Weekly Magazine* in 1909 and created the National Progressive Republican League in 1911. In 1912, La Follette hoped to prevent the conservative wing of the Republican Party from nominating President WILLIAM HOWARD TAFT for a second term; but when former president THEODORE ROOSEVELT announced his candidacy, most of La Follette's progressive supporters decided to back Roosevelt in his unsuccessful bid.

La Follette was a leading isolationist and one of the few senators to vote against American entry into WORLD WAR I. His presidential aspirations surfaced again in 1924 when he received the nomination to head the Progressive Party ticket. Supported by progressives and organized labor, La Follette garnered a respectable 17 percent of the vote. The campaign, however, proved exhausting. By the summer of 1925, La Follette was dead. One of the leading progressive politicians of his day, he fought for tax reform, corporate responsibility, the rights of organized labor, farmers, civil service reform, and for a greater federal and state role in regulating the railroads and industry.

See also PROGRESSIVISM.

Further reading: David P. Thelen, *Robert M. La Follette and the Insurgent Spirit* (Madison: University of Wisconsin Press, 1986); Nancy C. Unger, *Fighting Bob La Follette: Righteous Reformer* (Chapel Hill: University of North Carolina Press, 2000).

— Robert Gordon

Lawrence Strike (1912)

One of the first major, successful strikes of immigrant workers in a mass production industry, the Lawrence Strike led many labor leaders to believe that a new age of labor was on the rise. From January 11 to March 14, 1912, textile workers in Lawrence, Massachusetts, struck against the American Woolen Company and other smaller mills to protest a pay cut. The strike became national news. At the time, observers believed the strike had important implications for the future of labor in America. The strikers' use of mass picketing, their ethnic diversity and working-class unity, and the ability of workers to strike together across skill lines made the Lawrence Strike a model of the NEW UNIONISM. By March, the workers had won their demands for an increase in the piece rate they were paid, and the INDUSTRIAL WORKERS OF THE WORLD (IWW) had emerged as a new force in the American Labor movement.

The Lawrence Strike began when a Massachusetts law went into effect that lowered weekly working hours for women and children to 54. The mill owners announced that all workers would work the 54-hour week. Workers were paid according to the number of pieces they produced or finished. They knew that, if their hours were cut, their weekly pay would also decline unless they received an increase in the piece rate. The mill owners gave no indication they would increase piece rates, so as the date for the first pay day of 1912 drew near, Lawrence was filled with tension.

After receiving their first paychecks, workers moved through the mills. Based on old piece rates, the checks reflected deep cuts in their total pay. They broke windows and equipment before moving into the streets to join workers from other mills. The city and state officials quickly reacted by calling out the town's police force to prevent further destruction of property.

The IWW sent organizers Joseph Ettor and Arturo Giovannitti to Lawrence to support the strike. By the second day of the strike, they had organized the strikers to demand a 15 percent wage increase and double pay for overtime. The organizers also set up a central strike committee, which had three representatives from each ethnic group in the city, to run the strike.

Throughout the strike, unions battled over the future direction of the American labor movement. The conflict arose between the IWW, which advocated industrial unionism, and the United Textile Workers (UTW), a craft union affiliated with the AMERICAN FEDERATION OF LABOR. The UTW had earlier failed to organize the textile workers in Lawrence. Its native-born leaders did not reach out to the largely immigrant unskilled workforce. During the strike, the union set up relief stations, and its leaders spoke frequently of the dangers posed by the IWW. They tried to convince workers that their interests would best be served through craft unionism. Despite these efforts, the UTW failed to attract Lawrence textile workers.

The strike became a national cause among unions and attracted the attention of the major newspaper, media, and senators and representatives. Two specific events gained public support. First, the local police arrested the IWW organizers, Ettor and Giovannitti, on false murder charges. In response to the arrests, the IWW sent its best-known leaders, WILLIAM D. ("Big Bill") HAYWOOD and ELIZABETH GURLEY FLYNN, to take the place of the arrested organizers. Second, the police arrested a group of women and children, the wives and children of strikers, who were boarding a train in the organized effort to escape the deprivation they faced as a result of the strike. The IWW hoped to use the evacuation to evoke sympathy for their cause. The arrest of the women and children led to a nationwide outcry over police brutality and to government investigations. The threat that bad strike publicity might threaten the wool tariff pushed the American Woolen Company to settle with the strikers. The company granted a 5 percent increase in the piece rate, an increase in the wage scale that raised the wages of the lowest paid workers 20 percent, and overtime pay. It further promised that the company would not retaliate against strike leaders.

The strike thrust the IWW onto the national scene and appeared to vindicate its strategy of organizing American labor on an industrial basis. The IWW's National Industrial Union of Textile Workers membership increased to 18,000 in the aftermath of the strike, leading people to talk of the New Unionism as a force for social change.

Further reading: Ardis Cameron, *Radicals of the Worst Sort: Laboring Women in Lawrence, 1860–1912* (Urbana: University of Illinois Press, 1993).

— Michael Hartman

League of Nations

Envisioned as an assembly with seats for all nations and a council to be controlled by the "Great Powers," the League of Nations was established in 1919 by the TREATY OF VERSAILLES. It was the brainchild of President WOODROW WILSON, who sought to safeguard the self-determination of nations with the league and use it as a means of preventing another world conflict. Presented to Congress in 1918 as one of Wilson's Fourteen Points, the league was envisioned as a general association of nations. Wilson's plan formed the basis of the Covenant of the League of Nations, which centered on 26 articles and served as operating rules for the organization. The covenant was then formulated as part of the Treaty of Versailles, which ended WORLD WAR I.

The League of Nations was the predecessor of the United Nations. The purpose for its establishment was to maintain peace. Members agreed not to go to war and to submit disputes to World Court arbitration. The league existed from 1920 to 1946. The first meeting was held in Geneva on November 15, 1920, with 42 nations represented. The last meeting was held April 8, 1946.

Prior to the First World War, there were movements that pointed toward the establishment of a world association for peace. From the close of the Napoleonic Wars and the Congress of Vienna in 1815, popular support for peace societies and a concern for international law enabled national leaders to solve differences through arbitration.

In 1899, and again in 1907, Russia's Czar Nicholas called a conference at The Hague to discuss the limitation of arms and peaceful settlement of international issues. A Permanent Court of Arbitration was set up to resolve issues. Three conflicts between the Great Powers of Europe were settled this way before war broke out in 1914.

In the spring of 1914, President Wilson sent his friend and adviser, Colonel Edward House, to Europe as an unofficial ambassador for peace. House met with German officials and outlined concerns of Britain that Germany's navy was growing. Then he met with officials from France and Britain. House's mediation did not prevent the escalation of tensions that led to war.

In England, a League of Nations Society was founded in May 1915. In the United States, several branches sprang up. Senator HENRY CABOT LODGE early emerged as a great opponent of the idea, and he warned America not to get "entangled" with Europe. Wilson answered that "the nations of the world must in some way band themselves together to see that right prevails as against selfish aggression." He promoted three principles to govern such a league: one, sovereignty over self; two, right to territorial integrity; and three, that the world and its people should be protected against aggression. Wilson proposed that the United States start a movement for a universal association of nations. While speaking at West Point, he contrasted the "spirit of militarism" to the "citizen spirit." He contended that the civilian spirit was meant to dominate the military, which was why he was commander in chief of the armed forces.

The United States entered World War I in April 1917, but it was a year before many soldiers were fighting in France. That summer Wilson appointed a committee to study Europe and its laws, peoples, and economies. Utilizing this research, Wilson formulated a list of war aims and peace suggestions, and he presented them to Congress as the "Fourteen Points." The Fourteen Points argued specifically for a safer world run by self-governing nations. Wilson declared that the United States would be willing to fight for principles of international justice, which it adopted as the basis for peace. On October 6, 1918, the German government requested peace negotiations. The Germans agreed to disarm and relinquish their monarchical military leadership. They wanted a peace according to the points made in President Wilson's speeches. After the Armistice, the Paris Peace Conference was held, out of which came the Treaty of Versailles.

The idealist Wilson faced a serious challenge from European diplomats, who were determined to gain all they could for their national interests. Lloyd George of England had just been reelected with the slogan, "be tough on Germany." Clemenceau of France also wanted a weak Germany. The Italians and Japanese wanted specific territories. President Wilson introduced the League of Nations draft to the Peace Conference with an address on February 14, 1919. The day after the draft was accepted by the plenary session, the president departed for the United States, where he set to work on gaining public support for the league treaty and the League of Nations.

Political conflict kept the United States out of the league. The United States, Germany, and, initially, the new Soviet Union did not join the League of Nations. United States isolationists were against involvement. The United States, consequently, never ratified the Treaty of Versailles. As a consequence of the war, supervision of territories that had been colonies and possessions of Germany and Turkey before the war was awarded to league members in the form of mandates. These territories were issued varying degrees of independence depending on their stage of development. The Soviet Union and Germany both joined the league years after its inception.

As established, the league gave each nation one vote. Either party to a dispute could submit an issue to the league's executive committee. The debate could then be drawn out of the executive committee to the larger body of delegates, which ensured the moral force of international public opinion. If moral force failed, physical force remained in reserve. The helpless people of the world, it was thought, could expect a new light and a new hope.

The League of Nations achieved some of its goals in stemming the tide of international traffic in narcotics and prostitution, aiding war refugees, and surveying and improving on health and labor conditions in the world. During the 1920s, the league assisted in settling some minor disputes, but it was hampered by the non-membership of the United States. Ultimately, the failure of the league to prevent Japanese military ambitions in Manchuria and China, Italy's takeover of Ethiopia, and, finally, Hitler's renunciation of the Treaty of Versailles, discredited it as an international authority. Although it was not effective as a peace-keeping body, the League of Nations did lay the groundwork for international cooperation in its successor, the United Nations, which was founded in 1946.

See also FOREIGN POLICY.

Further reading: F. S. Northedge, *The League of Nations: Its Life and Times* (New York: Holmes and Meier, 1986); Thomas J. Knock, *To End All Wars: Woodrow Wilson and the Quest for a New World Order* (New York: Oxford University Press, 1992).

— Annamarie Edelen

Leo Frank case

The case of Leo Frank involved a 1914 murder and trial in Atlanta, Georgia, that became a national affair. On April 27,

1913, 14-year-old Mary Phagan was found murdered in the basement of a pencil factory in Atlanta, Georgia. The grisly murder shocked the community. Public dismay was heightened by the fact that the scene of the crime had been a factory, a symbol of the encroachments of capitalist industrial economy in the South. Outrage over Phagan's death quickly turned to a public demand that her killer be caught. Suspicions first settled on the factory's night watchman, an African American named Newt Lee. The evidence initially implicating Lee, however, turned out to be weak. Prosecutors' suspicions then turned to the superintendent of the factory, Leo Frank.

The prosecutors built a case against Frank based on circumstantial evidence and rumor. Many of the rumors were later proven false. The evidence against Frank centered on his being one of the few people in the factory on the day of the murder and his inability to provide a persuasive account of where he was when the murder occurred. Other accusations focused on Frank's alleged sexual perversity. Some women factory workers claimed that Frank had made sexual advances to them. A madam of a local bordello charged that he frequented her establishment. Despite the lack of evidence, the Atlanta newspapers seized every new development as proof that Frank was the killer. His trial thus took place amid the public perception that he was guilty.

The Frank case also took on other implications because of what Frank represented in the South. To many, Mary Phagan's death was proof of the dangers that industrial capitalism would bring to the South. The small family farm was in decline while industry was spreading. Many southern farmers were forced to send their wives and daughters to work in the new factories. Southerners thus saw factories not only as a symbol of the power of industrial capitalism, but also as a threat to their wives and daughters. To add to public fears, Leo Frank was Jewish, which made him suspect in the eyes of many. Anti-Semitism was prevalent in American culture. Racial prejudice characterized Jewish American men as sexual predators who preyed on innocent women. Leo Frank thus became to many a symbol of market power and a danger to the southern way of life. Combined with the predatory character of capitalism in the eyes of southerners, anti-Semitic feelings created an explosive situation that ended in a lynching.

Frank was found guilty. After the trial, many people started to question the verdict. Some of the evidence against Frank was revealed as false. When it appeared that Frank might be granted a lenient sentence, or even worse a new trial, many southerners denounced the possibility as due to his position and wealth. Frank did not, however, live long enough to see another trial. First, another inmate assaulted Frank and slit his throat, a wound from which he was recovering when a lynch mob broke into the jail, removed Frank, and lynched him. The Leo Frank case was one of the last and most visible public lynchings of the Progressive Era. For some traditionalists in the South, his death at the hands of a lynch mob was seen as a kind of urban frontier justice. For advocates of a New South, however, the Frank lynching was a painful reminder of how far southern justice had to travel to become modern.

Further reading: Albert S. Lindemann, *The Jew Accused: Three Anti-Semitic Affairs (Dreyfuss, Beilis, Frank), 1894–1915* (New York: Cambridge University Press, 1991).

— Michael Hartman

Leopold and Loeb (1924)

In a 1924 murder trial that captured the nation's attention, Nathan Leopold and Richard Loeb were convicted and sentenced to life in prison for the murder of 14-year-old Bobby Franks. The trial of Leopold and Loeb captured the nation's attention for a number of reasons. First, they were both teenagers. To many observers, the fact that two teenagers would plan and carry out a murder as cold-blooded as the murder of Bobby Franks served as an indictment of modern youth. At a time when many Americans were seeking advice on rearing children in the new corporate-industrial age, the fact that Leopold and Loeb came from wealthy families demonstrated to many that overindulged youth posed a threat to society. The trial captured the nation's attention because CLARENCE DARROW, the country's best-known trial attorney, represented the defendants. The trial was also significant because Darrow used the testimony of psychologists in arguing that the two had lived abnormal upbringings that shaped them into murderers. By doing so he successfully avoided the death penalty.

Leopold and Loeb were highly intelligent teenagers who graduated from college before they were 18 years old. Together they committed a series of crimes ranging from petty thefts to auto thefts. They apparently planned to murder someone for the intellectual challenge of literally getting away with murder. Planning the killing without a specific victim in mind, they developed a plan and waited for a victim to show up on the scheduled day. On May 21, 1924, Bobby Franks simply ended up in the wrong place at the wrong time. He was a neighbor of both Leopold and Loeb. On his way home from a football game at school, Franks accepted a ride from them. Although it was never determined for certain which of the two killed Franks, one of them knocked him unconscious with ether and beat him to death with the handle of a chisel. The two killers then left his body in a drainpipe in a wilderness area south of Chicago.

Leopold and Loeb then attempted to make the killing look like a kidnapping by contacting Franks' family to demand a ransom. Before they could follow through on the kidnapping plot, however, Franks's body was discovered. During the manhunt for the killers, Leopold and Loeb even went so far as to help two friends who were journalists try to track down the killers. The case broke when a pair of eyeglasses was found at the scene that turned out to belong to Leopold. Faced with the overwhelming evidence against them, the pair pleaded guilty.

Clarence Darrow took the case partly because he opposed the death penalty and saw it as an opportunity for a public forum to argue against it. The defendants pleaded guilty in order to avoid a trial by jury, which Darrow believed would end in the death sentence. Before a judge in the sentencing hearing, he introduced lengthy testimony by psychologists. Their testimonies were the first time that many of the emerging psychological theories were introduced into a court of law. They testified that Leopold and Loeb suffered through abnormal childhoods that included excessive fantasizing, excessive reading of detective fiction, drinking alcohol at an early age, associating with people much older than themselves, and, in the case of Leopold, sexual abuse by a governess and the death of his mother when he was 14. Darrow did not argue that Leopold and Loeb were insane due to their upbringing. He argued that, due to their childhoods, they developed abnormally and therefore should not be sentenced to death for their crime. The judge agreed that their upbringing mitigated the circumstances of their crime and sentenced them to life in prison. Richard Loeb was killed in prison in 1936. Nathan Leopold was paroled in 1957 and died of natural causes in 1971.

Further reading: Paula S. Fass, "Making and Remaking an Event: The Leopold and Loeb Case in American Culture," *Journal of American History* 80:3 (December 1993): 919–951; Hal Higdon, *Leopold and Loeb: The Crime of the Century* (Chicago: University of Illinois Press, 1999).

— Michael Hartman

Lindbergh, Charles Augustus (1902–1974)

As the pilot who flew the first solo nonstop flight across the Atlantic Ocean on May 20–21, 1927, in his airplane *The Spirit of St. Louis,* Charles Lindbergh was heralded as the "Lone Eagle" and "Lucky Lindy." He gained international renown for his solo flight. Lindbergh was born February 4, 1902, in Detroit, Michigan, and grew up in Little Falls, Minnesota. His father was Charles Augustus Lindbergh, Sr., a lawyer and U.S. congressman from Minnesota from 1907 to 1917. His mother was Evangeline Land Lodge.

Charles Augustus Lindbergh standing beside the *Spirit of St. Louis* *(Library of Congress)*

Interested in mechanics as a boy, Lindbergh attended the University of Wisconsin's engineering program for two years but left it to enroll in a flying school in Lincoln, Nebraska. He then became a barnstormer pilot, performing stunts for audiences at fairs, before he joined the U.S. Army as a pilot in the Army Air Service Reserve. After additional training, he graduated from flight school and transported mail between St. Louis and Chicago for the Robertson Aircraft Corporation.

Lindbergh's ambition was to make the solo transatlantic flight. Nine St. Louis businessmen whom he persuaded to support the effort financed his plane, the *Spirit of St. Louis.* He sought to win a prize of $25,000 for one flight offered by New York City hotel owner, Raymond Orteig. The winner would be the first aviator to fly nonstop from New York to Paris. Lindbergh helped design the plane, which successfully made the record-setting trip in 20 hours and 21 minutes. "Lucky Lindbergh" landed at Le Bourget Field near Paris to be greeted by thousands of

cheering fans. He became an instant hero. When he came home to America, he was aboard the USS *Memphis,* and President CALVIN COOLIDGE welcomed him home personally. Four million other people greeted him for a New York parade before his return to St. Louis for a rest. Lindbergh was awarded the Congressional Medal of Honor and the Distinguished Flying Cross.

Lindbergh's fame allowed him to promote both aeronautics and international goodwill. He wrote a book about his flight entitled *We,* referring to the author, his plane, and their experiences on the transatlantic flight. Lindbergh then traveled throughout the United States promoting aeronautics for the Guggenheim Fund. In a three-month nation-wide tour, he flew the *Spirit of St. Louis.* He visited 49 states and 92 cities and gave 147 speeches.

Lindbergh became interested in the research of the scientist Robert Goddard, who was conducting experimental research on missiles, satellites, and rockets. He drew the attention of the Guggenheims to Goddard's research efforts in order to help him in funding further projects. Lindbergh also flew to various Latin American countries in 1927 fostering goodwill between America and Latin America. It was on the Latin America tour that he met Anne Morrow, daughter of the American ambassador to Mexico. He married Morrow in 1929. After teaching her to fly, the couple undertook flying expeditions throughout the world.

After the kidnapping and death of their son, Charles, Jr., the Lindberghs fled to Europe to seek privacy and safety. While in Europe, Lindbergh was invited to tour various aircraft industries. He was particularly impressed with the advanced aircraft industry of Nazi Germany. After returning to the United States, Lindbergh spoke out against American intervention in any European war, supported pro-Hitler German-American groups, and criticized the policies of Franklin Delano Roosevelt. After Roosevelt denounced him, Lindbergh resigned his commission in the Army Air Corps. Refraining from his non-interventionist activity after Pearl Harbor, Lindbergh once again undertook military duties. In 1944, he flew about 50 combat missions in the Pacific despite his status as a civilian.

Lindbergh spent the rest of his life as a consultant, writer, and traveler. In 1954, President Eisenhower restored his commission and appointed him brigadier general in the U.S. Air Force. Lindbergh worked for Pan American World Airways advising on jet purchases, and eventually helped design the Boeing 747. Before dying of cancer in 1974, he spoke out for the conservation movement. He was particularly interested in campaigning for the protection of humpback and blue whales. He lived at this time of his life in Maui, Hawaii, where he published his collection of writings entitled *The Autobiography of Values.*

See also AVIATION.

Further reading: Scott Berg, *Lindbergh* (New York: G.P. Putnam, 1998).

— Annamarie Edelen

literature

The literary culture of the United States, much as its religious culture, experienced a tremendous shift in the years between 1900 and 1930. The genteel tradition of American letters that had been carefully cultivated over the course of the 19th century was in the midst of a commercial revolution. While Henry James, one of the major figures of the nation's literary renaissance, continued to publish in works such as *Wings of the Dove* (1902), *The Ambassadors* (1903), and *The Golden Bowl* (1903), he was supplanted by other voices. The elite world of letters in which he had made his mark gave way to the influence of commercial media in new literary journals like *Collier's* and *McClure's,* and in alternative journals like Harriet Monroe's *Poetry,* Margaret

Anderson's *The Little Review,* and H. L. Mencken's *American Mercury.* A new generation of small publishers like Modern Library, Horace Liveright, and Alfred Knopf proved more willing to publish new authors and risk violating the censorship laws. The flourishing of a RADICAL PRESS that gave space to new cultural trends, as well as alternate politics, opened the doors for diversity in literary voice, range, and genre.

The literary world imagined itself immune to commercial pressures, but neither academic literary criticism nor high art engaged new consumers of fiction. Innovative writers in the early 20th century did respond to increased demand fueled by new marketing techniques and lower subscription prices. With ties to mass journalism and experience in magazine publishing, authors such as Theodore Dreiser, UPTON SINCLAIR, and Frank Norris brought vivid naturalist prose and social criticism to the educated middle-class public. Rebelling against the politeness of older literature, they introduced language, imagery, and narratives that bore little resemblance to the genteel tradition or the literary realism of James and William Dean Howells. Literary naturalism assumed that characters were the product of a dehumanizing environment. Individual trajectories of success or failure had little to do with individual qualities. Dreiser's *Sister Carrie* (1900) shocked readers with its story of a young woman who, after she is sexually betrayed, sets out to make her own conquest. His novels *Financier* (1912), *Titan* (1914), and *An American Tragedy* (1925) similarly exposed the social forces that led to success or failure. Frank Norris's brutal portrayals of corporate and political bosses in *McTeague* (1899) and *The Octopus* (1901) and Jack London's social novels *The Iron Heel* (1907) and *Martin Eden* (1909) resonated with the same naturalistic sensibility. With such books as *The House of Mirth* (1906) and *Ethan Frome* (1911), Edith Wharton brought naturalism to the study of the upper classes. Willa Cather similarly brought serious themes of immigration, community, and the impact of environment on character to her readers in *O Pioneers!* (1913), *My Ántonia* (1918), and *Death Comes for the Archbishop* (1927).

Coined as a term in 1890s Germany, MODERNISM first emerged in the United States shortly before WORLD WAR I. Allied with literary experimentation and the cultural radicalism of artist colonies like GREENWICH VILLAGE and Provincetown, modernism in art and literature represented a break from the past. The modernist sensibility also rebelled against rigid Victorian sexual mores and the unquestioning belief in the virtues of progress. Gertrude Stein, one of the most famous American writers living abroad, argued that the United States had become the first modern, and thus the oldest, nation in the world. The rest of the world was forced to catch up. Stein was known as an unconventional writer who experimented with language, subject, and genre. She and her generation of writers were among the first to give voice to the new stresses and pleasures of the age. Honesty was their hallmark. Modernist photographer Alfred Stieglitz wrote that art must embrace "honesty of aim, honesty of self-expression, and honesty of revolt against the autocracy of convention." The primitivism that animated modern art sometimes prevailed in literature as well. Moving beyond literary naturalism, modernist writers experimented with language, abandoned metered verse, and broke conventions of plot and genre. In poetry, imagist writers such as Ezra Pound, H. D. (Hilda Doolittle), and Amy Lowell challenged the idea of poetry as a direct representation of feeling; other modernist poets such as T. S. Eliot, William Carlos Williams, and Gertrude Stein pushed free verse into new territory with experiments in form and language. Dramatists such as Eugene O'Neill told similarly experimental tales of sexuality and race in his plays *Emperor Jones* (1921), *The Hairy Ape* (1922), and *Desire under the Elms* (1924). Modernist writers such as John Dos Passos in *Three Soldiers* (1920) and e. e. cummings in *The Enormous Room* (1920) worked against the conventions of unitary narrative to create collages within the structure of their novels.

In historical writing, similar commitments surfaced to a modernism that challenged older ideals of objectivity and the legitimate subject of historical study. Led by progressive writers such as Charles and Mary Beard and Vernon Parrington, historians read and critically challenged the basis of positivist historical science. Historian and sociologist Lucy Maynard Salmon in many respects led the way with her unconventional history of the backyard and her study of domestic service. Not only historians but also sociologists such as William Graham Sumner, Lester Ward, Thorsten Veblen, and George Herbert Mead attacked the ideal of objectivity in the human sciences to address directly the social construction of reality. This modernist social science was far from an academic pursuit. The Beards' history of the United States was, by illustration, an important and widely popular book in its day; so too were the writings of Sumner and Ward, among others. By 1909, the writings of SIGMUND FREUD also made their appearance in American bookstores.

The destruction of World War I intensified the trend toward modernism in literature and social science. The war had distorted the perception of time, altered the nature of personal identity, and warned of the dangers of technology and the price of nationalism. In its aftermath, American writers confronted their national culture and discovered new influences and legacies. As literary historian Ann Douglas characterized it, the LOST GENERATION of 1920s intellectuals adopted new values of blunt honesty and pluralism in their art. Having cast aside the genteel culture of the Victorian age, they sought to cast off conservative ideas and

racial prejudices as well. The writers of the 1920s embraced instead the influence of African-American culture and the cynicism of postwar society. They emphasized the discovery of "truth" in art.

The postwar generation of writers provided a running critique of the weaknesses and strengths of American culture. In such publications as *The New Yorker*, writers Dorothy Parker and Robert Benchley and theater critic Alexander Woolcott ridiculed elite culture, old-fashioned social norms, and the provincialism of American life, as did H. L. MENCKEN in *The Smart Set* and *American Mercury*. Urbane humor competed for center stage with serious political and cultural criticism. At the same time, popular novelists such as Edna Ferber reached a broad audience with stories probing the private side of the American dream and the place of women within it. Her novel, *Show Boat* (1926), offered to popular audiences some of the seamier and more subversive relations between the sexes and among races. Abroad, writers F. Scott Fitzgerald and Ernest Hemingway revealed the underside of American masculinity in such characters as Jay Gatsby and Jake Barnes. The gallant and romantic Gatsby was what every

Sinclair Lewis *(Library of Congress)*

businessman was at heart—a gangster, as Fitzgerald saw it, while Jake in *The Sun Also Rises* (1926) is physically and emotionally disabled. In John Dos Passos's *Three Soldiers* (1922) and William Faulkner's *Soldier's Pay* (1926), disillusioned war veterans feel a loss of self and power in the materialistic postwar world.

The modernist turn coincided with a general American cultural revival. At the center was an emerging generation of African-American writers, artists, and performers in what has been called the HARLEM RENAISSANCE. This explosion of creativity was not so much a rebirth of African-American literary expression as its integration into mainstream modern literature and art. With the 1920s, audiences across the racial divide were newly exposed to the mythology, language, and musical traditions of African Americans. The GREAT MIGRATION had brought with it a southern black literature, which attracted new audiences and brought increased patronage to African-American writers and artists. Among the writers associated with this cultural flowering were Langston Hughes, Jean Toomer, ALAIN LOCKE, Claude McKay, Nella Larsen, and Zora Neale Hurston. Hughes in particular would become the voice of the black community, moving from cultural modernism in the 1920s to the sharper social and political critique of his depression-era writings. All of the writers shared the concern of defining African-American identity as dualistic, a product of both African and American experience. They sought to explore the dimensions of racial life and consciousness in such books as Toomer's *Cane* (1923), Locke's *The New Negro* (1925), Larsen's *Passing* (1929), and Hughes's *Not Without Laughter* (1930).

The intellectual community was similarly open to broadening cultural perspectives. In *Culture and Democracy in the United States* (1924), Horace Kallen first launched the idea of an American democracy dependent not on the suppression, but on the celebration, of ethnic diversity. During this decade, his work was echoed by a school of anthropologists working with FRANZ BOAS. Boas and his students—MARGARET MEAD, Ruth Benedict, Edward Sapir, Zora Neale Hurston, and Melville Herskovits—helped to undermine belief in Anglo-American superiority and to dismantle scientific racism. Their works were incredibly popular treatments of life in different cultures and further called into question American culture. In *Coming of Age in Samoa* (1928), Margaret Mead showed that child-rearing practices of another culture were not only different but also led to healthy attitudes toward self, community, and sexuality. *Growing Up in New Guinea* (1930) revealed how men's involvement in child care and the education of youth positively reaffirmed masculine identity in the community. Other studies of northern migrants, southern folklore, and Native American culture

suggested that there was no one right culture nor any scientific basis for a belief in racial differences in intelligence and ability. The modernist sensibility, first expressed in literature and art, began to infiltrate the social sciences and the politics they inspired.

See also ART; JOURNALISM; POPULAR CULTURE.

Further reading: Ann Douglass, *Terrible Honesty: Mongrel Manhattan in the 1920s* (New York: Farrar, Straus, and Giroux, 1995); Emory Elliott, ed., *Columbia Literary History of the United States* (New York: Columbia University Press, 1988); June Howard, *Form and History in American Literary Naturalism* (Chapel Hill: University of North Carolina Press, 1985); Bonnie G. Smith, *The Gender of History: Men, Women and the Historical Profession* (Cambridge, Mass.: Harvard University Press, 1999).

lobbying and interest groups

In the first three decades of the 20th century, the rise of interest group POLITICS brought new lobbies and organizations into the political arena. These groups included avowedly nonpartisan organizations such as the League of Women Voters and the Good Government League, as well as professional organizations like the American Medical Association and the American Farm Bureau, and such partisan groups as the Anti-Saloon League, the National Mothers' Congress, the AMERICAN LEGION, and the KU KLUX KLAN, which ran its own candidates for political office.

Businesses also were committed to using public interest groups such as chambers of commerce and trade associations. Interest groups lobbied for legislation, raised funds, mobilized voters and letter writers, and created political conditions favorable to their own—and, they argued, the public's—interests. Their emphasis on marshaling the resources of government to stimulate business growth, as well as to restrict government intervention in taxes and regulation, paid off in the business prosperity of the era. It had a negative impact, however, in the overall economic picture. While federal debt declined due to economy in spending, state and municipal debt mounted. Unequal distribution of income and wealth led to a weakening of consumer demand and personal indebtedness.

Although labor unions were weak throughout the period, the AMERICAN FEDERATION OF LABOR worked for significant federal legislation and, under the presidency of WOODROW WILSON, succeeded to a certain extent. The creation of a Department of Labor, and the passage of the CLAYTON ANTITRUST ACT and the ADAMSON ACT, gave witness to the power of organized labor. The AFL lobbied for immigration restriction, special laws for seamen and sailors (as well as government workers), and relief from antitrust laws and labor injunctions.

More powerful than organized labor were political organizations that represented American farmers. Developing out of 19th-century organizations such as the Grange, new groups like the American Farm Bureau became effective political agents for the mass of farmers. Unlike labor, which represented at the time about 6 percent of all wage workers, the Farm Bureau could claim to represent all farmers, who constituted about 25 percent of voters in the United States. Begun in 1919, the Farm Bureau had more than a million members by 1921. With claims such as that, it was able to have a substantial impact on legislation, particularly as it organized the Farm Bloc in Congress. The Farm Bureau helped secure the passage of legislation favorable to farmers, including the CAPPER-VOLSTEAD ACT (1922), which protected farm cooperatives from antitrust suits and other laws that increased tariffs and extended farm credits. The MCNARY-HAUGEN FARM BILL, a failed attempt to raise the prices of agricultural commodities, was a favorite item on the Farm Bloc's agenda. In addition, the Farm Bureau and other farm advocates sought relief from state and local property taxes, which laid an unfair tax burden on farmers and cut into declining farm income.

Among interest groups, African Americans represented themselves in a range of organizations, but racial hostility and discrimination weakened their power. The NATIONAL ASSOCIATION FOR THE ADVANCEMENT OF COLORED PEOPLE (NAACP) had small influence in governmental matters, despite the active participation of African Americans as members of the REPUBLICAN PARTY and as soldiers in WORLD WAR I. Its efforts to pass an anti-lynching bill were stymied in 1922.

Despite the claim that public interest groups supplanted the power of political parties, it was party politics that benefited from their growth. Older party structures lacked both the constituency and the resources to manage the country's politics and government on their own. New forms of direct democracy such as initiative, referendum, and recall required parties to have a dependable way of mobilizing voters. Interest groups thus provided the services and resources that kept alive the party system in a time of declining party loyalty.

See also ELECTIONS.

Further reading: Elisabeth S. Clemens, *The People's Lobby; Organizational Innovation and the Rise of Interest Group Politics in the United States, 1890–1925* (Chicago: University of Chicago Press, 1997); Sara Hunter Graham, *Woman Suffrage and the New Democracy* (New Haven, Conn.: Yale University Press, 1996); Peter Odegard, *Pressure Politics* (New York: Columbia University Press, 1928).

Lochner v. New York (1905)

The decision of the United States Supreme Court in *Lochner v. New York* is considered one of the most controversial in its history. Critics of the judgment view it as an example of blatant judicial activism, in which the Court used its power of judicial review to protect conservative economic policies against an era of regulatory reform. Labor reformers had concentrated their attention on legislative solutions to industrial ills. Long hours, low wages, and corrosive working conditions led to child labor laws, maximum hours and minimum wage legislation, and new safety standards. By 1905 many states had enacted statutes to protect workers. Despite the reputation for being conservative, most courts upheld the reform legislation. In *Lochner v. New York,* however, the Supreme Court struck down a maximum hours law. At the very least, the ruling in *Lochner* showed a lack of consistency in the court's decisions.

In 1893, New York passed the statute that became the point of contention in Joseph Lochner's litigation. The Bakeshop Act limited the number of hours bakers could labor to 10 a day and 60 a week and included provisions setting minimum standards for sanitation in all bakeries. Earlier, journeymen bakers in the state had organized the Baker's Progressive Union. It had been active in securing the Bakeshop Act, but the baker's union was not powerful throughout the state. Only in areas where the union was strong could the 1893 act be enforced. Lochner owned a small nonunion bakery in Utica, New York. He ignored the Bakeshop Act by requiring his workers to labor more than 60 hours a week. The town's journeymen bakers lodged a complaint against Lochner. He was found guilty of violations and fined. He appealed his conviction, and his case eventually reached the U.S. Supreme Court.

The Supreme Court decision in *Lochner* has been characterized as a conflict of competing ideals. At odds were conceptions of laissez-faire economic theory and the nation's reform agenda. Reform advocates based regulatory statutes like the Bakeshop Act on the state's police powers. By this authority, a state can act in ways necessary to protect the health, safety, and welfare of its citizens. What exactly constituted a valid use of the state's police powers was vague. In general, a law based on the state's police powers had to regulate specifically to clearly recognized health or safety objectives, which reformers believed that industrial conditions threatened the state's welfare and warranted using these powers.

On the other side, proponents of laissez-faire economic theory believed that maximum hours legislation was an unwarranted intervention into an individual's right to contract. The Supreme Court had previously ruled that the liberty of contract was protected by the Fourteenth Amendment to the Constitution, which guaranteed that no "State [shall] deprive any person of life, liberty or property, without due process of law." Adherents held that a worker had a right to property in his labor. State regulation would limit a laborer's ability to make contracts and therefore limit his ability to utilize his property. But liberty of contract assumed an equal playing field between employer and employee, which simply didn't exist.

Based on precedent, the Supreme Court should have ruled against Lochner. In *Holden v. Hardy,* the Supreme Court upheld legislation that limited mine work to eight hours a day as a reasonable use of the state's police powers. Furthermore, it dismissed the liberty of contract argument, stating that the employer and employee were not bargaining from equal positions. But in *Lochner v. New York,* the Supreme Court held that the New York Bakeshop Act was unconstitutional. Justice Rufus Peckham wrote for a bare 5–4 majority. It held that the law was not a valid exercise of the state's police power, because the number of hours of a baker's labor did not affect the public health. He declared that such acts are, "mere meddlesome interferences with the rights of the individual." Interestingly, Justice OLIVER WENDELL HOLMES disagreed with the Court's decision and wrote a brief but powerful dissent. Pointing to the underlying issues, Holmes wrote, "This case is decided upon an economic theory which a large part of the country does not entertain . . . The Fourteenth Amendment does not enact Mr. Herbert Spencer's *Social Statics.*"

Both the *Lochner* decision and its legacy reveal a lack of consistency in the Supreme Court's decisions in this era. Historians point out that the various courts tended to uphold reform legislation, but they were consistently hostile to laws that supported unions. Justice Peckham did not broach the issue of unions, but he was fearful of increasing government intervention in labor regulation. This decision might explain why the Court moved away from the precedent. In the end, many state courts disregarded the Lochner decision, and its effects at the federal level were uneven. Still, it remained prevailing law for almost 30 years.

See also *MULLER V. OREGON.*

Further reading: Paul Kens, *Judicial Power and Reform Politics: The Anatomy of Lochner v. New York* (Lawrence: University Press of Kansas, 1990); Melvin Urofsky, "State Courts and Protective Legislation during the Progressive Era: A Reevaluation," *Journal of American History* 72 (1985): 63–91.

— Debra A. Viles

Locke, Alain LeRoy (1886–1954)

An author, intellectual, and educator, Alain Locke was best known as the intellectual voice of the HARLEM RENAISSANCE. Born in Philadelphia, Locke entered Harvard University in 1904 and became the first African-American Rhodes Scholar in 1907. After attending Oxford University in England, he went to the University of Berlin. In 1911 he returned to the United States and began his career as an African-American spokesman and educator at Howard University in Washington, D.C.

Heavily influenced by the work of anthropologist FRANZ BOAS, Locke argued that race was not biological but historical. He went further than Boas by removing any hereditary factors from his view of race in favor of a pure environmentalism. Race and racial relations were determined by the historical circumstances of a time. Instead of races creating cultures, Locke argued that cultures created races. In support of his position, he pointed to ethnic relations and conflict in eastern Europe. He argued that the conflict between ethnic groups in Europe was not different from the conflict between whites and blacks in the United States, but was determined by a different set of historical circumstances. Locke's most important insight was that race relations pass through definitive stages in relation to political, economic, and demographic change. Thus, there was nothing static about race and relations between races. These views influenced historians of African-American history for years. Locke also recognized that race was an ideology that masked other interests. He was particularly interested in how class interests were covered by racism. Locke did not, however, accept the beliefs of those intellectuals who equated race prejudice with class conflict. He argued that racism had begun as a class construct but had taken on a cultural meaning separate from any class meaning.

His embrace of the importance of culture in race relations and formation led Locke to champion the development of an African-American culture. He argued that one could recognize that cultural differences existed without accepting racist beliefs. In fact, African Americans should use race, Locke argued, as a means to empowerment. They could build self-esteem and solidarity that would help them in the competitive society in which they lived. Locke pointed to literature and the arts as a way to build race consciousness without threatening white America. By doing this, African Americans also would disprove racist myths that held that African Americans did not possess any real culture of their own. This belief that African Americans could use art and literature became the basis for his advocacy of the Harlem Renaissance.

His 1925 book, *The New Negro: An Interpretation,* solidified his identity as a spokesman for the Negro Renaissance. In this work, Locke argued that the artistic and literary innovations occurring in Harlem offered a basis for the cultural development of the New Negro. This was all made possible by the migration of African Americans from the South to the urban areas of the North. These urban concentrations of African Americans were giving rise to a new culture based on a common racial past both as Africans and as African Americans.

See also RACE AND RACIAL CONFLICT.

Further reading: Jeffrey C. Stewart, ed., *Race Contacts and Interracial Relations* (Washington, D.C.: Howard University Press, 1992).

— Michael Hartman

Lodge, Henry Cabot (1850–1924)

Tenacious opponent of President WOODROW WILSON, Henry Cabot Lodge opposed the social reform movement of Wilson's era and the nation's lack of military preparedness after 1914. Lodge criticized the government for its slow mobilization, shortages of equipment, failure to prevent strikes, and delays in production during WORLD WAR I. He and the former president, THEODORE ROOSEVELT, led the PREPAREDNESS movement that sought to persuade the Wilson administration and the population of the United States that the nation must prepare itself for war. Later, as chairman of the Senate Committee on Foreign Relations, Lodge led the campaign against the ratification of the TREATY OF VERSAILLES and U.S. participation in the LEAGUE OF NATIONS.

Lodge was born in Boston, Massachusetts, on May 12, 1850. Graduating from Harvard in 1871 and from its law school in 1874, he was awarded a Ph.D. in 1876. Lodge taught American history at Harvard and edited *The North American Review* and *The International Review* until entering politics in 1879. He served two years in the Massachusetts House of Representatives and six years in the U.S. House of Representatives. He was elected to the U.S. Senate in 1893, where he remained for the rest of his life.

Lodge's influence was exerted through chairmanship of the powerful Senate Foreign Relations Committee from 1896 on. In international affairs, Lodge believed that a large modern navy and a dominant influence in the Caribbean and the Pacific were vital to the country's security. His beliefs were based on the theories of Admiral Alfred Thayer Mahan, who had advanced the idea that sea power was the determining factor in international affairs. As a result of Mahan's influence, Lodge favored U.S. entry into the Spanish-American War and favored the acquisition of the Philippines. Being a conservative, he supported the gold standard and high protective TARIFFS.

Immediately after Europe became embroiled in hostilities leading to World War I, Lodge became a proponent of military preparedness. He pointed out that the United States could no longer depend on its geographic advantages and distance from the European continent as a safeguard from invasion. Like others in the preparedness movement, Lodge advocated a build-up of the army and navy and additional funding for training and equipment. Eventually, President Wilson would be drawn into the effort to mobilize the military resources of the nation, despite his promise to keep the country out of the war.

When Germany sued for peace in 1918 and world leaders attended the peace conference in France, Wilson joined the conference with a select group of experts but failed to invite anyone from the Senate, including Lodge. His failure to indulge Senator Lodge caused irreconcilable differences between them, which resulted in the Senate refusing to ratify the Treaty of Versailles. Specifically, Lodge opposed Wilson on American participation in the League of Nations; he felt that the league clauses would involve the United States too deeply in European affairs. Wilson tried to take his case to the people, but he was overcome with sickness. Lodge later also opposed U.S. participation in the World Court. In 1921, Lodge was the U.S. delegate to the WASHINGTON CONFERENCE ON NAVAL DISARMAMENT in 1921. He died on November 9, 1924.

Further reading: William C. Widenor, *Henry Cabot Lodge and the Search for an American Foreign Policy* (Berkeley: University of California Press, 1980).

— Annamarie Edelen

Lone Wolf v. Hitchcock (1903)

In the late 19th century, U.S. policy toward NATIVE AMERICANS focused on dismantling tribal authority and assimilating Native Americans into mainstream society. The program hinged on the allotment of tribal lands from reservations to individual members and families and selling off "surplus" land to white settlers. The process of allotment began with the Dawes Severalty Act of 1887, but it was carried on through the Bureau of Indian Affairs, federal and state courts, and a series of laws that continued to loosen the restrictions on the lease and sale of Native American land. Few tribes escaped the impact of allotment, but the worst abuses of the land policy occurred in the Indian Territory of what is now Oklahoma, where reservations were forcibly dismantled and the land leased or sold, much of it under the guise of white guardianship of Native Americans and their land.

Kiowa chief Lone Wolf, and other Kiowa, Comanche, and Apache, sought to stop the forcible allotment and alienation of tribal land in the case of *Lone Wolf v. Hitchcock.* Basing their suit on the Treaty of Medicine Lodge signed in 1867, the Kiowa argued that the treaty required that all land transfers have the consent of the majority of adults on the reservation. The Medicine Lodge Treaty had already drastically reduced tribal holdings from 90 million acres to the 2.7 million acres of then-current reservations.

The policy of allotment promised to strip all resources from the tribes and reduce their members to poverty on small plots of land. Further, the allotments given to Lone Wolf and other Kiowa had not earned the requisite support from tribal members, and the transfer of land was, therefore, invalid. Reversing its traditional stand on the importance of property rights and contract law, the Supreme Court in 1903 held against the Kiowa and accepted the sale of surplus land as valid. They accepted the argument of the defendant that the majority of Kiowa had agreed to transfer land for money in 1892. The court case also revealed the tangled alliances that made both allotment and the court case possible. On the one side, reformers seeking to assimilate Native Americans pushed for the division of land and their integration into white farming regions. On the other side were the "implacables," who resisted white society and modernization, and their allies, the cattle ranchers who wanted to lease Native American land and resisted farm settlement. Allotment won out.

The Court's decision, which essentially denied Native American tribal sovereignty, had ramifications beyond Oklahoma. It made legal the U.S. violation of any and all treaties with Native Americans and set the parameters of Native American land policy for the next five decades. It underlined the dependent status of Native Americans under law and allowed the policy of allotment to forge ahead unaffected by formal agreements or governmental treaties. For these reasons, *Lone Wolf* became the most frequently cited court case in Native American law. It was only in 1955 that the Indian Land Claims Commission granted the Kiowa, Comanche, and Plains Apache $2 million as compensation for the illegal sale of land.

See also BURKE ACT.

Further reading: Blue Clark, *Lone Wolf v. Hitchcock: Treaty Rights and Indian Law at the End of the Nineteenth Century* (Lincoln: University of Nebraska Press, 1994).

Lost Generation

No group of artists and intellectuals had a greater impact on early 20th-century American literature than the group that came to be known as the Lost Generation. Associated with the alienation over WORLD WAR I, they became disenchanted with crusades at home and abroad. They saw the failures of America's involvement in the war and its futile PROHIBITION effort at purging alcoholic drink as symptoms of a society that was sick. The Lost Generation also embraced trends toward MODERNISM and rebelled against literary convention.

Gertrude Stein coined the term, "the Lost Generation," in reference to the young Americans who had survived World War I. In an epigraph to Ernest Hemingway's

The Sun Also Rises, she noted, "you are all a lost generation." The perceived futility of the war led a growing number of Americans to abandon WOODROW WILSON's idealistic vision of a world that was safe for democracy. The magnitude of the war effort and its human cost undermined faith in government and society. Americans increasingly saw the war as a cruel hoax in which Americans were betrayed into suffering and death. The young Americans who went off to fight did not come back as heroes. They came back as poor duped innocents whose sacrifices were in vain. The Lost Generation symbolized and championed this growing sense of disillusionment.

These young writers were one of the first artistic cohorts to be viewed as a distinctive generation. What made them distinct was that their youth coincided with the war and the great influenza outbreak. Those living in the 1920s were divided into separate and distinct categories. There were those who came of age before, during, and after the war. Most of the men termed members of the Lost Generation came of age in the immediate postwar period. They challenged the path that the previous generation had trod.

Ernest Hemingway (1899–1961) was one of the most celebrated of the group. His 1929 novel, *A Farewell to Arms,* summed up the emerging attitude toward war. The hero of the story was not a man who won his acclaim on the battlefield. It was his disdain for the conflict that made him a hero. His defining act, which Hemingway applauded, was abandoning the war effort in search of love with a nurse that he met in a war hospital. The needs and the wants of the individual seemed to trump that of an undefined conflict.

John Dos Passos (1896–1970) and Edward Estlin Cummings (e. e. cummings; 1894–1962) were two other notable men who were considered members of the Lost Generation. In Dos Passos's great trilogy, *USA* (1937), he depicted American life up to 1929. He shared Hemingway's concern for the direction of society. In *USA* he attacked American materialism, pettiness, and hypocrisy. In a similar fashion, Cummings used poetry to challenge what he saw as restrictive convention. He challenged all accepted conventions, even language and punctuation. Using wit and satire, he challenged social norms and customs. Both writers shared the conviction that crusading idealism was not the solution.

More than any other novel, F. Scott Fitzgerald's *The Great Gatsby* came to define the literary movement. Jay Gatsby, the book's protagonist, attempted to win the love of a woman whom he admired by attaining immense wealth and fortune. When he achieved all that he aspired to, he finally realized that the world is built on fraud, cruelty, and deception. This world, which he adopted in the pursuit of wealth, eventually killed him. The book was a fitting metaphor not only for the times, but also for the life of

F. Scott Fitzgerald and Zelda Fitzgerald *(Hulton/Archive)*

Fitzgerald himself. He was immensely popular and achieved the acclaim of which others merely dream, but it was not enough. He longed for substance and meaning.

Many of the members of the Lost Generation abandoned the United States in search of meaning. Some moved to France. As a result, Paris became the home for many American writers. Others found their sanctuary in the primitive surrounds of the American West. No matter how far they moved from the society that seemed to alienate them, they could not escape. The world war and its consequences haunted society and reshaped American culture.

See also LITERATURE; MODERNISM.

Further reading: John Dos Passos, *USA* (New York: Library of America, 1996), F. Scott Fitzgerald, *The Great Gatsby* (New York: C. Scribner's Sons, 1925), Ernest Hemingway, *The Sun Also Rises* (New York: C. Charles Scribner's Sons, 1953).

— Steve Freund

Ludlow Massacre (1919)

One of the longest and most violent labor disputes in the 20th century, the Ludlow Massacre occurred in 1914 when private security forces and National Guard troops attacked striking mine workers in Ludlow, Colorado. The miners were living in a tent city after the Colorado Fuel and Iron Company had evicted them from company-owned homes. The attack left 32 people dead, including nine children. The incident sparked public outcry against employer violence and prompted government investigations into workplace violence.

Labor violence was a common occurrence in the turn-of-the-century United States, but nowhere was it more prevalent than in the nation's mines. Mine operators, intent upon maximizing profits, worked to increase production and keep labor costs as low as possible. Efforts to introduce new technology and to aggressively resist organized labor accomplished the task. Hostility between mine workers and mine operators was particularly intense in western mining communities.

The Ludlow conflict began when the UNITED MINE WORKERS OF AMERICA (UMWA) began an organizing drive at the Colorado Fuel and Iron Company, owned by JOHN D. ROCKEFELLER, Jr. Faced with competition from the more radical Western Federation of Miners and the INDUSTRIAL WORKERS OF THE WORLD, the UMWA found organizing western miners difficult. Union leaders, however, were determined to organize in the West and steadily gained new members between 1900 and 1913. Relations between workers and mine operators in Ludlow had been strained for more than a decade. Company officials resisted attempts to organize and brought in immigrant workers to divide miners along racial and ethnic lines. Living conditions were made more difficult, because workers were required to live in company housing and shop at the company-owned store at inflated prices. Many miners found themselves perpetually in debt.

In September 1913, miners ignored the pleas of union officials for moderation and voted unanimously to go on strike. Company officials responded to the strike by evicting between 11,000 and 13,000 workers and their families from company housing, forcing them to live in a makeshift tent colony just as the harsh Colorado winter set in. The company proceeded to attempt to undermine the strike by hiring replacement workers and an armed private security force from the Baldwin-Felts Detective Agency. Colorado's governor, Elias Ammons, attempted to keep the peace by calling in the National Guard, but the miners quickly grew suspicious of the troops when company officials agreed to pay for their expenses. In exchange, troops protected strikebreakers and harassed and intimidated striking miners. The arrest and deportation of legendary labor leader Mother Jones intensified the conflict. Over the course of the long winter, numerous fatalities occurred, prompting Governor Ammons to remove all but a company of troops.

The troops that remained in the spring of 1914 were under the direction of Lieutenant Karl Linderfelt. Intent upon breaking the strike and punishing Louis Tikas, one of the strike leaders, Linderfelt and his National Guard troops attacked the tent colony on April 20. Facing gunfire throughout the day, miners and their families attempted to flee or take shelter. Linderfelt entered the colony and ordered his troops to set fire to what remained of the tents. When the smoke cleared the next day, the tent colony lay in ruins. Thirty-two miners had been killed, including two women and nine children who had been smothered by the blaze as they attempted to hide. Although Linderfelt and others involved in the massacre eventually were found guilty, their punishment amounted to no more than a slap on the wrist.

Throughout the country, workers and the general public were outraged. The UMWA pleaded with others in the labor movement to come to the defense of the striking miners. Guns, ammunition, and money flooded in, as did armed miners from the entire region. Violent clashes continued throughout the month until President WOODROW WILSON sent federal troops into the region and ordered both sides to disarm, ending the violence. Despite scathing criticism and a congressional investigation, mine owner Rockefeller insisted that, while the loss of life was regrettable, the goal of maintaining the OPEN SHOP justified the actions of company officials and the National Guard. The Wilson administration, though shocked by the behavior of the National Guard and Rockefeller, refused to side with the striking workers. In December 1914, more than a year after it began, the strike ended in defeat. The violence used to defeat the striking miners is indicative of the difficulties that faced workers and the labor movement throughout the Progressive Era.

Further reading: Philip S. Foner, *History of the Labor Movement in the United States,* vol. 5 (New York: International Publishers, 1980).

— Robert Gordon

Lusitania (1915)

At 2:15 P.M., on a clear but cold day off the Old Head of Kinsale in Ireland, near Queenstown, HMS *Lusitania* was struck amidships on the starboard side by a torpedo fired from a German submarine. Eighteen minutes later, the ship rolled on her side amidst a great burst of steam and quickly slid beneath the surface, taking 1,198 passengers and crew with her. The sinking of the *Lusitania* was one of the major incidents that aroused public sentiment against Germany during WORLD WAR I and helped prompt the U.S. entry into the war.

Owned by the British Cunard Line, HMS *Lusitania* was built in 1907. She weighed 31,950 tons, and won the Transatlantic Blue Ribbon on her maiden voyage with a cruising speed of 25.88 knots. The ship's lines and speed inspired her description as "Greyhound of the Seas." With the advent of World War I, the *Lusitania* continued her transatlantic sailing under the auspices of the Cunard Line, but, under a 1902 agreement with the British government, the ship had been modified to take up her role as an armed cruiser beginning in May 1913.

On May 1, 1915, the *Lusitania* set sail from New York City for Liverpool, England. On the shipping news pages of many newspapers, the Imperial German Embassy in Washington had printed the famous warning of Germany's unrestricted submarine warfare with the now-tragic caveat of "travelers sailing in the war zone on ships of Great Britain's on her allies do so at their own risk." Submarine warfare represented a sharp departure from past practices of sea warfare and a violation of international law. The rules of warfare required belligerent ships to stop their prey at sea and confiscate or destroy contraband. Belligerent ships had no right to destroy a ship if it was neutral, and naval officers were required to assure the safety of all aboard. Germany, in its own defense, claimed that British ships could easily target its U-boats, if they surfaced.

Approaching the coast of Ireland six days after setting sail from New York, the *Lusitania* was warned by the British Admiralty of submarine activity. Captain William Turner received six warnings in all, the latest at 11:52 A.M. on May 7. The ship failed to avoid headwinds, steer a mid-channel course, and operate at full speed. By 1:20 P.M., Captain Walter Schwieger, commanding the *U-20*, sighted the *Lusitania* and fired upon the ship. A little over an hour later, the lives of over a thousand people, including 120 Americans, were lost. The incident was particularly significant because it sparked an incredible wave of anti-German resentment in the United States and helped draw the United States into a war to protect American interests and honor.

Further reading: Thomas A. Bailey, *The Lusitania Disaster: An Episode in Modern Warfare and Diplomacy* (New York: Free Press, 1975).

— Paul Edelen

lynching See Volume VI

M

Mann Act (1910)

One of the first federal laws that granted police powers to the federal government, the Mann Act sought to outlaw the transportation of women across state lines for the purpose of prostitution. Officially known as the White Slave Traffic Act, the Mann Act became known under the name of its sponsor in the House of Representatives, James Mann of Chicago. The act made it a felony crime to transport knowingly any woman or girl in interstate commerce or foreign commerce for the purposes of prostitution or debauchery or for any other immoral purpose. It also made it a crime to procure or obtain a ticket to be used by a girl or a woman for prostitution or immoral purposes. A third provision made it a felony to coerce a woman or girl for immoral purposes and imposed a stiffer penalty if the victim was less than 18 years old. The final provision stated that any person who kept, maintained, controlled, or harbored a foreign-born girl or woman for prostitution or immoral purposes, within three years after she entered the United States, was required to file a statement with the U.S. Commission of Immigration and Naturalization.

In passing the Mann Act, Congress was responding to a sense of crisis that existed among reform-minded organizations and people. Many Americans believed that young women were being forced into prostitution in America's large cities. This fear became acute during this era because young women were moving from rural areas to America's cities in search of jobs. This movement occurred at the same time as the tremendous increase in emigration from southern and eastern Europe, an increase that went predominately to cities and so increased the fear of cities in the minds of many Americans. Cities seemed even more frightening and dangerous than ever before because of the foreign nature of their inhabitants. A series of articles in newspapers and magazines detailed stories of women who were abducted and forced into prostitution after coming to the city. The usual story line was that a young woman accepted a drink from a stranger that turned out to be drugged. In most of the stories, the man or woman who drugged the victim was foreign-born. When the woman awoke, she found herself captive in a brothel where she was forced to live the life of a prostitute. The white slavery panic was built on sensationalist accounts of these episodes. Despite the fact that there was little hard evidence to support claims that an organized conspiracy to enslave young white women existed, reformers called for the creation of laws aimed at combating a supposed conspiracy.

The power of the white slavery panic led lawmakers to override their fears of the expansion of federal law enforcement powers. The Mann Act was passed on the basis that the commerce clause of the Constitution granted the federal government the power to regulate the transportation of prostitutes across state lines. Initially the bill faced opposition from southern congressmen who feared the imposition on states' rights, but many who initially opposed the bill voted for its passage because they believed that the threat to America's young women outweighed their concerns about states' rights. The U.S. Supreme Court found the Mann Act constitutional in a 1913 decision, based on the power granted to the federal government by the commerce clause.

Because the act included the ambiguous phrases "immoral purposes" and "debauchery," law enforcement officials were able to interpret the act and apply it to many actions that did not involve forcible coercion into prostitution. Many local officials used the law to punish people who they believed were challenging the accepted norms of behavior. In the 1910s, many cases were prosecuted in which no prostitution was involved, but in which law enforcement officials had decided that transportation across state lines for immoral purposes had occurred. Some of these came before the Supreme Court and in each case the Court upheld the right of law enforcement officials to interpret the act to include these offenses. In the most public and infamous case of the era, heavy-weight boxing champion Jack Johnson, an African American, was charged in 1912 for bringing a white woman from Minneapolis to Chicago to become his mistress. These charges were dropped for lack of evidence, but the Department of Justice's Bureau of Investigation tracked down another companion of Johnson's who had crossed state lines with him. Based on this evidence, the court convicted Johnson and sentenced him to prison.

Further reading: Frederick K. Grittner, *White Slavery: Myth, Ideology, and American Law*, (New York: Garland Publishing, 1990).

— Michael Hartman

Mann-Elkins Act (1910)

The Mann-Elkins Act was part of the Progressive Era effort to regulate destructive competition and unfair trade practices. In the spirit of PROGRESSIVISM, President THEODORE ROOSEVELT had promised a Square Deal for ordinary Americans in his presidential election campaign of 1904. Previously, he had shown his willingness to rein in corporate abuses of power when he used his executive power to intervene in the ANTHRACITE COAL STRIKE of 1902. The threat of sending federal troops resulted in a compromise between the UNITED MINE WORKERS OF AMERICA and the mine owners, which gave the workers a wage increase and nine-hour day but did not demand recognition of the union. While the government had a practice of acting primarily on behalf of employers in industrial disputes, the Roosevelt administration's threat to seize the mines and continue coal production signaled a major shift in the role of the federal government as an impartial arbitrator. It also marked a change in government regulation of the railroad industry, which owned most of the anthracite mines.

The history of railroad regulation was an inconsistent one. By the 20th century, a series of legislative acts, passed to regulate railroads, were largely unenforceable. Yet the legislation demonstrated the enlarged federal power to regulate corporations. In 1887 Congress had passed the Interstate Commerce Act, which established the Interstate Commerce Commission (ICC) to regulate railroads, but the ICC's powers had been constrained by the courts over the years. In 1903 Roosevelt pushed the ELKINS ACT through Congress, which prohibited discriminatory railroad rebates. In 1906 Congress passed the HEPBURN ACT, which empowered the ICC to set maximum rates once a shipper filed a complaint.

Roosevelt's successor, WILLIAM HOWARD TAFT, worked to attain the previous administration's unfulfilled goals, in particular, railroad regulation. Taft signed the MANN-ELKINS ACT of 1910, which strengthened the regulatory power of the ICC. Extending the ICC's power over railroads, the act gave the ICC the authority to suspend rate increases without waiting for complaints from shippers. It set up the Commerce Court to hasten the settlement of railroad rate cases. In addition, the act placed telegraph, cable, and telephone companies under ICC control.

Railroad regulation had enlarged federal power over the industry. Ultimately, however, the ICC's record of enforcement remained unsatisfactory. By 1910, the railroads' voluntary efforts, not federal regulation, had curbed unfair rate-setting practices—the companies agreeing among themselves to set uniformly higher rates.

Although Taft supported regulatory legislation that Roosevelt had been unable to pass through Congress, Taft thought that Roosevelt had abused executive power. Because he refrained from using the tactics of Roosevelt and had a hands-off style of leadership, Taft was viewed as a less effective president. Despite the public perception of a weakened administration in the White House, Taft managed to pass the Mann-Elkins Act, a law that increased the power of the federal government to regulate the railroad industry.

Further reading: Lewis J. Gould, *Reform and Regulation: American Politics from Roosevelt to Wilson*, 2nd ed. (New York: Alfred A. Knopf, 1986); Albro Martin, *Enterprise Denied: Origins of the Decline of American Railroads, 1897–1917* (New York: Columbia University Press, 1971).

— Glen Bessemer

marriage and family life

In 1899, many Americans were shocked by the news that the United States had the highest divorce rate in the world. To many observers, the news was a sign that the American family was in danger. If the family was at risk, then America's entire social order faced uncertainty. Much of the fear surrounding the family arose from the profound changes taking place in the first decades of the 20th century. Many Americans believed that the family was in crisis. Industrialization, urbanization, immigration, feminism, and the expansion of the state led to changes in the roles of men, women, and children in the family. Despite the shrill pronouncements of many observers, ordinary people were not denouncing the family. They had simply begun to change their behavior and to ignore what had become an outdated family ideal.

Many of the changes that occurred after 1900 were a result of tensions between family ideals and practical realities. Family form and functions changed in response to a complex set of circumstances, chief among which were the effects of economic class and ethnicity. Thus, middle-class families in which the husband worked in a profession might have differed greatly from a working-class family in which both the husband and wife worked.

Most of the fears in regard to families arose from the middle class. The middle-class family ideal popular at the turn of the century centered on the home as a refuge from the world of commerce and trade. Ideally, men were to venture forth into the immoral and dangerous world to support the family, while mothers and children were to stay in the home and thus be protected from the world. This ideal of the middle-class family rested on the woman as the moral center of the family. It was her role to exert a moralizing influence on her husband and to raise her children. Many observers proclaimed that the middle-class family, which—they argued—formed the backbone of the American social order, faced imminent danger from a variety of forces acting to pull it apart.

The new family ideal of the early century emerged from a rapidly changing economic environment. Large-scale industrialization and commercialization were reshaping the work lives of many Americans. For non-farm families, work was completely removed from the home, which meant that workers of all classes were out of their homes and apart from their families for most of the day. At the turn of the century, for example, a typical industrial laborer worked 59 hours per week. Long hours often had a negative effect on family life. Fathers and—in the case of many working-class families—mothers were not always present in the home to parent their children. In middle-class families, the new wage economy meant that the mothers were in charge of raising the children. For some working-class families, the mother filled the same role. In the working-class families, care for children was often undertaken by older siblings or neighbors. The new economy also provided greater job opportunities for young women. Teenaged women could work in the factories, the newly created department stores, or in clerical jobs. Paid work opened up a new world for young women who traditionally had remained in the home to help out with domestic work. Their new independence often led to tension between the young women and their families.

The expanding cities that accompanied industrialization shaped family life. Cities offered new social opportunities for children outside their families. Commercial dance halls, pool rooms, amusement parks, and movie theaters provided space where youths could meet and socialize away from their parents. In these new venues, youths developed their own subcultures based on their shared values. In turn, they distanced themselves from their families. It was not only large cities, however, that experienced these changes. Age-segregated leisure surfaced even in small cities, like the Muncie, Indiana, of MIDDLETOWN.

The tremendous increase in immigration affected the family. Middle-class Americans feared that the increase in immigration, particularly from eastern and southern Europe, would overwhelm native-born, white American families. The declining birth rate among white native-born Americans contributed to the fear that uneducated immigrants eventually would outnumber and overrun the educated population. The idea of "race suicide" helped spur anti–BIRTH CONTROL campaigns aimed at convincing native-born, middle-class women to have more children. Despite these campaigns, the birth rate continued to drop, and birth control use increased.

The birth control campaigns were a reaction to new, emerging roles for women. As more middle-class women went to work outside the home, observers feared that America's children were endangered. Between 1890 and 1910, women's enrollment in colleges tripled. Their participation in the workforce doubled between 1890 and 1900, and it increased by 50 percent between 1900 and 1910. In addition, women expanded their public activity by creating women's clubs and other organizations that played an important role in the reform movements of the Progressive Era. The WOMAN SUFFRAGE movement lobbied for women to have expanded rights. It succeeded in passing and ratifying the Nineteenth Amendment, which gave women the right to vote, in 1920. Critics of the women's movement argued that women's participation in public life threatened the future of the country. If women were working or engaging in social reform activities, they could not be at home with their children. Children, the critics claimed, were growing up without proper guidance and socialization.

In response to these changes, many states sought to toughen their divorce laws. Throughout the 19th century, states had made getting a divorce easier, but others allowed divorce only on account of adultery, desertion, or physical cruelty. South Carolina outlawed divorce all together. In the Progressive Era, these laws became stricter, and many states tried to prevent divorces by preventing bad marriages. States passed laws outlawing marriages between men and women who suffered from drunkenness, venereal disease, addiction, and mental defectiveness. Other states raised the age of consent. These laws did not have the desired effect. Men and women seeking a divorce simply pretended to meet the requirements set down in the laws. Thus the divorce rate continued to rise even after the tightening of restrictions.

Government intervened in private life in new ways in an effort to save the American family. Most of these interventions focused on promoting the nuclear family ideal in which fathers worked, mothers were housewives, and children went to school until they were 15 or 16 years old. Most states passed women's maximum hour laws that restricted the hours women could work. The purpose of these laws was to ensure women's health, but a side benefit was that mothers might be able to be at home more frequently, particularly when children were home from schools. Many states began to offer MOTHERS' PENSIONS, which supplemented women's income as a means of keeping widow's families together. Although these programs had little impact, they demonstrated the commitment that Americans felt toward saving the American family.

States intervened in the lives of children in other ways to promote the nuclear family. They passed CHILD LABOR laws and compulsory school attendance laws so that working-class children were required to attend school. Compulsory schooling laws were partly an attempt to remove immigrant children from their homes, because educators believed that the schools provided a better environment for socializing children. Teaching children appropriate values in home economics was one way to shore up the family. These efforts failed to engender the nuclear family ideal. The inability of many working-class men to earn enough money to support their families was the major reason. Women and children often worked, therefore, out of necessity.

Family life was affected by mass-production industry in a different way. The increase in industrial jobs led to a decrease in the number of women who were willing to work as domestic servants. Many middle-class families had employed servants in their homes. Domestic service jobs were not as appealing, however, as jobs in factories and stores. Middle-class families faced a shortage of domestic servants, which meant that middle-class women had to do housework themselves. The shortage of domestic help led to efforts to professionalize domestic labor and increase public education in the domestic arts. Advocates hoped that professionalizing housework would convince women to remain home rather than work for wages. It further led to the rationalization and scientific organization of housework by introducing home appliances in order to reduce the labor involved in housework. New appliances such as electric vacuums and washing machines did not, however, release American women from housework. As appliances made cleaning more efficient, standards of cleanliness and hygiene were raised. American women experienced an increase in the time spent cleaning their homes. While work hours dropped, men did not engage in any new domestic labor. Thus, a majority of American mothers maintained their role as the principal provider of home labor.

The family ideal changed in regard to the purpose and place of family life. Families had been stripped of many of their educational, economic, and welfare functions. In their place, society assigned the family primary responsibility for fulfilling emotional and psychological needs of its members. This shift gave rise to a model of marriage called companionate marriage. Before this time, religious obligation, economic need, or moral pressures often held together marriages. Companionate marriage was to be held together by romance, equal rights, and affection. Psychologists, educators, and social service professionals popularized the new conception of marriage early in the 20th century. Relation-ships between parents and children also changed. Families were still supposed to provide a stable environment for children but added to this traditional role was emotional satisfaction. Children gained the right to express their feelings and to interact freely with their peers. The family ideal thus centered on nurturing emotional well-being in its members.

Paradoxically, as families grew closer emotionally, older children were gaining freedom outside their families. The creation of youth subcultures gave children the ability to define themselves outside of their family. By the 1920s, children identified more with peer groups than with families. This was particularly true for middle-class teenaged children, for whom high school education became universalized. High schools became the site in which youth subcultures were created and expressed. Working-class youths also enjoyed more freedom from family control. Many working-class parents allowed their children to keep some of their pay, rather than demanding that they turn over the entire paycheck to the family. The practice gave youth money with which to pursue leisure activities. Younger members of the family, therefore, were breaking away from the family.

Younger children faced a changing environment as well. In the Progressive Era, experts on children published countless books and articles on the proper care and rearing of children. They recommended that parents set strict sleeping and eating schedules for young children and advised parents to wean and toilet train their children early. Experts told mothers not to play with or fondle their children, because it would instill a desire for sensual gratification that would place a strain on a child's nervous system. By the 1920s, a new set of experts emerged who strongly rebuked the rationalized style of childrearing. They advocated a more permissive style of parenting. Parents were encouraged to use a reward system to encourage proper behavior. Many experts still recommended, however, that parents—and particularly mothers—avoid too much affection, for the fear that it would spoil children. In the 1920s, a third group of experts argued that childrearing should be aimed at developing well-adjusted personalities. They warned that stifling childish instincts and actions could permanently damage a child. Educators such as JOHN DEWEY and Maria Montessori argued that children's innate curiosity and independence should be encouraged.

By the end of the 1920s, the emergence of mass media, the common experience of living in an industrial society, and the rise in real wages for many workers led to a more homogeneous family model across class lines. The nuclear family became the ideal family. Although there was never a time when every family in America fit into that model, it was becoming more widespread.

See also EDUCATION; POPULATION TRENDS; SEXUALITY.

Further reading: Steven Mintz and Susan Kellogg, *Domestic Revolutions: A Social History of American Family Life* (New York: Free Press, 1988).

— Michael Hartman

The Masses

Associated with the Bohemian SOCIALISM of GREENWICH VILLAGE, *The Masses* was a radical journal that reflected the political and cultural changes of its time. The political, economic, and social turmoil of the early 20th century was transforming American society. Between the end of the Civil War and the end of WORLD WAR I, the country went from being a largely rural agrarian society to an increasingly urban industrial one. These transformations helped give rise to a variety of progressive, socialist, and radical political movements in the early decades of the new century. Changes in print media also played an important role in enabling these radical political movements to get their message to an increasingly large audience.

The most significant transformation in print media was the emergence of investigative journalism, associated with the MUCKRAKERS. Magazines and journals such as *Collier's, McClure's, Everybody's,* and *The Nation* began running articles exposing political and corporate corruption. They became immensely popular among the general public and pressured politicians and business leaders to enact important reforms. The popularity of the new political magazines skyrocketed. By 1906 circulation among the 10 most popular magazines publishing investigative reports topped 3,000,000.

Socialist and radical groups, with whom many investigative journalists had close connections, quickly realized the potential the print medium had to vastly expand the audience they were able to reach. Among the most well-written and effective magazines in the newly emerging radical press was *The Masses.* Established in 1911 by Piet Vlag, *The Masses* largely reflected the views of its Marxist editor, Max Eastman. Between 1911 and 1914, a veritable who's who of the political Left published in the pages of *The Masses.* The journal quickly became one of the leading progressive voices in the country. Contributors to the magazine included UPTON SINCLAIR, JOHN REED, Mabel Dodge, Randolph Bourne, and others. Eastman and others on the staff believed that the war in Europe was nothing more than a conflict between competing factions of capital. Between 1914 and 1917, its writers lampooned both the Allied and Central powers and strongly advocated that the United States remain neutral.

After the United States entered World War I, the magazine's editors came under intense pressure to change its stance on the war. When Eastman refused, the post-master general banned the magazine's distribution, and legal action was initiated aimed at shutting the magazine down permanently. Other radical and progressive magazines, such as *The Nation,* found themselves under intense pressure to support the nation's war effort. Even after the war ended, the federal government continued to place radical and progressive magazines under surveillance for their support of the RUSSIAN REVOLUTION, sexual radicalism, and outspoken criticism of the United States. *The Masses* and the RADICAL PRESS tapped into a strong undercurrent of social inequality and utilized innovations in the print media to achieve an unprecedented level of exposure and support for radical and progressive causes.

Further reading: William L. O'Neill, *The Last Romantic: A Life of Max Eastman* (New York: Oxford University Press, 1978).

— Robert Gordon

mass production

The introduction of the mass production of consumer goods fundamentally transformed virtually every aspect of American society between 1900 and 1930. Mass production allowed manufacturers to create economies of scale. In other words, they were able to make larger profits from selling more goods at a lower price than by selling goods at the highest price possible. Mass production also emphasized the use of machinery to produce interchangeable parts. These machine-produced parts and products created goods of uniform quality. Prior to the introduction of mass production, goods were frequently created by hand one at a time and varied greatly in quality. The concept of mass production was hardly new. Eli Whitney had adopted it in the manufacturing of flintlock guns in 1798. What was new at the turn of the century, however, was the extent to which American industry was committed to the idea of mass production. When the idea of mass production was joined with new ideas about SCIENTIFIC MANAGEMENT, the result was a revolution in the way goods were produced and the economy functioned.

Beginning in the late 1890s, American manufacturers were determined to implement the ideas of FREDERICK WINSLOW TAYLOR. Often referred to as the father of scientific management, Taylor argued that if manufacturers streamlined their operations, eliminating any waste or inefficiency, they could dramatically reduce the time it took to produce goods. This in turn would enable them to reduce the cost of the products. Taylor and his team of university-trained experts used stopwatches to time every aspect of the production process and then recommended ways to improve efficiency. At the same time, Taylor encouraged manufacturers to break down the production process into repetitive tasks. The performance of these tasks required some skill, but it did not require workers to understand or master the entire process.

The introduction of scientific management to mass production resulted in numerous advantages. Mass-produced goods often had interchangeable parts. This made it easier for consumers to repair broken items. In addition, the division of work into isolated and repetitive tasks allowed employers to exert greater control over the entire production process and the workforce. Prior to the widespread use of mass production, skilled artisans, who often took years to learn their craft, produced goods. Watchmakers, for example, created an entire watch step-by-step. Control over the pace and quality of the work was largely in the watchmaker's hands. When watches began to be mass-produced, workers used machines. Responsible for producing only one part of the watch, they now

repeated the same task over and over. The loss of specialized skill and knowledge, often referred to as deskilling, weakened the position of skilled workers.

Automobile manufacturer HENRY FORD perfected the mass production system. Obsessed with mass-producing affordable automobiles, Fords spent years streamlining and routinizing his assembly line production process. Instead of having workers assemble one car at a time, Ford employees assembled the car in the stages, as conveyor belts brought the automobile through various workstations. After years of experimentation, the opening of the Highland Park plant in 1910 was the culmination of Ford's efforts and set a new standard other manufacturers quickly attempted to imitate. The results were startling. With the opening of the Highland Park plant, the time it took to produce a finished Model T Ford dropped from 12 hours to an hour-and-a-half. Ford now turned out 600 new Model Ts a day. The result was that Ford was able to sell a high-quality automo-

Ford's first moving assembly lines at Highland Park *(Hulton/Archive)*

bile at a lower price than his competitors. By 1921, the company controlled 55 percent of the automobile market. Other manufacturers rushed to follow suit, forever altering the way goods were produced.

The widespread use of mass production transformed the economy. Consumers could now afford to purchase high-quality products at affordable prices. The Model T Ford, for example, was well built and sold for only $850 when it was introduced in 1908. As Ford continued to streamline production and manufacture and sell more cars, the price of the Model T continued to drop until it cost only $290 in 1927, making it affordable to all classes. In some ways, mass-produced goods helped create a more homogeneous society. Customers who bought a Model T got the same black, four-cylinder, no-frills automobile in Maine as they did in Michigan. Mass production also changed the American workplace. The pace of work increased dramatically as machine operators performed routine tasks over and over. Industrial jobs became faster-paced and more tedious. Finally, companies that mass-produced their goods were able to realize an advantage over their competitors and to quickly dominate entire industries.

Further reading: David A. Hounshell, *From the American System to Mass Production, 1800–1932: The Development of Manufacturing Technologies in the United States* (Baltimore: Johns Hopkins University Press, 1984); Robert Asher and Edsford, Ronald, eds. *Autowork* (Albany: State University of New York Press, 1995).

— Robert Gordon

McKinley, William See Volume VI

McNary-Haugen Farm Bill (1926)

Supported by the powerful Farm Bloc in Congress, the McNary-Haugen Farm Bill was designed to increase government support of farm commodity prices during the long farm depression of the 1920s. During that decade, the agricultural sector experienced a sustained economic decline. Farm commodity prices dropped not only from wartime highs but also from the stable prices of the period between 1909 and 1913. Farm bankruptcy and tenancy rates were on the rise. Each year, farmers improved less land and cultivated fewer crops, despite their economic dilemma. Farm organizations such as the American Farm Bureau added thousands of members, but they—like their urban counterparts—had little leverage in determining the price of commodities or methods of distribution. Organized farmers began to clamor for some form of government intervention in the guise of loans, price supports, or government regulation of the market.

The goal of radical farm organizations in the 1920s was to achieve parity pricing (prices equal to prewar prices) through government intervention. Working with Secretary of Agriculture Henry C. Wallace, Senator Charles McNary of Oregon and Representative Gilbert Haugen of Iowa introduced a bill to raise farm prices in 1924. Known as the McNary-Haugen Farm Act, the bill proposed that a Federal Farm Board be created to buy agricultural surpluses and hold them off the market until prices rose. The bill also empowered the new Farm Board to sell goods overseas, should prices remain stagnant. The problem with AGRICULTURE, the sponsors argued, was that postwar deflation of prices and increased debt loads had endangered the family farm, the backbone of American democracy. Farm bankruptcies and growing farm tenancy were signs of the overall decline in the agricultural economy. Introduced into CONGRESS in 1926, the McNary-Haugen bill featured government price supports of agricultural commodities to equalize farm prices by selling surplus agricultural commodities on the world market at lower prices than they would receive domestically. The measure was defeated.

In 1927 and in 1928, Congress narrowly passed the McNary-Haugen bill. Although his own secretary of agriculture helped to author the bill, President CALVIN COOLIDGE vetoed it both times, arguing that it illegitimately put into place a system for fixing agricultural prices. It was, he argued, "calculated to injure rather than promote the general welfare." He objected in particular to the provisions of the bill that charged farmers fees for government expenditures in purchasing farm surpluses. Introduced once again in 1929, the bill was vetoed by the new president, Herbert Hoover. There were not enough votes to pass it, even when farm prices began to drop again in the late 1920s. Within the Farm Bloc itself, extensive intervention in commodity markets was a divisive issue. The Farm Bureau, like the AMERICAN FEDERATION OF LABOR, often preferred voluntary economic solutions, rather then government ones. As a result, while the McNary-Haugen Farm Bill drew support from various sectors, the direction of farm policy remained limited to government support for farm cooperatives and marketing, in such laws as the CAPPER-VOLSTEAD ACT of 1922 and the AGRICULTURAL MARKETING ACT of 1929.

See also LOBBYING AND INTEREST GROUPS.

Further reading: Peter Harstad, *Gilbert N. Haugen: Norwegian-American Farm Politician* (Iowa City: State Historical Society of Iowa, 1992).

McPherson, Aimee Semple (1890–1944)

A popular evangelist and founder of the International Church of the Four-Square Gospel, Aimee Elizabeth

Aimee Semple McPherson *(Library of Congress)*

Semple McPherson was born in Salford, Ontario, Canada, on October 9, 1890. She was the daughter of James Morgan Kenney, a Methodist farmer, and his second wife, Minnie, an orphan who had been raised by a Salvation Army family. In 1908, at age 18, Aimee married Robert Semple, an Irish Pentecostal evangelist. She converted to Pentecostalism and joined her husband on tour. On a mission to China in 1910, Robert took ill and died, and Aimee became a widow. She gave birth to a daughter, Roberta Star, shortly thereafter. In 1912, Aimee Semple married Harold McPherson, an accountant. After she gave birth to a son, Rolf, in 1913, Aimee became depressed. Believing herself called to preach, she left McPherson to become a traveling evangelist. She believed that she heard voices

calling her to the ministry, and her experience of baptism in the Holy Spirit and speaking in tongues gave her the authority. In 1919, she moved to Los Angeles with her mother and two children. For the next few years, she remained a road evangelist and traveled with her mother Minnie across the country.

McPherson's ministry offered her followers a new version of Pentecostalism. She preached on the four roles of Jesus Christ as healer, baptizer, savior, and returning king. With this message, McPherson gained the financial support and personal loyalty of thousands she converted and others who found her a compelling personal presence. In 1923, after years of preaching in tent revivals on the road, McPherson opened her Angelus Temple with 5,300 seats in Los Angeles. She continued to draw large crowds to her services, and she finally incorporated her church as the International Church of the Four-Square Gospel in 1927.

McPherson's popularity was based in part on her relentless innovation. Drawing upon new technologies to "get out the word," she traveled the country in her revival days in the "Gospel car." She used the vehicle as part-pulpit and part-advertising billboard, and it carried her message: "Jesus is coming soon; get ready." McPherson also integrated jazz music, stage theatricals, and even opera into her services, and she became one of the first evangelists to use the RADIO as a "wireless telephone" to reach the masses. She opened a Bible school in 1923, to preach her own version of the Pentecostal gospel. In 1924, she bought a radio station, which she dubbed KFSG for "Kall Four Square Gospel."

In 1926 McPherson disappeared while on holiday. When she reappeared a few days later, she claimed to have been abducted. Newspapers reported that they had discovered a love nest in Carmel, California, which McPherson shared with a former KFSG radio engineer, Kenneth Ormiston. Put on trial under the charge of perjury, McPherson convinced the jury that she had been telling the truth about the kidnapping. She was acquitted, but never again did she have the same popularity. During the Great Depression, she opened a soup kitchen at her church and did other community work. McPherson continued her ministry for the rest of her life. She died in 1944, the victim of an accidental overdose of sleeping pills.

See also BILLY SUNDAY; RELIGION.

Further reading: Daniel Mark Epstein, *Sister Aimee: The Life of Aimee Semple McPherson* (New York: Harcourt, Brace, Jovanovich, 1993).

Mead, Margaret (1901–1978)

One of the most important public intellectuals of the 20th century, anthropologist Margaret Mead was and is a figure of both admiration and controversy. She was a prolific writer of 44 books and hundreds of articles, many written for popular audiences. Mead became best known for her work on adolescence and child care in other cultures. In landmark books, she advanced the argument that culture, not biology, determined gender identity and sexual behavior. Mead balanced her intellectual courage with wit and humor, making her a sought-after public speaker. By the end of her life, as much cultural icon as intellectual, she appeared on radio and television and published widely in the popular press.

Born on December 16, 1901, the oldest of four children, Mead was the daughter of economist Edward Sherwood Mead of the University of Pennsylvania and Emily Fogg, a sociologist and social reformer. Home-schooled prior to high school, Margaret took her bachelor's degree in psychology at Barnard College in 1923 and her M.A. and Ph.D. at Columbia University (1928). While in graduate school, she married theology student Luther Cressman. They were divorced in 1928.

A student of anthropologists FRANZ BOAS and Ruth Benedict, Mead did fieldwork in American Samoa for her dissertation. The study, later published as *Coming of Age in Samoa* (1928), argued that the experience of adolescence varied across cultures. A best-seller later translated into several languages, it asserted that the more relaxed child-rearing practices of Samoan culture made adolescence and sexual development less conflict-ridden and problematic than in the West. Indirectly, *Coming of Age in Samoa*, like much of Mead's later work, challenged the idea of Western cultural superiority by showing how the West might learn from other cultures.

In subsequent years, Mead returned to the South Pacific. With her second husband, psychologist Reo Fortune, she went on a fieldwork expedition to New Guinea in 1928–29. Mead studied the play and imagination of young children in the region. Based on her research, she published *Growing Up in New Guinea* in 1930. Mead divorced Fortune in 1935. A year later, she married British anthropologist Gregory Bateson, with whom she conducted research in Bali. Together, they wrote a study, *Balinese Character* (1942), which utilized photography in its analysis of culture. Mead gave birth to a daughter, Mary Catherine Bateson, in 1939. Mead later divorced Bateson.

Throughout her career, Mead chose to work at the intersection of academic and popular institutions. In 1926, she took a position with the anthropology department of the American Museum of Natural History in New York City. She worked there for over 40 years, first as assistant then as associate curator (1942–64), and finally as curator from 1964 to 1969. She joined the Columbia University faculty as director of research in contemporary cultures (1948–50) and adjunct professor of anthropology in 1954.

In 1968, she was appointed head of social sciences and professor of anthropology at Fordham University. She served in both official and informal capacities on federal commissions and in international associations, and she testified before Congress and other government agencies.

Mead saw her work as curator of museum collections and exhibits as being on an equal par with her publications and teaching. She was an enthusiastic advocate for women's rights, the environment, child development, and education. A strong believer in interdisciplinarity, she is given credit for combining for the first time psychology with anthropology. Her later works, including *Sex and Temperament in Three Cultures* (1935), *Male and Female* (1949), *New Lives for Old* (1956), and *Culture and Commitment* (1970), kept her ideas before the public. Believing that racism, warfare, and a lack of respect for the environment were learned behaviors, Mead argued that humans had the capacity to modify their paths and create different futures. She published her memoirs, *Blackberry Winter*, in 1972. Her anthropological work was tremendously influential in shaping the opinion both of scholars and of the general public. Mead died in 1978.

Further reading: Mary Catherine Bateson, *With a Daughter's Eye; A Memoir of Margaret Mead and Gregory Bateson* (New York: William Morrow, 1984); June Howard, *Margaret Mead; A Life* (New York: Simon & Schuster, 1984).

Meat Inspection Act (1906)

The Meat Inspection Act of 1906 was an attempt to regulate the meatpacking industry and to assure consumers that the meat they were eating was safe. By 1900, industrialization had changed food production in the United States. Throughout much of history, ordinary people either raised and slaughtered their own meat or purchased it from local butchers. As the nation became more urban and industrial, however, a national meatpacking industry emerged to capture the market. By 1900, livestock was being raised on large-scale farms and ranches and driven to centralized slaughterhouses in Kansas City and Chicago. Once slaughtered, the livestock was then divided into various cuts of beef and pork, and shipped across the country on refrigerated railroad cars. MASS PRODUCTION and the assembly line were introduced into meatpacking, and livestock was brought to slaughterhouse employees by conveyor belts. As the meatpacking industry changed, giant corporations such as Armour, Wilson, and Swift quickly came to dominate the industry. These large-scale producers attempted to maximize profits by introducing technological changes to increase efficiency and by pushing employers to work more quickly.

Working conditions and the cleanliness of the industry deteriorated as meatpacking companies attempted to increase profits at a time when food prices were steadily declining. Those calling for closer scrutiny of the food processing industry included the American Medical Association and journalists Samuel Hopkins Adams and UPTON SINCLAIR. In 1904, Sinclair published a series of articles in *McClure's* magazine exposing hazards facing slaughterhouse workers and the unsanitary conditions in the stockyards of Chicago. Later that year, he published *The Jungle* (1906), a novel based on his research. The conditions of the Chicago stockyards horrified consumers across the country and led to demands that the government take action to ensure the quality and purity of the nation's meat supply.

Ironically, Sinclair had focused his attention on the hazardous working and living conditions of slaughterhouse employees. The public turned out to be more concerned about the food they were eating. Pressure on the federal government mounted. The Neill-Reynolds report, a Department of Agriculture inquiry into the working conditions and sanitation of the industry, convinced many politicians of the need to act. The proposed legislation, however, was not without its critics. Conservatives in Congress, including Speaker of the House JOSEPH CANNON, argued that the Constitution did not grant the federal government the authority to regulate industry. The meatpacking industry lobbied aggressively to get the legislation blocked. Public concern, however, convinced President THEODORE ROOSEVELT and progressive congressmen of the need to act. The Meat Inspection Act and the PURE FOOD AND DRUG ACT were both passed in 1906. Concluding that distribution of meat constituted interstate commerce and hence fell under federal jurisdiction, Congress prohibited the sale of tainted meat and authorized the Department of Agriculture to investigate meatpacking plants. The momentum generated by the passage of the Meat Inspection Act helped secure the passage of the Pure Food and Drug Act, which had been stalled in Congress since 1905. With these two pieces of legislation, the federal government took important steps to assure the public that the food they were eating met minimum safety standards and, in the process, restored public confidence.

Further reading: Lewis L. Gould, *The Presidency of Theodore Roosevelt* (Lawrence: University of Kansas Press, 1991).

— Robert Gordon

medicine

Between 1900 and 1930, significant changes in the medical profession, medical practice, and medical knowledge transformed the health care system in the United States. At the turn of the century, the American Medical Association (AMA) was in its infancy. Only about 7,000 doctors (or 6 percent of medical doctors) belonged to AMA, and most doctors remained independent of professional ties. Jealous medical professionals fought the encroachments of PUBLIC HEALTH departments and competed with each other for patients. Medical licensing was neither widespread nor uniform, and medical education was haphazard. American medical knowledge lagged behind the advancements in Europe and compared badly to Germany, where laboratory SCIENCES were revolutionizing medical diagnosis and treatment. The hospital, long thought to be a house of death, was only beginning its transformation into an institution for the diagnosis, treatment, and cure of disease. By 1930, medicine in the United States would be transformed into the modern system of health care that prevails today.

The turn of the century was a time of great medical discoveries. New bacteriological studies had uncovered the cause of many infectious diseases, including tuberculosis, diphtheria, cholera, typhoid, and rabies. Public health officials attuned to the need for prevention and treatment had begun to clean up city sanitation and educate the public in new standards of personal hygiene. Surgery, which was scarcely practiced through most of the 19th century, came into its own as a field of medical practice. During this period, antiseptic procedures in surgery sharply reduced patient mortality in operations. By the turn of the century, abdominal surgery had become more frequent as had new surgical operations on the lungs, nervous system, and heart.

A central tension in the development of medicine in the 20th century was the competition that existed between public health needs and the medical profession. Doctors and medical practitioners faced the dilemma of having a professional creed (the Hippocratic oath) that obligated doctors to provide care mated with the economic self-interest of a newly powerful profession. As medical knowledge and treatment improved, doctors were in greater demand. They sought and slowly gained higher fees and salaries, but the problem remained of how to elevate the status and income of the profession, long seen as a mixture of concerned practitioners, traditional homeopaths, and outright quacks and charlatans who promised miracle cures. The only way, in the view of many physicians, was to reduce the supply of doctors and thus increase demand and reward. Doctors sought to achieve this goal by collective organization (the AMA), improvement of medical education and the discrediting of commercial medical schools, and licensing. The AMA reorganized in 1901 in order to create a more efficient system of governance. At the same time, it put pressure on state medical associations to reorganize and coordinate their activities with the national AMA.

The key to controlling entry into the profession, while at the same time improving medical care, was to radically reform medical education in the United States. The first tentative steps in this direction were made in the training of nurses. Reform in nursing education began as early as the 1870s and progressed into the 20th century. The dearth of trained nurses was solved, as the number of nursing schools increased from three in 1873 to 432 in 1900 and 1,129 in 1910. Nursing education came to include many of the same elements of medical schools, including student training in hospitals. The 1923 Carnegie Foundation report on *Nursing and Nursing Education in the United States,* which social investigator JOSEPHINE GOLDMARK helped to write, furthered these trends.

During the 1870s, there was a similar movement to reform doctor education. Harvard University led the way in professionalizing medical education beginning in 1871. Under President Charles Eliot, the university completely revamped its medical school, instituting training in the laboratory sciences of physiology, pathological anatomy, and chemistry, and integrating clinical work. The 1893 founding of Johns Hopkins University Medical School and its hospital was another step forward. The Johns Hopkins program focused on research in the laboratory sciences as well as clinical work and hospital internships. It was at Johns Hopkins that the term "residency" was first coined when the school implemented the practice of assigning newly educated doctors to practical training.

Drawing on European models, the innovative medical schools at Harvard and Johns Hopkins led the way for changes in medical education as a whole. The AMA put pressure on state legislatures to implement new standards of medical licensing of doctors and medical schools that required a higher level of both laboratory and clinical education. The elite schools also stretched the requirements for a medical degree from two to five and then eight years, including a hospital internship. The cost of laboratory equipment, adequate library resources, and hospital facilities put many small proprietary medical schools out of business.

The final blow for smaller commercial medical schools was a report issued in 1910. That year, the Carnegie Foundation for the Advancement of Teaching hired Abraham Flexner, an educational reformer, to conduct a survey of medical schools in the United States. Visiting medical schools across the country, Flexner found that there were many smaller medical schools that had only made gestures toward meeting the new educational standards. They lacked laboratory facilities to educate students in the clinical sciences of physiology and anatomy. Their libraries lacked books and journals; their faculty largely busied themselves with outside practice. Within a few years, the new state licensing boards, coupled with Flexner's report, had their desired effect. The number of medical schools declined from 161 in 1900 to 81 in 1922. With new and higher standards and strengthening of medical education,

the AMA shored up its prestige and the financial rewards of being a doctor, as income steadily increased throughout the period.

As both a school for the clinical training of physicians and as an institution for the treatment of disease, the American hospital went through several changes in the early 20th century. Early hospitals had been places where the poor went for refuge and free treatment and the terminally ill went to die. Most men and women preferred seeing private doctors in offices or homes. Surgery often was performed in kitchens, and doctors oversaw childbirth in the mother's home. In rural regions and poor city neighborhoods, midwives still watched over and sometimes intervened in births. After 1900, the hospital became the venue of choice for an increasing number of middle-class and even working-class patients. Their chief problems had been the lack of trained doctors and the high rate of infection in hospital wards. New antiseptic procedures and greater demand for hospital space by trained physicians changed the profile of the hospital. Reform of medical education made the hospital the place where new medical graduates did their internships, and doctors increasingly used hospital to place seriously ill patients and candidates for surgery. With these changes, there was greater specialization, as hospitals divided labor according to the level of training, years of practice, and reputation of doctors. Modern hospitals no longer depended on availability to attract doctors but rather began to pay fees to private doctors and salaries to those on staff. Moreover, many hospitals became profitmaking enterprises.

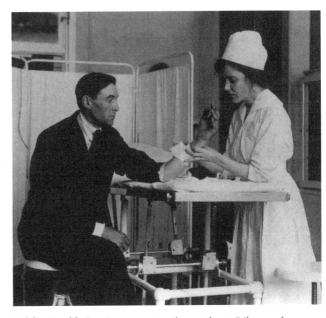

Public Health Service nurse treating patient *(Library of Congress)*

The modernization of American medicine came at a cost. The constant tension between private doctors and public health departments severely limited the provision of free public health care and truncated many community health initiatives. At the same time, public health programs such as free laboratory testing for diphtheria and tuberculosis and school health programs to diagnose hearing and eye problems and infectious diseases indirectly subsidized medical care. The desire for greater income and higher status for the profession led doctors to close down commercial medical schools that had trained doctors for working-class immigrant, rural, and African-American communities. In general, doctors gravitated to wealthy areas. As one AMA study showed, more than a third of small towns that had doctors in 1914 had lost them by 1925. In 1906, there was one doctor for every 590 persons; by 1923, this had increased to 910. In large cities, there had been little growth in the numbers of doctors per capita. The shortage of doctors was particularly acute among African Americans. The new standards for accreditation of medical schools had reduced the number of medical schools enrolling African-American students from seven to two. Within a few years of the 1910 report, only Howard and Meharry remained. The consequence for medical care in African-American communities was devastating. In Mississippi, for example, where medical care was segregated by race, there was only one physician in 1930 for every 14,634 African-American residents.

Women in the medical profession were also casualties of the new emphasis on research science and elite medical education. Where the United States once had the highest number of trained women physicians in the world and a relatively high percentage of women went to medical school, after 1910 most medical schools limited the proportion of women students admitted to 5 percent of classes. The number of women medical students dropped by nearly a third. At the same time, professional hostility toward women increased. The AMA, like many professional and academic associations, marginalized or excluded women in its ranks, which meant women received fewer medical referrals, had to pay more in malpractice insurance, and—without AMA support—might never receive, or eventually lose, their license to practice medicine.

With these changes, American medicine entered a new era of medical discovery, treatment, and care. It also faced a future in which private practice and private medical insurance, not public health care and national health insurance, was the dominant mode. It would be decades before development of a health system that reached the mass of the population with preventative treatment and regular care.

Further reading: Judith Leavitt and Ronald Numbers, eds., *Sickness and Health in America: Readings in the History of Medicine and Public Health* (Madison: University of Wisconsin Press, 1978); Paul Starr, *The Social Transformation of American Medicine* (New York: Basic Books, 1982).

Mellon, Andrew William (1855–1937)

Andrew Mellon was one of the most influential bankers and conservative politicians of the 1920s. He served as secretary of the treasury throughout the decade and earned a reputation for cutting taxes and trimming the federal budget. Born in Pittsburgh in 1855 as the son of Thomas Mellon, a successful banker, Andrew went to school at what is now the University of Pittsburgh. He left college early to enter into business and soon joined forces with his father and brother Richard to found the firm Thomas Mellon and sons. In 1889, Andrew Mellon established the Union Trust Company of Pittsburgh, which was destined to become one of the largest financial institutions in the United States. Mellon also invested widely and had holdings in the oil, locomotive, bridge construction, electric, coal, public utility, steel, and insurance industries.

In 1921, he resigned as president of the Mellon National Bank to become secretary of the treasury under WARREN G. HARDING, an appointment he held until 1932. As treasury secretary, Mellon had the dismantling of the war-built tax structure as his principal goal. He argued that the nation was "staggering under the existing burden of taxation and debt" and clamored for "gradual relief from war taxation." He reiterated his proposals to a special session of Congress in 1921, recommending repeal of the excess profits tax. He also called for the reduction of individual and corporate income taxes and surtaxes on income. In the Revenue Act of 1921, Congress repealed the excess profits tax. It further lowered income tax rates in 1921, 1924, and again in 1926. Taxes were reduced from a maximum of 73 percent to 40 percent on income for 1921 and 33 percent thereafter. He published *Taxation: The People's Business* in 1924 to express his tax philosophy.

Despite drastic tax cuts throughout the decade, Mellon's budgetary advice helped to reduce the national debt from over $24 billion in 1920 to $16 billion in 1930. His tight budget philosophy, however, had other, negative consequences. When the Great Depression began in 1929, his distaste for deficit spending reinforced President Herbert Hoover's conservative approach to the crisis. As the economy went into a tailspin following the Stock Market Crash of 1929, neither the president nor Mellon could find any justification for federal relief for farmers or the unemployed.

By the end of Hoover's presidency, Mellon had already begun to withdraw from political life. He served briefly as ambassador to Great Britain and left the position when Franklin Delano Roosevelt was elected in 1932. In private life, Mellon had a reputation as a philanthropist. He donated $10 million to the founding of the Mellon Institute for Industrial Research in Pittsburgh, and later he donated his art collection, and funds for a building to house it, to the federal government. Mellon died in 1937.

Further reading: Philip H. Love, *Andrew Mellon, The Man and His Work* (Baltimore: F. H. Coggins, 1929); Robert K. Murray, *The Politics of Normalcy: Government Theory and Practice in the Harding-Coolidge Era* (New York: Norton, 1973).

Mencken, Henry Louis (1880–1956)

Henry Louis Mencken (H. L.) was born in Baltimore on September 12, 1880. The son of August Mencken, a prominent cigar maker, Henry Mencken was groomed by his father to become a cigar maker, but he had different plans. The two years that he spent working for his father were the worst years of his life. Only two weeks after his father died, Mencken applied for a position with the Baltimore *Herald.*

Living the life of a cigar worker would have been difficult for Mencken. From early on it was clear that he was exceptionally bright and perceptive. Even during his formative years, he showed a promise that led to his appointment as his high school's valedictorian in 1896. His intelligence and curiosity led him to a career as a journalist. Just three years out of high school, in 1899 he became a reporter for the Baltimore *Herald.* In 1906 he moved on to the Baltimore *Sun* where he worked, on and off, for the remainder of his life.

In 1914 Mencken and George Jean Nathan began editing *The Smart Set,* a witty urban magazine that was a precursor to the *American Mercury,* which Nathan founded in 1924. Mencken was a primary contributor and edited the magazine until 1933. *The Smart Set* and *American Mercury* were two of a growing number of publications that came to symbolize the LITERATURE of the era. They challenged conventional norms with satire and humor. They helped to usher in one of the most noteworthy eras in American literature.

Mencken became one of the foremost social critics of the era. He ridiculed organized religion, pretension, provincialism, and businessmen. In one of his most infamous critiques, he referred to American middle-class businessmen as the "booboisie." He refused to accept the popularly held notion that successful businessmen were, by definition, better people. This placed him at odds with stalwart defenders of American capitalism. For many, he challenged society itself. On the heels of a scathing critique of American culture, Mencken was asked why he bothered living in a society that he held in such disdain. He simply remarked "for the same reason that people go to the zoo." Few were free from the wrath of his pen. In an unveiled attack on both American government and lawyers, he complained that "all the extravagance and incompetence of our present Government is due, in the main, to lawyers, and, in part at least, to good ones. They are responsible for nine-tenths of the useless and vicious laws that now clutter the statute-books, and for all the evils that go with the vain attempt to enforce them."

Mencken criticized the foundations of American society. He did not believe in democracy as it was practiced in the United States. The government, he believed, did not exist to help its citizens. It, he assured his readers, existed only to promote its own existence and expansion. It was apparent to many readers that Mencken had little respect for the so-called sacred institutions and he thought that Americans, and people in general, were ignorant and selfish. He once noted that, "No one has gone broke underestimating the intelligence of the American public."

The SCOPES TRIAL proved to Mencken that the American public was unfit for self-governance. Throughout the trial, he lambasted the American people for their ignorance and hatred. He was especially appalled by the fact that Americans seemed to have more faith in what he believed to be the incoherent ramblings of WILLIAM JENNINGS BRYAN than in the poignant, well-articulated arguments made by CLARENCE DARROW. The trial proved to Mencken that the American public was unwilling to accept the truth that was often before them, and therefore unfit to govern themselves. His opinions reflected many of the rural-urban tensions of the time as, in many respects, he exaggerated the strength of support for Bryan's position.

According to Mencken, PROHIBITION was an even more appalling example of the lack of judgment by the American people. He was convinced that unthinking, self-righteous individuals thrust Prohibition upon society. He was one of the first writers to point out the shortcomings of the amendment. In an article citing many of the failings of Prohibition, he sarcastically acknowledged one of its benefits. He noted that, "five years of Prohibition have had, at least, this one benign effect: they have completely disposed of all the favorite arguments of the Prohibitionists."

Mencken's wit and brilliance helped him to forge a literary genre that remains powerful even today, but he was more than one of the most popular writers of the era. He became a celebrity and wrote a number of books. Throughout his life, he remained a steadfast critic of American society. His criticisms were poignant and well articulated, but intolerance, mistrust, racism, and ANTI-SEMITISM also colored them. Mencken had a stroke in 1948 and died in 1956.

See also JOURNALISM.

Further reading: Richard J. Schrader, *H. L. Mencken : A Documentary Volume* (Detroit: Gale Group, 2000).

— Steve Freund

Mexican immigration

The migration of Mexicans north into the United States steadily increased between 1900 and 1930. The number of Mexican immigrants officially recorded as entering the United States grew from 49,000 between 1901 and 1910 to 219,000 from 1911 to 1920, and 459,000 in the 1920s. The ease in crossing the border between the United States and Mexico has always made it difficult to have an accurate count. Between 1900 and 1930, the number of Mexicans entering the United States far exceeded the "official" count. While a number of factors contributed to the movement of Mexicans north after 1900, much of the migration had its origins as a response to economic development in Mexico under President Porfirio Díaz during the last quarter of the 19th century.

Upon becoming president in 1876, Díaz faced two options for national development: either reorganize the agrarian sector to raise capital internally or leave domestic agriculture alone and turn instead to foreign investors for capital. Díaz favored the latter option. He quickly worked to improve the image of Mexico in an effort to increase foreign investment. In his first major initiative, Díaz expanded the national railroad system. Financed largely by American investors, this project linked the Mexican economy to the world market. Ignoring internal demands for an east-west railroad network, U.S. capital instead built in Mexico rail lines running north-south to ensure better American access to Mexico's cheap raw materials. The mining district of Sonora, for example, became better linked to the United States than to Mexico City. Moreover, the rail network facilitated the northward movement of Mexican workers displaced from the Mexican countryside. In his effort to modernize the country, Díaz established an export-based economy, making the country dependent on world market conditions. His program of development offered limited benefits to the country as a whole. Rather, the small economic elite received the major economic benefit of Díaz's policies. By 1910, the country sent 80 percent of its exports to, and received 66 percent of its imports from, the United States.

Although the expansion of Mexico's foreign trade brought new consumer goods and economic opportunities, widespread dissatisfaction appeared throughout the country. In urban areas, the growing wage labor force worked under extremely poor conditions, and the middle class resented the extent to which foreigners filled new professional jobs. Because the peasant population suffered large losses of land to foreign investors and Mexican elites, they lost their capacity for self-sufficiency. By 1910, the transformation affected nearly all of the rural population, creating an enormous, landless workforce and stimulating a massive migration of rural individuals to Mexican cities. While Díaz's program of foreign investment increased the wage labor sector, it failed to provide adequate resources or opportunities for laborers and the new landless class. Mexico's export-based economy further prevented the emergence of a substantial industrial sector that might have absorbed rural to urban migrants. In addition, the country's population grew by 50 percent between 1875 and 1910. This growth contributed to the limited wage labor opportunities available within Mexico.

The frustration caused by this economic development contributed to the outbreak of the MEXICAN REVOLUTION in 1910. Subsequent political instability motivated many Mexicans to migrate to the United States. Concurrently, the American Southwest (principally Texas, Arizona, and California) experienced rapid economic growth, largely in the labor-intensive areas of agriculture, mining, and railroads. In order to compete in the national market, industries sought ways to minimize their production costs. Because Díaz's economic development had resulted in better transportation connections between the United States and Mexico, American employers increasingly relied on Mexico as a cheap reservoir of both labor and raw materials. By the 1920s, the promise of higher wages easily attracted Mexican laborers to the United States. The average daily wage differed substantially between the two countries. In 1910, male agricultural workers in Mexico could anticipate making between 20 and 25 cents daily while their peers in the United States could expect to earn between 50 cents and one dollar per day. By 1920, the daily wage in the United States had risen to between $1 and $2, while in Mexico it remained virtually unchanged.

Higher wages were not the sole reason for the steady increase of Mexican immigrants to the United States during the 1920s. While the federal government enacted legislation that capped the total number of immigrants allowed to enter the United States annually, emigration from within the Western Hemisphere remained untouched by the QUOTA ACT of 1921 and the NATIONAL ORIGINS ACT of 1924. Over 450,000 Mexicans entered the United States during the 1920s, representing nearly 11 percent of the total immigrant population for the decade. In addition, thousands more took advantage of the relatively porous border and entered without the necessary visas. Although the 1924 National Origins Act did not apply any quotas on the number of Mexican immigrants, it did establish the Border Patrol under the authority of the U.S. Bureau of IMMIGRATION. Nevertheless, migrants still found ways across the border under the assistance of "coyotes," as the border-crossing experts came to be known.

For the most part, Mexican immigrants settled in Texas, Arizona, and California. The bulk of the American population was either unaware or unconcerned with this group. Through the 1920s, the response to Mexicans was varied, but it never reached the level of hostility that had been witnessed by Asian immigrants. The volume of Mexican immigration to the United States declined around 1928 as American consulates in Mexico started to enforce the literacy requirements of the IMMIGRATION ACT OF 1917. More than this stricter enforcement, the Great Depression brought a noticeable halt to the movement of Mexicans into the United States. Not only did large numbers of Mexicans voluntarily decide to return home, but also the United States forcibly repatriated many Mexicans who did not hold the proper documentation when many localities argued that immigrants were a drain on limited resources. The patterns of Mexican migration to fill the employment needs of such industries as agriculture, were well developed from 1900 to 1930. Following the Great Depression, employers in the southwest quickly turned to the federal government to create programs to supply them with sufficient numbers of employees from across the border in Mexico.

See also ETHNIC ORGANIZATIONS; RACE AND RACIAL CONFLICT.

Further reading: David Gutierrez, *Walls and Mirrors: Mexican Americans, Mexican Immigrants, and the Politics of Ethnicity* (Berkeley: University of California Press, 1995).

— David R. Smith

Mexican Invasion (1916–1917)

As an unsuccessful attempt to capture and punish Francisco "Pancho" Villa, a leader of the MEXICAN REVOLUTION, the Mexican invasion proved to be a costly embarrassment to the U.S. government and to President WOODROW WILSON. From March 1916 to January 1917, 6,000 U.S. Army troops under the command of General JOHN "BLACKJACK" PERSHING searched for Villa to punish him for the killing of Americans by his forces. Ultimately the expedition returned to the United States without ever finding Villa.

Pancho Villa was a leader in northern Mexico during the Mexican Revolution. He hoped to institute radical economic change that would benefit Mexico's industrial workforce and its agricultural workers. He initially courted U.S. support during the revolution and did not protest in 1915 when the U.S. Navy occupied Veracruz in an effort to determine the outcome of the revolution. When Woodrow Wilson threw his support behind a competing revolutionist, Venustiano Carranza, Villa launched an effort to punish the United States and Wilson in retaliation for what he saw as betrayal.

Villa forces first struck in January 1916 in northern Mexico by pulling 15 U.S. mining engineers from their train and murdering them. In March 1916, he sent nearly 500 men to attack Columbus, New Mexico. Villa's men terrorized the town for hours, killing 18 people, injuring scores more, and burning the town to the ground. The 13th Cavalry eventually drove Villa's forces out of New Mexico.

Demands for U.S. intervention to punish Villa were immediate. Some called for all-out war and occupation of Mexico. President Wilson avoided talk of war. Instead, he sent an expedition under General Pershing to capture Villa. Unfortunately for the United States, the organization of the expedition took one week. By the time the troops entered Mexico, Villa and his troops had covered their tracks. The U.S. Army wandered around Mexico looking for Villa. As they did, they met opposition from rural Mexicans who were the base for Villa's revolutionary movement. As they moved south, the Carranza government, which Wilson helped bring to power, began to see the American troops as a threat and ordered them to withdraw. In fact, the only confrontation during the invasion was between U.S. troops and the Carranza government's troops.

Despite their inability to capture Villa, the U.S. Army had weakened his position in the struggle for power in Mexico. While Villa fled Pershing's troops in northern Mexico, Carranza consolidated power in Mexico City. Preoccupied with Pershing's troops, Villa was unable to challenge Carranza for control of the Mexican government. The Mexican Invasion therefore played a role in the outcome of the Mexican Revolution by helping the pro-U.S. Carranza government consolidate power.

Further reading: Michael C. Meyer, and William L. Sherman, *The Course of Mexican History*, 3rd ed. (New York: Oxford University Press, 1995).

— Michael Hartman

Mexican Revolution (1910–1917)

The Mexican Revolution refers to a series of armed struggles that occurred from 1910 to 1917 and resulted in the creation of a new constitution under the government of Venustiano Carranza. The United States played an important role in both the cause of the revolutions and the outcome. The hardships created by the revolution also led many Mexicans to immigrate to the United States.

There were many political, economic and social causes of the revolution. Politically, widespread opposition to the 33-year dictatorship of Porfirio Díaz existed. Mexico's rapidly industrializing economy had created severe dislocations for many Mexicans. Díaz's government had pursued industrialization through agreement with foreign corporations, mainly from the United States and Great Britain. By 1911, for example, foreign companies owned the 80 largest commercial and industrial companies in Mexico. Companies from the United States controlled essential industries

Federalists watching the advance of rebels at Ojinaga, Mexico *(Library of Congress)*

such as mining, the railroads, oil, electric power, and the telegraph. Many Mexicans believed that the foreign corporations controlled too much of their country's economy.

The expansion of the railroad also played a key role in disenchantment with the Mexican government. As railroads infiltrated new areas, they brought industrial goods and opened up new markets for agricultural goods. This simultaneously put local producers out of business and led to an increase in agricultural production for export, both of which refocused the economic lives of millions of Mexicans from local concerns to international. These developments caused severe dislocations in rural Mexican society. Simultaneously, the new industrial workers laboring in foreign-owned factories were unhappy with their working conditions and wages. Many members of the middle class also resisted Díaz's economic policies. Business owners disagreed with his policies favoring foreign companies. They wanted both the economic benefits that industrialization brought and the independence from foreign control of their economy. The Mexican Revolution became, therefore, a many-sided affair.

The immediate cause of the revolution was an economic depression that began in 1907. The depression destroyed many businesses, leading to unrest among the middle classes who formed one of the most powerful groups in Mexico. In response to the unrest, Díaz called for presidential elections in 1910. Reversing his earlier

promise not to run for president again, he announced his candidacy and arrested his chief rival, Francisco Madero. Madero escaped police custody and fled to the United States, where he called for an armed insurrection against Díaz's government. Mexicans in several regions immediately took up arms.

The forces seeking the overthrow of Díaz coalesced around three leaders: Madero, Francisco (Pancho) Villa, and Emiliano Zapata. All three were fighting for the overthrow of Díaz but with different goals in mind. Villa, whose support came from the industrial north, sought radical economic change to benefit industrial workers. Zapata, who was based in the agricultural south, wanted agrarian reform. Madero and his supporters came from the middle class and hoped to gain control of the economy.

Faced with insurmountable opposition to his regime, Díaz signed a treaty with Madero that called for a new election in October 1911. Madero won the election and became president. He and his military commander, General Victoriano Huerta, quickly cracked down on their former allies in the revolution, killing and imprisoning many of Zapata and Villa's supporters. The military crackdown led to a rebellion against the government by workers and peasants. In 1913, feeling that Madero was not doing enough to quell the violence, Huerta led a coup that ended in the president's assassination. Huerta then assumed the presidency.

Huerta's violent takeover led to another round of violence as different factions fought to overthrow his illegitimate presidency. Villa and Zapata now directed their forces against Huerta. A third force emerged led by Venustiano Carranza, a former governor under Díaz, who sought to protect constitutional government and democratic rights. His followers became known as the Constitutionalists.

At this point, the United States got involved. President WOODROW WILSON enacted a financial blockade and arms embargo against Huerta's illegitimate government. The United States also aided the anti-Huerta forces, particularly the Constitutionalists. In 1914, the United States intervened even further by invading the half of Mexico port of Veracruz to stop a shipment of arms from reaching Huerta's forces. For a variety of reasons, U.S. intervention helped the Constitutionalists more than Zapata and Villa. Facing hostile forces from four sides, Huerta resigned on July 8, 1914. Reaching Mexico City first, Carranza and the Constitutionalists reached an agreement with Mexico's largest labor union that gave them overwhelming numerical strength. Carranza was thus able to proclaim himself president.

The revolution then entered a third and final phase that saw conflict between the Carranza government and the forces of Zapata and Villa. With aid from the United States, the government defeated the two rebel forces. The Mexican Revolution left Mexico with a government that came to power with the aid of the United States. Thus, a revolution that began partly as an attempt to reduce the influence of U.S. corporations ended with a government that owed the United States its victory. The revolution also played a significant role in enlarging the Mexican-American population of the United States as many Mexicans fled the inflation, violence, and social chaos of the revolution by immigrating to the United States.

See also MEXICAN INVASION.

Further reading: Michael C. Meyer and William L. Sherman, *The Course of Mexican History,* 3rd ed. (New York: Oxford University Press, 1995).

— Michael Hartman

Middletown (1929)

In 1929, sociologists Robert and Helen Merrell Lynd published the groundbreaking study, *Middletown: A Study in Modern American Culture.* The Lynds used sociological methods to examine the lives of ordinary American citizens in a midwestern city, Muncie, Indiana. One of the first community studies, *Middletown* served as a model for sociological research for generations to come. Robert Lynd, a Protestant minister, was committed to the ideas of the Social Gospel, a social movement within American Protestantism concerned with social justice and redeeming the nation's cities. The Lynds' concern about the influence of the modern urban world on traditional Protestant values thus became central to the study of *Middletown.*

The Lynds' study of Middletown was intended to explore how industry, urbanization, and consumption influenced traditional American values in the 1920s. They chose Muncie as their site for research because it appeared to be less affected by these modern forces. Initially funded by the Institute for Social and Religious Research, a John D. Rockefeller foundation dealing with the preservation of traditional American values, the Lynds purposefully did not choose an ethnically diverse city. Instead, they studied a "traditional vanishing white, Anglo-Saxon, Protestant city, which was . . . the center of old-fashioned American virtue." The Lynds thought, "The hope for social progress and moral reawakening resided . . . within the original American spirit, the adventurous, strong spirit of the Protestant pioneers of the Midwest." But when the Lynds found that dramatic changes in traditional American values had already transformed Muncie, the institute distanced itself from the publication of *Middletown.*

The Lynds found varying institutional adaptations to the modernizing forces at work in *Middletown.* They claimed that the highest degree of change had occurred in earning a living and leisure-time activities. Both changes were attributed to technological innovations. In the case of work, the rise of the industrial system created two major groups, the working and business classes. Meanwhile, greater organization of leisure time resulted from such technological developments as the automobile and moving pictures. While the informal contact of the past had encouraged the development of close-knit ties between people in the midwestern city, the technological changes in leisure-time activities were creating a highly mobile and organized group life that left residents more isolated in *Middletown.*

The Lynds found that consumer values had begun to replace the older Puritan values of frugality, austerity, and civic-mindedness. They believed that community members in Muncie, no longer each other's moral keepers, still retained a strong belief in competitive individualism. In addition, the community was characterized by a class system, divided between the "business class" and the "working class." The Lynds' examination of how competitive individualism replaced the older values of white, Anglo-Saxon, Protestant culture was a significant contribution that influenced a whole generation of sociologists.

By focusing on traditional American values, the Lynds ignored important trends that were part of Muncie's development. For example, southern "hillbillies" and African Americans were absent from the study, even though both groups already had become significant minorities in

Muncie by the 1920s. In addition, critics have pointed out that Muncie's dominant industrial family, the Ball brothers, were missing from the study as well. Evidently, the Lynds viewed such a dominant family as the norm and not of any special importance worthy of study. Even though their analysis of the class system was innovative, their examination of the decline of Protestant values obscured some of the demographic and cultural subtleties that transformed Muncie. In 1937, the Lynds returned to Muncie to see how the city had changed during the Great Depression. In *Middletown in Transition,* they concluded that not much had changed. Finding the values of the citizens of Muncie relatively unaffected by the economic crisis, the Lynds wrote, "The texture of Middletown's culture has not changed . . . Middletown is overwhelmingly living by the values by which it lived in 1925."

Further reading: Rita Caccamo, *Back to Middletown: Three Generations of Sociological Reflections* (Stanford, Calif.: Stanford University Press, 2000); Robert S. Lynd, and Helen Merrell Lynd, *Middletown: A Study in Modern American Culture* (New York: Harcourt, Brace & World, 1929).

— Glen Bessemer

Mitchell, John (1870–1919)

John Mitchell was one of the first presidents of the UNITED MINE WORKERS OF AMERICA (UMWA) and helped establish the organization as one of the most effective and progressive unions in the country. Born in Braidwood, Illinois, on February 4, 1870, Mitchell was orphaned at the age of six. He attended school only irregularly and began working in the mines at the age of 12. When not toiling underground, Mitchell spent his time reading and taught himself history, economics, and the law. In 1885, at the age of 15, he joined the Knights of Labor. Frustrated by the decline of the Knights and its inability to conduct successful strikes, Mitchell joined the UMWA shortly after the union was formed in 1890. Between 1890 and 1900, the union had considerable success at organizing the nation's bituminous miners. As the union grew, Mitchell moved up the ranks, becoming vice president in 1898 and president in 1899.

For a variety of reasons, the UMWA had not been able to organize anthracite miners. Anthracite mines had a greater variety of job categories, operated on a larger scale, and had greater ethnic diversity among their workers. The union had, without success, tried to organize anthracite miners on several occasions. In 1897, the UMWA initiated another organizing effort and quickly had widespread success. Employer opposition, however, remained intense and the organizing drive came to a head in 1902. In April and

May of 1902, Mitchell met with mine operators and railroad executives in an attempt to avoid an industry-wide walkout. When the companies refused to grant any concessions, the miners voted 57 percent to 43 percent to go out on strike. The ANTHRACITE COAL STRIKE idled over 140,000 miners and lasted five months. As the strike lingered on and the nation's supply of coal dwindled, President THEODORE ROOSEVELT intervened and appointed an Anthracite Coal Strike Committee to resolve the differences between the workers and the mine operators.

Roosevelt, who was attempting to establish a reputation as a critic of business monopolies, and Senator Mark Hanna of Ohio who sought organized labor's support of the REPUBLICAN PARTY, saw the 1902 strike as an opportunity to rebuke coal and railroad operators. Roosevelt ordered striking workers back into the mines while the Anthracite Coal Strike Committee gathered information about the dispute. After five months of deliberation, it called for a 10 percent pay increase and a reduction in the workday from 10 hours to nine. The successful conclusion of the strike made Mitchell a national hero for many workers.

The strike and negotiations, however, had left Mitchell exhausted. He had a nervous breakdown in 1906 and resigned as head of the UMWA in 1908. Mitchell remained active in the labor movement, serving on commissions and giving public lectures, until his death from pneumonia in 1919. As head of the UMWA, Mitchell navigated a path between the more conservative AMERICAN FEDERATION OF LABOR and the more radical INDUSTRIAL WORKERS OF THE WORLD. He was not hesitant to resort to strikes and direct confrontations when employers proved reluctant to negotiate. Yet, he also cooperated with business and political leaders in such joint efforts as the NATIONAL CIVIC FEDERATION in order to settle disputes. As a result, Mitchell was able to build the UMWA into one of the strongest unions in the country.

Further reading: John H. M. Laslett, ed., *The United Mine Workers of America: A Model of Industrial Solidarity?* (University Park: Pennsylvania State University Press, 1996); Melvyn Dubofsky and Warren Van Tine, eds., *Labor Leaders in America* (Urbana: University of Illinois Press, 1986).

— Robert Gordon

Mitchell, William (Billy) (1879–1936)

If, in the annals of American military history, men such as John Ericsson and George Patton are viewed as visionaries, then the name of Billy Mitchell should be a part of that class. His visionary adroitness and crusader zeal made possible not only the creation of the U.S. Air Force, but also set the strategic underpinnings of air power's role in future wars. Billy Mitchell, son of a future U.S. senator from Wisconsin, was born in Nice, France, in 1879. Raised in Milwaukee, Wisconsin, he was educated at both Racine College and George Washington University. Upon the outbreak of the Spanish-American War, Mitchell enlisted in the U.S. Army as a private in 1898. Within six weeks, he received a commission as a Signal Corps officer. In addition to service in Cuba, he saw action during the Philippine insurrection and the Mexican expedition against Pancho Villa.

As early as 1906, Mitchell prophesied that "conflicts, no doubt, will be carried out in the future in the air." After the army purchased its first aircraft, he wrote several articles stressing the importance of aircraft in war. He argued that airplanes would be useful for reconnaissance, for preventing enemy forces from conducting reconnaissance, and for offensive action against enemy submarines and ships. Due to the advances being made in aeronautical technology, Mitchell argued, the United States was being drawn ever closer to its enemies, and that distance would soon be measured in time not miles. These facts underlined the importance of developing air power. He was assigned to the Army General Staff in Washington in 1912 as a captain.

After being promoted to major, Mitchell was too high ranking and too old for flight training. Firmly believing that the future lay in aviation, however, he paid for his own flight training at a civilian flight school. When the United States entered WORLD WAR I, Mitchell quickly rose to the rank of colonel. He was appointed to General JOHN PERSHING's staff as an aviation officer. His actions in France culminated with his command of a 1,481-plane air attack, the largest of the war, during the St. Mihiel offensive of September 1918. In 1919, Mitchell returned to the United States a much-decorated officer and was appointed assistant chief of the U.S. Army Air Service. By 1920, he was promoted to the rank of brigadier general.

The postwar years, however, saw the parochial interests of army generals and navy admirals supersede Mitchell's dream of a prepared and well-equipped Air Service. In June and July 1921, Mitchell took on the Department of the Navy and demonstrated his theory of air power by sinking several battleships, including the German battleship *Ostfriesland,* off the Virginia coast. Never at a loss for words, Mitchell pronounced that "no surface vessels can exist wherever air forces acting from land bases are able to attack them." This and other declarations concerning the preeminence of air power earned him the undying enmity of generals and admirals alike.

In 1924 Mitchell continued his crusade by attacking his superiors and the foes of air power in both print and speech. It is little wonder that he was not reappointed to the Air Service when his term expired in 1925. Reduced to the rank of colonel and exiled to Fort Sam Houston in Texas, it was hoped that the last had been heard about and from Billy Mitchell.

Fortunately for his country and unfortunately for Mitchell, this was not to be the case. In September, two aviation accidents occurred. The first was the loss of a naval seaplane on a nonstop flight from San Francisco to Hawaii. The second was the crash of the dirigible *Shenandoah.* Mitchell's acerbic pen struck a scathing attack upon both the U.S. Navy and the War Department, accusing them of incompetence and criminal negligence.

Secretary of War Dwight F. Davis was outraged at Mitchell's attack. A court-martial board was convened in Washington on October 28, 1925. After seven weeks, the board found Mitchell guilty of the charge of insubordination. Mitchell resigned from the army on February 1, 1926. After many tireless years of sounding the alarm from the wilderness, Mitchell died in New York on February 19, 1936, at the age of 56. He was laid to rest in Milwaukee. The events of World War II vindicated Mitchell's vision and even though his conviction was never overturned, he did receive a special Congressional Medal of Honor "in recognition of his outstanding pioneer service and foresight in the field of American military aviation."

Further reading: Isaac Don Levine, *Mitchell: Pioneer of Air Power* (New York: Duell, Sloan, and Pearce, 1958); Alfred F. Hurley, *Crusader for Air Power* (Bloomington: Indiana University Press, 1975).

— Paul Edelen

modernism

Modernism was an intellectual and cultural movement that began at the turn of the 20th century and lasted until the end of World War II. As a term, modernism was first used in Germany during the 1890s and spread across Europe. The continued strain of technological innovation, the introduction of SIGMUND FREUD's theories of the unconscious, dream interpretation, and free association, and the growing sense of individual fragility in the face of modern society fueled a cultural rebellion against genteel culture and its rigid moral code and also against convention and tradition. Nonrepresentational or abstract art, free verse, and indirect imagist techniques in poetry and novels were central to this new artistic vision.

In the field of visual art, painters began to explore form and substance, rather than concentrate on fine-tuning realist techniques that were better reproduced with photography. Prevalent artistic movements within modernism included Art Nouveau, fauvism, and expressionist, futurist, cubist, dadaist, and abstract ART. In each case, there was a movement away from representation to using indirect and abstract forms. In the United States, modernism gained its first national notice with the experimental ARMORY SHOW of 1913, which brought to American artists the work of European impressionists and expressionists.

The movement toward modernist poetry had one of its chief centers in Chicago with Harriet Monroe's *Poetry: A Magazine of Verse,* first published in 1912, and Margaret Anderson's *The Little Review,* which began publication in 1914. Anderson drew on the modernist circle that formed in GREENWICH VILLAGE and included writers and social critics such as Max Eastman, Mary Heaton Vorse, Hutchins Hapgood, JOHN REED, and Eugene O'Neill. Monroe turned *Poetry* into the first imagist showcase when she wrote to Ezra Pound to persuade him to recruit his circle of poets to publish in the journal. Other modernist poets such as Thomas Stearns Eliot, H. D. (Hilda Doolittle), Gertrude Stein, e.e. cummings, and William Carlos Williams contributed to the growing acceptance of free verse and indirect representation of feeling through images associated with modernism.

The modernist impulse similarly influenced historical LITERATURE and the genre of the novel, particularly in the years after WORLD WAR I. While historians Charles and Mary Beard and Carl Becker reworked historical narrative and questioned historical objectivity, novelists such as John Dos Passos experimented with introducing multiple narrative lines and collage-like prose. Most importantly, the ideals of honesty and rebellion against convention brought new, diverse voices into art and literature. Among the artistic movements in the United States associated with modernism was the HARLEM RENAISSANCE that brought African-American traditions and racial experience to the forefront of American culture.

See also MUSIC.

Further reading: Abraham A. Davidson, *Early American Modernist Painting, 1910–1935* (New York: Harper & Row, 1981); Barbara Haskell, *Art & Culture, 1900–1950* (New York: W.W. Norton, 1999).

— Marcia M. Farah

Mooney-Billings case

Heightened class conflict in the Progressive Era sometimes involved the direct intervention of the government. In the Mooney-Billings case, political protests against military preparedness led to the conviction of two labor leaders for murder. The case became a celebrated cause for labor and radical reformers. On July 22, 1916, a bomb went off at a Preparedness Day parade in San Francisco, California. The Pacific Coast Defense League had sponsored the parade, following a successful one in New York City, to strengthen public support for military armament during WORLD WAR I.

Local newspapers estimated that the parade in San Francisco had over 50,000 participants. Ten people were killed and 40 seriously injured in the bombing. The police responded inconsistently. It was not until two and a half hours later that police roped off the scene, and authorities did not supervise the collection of evidence. Consequently, souvenir hunters combed the site, destroying relevant evidence along the way. As a result, the police department later had to publish a request for the return of evidence found at the scene to authorities.

In a climate of wartime hysteria, city leaders and newspaper editors accused PREPAREDNESS opponents and anarchists of the bombing. With irresponsible JOURNALISM feeding public outcry, five local radicals were arrested and indicted for murder. Out of the four that were tried, two were convicted. The men who were convicted, Warren Billings and Tom Mooney, were left-wing activists who had participated in local labor struggles over the years. Billings received a sentence of life imprisonment, Mooney death by hanging.

Evidence soon emerged that perjury had been committed and that the prosecution had withheld evidence. After his conviction, Mooney became internationally famous as a martyr for radicals, organized labor, and defenders of civil rights. Representing over 50 labor and radical organizations in San Francisco, the International Workers Defense League, of which Mooney was an active member, petitioned and lobbied for the pardon of Mooney and Billings. They also sent organizers around the country to raise funds and awareness for the legal defense of the two men. Some people, however, saw the two men as a radical threat to patriotism and law and order during World War I. In March 1918, the California Supreme Court upheld Mooney's conviction. Two weeks before Mooney was scheduled to hang, Governor William D. Stephens commuted his sentence to life imprisonment. Stephens said that President WOODROW WILSON had made repeated requests for him to do so and that new evidence had emerged in the case, though the governor failed to mention what the evidence was.

Radicals and organized labor supported Mooney's cause for another two decades. In 1939 Governor Culbert L. Olson declared that he believed Mooney was innocent and pardoned him, stating that the conviction had been based on perjured testimony. Billings, however, remained in prison for 10 more months after Mooney's pardon. Olson could not pardon Billings without the approval of the unsympathetic state supreme court in California. When the court repeatedly voted against pardoning Billings, Olson commuted his sentence to time served. In a ceremony the day after Billings was released, Olson apologized for not being able to pardon him, noting that he thought that Billings was innocent. In 1961, 45 years later, Governor

Edmund G. Brown gave Billings a complete pardon after he received the approval of the state supreme court.

Further reading: Richard H. Frost, *The Mooney Case* (Stanford, Calif.: Stanford University Press, 1968); Curt Gentry, *Frame-up: The Incredible Case of Tom Mooney and Warren Billings* (New York: W. W. Norton, 1967).

— Glen Bessemer

Morgan, John Pierpont   See Volume VI

mothers' pensions

Mothers' pensions were state-level relief benefits designed to support the children of widowed mothers. The forerunner of the Aid to Dependent Children program developed under the New Deal, mothers' pensions provided small cash grants to supplement the income of impoverished widows who supported themselves through wage-earning but needed additional funds. Advocates of mothers' pensions believed that the income supplement would encourage women to keep their children at home, rather than send them to orphanages. They also argued that the pensions would persuade widowed women to take jobs or engage in home work that allowed them to spend the maximum amount of time at home.

An early attempt to pass a statute for the support of widowed women took place in New York in 1897. The state legislature nearly passed a Destitute Mothers' bill, which would have given deserted women a right to public relief. The timing, however, was wrong. Social work advocates were only just beginning to shake off the legacy of scientific charity, and opponents of the bill could count on public opposition when they nicknamed the measure "the Shiftless Father's Act." By 1910, the political climate had changed. Mothers' pensions can be seen as part of the larger campaign of "child saving" in the Progressive Era. Linked to other reforms in education, the playground movement, child labor laws, and juvenile justice, the mothers' pension program sought to provide the best care for poor and working-class children. The same ideal of scientific motherhood that inspired the reformers of the CHILDREN'S BUREAU shaped the mothers' pension program. Financial support of women's role within the family, it was hoped, would give incentives to mothers to provide better parental care and supervision.

Juvenile court judges were among the first advocates of mother's allowances. Judge E. E. Porterfield of Kansas City lobbied the Missouri legislature to pass a measure giving mothers' aid to women in Jackson County. Illinois created the first statewide program for mothers' pensions in early 1911. Supported by divergent groups such as the National Congress of Mothers, the General Federation of Women's Clubs, and settlement house workers, the push for mothers' aid spread quickly through northern, midwestern, and western states. Within two years, 20 states had passed mothers' aid laws. By the 1920s, 40 states and hundreds of counties in the United States had mothers' pensions programs.

Despite the best intentions of its advocates, the mothers' pensions system failed to live up to its purpose of alleviating the plight of poor children and protecting motherhood. Most states and counties did not have the funds or the political support to expand the mothers' pension program beyond its modest beginnings and could not raise enough public monies to fund the system. States failed to fund existing mothers' pensions adequately, due to popular resistance to new property taxes and the absence of any alternatives. Further, many localities refused to develop new agencies and programs for widows. Even in terms of its original modest aims, the mothers' pension movement had severe drawbacks. Limited in its coverage, it did not fund women who were either deserted or divorced, and its provisions barred unwed mothers from eligibility.

Framed in the language of sacred motherhood, the mothers' pension effort dictated that its recipients be the moral and deserving poor. Those who received pensions were under moral scrutiny both when they applied and while they received the pension. At the same time, the program demonstrated racial and ethnic exclusivity, especially in the South. Most early recipients of the mothers' pensions were white, native-born women. Finally, as a state-level program, mothers' pensions never became the deserved "pension" for mothers that its most radical advocates desired. Mothers' pensions were tied to the number and age of children. No support was provided for the widow herself, and the stigma of poor relief, with its moral supervision and public disdain, remained.

In the 1930s, the collapse of local relief agencies and the lack of funding, combined with the new policy initiatives, provided the impetus for the development of a federally funded program in 1935 called Aid to Dependent Children. This program also suffered from the failures and limitations of its parent program. State-level administration, miserly grants, chronic lack of funds, moral supervision, and the stigma of relief continued to hobble efforts to provide single mothers, whether divorced, deserted, or widowed, with decent income support in hard times.

Further reading: Joanne Goodwin, *Gender and the Politics of Welfare Reform: Mother's Pensions in Chicago, 1911–1929* (Chicago: University of Chicago Press, 1997); Linda Gordon, *Pitied but Not Entitled; Single Mothers and the History of Welfare, 1890–1935* (New York: Free Press, 1994).

movie industry

The emergence of the motion picture industry was one of the most important social, cultural, and economic developments of the early 20th century. It helped to define and mold social values and norms. It assisted in the homogenization of American culture, and it provided accessible and affordable entertainment to the general public. In contrast with European film, which was viewed as an elite art form, movies in America were geared toward a mass audience.

When movies first emerged as a form of entertainment, they were hampered by limitations in technology. The most significant limitation was the inability to successfully integrate sound into moving pictures. It had a democratizing effect on the population. Language barriers, which often hampered immigrants' ability to fully enjoy English-language theater, were not a factor for silent films. Immigrants unable to speak or understand English were able to enjoy the comedy of Charlie Chaplin and the tragic genius of Rudolph Valentino and Greta Garbo.

Movies did not emerge overnight. The movie camera was developed in the late 19th century. Thomas Edison Laboratories created the first successful camera in 1889. Five years later, Edison's technicians perfected the Kinetoscope, a large wooden box with a peephole at the top through which customers could view the pictures. Edison, however, did not take adequate steps in protecting his

Charlie Chaplin in *A Dog's Life,* with Edna Purviance *(Library of Congress)*

invention. He filed only for American patents. As a result, his two assistants, W. K. Laurie Dickson and Eugene Lauste, broke away and patented their own inventions. They formed the American Mutoscope and Biograph Company, backed by a number of influential Americans. The most notable of their backers was Ohio governor and future president, William McKinley.

The development of the motion picture marked much more than a technological innovation. It signaled the beginning of an industry that would redefine American art and culture. The industry began slowly. At first, it was seen only as a source of amazement. To address the public fascination with the technology, movie producers focused on the appeal of the technology; the development and production of stories was a mere afterthought. Early novelty films were little more than still pictures put into motion.

As the technology improved, so too did the scope of films. Edwin Stratton Porter (1870–1941), who began his career in 1896, was instrumental in the development of the motion picture from novelty to art form. Porter was a Scotsman who settled in America with no theatrical experience. He eventually became the master of the edit. Through the editing process, he was able to modify films and in the process distort perceptions of reality. In late 1902 or early 1903, he created *Life of an American Fireman.* It was his first real motion picture. Later in 1903, he realized his sophomore work, *The Great Train Robbery,* the first of a long line of classic Western movies.

D. W. GRIFFITH further developed the idea of a motion picture not only telling stories but also defining reality. He was introduced to film in Porter's *Rescue from an Eagle's Nest* in 1907. He played the father hero. Even then, Griffith did not see himself as an actor. In fact, in order to save his name for greater endeavors, he went by the alias Lawrence Griffith. Griffith envisioned himself as a great theatrical producer, but success in the theater eluded him. His first and last theatrical production was a flop. In 1908 he directed his first film, *The Adventures of Dollie.* Less then a decade later, in 1915, he released the most ambitious movie of his time, BIRTH OF A NATION.

Unlike many films released in Europe, movies made in the United States were extremely short. *Birth of a Nation* challenged this idea. It was among the first full-length American feature films. It also changed the rules of how movies would be shot. Griffith moved the camera up close, which allowed for the development of intimacy between camera and audience. He integrated these with medium and distance shots. From this point on, movies became a way to convey thought and emotion. Innovation of filming techniques, however, was not the most notable accomplishment of the movie. One of the most noteworthy results of the movie was the response it provoked from different people. While large segments of society boasted of its sheer greatness, others protested its message. The release of *Birth of a Nation* made it clear that movies could and would influence the way people viewed certain events. The movie portrayed the Reconstruction era of American history in such a way that large segments of society, especially blacks, found it offensive. It degraded African Americans, insulted northerners, and idealized the KU KLUX KLAN.

The political possibilities of movies were evident even before the release of *Birth of a Nation.* One of the first Edison films to be shown in April of 1896 was *The Monroe Doctrine and Cuba Libra.* It was the first overtly political film. Politics, however, was only one of the many topics that films embraced. Another, as exemplified in *Birth of a Nation,* was history. The most recognizable of the history films were the stories of the American West. In the 1920s, epic Westerns became the films of choice. Like *Birth of a Nation,* these films were developed upon a loose interpretation of American history. Savage Indians forced the brave and heroic settler to fend off attacks. The *Covered Wagon* (1923) was just one of the many movies of the era that championed this perception of American history and cinema.

Alongside the development of dramatic pictures came comedies. Mack Sennett (1884–1960) released his version of an epic Western, *The Uncovered Wagon,* which, like his other films, displayed the comic side of life. Sennett was a former coworker of Griffith's. He took the comic film to new level through the development of slapstick comedy. Sennett's Keystone Kops came to represent this new form of entertainment. He understood that slapstick comedy was as natural for the movie industry as action and melodrama, because all three topics unutilized motion and timing.

The greatest comic actor of the era was Charlie Chaplin. Chaplin was born in England in 1889. He toured the United States with his family in 1910 and returned in 1912. The following year, he joined Sennett's comedy team. Chaplin's early shows were one- and two-reelers such as *The Pawnshop* (1916) and *Easy Street* (1917). He later stared in a number of medium-length films, such as *Shoulder Arms* (1918) and *The Kid* (1921). His major films were *The Gold Rush* (1925) and *City Lights* (1931). Chaplin's career lasted more than three decades. He entered the industry only a few years after Griffith, but he was still producing and directing films 30 years after Griffith's last major production.

During the first decades of the 20th century, the center of the movie industry moved from the East Coast to the West Coast. In 1910, D. W. Griffith and Cecil B. De Mille (1881–1959) helped to transplant filmmaking to California, where the land was cheap and the climate and scenery ideal for developing motion pictures. The fact that Los Angeles had a reputation as a staunch anti-union town further heightened its appeal.

WORLD WAR I proved to be a true catalyst to the development of the American movie industry. The United States was the only leading film-producing country (except for Italy) that did not enter the war in 1914. When the United States finally did enter the war, its participation was on a smaller scale than that of other nations. The American film industry never experienced the restrictions or lack of supplies that the filmmakers in European nations experienced. Not even European movie stars like Max Linder were excused from the war effort. The war devastated the European film industry and provided a vacuum that American film producers could fill. As a result, the United States was producing 90 percent of the world's movies by war's end.

When movies first emerged, they were targeted to the widest audience possible. John P. Harris and Harry Davis opened the first nickelodeon in Pittsburgh in 1905. Patrons could view a movie for five cents. It was well within the means of typical working-class people. As a result, the industry spread rapidly. Less than 12 months after the first nickelodeon appeared in Pittsburgh, there were more than 100 such enterprises in that city alone. By 1908 the number of nickelodeons in the United States had reached an astounding 10,000.

The movie industry did not remain fully faithful to its working-class origins. The discretionary income of the middle class made them a coveted target. As a result, movies became big business. The emergence of major movie studios allowed for full development of the industry. Large studios such as Metro-Goldwyn-Mayer made movies of increasing cost and complexity. With the added cost, only the biggest producers could take on such tasks. Actors too began to charge more for their work. It was clear that movies were indeed big business.

In the late 1920s, the major studios converted their production facilities from silent movies to talkies. These new movies had substantial commercial success. *The Jazz Singer,* produced by Warner Brothers, was the first feature-length movie to incorporate talking and sound and music effects. *The Jazz Singer,* starring Al Jolson, redefined the industry. In order to survive, movie industry moguls had to produce films with sound. It made the industry even more capital intensive, but it did not slow the growth of the industry. By the end of the 1920s, the nation had more than 22,000 movie theaters, and movie attendance rose to 90 million by 1930. Movies became the chief form of entertainment for the mass audience.

Further reading: D. J. Wenden, *The Birth of the Movies* (New York: Macdonald, 1974); Robert M. Henderson, *D. W. Griffith: His Life and Work* (New York: Oxford University Press, 1972).

— Steve Freund

muckrakers

Muckraker was the name given to investigative journalists in the Progressive Era. They were responding to concerns about the urban crisis, excessive corporate power, and political corruption. Following in the footsteps of reform journalists of an earlier day, they sought to make the truth about poverty, vice, and injustice known. Once the public was informed, they would demand that government address the problems of influence-peddling, monopoly practices, and employer negligence. Progressive and left-wing organizations such as the INDUSTRIAL WORKERS OF THE WORLD, the Socialist Party of America, and the PROGRESSIVE PARTY, which had their roots in the political turmoil of the 1890s, emerged full-force in the first decade of the new century. Key to the ability of alternative political parties to gain a foothold in American politics were advancements in communication and the spread of national newspapers and journals that specialized in investigative reporting.

Between 1900 and the outbreak of WORLD WAR I, a loosely aligned group of progressive and radical journalists began warning that the nation's excesses and inequalities were creating a crisis in American society and had to be brought under control. Labeled muckrakers by President THEODORE ROOSEVELT, these writers and journalists elevated the use of investigative journalism and political fiction to new heights. The most prominent muckrakers exposed political and corporate corruption. In so doing, they developed a widespread readership and helped establish investigative journalism as an influential medium of communication. The work of muckrakers began appearing in an ever-increasing number of newspapers, journals, and books.

From publicly elected officials to the nation's most influential boardrooms, no prominent entity in American life escaped the scrutiny of the new generation of reform journalists. In *The Shame of the Cities,* LINCOLN STEFFENS railed against political machines and the power of business, which—he argued—were lining their pockets, undermining democracy, and corrupting the nation's political, legal, and economic systems at the expense of the common man and traditional values. In 1902, IDA TARBELL exposed how JOHN D. ROCKEFELLER had ruthlessly created a monopoly through his company, STANDARD OIL. In 1904, Tarbell's articles were consolidated in *The History of the Standard Oil Company.* Her attacks on Rockefeller helped create public support for federal antitrust action against Standard Oil that finally broke the company apart in 1911. In a different vein, journalist and author David Graham Phillips addressed political corruption at the highest levels in a 1906 series of articles in *Cosmopolitan,* which he later published as *The Treason of the Senate.* Nor did muckrakers ignore the labor movement. During the 1902 ANTHRACITE COAL STRIKE, Ray Stannard Baker examined the other side of labor in "The Right to Work."

It was the growth of the magazine industry that offered muckraking journalists a forum for their reform crusade. *McClure's Magazine,* founded in 1893 and published until 1929, was the early home of many muckrakers. Lincoln Steffens edited *McClure's* between 1902 and 1906. Determined to make the magazine a financial and political success, Steffens hired a staff of progressive writers and journalists. As editor, Steffens transformed *McClure's* into the leading political magazine in the country. Under his leadership, sales of the magazine expanded, as did its influence among progressives, radicals, socialists, and communists. In 1906 Steffens, along with Tarbell and Baker, decided to leave the magazine to form a new, more radical journal, *American Magazine.*

Between 1900 and 1916, muckraking journalists played an important role in exposing fraud and corruption and in pressuring politicians to make progressive reforms. Public outrage following the publication of UPTON SINCLAIR's muckraking expose of meatpacking in 1906 prompted an investigation of the industry. It convinced Congress and President Theodore Roosevelt of the need for federal intervention and led to the passage of the MEAT INSPECTION ACT (1906) and the PURE FOOD AND DRUG ACT (1906). Other reform legislation influenced by progressive journalists included the HEPBURN ACT (1906), CLAYTON ANTITRUST ACT (1914), ADAMSON ACT (1915), WORKMEN'S COMPENSATION ACT (1916), and the child labor, KEATING-OWEN ACT (1916).

See also JOURNALISM; RADICAL PRESS.

Further reading: Carl Jensen, *Stories That Changed America: Muckrakers of the 20th Century* (New York: Seven Stories Press, 2000); Justin Kaplan, *Lincoln Steffens: A Biography* (New York: Simon & Schuster, 1974); Kathleen Brady, *Ida Tarbell: Portrait of a Muckraker* (New York: Seaview/Putnam, 1984).

— Robert Gordon

Muller v. Oregon (1908)

The U.S. Supreme Court decision in *Muller v. Oregon* upheld maximum hours legislation for women. It was an important victory for many female activists. Progressive reformers had concentrated their attention on industrial ills. Their agitation led to enactment of child labor laws, maximum hours and minimum wage legislation, and minimum sanitation and safety standards in a variety of work places. Initial attempts at labor legislation met with mixed reviews from the state and federal courts. The earliest successful campaigns centered on regulating child labor. The special leeway accorded to children soon opened the door for women, who were perceived as similarly disadvantaged. In the long run, the *Muller* decision allowed states to limit the hours of male contractors on state jobs, and then maximum hours legislation for all. Female activists heralded *Muller* as a victory not because of its future impact on men's hours, but rather because they believed that such legislation was necessary to protect women workers. The victory came, however, at the cost of reinforcing women's status as a protected and dependent class.

The issue in *Muller v. Oregon* was a 1903 Oregon act that made it illegal to employ laundresses for more than 10 hours a day. The question was whether the act violated a woman's freedom to contract her own labor. In September 1905, laundry-owner Curt Muller was fined for requiring Emma Gotcher, a laundress and labor activist, to work more than 10 hours on Labor Day. Muller's attorney, William Fenton, was confident that the courts would rule in his client's favor, given recent court decisions in *Ritchie v. People* (1895) and LOCHNER V. NEW YORK (1905). The Illinois Supreme Court in *Ritchie* had invalidated a law that would have limited the time a woman could be employed in factories or workshops to no more than eight hours a day. Similarly, in *Lochner*, the U.S. Supreme Court struck down a law that would have set a maximum hours standard for male bakers. In both cases, the courts decided the legislation was an inappropriate usage of the state's police powers and restricted an individual's right to contract without due process of law. In his arguments before the Supreme Court, Fenton reiterated that women were persons and citizens with the same rights as men and therefore had the same right to labor and liberty of contract.

When the *Muller* case was sent on appeal to the U.S. Supreme Court, the National Consumers League approached LOUIS BRANDEIS to defend the maximum hours statute. The league sought to educate the public, lobby legislatures, and pressure employers in order to improve workplace conditions. It also tracked the court battles surrounding the regulatory statutes in which it took interest. As part of their agreement, the league supplied massive amounts of data to support the Brandeis brief in the case.

The famous Brandeis Brief consisted of two pages of legal citations, most of which rested on the *Lochner* precedent. Louis Brandeis believed that the *Lochner* decision allowed that, if a valid reason could be found to justify regulating hours of labor, a statute would withstand judicial scrutiny. Accordingly, Brandeis and the National Consumers League collected employment statistics from Europe and the United States documenting the effects of long hours and hazardous conditions on women workers. Brandeis based his defense of the Oregon law on the state's police powers, the delicate physical condition of women, and their special role as the bearers of children. The health

of children, and therefore society's general welfare, depended on protecting women as mothers or future mothers from overwork.

The Supreme Court agreed with Louis Brandeis. Justice David Brewer wrote the Court's unanimous opinion upholding the constitutionality of the Oregon law. Brewer found that, "As healthy mothers are essential to vigorous offspring, the physical well-being of woman becomes an object of public interest," thereby justifying Oregon's use of its police powers. The Court also found that "woman has always been dependent upon man," and because of this, "she is not an equal competitor with her brother." Protective legislation that put unacceptable limits on men's liberty of contract thus could be sustained for women. In concluding, the Court specifically stated that the *Muller* ruling did not overturn the decision in *Lochner v. New York*. The *Muller* decision validated only sex-specific economic protection based on a woman's inherent maternity. Still, the National Consumers League accepted the ruling as a signal victory. It also established a permanent committee in defense of labor laws, and turned its attention to securing minimum wage legislation for women.

See also ADKINS V. CHILDREN'S HOSPITAL; JOSEPHINE GOLDMARK; FLORENCE KELLEY; WOMEN'S STATUS AND RIGHTS.

Further reading: Nancy Woloch, *Muller v. Oregon: A Brief History with Documents* (Boston: Bedford/St. Martin's Press, 1996); Melvin Urofsky, "State Courts and Protective Legislation during the Progressive Era: A Reevaluation," *The Journal of American History* 72 (1985): 63–91.

— Debra A. Viles

music

Modern American music emerged in the years between 1900 and 1930 as a product of diverse cultural influences. From western European formal composition and the music of eastern European Jews to the broad influences of African-American gospel and blues music, both popular and classical music took on different sounds in these years. Innovations in the technology of music such as the mass marketing of machine recordings and the widespread adoption of RADIO changed the cultural economy of music as did the influence of TIN PAN ALLEY music publishers in New York, the national tours of VAUDEVILLE acts and Broadway musicals, and the MOVIE INDUSTRY. While New York and Chicago became music centers during the period, several other cities, such as New Orleans, Memphis, and Los Angeles, became important both in the development of new musical styles and in the diffusion of music to the national market. The new genres of BLUES and JAZZ and the development of modern classical music incorporated vernacular music from rural and immigrant communities into distinctive American sounds.

At the turn of the century, the music publishing industry of Tin Pan Alley launched songs that became commercial bestsellers and hallmarks of the era. Crossing the line of strict Victorian morals to erotic suggestion, songs like "A Bird in a Gilded Cage" (1900), "In the Good Old Summertime" (1902), "Sweet Adeline" (1903), "Meet Me in St. Louis, Louis" (1904), and "Wait 'Til the Sun Shines, Nellie" (1905) were but a few of the anthems that sold millions of copies of sheet music. The popularity of this music cemented the reputation of New York as the capital of POPULAR CULTURE. Later, composers such as Irving Berlin and GEORGE GERSHWIN started their careers plugging songs at music stores, in restaurants and saloons, and after shows. Audiences were eager for fare as diverse as arias from operas and operettas, folk songs, and spirituals.

Tin Pan Alley linked popular music to the developing musical stage. By the early 1900s, the musical stage, in particular vaudeville and operetta, was the vehicle for new music. With contemporary language, energetic choruses, and sweet melodies, the operetta took off in popularity. The 1907 production of Franz Lehár's *Merry Widow* spun off several road companies that performed the show over 5,000 times between 1907 and 1908. Sheet music, wax cylinders for phonographs, and piano rolls carried the show songs to a broad national audience. Between 1907 and 1914, operetta held sway on the musical stage. The work of Rudolph Friml (*Rosemarie* [1924] and *The Vagabond King* [1925]) and the prolific Victor Herbert (who wrote 40 operettas during his long career) in *Babes in Toyland* (1903), *The Red Mill* (1906), and *Naughty Marietta* (1910) attracted large followings. African-American musical theater also made a showing with the production of William Marion Cook's *Dahomey* in 1902. Eubie Blake contributed his own shows throughout the 1920s. Broadway musicals also provided material for popular music tastes from such composers as Gershwin, George M. Cohan, Jerome Kern, and Cole Porter.

African-American music made its way to Tin Pan Alley in the form of dance music such as the cakewalk and the two-step, dances that further evolved into the Bunny Hug, the Fox Trot, and the Grizzly Bear. Ragtime, which had its origins in the 1890s, continued to have a popular appeal that influenced much of the music coming out of Tin Pan Alley. Ragtime's greatest composer, SCOTT JOPLIN, popularized its rhythms in "Maple Leaf Rag," "Gladiolus Rag," and "The Entertainer." Its influence also appeared in show music such as Berlin's "Alexander's Ragtime Band," published in 1911. The syncopation of ragtime provided the impetus for innovation in music, first through the sweet sound of Dixieland jazz and later in modern jazz music.

In the period between 1910 and 1920, blues began to gain in popularity. W. C. Handy, considered "the father of the blues," was trained as a professional musician but was first exposed to folk blues when playing with a band in Cleveland. Drawing on the folk tradition, Handy composed his own melodies, notably "St. Louis Blues" (1914). By 1910, blues had begun to develop distinctive regional styles; some retained a down-home blues style, accompanied chiefly by slide guitar, and others an urban style (Chicago and Memphis) that relied on a wider range of instruments, including piano, and had a narrative shape not found in folk blues. Urban blues often featured female vocalists, among them Gertrude "Ma" Rainey, Alberta Hunter, and Bessie Smith. Mamie Smith made the first blues recording with her "Crazy Blues" in 1920, which sold 75,000 copies in a few months. The recording industry capitalized on blues popularity in the African-American community with "race records" of both down-home and urban blues.

Influenced by ragtime origins and blues melodies, along with European-style elements, jazz emerged in the late 1910s as a distinctive style. The Original Dixieland Jazz Band, a white band from New Orleans, made the first jazz recordings in 1917. Jelly Roll Morton's piano compositions were first recorded at about the same time. Hotter jazz, the result of introducing blue notes into ragtime's syncopation and incorporating solo improvisations, developed by the 1920s. First heard in the recordings of Chicago-based "King" Oliver's band, with its talented trumpeter Louis Armstrong, jazz quickly spread to Harlem and contributed to the HARLEM RENAISSANCE revival of African-American cultural forms.

Classical music similarly showed vitality at the turn of the century. Major cities spent the decade cultivating classical music by organizing orchestras and building concert halls. In New York, Carnegie Hall was completed in 1891. Boston followed with Symphony Hall in 1900, and Chicago built Orchestra Hall in 1904. Cincinnati, Cleveland, Minneapolis, Pittsburgh, and Philadelphia established orchestras in the same period of time. Playing largely European music, symphony orchestras and opera companies spread its popularity while encouraging the development of American music. In the early years of the century, academic composers such as Horatio Parker and Charles Cadman added to the operatic and symphonic repertoire. With the spread of phonograph technology, classical music came into average homes. The music industry tapped artists such as maestro Arturo Toscanini and opera singer Enrico Caruso for recordings that made classical music available to listeners from all classes. The new medium of radio and national broadcast networks also created new audiences for what had previously been restricted to the affluent and the professional.

Enrico Caruso *(Library of Congress)*

The first modern composer in the United States was Charles Ives (1874–1954), whose use of modern techniques of composition predated the two most important European modernist composers, Igor Stravinsky and Arthur Schoenberg. Dissonant harmonies, use of vernacular music, and major-minor tonal structure characterized some of his most important work. A talented musician, Ives gave up professional music and worked in the life insurance industry. After a heart attack caused him to retire in 1918, Ives self-published his early work, including his *Concord Sonata* for piano and his *114 Songs,* an idiosyncratic anthology with a range of musical styles. By 1925, however, Ives stopped composing original work and withdrew from the public. It was only in 1939 when his *Concord Sonata* was performed that his work attracted a wide following among composers and listeners. Ives won the Pulitzer Prize for music in 1947.

The abstraction of Charles Ives's atonal music had little appeal for classical audiences of the time. A more fruitful and popular path came in the work of George Gershwin, who brought together his own mastery of vernacular music with classical composition. His *Rhapsody in Blue* (1924) showed the influence of both popular song and the rhythms of jazz. *An American in Paris* (1928) and the

opera *Porgy and Bess* (1935) showed Gershwin's virtuosity in moving back and forth across cultural and artistic lines. His marriage of folk and classical themes set the stage for the later work of composers Aaron Copland, Marc Blitzstein, and Leonard Berstein. Copland's own career took off with the publication of his *Music for the Theatre* in 1925 and his *Piano Concerto* in 1926.

Beyond the classical realm, there were three important developments in music during the 1920s. First, the sheet music industry centered in Tin Pan Alley began to decline, due to a drop in sales and to rising costs of production. Wartime paper shortages and printers' strikes had driven up the price of sheet music. Sheet music sales also began to fall due to another development. Radio broadcasts, first local and then on the new national networks of NBC and CBS, began to supplant sheet music as a means of reaching the popular audience. Third, sound motion pictures, which were produced beginning in 1927, substituted for touring Broadway productions as a means of introducing songs to the public. In dance clubs, speakeasies, and concert halls, new music, influenced by ragtime and blues, was spread to an ever-widening audience.

African-American music gained in popularity throughout the 1920s. Jazz and urban blues made their "mainstream" cultural breakthrough in the period. New recordings made the transition from "race records," sold to a small segment of the market, to major-label recordings, as Black Swan and Okeh gave way to RCA Victor and Columbia Records. Singers Ma Rainey, Bessie Smith, and Ethel Waters sang of urban love and trouble in songs such as "It Ain't Nobody's Business If I Do" and "Prove It on Me Blues." Blind Lemon Jefferson, Blind Blake, and other blues greats could be heard on the airwaves and phonographs singing songs of chain gangs, poverty, and misfired love, and Louis Armstrong made his classic Hot Five and Hot Seven recordings (1925–28) featuring his dazzling solo improvisations. Fletcher Henderson and Edward "Duke" Ellington started jazz orchestras during the 1920s and built audiences for "hot" jazz (later called swing) in Harlem at the Cotton Club and Connie's Inn and Plantation and the Roseland Ballroom uptown. At the same time, white musicians such as Paul Whiteman and his orchestra were able to translate jazz music by sweetening the music with softer tones and formal arrangements designed to appeal to white middle-class listeners.

The cultural character of modern American music had its origins in the decades prior to the Great Depression. By the end of the 1920s, jazz, once exclusively linked to African-American musicians, became the preferred music for up-and-coming white musicians, and vernacular gospel and blues music invaded the realm of high art in the classical compositions of Gershwin and Copland. Modernism in music, like modernism in art and literature, challenged the strict formalism and cultural segregation of the 19th century to produce an art representative of the broad cultural range of urban industrial society.

See also ENTERTAINMENT, POPULAR; YOUTH.

Further reading: Richard Crawford, *America's Musical Life; A History* (New York: Norton, 2001); D. Nicholls, ed., *The Cambridge History of American Music* (Cambridge, U.K.: Cambridge University Press, 1998); I. Sablosky, *American Music* (Chicago: University of Chicago Press, 1969); Arnold Shaw, *Jazz Age; Popular Music in the 1920s* (New York: Oxford University Press, 1987).

Narcotics Act (1914)

Passed by Congress in 1914, the Narcotics Act was the culmination of a Progressive Era effort to reduce drug addiction in the United States. In the final decades of the 19th century, a growing number of Americans were gripped by the fear that narcotics addiction was undermining society. Influenced by new theories regarding the ways in which drugs affected the body and mind, they sought to control drug use. While the intense focus of the anti-drug forces was somewhat novel, the perception that drugs were dangerous was nothing new. Social critics had a long history of battling drugs. For the most part, however, they had focused on the evils of alcohol use and abuse. It was not until the 1870s that a number of social reformers began to target narcotics.

Like the battles that were being waged over "demon rum," class and race played a significant part in the promotion of legal restrictions on narcotics. While the public discussion regarding the "drug problem" focused on southern blacks, the urban poor, and the Chinese, men and women from all levels of society increasingly used narcotics. By the turn of the century, narcotics addiction had spread throughout the social strata. The perceived pervasiveness of the problem led to a more unified call for government regulation.

Police officers and others concerned with the promotion of law and order often blamed drug addicts for increases in criminal activity. They believed that without narcotics use and abuse there would be significantly less crime. Doctors, initially cool to the idea of government regulation, soon joined the chorus of reformers who voiced their concern over the use and abuse of narcotics. As the medical profession became more organized and structured, doctors sought to promote regulation to thwart the distribution of patent medicines. Many doctors viewed unlicensed peddlers of narcotic elixirs as a threat to society and a challenge to their professional standing. Competition was a main reason for medical professionals to support legal restrictions on narcotics. Fear of competition from patent medicines should not, however, be viewed as the only reason that drug legislation won doctors' endorsement. Doctors saw firsthand the dangers of addiction among some of their patients and colleagues.

Local laws prohibiting the use of narcotics seemed to be incapable of stemming their use. This realization led to a unified call for national regulation. Federal regulation of narcotics was nothing new. The federal government had regulated opium through import taxes, but that was a far cry from federal regulation of what had previously been considered a local problem. In 1906, the federal government took a significant step toward stemming narcotics use with passage of the PURE FOOD AND DRUG ACT. The law challenged the patent medicine industry by requiring that it list all ingredients. In 1909, Congress stepped up its efforts by restricting the importation of opium except for certified medical uses.

In 1914, Congress passed the Harrison Anti-Narcotic Act. This law did more than regulate the narcotics industry. In effect, it prohibited the use of a number of popular narcotics. The Harrison Act required surveillance of narcotics production, greater record keeping, and general supervision of doctors who prescribed narcotics. Soon after, the courts validated congressional authority to regulate the drug industry. The law favored incarceration over treatment. It turned addicts into criminals. For the next three-quarters of a century, addicts would be treated as threats to the social structure and thus often were incarcerated. By the end of 1920s, public angst regarding narcotics abuse faded.

Many Americans believed that the Harrison Act was effective in stemming the use and abuse of narcotics. In the years that followed, the act was strengthened. Heroin was banned in 1929. In the 1930s, laws banning marijuana followed. While intense regulation and prohibition were the two most significant forces used by the government to combat drug abuse, they were not the only methods used. The government also began to operate hospitals that aimed at curing those suffering from addiction. These efforts, however, paled in comparison to those that sought to punish drug offenders. At the same time, the combination of legal restrictions and medical treatments allowed most citizens to believe, at least for a number of generations, that the government was winning its war on drugs.

Further reading: Wayne H. Morgan, *Yesterday's Addicts: American Society and Drug Abuse, 1865–1920* (Norman: University of Oklahoma Press, 1974).

— Steve Freund

National American Woman Suffrage Association (NAWSA)

Formed in 1890, the National American Woman Suffrage Association was the result of merging two early associations—the American Woman Suffrage Association, originally led by Lucy Stone and Henry Blackwell, and the National Woman Suffrage Association, which Elizabeth Cady Stanton and Susan B. Anthony organized. The formation of NAWSA signaled the end of a long debate in the WOMAN SUFFRAGE movement about how to obtain the vote for women. The American association had preferred to work for state suffrage amendments, while Stanton and Anthony's group had focused on court challenges and national campaigns directed at a woman suffrage amendment to the Constitution. Susan B. Anthony, one of the last remaining suffrage pioneers, became president of the new association. In the next decade, there were few victories apart from the recruitment and training of the next generation of suffrage leaders. In the words of suffrage historian Eleanor Flexner, NAWSA suffered "the doldrums," an inability to build majority support for state suffrage.

With Anthony's retirement from NAWSA in 1900, her chosen heir, CARRIE CHAPMAN CATT, began a series of new campaigns and strategies to further the suffrage cause. First, she tackled the problem of public opinion by cultivating the support of wealthy and well-respected women. She also created a suffrage history to back the movement. Memorials for Susan B. Anthony's leadership, and the simultaneous decline of the more radical Stanton's reputation, educated a new generation of suffragists in the traditions of the women's rights movement.

Between 1900 and 1905, Carrie Catt ably led NAWSA, but her husband's terminal illness led her to resign as president. For the next 10 years, minister, orator, and suffragist Anna Howard Shaw served as head of the organization. Her lack of organizational skill and the continued sense that NAWSA was drifting led Catt, who had worked in New York State for suffrage, to return as head of the organization. When she did, she came back with a highly centralized plan, "the Winning Plan," to garner support for the passage of a federal amendment giving women the right to vote. NAWSA would now subordinate all state-level efforts to a national campaign. Only by coordinating resources, Catt insisted, could it obtain the needed support for passage and ratification.

As the dominant suffrage organization, NAWSA was able to garner the political and financial support of many wealthy women. At a time when it was most needed to grease the political wheels, NAWSA received a large bequest from the widow of publisher Frank Leslie. The Leslie Fund gave NAWSA an endowment to be used in its suffrage battles. Under Catt's leadership, this money, and growing congressional support, reenergized the suffrage movement and put the cause of women's right to vote constantly before the public.

When the Nineteenth Amendment granting women the right to vote was ratified in 1920, many asked what goal the women's rights movement should tackle next. For those women moved by the carnage of WORLD WAR I, it was the cause of peace. Many joined the WOMEN'S INTERNATIONAL LEAGUE FOR PEACE AND FREEDOM. For others, such as ALICE PAUL, a former NAWSA member and head of the NATIONAL WOMAN'S PARTY, it was to work for passage of an EQUAL RIGHTS AMENDMENT to fight for women's full political and economic rights. Catt directed her own efforts toward building the League of Women Voters, a nonpartisan organization to educate and mobilize voters on issues of public interest.

Further reading: Eleanor Flexner and Ellen Fitzpatrick, *Century of Struggle: The Women's Rights Movement in the United States,* enl. ed. (Cambridge, Mass.: Belknap Press, 1996); Sara Hunter Graham, *Woman Suffrage and the New Democracy* (New Haven, Conn.: Yale University Press, 1996).

National Association for the Advancement of Colored People (NAACP)

Founded in New York City in 1909 by African-American and white social reformers and intellectuals, the National Association for the Advancement of Colored People became the dominant civil rights organization in the United States. In response to a 1908 Springfield, Illinois, lynching, a group came together for "the discussion of present evils, the voicing of protests, and the renewal of the struggle for civil and political liberty." Meeting in 1909 on the centennial of Abraham Lincoln's birth, the gathering included many of the leading white social reformers of the day—JANE ADDAMS, JOHN DEWEY, LINCOLN STEFFENS, and LILLIAN WALD. Six African Americans attended, including W. E. B. DU BOIS and Ida B. Wells-Barnett, chairwoman of the Anti-Lynching League. The participants made plans for a permanent organization that began operation the next year. They pledged themselves and the organization to working toward the elimination of segregation, for African-American voting rights, and for enforcement of the Fourteenth and Fifteenth Amendments, which guaranteed equal protection before the law and the right to vote.

The NAACP merged two earlier civil rights groups, the Constitutional League, which was a white organization, and the NIAGARA MOVEMENT, an African-American organization. Despite having both white and African-American members, whites dominated the NAACP leadership. Some African-American members expressed concern over this, but Du Bois, the only African American on the first slate of officers, praised the dedication of the experienced social reformers to the African-Americans' cause. In addition to their commitment, white supporters lent significant financial support and raised funds for the organization.

The NAACP's first goal was to bring the plight of the African Americans to the attention of white America. It began a campaign of speechmaking, lobbying, and publicizing. In 1915, for example, the NAACP led a boycott of the film, BIRTH OF A NATION. The film used offensive racial stereotypes to tell the story of Reconstruction in the South after the Civil War. To help get their message out, the NAACP started a magazine, *The Crisis*. W. E. B. Du Bois served as editor from 1909 to 1934 and used his position to expound on the causes he believed important. Given his own growing political radicalism and opposition to Booker T. Washington, Du Bois set forth positions on issues in *The Crisis* that sometimes made board members uncomfortable. It strained the relationship between Du Bois and the rest of the leadership and eventually led to his ouster in 1934. For 25 years, however, he used his position within the NAACP to shape the debate over civil rights.

The NAACP leadership realized that equal rights called for more then just publicity. In the 1910s, they began to attack racial inequality and segregation in the courts. In 1915, for example, they took on the grandfather clause used by many southern states to disenfranchise African Americans. In 1917, they successfully challenged a Louisville ordinance that required African Americans to live in segregated sections of the city. The NAACP then attacked and won a ruling against restrictive covenants in real estate deeds, which were used to prohibit African Americans from buying certain property. In 1923, it helped bring a case before the courts that ended with a decision that declared unconstitutional the exclusion of African Americans from juries solely due to race. In 1927, the NAACP again attacked the efforts of southern states to prevent African Americans from voting and won a Supreme Court ruling that outlawed the all-white primary.

In 1916, James Weldon Johnson, who later became the first African-American NAACP executive secretary, began a campaign to spread the NAACP into the South. By 1920, nearly half of the organization's members lived there. The NAACP's major campaign in the South was to gather support to pass federal legislation outlawing lynching. To publicize the horrors of lynching, NAACP members undertook an exhaustive investigation into southern racial violence. In 1919, the organization issued a report titled *Thirty Years of Lynching in the United States, 1889–1918*, which listed the details of every incident of lynching it could find. Efforts to push through anti-lynching legislation failed, but the light of publicity helped reduce lynching.

By 1930 the NAACP had become the dominant civil rights organization in the United States. It has continued to use the techniques developed in its early years of attacking racial discrimination—through publicity, legislation, and the courts—to improve the lives of Americans.

See also RACE AND RACIAL CONFLICT.

Further reading: Langston Hughes, *Fight for Freedom; The Story of the NAACP* (New York: Norton, 1962); Robert L. Zangrando, *The NAACP Crusade against Lynching, 1909–1950* (Philadelphia: Temple University Press, 1980).
— Michael Hartman

National Association of Colored Women

The National Association of Colored Women was established in 1896 to further the community support and political efforts of African-American women. By the 1890s, there was a thriving women's club movement that established and maintained institutions for charity, education, health, and social uplift in African-American communities. Combining a mission to help "uplift the race" with a concern for women's progress, such groups differed from white women's clubs by their pointedly political agenda. Faced—like men of their communities—with racial hostility and discrimination in the segregated South and urban North, African-American women sought to find ways to address racial inequality that went beyond pleas for accommodation. The anti-lynching campaign of Ida B. Wells-Barnett, herself an ardent clubwoman, expressed for many their own instinct to challenge the system and fight back against extralegal violence. When the white press in 1895 attacked Barnett and African-American women for "having no sense of virtue and being altogether of no character," social reformer Josephine St. Pierre Ruffin issued a call for national organization.

At that meeting, women in the Northeast formed the National Federation of African American Women under the leadership of Margaret Murray Washington. At the same time in Washington, D.C., educator MARY CHURCH

TERRELL and others created the National League of Colored Women. At a national convention in Washington in 1896, the groups merged to form the National Association of Colored Women (NACW). Taking as its motto, "Lifting as We Climb," the organization had as its goal furthering the work of African-American women's clubs by using their collective political clout to pressure governments and private businesses to address racial inequality. Terrell was elected the NACW's first president in 1896.

The work of the league stretched along the lines of charitable drives, civic improvement, public education, and WOMAN SUFFRAGE campaigns. Inspired by Terrell's words that "Self preservation demands that [we] go among the lowly, the illiterate, even the vicious, to whom [we] are bound by ties of race and sex . . . to reclaim them," the NACW helped to organize and support African-American women's club efforts nationwide. It recruited thousands of members with the goal of bringing women's influence to bear on race politics. By 1914, the black women's club movement had grown to more than 50,000 members in 28 federations and over 1,000 clubs.

The NACW strongly supported woman suffrage as an extension of its goals. Excluded at various times from the work of the NATIONAL AMERICAN WOMAN SUFFRAGE ASSOCIATION due to racial prejudice, the NACW developed its own suffrage strategies and campaigns. As NACW member Adele Hunt Logan proclaimed, "If white American women with all their natural advantages need the ballot . . . how much more do black Americans, both male and female, need the strong defense of the vote to help secure their right to life, liberty, and the pursuit of happiness?" The NACW built support among African Americans, who demonstrated greater support for woman suffrage than in the population at large.

The NACW continued to expand its mission and activities in the years after the granting of woman suffrage in 1920. Working toward the abolition of the poll tax in the South, lobbying for the passage of an anti-lynching law, and maintaining its efforts in relief, education, and civic improvement, the NACW remained a major force in African-American political and social life throughout the first three decades of the 20th century.

Further reading: Paula Giddings, *Where and When I Enter: The Impact of Black Women on Race and Sex in America* (New York: Morrow, 1984); Rosalyn Terborg-Penn, *African American Women in the Struggle for the Vote, 1850–1920* (Bloomington: Indiana University Press, 1998).

National Association of Manufacturers (NAM)

The economic collapse of 1893 shook American industry to its knees and convinced many financiers and industrialists of the need for more stable markets, less competition, more efficient production, and greater influence on federal and state governments. In 1895, a group of 583 industrial manufacturers from all over the country met in Cincinnati, Ohio, and formed the National Association of Manufacturers (NAM). Under the leadership of Thomas Eagan, the NAM stated that its objectives included the expansion of foreign trade, support for the construction of a PANAMA CANAL, the improvement of domestic transportation, and support for creating a Department of Commerce.

Although the NAM was ostensibly created to promote domestic development and foreign trade, by 1903 it had become vociferously anti-union. Industrial organizing drives by the UNITED MINE WORKERS OF AMERICA, the INDUSTRIAL WORKERS OF THE WORLD and, to a lesser extent, the AMERICAN FEDERATION OF LABOR (AFL) had resulted in increased union membership in the nation's factories and mines. In response, the NAM began warning about the deleterious impact of organized labor and encouraging employers to resist organizing initiatives. In particular, the NAM encouraged employers to resist union efforts to establish closed union shops, in which employees were required to join the union as a condition of employment. Arguing that the closed shop was unconstitutional and un-American, the NAM supported an OPEN SHOP policy, in which workers, they argued, could chose whether or not they wanted to join a union and pay union dues. Under such a system, however, there were no guarantees of workers' right to organize. The NAM also supported the use of yellow dog contracts, which prohibited employees from ever joining a union.

Between 1900 and 1910, Samuel Gompers and the AFL proved willing to try to work with employers to avoid strikes and keep more radical unions like the IWW at bay. These cooperative efforts, however, proved short-lived as employers and the NAM launched a counteroffensive against organized labor that was halted, only briefly, by the outbreak of WORLD WAR I. With the end of the war, the NAM helped launch an all-out offensive against radicals, socialists, and organized labor. It led the charge in the drive for the Open Shop, effectively eviscerating labor's wartime gains. Union membership, which had grown from 2 million in 1904 to 5 million in 1921, plummeted over the course of the 1920s. It declined to 3.5 million in 1929, despite the fact that there were millions more industrial workers than in 1904. By 1930, the NAM, which had its roots in coordinating industrial production and the expansion of foreign trade, had become one of the most conservative, anti-union, and influential trade associations in the country.

Further reading: Melvin Dubofsky, *The State and Labor in Modern America* (Chapel Hill: University of North Carolina Press, 1994); David Montgomery, *The Fall of the*

House of Labor: The Workplace, the State, and American Labor Activism, 1865–1925 (New York: Cambridge University Press, 1987).

— Robert Gordon

National Civic Federation

Formed in 1901 as the brainchild of Chicago newspaperman Ralph Easley, the National Civic Federation had as its purpose creating more harmonious relationships between employers and workers. Taking on issues of labor conflict, employers' liability, workers' compensation, and WELFARE CAPITALISM, the NCF became a leading influence in employee relations and social policy. The NCF had its origins in the Chicago Civic Federation, which had formed in response to the Pullman Strike of 1894. Easley, however, had a broader national vision, and he recruited some of the major business, financial, and political leaders of the day to support the NCF in its mission. Such men as Marcus Hanna, the Republican politician; August Belmont, the railroad magnate; and banker J. P. Morgan were all members of the NCF. A third party in the creation of the NCF was organized labor. Beginning with the ANTHRACITE COAL STRIKE of 1902, the NCF sought the participation and support of major labor leaders such as Samuel Gompers, president of the AMERICAN FEDERATION OF LABOR, and JOHN MITCHELL of the UNITED MINE WORKERS.

Labor too saw the advantages of working in coalition with corporate leaders. Faced with the open hostility of organizations like the NATIONAL ASSOCIATION OF MANUFACTURERS and the American Anti-Boycott Association, it had to contend with the constant threat of labor injunctions, expensive court cases, and employer resistance. In order to pass employer liability and workers' compensation laws, the labor movement needed allies. It was in the interest of corporate leaders to find common cause with labor on these issues. They, too, sought protection from civil suits in court, and organized labor, ever pragmatic, wanted to find a compromise solution. Finally, the conservative AFL faced the threat of militancy among the working class, including new organizations such as the INDUSTRIAL WORKERS OF THE WORLD and the Socialist Party of America, which served as voices of the NEW UNIONISM.

Not all labor leaders were supportive. Socialist labor leader EUGENE V. DEBS described the NCF as "a beast of prey, which always tells its victims, 'our interests are one,' and then devours them." Still, the Civic Federation gave labor leaders Samuel Gompers and John Mitchell unprecedented access to the attention and support of corporate leaders. The attorney who defended Gompers in the *BUCK'S STOVE* case, Alton B. Parker, was a corporate lawyer. State legislatures passed workers' compensation laws that

were in part the result of the NCF's work. The NCF also supported mediation between the skilled trades and employers, although most of its business members resisted unionism in their own factories.

The relatively harmonious relations between labor and business in the NCF were short-lived. By WORLD WAR I, founder and NCF secretary Ralph Easley and NCF president Seth Low had moved away from seeing organized labor as a sympathetic ally. The massive strike wave during and after the war prompted many business leaders, including Easley, to greater hostility toward, and opposition to, the organized labor movement. They saw little difference between skilled workers in the AFL and the mass of factory workers who did not belong. Organized workers of any sort constituted a threat. The NCF joined other employer organizations in supporting the suppression of labor in the RED SCARE of 1919–20.

Further reading: Gerald Kurland, *Seth Low; The Reformer in an Urban and Industrial Age* (New York: Twayne, 1971); James Weinstein, *The Corporate Ideal in the Liberal State, 1900–1915* (Boston: Beacon Press, 1968).

National Consumers League   See Goldmark, Josephine Clara; Kelley, Florence

National Defense Act (1916)

Once European nations went to war in 1914, the question of military preparedness arose in the United States. The National Defense Act, passed in 1916, was the first attempt to address the nation's need for greater defense. After the LUSITANIA was sunk in May 1915, President WOODROW WILSON dropped his opposition to an American military build-up. In 1916, he toured the country to urge support for preparedness even though he campaigned on the slogan, "Vote for Wilson—Peace with Honor." He declared, "there is such a thing as a man being too proud to fight."

Many, including Wilson's notable opponents, THEODORE ROOSEVELT and HENRY CABOT LODGE, were enraged by Wilson's comments. They had supported preparedness early on. Roosevelt had decried the "Flubdubs and Mollycoddles" who refused to acknowledge the need to strengthen the ARMED FORCES. He and Henry Stimson fought for the expansion of the army under the National Security League.

As early as 1914, the Army War College had composed a "Statement of a Proper Military Policy for the United States." In it the War College pointed out that the United States could no longer depend on its geographic advantages and distance from the continent as a safeguard from invasion. The speed and carrying capacity of ocean vessels, the submarine's capacities, and the wireless all lent increasing access to our coasts. War College analysts cried out for a standing army of at least 500,000 backed by an equipped reserve of equal size. They felt that 18 to 24 months was needed to prepare such an army—and additional time was needed to train them.

In 1916 Wilson's secretary of war, Lindley Garrison, and his assistant, Henry Breckenridge, drew up their own national defense plan. Supported by Wilson, it called for the establishment of a large, volunteer "Continental Army." This army would reach 400,000 men (an increase of 40 percent) who would serve on active duty for two months a year for three years and then become part of a reserve force. When Congress rallied against this idea, Wilson withdrew his support. Garrison and Breckenridge resigned.

In June 1916, Congress passed the National Defense Act. It allowed the president to commandeer factories and establish a government nitrate plant. It further permitted the army to double its size by adding 11,450 officers and 223,580 enlisted men in annual increments over five years. The National Guard could expand to 17,000 officers and 440,000 men.

In spite of the National Defense Act, the nation was unable to recruit to its authorized strength before war intervened. In April 1917, the regular army consisted of only 5,791 officers and 121,797 enlisted men. The idea that the United States did not need a standing army had a long tradition. Militia and state forces, it was believed, could handle any emergency. Once the nation was in danger, volunteers would show up. Because the nature of warfare had changed, however, both a military draft and training were required. Only the passage of the SELECTIVE SERVICE ACT of 1917 gave the United States the army it needed.

See also ARMED FORCES; CONSCRIPTION.

Further reading: David M. Kennedy, *Over Here: The First World War and American Society* (New York: Oxford University Press, 1980).

— Annamarie Edelen

National Origins Act (1924)

Despite growing support for restrictive immigration policies in the early 20th century, some 800,000 immigrants, many from eastern and southern Europe, entered the United States in 1921. Two major pieces of legislation were aimed at restricting this immigration—the IMMIGRATION ACT OF 1917 and the QUOTA ACT of 1921—but the proportion of southern and eastern Europeans remained high. The 1921 Quota Act had attempted to severely limit the number of immigrants that annually could enter the United States. Many in Congress however, felt that the restrictions did not go far enough. By the early 1920s, many

Americans felt that the country could no longer accommodate the nearly one million immigrants that had been arriving each year since the 1880s. Moreover, when northern industrial cities received a new source of labor with the influx of African Americans in the GREAT MIGRATION that followed WORLD WAR I, industrial leaders were no longer as apt to push for open immigration policies. Accordingly, one of the chief proponents of restrictive immigration policies, Senator Albert Johnson of the state of Washington, secured passage of far more restrictive legislation in 1924.

The NATIONAL ORIGINS ACT of 1924, also known as the Johnson-Reid Act, reduced the admissible number of immigrants from outside the Western Hemisphere annually to 165,000, less than a fifth of the average prewar level. The sponsors of the 1924 legislation essentially agreed with the findings of the DILLINGHAM COMMISSION, which contended that certain immigrant groups were better suited to assimilating into American society. In particular, the sponsors of the 1924 legislation argued that British, Germans, and Scandinavians were racially superior to other immigrants, and that, consequently, these groups should be allowed to enter the United States in greater numbers.

The 1921 Quota Act had attempted to control the origin of immigrants to the United States by using 1910 as the base year for determining the number of immigrants from each country allowed to enter the United States. But by 1910, the number of southern and eastern Europeans already in the United States had reached such a level that the quotas did not achieve the results desired by anti-immigration forces. Accordingly, the Johnson-Reid legislation pushed the base year back to 1890. In crafting this new piece of legislation, lawmakers had selected 1890 because they knew that immigrant ranks then had been dominated by groups from Great Britain, Germany, and Scandinavia. Immigrants from Italy, Greece, Poland, and other areas were poorly represented. Under the 1924 National Origins Act, each nationality group was given a quota of 2 percent of its population in the United States according to the official census of 1890, with up to 160,000 total individuals (from all countries) allowed to enter the United States annually. In addition, the 1924 Johnson-Reid Act continued the long-standing policy of excluding Chinese immigrants. It added Japanese and other Asians to the list of ethnic groups that were altogether barred from entering the United States. This new formula for determining the number of immigrants eligible quickly achieved the results that the proponents of immigration restriction had been lobbying for since the early part of the century.

Further reading: John Higham, *Strangers in the Land: Patterns of American Nativism, 1860–1925* 2nd ed. (New Brunswick, N.J.: Rutgers University Press, 1988).

— David R. Smith

National Park Service (1916)

In 1916, President WOODROW WILSON signed the bill that established the National Park Service. It was charged with managing and maintaining the nation's system of federal parks and wilderness areas. The Park Service grew out of public concerns about conserving the nation's natural resources and preserving some of the remaining wilderness areas, such as Yellowstone National Park. Yellowstone, the first national park, was established in 1872. The founding of Yosemite National Park followed in 1890. By 1900, the country's national parks included Yellowstone, Yosemite, Sequoia, and Mt. Rainier. They were officially under the control of the U.S. Army. The task of managing the parks was compounded between 1901 and 1909 when President THEODORE ROOSEVELT added 16 million acres of national parkland, some of it through the ANTIQUITIES ACT. After Roosevelt left office in 1909, many of the parks fell into disrepair as no money had been set aside to protect the parks. The result was that poachers and illegal timber operations frequently vandalized the parks. In 1913, Secretary of the Interior Franklin Lane appointed Horace Albright to be the assistant for parks; but without sufficient resources, the parks continued to deteriorate.

Although pressure to protect the parks had been mounting since 1908, it wasn't until businessman and naturalist Stephen Mather became involved that there was a concerted effort to improve the park system. He spent much of his free time touring the various national parks and became increasingly alarmed at their condition. He expressed his concerns to Secretary Lane in 1914. Lane wrote back, "Steve, if you don't like the way the national parks are being run, come on down to Washington and run them yourself." Mather took Lane up on the offer and went to Washington to lobby for the creation of a National Park Service. Mather used his wealth and influence to convince Congress and President WOODROW WILSON to pass the National Park Service Act in 1916 and to name him its first director. The Park Service's mandate reflected the dual themes of conservationism and public recreation, which have subsequently shaped how the national parks have developed.

In the decades following its formation, the National Park Service continued to struggle to maintain the parks. The National Park Service Act was mandated only a small budget, and Mather found it difficult to both keep the parks maintained and to have them accessible to the public. He and Park Assistant Albright launched an aggressive and ultimately effective campaign to protect the parks by promoting tourism. Automobile ownership and tourism became increasingly common in the 1920s; and by 1930, the national parks began to attract millions of visitors each year.

See also CONSERVATIONISM.

Further reading: Ronald Foresta, *America's National Parks and Their Keepers* (Baltimore: Johns Hopkins University Press, 1984).

— Robert Gordon

National Reclamation Act (Newlands Act) (1902)

The National Reclamation Act of 1902 attempted to resolve long-standing disputes involving control and distribution of water in the American West. Between the end of the Civil War and 1900, hundreds of thousands of Americans moved westward, permanently altering the western landscape and creating conflict over land ownership and control over the region's most precious asset—water. Because much of the western United States is semi-arid, water was and is a scarce commodity. As Anglo settlers and recently arrived immigrants moved into the West, conflicts over water and control of land were inevitable. By 1900, largely because of the scarcity of water, large-scale farming operations had gained the upper hand over small, freehold farmers. Nevertheless, conflicts over water remained and persistently threatened to undermine the viability of small- and large-scale farms.

The scarcity of water, when combined with several decades of falling food prices, placed many western farms in a precarious position by the turn of the century. Pressure on the federal government to intervene mounted. In 1901, Democrats in Congress introduced legislation aimed at ensuring that western farmers had the funds to secure enough water. Senator Francis G. Newlands (D–Nevada) sponsored the legislation. He had come to power in Nevada through land speculation and championing the construction of dams and water projects. President THEODORE ROOSEVELT and his secretary of the interior, Ethan Allen Hitchcock, also supported the reclamation bill, but other Republicans, including the influential Speaker of the House, JOSEPH CANNON, opposed its passage.

Largely due to Roosevelt's support, the legislation passed the House and Senate, and it was signed into law in 1902. In its final version, the legislation pooled the proceeds from the sale of public land in 16 western states into a fund that would then be used to build irrigation projects throughout the West. The Reclamation Act gave final responsibility and authority over the construction of these large-scale projects to the federal government. It was hoped that, once the projects were completed, farmers and landowners would be responsible for their maintenance and upkeep and that within 10 years the proceeds from land sales and water usage rights would offset any construction costs. The bill's authors thought that limiting land sales to 160-acre parcels would encourage settlement and family farming. Because of the size and expense of the irrigation projects, however, the expense and upkeep frequently fell to the federal government and the newly created Federal Bureau of Reclamation. Several projects began almost immediately after the legislation was enacted, including the Newlands Project and construction of the Salt River Dam.

Over the long term, the Reclamation Act had a tremendous impact on the development of the modern West. It paved the way for the construction of aqueducts and massive dams, including the Hoover Dam in Colorado, the Grand Coulee Dam on the Columbia River, and the Glenn Canyon Dam in Dinosaur National Park. In addition, because the acreage limitations were not strictly followed and access to inexpensive water never materialized, its impact on family farming remained limited. Instead, the construction of these aqueducts and dams enabled large-scale corporate farmers to secure a sufficient water supply for crops hundreds of miles away, giving them a competitive advantage over small, independent farmers.

Further reading: Marc Reisner, *Cadillac Desert: The American West and Its Disappearing Water* (New York: Viking, 1986); William D. Rowley, *Reclaiming the Arid West: The Career of Francis G. Newlands* (Bloomington: Indiana University Press, 1996).

— Robert Gordon

National War Labor Board (NWLB)

The National War Labor Board (NWLB) was created in 1918 by President WOODROW WILSON in an attempt to formalize a federal policy for dealing with organized labor during WORLD WAR I. When the United States declared war on Germany, the Wilson administration, business leaders, and others believed it essential to create a war labor board to ensure that labor disputes did not disrupt war preparations. Prior to this time, the federal government's involvement in labor disputes tended to be limited to enforcing injunctions, breaking strikes, and keeping surveillance on labor radicals. Samuel Gompers and the conservative AMERICAN FEDERATION OF LABOR (AFL) hoped that would change with American entry into war. War and its dependence on defense production, Gompers believed, offered a golden opportunity to ensure that responsible craft unions were allowed to organize and negotiate contracts supported by the federal government. Other labor leaders and progressives supported American participation in the war, believing the Wilson administration's rhetoric that it was a war to make the world safe for democracy.

With the creation of the NWLB in 1918, the AFL and the Wilson administration had worked out a blueprint that would last throughout the war. The AFL agreed to a no-

strike pledge and the maintenance of OPEN SHOP, non-union workplaces. In exchange, business leaders agreed to pay union wages and refrain from the worst forms of anti-labor behavior that had been typical before the war. The two most prominent members of the NWLB were former president WILLIAM HOWARD TAFT and labor progressive Frank Walsh. Initially the NWLB had a fairly positive impact on organized labor as the board did in fact curtail some of the most flagrant anti-union practices, such as forcing workers to sign yellow-dog contracts that prohibited them from joining unions. Although the NWLB acted decisively in only a few dozen cases, its support of organized labor in some rulings was almost unprecedented. The impact of the NWLB, however, was short-lived. The end of World War I in November 1918 brought with it immediate employer demands for the return of prewar labor relations. Specifically, employers insisted that since the nation was no longer dependent upon defense production, it was not appropriate for the federal government to intervene on behalf of workers and organized labor. Wartime agreements in such industries as meatpacking were soon invalidated. By December 1918, the power of the NWLB had been effectively demolished.

Further reading: Joseph McCartin, *Labor's Great War: The Struggle for Industrial Democracy and the Origins of Modern Labor Relations, 1912–1921* (Chapel Hill: University of North Carolina Press, 1997).

— Robert Gordon

National Woman's Party (NWP)

The National Woman's Party was organized in 1916 as a by-product of the Congressional Union for Woman Suffrage. Led by ALICE PAUL, the NWP focused on securing a federal amendment for WOMAN SUFFRAGE. Unlike the NATIONAL AMERICAN WOMAN SUFFRAGE ASSOCIATION (NAWSA) for which Paul once worked, the NWP adopted radical tactics of direct action. Devoted to a federal campaign rather than local and state efforts, the NWP spent most of its energies lobbying CONGRESS, running political campaigns, and organizing public protests. Influenced by British suffragists, the NWP pioneered in dramatic methods to draw attention to woman suffrage. The women of NWP stepped into such male arenas as union halls and lumber and mining camps to ask support for women's right to vote. Their most controversial activities, however, occurred in the nation's capital. From January 1917 to mid-1918, NWP representatives held ongoing picket lines, complete with clever slogans and photo placards, outside the White House and Congress.

The NWP drew national attention, especially after the United States entered WORLD WAR I, as its pickets became the targets of counter-protests. The NWP's "silent sentinels" outside the White House were arrested for disturbing the peace, and 168 served sentences. In jail, Alice Paul and others went on a hunger strike. Violence against suffragists escalated, culminating in the November 1917 "Night of Terror," during which suffragists, including Dorothy Day, were attacked and beaten by jail guards. Pickets continued unabated. In fact, suffragists employed increasingly dramatic tactics such as burning copies of President WOODROW WILSON's speeches in ceremonies in Washington, D.C., in order to humiliate the president for not supporting woman suffrage.

The NWP's philosophy and tactics drew criticism from the more genteel suffragists of the NAWSA, who condemned NWP for alienating potential supporters and opposing the nation's war effort. NWP's tactics and political positions, however, made NAWSA appear much more respectable to suffrage supporters in Congress. In early 1918, Wilson finally came out in support of woman suffrage. In June 1919, the Senate passed the Nineteenth Amendment, giving women the right to vote. It joined the House, which had already done so in 1918. The amendment was ratified in 1920.

Although NAWSA accepted the credit for passage of the woman suffrage amendment, the impact of the NWP cannot be dismissed. Its demands, leadership, and methods rendered woman suffrage a national issue. Male politicians could no longer ignore or ridicule suffragists; they now had to respond to them out of fear that the NWP might target them with protests or electoral opposition.

After securing women's right to vote, the NWP turned its attention to the EQUAL RIGHTS AMENDMENT, which was first introduced in Congress in 1923. The party sought to end legal and economic discrimination based on sex, an issue that brought it into conflict with progressive activists who wanted to preserve legislation for women. The party's focus on the ERA set the stage for future feminist challenges to the economic and political status quo based on women's demands for equality. As second-wave feminism emerged, new calls for the ERA were heard in the 1960s and 1970s. By that time, the NWP was no longer a prominent voice.

Further reading: Christine Lunardini, *From Equal Suffrage to Equal Rights: Alice Paul and the National Woman's Party, 1910–1928* (New York: New York University Press, 1986).

— Natalie Atkin

National Women's Trade Union League (NWTUL)
The Progressive Era saw the flourishing of women's organizing on a wide range of issues. One of the most fertile

areas was the plight of working women. Facing poverty, poor working conditions, and personal danger in the workplace, as in the city streets, women workers had few means with which to combat inequality. Organized labor, long the recourse of skilled workingmen, was noted for its hostility toward women in the workplace and in the union. With few allies, working women often had to rely on their own scant resources. In Great Britain at the turn of the century, middle-class and elite women organized a support group for women workers and their unions called the Women's Trade Union League. Following their example, American socialists, among them William English Walling and Mary Kenney O'Sullivan, sought to organize a similar association. At two meetings in Boston in 1903, settlement house workers, labor union leaders, and others formed the National Women's Trade Union League (NWTUL). The league's first president was Mary Morton Kehew; Jane Addams was first vice president, and Mary O'Sullivan first secretary. Labor reformers in Boston, Chicago, and New York quickly formed local branches of the league to address the poor conditions and poverty faced by women in the workplace. In 1906, Mary Dreier Robins, a labor reformer and wife of Chicago settlement house worker Raymond Robins, became NWTUL president. She remained in the office until 1922.

Built on a model of cross-class solidarity, the NWTUL brought working women and middle-class women together to improve the condition of women in the workplace. In this effort, they had a range of tactics—public education, social investigation, support for unions in organizing drives and strikes, and lobbying state legislatures and Congress for protective labor laws. During the league's first two years, it supported strikes in Chicago; Troy, New York; and Fall River, Massachusetts.

The event that catapulted the NWTUL to national attention was the 1909–10 SHIRTWAIST MAKERS STRIKE in New York City. During that strike, the NWTUL raised money for strikers' relief and bail, helped to revitalize local 25 of the INTERNATIONAL LADIES' GARMENT WORKERS UNION, and organized mass meetings and picket lines. Early on, reports of the arrest of women pickets and police harassment fueled public outrage at the treatment of the young workers. When middle-class women allies, including the New York Women's Trade Union League president Margaret Dreier, were jailed for participating in the picketing, public pressure on garment firms to settle the strike increased.

In the midst of the shirtwaist strike, NWTUL members William Walling, Mary Dreier, Helen Marot, Leonora O'Reilly, and LILLIAN WALD helped found the NATIONAL ASSOCIATION FOR THE ADVANCEMENT OF COLORED PEOPLE, a move that helped solidify support for the strikers and avoided the possibility of African-American strikebreakers.

Still, larger firms proved resistant to public pressure to settle the strike. The strike ended when garment manufacturers broke down worker resistance, and many returned to work. Despite the loss, the NWTUL took credit for solidifying its goals by reviving ILGWU labor organizing in the garment trade.

The national NWTUL progressively worked to investigate working conditions, conduct union organizing campaigns, and support women workers in strikes across the nation. Its support of the organizing campaign in men's clothing led to the founding of the Amalgamated Clothing Workers. The league also understood the need for publicity and education for the public. Its journal, *Life and Labor*, edited by Australians Alice Henry and Stella Franklin, served as a forum to educate women workers in citizenship, labor history, and union practice. Once the NWTUL came out in support of WOMAN SUFFRAGE, the journal also informed its readers about the progress of suffrage campaigns. Beginning in 1915, the Chicago branch of the NWTUL formed a leadership school that recruited women workers nationally. As union membership began to decline in the 1920s, the NWTUL turned its primary attention to protective labor legislation, especially minimum wage and maximum hour laws for women. This turn cost the league members and relegated much of its activity to lobbying. Under Rose Schneiderman, its next president, the league continued to press for labor legislation throughout the 1920s.

Further reading: Nancy Schrom Dye, *As Equals and as Sisters: Feminism and the Labor Movement in the Women's Trade Union League of New York* (Columbia: University of Missouri Press, 1980); Robin Miller Jacoby, *The British and American Women's Trade Union Leagues, 1890–1925; A Case Study of Feminism and Class* (Brooklyn, N.Y.: Carlson, 1994).

Native Americans

In the late 19th century, reformers responding to the devastation of the Native American population began to formulate policies aimed toward assimilating native peoples. In some ways, their campaign to bring "civilization" to their charges was well-intentioned. They thought that education, property ownership, and religious conversion were the means by which Native Americans could achieve equal citizenship. At the same time, support for assimilation was deeply colored by misunderstanding and even fear and hatred of Native American language, religion, and cultural practices. In their challenge to Native American tribalism, with its collective land ownership, nomadic ways, and animistic religion, reformers cooperated with others whose main purpose was to use and exploit Native American land and resources.

A threefold plan to assimilate Native Americans became the major driving force behind the U.S. government's policy in the Bureau of Indian Affairs. Through allotment policy, the government assigned individuals' plots of land from the reservation and sold the surplus. It developed a system of BIA boarding and day schools to educate Native American children in English and in industrial and agricultural skills; and it replaced tribal authority in criminal trials with federal, state, and local courts. The undermining of tribal government effectively ended tribal sovereignty. By granting Native Americans citizenship in conjunction with allotment and military service, or in the comprehensive Indian Citizenship Act of 1924, the U.S. Congress finally and forcibly integrated Native Americans into the nation. However, it was not until after World War II that some states granted Native Americans the right to vote or equal political rights.

After 1900, the policy of allotment, first begun under the Dawes Severalty Act (1887), began to take its toll on Native American land ownership. The original legislation had put breaks on the ability of land speculators and corporations to take advantage of the allotment system and buy or lease the millions of acres of Native American reservation land. Allotted land had been put in trust for 25 years to ensure that it would not be sold wholesale to non-Native Americans. Each land sale or lease had to be approved by the Department of the Interior. Under pressure from railroad corporations, who sought the right-of-way on reservations, from oil and mining companies looking for mineral leases, and from timber companies and cattle syndicates, the Congress responded with a new series of laws that speeded up the allotment of land. In 1898, the Curtis Act ended tribal sovereignty in the Indian Territory. In 1902, the Dead Indian Land Act gave the right to Native Americans to sell inherited property, and the BURKE ACT put more Native American land at risk by eliminating the 25-year trust period. Over 90 million acres of reservation land were transferred to non-Native Americans between 1887 and 1932. While more than 100,000 Native Americans had received individual allotments, most of the land had been sold as "surplus" to non-Native American owners.

Connected to the policy of allotment was the transfer of criminal and civil legal cases from tribal authority to the federal and state court system. In part the transfer was designed to dismantle tribal authority and the separate sovereignty of Indian nations. Another consequence was that the shift to state courts aided the transfer of Native American land to white authorities. County courts soon provided supervision for, and later guardianship of, Native American lands, and the practice led to abuses. There was no compensation for the loss of tribal sovereignty. Few states accepted that Native Americans had equal political or civil rights, and in some states, Native Americans were denied the right to vote. This left them vulnerable to state and local courts. By declaring its owners legally incompetent, for example, courts and lawyers in the former Indian Territory of Oklahoma simply usurped control over Native American land and sold or leased it to mining, oil, timber, and cattle corporations. Court challenges to the forcible allotment of land, such as *LONE WOLF V. HITCHCOCK*, only confirmed the second-class status of Native Americans under the law.

Along with allotment came the creation of a federal school system for Native Americans. In the schools, native languages, religious practices, dances, and chants were forbidden, as they were on many reservations under government supervision. Despite substantial resistance to Christianity and white education, however, the Bureau of Indian Affairs continued to push for its agenda of assimilation. In 1918, Congress passed a law granting citizenship to Native Americans who served their country in the military during the war; and in 1924, the Indian Citizenship Act

granted citizenship to all Native Americans who had not yet been naturalized.

Despite the assault on tribal land and authorities, many Native American communities proved resilient to the threat of federal and state policies. Not only through formal organization but also by retaining tribal independence, such tribes as the Navajo, Yuma, Pueblo, Hopi, Seneca, and Seminole successfully sidestepped allotment and the destructive policies of the period. For other reasons, the cessation of warfare, improvement in health care and nutrition, in particular the decline in the incidence of tuberculosis, and the creation of stable communities, the Native American population, in decline for hundreds of years, began to show signs of recovery and revival. From a low of 237,000 in the Bureau of Indian Affairs census of 1900, there was a slow growth in population to nearly 335,000 in 1930. Changes in Native American mortality were central to this growth. Life expectancy for Native Americans in 1900 was 30 to 35 years on average, significantly lower than

A group of young Native American men and women at the U.S. Indian School, Carlisle, Pennsylvania, participate in an art class. *(Library of Congress)*

the 50 years for the general population. Fertility also increased, as the population received better health care.

There were signs of a significant political revival as well. New groups, often coalitions of Native Americans and their white allies, took on the issues of Indian rights after 1910. The Four Mothers Society, the Society of American Indians (later the American Indian Association), the Indian Rights Association, and the American Indian Defense Association fought to stop the illegal seizure of lands attempted by Albert Fall, the secretary of the interior responsible for TEAPOT DOME, and supported legislation such as the Pueblo Lands Act, which defended land ownership and pushed for additional compensation for lands already lost. These groups also lobbied Congress to study Native American policies and conditions on reservations. In a 1924 report, *The Indian Problem,* a committee of 100 reviewed federal policy and upheld the land rights of Native Americans. In 1928, the Merriam Report on the Problem of Indian Administration directly linked allotment policy to the widespread poverty, high infant mortality, and low life expectancy of Native Americans. The Merriam Report called for the reorganization of the Bureau of Indian Affairs and improvement of living conditions. By the 1930s, with the Native American population recovering and the advent of a new, more sympathetic administration under Secretary of the Interior John Collier, the policy of assimilation ground to a halt.

Further reading: Frederick E. Hoxie, *A Final Promise: The Campaign to Assimilate the Indians, 1880–1920* (Lincoln: University of Nebraska Press, 1984); James C. Olson and Raymond Wilson, *Native Americans in the Twentieth Century* (Provo, Utah: Brigham Young University Press, 1984); Nancy Shoemaker, *American Indian Population Recovery in the Twentieth Century* (Albuquerque: University of New Mexico Press, 1999).

nativism

During the years from 1900 to 1930, the United States experienced several pronounced episodes of nativism, or anti-immigrant sentiment. A number of factors contributed to the nativism that characterized the time. In particular, as the United States witnessed major economic changes at the turn of the century, new immigrants from southern and eastern Europe often became the scapegoat for the nation's social and economic problems. Further influencing the nativist sentiment in the United States was the outbreak of WORLD WAR I, and President WOODROW WILSON's concerted effort to achieve "national unity" for bringing the United States into the conflict on the side of Britain and France. Xenophobia, or nativism, was not new to the United States, but the rapid increase in immigration only

provoked the latent anti-foreigner feelings that had come to characterize much of the nation. Throughout the war years, the Wilson administration expanded the powers of the government to promote (and in some cases, force) national unity. As President Wilson commented, "There are citizens of the United States, I blush to admit, born under other flags but welcomed under our generous naturalization laws to the full freedom and opportunity of America, who have poured the poison of disloyalty into the very arteries of our national life. Such creatures of passion, disloyalty, and anarchy must be crushed out. The hand of our power should close over them at once."

The rising spirit of nativism and Americanism, accordingly, was solidified in two concrete ways. First, nativists moved to restrict the ability of immigrants to enter the United States. Although Congress enacted legislation that restricted Chinese immigration in 1882, emigrants from other Asian countries faced relatively few restrictions on their ability to enter the United States before the outbreak of the First World War in 1914. With an Open Door policy in immigration and steady improvements in transatlantic transportation, European migrants were able to reach the United States in ever-increasing numbers and from a wider range of areas. Some 788,922 immigrants entered the United States in 1882 and 1,285,349 in 1907. As the volume of immigrants steadily increased, so too did the number of their religions and national diversity. By 1907, in contrast to earlier decades, nearly 75 percent of the immigrants who arrived in the United States were from Russia, Austria, Hungary, Balkan countries, and Italy. Despite numerous attempts to push Congress to close the doors on immigration, the nativist movement enacted only a few pieces of legislation to restrict the migration of individuals to the United States prior to 1907.

In 1907, the Expatriation Act granted the Immigration and Naturalization Service the right to bar immigrants who were suspected radicals. The act also, for the first time in American history, took citizenship away from women who married foreign nationals. The GENTLEMEN'S AGREEMENT of the same year informally stopped the flow of emigrants from Japan. And in 1917, the IMMIGRATION ACT first instituted a literacy test for immigrants and prescribed health standards.

By the early 1920s, many Americans felt that the country could no longer accommodate, especially in the face of growing labor radicalism, the nearly one million immigrants that had been arriving each year since the 1880s. A renewed effort was put into place to curtail immigration to the United States. The resulting laws—the QUOTA ACT of 1921 and the NATIONAL ORIGINS ACT of 1924—adopted a racist formula for determining the number of immigrants allowed into the United States annually for individual nations. In particular, the legislation adopted the idea that certain immigrants were more prone to Americanization. As such, they should be permitted into the United States, while other nationalities should be excluded because of their supposed inability to adopt American ways.

The move to "Americanize" the foreign-born, particularly during the First World War, represented the second major way in which nativism surfaced in the United States. Anti-Chinese and anti-Japanese sentiments had already placed all Asians, whether foreign-born or native-born, beyond the bounds of American identity. Attempts in San Francisco to segregate Japanese-American schoolchildren in 1907 and the successful drive to bar Japanese ownership of agricultural land were but two examples of how Asians were excluded from American rights. The anti-immigrant activities of the KU KLUX KLAN also revealed how immigrants were excluded and vilified. Patriotism and national unity efforts during the world war culminated in increasing and systematic efforts at the Americanization of immigrants. The move to make 100-percent Americans of the foreign-born was a concerted attempt to create a homogeneous national identity. Various institutions were involved in these efforts. They ranged from the efforts of employers like HENRY FORD to "melt" the foreign-born into unhyphenated "Americans" through workplace programs to public school education. Despite pleas by some social scientists such as Horace Kallen that to strip immigrants of their cultural identity was undemocratic, federal, state, and local governments made Americanization among their top priorities after 1917.

As labor radicalism erupted in the United States, many contended that Americanization was not a sufficient means to obtain national unity. As a result, the effort to secure restrictive immigration laws gained renewed support. The anti-immigrant supporters argued that only by closing the door on undesirable nationalities would the United States be able to achieve the nativist goal of Americanization. By 1924, Congress had enacted legislation that effectively closed the door to emigrants from countries outside of northwest Europe and the Western Hemisphere. This restrictive legislation remained the basis of American immigration policy until the administration of President Lyndon Johnson revised it in the 1965 Immigration Act.

Further reading: John Higham, *Strangers in the Land: Patterns of American Nativism, 1860–1925,* 2nd ed. (New Brunswick, N.J.: Rutgers University Press, 1988).

— David R. Smith

Naval Disarmament Conference (1927)

In 1927 the major powers met at the Geneva Conference on Naval Disarmament to negotiate for more extensive reductions in naval armaments than they had agreed to at the WASHINGTON CONFERENCE ON NAVAL DISARMAMENT of 1921–22. Competing national interests frustrated their efforts. Failing to reach an agreement at the Geneva Conference had important consequences for the future of peace and stability around the world. Although at first the United States stayed out of an arms race for budgetary reasons, Japan and Great Britain competed in a naval buildup that eventually helped to bring about World War II.

The limitation of naval armaments seemed like a realistic possibility in the 1920s. The major powers first successfully concluded a round of agreements at the Washington Conference on Naval Disarmament in 1922. At the same time, the LEAGUE OF NATIONS had been working, without the participation of the United States, for limitations of both land and sea armaments. Although the TREATY OF VERSAILLES had limited only German armaments, it reiterated the need for general limitations among the major powers.

Under the administration of President CALVIN COOLIDGE, the United States hoped to reach agreements that would lead to broad-based naval disarmament. Although the Washington Conference had set limits on the size of warships and aircraft carriers of the major powers, it left a loophole for smaller ships. The naval powers used the loophole to strengthen their military on the seas. In 1927 the Coolidge administration called for another conference, hoping to reach an expanded naval agreement. Meetings between the United States, Britain, and Japan took place in Geneva, but the French and Italians refused to participate in the conference. The French were disgruntled at being placed in the same class of military power as Italy at the 1921–22 conference. The Italians would not attend if the French did not show up. Meanwhile, Britain and Japan refused to stop their naval arms race in cruisers. After meeting for several months, the conference ended without an agreement. After the failure of the Geneva Conference, the U.S. Congress passed legislation that, in effect, placed the United States in the arms race. A few weeks before Coolidge left office in 1929, Congress passed a bill that provided for the construction of 15 heavy cruisers and an aircraft carrier.

Representatives of the major powers met once again for a naval disarmament conference in 1930 as they faced a world economic crisis. Facing an international economic depression, governments recognized that a reasonable place to cut costs significantly was in spending on their navies. The conference agreed to extend the limits of the 1922 Washington agreement to lighter ships. In addition, America, Britain, and Japan agreed to limit their navies at a 5:5:3 ratio. Italy and France signed the agreement as well. Although the two countries could not agree on a ratio between them, they agreed to resolve the dispute within two years. As international tensions heightened in the

1930s, due to Japan's expansion in Asia and the continued British presence, no agreement could be reached.

Further reading: Richard W. Fanning, *Peace and Disarmament: Naval Rivalry and Arms Control, 1922–1933* (Lexington: University Press of Kentucky, 1995).

— Glen Bessemer

neutrality

Neutrality is a legal concept whereby a nation seeks to avoid military involvement in armed conflicts between belligerent states. Neutral powers are permitted to engage in all legal international trade and transactions. Laws concerning the rights and duties of neutrality are contained in the Declaration of Paris of 1856, Hague Convention V (1907) under "neutrality in land war," and the Hague Convention XIII (1907) under "neutrality in maritime war." Neutral parties are required to issue either a general or a special declaration when hostilities break out, although the declaration of neutrality may be repealed or modified.

Certain rights are implicit in a country's declaration of neutrality. One of these is the right to territorial integrity. Territory may be defined as air space, water, or land. Those who are engaging in a war may not use a neutral's territory as a base of operations or engage in hostilities on or in it. A neutral also has the right to maintain diplomatic communications with other neutrals and with the warring parties, the right to demand compliance with domestic regulations set to secure neutrality, and the right to demand warring parties not interfere with commercial endeavors of its citizens.

Early on, the American Republic had struggled with issues of neutral rights in a world rife with European conflicts that often disrupted trade. As a commercial nation, the United States embraced the concept of "free ships, free goods." This concept held that the nationality of a ship determined the status of its cargo and that only contraband (forbidden goods) on neutral ships would be subject to capture. The issue was fought over with France in the "Quasi-war" in 1797, during the Napoleonic Wars, and finally in the War of 1812. Only in 1856 did the European powers guarantee "free ships, free goods" to neutral powers in wartime.

After WORLD WAR I began in 1914, Britain greatly expanded its contraband list. It intended to enforce a "continuous voyage" doctrine. Under this doctrine, a nation at war could seize a ship en route from one neutral port to another if its cargo were destined for an enemy nation. President WOODROW WILSON immediately protested Britain's actions as a violation of a neutral power's rights. Germany added to the problem when it declared that the waters around Britain were a war zone in which all ships, even neutral ones, could be sunk without warning. Wilson threatened war in the eventuality that any American ship was sunk without warning or without thought for the safety of passengers and crew. Between 1914 and 1917, Wilson successfully kept the United States neutral by maintaining trading rights with Britain while not provoking Germany.

When the war dragged on into its fourth year, the Germans called Wilson's bluff. He broke off diplomatic relations with Germany, but he refused to declare war unless Germany were to undertake "overt" acts against American lives and property. Wilson proposed instead that American ships be armed, but a filibuster of isolationist congressmen prevented this. The ZIMMERMANN TELEGRAM, in which the German foreign secretary proposed a secret Mexican-German alliance, was published in March 1917. It produced the predictable ill will toward Germany. Even worse, the long dreaded "overt" acts directly followed the publication of the telegram when Germany sank four unarmed American merchant vessels.

German violations of American neutrality rights forced Wilson's hand. On April 2, 1917, he asked Congress for a declaration of war. German U-boats had now pushed a wavering country to enter the war. Six senators and 50 representatives voted against overcoming neutrality and going to war, but the goal of making the world safe from the submarine was not compelling enough to inspire the country's patriotism. In his declaration of war, Wilson transcended commerce and widened the scope of the war to include making the world safe for democracy. His idealistic vision won the support of a majority of Americans.

See also LEAGUE OF NATIONS.

Further reading: John W. Coogan, *The End of Neutrality: The United States, Britain, and Maritime Rights, 1899–1915* (Ithaca, N.Y.: Cornell University Press, 1981).

— Annamarie Edelen

New Freedom

Writing about his new reform program or the "New Freedom," President WOODROW WILSON wrote, "the concern of patriotic men is to put our government again on its right basis by substituting the popular will for the rule of guardians, the processes of common council for those of private arrangement." To do this, the Wilson administration would let the light in on all government affairs. Wilson sought to substitute public for private machinery in overseeing the economy and society. In the 1912 election Wilson voiced his program of reform as the "New Freedom," hearkening back to the American ideal of family farms and small businesses and fair competition. Roosevelt, his major opponent, called for a New Nationalism of increased federal government power. Wilson won the day.

The DEMOCRATIC PARTY regained the presidency under Wilson in 1912 due, in great part, to divisions within the REPUBLICAN PARTY. THEODORE ROOSEVELT's decision to establish the PROGRESSIVE PARTY cost the incumbent WILLIAM HOWARD TAFT the presidency. Wilson's own progressive policy, the "New Freedom," concentrated on opening the processes of politics and capital.

Wilson's hallmark "New Freedom" legislation included tariff, currency, election, banking, and child labor reform. The Wilson administration's first attacks on the domestic front were on TARIFFS, the banks, and the trusts, known as the "triple wall of privilege." Wilson personally presented his appeal to Congress for the Underwood Tariff Bill, which instituted a large reduction in rates and import fees. Many thought Wilson was committing political suicide, but he felt that the existing tariff placed undue hardship on average Americans. Wilson was successful in his lobbying efforts on the bill. A related measure was the new progressive income tax attached to the bill.

A second area of interest for Wilson's New Freedom was the banking system. Once again, Wilson took his appeal to the "sovereign people" and won. In 1913 he signed the FEDERAL RESERVE ACT. This act created the new Federal Reserve Board, which controlled 12 regional reserve districts, each with a central bank. They issued federal reserve notes backed by paper money, thus controlling the amount of currency. Trusts also were targeted with the FEDERAL TRADE COMMISSION ACT of 1914. This commission focused on monopolies and tried to prevent unfair trade practices. Other progressive measures put forth under Wilson included the FEDERAL FARM LOAN ACT of 1916, making credit available to farmers at low interest rates; the WORKMEN'S COMPENSATION ACT of 1916 for federal civil service employees; and the ADAMSON ACT of 1916, establishing an eight-hour day for railroad workers. In 1916 the child labor, KEATING-OWEN ACT was passed, which prohibited the shipment of products that had been made by workers under 14 years of age for some products and 16 for others. A Supreme Court decision later declared the act unconstitutional, but it was an important first step toward barring child labor.

Finally, the Seventeenth Amendment to the Constitution, which provided for the DIRECT ELECTION OF SENATORS and was considered a move toward more democratic representation, was passed during the Wilson years. It was designed to take away the influence of "party machines" and other threats to democratic elections. Wilson strove to give selection of candidates over to direct primaries and elections and get it out of the hands of "small groups of men." Wilson had wanted to leave a legacy more concerned with human rights than property rights.

Further reading: Kendrick A. Clements, *The Presidency of Woodrow Wilson* (Lawrence: University of Kansas Press,

1992); Arthur S. Link and Richard McCormick, *Progressivism* (Arlington Heights, Ill.: Harland Davidson, 1983).

— Annamarie Edelen

New Nationalism

During his first term in office, President THEODORE ROOSEVELT became increasingly aware of the power of corporations in public life. He targeted the large trusts, specifically Northern Securities and STANDARD OIL, for the worst abuses of the monopoly power to distort the market and corrupt the political process. For Roosevelt, however, the size of corporations was not the issue; it was how corporations used their power. To keep monopoly in check, what was needed was for government to regulate the large trusts. If the United States was to become a world power, it needed both powerful corporations and a strong, centralized federal government. Shared by many progressive reformers, this philosophy became known as the "New Nationalism." The New Nationalism took as its manifesto Herbert Croly's book, *The Promise of American Life* (1909). Croly argued that the major aim of progressive reform should be "to secure the maximum production from a private system with the most widespread diffusion of benefits as possible." Roosevelt agreed. As he announced to an audience in Osawatomie, Kansas, in 1911, true progressives would "recognize the inevitableness and the necessity of combinations in business and meet it by a corresponding increase in governmental power over big business." A year later, at the PROGRESSIVE PARTY convention, Roosevelt further developed these ideas, targeting the federal courts for criticism and arguing for greater federal power to regulate. He observed that it would take a powerful central government to control the force of Big Business. What was more, as federal courts continued to decide that new state legislation was unconstitutional, Roosevelt sided with those who viewed the courts as major obstacles to progressive reform. As he later asserted, the courts had created a safe neutral zone for corporate "lawlessness," in which neither state nor federal governments could act. He based his arguments on the claim that communities had the power to regulate property for the public good.

Roosevelt's political philosophy stood in stark contrast to those for whom small businesses, family farms, and voluntary organization were the primary means of securing American democracy. While he listened to their rhetoric, he characterized their belief as "rural toryism." They wished, he believed, to "attempt the impossible task of returning to the economic conditions that obtained sixty years ago." In the election of 1912, the divided soul of PROGRESSIVISM was on display. While Roosevelt and his party embraced the growth of government, Democratic candidate WOODROW WILSON and his supporters, including

WILLIAM JENNINGS BRYAN and future Supreme Court justice LOUIS BRANDEIS, echoed their fears that a powerful government could overshadow competition in the marketplace and individual liberty. As Roosevelt thundered about the New Nationalism on the campaign trail, Wilson articulated his beliefs and those of others as the NEW FREEDOM. In many ways, the election of 1912 and the battle over the role of government marked the first modern election. At the same time, the irony of the debate was that Wilson, the voice of the New Freedom, became an even more powerful president than Roosevelt, as his administration faced participation in WORLD WAR I. By virtue of his wartime government, Wilson took on the powers of a strong federal government for which the New Nationalism had clamored.

See also NORTHERN SECURITIES CASE.

Further reading: George Mowry, *The Era of Theodore Roosevelt, 1900–1912* (New York: Harper, 1958).

New Unionism

New Unionism refers to efforts to organize American workers in ways that sharply contrasted with the more conservative methods of the AMERICAN FEDERATION OF LABOR (AFL). Led by Samuel Gompers, it focused its organizing efforts on forming trade unions among skilled workers who were overwhelmingly white, male, and native-born. The AFL became the nation's first firmly established and influential labor organization and solidified its position by eschewing radical politics and labor violence. At times, it worked cooperatively with employers both in the workplace and through organizations such as the NATIONAL CIVIC FEDERATION.

Despite the AFL's success, the vast majority of American workers remained unorganized and poorly paid. Among the reasons for this failure were the increasing use of SCIENTIFIC MANAGEMENT techniques in MASS PRODUCTION and the wave of new immigrants from eastern and southern Europe, who competed with each other for factory jobs. The nature of work itself also was changing. Receding were the days when skilled craft workers enjoyed positions of privilege, prestige, and power because of their specialized knowledge. With the introduction of interchangeable parts and assembly line production, many employers no longer required highly skilled craft workers. Finally, the number of industrial workers increased dramatically, as the automobile, steel, mining, and oil industries built massive plants and refineries and employed hundreds, even thousands, of workers.

When the AFL failed to organize these unskilled and semi-skilled industrial workers, other organizations stepped into the breach. Where the AFL had restricted its efforts to organizing only highly skilled workers, many of the new unions attempted to organize workers throughout entire industries. One of the early examples of this was the UNITED MINE WORKERS OF AMERICA (UMWA). Led by JOHN MITCHELL, the UMWA attempted to organize mine workers regardless of their job classification within the industry. It was successful in recruiting new members in both bituminous and anthracite coal in the eastern fields and began to recruit in the West. Other unions, such as the INDUSTRIAL WORKERS OF THE WORLD (IWW), had as their purpose the organization of workers on an industrial basis, regardless of their gender, race, ethnicity, or occupation.

These new unions also differed from the AFL in that they were more progressive and even radical in their politics. Some had strong socialist influences and sought state intervention in labor relations; others looked toward direct action in the workplace as a cure for workers' ills. They were more willing to confront employers to gain recognition or secure their demands. When the UMWA encountered resistance to its attempts to organize the Pennsylvania miners, 140,000 miners walked off the job in the 1902 ANTHRACITE COAL STRIKE, one of the nation's largest. Led by WILLIAM "Big Bill" HAYWOOD, ELIZABETH GURLEY FLYNN, and others, the IWW pursued its goals through work stoppages, general strikes, boycotts, strikes, and other forms of direct action in eastern textile and electrical manufacturing, midwestern agriculture and timber, and at the iron ore deposits of the Mesabi Range in Minnesota and Michigan. Some of the most dramatic demonstrations of the New Unionism were in the SHIRTWAIST MAKERS STRIKE of 1909–10 and the LAWRENCE STRIKE of 1912.

One result of the rise of new unionism was that the labor movement grew in size and strength between 1900 and 1920. Union membership increased from 2 million in 1904 to 5 million in 1920. Throughout the country, workers were organizing unions and demanding pay increases, shorter workdays, and improved working conditions. The burgeoning labor movement also began flexing its political muscle, securing passage of the CLAYTON ANTITRUST ACT (1914) at the federal level and workmen's compensation laws at the state level. Through the INDUSTRIAL RELATIONS COMMISSION, the organized labor movement for the first time played an active role in shaping federal policy on labor relations. Despite the growing influence of the New Unionism, employers continued to resist bitterly the more radical new unions, especially the IWW, preferring to work with the more conservative AFL or to resist with private and state action all labor unions. Between 1914 and 1919, the AFL was the chief beneficiary of the increased power of the labor movement and worked closely with WOODROW WILSON's administration to support the American effort during WORLD WAR I.

The end of the war also brought an end to cooperation between the labor movement and the federal government. It resulted as well in severe repression of the new unionism. Across the country, workers frustrated by pledges not to strike during the war, by low wages, and by rampant inflation, walked off the job in one of the largest waves of strikes in the country's history. The STEEL STRIKE OF 1919, which began on September 22, and lasted until January 8, 1920, involved 365,000 steelworkers and marked the end of the uneasy labor accord reached during the war. The backlash against the strike wave and the labor movement was swift and widespread. Attorney General A. MITCHELL PALMER was convinced that many of the new unionists were supporters of the RUSSIAN REVOLUTION and were plotting to overthrow the federal government. With the backing of the AFL and many employers, Palmer launched a series of raids against suspected radicals, which became known as the RED SCARE. As one of the chief targets of the Red Scare, the IWW had its offices raided on several occasions. Big Bill Haywood and 165 other IWW leaders were arrested and convicted under the ESPIONAGE ACT of 1917 for hindering the war effort. Similar repression took place throughout the Northwest, where the IWW had been strongest. By the end of 1920, the organization was in total disarray and ceased to be an effective force in the American labor movement.

The demise of New Unionism severely undermined the strength of the labor movement and ensured that it remained in a weakened state throughout the 1920s. New industrial and mixed unions had brought thousands of previously unorganized workers into the labor movement, challenged the supremacy of employers, and criticized conservative state and federal policies toward organized labor. The massive post–World War I strike wave indicated the extent to which new ideas and a willingness to take direct action had taken root among American workers, but the divisions between the new and more radical unions, such as the IWW and the older, more conservative AFL, undermined the effectiveness of the strike wave and helped ensure the demise of the new unionism.

See also LABOR AND LABOR MOVEMENT.

Further reading: David Montgomery, *The Fall of the House of Labor: The Workplace, the State, and American Labor Activism, 1865–1925* (New York: Cambridge University Press, 1987).

— Robert Gordon

New Woman

The New Woman is a term that referred to women's more prominent role in the public arena in the late 19th and early 20th centuries. Women's greater visibility manifested

Satirizing modern role reversals, a woman wearing knickers and smoking a cigarette observes a man doing laundry (*Library of Congress*)

itself in colleges, the professions, and reform movements. Economic and social transformations in the mid- to late 19th century contributed to new and different roles for women, particularly women of the upper and middle classes. Social restrictions on middle-class women eased as a market economy changed the dynamics of the household and the relationship of households to the rest of society.

Middle-class white women's lives were shaped not only by circumstances, but also by their changing status. For one, they chose to have fewer children, a fact that contributed to their growing power within the family and allowed them greater time and flexibility to pursue activities outside of the home. Once the children of married middle-class women were in school, women could devote their energies to a variety of causes. Temperance, social reform, church activism, and the club movement among others provided women with the opportunity to "work" outside the home and in same-sex organizations.

Colleges served as a politicizing and socializing force for the emerging New Woman. As more colleges began accepting women and more women's colleges were established, opportunities expanded for women. Women's colleges in particular allowed women to establish their own social networks that eventually served as stepping stones into the public arena.

Education provided professional opportunities that characterized the New Woman's elevated status. The New

Woman was often a college graduate who worked as a settlement worker, teacher, or librarian. Previously, female jobs such as nursing did not require a college education, but nursing became increasingly professionalized early in the 20th century. Despite these changes, female college graduates still worked in traditional female occupations believed to require women's innate skills of nurturing and compassion.

Other characteristics of the New Woman included delaying marriage or remaining single. Delaying or avoiding marriage grew more acceptable by society as long as women devoted themselves to a calling deemed socially valuable, such as charitable or reform work. The women's club movement channeled some of women's activism in these areas. Beginning in the 1890s, women began forming women's organizations for the purpose of coordinating volunteers on issues of social concern. Although these groups had precedents, not until the Progressive Era did such activity become widespread. In 1892, there were 100,000 members associated with the newly formed General Federation of Women's Clubs; by WORLD WAR I, there were over a million. Initially, most women's clubs engaged in cultural discussions, but many soon adopted a reformist, and even radical, agenda, including advocating for WOMAN SUFFRAGE. Women's clubs were a reflection of both women's growing politicization and their political limits. The women's club movement staked a claim in the public arena using domestic arguments that women needed to extend their sphere to improve society.

Other movements associated with the New Woman made similar arguments. Temperance galvanized hundreds of thousands of women in the late 19th and early 20th centuries. The Women's Christian Temperance Union was the largest women's organization of the period. It not only worked to eliminate the evils associated with alcohol, but also sought to eradicate ills associated with men, including prostitution and political corruption. As such, it was a political association that located women's position as moral arbiter in public life. The movement's foot soldiers tended to be white middle-class women, many of whom later converted to the suffrage cause for many of the same reasons that they initially became involved in temperance.

Suffrage, like temperance and the club movement, drew primarily from a middle-class constituency. Arguing that society's problems could be remedied by women's influence, suffragists began agitating in earnest for the vote by the 1890s. The movement reflected the New Woman's emphasis on female organizations and networks to support reform and women's entrance into previously male domains. Despite these arguments, suffragists were regularly derided by their foes for allegedly acting against nature in attempting to enter politics. Opponents of women's education made similar claims that women did not have the mental and physical capacity to engage in learn-ing. Intellectual activity, some male physicians maintained, drained blood from a woman's reproductive organs. Nativists feared that, if native-born American women were educated, they would have less interest in children, causing immigrant women and children to outpace native-born families. Race suicide, they claimed, was the inevitable result of women's education.

JANE ADDAMS, who founded Hull-House in Chicago, was the model for this generation of New Woman. She came from a prominent Illinois family and attended college. Later traveling to Europe, she was influenced by the settlement house movement there. Never considering marriage an option, Addams returned to the United States to devote herself to uplifting urban immigrants as well as herself, as she had long been searching for a purpose in life. In her autobiography, *Twenty Years at Hull-House,* she argued that women needed to relinquish "the family claim" on their lives and find "salvation" in attending to social needs.

Addams represented the cross-class activism that many New Women pursued. The NATIONAL WOMEN'S TRADE UNION LEAGUE embodied the reform spirit of the New Woman in labor struggles. Many female reformers worked with poor urban immigrants who labored in hazardous working conditions. The NWTUL was formed in 1903 as a vehicle for upper- and middle-class women to support working-class women. In one of the most famous strikes of the period, the NWTUL lent its moral, financial, and legal resources to thousands of striking garment workers in 1909, raising awareness of the female immigrants' plight and forging a cross-class alliance that the male labor movement would not.

The New Woman herself was a bridge between Victorian social mores and modern life. She opened up doors to economic, social, and political advancement through single-sex networks and by using society's sexual divisions to her advantage. The New Woman was one of the most important constituent groups engaged in Progressive Era reform. After such victories as the Prohibition and suffrage amendments, reform waned in the period after World War I, as did many of the women-based groups that had spearheaded reform. As an image of its time, the New Woman was retired, as "modernity" became the new watchword of the age.

See also WOMEN'S STATUS AND RIGHTS.

Further reading: Nancy Cott, *The Grounding of Modern Feminism* (New Haven, Conn.: Yale University Press, 1987).

— Natalie Atkin

Niagara Movement

A civil rights organization founded by W. E. B. DU BOIS in 1905, the Niagara Movement sought to provide a voice for militant action against racial discrimination in the United States. It suffered due to organizational weakness, the opposition of other African-American leaders, and the opposition of whites, and disbanded by 1911. The Niagara Movement's legacy of black militancy lived on in the NATIONAL ASSOCIATION FOR THE ADVANCEMENT OF COLORED PEOPLE.

Du Bois called the first convention at Niagara Falls, Ontario, in the hope of creating a militant voice that would challenge the prevailing racial system in the United States. Du Bois and the other founding members disagreed with the teachings of Booker T. Washington, who at the time was the best-recognized leader among African Americans. Repudiating Washington, Du Bois and the others believed that African Americans should fight for immediate political and civil rights. Rejecting Washington's argument that white Americans would accept African Americans once they proved themselves to be upstanding and useful citizens through hard work, Du Bois and the others proclaimed that only through immediate and militant action could the African Americans force white Americans to change.

The Declaration of Principles written after the first convention indicated the radical protest that the founders supported. The principles demanded immediate suffrage and civil rights. It protested the "peonage and virtual slavery" that existed in the South. The principles included complaints against the policies of employers in using African-American workers against white workers and against labor union discrimination. They demanded free and compulsory education through high school and the end of discrimination in colleges and trade schools. The Niagara group attacked segregation in churches and streetcars. To right these wrongs, the Niagara Movement urged national education and legislation to secure enforcement of the constitutional amendments guaranteeing equal rights.

The movement never became the force its founders envisioned. Although it gained members in its first two years, it did not establish itself financially and never effectively found its voice. This was due to a number of reasons. First, Booker T. Washington actively discouraged white and conservative African-American donors from supporting the Niagara Movement. Second, its militant tactics repelled some supporters and it faced a severe backlash from its critics. Third, Du Bois and the others never made the movement into a mass organization. It remained an organization of the educated elite. Fourth, the leadership continually fought over tactics.

By 1911, the Niagara Movement had collapsed beneath all these pressures. Its legacy lived on in the National Association for the Advancement of Colored People (NAACP). Du Bois and several other Niagara leaders helped found the NAACP and brought to it a dedication to militant, direct agitation in the pursuit of civil rights.

See also RACE AND RACIAL CONFLICT.

— Michael Hartman

Nineteenth Amendment   See woman suffrage

Non-Partisan League

Founded in 1915 in North Dakota, the Non-Partisan League (NPL) became a leading force in state and regional politics for the next decade and the sponsor of experiments in public ownership and socialist governance. Dedicated to a non-partisan strategy and the Populist tradition of agrarian radicalism, the league sought to create a future of cooperative production within a state-controlled economy that favored small farms and small firms. NPL adherents organized not as a third party but as a political force that could support and influence progressive factions of the two major parties. It backed candidates who supported its progressive program and sought to work as a balance of power in both state and, eventually, national politics.

Situated in a largely rural state, the Non-Partisan League's program promoted an agenda of a "New Day" for North Dakota. It directed its efforts at revitalizing the rural economy and protecting ordinary people from the power of corporations. It flourished in the context of a political culture that provided its members with public education, social and political events, and material symbolism. Under the leadership of league president Arthur C. Townley, Socialist Party organizers and members of the Equity Society, an organization for farm cooperatives, spread the word of the Non-Partisan League. They supported league efforts to take control of the North Dakota state government in 1916. By 1918, the NPL had defeated most of its rivals in new elections and proceeded to enact its program in the state legislature, seeking to establish a state bank to provide rural credit and state-owned grain mills and grain elevators, state-funded crop and farm insurance, workers' compensation, and subsidized housing for workers, as well as greater state regulation of transportation.

Tapping into a regional political culture, the Non-Partisan League spread through the Midwest and the northern plains. As a social movement rooted in rural life with its dependence on the labor of women as well as men, the NPL recruited large numbers of women into its ranks and supported women's right to vote and participate. The league had its greatest success in Minnesota, where a state Non-Partisan League joined farmers and workers in new political efforts and laid the groundwork for the founding of the Farmer-Labor Party in 1922. The league also had influence on the politics in Montana, Idaho, Wisconsin, and Colorado as well as supporters in 13 other states.

Opposition to the league from North Dakota's small urban population, middle-class farmers, and business came together in the Independent Voters' Association, which openly challenged the NPL through investigation of league finances, accusations of corruption, and charges of anti-Americanism. The NPL's opposition to the U.S. entry into WORLD WAR I also cost the league supporters and brought with it government surveillance. Before the war, many German-American farmers held aloof from the Non-Partisan League, in large part due to its rhetorical support of temperance. Now, however, the NPL's position against the war attracted the support of German-Americans who felt embattled. Their growing support added weight to the charge that the NPL was pro-German and anti-American. By 1919, these charges had eroded league support and cost it political office. By 1925, factionalism within the league, its declining membership, and government prosecution effectively destroyed the NPL as a mass organization. It lingered on as a force in North Dakota politics for another two decades, reviving itself under a more conservative banner in the 1930s. In contrast, its heir, the Farmer-Labor Party of Minnesota, grew to become a major state power in the same decade.

See also FARMER-LABOR PARTY; RADICALISM; SOCIALISM.

Further reading: Robert L. Morlan, *Political Prairie Fire: The Non-Partisan League, 1915–1922* (Minneapolis: University of Minnesota Press, 1955).

Northern Securities case (*Northern Securities Co. v. U.S.*) (1904)

A landmark court case in the antitrust movement of the Progressive Era, the Northern Securities case pitted the interests of a newly formed railroad conglomerate against the federal government's authority to regulate and restrict monopoly in national markets. In its 1895 decision in *U.S. v. E.C. Knight*, the Supreme Court held that holding companies, corporations that held a controlling interest of stock in more than one corporation, did not violate antitrust laws. Under this loose interpretation of the Sherman Antitrust Act, industrial and transportation giants such as U.S. STEEL and STANDARD OIL sought to combine the vertical and horizontal functions of industry within a single company, which both created a monopoly within an industry and gave them competitive advantages in the marketplace. Using the form of a holding company, railroad magnate James J. Hill and financier J. P. Morgan

sought to form a railroad monopoly. They merged the Great Northern Railroad and the Northern Pacific Railroad into a new corporation known as Northern Securities, with its headquarters in New Jersey. With capital of over $400 million, Hill and Morgan acquired majority stock in the large railroads and indirectly controlled the smaller Chicago, Burlington and Quincy. Outside observers noted that the stock was about 30 percent water, noting the practice of overvaluing corporate stock. Under the umbrella of the Northern Securities holding company, Hill and Morgan essentially acquired a monopoly in rail transportation in the Pacific Northwest.

Joining the ranks of large American corporations, Northern Securities attracted the attention of trust-busting president THEODORE ROOSEVELT in 1904. Under his administration, the Justice Department filed an antitrust suit against the company, charging it with antitrust violations. In the Supreme Court case, the high court decided against Northern Securities. It found that the creation of the Northern Securities holding company was a clear violation of the Sherman Antitrust Act. The company had created an illegal monopoly that restrained trade and undermined the competitive working of the market. Although Northern Securities' lawyers argued, using the *Knight* precedent, that the Sherman Act did not apply to holding companies, the Court responded that "If Congress had not, by the words used in the Act, described this and like cases, it would, we apprehend, be impossible to find words that would describe them." The company had to disband.

Northern Securities Co. v. U.S. was the first successful prosecution of a holding company under the antitrust laws. After the decision, Roosevelt declared that the Supreme Court had returned to the federal government the power to regulate corporate monopolies and illegal business combinations. He had, however, overstated the case. Although the government's victory put an end to the turn-of-the-century merger movement, holding companies were still in their infancy as a business practice. While they were no longer subject to government regulation, federal antitrust laws had little long-term effect on corporate use of the holding company to form monopolies. The 1911 Standard Oil decision did not alter the environment for big corporations, and trusts such as Amalgamated Copper, American Smelting and Refining, American Sugar, and U.S. Steel continued to thrive. In the 1920s, the use of holding companies spread to the utilities industry, as local utility companies began to form new monopoly enterprises.

Further reading: Arthur Link and Richard L. McCormick, *Progressivism* (Arlington Heights, Ill.: Harlan Davidson, 1983).

O

oil industry

The oil industry in the United States expanded rapidly between 1900 and 1930 as it tried to keep pace with the nation's energy demands. In particular, the expansion of industrial production and the widespread ownership of automobiles resulted in an insatiable demand for oil and gasoline. An important part of the nation's industrial development in the 1860s and 1870s, oil was first drilled in the United States in 1859 in Titusville, Pennsylvania. Initially, the oil refining industry was centered in three locations— Cleveland, Pittsburgh, and Philadelphia—and characterized by numerous small competitors. The crude oil was pumped from wells, chemically refined into kerosene, and then used primarily in the growing illumination industry. In 1867, JOHN D. ROCKEFELLER formed the STANDARD OIL Company and quickly began to dominate the industry. Rockefeller was determined to control every aspect of the industry including drilling, refining, transportation, sales, and distribution. As Standard Oil grew larger, Rockefeller used the company's power and wealth to buy out competitors and secure preferential transportation rates from the railroads. In 1872 Standard Oil controlled 10 percent of the industry. A decade later, the company controlled 90 percent. In 1882, Rockefeller combined all of the companies he had purchased to form the Standard Oil Trust. Less than a decade later, Rockefeller had expanded his oil empire to include ownership of oil wells, railroads, refineries, and distribution facilities throughout the country and could set oil prices at whatever level he desired.

By 1900, Standard Oil dominated the oil industry as one of the most powerful companies in the country. The way in which Rockefeller controlled the industry, determined prices, and eliminated competition worried muckraking journalists and progressive reformers. In 1904, *McClure's Magazine* published a series of articles by IDA TARBELL that exposed the way in which Rockefeller built his oil empire and the ruthless way in which he maintained it. Collectively published in 1904 as *The History of Stan-*

dard Oil, the articles helped convince the federal government to investigate possible antitrust violations. President Theodore Roosevelt had promised to enforce the Sherman Antitrust Act of 1890 and take an aggressive stand against illegal trusts and monopolies. In 1906, Roosevelt,

Oklahoma well strikes oil *(Library of Congress)*

217

claiming Standard Oil was 20 times larger than its nearest competitor, instructed the federal government to take action against the corporation. The case wasn't resolved until 1911 when the Supreme Court ruled that the company had in fact violated federal antitrust laws and ordered that, in order to spur competition, the company be broken into smaller, independent parts.

Between 1900 and 1930, oil became more and more profitable. As it did, oil companies began investing vast sums of money in exploration and development. No longer able to meet demand by finding oil reserves that had seeped to the earth's surface, companies began drilling deep underground. Oil companies hired university-trained scientists and geologists to analyze soil samples and rock formations in order to predict the location of new underground reserves. When a huge underground "gusher" was discovered in Beaumont, Texas, in 1901, it started an oil boom that lasted until the onset of the Great Depression. The new crude oil discovered in California and on the Gulf Coast of Texas yielded extremely high levels of fuel oil. After the discovery of the Beaumont gusher, the center of the domestic oil industry shifted to Texas.

Demand for oil was at an all-time high as industrial production increased. Factories, which had once been little more than small workshops, grew in size and complexity. The Ford Highland Park auto plant, for example, opened in 1910 and by 1917 employed 36,000 auto workers. The plant was highly automated, and it used massive amounts of gasoline and oil. The spread of the assembly line and mass production resulted in a corresponding growth in the oil industry. By 1919, gasoline had become the oil industry's best-selling product, accounting for approximately 45 percent of all sales. Technological innovations increased the purity of the gasoline produced. In 1914, Standard Oil of Indiana developed a "cracking" process that yielded a higher-octane gasoline. By eliminating impurities, automobile manufacturers were able to develop more powerful and efficient engines.

For a period of time, the Supreme Court's decision to break up Standard Oil had the desired impact. Even before the Court's ruling, it had become clear that the company's domination of the industry had begun to wane. Several new competitors entered the field before 1911, including Texaco (1902), Shell (1907), and British Petroleum (1909). By the time it was dissolved, Standard Oil controlled only 65 percent of the industry. The Supreme Court ruling against Standard Oil broke the giant into 34 smaller companies. Eventually, however, several large corporations dominated the industry. Known as the Seven Sisters, Esso (So = Standard Oil), Shell, Amoco, Chevron, Atlantic Richfield, British Petroleum, and Texaco extended their control over all aspects of the industry, both in the United States and around the world.

While industrial expansion helped spur the growth of the oil industry, it was the development of widespread automobile ownership that made the industry one of the wealthiest and most important in the country. In 1900, there were fewer than 2,500 registered automobiles. By 1929, the number had jumped to a staggering 26.7 million. Throughout the country, the local filling station became as common and as essential as the local bank.

The impact the oil industry had on the nation between 1900 and 1930 is impossible to overstate. ELECTRICITY, a rarity prior to 1900, also had become commonplace in most cities and spread rapidly to rural areas as well. By 1930, the country had become completely dependent upon gasoline and electricity. Homes were lighted and heated by gas and electricity. Food was stored and prepared using gas and electricity. In fact, by 1930, oil companies in the United States were producing over 3 million barrels of oil per day, and every aspect of daily life and the health of the American economy had become dependent upon oil.

Further reading: Daniel Yergin, *The Prize: The Epic Quest for Oil, Money, and Power* (New York: Simon and Schuster, 1991); Anthony Sampson, *The Seven Sisters: The Great Oil Companies and the World They Shaped* (New York: Bantam Books, 1976).

— Robert Gordon

Open Door Policy (1899, 1900)

As a summary of American foreign policy toward Asia, the Open Door policy was first articulated at the turn of the century in a bid for greater access to Asian economic markets. American interest in protecting these markets increased after the United States took control of the Philippines in the war with Spain in 1898. Government officials feared that they would be cut out of plans by the European imperialist powers to carve up China for themselves. By 1900, England, France, Germany, Russia, and Japan had already taken territory in China. In response, the United States hoped to persuade the major powers through diplomacy to maintain the territorial status quo and thus keep open economic access to Asia.

President William McKinley issued a statement in September 1898 stating that the United States wanted to protect the political and administrative integrity of China as well as have access to the country: "Asking only the open door for themselves, we are ready to accord the open door to others." In 1899, Secretary of State John Hay sent out a similar message, which was later called the "Open Door notes," to the major powers in Europe and Japan. In the messages, Hay asked England, Germany, Russia, France, Japan, and Italy to abide by three principles. First, he asked that each nation with a sphere of influence in China respect the rights of other nations in its sphere. Second, he asked that Chinese officials continue to collect tariff duties in all the spheres. Third, he asked for nondiscrimination by nations in levying port dues and railroad rates against other nations. U.S. officials hoped that the principles would protect free trade in China. In addition, they wanted to prevent the formal partition of China by European powers while avoiding military involvement.

Europe and Japan reacted coolly to the Open Door proposals, noting that they would be unable to act unless all the other powers agreed as well. Despite the weak reception to the Open Door policy, Hay announced that all major powers had accepted the American principles. In practice, any nation could violate the Open Door, unless the United States was willing to go to war over the policy.

Almost immediately the Open Door was tested by a revolt that broke out in China. In the BOXER REBELLION, nationalists laid siege to the entire foreign diplomatic corps, most of whom had retreated to the British embassy in Beijing. As a result the imperial powers, including the United States, sent an international expeditionary force into China to rescue the diplomats. The international force broke the siege in August 1900.

President McKinley ordered the military to participate in the expeditionary force so that the United States could prevent the partition of China by Japan and the European powers. After the Boxer Rebellion, England and Germany agreed to abide by the Open Door Policy. In addition, Hay persuaded the major powers to agree to China compensating them for damages accrued during the rebellion. At least in theory, the United States achieved its goals of maintaining access to free trade and of protecting the sovereignty of China. In practice, the United States was unable to prevent the country's dismemberment by European countries, because the United States was ultimately unwilling to use military force against the major powers to protect China.

During the Boxer Rebellion, Russia had positioned 175,000 troops in Manchuria, a province of China over which Russia and Japan vied for control. It demanded exclusive rights and a commercial monopoly in China. President THEODORE ROOSEVELT and Hay, unable to stop Russian encroachment on Chinese sovereignty, stated that they recognized the privileged role of Russia in the region but that the administration wanted to preserve the commercial freedom of the United States. Roosevelt backed down from the Open Door Policy of 1900, because he thought that Americans were not willing to fight in a remote area of Asia for the abstract idea of Chinese sovereignty in Manchuria. According to historian Akira Iriye, Roosevelt realized the futility of trying "to play the role of an Asian power without military power."

In 1904, Japan attacked the Russian fleet at Port Arthur in Manchuria. In 1905, President Roosevelt agreed to mediate the RUSSO-JAPANESE WAR that had broken out as a result. At a peace conference, Roosevelt reached an agreement between the powers. The Russians agreed to recognize Japanese territorial gains in exchange for the Japanese agreeing to cease their fighting and expansion. Roosevelt also reached a secret agreement with the Japanese, ensuring that the United States could continue its free trade in the region. With the Russian fleet destroyed at Port Arthur, however, Japan became the dominant naval power in the Pacific, and began excluding American trade from the territories it controlled.

In the end, the United States persuaded some of the European powers to enforce the Open Door. Having intervened in the affairs of nations outside the Western Hemisphere, the Open Door policy was symbolic of the rise of the United States as a world military power early in the 20th century. Yet, both the war with Spain and the relative ineffectiveness of its diplomacy in the Open Door notes revealed the inadequacy of the American military. The experience of expansion spurred national reforms to build a modern military system in the United States.

Further reading: Michael H. Hunt, *The Making of a Special Relationship: The United States and China to 1914* (New York: Columbia University Press, 1983); Akira Iriye, *Pacific Estrangement: Japanese and American Expansion, 1897–1911* (Cambridge, Mass.: Harvard University Press, 1972).

— Glen Bessemer

open shop movement

The open shop movement was an attempt on the part of corporations, trade associations, chambers of commerce, and their political supporters to weaken the organized labor movement by requiring employees to work in an open or nonunion workplace. Gains in labor union membership in the early 20th century prompted sharp responses from employers and businessmen, and antiunion organizations such as the NATIONAL ASSOCIATION OF MANUFACTURERS and the American Anti-Boycott Association organized campaigns at both the local and national level aimed against strikes, boycotts, and political action among workers. Although the majority of employers had long opposed labor unions and resisted the closed or union shop (whereby workers were required to join the union as a condition of their employment), the open shop movement began in earnest in response to the wave of labor unrest that followed WORLD WAR I.

The labor movement gained strength between 1900 and 1918. Union membership increased from 2 million in 1904 to 5 million in 1920. As the power of the labor movement increased, unions began demanding closed or union shops. The main advantage of the closed shop was that unions did not have to continually recruit new employees in order to maintain their presence. Most employers resisted any form of organized labor, and they especially opposed the closed shop. The wave of labor unrest that followed the end of the war, most notably the massive STEEL STRIKE OF 1919, convinced business leaders of the need to fight labor with a united front.

At a 1919 meeting on industrial relations called by President WOODROW WILSON, business leaders such as Henry Clay Frick, Judge Elbert Gary, and JOHN D. ROCK-EFELLER, Jr., came up with a plan to roll back the gains made by organized labor. Dubbed the AMERICAN PLAN, it encouraged employers not to negotiate with labor unions and launched a campaign to convince the American public that the closed shop and the labor movement in general were "un-American." Tapping into the patriotism unleashed during the war, backers of the open shop movement insisted that, because employees were required to become union members, the closed shop was unfair and undemocratic. NAM president John Edgerton stated "I can't conceive of any principle that is more purely American . . . than the open shop principle."

By 1920, a network of open shop organizations had spread throughout the country and the labor movement was on the defensive. Although the open shop movement was couched in patriotic terms, in reality it was little more than a concerted effort to roll back many of the wartime gains made by organized labor. Many employers who publicly championed the open shop as a workplace that welcomed both union and non-union employees were bitterly opposed to any union presence. U.S. STEEL, for example, had endured a five-month-long strike in 1919 rather than negotiate a contract with the National Committee for Organizing Iron and Steel Workers. Throughout the strike and even after, its president insisted that he would close every steel mill he owned before he agreed to a union contract. When combined with the RED SCARE, the open shop movement had a devastating impact on the labor movement. By 1929 union membership had fallen to 3.5 million.

Further reading: Irving Bernstein, *The Lean Years: A History of the American Worker, 1920–1933* (Boston: Houghton Mifflin, 1960).

— Robert Gordon

P

Palmer, Alexander Mitchell (1872–1936)

A. Mitchell Palmer was the attorney general who spearheaded the post–WORLD WAR I raids against suspected socialists, communists, radicals, and others who had opposed American entry into the war. Born in Moosehead, Pennsylvania, in 1872, Palmer was brought up in a strict Quaker family. After attending Swarthmore College, he joined the Pennsylvania Bar in 1893 and became involved in Democratic Party politics. He used his legal and political connections to launch his own political career. He was elected to the House of Representatives in 1909 and held his seat until 1915. As a member of the House, Palmer was an early supporter of WOODROW WILSON's presidential campaign in 1912, but his political career suffered a serious setback in 1916 when he was defeated in his bid to win a seat in the Senate.

During the time he spent in Congress, Palmer was closely identified with the progressive wing of the DEMOCRATIC PARTY and earned a reputation as a defender of woman suffrage and labor unions. His political career was revived in 1919 when Woodrow Wilson, rewarding Palmer's long-standing support, nominated him to become attorney general. American involvement in World War I had caused a serious rift among progressives, socialists, and pacifists, between those who supported American entry into the war and those who opposed it. Concerned about the public's long-standing isolationism, the Wilson administration was determined to rally public support for the war effort. Key components of its efforts to ensure public support were an all-out public relations campaign, spearheaded by the COMMITTEE FOR PUBLIC INFORMATION, and the silencing of anti-war critics, best exemplified by the passage of the ESPIONAGE ACT (1917) and the SEDITION ACT (1918). The fact that some progressives supported U.S. entry into World War I made it easier for the administration to crack down on those who dissented. Even though the war ended in November 1918, the outbreak of the RUSSIAN REVOLUTION had convinced many in the government of the need for even greater vigilance and suppression of political dissent.

By the time Palmer became attorney general, he was convinced that the Bolsheviks were intent upon launching a worldwide revolution and overthrowing the American government. In response, Mitchell hired J. Edgar Hoover as his special assistant. The Justice Department used the Espionage and Sedition acts to silence radical and left-wing dissent. Nevertheless, political and labor unrest escalated after the war. By the fall of 1919, Palmer was convinced that domestic and international communists and anarchists were determined to overthrow the American government. In response, on November 7, 1919, he authorized the arrest of more than 10,000 suspected communists, radicals, anarchists, immigrants, and dissidents. Many of those arrested during the first Palmer Raid were detained for days without a trial. A second raid took place in January 1920, with the INDUSTRIAL WORKERS OF THE WORLD as its main focus. Although most of those arrested in the Palmer raids were eventually released and no charges filed, several hundred were ultimately deported from the country.

By early 1920, when it became clear that no revolution or uprising had ever been in the works, public opinion turned sharply against Palmer and the Wilson administration. The Palmer Raids and the RED SCARE of 1919–21 not only devastated the already weakened labor movement but also established a long-standing tradition of hostility and paranoia toward the political left.

Further reading: Stanley Coben, *A. Mitchell Palmer: Politician* (New York: Columbia University Press, 1963).

— Robert Gordon

Palmer Raids   See Red Scare

Panama Canal

The United States built the PANAMA CANAL, a channel 50 miles in length, to cut through the Central American nation of Panama and link the Atlantic and Pacific Oceans. The construction of the canal reinforced the rise of U.S. naval power and economic dominance in the Western Hemisphere, fulfilling a long-held dream to create a route that allowed ships to move freely between the two oceans.

The Clayton-Bulwer Treaty of 1850 had already provided for the joint construction of any Central American canal by Britain and the United States. By the turn of the century, the United States wanted sole control over the canal zone. After its victory over Spain, President William McKinley came to an agreement with Britain in February 1900. The Hay-Pauncefote Treaty allowed the United States to build a canal on its own but did not permit its fortification.

The hero of the SPANISH-AMERICAN WAR of 1898, THEODORE ROOSEVELT, opposed the treaty, because it forbade the United States from fortifying the canal. He led a campaign that defeated the Hay-Pauncefote Treaty in the Senate. On November 18, 1901, Hay and Pauncefote signed a treaty that Roosevelt, who had become president of the United States after William McKinley's assassination, found acceptable.

At the same time, a two-year investigation under the Walker Isthmian Canal Commission found that Nicaragua would be a more suitable route for the canal. The report found that purchasing the rights for a route through Panama would be too expensive. A French-chartered firm, the New Panama Canal Company, which held the canal rights, estimated its assets on the Panamanian isthmus at $109 million. Following the recommendations of the Walker Commission, the U.S. House of Representatives passed the Hepburn Bill on January 8, 1902, authorizing a canal through Nicaragua.

Lawyers representing the New Panama Canal Company waged an intense lobbying effort in Washington, D.C. The Walker Commission estimated the value of the New Panama Canal Company at $40 million. In addition, the

The Panama Canal under construction *(Library of Congress)*

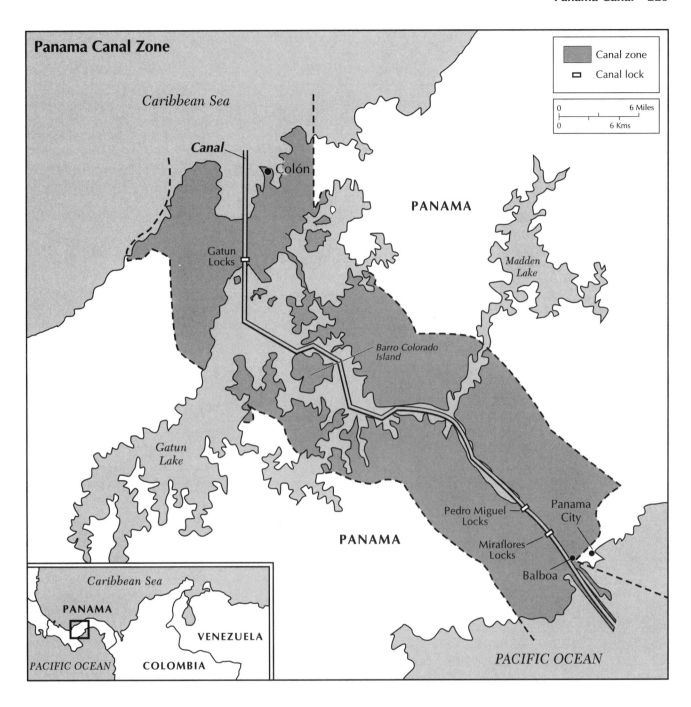

Panama Canal Zone

Caribbean Sea

Canal

Colón

PANAMA

Gatun
Locks

Madden
Lake

Barro Colorado
Island

Gatun
Lake

PANAMA

Pedro Miguel
Locks

Panama
City

Miraflores
Locks

Balboa

PACIFIC OCEAN

Canal zone
Canal lock

0   6 Miles
0   6 Kms

Caribbean Sea

PANAMA

VENEZUELA

PACIFIC OCEAN

COLOMBIA

Walker Commission, noting that the company was willing to sell the rights to the canal at the lower price, reversed itself on January 18, 1902, to favor the canal route through Panama. Five months later, Congress passed the Spooner Act, which authorized the route in Panama. On January 22, 1903, Secretary Hay and Colombian chargé d'affaires, Tomas Herrán, signed a treaty that provided Columbia with an initial payment of $10 million and $250,000 annually. In return, the United States gained control over the canal zone for 100 years, an option renewable in the future only by the United States.

Although Colombia wanted the United States to construct the canal, a costly civil war created an urgent need for funds. The Colombian government tried to exact $10 million from the New Panama Canal Company as a payment for transferring its assets to the U.S. government. In addition, the Bogotá government attempted to get a higher initial payment of $15 million from the United States.

President Roosevelt refused to make the higher payments. In addition, the Colombian senate balked at the American encroachment on Colombia's sovereignty over Panama. The Colombian senate unanimously rejected the treaty on August 12, 1903.

When Colombia's rejection of the treaty seemed imminent, Roosevelt considered either taking Panama by force or providing any revolutionary regime in Panama with immediate recognition and support. With an uprising appearing likely, Roosevelt chose the second option. On October 16, 1903, Secretary Hay informed Philippe Bunau-Varilla, a Frenchman who had fought for a Panamanian canal and agitated for Panamanian independence from Colombia, that the United States was sending warships to the isthmus.

Bunau-Varilla notified the revolutionaries when the American ships would be arriving. On November 2, the USS *Nashville* reached Colón. Acting Secretary of State Francis B. Loomis had ordered the commanding officer of the *Nashville* to "make every effort to prevent [Colombian] Government troops at Colon from proceeding to Panama." However, the transmission to the *Nashville* had been delayed, and the commander of the *Nashville* did not interfere with the landing of Colombian troops. The revolutionaries, forced to fend for themselves, successfully took control of Panama and formed a provisional government.

On November 18, 1903, less than two weeks after the U.S. administration recognized the new government of Panama, the two countries signed the Hay-Bunau-Varilla Treaty, which permitted the United States government to construct, fortify, and run a canal connecting the Atlantic and Pacific Oceans. Upon the urging of Roosevelt, the Congress quickly ratified the Hay-Bunau-Varilla Treaty. Construction of the canal began in 1904.

In 1911, former president Roosevelt was widely reported as saying, "I took the Canal Zone and let Congress debate; and while the debate goes on the Canal does also." After a decade of construction, the Panama Canal opened to traffic on August 15, 1914. In 1922, the United States paid $25 million to Colombia for the canal zone. Vital to the strategic and economic interests of the United States in the Western Hemisphere, the Panama Canal Zone allowed for the free movement of shipping between the Atlantic and Pacific Oceans. The U.S. presence at the Panama Canal was symbolic of the rise of American economic and military power in the region.

See also BIG STICK DIPLOMACY; FOREIGN POLICY.

Further reading: J. Michael Hogan, *The Panama Canal in American Politics: Domestic Advocacy and the Evolution of Policy* (Carbondale: Southern Illinois University Press, 1986); Walter LaFeber, *The Panama Canal: The Crisis in*

Historical Perspective (New York: Oxford University Press, 1978).

— Glen Bessemer

Passaic Strike (1926)

The economic recession after WORLD WAR I, the loss of massive postwar strikes, and the RED SCARE took a severe toll on the labor movement. In the following decade, labor unions suffered steep declines in membership, particularly in the ailing textile and mining industries. By the mid-1920s, however, these industries began to recover from the postwar crisis and witness the stirrings of worker protest that included the Passaic strike of 1926. As cotton and woolen textile manufacturing increased, so too did the willingness of workers to demand their due. The wage cuts, mandatory overtime, bad working conditions, and increasing workloads that had followed the war set the stage for strikes in textile factories in the Northeast and the South.

During these years, craft unions continued to dominate the labor movement. They had little incentive to organize industrial workers. New initiatives from within the COMMUNIST PARTY gave priority to organizing mass industry. Its work in the textile industry played a crucial role in organizing drives in the woolen industry in Passaic, New Jersey. Workers in the woolen mills in Passaic and surrounding towns were first and second generation ethnics, many of them women. Like the workers in the LAWRENCE STRIKE of 1912, they spoke a wide array of languages, including Polish, German, Hungarian, Russian, and Italian. These differences kept them divided. Their employers had sharply cut wages and frequently laid off workers during the early 1920s. Recovery brought the hope that workers would no longer be asked to accept deteriorating conditions.

On January 25, 1926, 6,000 workers struck the Botany Woolen Mill in Passaic. The strike quickly spread to mills in Garfield, Clifton, and Lodi. Within a few weeks, over 20,000 woolen workers were on strike. The strikers demanded that their employers rescind a 10 percent wage cut, limit hours to 44 per week, and improve working conditions. They also asked that the union be recognized. The Passaic City Council passed an ordinance to prohibit workers from picketing, but strikers continued to protest outside the plants. There were many arrests. The strike attracted national publicity and the support of liberal and left-wing organizations, and the relief committee raised over $500,000 to aid strikers.

By summer, however, the long strike was beginning to take its toll. The Communist Party decided to turn control of the strike over to the United Textile Workers, an AFL union. The UTW took over the direction of the strike on the condition that Communist labor organizer Albert

Weisbord leave his leadership position. Once he withdrew, the strike began to fall apart. Relief funds slowed, and the UTW began to negotiate with employers. In late 1926 and early 1927, some of the mills came to terms with the strikers. The wage cut was stopped, but workers failed to gain union recognition. That failure left them, and the organized labor movement, without recourse to collective bargaining in the textile industry.

The Passaic strike foreshadowed organizing drives in the textile industry between 1928 and 1932, especially the GASTONIA STRIKE. The conservatism of the labor movement and the resistance of craft unions to industrial unionism meant that workers in mass production industry failed to establish stable unions during this crucial decade.

See also LABOR AND LABOR MOVEMENT.

Further reading: David J. Goldberg, *A Tale of Three Cities: Labor Organization and Protest in Paterson, Passaic, Lawrence, 1916–1921* (New Brunswick, N.J.: Rutgers University Press, 1989).

Paterson Strike (1913)

A crucial test of the strength and durability of the early industrial unionization movement, the Paterson Strike led to the decline of industrial unionization as a strategy and weakened the INDUSTRIAL WORKERS OF THE WORLD (IWW). From February 25 to mid-July of 1913, nearly 25,000 silk workers joined in a general strike in Paterson, New Jersey. By the time all the workers trickled back into the silk mills in July, the strikers had largely failed to achieve their goals. In addition, the failure led many workers to question the efficacy of industrial unionization and the leadership of the IWW.

After their victory the previous year in the LAWRENCE STRIKE, the IWW had won a number of other small victories. This led them to believe that they were building the future of unionism in the United States. The IWW's textile union had gained members since the Lawrence strike and had become more popular among textile workers in Paterson than the craft-based Union of Textile Workers, which was affiliated with the AMERICAN FEDERATION OF LABOR. When in February 1913, weavers in one mill went on strike over the number of looms they were required to work, the IWW took action to expand the strike to all mills in Paterson. They did this because one mill owner would not be willing to give in to the union's demands if its competitors had not. In making the strike a general strike, the IWW avoided making specific demands. It feared that a strike based on a set of specific demands might not appeal to all workers. Instead, the IWW called for a general strike to protest working conditions throughout the Paterson silk industry.

The IWW used many of the same tactics that it had used successfully in Lawrence but did not achieve the same results. It again called in its best-known leaders, WILLIAM D. ("Big Bill") HAYWOOD and ELIZABETH GURLEY FLYNN, who organized a central strike committee made up of members of all the local unions. The IWW also tried to gain sympathy by evacuating the children of strikers, claiming that their lives were in danger because of the hardships faced by the striking workers. The town authorities and mill owners successfully counteracted the IWW's actions by remaining calm. They did not use the police to harass strikers to the extent that their counterparts in Lawrence had. Most importantly, they ignored the evacuation of the children. Without a violent reaction from the authorities, the evacuation gained the strikers little sympathy from outside observers. The mill owners thus won the propaganda war.

In what became a controversy, the strike leaders attempted to win the propaganda battle by producing a play to publicize the plight of the silk workers. Performed in New York City's Madison Square Garden, the play attracted a large audience but ultimately contributed to the failure of the strike. Financially, the play was a failure. Promoted to the strikers as both a publicity stunt and a money raiser, the play raised just a few hundred dollars. There were many accusations that IWW leaders embezzled funds. Although no credible evidence was produced to support the charges, the efforts to produce the play diverted energy from the situation in Paterson. Subsequently, many of the striking workers felt that the IWW leaders were too preoccupied with the play to effectively lead the strike.

Ultimately, the strike failed due to divisions among the workers who held a variety of jobs and had, therefore, differing demands. General demands for improvements in working conditions were not enough to hold the strikers together. The strike effectively ended the IWW's influence in the eastern United States and seriously damaged the industrial union movement.

Further reading: Anne Huber Tripp, *The I.W.W. and the Paterson Silk Strike of 1913* (Urbana: University of Illinois Press, 1987).

— Michael Hartman

Paul, Alice (1885–1977)

Born on January 11, 1885, into a Quaker family in Moorestown, New Jersey, Alice Paul became one of the most formidable voices in the movement for a federal woman suffrage amendment. Paul attended Swarthmore College and the New York School of Social Work. She relocated to Britain, where she continued her studies and became involved in that country's suffrage movement. It was there that Paul developed an appreciation for militant protest techniques such as civil disobedience and hunger strikes. Such tactics would catapult her into the national spotlight and bring her into conflict with other suffragists when she returned to the United States.

Alice Paul became involved with the NATIONAL AMERICAN WOMAN SUFFRAGE ASSOCIATION (NAWSA) in 1912. Earning a reputation as a tireless and demanding activist, Paul organized teams of women from around the country to lobby representatives in Washington, D.C. In March 1913, she organized an 8,000-strong suffrage parade, timed to coincide with President WOODROW WILSON's first inauguration, in the nation's capital.

Paul's tenure at NAWSA was short-lived, as her tactics were seen as too radical and counterproductive. She did not defer to male politicians. Her single-minded focus on a federal amendment, furthermore, was at odds with NAWSA's combined state and federal approaches to woman suffrage.

In 1916, Paul and other radical suffragists formed the NATIONAL WOMAN'S PARTY to fight for a federal suffrage amendment. The NWP targeted Wilson and his party by picketing the White House daily after January 1917 and campaigning against anti-suffrage politicians. NWP activists also appealed to women in enfranchised states to vote against the party in power, the Democratic Party, to hold them responsible for the failure to pass woman suffrage. The pickets, called Silent Sentinels, garnered national attention as women of all ages protested, regardless of weather conditions. The picketers were treated inconsistently but sometimes violently by authorities. Alice Paul herself went on a hunger strike while in custody, prompting officials to force-feed her for two weeks.

The efforts of Alice Paul and other suffragists finally paid off as Wilson realized that not only could the suffragists no longer be ignored, but also woman voters, he learned, might actually benefit his party. Wilson publicly supported woman suffrage in 1918. The House of Representatives passed the Woman Suffrage Amendment that same year and the Senate in 1919. The Nineteenth Amendment was ratified in 1920.

After the ratification of the Nineteenth Amendment, Alice Paul concentrated on presenting an EQUAL RIGHTS AMENDMENT to Congress, which she did in 1923. After conflicts with other female activists over the ERA, Paul began work on women's issues at the international level. She cofounded the World Party for Equal Rights for Women, also known as the World Women's Party, to pressure governments to expand women's rights through international organizations such as the LEAGUE OF NATIONS and its successor, the United Nations. In the United States, she continued to be associated with the NWP and the struggle for an ERA after World War II. Alice Paul died in 1977 in her hometown, Moorestown, New Jersey.

Despite her impressive legacy in the fight for female suffrage and the ERA, Alice Paul was not without controversy. Like many white suffragists active in the Progressive Era, Paul was less willing to fight for the rights of African-American women. After the ratification of the Nineteenth Amendment, she still did not think the time was appropriate to support black female voting rights. Her support for an Equal Rights Amendment, while far-sighted, caused a rift in the women's rights movement. Her dependence on contributions to support the struggle kept her from reaching out to women across class barriers. Despite these shortcomings, Paul is remembered as a primary mover for women's rights.

Further reading: Christine A. Lunardini, *From Equal Suffrage to Equal Rights: Alice Paul and the National Woman's Party, 1910–1928* (New York: New York University Press, 1986).

— Natalie Atkin

Payne-Aldrich Tariff Act (1909)

The increased duties of the Payne-Aldrich Tariff Act marked a shift in the policies of President WILLIAM HOWARD TAFT from progressive reform toward a more conservative, business-oriented politics. Upon leaving the office of president, THEODORE ROOSEVELT had charged Taft, his chosen successor, with continuing the progressive reform agenda that he had initiated during his two terms as president. When Taft entered office in 1909, he continued many of the progressive reforms that his predecessor had established, but he was not entirely comfortable in the role of reformer. A natural conservative, Taft sanctified private property and revered the process of the law. Still, President Taft was aggressive in attempting to deflate in one term the power held by trusts that Roosevelt had attempted in his two terms as president.

By 1909 the REPUBLICAN PARTY was torn on how to respond to the demands of the Progressive movement. While the movement lacked a coherent, unifying element, it tended to speak for the need to better regulate and control the economic power held by the corporate elite. Progressives considered protective tariffs a major factor in the consolidation of economic power that had contributed to the decline of competition in the American marketplace. Instead of protective tariffs, which often closed the American market to less-expensive imported products, Progressives argued for a revenue tariff that would allow the federal government to generate needed revenues but that did not entirely close the American market to foreign products. Despite advocating a progressive agenda during his presidential campaign, President Taft annoyed many Progressives when he signed the Payne-Aldrich Tariff in 1909.

When he entered office, Taft had favored lowering tariffs on a broad range of commodities. In a relatively short amount of time, the House passed a bill that lowered the tariff on a number of products and goods, but the Senate took a different position from the House. The chair of the Senate Finance Committee, Nelson W. Aldrich, guided through the Senate a bill that drastically revised and enlarged the tariff on more than 800 items. The tariff created an acrimonious debate in the Senate, with Midwestern Republicans charging that the legislation was a throwback to the days when the Republican Party served the interests of industry without question. Taft, who had initially supported lowering the tariff, came to support the Payne-Aldrich Tariff for fear that, if he did otherwise, it would cause a split within the Republican Party. Unwilling to interfere in the legislative process, Taft signed the bill and steadily drifted into the orbit of the Republican Old Guard. Accordingly, President Taft quickly alienated the progressive wing of his party, causing it to actually split, with the formation of the PROGRESSIVE PARTY, by the next presidential election in 1912.

See also PROGRESSIVISM.

Further reading: Edward S. Kaplan, *Prelude to Trade Wars: American Tariff Policy, 1890–1922* (Westport, Conn.: Greenwood, 1994).

— David R. Smith

Pershing, John Joseph (1860–1948)

Commander of the AMERICAN EXPEDITIONARY FORCE (AEF) in Europe in WORLD WAR I, John Pershing preserved the unity of the American army in the face of pressure to divide it among the allied forces. The European allies had suggested dispersing American units as well as limiting their participation. A desperate need for troops on the European front gave General Pershing the power to insist on independence, and the AEF became a central force in the last year of the war.

Pershing was born in Linn County, Missouri, on September 13, 1860. His father, John Fletcher Pershing, was a tracklayer for the North Missouri Railroad at Warrenton, Missouri. He married Ann Elizabeth Thompson on March 22, 1859. Once the Civil War began, Pershing's father bought a general store, two farms, and a lumberyard. He would later lose most of the farmland. John Joseph Pershing worked on his father's land, attended school, and later taught school. After attending Normal School from 1880 to 1882, Pershing won an appointment to West Point.

On graduating from West Point in 1886, Pershing began his army career in the Apache and Sioux campaigns of 1886 and 1890. In Cuba, during the Spanish-American War, he served throughout the Santiago Campaign. He

fought at San Juan Hill, for which he was awarded the Silver Star. Pershing was assigned to the Philippines in 1899. There he helped suppress the Moro Insurrection. His return to Washington allowed his introduction to Helen Frances Warren, a daughter of the senator from Wyoming. They were later married in 1905. Pershing commanded American forces in Mexico during the pursuit of Pancho Villa in what became known as the MEXICAN INVASION. He was promoted in September of that year to major general.

In 1917, General Pershing was one of the few American generals with battle experience. He knew the United States needed a huge army to make a difference in the stagnating war in Europe. The military draft brought millions into the army, but they needed to be trained. As a result of Pershing's efforts, great numbers of American soldiers began to arrive in France in early 1918. Despite problems with supplies, training, and equipment, the American soldiers were fresh as compared with the war-weary French and British. Pershing sent AEF divisions into action in March. He led the first major American offensive of the war in September. In the fall, the AEF fought its largest offensive in the Argonne Forest. During the course of the war, the American Expeditionary Force saw only 150 days of combat; but in that time, it seized 485,000 square miles of enemy-held territory and captured 63,000 prisoners, 1,300 artillery pieces, and 10,000 mortars and machine guns.

After the war, Pershing became chief of staff for the U.S. Army. He died at Walter Reed Army Medical Center in Washington, D.C., on July 15, 1948. He was buried in Arlington Cemetery, his grave marked only by a simple marker, as was his wish, near other soldiers from World War I.

Further reading: Donald Smythe, *Pershing, General of the Armies* (Bloomington: Indiana University Press, 1986); Gene Smith, *Until the Last Trumpet Sounds: The Life of General of the Armies John J. Pershing* (New York: Wiley, 1998).

— Annamarie Edelen

Pinchot, Gifford (1865–1946)

Gifford Pinchot was one of the leading naturalists and conservationists of the 20th century and played a crucial role in the development of the conservation movement. From 1893 to 1910, he headed the U.S. Forest Service, during which time he had tremendous influence on President THEODORE ROOSEVELT's conservation policies. Under Roosevelt's administration, the number of national forests increased from 32 to 149, covering 193 million acres. The son of a New York businessman, Pinchot became interested in forestry and CONSERVATIONISM at an early age. After graduating from Yale in 1885, he spent several years studying forestry in Europe. Pinchot's rise to prominence began when he was appointed to the National Forest Commission in 1897. Because of his service on the commission, President William McKinley named him chief forester of the United States in 1898.

By the 1880s and 1890s, the nation's appetite for natural resources, particularly timber, had become insatiable; and vast tracts of forest were rapidly disappearing. Where preservationists such as John Muir believed that some regions of the country and some natural resources ought to be off-limits to growth and development, Pinchot and other conservationists concluded that it was neither realistic nor desirable that commercial use of natural resources be curbed or eliminated. If the nation's economy was to continue growing, it needed a constant supply of resources. For these reasons, Pinchot pushed the federal government to become actively involved in land use management. He argued that the government had to ensure that the nation's resources were not squandered and wasted by inefficient and careless use. By 1910, two years after WILLIAM HOWARD TAFT became president, Pinchot concluded that the government had abandoned its commitment to conservationism. After filing suit against Richard Achilles Ballinger, Taft's secretary of the interior, Pinchot was dismissed as head of the Forest Service.

After he left the federal government, Pinchot launched a successful career as a progressive Republican politician. In 1914, he ran for and lost the Senate seat in Pennsylvania. His platform included support for women's right to vote, a graduated income tax, a workmen's compensation law, and the right of workers to form legally recognized labor unions. After this initial setback, Pinchot went on to win the Pennsylvania governorship in 1922 and again in 1930. As governor, he instituted numerous bureaucratic and legislative reforms and recruited women, African Americans, and Jews to serve in his administration. In addition, Pinchot helped to establish rural electrification and anti-poverty programs and frequently sided with organized labor, using his office on several occasions to resolve protracted labor disputes.

Although an important progressive Republican, Pinchot's lasting contribution came from his views of land use and the conservation of natural resources. His views played an important role in shaping both the conservation movement and the federal government's approach toward land use from the turn of the century until the rise of the modern environmental movement of the 1960s. Conservationism provided a much-needed balance to the dominant free market approach toward natural resources and the environment, but it also served to mute the preservationist impulse and legitimized the nation's insatiable use of natural resources under the guise of wise and efficient use.

Further reading: Char Miller, *Gifford Pinchot: The Evolution of an American Conservationist* (Milford, Pa.: Grey Towers Press, 1992).

— Robert Gordon

Pingree, Hazen   See urban reform

politics

Between 1900 and 1930, political life in the United States underwent a significant transformation. The character of the electorate, the rules and procedures for elections, and the way in which parties and politics were organized all changed. While electoral politics continued to be dominated by the DEMOCRATIC PARTY and the REPUBLICAN PARTY, the emergence of LOBBYING AND INTEREST GROUPS altered how parties and individuals influenced political outcomes. At a time of declining party identification and voter participation, the two parties continued to control the major governmental institutions of the presidency, CONGRESS, and the court system, in large part due to their ability to incorporate new public interest lobbies into the workings of party politics.

For most of the 19th century, historians have argued, politics ran along a divide between party and electoral politics on the one hand and a more issue-driven reform politics on the other. The principal tools of parties were the ballot and party organization; the principal means of pursuing reform politics were lobbying, petition, and public protest. By 1900, however, voters were increasingly alienated from party politics. New practices, such as split ticket voting and independent lobbying, reinforced a decline in party loyalty and an upsurge in independent political organization. Finding new ways to educate the public, inform legislators, and pass laws meant that the younger generation of active citizens was able to enter political life and significantly shift politics away from party agendas. Organizations such as the League of Women Voters emerged to educate and mobilize voters, and social organizations such as the National Mothers' Congress and the American Farm Bureau pursued their political agendas in new ways.

The shift toward interest group politics had contradictory results. Undertaken under the banner of greater democracy, political reforms such as the direct primary, initiative, referendum, and recall, and the DIRECT ELECTION OF SENATORS, along with the granting of woman suffrage, URBAN REFORM, and new voting laws, gave "the people" greater direct access to their representatives. Ironically, it gave the same or better access to corporate interests.

In the government, the electoral realignment of 1896 guaranteed Republican Party control of all three branches of the federal government. Between 1896 and 1932, the Republican Party won every presidential election except the elections of 1912 and 1916, when it was badly divided. The old competitive states such as Ohio, Indiana, and New York, which the two major parties had contested in election after election, now became solidly Republican. In Congress, the Republican Party dominated the House of Representatives between 1900 and 1911 and from 1919 until 1932 and the Senate from 1900 to 1913 and again from 1919 to 1932. Dominance over the office of the presidency also guaranteed control over the judiciary. At the national level, Republican presidents nominated 18 of the 21 Supreme Court justices appointed between 1898 and 1932. The lower federal courts were similarly slanted.

Despite the continued dominance of the two-party system, the years between 1900 and 1930 saw many political experiments come to the fore. Third parties launched successful campaigns at the state and local level and passed reforms governing political and economic life. At the forefront of change was the increasing influence of SOCIALISM, both in the writings of American socialists such as Edward Bellamy and CHARLOTTE PERKINS GILMAN and in the thought of European radicals Karl Marx and Frederick Engels. Public intellectuals such as JOHN DEWEY and William James began to rethink how society should organize public life, labor, community, and family. Progressive politicians such as ROBERT LA FOLLETTE and TOM JOHNSON integrated socialist ideas about land reform, municipal or public ownership of utilities, and transportation into their political agendas. The growing number of votes for socialist presidential candidate EUGENE V. DEBS and the success of local and state socialist candidates, shown in the election of more than 300 mayors, city council members, and state legislators, pushed mainstream politics to the Left. As the intellectual basis for PROGRESSIVISM, socialist thought helped reformers challenge relations between individuals and government, private interests and public welfare, and employers and workers. Socialist thought shifted the balance away from sovereign property rights to a new investment in human rights.

Demands for social change eventually hit the wall of conservatism within the political system. At the beginning of the 20th century, Congress was still the dominant branch of government. The Senate served as a break on the new reform measures passed by the popularly elected House of Representatives. The court system was an even greater obstacle to federal and state legislation, as both state and federal courts envisioned limited government and the primacy of property rights. Faced with these obstacles, Progressives arrived at a critique of how politics were organized. The lack of direct democracy, the concentrated power of business and banking interests in government, and the party system itself were at fault. As the MUCKRAK-

ERS discovered, many forces in American life were susceptible to corruption and vulnerable to the influence of large corporations. Money corrupted politics, and many progressives sought to curtail its influence in public life.

For one, Progressive politicians pushed for the reform of the party system and new forms of direct democracy. In several states, political reformers passed resolutions for direct primaries, substituting them for the "smoke-filled rooms" of party caucus and convention. West of the Mississippi, several states passed initiative, referendum, and recall, which allowed voters to initiate their own legislation, approve legislation passed by the legislature, and recall elected officials who were either incompetent or corrupt. In particular, there was an interest in recalling judges, for the judicial system acted to forestall and undermine progressive reforms. One of the most important democratic reforms of the day was to change the way senators were chosen. Prior to the passage of the Seventeenth Amendment, state legislatures appointed individuals to serve in the Senate. The process was rife with opportunities for bribery and corruption, and it tended to give greater power and weight to rural districts, which were more conservative. With the ratification of the amendment for direct election of senators, voters chose among individual candidates, usually nominated by major parties, for Senate seats. Urban reform measures, which gave some cities commission governments and took power out of the wards and the hands of political machines, were seen as the local complement of direct democracy. By shifting the balance of political power away from political parties and toward individual voters, it was hoped that the democratic will would prevail.

If these reforms seemed a democratization of earlier practices, they did not, on the whole, open up the process. Initiatives and referenda required party candidates or interest groups to endorse them. Further, these political reforms were mirrored by others, which both broadened (through woman suffrage) and narrowed (new voting regulations) the number of men and women eligible to vote. Done against the background of the ratification of the Nineteenth Amendment (granting women the right to vote) and the introduction of new voting and immigration laws (restricting entry to the United States and altering rules concerning citizenship and marriage), the voting regulations required longer periods of residency and stricter control over the ballot. These moves discouraged voters and prompted, over the course of a decade, precipitous declines in voter participation and party identification. It also promoted more independent voting. Finally, new women voters played a role. Apart from agitating for labor legislation and maternal health, women became more active in party politics. By 1933, many women had held public office, including two governors, one senator, 14 representatives, and thousands of state and local legislators and city and county officials.

In the realm of third party politics, the first three decades of the 20th century saw growth in the number of non-mainstream party votes. Several major party candidates ran on non-party platforms during the period. In 1912, the PROGRESSIVE PARTY nominated THEODORE ROOSEVELT, who received one of the highest total votes for a non-party candidate. The Progressive Party nominated Republican CHARLES EVANS HUGHES in 1916 (he narrowly lost to WOODROW WILSON), and in 1924, it put forth the progressive Republican, Robert La Follette, and the progressive Montana Democrat, Burton Wheeler, as the Progressive Party ticket. In addition, farmer-labor parties were active at the state and local level, as they were in the 1910s with the NON-PARTISAN LEAGUE and in the 1920s with the FARMER-LABOR PARTY. Lastly, parties on the Left thrived in small but significant numbers. Socialist Eugene Debs ran for president in a series of elections, and in 1916 and 1920 he earned over a million votes. The conservative backlash after WORLD WAR I culminated in the RED SCARE and put an end to the strong showing of third parties.

Parties began to suffer from the decline of voter participation but not more so than the party workers themselves. The decline of party machines and party patronage meant that political parties had to find new ways of financing political campaigns and staffing of the effort to get out the vote. In the wake of WOMAN SUFFRAGE, women, who on the whole had greater leisure time than men, became party members and performed much of the voluntary labor behind campaigns. Women winning the right to vote also meant the election of women to public office, which they did in significant numbers during the early to mid-1920s.

Despite the conservative turn of the 1920s, there were definitive changes in American politics that suggested a continuity throughout the period. While Republican presidents strove to maintain "normalcy" in government affairs, the period saw increased demands for government regulation and social provision. Not only did the regulatory state emerge from such initiatives as antitrust suits, the HEPBURN ACT, and the MANN-ELKINS ACT, but also the country witnessed the emergence of a social welfare state in state and national legislation for workers' compensation, the growth of mothers' pensions, and protective labor legislation. The invention of War Risk Insurance during World War I, the creation of the VETERANS BUREAU and programs for disabled veterans, and the SOLDIERS' BONUS of 1924 revealed greater public support for social provision under the right circumstances and with the correct constituency. Public opinion began to embrace a larger and more active government role in the arenas of public welfare and regulation of the economy. Even during the backlash against progressive reform during the 1920s, the federal budget grew. Politics continued to embrace a wide range of ideologies, agendas, institutions, and tactics, and opened the way for the realigning politics of the 1930s.

See also ELECTIONS.

Further reading: Paula Baker, *The Moral Frameworks of Public Life: Gender, Politics, and the State in Rural New York, 1870–1930* (New York: Oxford University Press, 1991); Elisabeth S. Clemens, *The People's Lobby: Organizational Innovation and the Rise of Interest Group Politics in the United States, 1890–1925* (Chicago: University of Chicago Press, 1997); Richard L. McCormick, *The Party Period and Public Policy: American Politics from the Age of Jackson to the Progressive Era* (New York: Oxford University Press, 1986).

popular culture

Between 1900 and 1930, American popular culture underwent a transformation characterized by the development of national popular culture and its commercialization. Popular culture refers to cultural activities and products that appeal to broad audiences. It includes popular LITERATURE, RADIO broadcasting, popular MUSIC, popular dance and theater, SPORTS and recreation, some decorative arts, and motion pictures. During the first three decades of the century, corporations increasingly turned out cultural productions for popular consumption to make a profit. This led to tensions between a popular culture created by people themselves and popular culture created by commercial interests. The transformation of popular culture into a broad-based national phenomenon occurred as a result of economic, social, demographic, and technological changes of the emerging industrial age.

The rise of modern popular culture was made possible by the tremendous growth of American cities, the emergence of the urban middle class, changing social values in regard to leisure, technological advances, and a rise in real wages for almost all workers. As the urban population exploded early in the 20th century, cities became the sites in which popular culture was created and consumed. Easy access to large audiences gave cultural producers such as movie makers and amusement park owners an economic incentive to produce products that catered to these new audiences. In addition, corporations were growing in size and required increasing numbers of white-collar workers. These workers, many of whom were children of immigrant parents, earned enough money to afford movies and plays, and they had the time in which to do so. A new ethos in regard to leisure activities also was emerging, as middle-class Americans rejected traditional beliefs that restricted their use of leisure time. Wage workers also were improving their standard of living. Better wages meant that, for the first time, many wage earners and their families could afford new public amusements. Finally, the improved abilities to transmit information over wire and through the air brought different regions into closer contact than had ever been possible. Chains of VAUDEVILLE theaters and national sports leagues gave many Americans common experiences. All of these developments helped transform popular culture into a national culture that often cut across ethnic, social, and regional groupings.

As producers of popular culture tailored their offerings to appeal to a broad audience, the cultural differences between these groups diminished. In doing so, popular culture helped Americanize the millions of immigrants who came to America. At the same time, some forms of popular culture reinforced group differences, as each group interpreted popular culture among themselves. Popular culture thus could simultaneously diminish cultural differences and help maintain them. In Vaudeville theaters, for example, audiences often consisted of a cross-section of urban society. Members of these audiences joined in a unifying activity that brought people of numerous backgrounds together. At the same time, there was a hierarchy of theaters determined by the cost of a ticket. The more expensive theaters tended to be downtown while less expensive theaters operated in working-class immigrant neighborhoods. The performances often catered to the audience, creating different versions of popular culture within the same cultural institution. The same dynamic occurred in public amusement parks such as Wonderland and Luna Park at Coney Island, New York. The crowds that streamed out of New York City to Coney Island consisted of all ethnic and class backgrounds, and they all shared some of the experiences at the parks. There were, however, different sections of Coney Island, differentiated by the

Luna Park at Coney Island, N.Y. *(Library of Congress)*

cost of food and lodging. Thus, a popular culture activity could be both unifying and divisive.

BASEBALL serves as an informative example of how popular culture emerged out of the new industrial urban environment. Americans had been playing baseball since before the Civil War. Only in the 20th century, however, did it become the national phenomenon that it still is today. Baseball's increased popularity was due to a variety of factors. First, the sheer number of urban residents who could attend games provided a potential audience. Second, it appealed to urban Americans as a throwback to simpler times. Going to a baseball field with its green grass provided an opportunity to spend the afternoon in an environment that reminded city residents of the recent rural past. The players came from a variety of backgrounds, which made it possible for any fan to find players that they related to because of their ethnic identity. Baseball's popularity rose from more than these factors, however. Seizing upon a money-making opportunity, the team owners built larger stadiums and relied on marketing to attract audiences. One marketing strategy was the creation of the star system in which team owners marketed their best players to attract audiences. It made many players household names.

Motion pictures emerged during this time to take their place at the center of popular culture. The first motion pictures to be marketed to a public audience purely for entertainment purposes were shown in nickelodeons in large cities. The nickelodeons were commercial spaces that contained anywhere from five to 50 viewing machines. Patrons dropped their five cents in a coin slot and watched a brief film. The subjects of these films ran anywhere from acrobatics and animal acts to films of men and women kissing. The films did not have sound. The nickelodeons quickly became the most popular form of entertainment in America's cities and provided the basis for the nascent MOVIE INDUSTRY. The novelty of the motion picture combined with the affordability appealed to a broad audience.

A combination of audience desire for longer films and entrepreneurs' realization of the money to be made led to the development of big screen films. The first films that were shown on a screen in front of audiences were exhibited as educational films in traveling shows. Entrepreneurs realized that there was money to be made from the urban audiences who attended vaudeville shows. Vaudeville theaters began to show motion pictures as part of the show. By the 1910s, movies had separated from vaudeville, and motion picture theaters began to spring up in cities.

Changes in the quality and type of films increased their popularity. Initially, films consisted of short clips. The appeal of these was limited, once the novelty wore off. To meet the demand for more meaningful films, filmmakers began to make films that told a story. The first film to tell a story was the 1903 *Great Train Robbery*. The quality of

early films in terms of technology and filmmaking left much to be desired. The 1915 BIRTH OF A NATION, a racist account of reconstruction after the Civil War, was a turning point in filmmaking. It used new lighting techniques and acting techniques to make a more realistic representation. It made more money than any film of its time and helped revolutionize filmmaking. By the 1920s, motion pictures had become the most popular form of entertainment in the United States. Movie stars such as Mary Pickford became household names as the movie studios used the same star system as baseball teams did to market their films and the entire industry.

Radio was another element of popular culture that developed from commercial interests. Although the technology was invented in the late 19th century, radio did not occupy a significant space in American culture until after WORLD WAR I when the commercial possibilities of radio were first realized. The first radio broadcasting stations were set up by the companies that manufactured radio equipment. GENERAL ELECTRIC, Westinghouse, and American Telegraph and Telephone all realized that they could sell more radio equipment if the public had something to listen to. Initially this was all done on a local basis. The radio owners living near Pittsburgh, for example, could listen to the first permanent station, KDKA, created by Westinghouse in 1920, but audiences outside of the listening area could not. In addition, all the programming was local, consisting of music, Broadway plays, and news among other things. The programming was sporadic, because the local stations did not have access to large amounts of music and other entertaining programs. Programming changed in the mid-1920s with the establishment of the network system. The National Broadcasting Corporation and the Columbia Broadcasting System provided their affiliate stations a certain amount of programming each day. The local stations filled the remaining airtime. The network system helped nationalize popular culture, because radio listeners all over were listening to the same program. Moreover, the national programs were sponsored by the manufacturers of certain products, which then became household names. This helped create a national market for some products. The first radio program to put all these trends together was the *Amos 'n Andy* show, which premiered in 1929. Thus the 1920s were only the beginning of radio's important role in popular culture.

A range of different genres characterized popular literature during the first decades of the century. As books became more affordable in soft covers and literacy spread, literature became more popular. Best-sellers came from a number of different genres. Sentimental novels such as *Pollyanna* and *Rebecca of Sunnybrook Farm,* religious books, historical fiction, westerns such as *The Virginian,* sensationalist exposés such as Upton Sinclair's *The Jungle,* and detective mysteries all found their way onto the best-seller lists. Pulp fiction also emerged as a form of popular literature. Named for the cheap paper stock on which they were printed, these magazines appealed to specialized audiences with serial and short stories off all sorts. They sold for 10 cents. Initially, they included a variety of story types, but by 1910 magazines began to specialize. Some were detective fiction magazines, others Westerns, while others published love stories. By the mid-1920s, some of the pulp magazines had circulations of 500,000.

Dance crazes were another form of entertainment that became a part of popular culture. The ability to publish sheet music in large quantities helped spread music and the dances that often accompanied specific songs. In the 1920s, radio helped spread both the songs and dances. Many of the dance crazes appealed to youths because they allowed them to engage in close physical contact. The dance crazes of the pre–World War I years included the turkey trot, grizzly bear, and the bunny hug, all of which allowed close physical contact. After the war, dances such as the Charleston and the Lindy Hop became national phenomena as Americans embraced the fast-paced dances that accompanied the fast-paced life-style that helped define the decade.

Changes in popular music accompanied the various dance crazes. The most significant development in music was JAZZ. Evolving from a combination of the blues, ragtime, and brass band music, jazz was America's only unique musical form. Prior to the rise of jazz, European orchestra music dominated the American music scene. A few American composers were writing pieces for orchestras, sentimental art songs, dances for keyboards, and songs for vaudeville. It was not until the rise of jazz, however, that an American form of music emerged. The GREAT MIGRATION of African Americans from the South to northern cities played an integral role in the development of jazz. The migration brought both musicians and an audience to the urban North, where commercial record producers helped popularize jazz.

By the end of the 1920s, popular culture had taken its modern form. Popular wants and commercial possibilities helped create a popular culture that was also a mass culture. This dynamic has led some to question whether popular culture rises from the people or is created by commercial enterprises seeking a profit from mass consumption. During the years from 1900 to 1930, commercial interests began to dominate the production of popular culture. It is important to remember, however, that the individual still made the daily choices that decided which cultural products and activities were truly popular.

Further reading: M. Thomas Inge, ed., *Concise Histories of American Popular Culture* (Westport, Conn.:

Greenwood Press, 1982); David Nasaw, *Going Out: The Rise and Fall of Public Amusements* (New York: Basic Books, 1993); Kathy Peiss, *Cheap Amusements, Working Women and Leisure in Turn-of-the-Century New York* (Philadelphia: Temple University Press, 1986).

— Michael Hartman

population trends

In the period between 1900 and 1930, the population of the United States continued to grow, albeit at a declining rate. In 1900, the total population was nearly 76 million; by 1930, it had grown to nearly 123 million. After experiencing high rates of natural increase early in the 19th century, a long decline in fertility finally began to show in population rates by the 1870s. A pattern of delayed marriage and low fertility associated with urban development continued to spread throughout cities early in the 20th century. Marriage rates climbed incrementally in these decades, with a slow decline in the number of people who never married. At the same time, the number of divorces rose rapidly from over 100,000 in 1914 to more than 205,000 in 1929. Better than one in seven marriages ended in divorce. More open divorce laws had made it possible for men and women to start new relationships when old ones failed.

Changing family patterns had an effect on fertility as well. First, there was an increased incidence of sex outside marriage. Before 1900, only 14 percent of women (about one in seven) admitted to having premarital sex before they were 35. Among women in the generation of the 1920s, however, more than one in three (36 percent) had experienced premarital intercourse. Delayed marriage and new methods of BIRTH CONTROL furthered the general decline in fertility. New birth control clinics now provided advice and contraceptive devices, so that by 1925, one study reported that more than 80 percent of middle-class women used birth control. In contrast, only about 36 percent of poorer women did.

Fertility during these decades declined significantly. For white women, the crude birth rate dropped from 30.1 births per thousand in 1900 to 20.6 per thousand in 1930. In addition, the median number of children per woman declined for whites from 3.56 in 1900 to 2.45 in 1930. For African-American women, there was an even steeper decline, from 44.4 births per thousand in 1900 to 27.5 per thousand in 1930. The median number of children an African-American woman had, dropped from 5.61 in 1900 to 2.98 in 1930. Much of the decline can be attributed to rural-urban differences, as a disproportionate number of African Americans lived in rural areas and farm fertility, for a number of reasons, remained high through the 1920s. At the same time, improvements in birth control, a rise in the age at marriage, and declining infant mortality created the conditions for a general drop in the fertility rate.

Between 1900 and 1920, the United States was at the high tide of IMMIGRATION with an average of 1 million immigrants entering the country every year. These immigrants, in contrast to earlier periods, were primarily from eastern and southern Europe. Arriving from the Austro-Hungarian Empire, Russia, Italy, and other southern European countries, they brought diverse religious and cultural practices to cities in the East and Midwest. The conflict of WORLD WAR I had a dampening effect on immigration to the United States. Obstacles to travel, from the national conscription to fear of submarine warfare, lessened the demand; fear of foreign subversion and radicalism, later expressed in the RED SCARE of 1919–21, brought about pressure for changes in immigration. Immigration laws such as the IMMIGRATION ACT OF 1917, the QUOTA ACT of 1921, and the NATIONAL ORIGINS ACT of 1924 introduced new restrictions ranging from literacy tests to national quotas. The new laws slowed the stream of European migrants into the United States, but migration from Canada and

Mexico continued unaffected until the economic crisis of the 1930s.

Mortality also declined due to a number of reasons. Better nutrition, health care, and public hygiene cut the rates of infection and mortality from common epidemic diseases such as diphtheria, measles, typhoid, and tuberculosis. Life expectancy improved as better nutrition and medical care reached the general population. The average life expectancy in the United States rose from 47.3 years in 1900 to 59.7 years in 1930. At the same time, improving health and life expectancy did not reach all populations. Among African Americans, poverty, lack of health care, and malnutrition continued to take a toll on the rate of population growth, despite a higher fertility rate than among the general population. Among NATIVE AMERICANS, however, the long decline in population had halted by the turn of the century. Tuberculosis, which had ravaged Native American populations, became more manageable, and better nutrition slowly improved health.

Internally, there were significant movements of population throughout the period. Among them was the movement

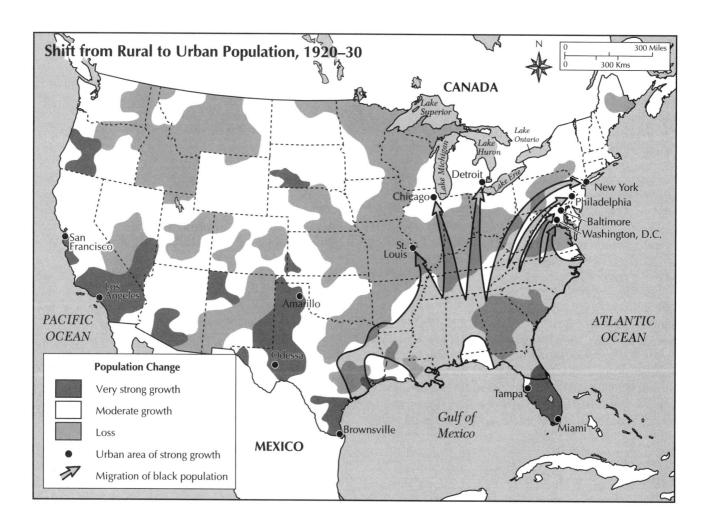

of African Americans from the rural South to the urban North known as the GREAT MIGRATION. Deteriorating race relations in the South and greater economic opportunity in northern cities brought a flood of migrants before and during World War I. From 1910 to 1920, the net migration of African Americans to cities was almost half a million. The pace of migration increased throughout the 1920s, with the net number of migrants numbering over 750,000.

A parallel development was the rural to urban migration that continued at an ever-increasing rate between 1900 and 1930. Rural to urban migrants had always been a substantial proportion of urban residents and contributed to the nation's becoming majority urban in 1920. The demand for labor during World War I had attracted southern migrants—both white and black—into northern industry. Cities such as Detroit and Chicago were transformed in the aftermath of the migration. But the greatest wave of rural to urban migration was due to the agricultural crisis of the 1920s, when many farm families and individual men and women left farms and rural towns to migrate to large cities. Lacking employment in the countryside and witnessing the decline of rural America, more than 19 million people made the trek from farms and small towns to cities during the decade. Not surprisingly, it was the disinherited youth who became the harbingers of change. One in four men and women ages 20 to 24 moved from rural areas to urban ones, where greater opportunities awaited them than in the depression-ridden agricultural regions of the Midwest and South.

By 1930, the United States was a nation that had reached demographic stability. Its population, while ethnically and racially diverse, grew at a steady but slow pace. The entry of European immigrants had slowed to a trickle due to new restrictive policies, and Mexican migration, while it increased in number over the 1920s, was not of the same magnitude. Fertility remained in a fairly steady decline that would deepen with the Great Depression, while improved PUBLIC HEALTH measures eroded mortality and morbidity rates.

See also MARRIAGE AND FAMILY LIFE; MEDICINE.

Further reading: Michael Haines and Richard Steckel, eds., *Population History of North America* (New York: Cambridge University Press, 2000), Walter Nugent, *Structures of American Social History* (Bloomington: Indiana University Press, 1981); Conrad Taeuber and Irene Taeuber, *The Changing Population of the United States* (New York: Wiley, 1958).

Preparedness

Before WORLD WAR I Preparedness became a movement to increase the military capacity of the United States as well as citizen support for war efforts. After the outbreak of European hostilities in 1914, organizations such as the National Security League, the Americans Defense Society, the League to Enforce Peace, and the American Rights Committee exerted pressure on an unwilling president WOODROW WILSON to strengthen military defenses. Wilson, who campaigned and won on keeping America out of the war, stood behind his pledge of NEUTRALITY until events forced the United States entry into the war in 1917.

THEODORE ROOSEVELT was a leading advocate of the Preparedness movement. He wrote *America and the World War* in 1915 and *Fear God and Take Your Own Part* in 1916, which appealed to the people of the United States to prepare for war. These books helped popularize the Preparedness movement. Roosevelt disdained those who, like Wilson, were "Flubdubs and Molycoddles" ignoring the fact that the country was unprepared to fight. The Preparedness movement took offense at occupied Belgium's fate and decried "German atrocities," which were said to be going on there.

In 1914, the Army War College issued a report entitled "A Statement of a Proper Military Policy for the United States," which warned of depending on isolationism as a policy. It warned that newer technology, such as the submarine, the airplane, and the wireless telegraph placed the United States within the sphere of action of hostile nations. No longer could the United States depend on distance and geography to protect it. War College estimates demanded a standing army of at least 500,000 with a reserve of equal force. It also called for arms and training programs.

One such program was initiated by General Leonard Wood, a medical doctor turned soldier. He was the senior officer in the army and commander of the Department of the East. Wood established a military training camp at Plattsburg, New York. There, he and other professional man trained to be reserve officers. Administered by regular army personnel, the course was five weeks long. The Preparedness movement, financed by wealthy financier BERNARD BARUCH, caught on, and around 16,000 business and professional men were trained as officers in eastern cities.

As the United States inched closer to war, the issue of military preparedness gained new urgency. Organizations including the National Security League, the American Defense Society, the League to Enforce Peace, and the American Rights Committee held activities and Preparedness Day parades to further promote their cause. After German submarine attacks, especially the sinking of the LUSITANIA in May of 1915, Wilson dropped his opposition to an American military buildup. In 1916 he toured the country to urge support for preparedness, even though this was in direct opposition to his campaign promises of "Peace with Honor."

In 1916, Wilson's secretary of war, Lindley Garrison, and his assistant, Henry Breckenridge, established a national defense plan with the support of Wilson that called for a "Continental Army." The plan would build up forces over a three-year period in a federal reserve army. Congress disapproved, and Wilson withdrew support. Garrison and Breckenridge resigned. In June of that year, however, Congress passed the NATIONAL DEFENSE ACT. It allowed the president to commandeer factories and establish a government nitrate plan, and it permitted the army to double its size by adding 11,450 officers and 223,580 enlisted men in annual increments over five years. The National Guard could expand to 17,000 officers and 440,000 men. A corresponding naval appropriations bill broadened the effect of the measure.

In spite of the National Defense Act, the nation was unable to recruit new troops up to the authorized strength. Militia and state forces had always been depended upon for emergency reserves. As a consequence, ground forces of the U.S. Army numbered only around 128,000 as America entered World War I in April of 1917. The SELECTIVE SERVICE ACT of 1917, which required that all men between the ages of 18 and 45 register in the Selective Service System, was used to bolster the military. A total of 24 million men registered, and the army was increased to 4 million soldiers. The Preparedness movement began to lose its raison d'etre following the National Defense Act and the accompanying increase in naval expenditure in 1917. The movement disappeared when mobilization began following U.S. entry into the war.

Further reading: Michael Perlman, *To Make Democracy Safe for America: Patricians and Preparedness in the Progressive Era* (Urbana: University of Illinois Press, 1984).

— Annamarie Edelen

Progressive Party

The Progressive, or Bull Moose, Party was formed in 1911 by members of the Republican Party dissatisfied with the leadership of President WILLIAM HOWARD TAFT. The nation had changed rapidly between 1900 and 1912, becoming more urban, more industrial, and more ethnically diverse. Economic changes further complicated the picture as large national corporations began dominating entire industries, and class divisions threatened to undermine American democracy. Finally, numerous segments of society, including women, organized labor, minorities, and reform journalists had become increasingly active in politics. These changes resulted in substantial political turmoil, as the DEMOCRATIC and REPUBLICAN PARTIES struggled to understand and take advantage of this new landscape. Many believed that progressive and even radical reforms

needed to take place if the nation was to remain unified and prosperous.

Progressive elements within the Republican Party had become convinced that President Taft was too conservative and unresponsive to demands for reform. They believed that the federal government needed to be more actively involved in regulating the economy and society. The roots of PROGRESSIVISM within the Republican Party can be traced to the presidency of THEODORE ROOSEVELT who, during his two terms in office (1901–09), had supported federal regulation of industry and promoted tax reform, labor law reform, and social legislation. Others within the party, particularly those in the urban North and Midwest, understood the appeal of progressivism and pushed the party in that direction. With Roosevelt's support, Vice President Taft won the Republican nomination and the general election in 1908. Once in office, however, Taft established strong ties with the party's conservative wing, the Old Guard Republicans.

Divisions began to emerge within the party as early as 1909 during debates on the PAYNE-ALDRICH TARIFF ACT. Wisconsin senator ROBERT M. LA FOLLETTE and other progressives were vehemently opposed to the tariff, because they believed that it kept prices artificially high and primarily benefited large industrialists and eastern financial markets. When Taft called for a special session of Congress to deal with the tariff issue, he planned to have them lowered; but the final version of Payne-Aldrich did the exact opposite. When Taft signed the tariff and announced that is was "the best bill the Republican Party ever signed," he created a split in the party.

Between 1909 and 1911, a series of controversies furthered deepened divisions in the party. Shortly after he took office, Taft refused to support progressives' attempts to unseat the autocratic Speaker of the House, JOSEPH CANNON. In 1909 Taft fired GIFFORD PINCHOT, head of the U.S. Forest Service and long-time Roosevelt supporter, after he disagreed with Secretary of the Interior Richard Ballinger. In August 1910, Roosevelt delivered a speech in which he criticized Taft and laid out the idea of the NEW NATIONALISM that would provide the framework for his 1912 presidential campaign. Finally, in the 1910 elections, Taft and the Old Guard Republicans attempted to unseat or block the nominations of congressional progressives, convincing La Follette to form the National Progressive Republican League. He announced his candidacy for the Republican nomination in June 1911. Initially Roosevelt refused to publicly side with either Taft or the progressive dissidents; but when Taft overruled some of Roosevelt's decisions, Roosevelt announced that he would seek the Republican nomination.

As president, Taft had complete control over the Republican Party machine. He was able to block challenges from both La Follette and Roosevelt, easily securing the Republican nomination. Convinced that they could defeat Taft and Democratic nominee WOODROW WILSON, dissidents in the Republican Party formed the Progressive Party. At their convention in August 1912 they selected Roosevelt as their presidential nominee and California governor HIRAM W. JOHNSON as their vice presidential candidate. The Progressive Party platform called for the abolition of CHILD LABOR, the creation of primary elections, the DIRECT ELECTION OF SENATORS, WOMAN SUFFRAGE, graduated income and inheritance taxes, limits on labor injunctions, an eight-hour work day, the use of collective bargaining in labor disputes, and the introduction of medical, retirement, and unemployment insurance.

The election of 1912 was tightly contested. The Progressives hoped they could lure enough votes away from both parties to secure a victory. In the end, while Roosevelt easily outpolled Taft, he failed to make significant inroads among Democratic voters to win. Wilson received 6,293,000 votes, Roosevelt 4,119,000, and Taft 3,484,000. The electoral vote was even more decisive, as Wilson received 435 votes to Roosevelt's 88 and Taft's 8. The Progressive Party attempted to maintain some semblance of unity and ran congressional candidates in 1914, but all besides Johnson were decisively defeated. By 1916, most Progressives were back in the Republican fold. When Roosevelt refused the party's nomination in 1916, it endorsed Republican nominee CHARLES EVANS HUGHES. In the long run, the decision to break with the party in 1912 proved disastrous for liberal Republicans. Roosevelt had outpolled Taft, but the party had failed to create an independent political base. By the time progressive Republicans returned to the party between 1916 and 1917, the conservative Old Guard had complete control.

Further reading: J. A. Gable, *The Bull Moose Years: Theodore Roosevelt and the Progressive Party* (Port Washington, N.Y.: Kennikat Press, 1978).

— Robert Gordon

progressivism
Progressivism, a loosely defined movement for social, political, and economic reform, gained political power and prestige during the first two decades of the 20th century. Progressives had a range of separate, even contradictory goals, which ranged from PROHIBITION, IMMIGRATION restriction, and the eradication of CHILD LABOR, to a complete overhaul of the political and social system. To add to its complexity, the umbrella of progressive reform sheltered conflicting ideologies used by men and women to justify their actions. Generally, they embraced new ideas of social justice and social order, but there were tendencies that

united the group. Progressives focused on reforming America's political, social, economic, and moral landscape. They had a seemingly unending faith in progress and believed that, through rational development, they could foster a society of unlimited potential.

The degree to which Progressives believed in participatory democracy is unclear. Some sought to empower those on the lower rungs of the socioeconomic ladder. While many believed in defending members of society whom they considered powerless and in need of support, few progressives challenged fundamental tenets of the capitalistic system. They sought to work within the system to create a more socially cohesive, rational, and just society. For some, their activism was a way to defend and improve the system. For others it was a way to uplift the downtrodden and provide social justice.

Progressive reformers championed democracy as more than an ideal political system. They believed that devotion to the tenets of democratic life produced desirable economic and social effects as well. As a result, they sought to promote their vision of democracy both at home and abroad. At home, they sought to reform the political system and sponsored political checks and balances such as initiative, referendum, and recall. They also called for the secret ballot, the DIRECT ELECTION OF SENATORS, and the direct primary. To further spread democracy, progressives supported the enfranchisement of women. These, along with hundreds of smaller measures, helped to revolutionize democracy at home. Progressives advocated the spread of democracy throughout the world, which culminated in WOODROW WILSON's Fourteen Points during peace negotiations after WORLD WAR I.

While few progressives dreamed of challenging the capitalistic system, many sought to make American capitalism more just and less costly in human terms. In an attempt to challenge the increasing power of the corporations, they sponsored legislation such as the Sherman Antitrust Act and the CLAYTON ANTITRUST ACT. Through these laws and other like measures, progressives sought to challenge the power of the large corporations. For the most part, however, these legislative acts did little to challenge the corporations' grasp on the political and economic reins of the American system. They often supported the status quo. Other forms of regulation such as the FEDERAL TRADE COMMISSION ACT were adopted in an effort to stem what was viewed as the uncontrollable growth of capitalistic enterprises.

As one wing of progressivism sought to regulate capitalist competition, another sought to develop the capitalistic model even more fully. Efficiency was the watchword. Progressives championed increased rationalization, and managers emerged to rationalize business and industry through SCIENTIFIC MANAGEMENT. Rationalization did not end at the corporation. Even cities underwent the transformation. In URBAN REFORM efforts, mangers took on many of the roles that were previously reserved for elected officials. New laws that increased residency requirements for voting and instituted new election laws promoted selective democracy.

No aspect of the Progressive movement was more salient than the search for social order. Prohibition, which called for a ban on the production and sale of alcohol, was the grandest of the Progressives' attempts at ushering in an era of social harmony. Prohibitionists were convinced that if they could stem the flow of alcoholic spirits, they could promote a society with unlimited potential. They believed that an amendment that made the production and distribution of alcoholic beverages illegal would eliminate pain, suffering, and poverty. In another attempt to eliminate urban poverty, progressives promoted public projects such as settlement houses, which integrated new social reforms in urban immigrant neighborhoods. Settlement workers were pioneers in developing new techniques of SOCIAL WORK and proposed new programs to benefit the poor, such as MOTHERS' PENSIONS and WORKMEN'S COMPENSATION.

Progressive reform was furthered through a new type of JOURNALISM. Professional journalists, known as MUCK-RAKERS, wrote exposés of social problems. They were nicknamed muckrakers due to their propensity to rake up the economic, political, and social muck that others chose to ignore. Jacob Riis began as a photojournalist in New York. It was there that he first witnessed the torments of the city. Riis's exposés told the story of "How the Other Half Lives." Riis was one of the most renowned, but he was far from the only muckraker of the era. UPTON SINCLAIR, LINCOLN STEFFENS, IDA TARBELL, and others kept the social inadequacies of American urban life at the forefront of newspapers.

Progressivism had its darker side. In the search for social order, many turned to reforms that would restrict access to political rights, narrowly define citizenship, and regulate private behavior. Advocates of immigration reform helped write and pass such laws as the IMMIGRATION ACT OF 1917, the QUOTA ACT of 1921, and the NATIONAL ORIGINS ACT of 1924, which greatly restricted the entry of new immigrants from southern and eastern Europe. In seeking to rationalize American citizenship, Progressives implemented their own racial, ethnic, and gendered views of what constituted true American democracy.

Progressivism developed into a full-blown political movement. The first PROGRESSIVE PARTY, known as the Bull Moose Party, was founded after a bitter fight for the Republican presidential nomination between the more moderate incumbent, President WILLIAM H. TAFT, and THEODORE ROOSEVELT. At the Republican convention in

June 1912, the nomination went to Taft. Unable to accept Taft's conservatism, Roosevelt helped to form the Progressive Party, which nominated him for president and the California governor HIRAM W. JOHNSON for vice president. Throughout the 1912 election, the tensions and divisions present in progressivism surfaced between Wilson's NEW FREEDOM and Roosevelt's NEW NATIONALISM. While the Progressive Party garnered more support than the Republicans in the election, the end result was a victory for the DEMOCRATIC PARTY's candidate, Woodrow Wilson.

Wilson's election marked a shift to a new visibility for progressive reform. He came to embody many of the ideals of the Progressives. He called for a country and a world that was "Safe for Democracy." In 1924 a liberal coalition, frustrated with conservatives in both major parties, formed the League for Progressive Political Action, also called the Progressive Party. The party nominated Senator ROBERT LA FOLLETTE for president and Montana Democratic senator Burton K. Wheeler for vice president. The party drew considerable support from left-wing progressives, socialists, and Farmer-Labor advocates. Many of its most committed members were socialists. They argued for government ownership of public utilities and labor reforms such as the right to collective bargaining. CALVIN COOLIDGE overwhelmingly defeated La Follette, who polled a respectable 4.8 million votes; he captured about 16.5 percent of the total ballots cast and 13 electoral votes.

This campaign was the final hurrah of the progressive movement. With the disenchantment that followed World War I and the deficiencies in social policies such as Prohibition, many Americans abandoned the crusading ideals of progressivism. But its legacy lived on in the careers of progressive reformers and in the New Deal, which brought about many of the reforms progressives had sought.

See also CRIMINAL JUSTICE; EDUCATION; FLORENCE KELLEY; JANE ADDAMS; specific reforms.

Further reading: Alan Dawley, *Struggles for Social Justice: Social Responsibility and the Liberal State* (Cambridge, Mass.: Belknap Press, 1991); Arthur S. Link and Richard L. McCormick, *Progressivism* (Arlington Heights, Ill.: Harlan Davidson, 1983); A. D. Shannon, ed., *Progressivism and Postwar Disillusionment, 1898–1928* (New York: McGraw-Hill, 1966).

— Steve Freund

Prohibition

Prohibition, the law that made the sale, production, and distribution of alcohol a crime, was one of the most profound social experiments in American history. Its proponents viewed it as a means of achieving true social enlightenment. They championed it as a way to attain polit-

Law officials raid a cellar during Prohibition *(Library of Congress)*

ical and social perfection through the elimination of suffering, poverty, and hardship. For its opponents, Prohibition was an attack on the rights of the individual. It was an overly aggressive attempt by the government to impose legal restrictions on private behavior. Regardless of perspective, Prohibition was an effort to fundamentally alter American political and social life.

Many Americans viewed alcohol use and abuse as an affront to the political system. While alcohol consumption was not confined to men, drinking became an important part of American men's personal and political identity. In the early decades of the 19th century, the connection between drinking and democratic citizenship grew to reinforce the maleness of both drinking and political activity. As a result, by the middle of the century, drinking and voting were combined into a single event—a celebration of political masculinity. Political and social reformers alike perceived this link between alcohol and democratic life as a real threat to the nation. Many of these concerned citizens viewed the saloonkeeper, who often functioned as a link between the political and social life for most immigrants, as a true enemy of society. Some social reformers came to view the saloon as the devil's headquarters on Earth. These views provided prohibitionists with ample weapons to attack not only the saloon, but also drinking in general.

No two organizations were more important in bringing about the passage of Prohibition than the Women's Christian Temperance Union (WCTU) and the Anti-Saloon League (ASL). The WCTU viewed drinking as a moral abomination that demeaned men, threatened women, and destroyed the family. The WCTU was extremely successful in popularizing the idea of a national prohibition amendment, but it was the ASL that bolstered the final drive toward national Prohibition. Howard Russell, the founder of the organization, noted that the league was more than the male counterpart of the WCTU. Many of its members believed that the WCTU relied too heavily on moral suasion and did not place enough focus on the enforcement of laws that were already in place. The ASL, in contrast, was a modern organization that benefited from a coherent business structure. In addition, its attacks on drinking were not strictly from a moral position. Its leaders challenged demon rum on a legal front. They began by demanding the enforcement of laws that were already on the books. Only later, when liquor dealers openly flaunted these laws, did they attempt to bring about national Prohibition.

WORLD WAR I provided the opportunity for which opponents of the saloon were looking. They used the war to challenge the saloon on two fronts. On the one hand, they claimed that brewers and distillers were wasting needed war supplies in the pursuit of profit. On the other hand, they challenged the loyalty of the predominantly German brewers. Against the wishes of President WOODROW WILSON, Congress in 1918 passed the Wartime Prohibition Act, banning the manufacture of beer and wine beginning in May 1919 and intoxicating beverages after June 30, 1919. It was to remain in effect until the end of hostilities. This vague terminology allowed the ban to be stretched out until formal Prohibition was adopted.

On the heels of wartime Prohibition, national Prohibition would be implemented. On December 18, 1917, Congress approved a constitutional amendment to prohibit the production, distribution, and sale of alcohol. Once again, the president opposed in vain, and the act was passed over his veto. President Wilson believed that the act's definition of intoxicating beverages—any beverage containing more that 0.5 percent alcohol—was too strict. He believed in the goal of the amendment, but he had his reservations about such a strict definition of alcoholic spirits. He was in favor of a law that allowed for the casual use of weaker wines and ales. His veto proved to be nothing more than a symbolic gesture.

Overriding the president's veto was only the first step toward amending the Constitution. The next step was winning approval in the states. At first it was believed to be a daunting task. But upon further assessment, it was not as difficult a task as once predicted. The Women's Christian Temperance Union, the Anti-Saloon League, and dozens of other pro-Prohibition organizations had been developing the local networks necessary to win support in the states. Twenty-five states already had dry laws. Prohibition forces received a boost when Detroit became the first large city to support the amendment. State by state, the amendment was ratified. On January 15, 1919, New Hampshire became the 36th state to ratify the amendment. One year later, on January 20, 1920, the law took effect.

One of the primary shortcomings of the Prohibition amendment was that it proved difficult to enforce. The concurrent enforcement from the states and federal government allowed both the federal and state governments to leave enforcement of the act to the other. In open defiance

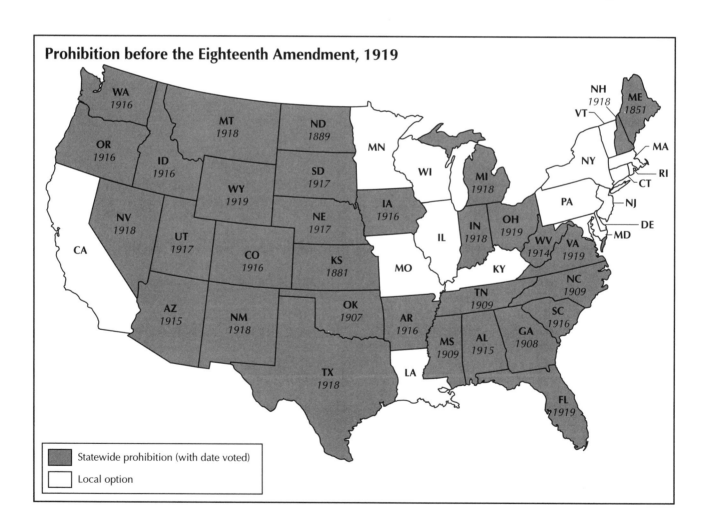

Prohibition before the Eighteenth Amendment, 1919

of the Volstead Act, the legislatures in New York, New Jersey, and Massachusetts passed laws in 1920 allowing for the production and sale of low-alcohol beer and light wines. Later in the same year, through national Prohibition cases, the Supreme Court crushed these efforts and set alcohol limits at .05 percent. These decisions did not win the support of reluctant states. Challenging the federal government, a number of states decided not to enforce national Prohibition.

In addition to problems with enforcing national Prohibition, criminal syndicates emerged to profit from the traffic in illicit spirits. Instead of decreasing criminal activity and misery, Prohibition seemed to be promoting criminal activity. Al Capone in Chicago, George Remus in Cincinnati, and dozens of other underworld figures made millions bootlegging illicit spirits. It sparked considerable violence. In Chicago alone, between 1920 and 1930, nearly 550 men were killed by rival gang members, while police killed hundreds of others during the era. These murders began to capture the attention of the American public. Gangsters, not liquor, became public enemy number one.

The saloon of the pre-Prohibition era had been viewed as a den of evil. What emerged in its place during Prohibition had a far less ominous reputation. The speakeasy came to supplant the local tavern. The speakeasy quickly gained a reputation for being a place where Americans went to have a good time. Even though it was illegal to frequent these establishments, going to a speakeasy was viewed as a victimless crime. Patronizing speakeasies was increasingly viewed as an innocent way to challenge the unjust law. Along the way, women joined in the rebellion.

In the years that led to the passage of the Eighteenth Amendment, women had been making slow but steady progress toward eroding the strictly male identity of the tavern. Women were demanding and, in some cases, receiving access to drinking establishments, but they were far from attaining an equal place within this male bastion. When they were admitted, women often needed to enter through "women's entrances," while only "questionable" women entered drinking establishments without male escorts. With the adoption of the Eighteenth Amendment, women's slow encroachment became a full-scale frontal assault. The emerging speakeasy came to represent something that was risqué but not necessarily immoral. And women increasingly found the doors to the speakeasies open. As women began to frequent the local speakeasies in greater numbers, they helped to redefine gender and drinking roles. Simultaneously, women were less domesticated and drinking more.

The Great Depression, more than any single event, challenged the future of Prohibition. For many Americans, Prohibition not only failed to end drinking, crime, or violence, it also failed to deliver on the promise of a more prosperous nation. In the depressed economic climate of the early 1930s, men and women were tired of devoting needed resources to fighting demon rum. They also wanted the added revenue that a revitalized alcohol industry might foster. The Association against the Prohibition Amendment (AAPA) and the Women's Organization for National Prohibition Reform (WONPR) had launched a serious challenge to Prohibition. Pauline Sabin, one of the leading forces behind WONPR, referred to herself as a "reformed Prohibitionist." She claimed to support the ideals of Prohibition but challenged the methods. She helped to promote that idea that it was acceptable for women to oppose Prohibition. By the middle of the 1920s, the AAPA had companies like General Motors and Standard Oil supporting them. Few predicted the repeal of national Prohibition. Morris Sheppard of Texas went as far as to note that, "There is as much chance of repealing the Eighteenth Amendment as there is for a humming bird to fly to the planet Mars with the Washington Monument tied to its tail." But after 13 years of the noble experiment, Americans decided that it was time for it to end. They repealed national Prohibition.

In some ways, the failure of Prohibition is a myth. Prohibition did reduce alcohol consumption in America. Whether due to Prohibition or not, drinking did not return to its pre- Prohibition levels until the 1970s. Most perceptions of Prohibition's shortcomings are based on its overly inflated objectives. It did not do what many had hoped. It did not wipe alcohol from the American landscape, nor did it end poverty and suffering. But it is difficult to imagine a scenario where Prohibition could have lived up to its promise. What is clear is that Prohibition was successful in putting an end to the reign of the old-time saloon. The drinking establishments that emerged in the wake of Prohibition were no longer the "Devil's den on Earth" that they had once been.

See also CRIMINAL JUSTICE; PROGRESSIVISM.

Further reading: Thomas Pegram, *Battling Demon Run: The Struggle for a Dry America, 1800–1933* (Chicago: Ivan R. Dee, 1998); Austin Kerr, *Organized for Prohibition: A History of the Anti-Saloon League* (New Haven, Conn.: Yale University Press, 1985); Catherine Murdock, *Domesticating Drink: Women, Men, and Alcohol in America, 1870–1940* (Baltimore: Johns Hopkins University Press, 1998).

— Steve Freund

public health

"The golden age of public health" dawned at the beginning of the 20th century. As social reformers and public officials increasingly accepted environmental and epidemiological factors as the causes of the commonly fatal diseases of tuberculosis, diphtheria, typhoid fever, and cholera, they turned toward medicine for the answer. Directing new attention toward epidemic disease and educating the public in social hygiene, states abandoned the old practice of politically appointed public health officers and instead relied on medical experts to establish new rules and procedures to protect public health. City and state governments created boards of health to intervene in epidemics and regulate sources of contagion and disease, such as water supply and sewage systems, commercial milk production, and workplace ventilation. They also strengthened their efforts to immunize children against ailments such as diphtheria, to quarantine affected populations, especially immigrants, and to treat infectious diseases such as tuberculosis through isolation in public sanitariums.

There was tension, however, between public health officials and the private practice of MEDICINE. In every attempt to open up public health services, whether in private maternity hospitals, public schools, or community clinics, the new power of the American Medical Association (AMA) made itself felt. Even as medical knowledge and practice expanded, the AMA's ability to lobby for new state licensing boards and higher standards of medical education stymied lay practitioners. Its growing control over prescription drugs and medical treatment also made itself felt. By the end of the 1920s, the medical profession had been able to turn public health programs from a threat to private practice to an indirect subsidy for private physicians.

Epidemic disease, however, was the one area in which public health reigned. The principal reason why governments gave new powers to public health departments was the medical discovery of the origin, course, and treatment of such diseases as tuberculosis and diphtheria. The importance of factors such as exposure to disease in the spread of contagion, and the impact of the urban environment, required new public measures. Successful treatment of these two diseases alone promised a decline in the mortality rate, as they were among the leading causes of death in the late 19th and early 20th centuries.

Campaigns to control tuberculosis led the way. In 1904, the National Association for the Study and Prevention of Tuberculosis took steps to conduct studies, educate the public, and broadcast findings about the disease. Local and state campaigns followed. A leader in this effort was the state of New York, where the State Charities and Aid Association formed a Committee for the Prevention of Tuberculosis. New findings about the contagious nature of the disease led to a demand for greater reporting and oversight, and in 1908, the New York state legislature passed a law mandating that physicians report tuberculosis cases. While it was rescinded, reporting on the disease increased; and overall the rate of infection slowed incredibly between 1907 and 1917. Improved nutrition, better general health care, and the pasteurization of milk provided a context for the decline of tuberculosis. Isolation of tuberculosis patients in newly established state sanitariums stopped the epidemic spread of the disease and forced a decline in tuberculosis as one of the major causes of death. Within the sanitariums themselves, the period saw little change in cure rates, as medical practitioners continued to experiment with treatments. The better food, fresh air, and personal rest that were offered to minimally infected patients probably aided their recovery, while the severely ill tended to die in isolation from their families.

The creation of the United States Public Health Service in 1902 was emblematic of new trends in public health and medicine. The United States had been slow to create a public health agency because, unlike European industrial states, the federal government had a vested interest in relying on private health care. Congress had created a National Board of Health in 1879 but abolished it only four years later. In 1902 and 1912, Congress finally expanded the Marine Hospitals for seamen into the Public Health Service. For the most part, however, it left medical authority in the hands of local and state governments and private organizations. Voluntary associations such as ethnic benevolent societies, fraternal organizations, unions, and private employers provided some measure of health care and diagnosis. Health insurance, even in the private sector, was underdeveloped. And dispensary medicine, long the refuge of the poor, was under siege from private medical doctors.

During the period, public health officials directed attention to those areas of public health shunned by private practitioners. They addressed the spread of sexually transmitted diseases such as syphilis (Paul Ehrlich invented salvarsan, for treatment of syphilis, in 1910; although only partly effective, it became available through public venereal disease clinics) and created new, if largely ineffective, laws that regulated or prohibited prostitution. During WORLD WAR I, concern over venereal disease led to increasing control of towns around military bases, sex education in military training, and the increased use of condoms. The war generally increased the willingness to allow state and federal interventions in public health matters.

The Influenza Epidemic of 1918–19, or Spanish Flu Epidemic, was a proving ground for the new powers of the state to regulate public health. Viewed in total numbers of lives lost, it was possibly the most devastating epidemic in history and claimed more than 25 million lives worldwide in a relatively short period of time. At least 12,500,000 people died in India alone; in Samoa 25 percent of the population perished in the epidemic. The magnitude of loss throughout the United States was such that some towns were decimated. The sudden onset of the flu, rapid loss of life, and the quick disappearance of the disease revealed the limitations of medical knowledge and public health measures as the disease spread rapidly and without any certain treatment.

There were three distinct waves to the outbreak of the epidemic. The first wave was thought to have originated in Kansas in March 1918. The cases were comparatively mild, and few Americans paid much attention to it. There were other, more pressing considerations at the time. The war in Europe, the TREATY OF VERSAILLES, and the RUSSIAN REVOLUTION captured the headlines more than the outbreak of flu. The second wave of cases, however, caused greater alarm. During the hot summer months, a lethal strain of the Spanish flu virus emerged. This more deadly strain worked extremely fast. It raced through both city and countryside. Unlike its relatively mild predecessor, this virus brought pneumonia soon after the initial infection. The flu strain struck the armed forces and the civilian population hard. The third and final wave of the flu surfaced the following winter, when it cost millions of citizens their lives. It was more deadly than either of its predecessors. It disappeared, however, as fast as it had appeared. By spring, the epidemic had run its course. The social effects of the epidemic were pronounced. Unlike most flu outbreaks, which affect the young and the aged, nearly half the victims of the Spanish Flu were men and women between the ages of 20 and 40. The epidemic thus added to the losses endured during WORLD WAR I. The wildfire spread of the flu also brought new caution to a medical field that could no longer know with certainty that infectious diseases could be cured. Epidemic disease revealed the real limitations of the nation's health care delivery system.

Another area of weakness was in the provision of medical care for war VETERANS. Over 300,000 veterans had returned from the war in Europe in need of care in hospitals, sanitariums, and asylums. Prior to the war, the U.S. Public Health Service had no responsibility for providing military health care. In 1919, however, Congress assigned the Public Health Service responsibilities for veterans with service-related disabilities, including tuberculosis, neuropsychiatric disorders, and general medical and surgical cases. Given the lack of facilities, the PHS opened to veterans the 20 marine hospitals under its supervision and leased other hospital facilities from the army and navy, bringing the number to 62 hospitals. Even these were inadequate to care for the thousands of disabled veterans. In 1921, under the administration of WARREN G. HARDING, Congress passed the first Langley Act, which authorized $18.6 million for veterans' hospital construction. It was in this period of time that veterans' medical care was moved from the Department of the Treasury to the VETERANS BUREAU. Medical care for disabled veterans had become a major investment in the public health care system.

In the case of pregnant mothers and young children, the health care system was engaged in an experiment with government-funded medical education. The interest of progressives in child welfare, evidenced in the creation of MOTHERS' PENSIONS, became the focus of women's organized efforts for a national health program under the Maternity and Infant Health Care Act, or SHEPPARD-TOWNER ACT, of 1921. Under the authority of the CHILDREN'S BUREAU, the program helped to nurture the public health nursing service and generally contributed to the continuing decline in infant mortality. Congress allowed the funding of the controversial program to expire in 1929. Competition between Public Health Service doctors and the nurse practitioners who provided health care under the Children's Bureau program had shadowed the program from the beginning.

The same competition that plagued publicly funded maternity and infant child care was an issue in the provision of BIRTH CONTROL as well. Between 1900 and 1920, radicals such as MARGARET SANGER and EMMA GOLDMAN battled for the right of poor women to have access to new birth control methods and safe abortions. Many in the medical profession, however, opposed methods of contraception both for reasons of personal belief and due to a lack of medical regulation. Sanger pushed for the adoption of the spring-loaded vaginal diaphragm, which she originally argued should be available at neighborhood clinics and from nurse-midwives. Seeking to pave the way for easily accessible birth control, Sanger eventually allied herself with the medical profession in creating Planned Parenthood, an organization dedicated to motherhood by choice. Not until the 1930s, however, did she succeed in getting birth control and fertility seen as a public health concern. By then, the medical profession had succeeded in limiting public health initiatives and expanding its role even in the provision of health care to the general public.

Further reading: John Duffy, *The Sanitarians; A History of American Public Health* (Urbana: University of Illinois Press, 1990); Paul Starr, *The Social Transformation of American Medicine* (New York: Basic Books, 1982); L. C. Taylor, *The Medical Profession and Social Reform, 1885–1945* (New York: St. Martin's Press, 1974).

Pure Food and Drug Act (1906)

Changes in the manufacturing, processing, and distribution of goods and services fundamentally altered the nation's food supply and the way in which food was prepared. Gone were the days when food was grown, cultivated, and sold locally. By the first decade of the 20th century, much of the food supply for urban America was grown at some distance, shipped in bulk, and sold at markets or grocery stores. Food producers learned lessons from the automobile industry and increasingly began producing food in mass quantities. This food was then shipped in newly designed, refrigerated train cars and trucks. Technological innovations also allowed food manufacturers to produce canned goods. These innovations came with mixed blessings. The price of food declined steadily while the supply and variety of food increased substantially. However, because it was largely unregulated, the quality of the nation's food supply declined as food purity frequently took a back seat to reducing costs.

The alarming conditions of food production were first exposed in muckraking journalist UPTON SINCLAIR's *The Jungle* (1906). In 1904, Sinclair was commissioned to investigate the living and working conditions of the largely foreign-born workers in the Chicago meatpacking industry. What Sinclair found was published in his book *The Jungle.* Sinclair's intent had been both to alert the public to the appalling lack of sanitation and to expose the low wages, hazardous working conditions, and substandard living conditions of the Chicago stockyard workers and their families. Although Sinclair would later complain, "I aimed at the public's heart and by accident I hit it in the stomach," *The Jungle* had a tremendous impact on an already wary public.

Concern about drug abuse and the purity of food products had been mounting since the 1890s. Dr. Harvey Wiley, the head of the Department of Agriculture, formed a "poison squad" to test food for chemical additives; and the American Medical Association, concerned that pharmaceutical drugs were being mislabeled and sold as health tonics, lobbied for the introduction of strict federal oversight. Intense lobbying on the part of progressive reformers and the medical community along with growing public concern prompted President THEODORE ROOSEVELT to order investigations into the meatpacking and pharmaceutical industries. These investigations resulted in the passage of the MEAT INSPECTION ACT (1906) and the Pure Food and Drug Act (1906). The Pure Food and Drug Act established strict controls on food and drug labeling and placed oversight responsibility with the Department of Labor, the Department of Agriculture, and the Department of the Treasury. The act has been extended and strengthened numerous times since 1906, most notably in 1938 when the Food and Drug Administration was created.

Further reading: Lorine Goodwin, *The Pure Food, Drink, and Drug Crusaders, 1879–1914* (Jefferson, N.C.: McFarland, 1999); Upton Sinclair, *The Jungle* (Urbana: University of Illinois Press, 1988).

— Robert Gordon

Q

Quota Act (1921)

The Quota Act of 1921 was the culmination of 25 years of lobbying for restrictive immigration laws. Through much of the 19th century, the United States had an "open door" immigration policy, which had allowed individuals and families to enter the country with relatively few restrictions. As the economy of the United States became more concentrated in urban areas and focused on industrial production, the volume of migrants steadily increased. The growing number of immigrants in urban centers quickly became an issue of concern and gave raise to a vocal anti-immigrant movement. Although CONGRESS moved to restrict the entry of Asian immigrants, particularly those from China, as early as 1882, it was not able to enact legislation that closed the door to immigrants from Europe prior to WORLD WAR I. Indeed, with steady improvements in transatlantic transportation, European migrants were able to reach the United States in ever-increasing numbers. In 1882, some 788,922 immigrants entered the United States, and 1,285,349 entered in 1907. Not only did the volume of immigrants steadily increase, but the countries of origin for immigrants dramatically shifted as well. New immigration from southern and eastern Europe predominated.

World War I brought a precipitous drop in the number of immigrants arriving in the United States, but the volume of people seeking entry quickly returned to near prewar levels following the cessation of hostilities in Europe. By 1921, some 800,000 immigrants had sought entry to the United States, and the proportion of southern and eastern Europeans among them remained high. In 1917, Congress had enacted a literacy test in the hope of restricting the entry of immigrants to the United States in the IMMIGRA-TION ACT OF 1917. Within only a few years, it became clear that this legislation would not have the desired effect. Accordingly, Congress moved to the next step and put into place legislation that limited the number of immigrants eligible to enter based on country of origin and the total number of immigrants that the United States accepted annually. The Quota Act of 1921 limited the annual number of entrants of each admissible nationality to 3 percent of that foreign-born nationality as recorded in the official census of 1910. The intended purpose of this legislation was to control the influx of immigrants. Immigration restrictionists thought that this legislation would effectively close the door on emigrants from southern and eastern Europe, who had quotas set at less than one-quarter the annual volume of immigration prior to World War I. Under this legislation, Congress continued to allow free emigration from its neighbors in the Western Hemisphere. Between 1907 and 1914, the average annual emigration from countries in northern and western Europe was nearly 177,000 while the same figure for emigrants from countries in southern and eastern Europe slightly exceeded 685,000. With the passage of the 1921 Quota Act, the volume and origins of immigrants to the United States dramatically shifted. Some 198,000 emigrants entered in 1922 from northern and western Europe, while only a little better than 158,000 emigrants from southern and eastern Europe were able to gain entry to the United States.

Further reading: John Higham, *Strangers in the Land: Patterns of American Nativism, 1860–1925*, 2nd ed. (New Brunswick, N.J.: Rutgers University Press, 1988).

— David R. Smith

R

race and racial conflict

During the first decades of the 20th century, Americans significantly changed the way they thought about race. At the turn of the century, many believed that numerous distinct races existed. They categorized Scandinavians, Slavs, Japanese, Germans, and Irish as separate races. By 1930, the modern conception of race based on skin color had developed, and all groups of Europeans were now defined as white. Because racial categorization depended on political, legal, and social boundaries between recognized races, changes in how race was categorized involved recognizing and maintaining new boundaries. Part of this change involved violence between whites and African Americans as whites tried to distance themselves from African Americans. At the same time, intellectuals shifted the terms of the debate about racial differences from biology to culture.

In the United States socially and politically powerful groups imposed racial categories for the purpose of maintaining their own power. Members of the dominant racial group enjoyed greater access to the benefits of American society, benefits that differed only by gender. Even before the modern racial categorization based on African ancestry developed, race was thought of in terms of color. The police and the courts were open only to white Americans. The best jobs were open to them. They could send their children to the best schools. Whites' votes gave them a say in the political and economic arenas. Asian immigrants and Native Americans were consigned to a category outside citizenship, and to be considered black meant being shut off from all or most of these opportunities. At the turn of the century, not all Americans of European ancestry were believed to be white. New immigrant groups were categorized as black, meaning they were not deemed worthy of the benefits enjoyed by the dominant racial group. Only after they had suffered through a probationary period, in which their worthiness for full citizenship was evaluated, did they gain access to broader social and political rights.

It was not unusual in the 1850s, for example, to refer to Irish Americans as blacks. Once an immigrant group gained political and economic power, it eventually was seen as white. It was not, however, until the 1920s that all Europeans, regardless of their country of origin, fell into that category.

Before that time, immigrants were categorized according to their country of origin. As IMMIGRATION to the United States increased in the late 19th and early 20th centuries, whiteness was fractured into a myriad of scientifically defined races. The immigration laws specifically allowed only "white persons" to enter the United States freely. Laws such as the Chinese Exclusion Act of 1882 and the GENTLEMEN'S AGREEMENT of 1907 restricted Asian immigration. People from these groups were not eligible, therefore, for even a probationary status in the eyes of white Americans. Despite the perceived inferiority of many groups, the exclusion of Asian immigrants gave every European immigrant some claim to whiteness. Many members of the socially and politically powerful groups within American society expressed the fear that immigrants, particularly those from southern and eastern Europe, threatened to dilute the purity of the white race. This fear led to a system of racial classification in which physical, mental, and emotional characteristics were attributed to individuals based on their nationally defined race.

The attempts of some Americans to redefine racial categories led to a debate over the nature of race. On one side were proponents of the pseudo-science of eugenics. Eugenics revolved around efforts to classify individuals into racial categories and to rank those races according to a set of criteria that favored northern Europeans. Many believed that Italians and Jews, for example, could be identified by their physical characteristics. Eugenicists used these racial classifications to argue that the whites were committing "race suicide" by allowing southern and eastern Europeans to settle. Eugenicists argued for changes in population policy, which ranged from sterilization of the poor and disabled to harsh anti-immigration measures. In his extremely popular 1916 book, *The Passing of the Great Race,* Madison Grant argued that the American melting pot was creating a lower race of people, as southern and eastern European immigrants bred with native-born white citizens. In opposition to the eugenicists, anthropologists such as MARGARET MEAD and FRANZ BOAS demonstrated that perceived differences among races were products of historical circumstance, not products of inherent physical and mental characteristics. Sociologists at the University of Chicago such as Robert Park also defied the efforts of eugenicists.

Among the general public and policy makers, the eugenicists' view of race predominated. As early as 1911, the DILLINGHAM COMMISSION reported that the immigrants coming to the United States were different from earlier groups. It recommended that immigration from eastern and southern Europe be restricted. In coming to its conclusion, commission members ignored most of the data they collected to report, instead, preconceived findings. The commission's recommendation gained the force of law in the 1921 QUOTA ACT and the 1924 National Origins Act, which established quotas that severely limited emigration from southern and eastern Europe. The new law had the effect of removing the threat of inferior white races, which allowed the immigrants and children of immigrants to gain white status. As all European Americans became white, the only racial distinctions remaining were those between whites and those defined as "other," specifically African Americans, Asian Americans, NATIVE AMERICANS, and, to a lesser extent, Hispanics. Thus, modern racial relations based on skin color developed.

As members of the few racial groups in the United States that never had the opportunity to become white, African Americans, Asian Americans, Native Americans, and Hispanics faced new efforts at codifying and strengthening racial discrimination. In this effort, many European Americans stressed the differences between themselves and African Americans, for example, through the ideology of white supremacy and the practice of SEGREGATION. Supporters of the idea of white supremacy developed the argument that non-European Americans were innately inferior to whites. At a time when mass-production industry was playing a larger role in American life, white supremacists constructed an image of African Americans, Native Americans, and Hispanics as pre- industrial and irrational peoples. In this scheme, whites were seen as rational for adopting time clocks in determining the pattern of their days. Eugenicists bolstered these arguments with purported scientific "facts" that non-Europeans belonged to more ancient, less developed racial groups. In the minds of many, if non-Europeans were not quite human, they did not need to be treated as such. Many proponents of educa-

tion for non-European Americans, for example, argued that they required only a basic education that focused on rudimentary vocational skills. In the Southwest, many of the same ideas were applied to Hispanic and Native American peoples, just as in the West, Asian Americans were viewed as products of a feudal society.

One outgrowth of white supremacy was the violation of non-European Americans' civil, political, and social rights through segregation, or the physical and legal separation of the races. The most systematic efforts to legislate racial prejudices came in the southern states. Beginning in the late 19th century, southern states launched an attack on African Americans that resulted in the passage of a myriad of oppressive laws known under the name of Jim Crow. By 1900, most southern states had passed laws restricting the voting rights of African Americans. The laws established either a property or literacy requirement for voting and then created loopholes through which white voters could vote. Most states also required payment of a poll tax.

After taking African Americans' voting rights, the southern states passed countless laws restricting the social and economic rights of African Americans. By 1910, every southern state had segregated railway stations in which African Americans and whites waited in separate rooms. Between 1901 and 1907, 10 states segregated their streetcars and trains, requiring African Americans to sit in the rear. States segregated hospitals, prisons, and parks. Theaters established separate entrances and seating areas. Even workplaces became segregated. A 1915 South Carolina law, for example, prohibited the races working together in the same room and required separate entrances, pay windows, doorways, toilets, and drinking water.

By 1920, 30 states had outlawed racial intermarriage. Most of these laws pertained to marriage between whites and blacks, but some states outlawed marriage between other racial groups. In 1905, for example, California outlawed marriage between Asians and whites. The movements to prohibit racial intermarriage led to the establishment of the "one-drop rule" of racial identification, which held that if a person had any ancestor considered to be of African descent, then they were considered black under the law. Some states also imposed the one-drop rule for Native American ancestry. The nature of race as a social construction was demonstrated in the 1924 Virginia Racial Integrity Act. The Virginia legislature established a "one-drop" law for determining African ancestry and outlawed all racial intermarriage. The legislature also sought to prohibit marriage between whites and Native Americans, originally proposing a "one- drop" law. A number of legislators and prominent citizens, however, traced their lineage to John Rolfe and Pocahontas. Any "one-drop" law would have applied to them. They therefore changed the law to allow citizens with up to one-sixteenth Native American ancestry to be considered white.

A complex racial etiquette accompanied the legal restrictions. In California, Japanese men were expected to be docile and deferential to whites. In the southern states, whites expected African Americans to demonstrate their inferior status by deferring to whites in public. African Americans were not to look whites in the eyes. When walking on the same sidewalks, African Americans were to move into the road to allow whites to pass. Southern whites reserved a special place in the racial etiquette for the relationship between African-American men and white women. A mythology surrounding African-American men existed in which they were supposedly interested in nothing but ravaging white women. These beliefs were spread through word of mouth and the new media of motion pictures. In 1915, the film, *The Nigger,* showed an African-American man attacking a white woman. D. W. GRIFFITH's film, *BIRTH OF A NATION*, claimed to tell the true story of Reconstruction in the South after the Civil War. Of special note was its portrayal of African Americans with white ancestry. Mulattoes, as they were known at the time, supposedly wanted what white men had—power and white women. The film included scenes of mulatto men degrading white women. The creation of the Jim Crow system was dedicated, many believed, to preserving the purity of white southern women.

The system of racial etiquette was backed by force. Any African American who violated the cultural rules faced punishment ranging from severe beating to death. A lynching was a mob action in which a group seized a person believed to have committed a crime and committed an extralegal murder by shooting or hanging the victim. Often the mob attacked and defaced the corpse. Between 1880 and 1930, white mobs lynched approximately 3,220 African Americans in the southern states. Sporadic lynching occurred in other regions as well. In the early 20th century, Japanese men faced beatings on the streets in California. Many African Americans in the South lived in fear that the slightest transgression could lead to death.

African Americans did not always stand idly by as they were attacked. In many instances, they fought back. In 1900, a New Orleans man refused to surrender to the police after an altercation with a white man. He ended up killing 10 white people before the police shot him. In 1906, African Americans in Mississippi took up arms on two separate occasions to defend themselves. The same year, whites in Atlanta were incited to riot by newspaper articles that alleged mobs of African-American men were roaming the city attacking white women. The whites took to the streets and began randomly to attack and murder African Americans. When the mob moved into the African-American neighborhood, blacks organized to defend themselves and killed several of the invaders.

Racial violence was not confined to the South. Race riots occurred in 1900 in New York City and Akron, Ohio. In 1908, white mobs took control of Springfield, Illinois, and attacked African Americans and their property. Racial violence in the northern states intensified after World War I. African Americans had migrated to the northern cities in great numbers during and after WORLD WAR I in the GREAT MIGRATION—with two effects. First, the growing populations of African Americans pushed against the boundaries of segregated neighborhoods. There was not enough housing in the traditional African-American areas, and migrants from the South sought housing in areas that whites saw as their own. Often an attempt by an African-American family to move into a new neighborhood led to an attack by whites. In Chicago between 1919 and 1921, for example, there were 58 bomb explosions, almost all of them related to African-American housing. Conflict erupted over control of other public spaces such as parks and beaches. One of the worst riots started when an African- American youth swam across the dividing line between black and white sections of a Chicago beach. Second, the African-American migrants came with the hope of securing an industrial job. Many white workers saw them as a threat. The use of African Americans as strikebreakers contributed to these anxieties, and economic crisis intensified white fears. An additional factor was the new, militant attitude of some African Americans returning from military service. They began to demand the rights and opportunities for which they had presumably fought.

All of these factors combined led to an outbreak of racial violence in the years immediately following the First World War. In the last six months of 1919, 25 separate incidents of racial violence erupted. In Chicago, conflict at a public beach flared into a riot that lasted almost a week and resulted in 38 deaths, 23 of which were African American. Countless others were injured and substantial amounts of property were damaged. In East St. Louis in 1917, tensions ran high over competition between African-American and white workers. On the night of June 30, 1917, a fight led to the shooting of a white policeman by an African American. White crowds gathered to avenge the police officer's death and attacked African Americans. Nine whites and 25 African Americans were officially counted as dead, but officials believed that more African Americans had died in fires set by attackers. In Tulsa, Oklahoma, in 1921 whites assaulted the African-American section of the city, burned most of it to the ground, and killed anywhere from 20 to 60 African Americans.

Ironically, racial violence peaked just as anthropologists such as Franz Boas presented new challenges to scientific racism. Still, these incidents of racial violence took place during a time of change in the way race was perceived in the United States and were partially the result of white American attempts to redefine themselves. Only with the broad changes in society and politics in the years between the wars did movements for racial equality begin to change Americans' perception of race.

See also ANTI-SEMITISM; ETHNIC ORGANIZATIONS.

Further reading: Allen D. Grimshaw, ed., *Racial Violence in the United States* (Chicago: Aldine Publishing Company, 1969); David G. Gutierrez, *Walls and Mirrors: Mexican Americans, Mexican Immigrants, and the Politics of Ethnicity* (Berkeley: University of California Press, 1995); Matthew F. Jacobson, *Whiteness of a Different Color: European Immigrants and the Alchemy of Race* (Cambridge, Mass.: Harvard University Press, 1998); Paul R. Spickard, *Mixed Blood: Intermarriage and Ethnic Identity in Twentieth-Century America* (Madison: University of Wisconsin Press, 1989); Ronald Takaki, *From Different Shores: Perspectives on Race and Ethnicity in America* (New York: Oxford University Press, 1987).

— Michael Hartman

radicalism

American radicalism played an important role in shaping the nation's political development between 1900 and 1930. Radicalism can be defined as opposition to the dominant economic, political, and social structures of the country. At the turn of the century, this meant opposition to the poverty and social inequality created by MASS PRODUCTION industry, free-market capitalism, and emerging consumerism. Radicalism in the United States had several different strains, including anarchism, socialism, labor militancy, feminism, and cultural radicalism. The upsurge in radicalism between 1900 and 1920 did not, however, result in an attempt to overthrow the government or the formation of a permanent third political party. Radicals tended to support gradual reform, rather than violent revolution. The RED SCARE and political repression in the 1920s kept radicals divided throughout the decade.

The radicalism of the early 20th century drew on the concerns and tactics of its predecessors. The emergence of the industrial revolution, urbanization, and the demise of small, independent farming resulted in social and political unrest in the 1880s and 1890s. Several political movements attempted to address the concerns of workers, farmers, and immigrants. In the 1880s, the Knights Of Labor attempted to organize the new industrial workers, southern African-American sharecroppers, and farmers struggling to maintain their independence. In the 1890s, the populists also attempted to address the plight of farmers by attacking the power of the railroads and the banks. Both the Knights and the populists advocated that the federal government play a larger role in ensuring social harmony by redistributing

wealth and property more equally, but they refrained from calling for the abolition of private property or from seeking violent means for social change. In the same period of time, women continued to organize for WOMAN SUFFRAGE and PROHIBITION, among other reforms.

A more class-based form of radicalism emerged at the dawn of the 20th century. Support for SOCIALISM grew rapidly among new immigrants, intellectuals, agrarian activists, and industrial workers. This new socialism was by no means confined to the working class, but it did highlight workers' concerns. Between 1890 and 1910, business and industry actively worked to suppress unionism by employing company spies to infiltrate unions, blacklisting suspected radicals and union supporters, forcing workers to sign anti-union contracts, and using labor injunctions to break strikes. Added to this were changes in the pace of work and how work was organized. As workers began to resist these changes, some found the efforts of the conservative AMERICAN FEDERATION OF LABOR (AFL) to be insufficient. Socialists, both in the labor movement and outside the labor movement, argued that industry and wealth should benefit all of society, not just a wealthy elite. In 1901, the Socialist Labor Party, led by Morris Hillquit and Daniel De Leon, merged with the Social Democratic Party, led by EUGENE V. DEBS, to form the Socialist Party of America (SPA). The SPA grew steadily between 1900 and 1912. Its goals were diffuse, from supporting political reform and labor legislation to municipal ownership of utilities and urban transportation.

Syndicalism, or revolutionary industrial unionism, was another form of socialism that gained support among workers. Its ultimate goal was to organize society and government on an industrial basis. THE INDUSTRIAL WORKERS OF THE WORLD (IWW), the leading voice of syndicalism in the United States, emerged in 1905 and quickly challenged the dominance of the AFL. In its most radical form, the IWW supported the general strike, producer cooperatives, workers' control of production, and the abolition of capitalism. More typically, the IWW directed its energies toward forms of direct action, including massive strikes at McKees Rocks in 1909 and the LAWRENCE STRIKE in 1912. Its membership grew steadily until WORLD WAR I, when it declined in the face of government repression under the ESPIONAGE ACT and SEDITION ACT and state criminal syndicalism laws, but it never seriously threatened the dominance of the AFL.

Anarchism, another form of radicalism, advocated extreme means of opposing capitalism and the status quo. Some individualist anarchists feared that the rise of modern, urban, and industrial society threatened to undermine individual rights. The majority of American anarchists were followers of Peter Kropotkin, a Russian communitarian anarchist. In general, they opposed centralized government, because it inevitably led to economic exploitation, militarism, and war.

Finally, some socialists, anarchists, and syndicalists gravitated toward communism, particularly after the RUSSIAN REVOLUTION of 1917. In 1919, two competing factions—the COMMUNIST PARTY and the Communist Labor Party—split from the Socialist Party and its international sections. Each claimed to be the legitimate representative of the worldwide communist revolution. The two factions merged in 1924. By 1929 the party was known as the Communist Party of the United States of America (CPUSA). Between 1919 and 1930, American communists focused their efforts on recruiting industrial workers in core industries such as steel, coal, and automobiles, and—to a lesser extent—organized among African-American sharecroppers. Prior to 1930, support for communism among union members remained very small.

Several key factors ensured that American radicalism failed to have the impact radicalism had in Europe. Judged by the absence of an independent working-class or labor politics, American radicalism failed. There were reasons for this failure. The national economy, despite cyclical depressions, grew at a faster rate than did the economies of Europe. Though workers and poorer Americans did not share equally in the nation's economic growth, many workers and recently arrived immigrants saw improvements in their standard of living. The result was that many ordinary men and women were reluctant to support efforts for greater state intervention in the economy, and indeed, there was a commonly held distrust of government among both working-class and middle-class Americans. Few advocated the abolition of private property. Socialists and Social Democrats, who generally advocated more moderate reforms, were able to generate much more widespread support. Even the million votes for EUGENE DEBS in 1912 could not compare in political dominance with the two mainstream political parties.

Possibly the most significant reason why radicalism failed to have a greater impact in the United States was that radicals encountered a coordinated resistance from the government, the courts, and employers. Employers fired and blacklisted suspected radicals. When violence did occur, judges sought to ensure that radical leaders were convicted and either deported or sentenced to long prison terms. Both federal troops and state militias as well as private corporate arming were used to violently repress strikes. Finally, at the outbreak of World War I, federal legislation made it illegal to criticize the government or to oppose American involvement in the war. Socialist Eugene Debs and anarchist EMMA GOLDMAN both were arrested and convicted of violating these laws. Attacks against radicals and radicalism continued after the end of the war in 1918.

The fear that radicals were behind the massive postwar strikes fueled the Red Scare of 1919–20. Led by Attorney General A. MITCHELL PALMER, the government launched a series of raids against radicals, which specifically targeted the offices of the IWW and the Communist Party. The largest raid took place on January 2, 1920, when approximately 10,000 suspected communists and communist sympathizers were arrested and held without bail. Many of those arrested, particularly those who were recent immigrants, were deported from the country. Afterward the labor movement and other radical political organizations were in a shambles; long-time SPA leader Eugene Debs was serving a prison sentence for treason, and fear of deportation and blacklisting silenced many immigrants and workers.

At the same time, radical ideas did change the way that government and society functioned in the United States. Socialist thought influenced the reform movement of PROGRESSIVISM and helped to shape legislation to regulate business and protect women and child wage earners. Reformers such as the National Consumer League's FLORENCE KELLEY and Social Gospel minister WALTER RAUSCHENBUSCH read socialist texts and moved to incorporate the more humanitarian strains of radical thinking. Feminist thinkers like CHARLOTTE PERKINS GILMAN and civil rights advocate W. E. B. DUBOIS contributed to both mainstream and radical social thought. Sexual mores, gender norms, and racial etiquette were altered by the radical culture of the early 20th century. When the Republican administrations of WILLIAM HOWARD TAFT and CALVIN COOLIDGE argued that it was time to return the country to normalcy and economic prosperity, they spoke of retaking the government. But as the radical revival during the Great Depression would show, radicalism did not die in the 1920s; it just shifted ground.

See also RADICAL PRESS; WOMEN'S STATUS AND RIGHTS.

Further reading: John Button, *The Radicalism Handbook: A Complete Guide to the Radical Movement in the Twentieth Century* (London: Cassell, 1995); Robert K. Murray, *Red Scare; A Study in National Hysteria, 1919–1920* (New York: McGraw-Hill, 1955); Sidney Lens, *Radicalism in America* (New York: Crowell, 1966).
— Robert Gordon

radical press

At the turn of the century, strong socialist and labor organizations supported a broad range of newspapers and journals across the United States. With membership in trade unions numbering in the millions after 1900 and socialist parties garnering hundreds of thousands of votes every year, journalists who explored radical causes found an audience for their own publications. The radical press ranged from the socialist *An Appeal to Reason* and *Solidarity,* published by the INDUSTRIAL WORKERS OF THE WORLD, of the *Woman Rebel* edited by feminist birth control advocate MARGARET SANGER. Radical publishing houses such as Haldeman-Julius and Charles H. Kerr supplemented newspapers and journals with books and pamphlets on social and political issues.

At a time when major newspapers dominated the urban markets, and printing costs were escalating radical, newspapers continued to thrive in rural areas, where they appealed to farmers as well as workers, as did the socialist *Appeal.* Inspired by progressive beliefs in the "Cooperative Commonwealth," and taking seriously the need for alliances across class and region, radical editors sought ways to influence public opinion far beyond the formal membership of socialist and labor organizations. Their investigative reporting on urban poverty and hazardous working conditions inspired the work of the MUCKRAKERS, reform journalists who directed their critical gaze at political corruption, business monopolies, and employer abuses.

Labor newspapers of the time ranged from the relatively conservative *American Federationist,* the journal of the AMERICAN FEDERATION OF LABOR, and *Labor,* published by the railroad unions, to the IWW's *Solidarity,* which embraced radical causes and promoted worker sabotage in the workplace. *Solidarity* was blessed with pungent humor and writing and with a wide range of perspectives from words to Joe Hill's labor anthems to the cartoon satire of Mr. Block. The image of labor in the period embraced a broad masculine labor, but its prose also revealed stories and viewpoints sympathetic to women workers. By the turn of the 20th century, there were literally thousands of union newspapers published by city labor federations and national trade unions. They had a readership that numbered in the hundreds of thousands. Along with conventional labor newspapers were a growing number of publications that crossed the lines to a new audience. From the NATIONAL WOMEN'S TRADE UNION LEAGUE, an organization that supported women workers and their unions, came *Life and Labor.* Edited by Australian feminists Alice Henry and Stella Franklin, the journal incorporated some of the best labor reporting, with editorial matter on citizenship, education, and politics.

Shifts in radicalism brought forth a new generation of radical newspapers and journals. By 1910, broadly defined radical publications such as THE MASSES and anarchist EMMA GOLDMAN's *Mother Earth* touted birth control, sexual emancipation, and Freudian psychoanalysis in addition to traditional working-class and populist issues. Experimental arts journals provided a new forum for modern poetry and criticism, with such publications as *Seven Arts*

and *Little Review* (edited by Margaret Anderson) leading the way. Edited by Harriet Monroe, *Poetry,* the premiere journal for modern poetry, published its first issue in 1911.

By 1910, there were over 300 socialist newspapers and journals alone. Every major city had labor-oriented socialist newspapers, including the *Milwaukee Leader,* the *New York Call,* and the *National Rip Saw* (St. Louis), as well as ethnic journals such as the *Arbeiter Zeitung* (New York). Under the editorship of writer Abraham Cahan, *The Jewish Daily Forward,* published in New York, became a national Yiddish newspaper with a circulation of over 200,000. Anarchist journals, from Alexander Berkman's short-lived *The Blast* to the *Freie Arbeiter Shtimme* drew an audience far beyond the small number of committed anarchists.

WORLD WAR I changed the political environment in which radical journals had thrived. Prior to the war, government censorship had focused largely on questions of sexual morality and language under the Comstock Laws. Comstockery, as it was lampooned, harassed editors and presses about the publication of works such as Theodore Dreiser's *The Genius* and James Joyce's *Ulysses,* which had been serialized in *The Little Review.* While publishers became more willing to take on the censors for the cause of Free Speech, government censorship had a dampening effect on publishing.

With the entry of the United States into the world conflict, the federal government turned radical newspapers during the war to suppress discussion of and opposition to military conscription and the war effort. Under the TRADING WITH THE ENEMY ACT, Congress assigned the U.S. Post Office the responsibility to censor private mail and deny mailing privileges to newspapers and journals critical of the war. It also required all foreign-language publications to submit translations before printing, a time-consuming and expensive requirement that forced many publications simply to close their doors. Under Postmaster General Albert S. Burleson, this broad-based authority was used to exclude publications not only for their opposition to the war but also for any content he construed as anti-American. During the war, *The Masses, International Socialist Review, Appeal to Reason,* and the *Milwaukee Leader,* among others, were denied mailing privileges and hence lost subscribers and revenue. Some were forced to stop publication.

After the war, the anti-radicalism of the RED SCARE shut down many radical and labor newspapers. The Bolshevik Revolution in Russia also changed the nature of radicalism in the United States. Newly formed communist parties, sympathetic to the Soviet Union, split off from older, more conservative socialist organizations. Labor unions divided along similar political lines, which rendered them ineffective in responding to the new conservativism. Anti-union activity both during and after World War I brought about a decline in union membership. All of these factors forced the closing of many small labor and radical publications. At the same time, a new generation of radical newspapers and journals, stimulated by new communist parties and the fomenting of revolution abroad, emerged on the scene.

In the 1920s, *Masses* editor Max Eastman joined with Floyd Dell to edit a new journal, *The Liberator.* V. F. Calverton, an intellectual affiliated with the Greenwich Village group, began his new journal, *Modern Quarterly,* which kept radical theory and avant-garde literature before the public. The Communist Party launched its *Daily Worker,* and radical labor groups began to publish infrequent numbers of newsletters and journals. City-centered labor unions, faced with steep declines in membership, still managed to keep their newspapers afloat. With the woman suffrage movement victorious, the old suffrage journals closed their doors, to be replaced with *The Woman Voter* (League of Women Voters) and *Equal Rights* (National Woman's Party). Neither attained the same loyal following as their suffrage predecessors. Only with the revival of radical fortunes in the wake of the Great Depression did the alternative press again thrive.

Further reading: Joseph Conlin, ed., *The American Radical Press, 1880–1960.* (Westport, Conn.: Greenwood Press, 1974); William O'Neill, *Echoes of Revolt: The Masses, 1911–1917* (New York: Quadrangle Books, 1966); Elliot Shore, *Talkin' Socialism: J.A. Wayland and the Role of the Press in American Radicalism, 1890–1912* (Lawrence: University of Kansas Press, 1988).

radio

The period from 1899 to 1930 was marked by two significant developments in the history of radio in the United States. In 1899, Guglielmo Marconi, the first inventor to successfully transmit and receive radio signals, demonstrated his invention for the first time to an American audience. By 1930, the *Amos 'n' Andy* radio program had set the standard by which all radio broadcasting would be developed. Between these two events, developments within the radio industry created the modern system of broadcasting in which stations are corporately owned, connected in a network, and made profitable by advertising.

During the first decade of the 20th century, the inventors and corporations involved in the development of radio technology hoped to develop an alternative to the use of wires in telegraph and telephone communications. Their goals were evident in the term used for the new technologies: radio telegraphy. Marconi's own company, which became Radio Corporation of America (RCA) in 1919, focused on developing applications such as ship-to-ship or ship-to-shore communications. The telephone company, AT&T, became involved in radio in the hope of discovering ways to better their phone service through wireless technology. The Westinghouse and General Electric companies also pursued radio technology in the hope that it would lead to large profits from the manufacture and sale of radio equipment. They assumed that once perfected, radio telegraphy would become essential for shipping companies, telegraph and telephone companies, and the U.S. government.

It was not until WORLD WAR I that any of these corporations saw the economic possibilities in transmitting voice signals over the air. Many other Americans had embraced voice transmission, or as it was known at the time, radio telephony. The first radio voice broadcast occurred in 1906. Radio telephony over the next decade was characterized by its amateur status. Thousands of radio enthusiasts throughout the country built their own transmitters and receivers and began to send signals. Some of them transmitted music, speeches, dramatic plays, and news. None of this was done for profit. The signals were weak and often interrupted by static.

When inventors improved the technology to send long distance signals that could be heard more clearly, the larger communication companies began to embrace radio telephony. In 1915, AT&T sent the first transatlantic voice transmission. This transmission attracted the U.S. Navy's attention, and it began to outfit its ships with radio stations capable of sending voice transmissions. United States involvement in World War I led the navy to seize control of the radio industry in the interests of national defense. Its demands for high-quality radio equipment favored the large companies. With the navy's help, the largest companies in radio joined in an organization known as the Radio Group for the purpose of sharing patent information. This combination of the companies helped speed the development of better radio equipment, but it had unintended consequences. Four companies—RCA, Westinghouse, General Electric, and AT&T—came to dominate the production of radio equipment and the operation of stations.

At the end of the war, the companies that dominated radio still did not see the future of radio broadcasting. They believed that radio telephony was best suited for point-to-point communication; but this began to change in the 1920s. The turn to radio broadcasting emerged out of the wartime agreement between the large radio companies that the U.S. government had brokered. As part of the agreement, the Westinghouse Corporation had given up its rights to operate voice transmission stations in return for the right to share the manufacturing market with General Electric. Having lost out on the lucrative market of voice communications, Westinghouse began to look for other ways to profit from its radio manufacturing business.

In 1920 Westinghouse came up with an idea that changed the nature of radio and its role in American society. Amateur radio broadcasts were becoming more sophisticated as equipment improved. More people were using their radio transmitters to send music and other programming over the airwaves. The number of radio sets also was increasing because there was more on the airwaves. In 1920, a Westinghouse official noticed that a Pittsburgh department store's newspaper advertisement for radio sets mentioned a specific radio program. Westinghouse decided that if an amateur program could sell radio sets, then professional radio broadcasts could help them sell their radio equipment. The desire to sell more radio equipment led to the first regular broadcast station in the United States.

On November 2, 1920, station KDKA, broadcasting from the Westinghouse factory in Pittsburgh, became the first radio station to institute regular broadcasting when it covered the Harding-Cox presidential election. After this first broadcast, KDKA broadcast a regular program every night. Originally only one hour in length, the program was a watershed in radio, because it was the first to be broadcast on a regular schedule.

Once Americans realized the power of radio broadcasting, the number of stations expanded dramatically. The stations were owned by a variety of businesses and organizations. Radio stores and equipment dealers started local stations in order to increase demand for their products. Local department stores used radio stations to advertise their products and increase demand for the radios they sold. Newspapers established stations in an effort to join the new media that might threaten their control over the news. Colleges and universities used stations as learning tools for their students. Westinghouse's success in radio broadcasting led the other giants in the radio industry to establish their own stations.

The explosion of radio broadcasting led to questions about how radio was to survive financially. Some people advocated government control of radio broadcasting supported by a tax, but the ultimate solution embraced a free market approach. By 1923, the AT&T-owned station WEAF in New York was broadcasting programs sponsored by commercial companies. WEAF used the revenue from these programs to improve its equipment, which made it possible to reach more radio listeners. In turn, the growing audience made the station more attractive to sponsors. WEAF's success led other stations to turn to sponsors for financing their programs, and the age of radio advertising was born. It was not until the end of the 1920s, however, that the true commercial possibilities of radio were recognized.

Programming in these early days was sporadic. Even the larger stations broadcast for only part of the day. Local stations often scrambled to find programming. Initially, broadcasters were able to attract musicians and other performers for free in return for the publicity. They also played phonograph records and read the news. In an effort to fill out programming, radio entrepreneurs established the network system. The network system was built around a single, high-powered station that provided high-quality programming (by recordings, when stations were beyond the reach of the network leader's transmitters) to its affiliates throughout the country. RCA and AT&T established the first networks in 1925. They did not, however, provide extensive broadcasting, but rather individual programs and special events. In 1926, in an effort to forestall competition that both companies saw as harmful, RCA and AT&T entered into an agreement in which AT&T sold its flagship station, New York's WEAF, to RCA, which gave RCA control of both radio networks. RCA created a new corporation to run its broadcasting system, and in January 1927, the National Broadcasting Company (NBC) began regular programming.

As the network system increased the quality and quantity of programs available, radio's popularity boomed. Between 1922 and 1928, the number of radio sets increased from 60,000 to 7,500,000. With approximately one-third of the U.S. population listening, radio became a powerful force in American society. The programs helped shape American tastes for music, for example. In the 1920s, music made up the bulk of radio programming; and most of it was classical music. As radio's popularity increased so did the popularity of classical music. The number of orchestras in the United States increased dramatically, along with the sale of musical instruments. Schools began to teach music as part of their regular curriculum. Some stations helped popularize other kinds of music. Radio stations that played jazz and hillbilly music helped spread these to northern cities. Radio stations also introduced the first variety acts during the 1920s.

Even with the success of their programming, radio stations and networks had difficulty convincing businesses that sponsoring radio programs was worthwhile. One radio program changed all that. In 1928, the *Amos 'n' Andy* program went on the air and changed radio forever. Created by two veteran radio performers, Freeman Gosden and Charles Correll, the program was based on the lives of two naïve African Americans living in Chicago. The comedy revolved around the African-American dialect and their continuous mishaps and misunderstandings, which stemmed from an inability to understand the complex world in which they lived. The 15-minute program was the first successful radio comedy with a continuous story line from show to show. The radio public eagerly anticipated each week's show to find out what happened to the two main characters. By the end of the 1920s, 40 million listeners—one-third of the U.S. population—tuned into *Amos 'n' Andy* each week.

The program's significance spread beyond its mere popularity. It made the commercial possibility of radio clear. Colgate Company, the program's sponsor, enjoyed a marked increase in sales of its toothpaste. With prospective audiences of 40 million, companies began to line up to sponsor programs. As network advertising revenue grew, they could broadcast more programs and increase their role in American radio broadcasting, leading to the system of media broadcasting that still exists today in television.

See also POPULAR ENTERTAINMENT.

Further reading: George H. Douglas, *The Early Days of Radio Broadcasting* (Jefferson, N.C.: McFarland, 1987); Susan J. Douglas, *Inventing American Broadcasting, 1899–1922* (Baltimore: John Hopkins University Press, 1987).

— Michael Hartman

Railroad Administration

In the winter of 1917–18, President WOODROW WILSON took over the railroads in the United States and created the Railroad Administration. In seeking to forge a war economy, Wilson most often preferred voluntary means. However, when the 2,905 companies that owned 397,014 miles of track refused to cooperate with each other and caused a standstill on the rails, the government acted swiftly. The railroads were just one part of the mobilization challenges facing the Wilson administration during WORLD WAR I. Because the United States was not prepared for its entry into global war, despite many warnings, its victory in the war could not be assured. Wilson, who had hoped for peace, had only belatedly joined in preparedness measures such as those in 1915 when he created the civilian Council on National Defense, which studied problems of economic mobilization.

Prior to the war, the railroads had functioned profitably. They had paid their workers low wages and had invested little in their operation costs. During wartime they had little interest in improving the system to upgrade service, even though they needed approximately 115,000 new railroad cars. The hard-won ADAMSON ACT ensured for railway workers an eight-hour day for all employees on trains in interstate commerce, with extra pay for overtime, but most workers were still unhappy with their lot. Other wartime industry jobs were more attractive and with better pay, leaving a critical shortage of railway workers.

Wilson strove to inspire all labor in the United States to put forth their best effort for the country with slogans like "Labor Will Win the War." Women picked up the slack by entering into industry and agriculture. The AMERICAN FEDERATION OF LABOR gave loyal support to the war effort. Most mobilization for the war effort was voluntary.

Railroad companies, however, refused to coordinate their efforts to ensure the transport of war materials, and acute shortages on the war front endangered American efforts. In the winter of 1917–18, 180,000 railroad cars sat idle. The Military Affairs Committee under Senator George Earle Chamberlain (R–Oregon) called for an inquiry. The railroads' lack of preparedness was apparent to committee members. Two weeks after the hearing, the railroads were taken over by presidential decree. Secretary of the Treasury William McAdoo became "tsar of the rails." He faced challenging weather conditions immediately as winter storms raged in the Northeast. By summer, however, the railroads were operating effectively.

Passed in May 1918, the Overton Act gave the president powers for the duration of the war and six months after. It allowed him to consolidate the six war agencies (fuel, food, shipping, railroads, war trade, and war industries) into a war cabinet. It also gave him power to disband, add, or reorganize any executive or administrative agency without the approval of Congress. Thus, by 1918, the United States had changed within one year from being a "free economy" to a managed one. Railroads became a major beneficiary of government support and regulation, due to their vital role in defense.

Further reading: David M. Kennedy, *Over Here: The First World War and American Society* (New York: Oxford University Press, 1980).

— Annamarie Edelen

Randolph, Asa Philip   See Volume VIII

Rauschenbusch, Walter (1861–1918)

Baptist minister and social reformer Walter Rauschenbusch was born in 1861. His father was a German immigrant clergyman in Rochester, New York, and Walter graduated from Rochester Theological Seminary in 1887. He went on to study economics, theology, and industrial relations in Germany and Britain in the 1890s. Named pastor of the Second German Baptist Church in New York City's "Hell's Kitchen," he witnessed the struggles of the urban immigrants firsthand. Rauschenbusch believed that industrialization eroded workers' religious commitment.

As a prominent figure in the Social Gospel movement of the Progressive Era, Rauschenbusch sought to apply the principles of Christianity to urban reform. Influenced by the Christian Socialism he saw in Germany and Britain, he critiqued the economic and social conditions that dehumanized urban immigrants and isolated them from religion. Broadening the context of sin, he saw social ills as a form of evil. Purifying democracy required Christians to infuse the spirit of Christ into the secular world. Like many other Social Gospel advocates, Rauschenbusch believed that the state should play a role in rectifying injustice. He also argued that Protestantism needed to become more socially relevant by addressing the problems of the urban poor. Salvation for the human race came through civic activism and social service.

Rauschenbusch was one of the first to undermine the social and intellectual assumptions of his time by arguing that Social Darwinism need not be a fierce competition among humans. Rather, evolution required the religious and social awakening of humanitarianism. In such works as *Christianity and the Social Crisis* (1907) and *A Theology for the Social Gospel* (1917), Rauschenbusch rendered religious social reform a mainstream movement in the United States. In his 1910 prayer book, *For God and the People* (1910), he declared the Lord's Prayer the great prayer of social Christianity. His works had a wide readership.

In 1897, Rauschenbusch left parish work to become a professor of church history at Rochester Theological Seminary and devoted himself to a career of writing, public speaking, and active social reform. It was only when WORLD WAR I stirred anti-German sentiment that he withdrew from public life. He died in 1918.

Further reading: Donovan E. Smucker, *The Origins of Walter Rauschenbusch's Social Ethics* (Montreal: McGill-Queen's University Press, 1994).

— Natalie Atkin

recreation

Recreation, defined as leisure-time activities pursued for pleasure, underwent significant change during the early 20th century. At the turn of the century, class largely determined recreational opportunities. Upper-class Americans who were not tied down by work schedules and were wealthy enough, enjoyed a variety of recreational activities ranging from bicycling to summer vacations. The growing middle class was beginning to engage in many of the same recreational opportunities, albeit on a less grand scale, by the turn of the century. Wageworkers, on the other hand, did not have the time or money to participate in recreational activities beyond trips to the saloon for men, informal interactions among neighbors, and church activities.

This pattern changed during the first three decades of the 20th century as recreation became democratized. Early 20th-century changes in the workplace led to decreased hours for wage laborers at a time when real income was rising. Although wage laborers were never able to afford the grand vacations undertaken by wealthier Americans, they enjoyed increased access to recreational activities. This in turn led to a tremendous increase in the number of

available recreational activities as entrepreneurs jumped in to take advantage of the new demand and reformers attempted to use recreation as a means to reform society.

Americans participated in a tremendous variety of different activities. Some involved an afternoon while others occupied an entire week or longer. While many spent their leisure time in their homes and neighborhoods, the 20th century brought a blossoming of recreational activities in places designed specifically for recreation. It was during this period that amusement parks first emerged, BASEBALL became a national phenomenon both as a spectator sport and as a game to be played, and cities throughout America created public playgrounds and parks, to name just a few of the new recreational activities. Some forms of recreation brought people of various backgrounds together to share a common commercial culture, and many public amusements became places where social differences lessened. Other activities maintained social distinctions. The one common characteristic shared by all Americans was an increase in time spent taking part in recreational activities, despite industries' increasing reliance on the time clock and systemization. Some activities helped workers escape for a brief time while others provided longer respites.

One of the most popular recreational activities was a trip to public amusement parks. These parks symbolized the cultural changes taking place. They helped challenge Victorian codes of behavior but did so in a safe, controlled environment. Modeling themselves on the 1893 Columbian Exhibition in Chicago and the 1901 Pan American Exposition in Buffalo, amusement parks opened in or near every major city in the first years of the 20th century. The first and best known parks—Steeplechase, Luna, and Dreamland—opened on Coney Island, New York, and set the standard for parks nationwide. Developers of these parks created fantasylands where city residents could escape for a day to experience thrills. The key to their popularity was the parks' easy access by rail from neighboring cities and their appeal to visitors of all classes, which they accomplished by offering a variety of attractions. The parks offered roller coasters and other thrill rides, theatrical performances, dance halls, animal shows and rides, sideshow performances, ostensibly educational performances, and disaster exhibitions demonstrating, for example, the floods that devastated Johnstown, Pennsylvania, and Galveston, Texas.

The amusements offered at the parks often challenged accepted modes of behavior by offering ribald attractions disguised as wholesome or educational entertainment. One park, for example, offered an exhibit of "The Streets of Cairo and Mysterious Asia," which included female dancers in states of dress that no proper audience would accept in other contexts. The parks also appealed to young men and women who were beginning to strain against Victorian codes of morality that prescribed a strict distance between

Thousands of Americans flocked to the seashore, as here on the New Jersey shore *(Library of Congress)*

the sexes. At the parks, men and women could interact socially with members of the opposite sex outside the supervision of their families. The rides were popular with youths, because the action of the rides often threw men and women together or forced them to hang on to one another for balance, thus allowing physical contact frowned upon in other settings.

New forms of recreation did not have to involve day-long excursions to amusement parks. Many young working-class and middle-class men and women attended dance halls at night, an urban phenomenon made possible by the tremendous increase in young single women drawn to the cities by available work. Men and women went to the dance halls for the chance to mingle with members of the opposite sex outside of parental supervision. Other men and women attended dances and concerts sponsored by such organizations as the YOUNG MEN'S CHRISTIAN ASSOCIATION AND YOUNG WOMEN'S CHRISTIAN ASSOCIATION.

Many types of recreation emerged during these years. The most significant was the motion picture. First made

available by one-person nickelodeons in which customers could watch a brief film clip by dropping a nickel into the slot and peering through a small viewer, motion pictures enjoyed great popularity even before they could be projected onto a screen. Once the technology improved to where films could be shown on a screen, films quickly became the most popular form of recreation. One reason for motion pictures' popularity is that they appealed to a wide audience. Ticket prices were low enough that practically anyone could attend as long as they followed the rules of behavior set forth by theater owners. Even when theater owners began to build ornate houses in central business districts in an effort to attract a wealthier clientele, working-class film lovers could still attend neighborhood theaters.

Americans of all classes also enjoyed SPORTS, both as participants and spectators. It was during the period from 1900 to 1930 that athletic contests witnessed by large crowds emerged. While the audiences were restricted by ticket prices and the fact that few games were played on

Sunday, the workers' only day off, attendance at sporting events skyrocketed. Between 1903 and 1908, for example, attendance at major league baseball games doubled. In response, several professional teams built new stadiums. College football also enjoyed tremendous popularity, and universities built football stadiums with capacities up to 80,000. In the early years of the century, critics had tried to outlaw boxing because of the brutality of some fights, but by 1927 it had rebounded to a point where 145,000 fans witnessed a title bout between Gene Tunney and JACK DEMPSEY at Chicago's Soldier Field.

People were doing more than just watching sports; they spent a great deal of time participating in them. Baseball's popularity extended to a myriad of amateur teams and leagues. Towns throughout America had amateur or semi-pro teams for both men and women, factories formed leagues, and baseball gear became standard issue for U.S. military units. Golf, tennis, and skiing also exploded in popularity among those Americans able to afford them. Holiday celebrations, such as union picnics on Labor Day, often included athletic contests in which participants competed for prizes. Cities built parks with playing fields to provide play space for their working-class citizens.

Most cities did not, however, build parks and simply turn them over to the people. Many reformers hoped to use recreation as a way to reform American society. Every large city in America created its own recreation department staffed by a team of experts who oversaw the use of the city's parks and playing fields. Many reformers believed that athletic contests and games had the power to connect participants to their proper place in the social order, but only if played in the proper way. Unfortunately for the reformers, the users of the parks and playgrounds had their own ideas of how to use them, and no amount of coaching or policing could make them follow the guidelines set by recreation departments.

Americans also participated in numerous recreational activities that did not involve athletics. There were crazes, for example, for ping-pong in 1913, mah-jongg in 1923, crossword puzzles in 1924, contract bridge in the 1920s, and miniature golf in 1930. As soon as they tired of one fad, people turned to new ways to spend their leisure time.

Citizens used their leisure time to make longer escapes from the city as well by going on vacations. In the early years of the 20th century, vacations were still enjoyed predominantly by the middle classes. Before the 1910s, any time off that wageworkers received was unpaid, which for the most part precluded taking any sort of vacation. The vacations taken by middle-class Americans usually involved trips to resorts and hotels at various waterfront locations. Many enjoyed their first vacation experience at camp revival meetings, where they immersed themselves in religious activity. Camping also became very popular, espe-

cially when the automobile became widely available. Families could hop in their car and tour the country, stopping to camp along the way. Automobiles provided a form of vacation that was affordable to many middle-class workers.

It was not until after WORLD WAR I that working-class Americans were able to take vacations in significant numbers, a change brought about by a number of developments. In the tightened labor market employers became more concerned with their employees' health and happiness, and studies showed that rest benefited both the workers and the employers. As a result, many more employers began to give paid vacations to wage workers. In addition, the cost of automobiles dropped considerably in the 1910s, putting them within reach of working-class Americans. Workers could, therefore, take their families on trips in their cars. Vacations still had to be cheap by necessity, but car trips to fishing and hunting spots, camping trips, and to visit relatives were within the financial means of many wageworkers. By 1930, the family vacation was well on its way to becoming the mass phenomenon that it is today. Between 1900 and 1930, many novel recreational activities became mainstream. Americans decided that recreation was integral to their happiness and therefore embraced a myriad of recreational possibilities. In doing so, they helped usher in many characteristics of our modern society.

See also POPULAR CULTURE.

Further reading: Cindy S. Aron, *Working at Play: A History of Vacations in the United States* (Oxford: Oxford University Press, 1999); David Nasaw, *Going Out: The Rise and Fall of Public Amusements* (New York: Basic Books, 1993).

— Michael Hartman

Red Scare

The Red Scare took place between 1919 and 1920 as a backlash against the recent successes, in Europe and the United States, of radicals and progressive who were calling for sweeping economic and political reforms. The peak of the Red Scare hysteria took place in January 1920 when Attorney General A. MITCHELL PALMER coordinated raids against numerous labor unions and political groups and arrested hundreds of suspected radicals. The primary impetus behind Palmer's actions was the recent upsurge in labor militancy and fear that the RUSSIAN REVOLUTION of 1917 would inspire similar actions in the United States.

The withdrawal of Russia from WORLD WAR I in 1918 and the Bolshevik call for the worldwide overthrow of capitalism resulted in suspicion of a broad range of labor and political activism in the United States. During the war, President WOODROW WILSON had attempted to keep labor disputes in check by creating an accord between labor and employers in which the federal government arbitrated disputes in exchange for labor's pledge not to strike. Labor unrest mounted as the war reached its conclusion. Workers and union leaders felt they had not received their fair share of wartime profits and that inflation, which reached 69 percent between 1914 and 1918, had largely eroded any gains they had made. When military expenditures and overtime pay came to a halt following the war, labor unrest increased. Frustrated by loss of real wages and wage cuts, and inspired by labor militancy in Russia and western Europe, more than 4 million American workers walked off the job in 1919. Nor was political unrest limited to the workplace, as progressives and socialists gained a significant following among middle-class men and women, the intelligentsia, working-class immigrants, and African Americans. Membership in labor unions and radical political organizations peaked between 1918 and 1920. By 1920, the Socialist Party of America had over 150,000 members, and Socialist Party presidential candidate EUGENE V. DEBS received almost 1 million votes. Membership in the UNITED MINE WORKERS OF AMERICA topped the 500,000 mark, and nearly 5 million workers belonged to labor unions.

Concern about RADICALISM and the growing strength of organized labor escalated following the war as a wave of strikes spread throughout the country, including strikes by miners, textile workers, a police strike in Boston, and the SEATTLE GENERAL STRIKE. The wave of unrest prompted Attorney General Palmer to conclude that a Bolshevik plot had been hatched to overthrow the country. He responded by launching an all-out effort to contain what he thought was a "Red Menace." After a series of bombings at the homes of Palmer and other government officials, he launched a series of raids against resident immigrant radicals, the INDUSTRIAL WORKERS OF THE WORLD (IWW), and factions of the COMMUNIST PARTY. The largest raid took place on January 2, 1920, when approximately 10,000 suspected communists and communist sympathizers were arrested and held without bail. Many of those arrested, particularly those who were recent immigrants, were deported. The Red Scare also directed attention toward African Americans. Opposition to Jim Crow laws and the lynching of African Americans intensified after World War I as thousands of black soldiers returned home with a renewed determination to bring the fight for democracy back home. Between April and October of 1919, there were 25 race riots and dozens of African Americans were lynched. For the Department of Justice, however, the real threat lay in organized resistance, and government surveillance of African Americans increased during and after the war.

The Red Scare of 1919–20 had a chilling effect on labor unions and progressive politics throughout the 1920s. Union membership, which reached an all-time high of 5 million in 1921, plummeted throughout the rest of the decade. Similarly, support for the IWW and the Socialist Party peaked in 1919–20. Within the course of the next decade, membership in radical organizations plummeted.

Further reading: Robert K. Murray, *Red Scare: A Study in National Hysteria, 1919–1920* (New York: McGraw-Hill, 1955); Peter H. Buckingham, *America Sees Red: Anticommunism in America, 1870s to 1980s* (Claremont, Calif.: Regina Books, 1988).

— Robert Gordon

Reed, John (1887–1920)

John Reed was one of the few American journalists in Russia during its 1917 revolution. Reed's *Ten Days That Shook the World* recounted for an appalled and fascinated American audience the revolution that brought the Bolsheviks to power. Reed was born in Portland, Oregon, grew up in a wealthy family, and attended Harvard University, from which he graduated in 1910. After spending several years as a struggling journalist and poet, Reed began to write for progressive and socialist magazines, including the *New Review* and *The Masses*. Gradually, Reed became a radical labor and political activist. In 1914 he was arrested for addressing a gathering of striking silk workers in Paterson, New Jersey. Reed also spent four months traveling with Mexican revolutionary Pancho Villa, and in 1914 he published his account of the MEXICAN REVOLUTION in *Insurgent Mexico*.

By the beginning of WORLD WAR I, Reed had established himself as one of the leading radical journalists and political activists in the country. He agreed to work as a war correspondent for *Metropolitan Magazine*. During the war, Reed met and became friendly with Bolshevik leader Vladimir I. Lenin. In 1917, when Lenin and the Bolsheviks decided to move against the provisional government that had overthrown Czar Nicholas II, Reed and his wife, journalist Louise Bryant, were eyewitnesses to the October Revolution. Reed's dispatches portrayed Lenin and the Bolsheviks in a very positive light. Carried first in the radical journal, THE MASSES, the dispatches were then consolidated into *Ten Days That Shook the World*. Reed's romanticized portrayal of the RUSSIAN REVOLUTION helped the American COMMUNIST PARTY recruit new members between 1917 and 1919, but it also earned him the hostility of American political leaders. Upon his return to the United States, Reed became increasingly active in the Communist Party; and in 1919, he became one of the leaders of the Communist Labor Party when it splintered off from the larger organization. Later that year, Reed was forced to flee the country when his affiliation with communism caused him to be charged with treason. He spent his exile helping Lenin and the newly created Bolshevik government to consolidate their power, resist Western invasions, and fight a bitter civil war. Less than a year later in 1920, Reed contracted typhus and died in Moscow at the age of 33. Reed's influence continued well after his death. His life was memorialized in 1981 when Warren Beatty portrayed Reed in the Academy Award-winning movie, *Reds.*

See also GREENWICH VILLAGE; RADICAL PRESS.

Further reading: James Wilson, *John Reed for the Masses* (Jefferson, N.C.: McFarland, 1987); Robert A. Rosenstone, *Romantic Revolutionary: A Biography of John Reed* (New York: Knopf, 1975).

— Robert Gordon

religion

Between 1900 and 1930, the once seemingly unified Protestant America became a nation diverse in its religious beliefs and practices and open to new religious thought along both liberal and conservative lines. For most of the 19th century, American political leaders referred to the United States not only as a democratic republic but also as a Christian nation, by which they meant its values were those of Protestant Christianity. With the influx of the new IMMIGRATION after 1900, it was clear that Americans faced a world in which religious diversity was increasing not only among Protestants and their dissenting sects but also in the growing number of Roman Catholic, Eastern Orthodox, and Jewish citizens. New scientific discoveries, especially the theory of evolution; biblical criticism and comparative religion; and new liberal theology seemed to shake more traditional churches to their core. Some of these trends toward religious liberalism had been underway since the late 19th century. Evangelical and Pentecostal sects, renewed religious revivals, and what came to be called Fundamentalism developed at the same time.

For many conservative religious leaders, the most troubling development at the turn of the century was the emergence of religious modernism. The scientific theory of evolution, and the life sciences and geology that supported the idea of a gradually evolving human species, threatened those who believed in the literal truth of the Bible. Liberal religious thinkers and biblical scholars expanded beyond human evolution to question the authority of biblical authors and to note contradictions in the sacred texts. They offered new interpretations about how the Bible, once thought to be the literal word of God, had been written. In addition, there was an increasing interest in world religion and in ecumenicalism, which focused on common ground among competing religious faiths. The World Parliament of Religions in 1893 led the way, but questions about the need

for creed- or doctrine-based religions led to the creation of the Federal Council of Churches in 1907. Unitarians, who were among the leaders of religious liberalism for over a century, had an impact on American theology out of proportion to the number of their adherents. They, like other churches, questioned both the soundness and the efficacy of petitionary prayer, the practice of invoking the direct intervention of God. While remaining primarily theistic (that is, expressing belief in a supreme being), liberal churches began to understand many traditional religious practices as historically—not divinely—determined.

Religious liberalism found practical expression in a social movement known as the Social Gospel. As religions shifted their focus away from the mission of God on Earth to the world's problems, many leaders such as WALTER RAUSCHENBUSCH advocated practicing religion through service. His book, *Christianity and the Social Crisis* (1907), became a primary text for the social gospel movement. Developing programs to tend to the needs of the poor and indigent, the working class and the disadvantaged, ministers and lay Christians organized institutional churches such as Charles Stetzle's Labor Temple in New York, which provided social services as well as religious ones. The influence of reforming religion could be felt in the settlement house movement, in which young socially concerned men and women moved into poor urban neighborhoods to provide a range of services, from soup kitchens and relief programs to education and political and social organizations. As JANE ADDAMS argued in her autobiography, *Twenty Years at Hull-House,* the "social necessity of settlements" was not only in providing for the burgeoning needs of a poor urban population but also in offering an opportunity for the secular salvation of the settlement workers themselves.

The emergence of religious liberalism among Protestants was paralleled by developments in Roman Catholicism and Judaism. In the case of the Catholic Church, the new scientific findings and greater social consciousness had led to an opening of the church under Pope Leo XIII. His 1891 encyclical, *Rerum Novarum,* was the basis of social activism among Catholic clergy and believers for the next 50 years. It inspired the work of social activist priests such as Father John Ryan, whose book, *A Living Wage* (1906), was a poetic call for social justice. The National Conference of Catholic Charities became an institutional voice to rival Protestant poor relief. The openness to scientific thought and scriptural criticism, however, faced opposition within both the Vatican and in the United States. The threat of theological and religious modernism provoked Leo XIII and his successor, Pius X, to issue the encyclicals *Testem Benevolentiae* in 1899 and *Pascendi Gregis,* in 1907, which warned against Americanism and dismissed the findings of the new science, threatened church sanctions, and reasserted the conservative stance of the Roman church. These policies caused a retreat in theological terms within the American church, even as social activism increased.

In the United States, Catholic immigrants continued to contribute to the growth of the church nationally. The number of parishes and parishioners increased dramatically, and church schools and social services expanded. In many ways, Catholicism became an ethnically defined religion, as neighbor and community churches reflected the folk practices of their national Catholic faiths, combining ethnic holidays with religious ones and shaping religious ritual with ethnic traditions. While there were some tensions among clergy who often served an ethnically diverse community of believers, the basic tenets of faith and services in Latin bound together Catholic believers beyond the church doors.

Among those of the Jewish faith, the turn-of-the-century wave of immigration brought both new growth and increasing division. In the 19th century, American Jews, the majority of German descent, had fostered Reform Judaism. Numbering only about 150,000 in 1870, they, like their Protestant counterparts, worked to incorporate the new science and commitment to social activism. Disengaged from its historic roots, Reform Jews founded Hebrew Union College and Seminary. A Reform rabbi, Stephen S. Wise, founded the Free Synagogue of New York in 1907 and later the Jewish Institute of Religion, a liberal seminary, in 1923, as a move to modernize Judaism. Arguing for absolute freedom of the pulpit, he was a well-known orator who also worked for reform causes. For new immigrants, however, much of Reform Judaism was alien in practice and belief. Nearly two million Jews from eastern Europe immigrated to the United States between 1870 and 1914, and more than half of these settled in New York City. They brought with them the traditional practices of the shtetl (or village), and their religious leaders adhered to these practices, despite the pressures to accommodate to secular American society. Conservative Judaism and a later Reconstruction movement existed as moderating influences between the forces of Reform and Orthodox Judaism.

The growth of immigration, religious expansion among non-Protestants, and the impact of liberal theology provoked a response among conservative religious leaders beginning in the 1910s. While they, along with religious liberals, had been active in social causes such as PROHIBITION, the belief that traditional religion was losing ground caused some conservatives, such as Baptist minister William Bell Riley, founder of the Northwestern Bible School, to call upon their peers to organize against the modernists. A series of pamphlets, called *The Fundamentals*, published between 1900 and 1930, addressed the threat of the new biblical criticism and other forces such as Roman Catholi-

cism and the study of comparative religion. At yearly conferences, conservatives laid the groundwork for the emergence of what came to be called Fundamentalism in all the major Protestant denominations. Central to its appeal was its ideological opposition to the new science, especially evolution, and its insistence on codifying religious creeds. The northern Presbyterians and Baptists faced the most serious challenge from religious reaction, but they soon defeated calls for them to abandon the historical independence of local congregations.

Fundamentalists were only one part of the evangelical revivals of the 1910s and 1920s. Holiness churches and Pentecostal sects grew rapidly, especially among Methodists and in the African-American community. The Holiness movement had its roots in late-19th-century reform within the Methodist Church. Its followers believed that sanctification, which in the Methodist Church was seen as a life-long process of salvation, could be granted immediately. The sinner would then be relieved of a life of sin. By the turn of the century, Holiness churches had become independent. One of the Holiness preachers, Charles Parham, pushed its ideas further, arguing that sanctification, or the baptism of the Holy Spirit, manifested itself in signs. In Kansas in 1901, Agnes Ozma, a student at Bethel College and Parham's follower, spoke in tongues. Another of Parham's students, William Seymour, the minister of an African-American Holiness church in Los Angeles, employed Parham's ideas in a revival that began in 1906. The Azusa Street Revival, which lasted until 1909, recruited thousands. This new evangelical turn identified itself as Pentecostalism, after the day when the Holy Spirit descended on Jesus's disciples. Speaking in tongues, faith healing, distrust of medical care, and puritanical social mores characterized the new religious movement. An interracial movement from its beginnings, Pentecostalism soon divided along racial lines. A 1914 meeting of white Pentecostals had as its mission the creation of a new religious organization and the election of leaders to the presbytery. White followers separated from the African-American Church of God in Christ to form their own denomination, later called the Assemblies of God.

The revival of Protestant evangelical religion inspired new religious activism in the political realm. Seeing a "moral breakdown" in American life, conservative Protestants called for a stop to attacks on the Sabbath, the family, moral purity, and "the right to teach our children in our own schools fundamental facts and truths." The teaching of evolution in schools led to the passage of several anti-evolution laws in states where fundamentalists were well organized. In 1925, the SCOPES TRIAL, in which fundamentalists technically won their case, had unexpected consequences, including rallying liberal Christians against the backlash of Fundamentalism. The causes for the revival of traditional religion, however, are unclear. Some reacted to fears about the impact of rural-to-urban migration, which caused a decline in rural church membership and the closing of many crossroads churches. A younger, more liberal clergy staffed new, consolidated churches that were located in larger towns. To a great extent, militant Protestant fundamentalism staged a comeback in both religious and political terms in order to survive.

Fundamentalist expressions drew from the surrounding consumer culture. Evangelists such as BILLY SUNDAY and AIMEE SEMPLE MCPHERSON relied on radio broadcasts, new forms of advertising, and the sale of religious literature to pay the costs of the religious life. While revivals continued to sprout in rural Protestant areas, many of the new revivalists were dependent on urban donations to sustain their ministries. Marrying new forms of Pentecostal religion to old-time Protestant faiths, McPherson and Sunday, the precursors of later-day revivalists, used faith healing, talking in tongues, and "miracles" of faith to recruit new members. They also used the language of business and sport to bring in converts.

The darker side of the fundamentalist insistence of Protestant Christian orthodoxy was its intolerance toward the beliefs of others. For some conservative Protestants, the social threat of difference led to the growth of organizations such as the KU KLUX KLAN, which merged a belief in white superiority, anti-Catholicism, and anti-Semitism, and general fears about strangers in American society with the language of fundamentalist Christianity. For others, the influence of religious liberals in secular life meant a conservative retreat from public activism. Not until the 1970s did fundamentalist Christians reemerge as a political force and seek to use public power to implement their religious principles.

By 1930, divisions within every major Protestant denomination, within the Catholic Church, and among Jews shifted religious disputation away from the differences among churches and toward the liberal/conservative divide in religious belief. For religious liberals, whether Protestant, Catholic, or Jew, rigorous textual criticism, an understanding of comparative religion, and social activism seemed to underline the secularization of society and the uses of religion in secular politics. For religious conservatives, the battle to retain religious influences in a secular world remained the principal challenge of the 20th century.

Further reading: Sydney E. Ahlstrom, *A Religious History of the American People* (New Haven, Conn.: Yale University Press, 1972); Robert T. Handy, *A History of the Churches in the United States and Canada* (New York: Oxford University Press, 1977), Rick Ostrander, *The Life of Prayer in a World of Science: Protestants, Prayer and American Culture. 1870–1930* (New York: Oxford University Press, 2000); Ferenc Morton Szasz, *The Divided Mind of Protestant America, 1880–1930* (University: University of Alabama Press, 1982).

Republican Party

Between 1900 and 1930, in both the White House and in Congress, the Republican Party was the dominant political party. The Republican Party's long domination of national politics began with the crucial realigning election of William McKinley in 1896 and his reelection in 1900. In both elections, he narrowly defeated his populist Democratic challenger, William Jennings Bryan. Bryan and the Democratic Party had strong support in the South and Midwest among farmers, agrarian radicals, reformers, and populists; somewhat less securely, the party also held the loyalty of many immigrant groups. While the Republicans also had support among agrarian reformers, their strength came from support in northern cities, among eastern financial and business interests, and among middle-class men.

Mark Hanna, the chair of the National Republican Committee, solicited large campaign contributions from financial and business leaders. Hanna and McKinley viewed the great industrialists as the country's natural leaders and gave them unprecedented access to the White House. Other financial conservatives, including Nelson Aldrich, Thomas Reed, and Thomas Platt helped shape the party's support of the gold standard, in opposition to Democratic support of silver and more lenient economic policies. The triumph of the fiscal conservatives came in 1900 with the passage of the CURRENCY (or Gold Standard) ACT; industrial and agricultural interests also placed maintaining protective TARIFFS on the Republican political agenda as a major priority. The support of the nation's financial and business communities was one of the consistent themes of the party's electoral success. The party also tended to oppose American involvement in foreign affairs, to be financially conservative, and to view the role of the federal government as one of supporting industry and the general prosperity.

Relying on these issues, the Republican Party dominated the presidency and Congress between 1900 and 1930. It won presidential elections in 1900, 1904, 1908, 1920, 1924, and 1928, losing only in 1912 and 1916 to Democratic candidate WOODROW WILSON. The party also controlled the House of Representatives between 1900 and 1911 and from 1919 until 1932 and the Senate from 1900 to 1913 and again from 1919 to 1932. The party often had a large majority in both the House and the Senate, which gave it complete control over both the executive and legislative branches.

The dominance over the legislature was matched by control over the judiciary. At the national level, the party had a tremendous impact on the make-up of the Supreme Court. Of the 21 Supreme Court justices appointed between 1898 and 1932, Republican presidents appointed 18. They had a similar impact on the appointment of federal judges. The party used this control to shape federal policies on a wide range of issues, including international trade, foreign policy, labor relations, conservation, and domestic affairs. In general the party tended to support protective tariffs, and Republicans authored the historic PAYNE-ALDRICH TARIFF ACT in 1909 and the Hawley-Smoot Tariff of 1930. In general, the party also tended to favor employers in labor disputes and made an effort to keep government intervention to a minimum.

The extent to which the party maintained the support of financial and business leaders varied. Under the presidencies of THEODORE ROOSEVELT and WILLIAM HOWARD TAFT, the party was at least partially responsive to progressive demands for restraints on the power of national corporations and the new industrial elite. Roosevelt earned a reputation as a trustbuster for taking on JOHN D. ROCKEFELLER and STANDARD OIL. Roosevelt also signed progressive federal legislation such as the MEAT INSPECTION ACT (1906) and the PURE FOOD AND DRUG ACT (1906). As president, Taft continued Roosevelt's policy of trust busting and presided over the passage of the Sixteenth Amendment establishing a FEDERAL INCOME TAX. Nevertheless, Roosevelt and Taft remained strong supporters of free enterprise and big business, advocating the use of executive powers to correct only the most flagrant abuses.

The extent to which the federal government sought to police industry, support reforms, and control the economy caused a rift in the party between 1908 and 1916. Prior to 1900, agrarian radicals and progressive reformers had for a long time influenced the party. During the presidency of Theodore Roosevelt, the party's midwestern progressives and eastern financial and business backers maintained an uneasy truce. Roosevelt supported business growth, but he sought to regulate monopolies and supported limited progressive reforms. Progressives grew increasingly frustrated, despite Roosevelt's tentative commitment to a program of reform. Conservative Old Guard Republicans maintained a firm control over Congress and blocked important reform legislation during much of the decade. A key obstacle was the conservative Speaker of the House, JOSEPH CANNON. Using his control over the Rules Committee, he controlled the House of Representatives with an iron fist from 1903 to 1911.

Between 1909 and 1913, William Howard Taft initiated even more antitrust suits than trustbuster Roosevelt, but progressives in the Republican Party quickly became disenchanted with Taft's leadership. When Taft fired the head of the U.S. Forest Service, GIFFORD PINCHOT, developed closer ties with the party's Old Guard, and refused to oppose Cannon's control over the House, progressives organized to take control of the party. In June 1911, Senator ROBERT LA FOLLETTE, California governor HIRAM W. JOHNSON, and others formed the National Progressive Republican League. La Follette prepared to challenge Taft for the party presidential nomination in 1912. By 1910, however, Roosevelt had become convinced that Taft was too closely tied to business interests and the Old Guard. When Roosevelt announced that he too would seek the Republican nomination in 1912, Taft used his control of the party machinery to gain the nomination. With Taft's renomination secure, progressives bolted the party and formed the PROGRESSIVE PARTY with Roosevelt as their presidential candidate. Roosevelt outpolled Taft in the general election, but Democratic candidate Woodrow Wilson won the presidency. Most progressives rejoined the party by 1916, although some defected again to cast their ballot for Progressive Party candidate La Follette in the presidential election of 1924.

With the 1912 election of Democrat Woodrow Wilson, the Republican Party lost control of the federal government for the first time since 1896. Wilson proved to be a very effective president, winning reelection in 1916 over Republican nominee CHARLES EVANS HUGHES. He helped the Democratic Party maintain control over the House and Senate until 1919. Republican opposition to Wilson's peace program following the end of WORLD WAR I revitalized the party. Led by HENRY CABOT LODGE, Old Guard Republicans and isolationists, including some western progressives, opposed the peace treaty. Fearing that international coalitions would serve only to entangle the country in foreign conflicts, they vehemently opposed the provision of the TREATY OF VERSAILLES that required the United States to join the new LEAGUE OF NATIONS. Republican opposition ensured that the peace treaty with Germany was not ratified (a treaty officially ending the war with Germany was not signed until 1921).

With the wave of labor disputes and the economic depression that followed the war, the Republican Party was able to regain control of Congress and the presidency by promising "a return to normalcy." WARREN G. HARDING handily defeated Democratic nominee James M. Cox, winning 60 percent of the popular vote. The Republican Party continued its national dominance throughout the 1920s, winning every presidential election and controlling both the House and the Senate. Republican presidents Harding, CALVIN COOLIDGE, and Herbert Hoover championed fiscal conservatism, a smaller role for the federal government, lower taxes, and an emphasis on continued industrial development and economic growth. On that platform, they retained power until the economic crisis of the 1930s.

Further reading: John D. Hicks, *The Republican Ascendancy, 1921–1933* (New York: Harper and Row, 1960); George H. Mayer, *The Republican Party, 1854–1964* (New York: Oxford University Press, 1964); Charles O. Jones, *The Republican Party in American Politics* (New York: Macmillan, 1965).

— Robert Gordon

Rockefeller, John Davison (1839–1937)

Born in Richford, New York, to Eliza Davison Rockefeller and William Avery Rockefeller, an itinerant medicine peddler, John D. Rockefeller attended country schools and spent a year at Owego Academy before his family moved to Ohio. He attended high school for two years in Cleveland and started his business career there in 1855, when he obtained a bookkeeping job after three months' training at a commercial college. When he was only 18, he became a partner in a commission house. In 1863, four years after oil was first tapped by a well in Pennsylvania, Rockefeller and two partners bought into the oil refining business. In 1865 Rockefeller and his partners established

John D. Rockefeller *(Hulton/Archive)*

their own refinery, where Rockefeller could be "daring in design" and "cautious in execution," a formula he used throughout his career. From the beginning, he kept careful records of costs and profits that informed him where his business stood.

Setting out to monopolize the petroleum industry, the partners added a second refinery. In 1870 they replaced their partnership with a joint-stock firm, the STANDARD OIL Company (Ohio). In 1882 it became the Standard Oil Trust, with 40 allied firms controlling 90 percent of American refineries. Its monopoly was declared illegal by the Ohio Supreme Court in 1892. Starting that year and ending in 1899, Standard Oil operated as a community-of-interest combination of 20 firms. From then until 1911 when the Supreme Court declared it in violation of antitrust laws, Standard Oil acted as a holding company, the Standard Oil Co. of New Jersey. Through the years, Standard Oil acquired its own warehouses, shipping facilities, tank cars, pipelines, and barrel-making plant and managed to cut the unit costs of refining oil almost in half, while extending the market for petroleum by-products.

The guiding genius behind Standard Oil, John D. Rockefeller pioneered the modern corporation. He has been called the "greatest business administrator America has produced." Although he often forced competitors to sell or to join his alliance, he seldom bankrupted them and occasionally treated them leniently. He paid his employees well and ruled his operation by consensus.

Efficient and benign within Standard Oil, Rockefeller's passion to bring order out of chaos in the infant oil industry made him ruthless in eliminating competitors. Although well informed, he often feigned ignorance of the tactics of terror and espionage employed against rivals by his underlings. Rebating was the most effective weapon Standard Oil used to force competitors to join it or be ruined. The huge volume of its shipments enabled it to secure from competing railroads discounts of up to 50 percent of the published freight rates. At times it even got "drawbacks," or rebates, on oil shipped by some competitors. Rockefeller's marketing practices ranged from shrewd to unscrupulous. By the 1890s the company marketed 84 percent of all petroleum products sold in America and produced a third of its crude oil. Later those percentages were reduced by new oil fields, stronger competitors, and more effective federal antimonopoly legislation.

Rockefeller was a man of contradictions. He was determined to be both rich and virtuous. He was both a predatory businessman, trying to prove he was the fittest by surviving his competitors, and a church-going Baptist who aimed "to promote the well-being of mankind throughout the world." He was devoted to his wife, Laura Celestia Spelman, whom he married in 1864, and to their children, four of whom lived to adulthood.

Tooth and claw business practices, however, made Rockefeller extremely unpopular, and his reputation and that of Standard Oil was further damaged by Henry Demarest Lloyd's *Wealth Against Commonwealth* (1894) and even more by muckraker Ida Tarbell in her 1902–03 series on Standard Oil, first published in *McClure's Magazine.* Having ignored hostility and been anonymous in his giving (for example, he established the University of Chicago and gave it $35 million with no strings attached), Rockefeller hired a publicist to broadcast his good works and tag his gifts with his name.

No longer active in his company's decisions after 1895, Rockefeller concentrated on his philanthropic work, giving away $550 million in his lifetime ($450 million of which went for medical research). Believing that the prevention of disease was more important than its relief, he was willing to fund pure research for generalized future benefits. In 1891 he endowed the Rockefeller Institute for Medical Research; the next year the General Education Board, which became the world's foremost educational foundation; in 1913 the Rockefeller Foundation, the world's largest grant-making foundation and the country's main sponsor of medical science, medical education, and public health; and in 1918 the Laura Spelman Rockefeller Memorial. Many of these programs were later consolidated in the Rockefeller Foundation. The benefits of Rockefeller-funded research were mind-boggling, even surpassing those of the later World Health Organization. Among them were the actual elimination of hookworm, the virtual eradication of yellow fever, and the revitalization of medical schools and medical research throughout the world. Rockefeller outlived his enemies and his reputation improved when his giving became public knowledge. He distributed over a billion and a half dollars, making Rockefeller the greatest philanthropist in American history.

Further reading: Ron Chernow, *Titan: The Life of John D. Rockefeller, Sr.* (New York: Random House, 1998).

— Olive Hoogenboom

Roosevelt, Theodore (1858–1919)

The son of Theodore Roosevelt and Martha Bulloch, future president Theodore Roosevelt, Jr., was born in New York City on October 27, 1858. Renowned as an advocate and exemplar of the mainly virtues of physical fitness, military action, and adventure, he came into the world as a small, asthmatic, near-sighted boy. As the younger Roosevelt matured, he became an amateur naturalist, an interest expressed later in his CONSERVATIONISM. In 1876 Roosevelt entered Harvard, where he was unpopular due to his enthusiasm for studies in natural science. After graduating, he published a naval history of the War of 1812, the

President Theodore Roosevelt (left) with John Muir *(Library of Congress)*

first of a long series of writings that would come from his pen. He was married twice, first to Alice Lee, the mother of his daughter Alice Roosevelt Longworth, and later to Edith Carow, who gave birth to their five children—Theodore, Kermit, Ethel, Archibald, and Quentin.

In 1882, Roosevelt began his political career when he was elected to the New York State Assembly on the REPUBLICAN PARTY ticket. He was a freshman representative but did not play the part. Roosevelt startled the assembly by calling for an investigation of the state's Attorney General Hamilton Ward and Supreme Court Justice T. R. Westbrook, who failed to prosecute millionaire Jay Gould for manipulating stock of the Manhattan Railway Company. While the subsequent inquiry into the Westbrook scandal revealed no wrongdoing, Roosevelt earned a reputation as a reformer.

The emotional devastation caused by the death of his wife Alice and his mother on February 14, 1884, forced him to relinquish his seat and retreat to his ranch in the Dakota Territory. Politics called him back east in 1886, when the Republican Party, fearing that independent candidate Henry George might lead New York to a second Paris Commune, tapped Roosevelt to run for mayor. On Election Day, Roosevelt finished last in a three-way race, with many Republicans voting for the Democratic candidate and winner Abraham Hewitt. His candidacy, however, laid the groundwork for later political races. In 1889,

President Benjamin Harrison appointed Roosevelt head of the Civil Service Commission, where he championed the merit system over the patronage system. Amazed that border patrolmen were tested for their spelling and arithmetic and not their riding skills and marksmanship, Roosevelt revised the Civil Service examinations to assess practical skills, rather than theoretical knowledge.

In 1891 Roosevelt published his *History of New York City*. Its publication attracted the attention of the reform mayor of New York City, William L. Strong, who appointed Roosevelt police commissioner in 1895. The New York Police Department of the 1890s was rife with corruption. To improve the force's morale Roosevelt established the practice of handing out medals for exemplary service. He also modernized the police communications by developing a telephone call box system. His zealousness proved to be his undoing. In an effort to stop police extortion, he vigorously enforced the city's blue laws, which forbade the sale of alcohol on Sundays. Many saw his efforts as a form of class prejudice and a war on working-class recreation. Public support evaporated. He was saved from being driven from office when the McKinley administration appointed him to the position of assistant secretary of the navy in 1897. At the Navy Department, Roosevelt was an ardent and unabashed expansionist. He took advantage of Navy Secretary John Long's frequent absences to reorganize the administration of the navy in preparation for war with Spain. While President McKinley considered how to respond to the sinking of the USS *Maine* at Havana, Roosevelt told the chief executive that war was the only option "compatible with national honor."

After the declaration of war on Spain, Roosevelt resigned his post and accepted the rank of lieutenant colonel in the First Volunteer Cavalry Regiment soon to be known as the Rough Riders. Although they were trained as mounted riflemen at their base in San Antonio, Texas, they arrived in Cuba bereft of their horses because of transport problems. After landing at Daiquiri, Cuba, they were instrumental in pushing the Spanish back in skirmishes at Las Guasimas and El Caney. Six days after landing, Roosevelt and his regiment distinguished themselves in action outside Santiago by helping to take Kettle and San Juan Hills. Due to heavy rifle fire, losses among the Rough Riders were heavy; but by that afternoon, the army was in possession of the two strategic hills. After the war ended, Roosevelt returned home a hero; and in 1899, he was elected governor of the state of New York. As the state's chief executive, he ran afoul of his chief sponsor, Senator Thomas C. Platt, by supporting the Ford Bill, which placed a tax on any corporation owning public franchises. After thwarting efforts by Platt's followers to bury the bill in committee, Roosevelt signed the bill into law. After serving one term as governor, Roosevelt was elected in 1900 as William

McKinley's vice president. The assassination of McKinley in 1901 elevated Roosevelt to the presidency.

Roosevelt's administration was known for its strong stands in favor of conservation, regulation of the trusts, and an assertive FOREIGN POLICY. Repudiating the country's tradition of isolationism, Roosevelt had lobbied for U.S. intervention in Cuba and the Philippines under McKinley's administration. As president, he moved to show American strength in Latin America and the Pacific by issuing the ROOSEVELT COROLLARY to the Monroe Doctrine, jockeying to build the Panama Canal, and sending the GREAT WHITE FLEET to Japan. In addition, he mediated an end to the RUSSO-JAPANESE WAR (for which he won a Noble Peace Prize) and disputes in Venezuela, the Dominican Republic, and Morocco; and he sought to guarantee American interests in Asia with the ROOT-TAKAHIRA AGREEMENT and the GENTLEMEN'S AGREEMENT with Japan that assured peaceful relations by eliminating school segregation of Japanese immigrant children in the United States in return for a voluntary cessation of emigration from Japan.

Roosevelt preferred to work out national problems and needs through cooperative arrangements between private and public interests and to strengthen the hand of the federal government in domestic affairs, a political philosophy that he called the NEW NATIONALISM, echoing progressive Herbert Croly. Domestically, Roosevelt's preference for a stable economy and a strong national government led to his intervention in the ANTHRACITE COAL STRIKE of 1902, the prosecution of monopoly trusts such as the railroad holding company in the NORTHERN SECURITIES CASE and STANDARD OIL, and the passage of government regulation of industry in the ELKINS ACT and HEPBURN ACT, the MEAT INSPECTION ACT, and the PURE FOOD AND DRUG ACT. Roosevelt's conservationism expressed itself in the passage of the ANTIQUITIES ACT, the NATIONAL RECLAMATION ACT, and the creation of the NATIONAL PARK SERVICE.

During his nearly eight years in the White House, Roosevelt expanded the powers of the office and became a model for the modern presidency. While he refused to run for a second term in his own right, Roosevelt's discontent with the conduct of his self-chosen successor, WILLIAM HOWARD TAFT, led to a failed presidential campaign as the PROGRESSIVE PARTY nominee in 1912. The death of his son Quentin during WORLD WAR I left Roosevelt devastated. He died in 1919.

See also BIG STICK DIPLOMACY; PROGRESSIVISM.

Further reading: Nathan Miller, *Theodore Roosevelt: A Life* (New York: William Morrow, 1994); Edmund Morris, *The Rise of Theodore Roosevelt* (New York: Coward, McCann & Geoghegan, 1979).

— Timothy E. Vislocky

Roosevelt Corollary

In an extension of the Monroe Doctrine, the Roosevelt Corollary claimed the right of the United States to intervene in the affairs of its neighbors in the Western Hemisphere if they were unable to preserve domestic order on their own. In an annual address to Congress in 1823, President James Monroe had articulated what became known as the Monroe Doctrine, stating that the United States would not permit European powers to colonize independent nations in the Western Hemisphere. In 1904, President THEODORE ROOSEVELT extended the Monroe Doctrine with his own corollary.

Roosevelt used the corollary as a rationale for his intervention in the crisis of the Dominican Republic. Even though revolutionaries had overthrown a corrupt government in the Dominican Republic in 1903, the new government still was unable to make payments on its $22 million debt to European nations. Citing the Roosevelt Corollary, the American administration took control of Dominican customs. Under American receivership, 45 percent of the country's revenues were distributed to Dominicans and the rest sent to foreign creditors. This arrangement lasted for more than three decades.

Having absorbed Cuba as a protectorate as a result of winning the Spanish-American War of 1898, the United States granted it independence in 1902. But Cuba became independent only after the new government agreed to abide by the Platt Amendment, which gave the United States the right to intervene in the affairs of Cuba if its independence were threatened by any foreign power. In 1906 Roosevelt intervened in Cuba when a rebellion undermined the stability of the country. American troops landed on the island, suppressed the rebellion, and stayed in the country for three years.

As an extension of Roosevelt's BIG STICK DIPLOMACY, the Roosevelt Corollary dramatically altered American foreign policy. It signaled a shift from merely intending to safeguard the Western Hemisphere against European intervention to openly promising U.S. intervention if Latin American countries were unable to keep their domestic affairs in order.

Further reading: Louis A. Perez, Jr., *Cuba under the Platt Amendment* (Pittsburgh, Pa.: University of Pittsburgh Press, 1988).

— Glen Bessemer

Root-Takahira Agreement

The Root-Takahira Agreement of 1908 came about as a result of the desire of the United States to protect its interests in Asia and to ease tensions between America and Japan. The RUSSO-JAPANESE WAR of 1904–05 had tested the resolve of American administrations to enforce the OPEN DOOR POLICY in Asia. At the time, Japan saw Russia's military presence in Manchuria as a direct threat to its own economic and territorial expansion. On February 8, 1904, the Japanese navy destroyed the Russian fleet in a surprise attack at Port Arthur. By 1905, the Japanese army had defeated the Russians at Mukden, where 97,000 Russian soldiers died, and the navy had sunk the Russian fleet in the straits of Tsushima. But Japan had drained its financial and military resources. On May 31, Minister Kogoro Takahira asked President THEODORE ROOSEVELT to negotiate a peace treaty with Russia and Japan.

Seeking a balance of power to protect American interests in the region, Roosevelt invited representatives from the two countries to meet at Portsmouth, New Hampshire, on August 9, 1905. In the Treaty of Portsmouth, the Russians acquiesced to most of the Japanese demands. They agreed to allow Japan to take over the Liaodong Peninsula and the railroad from Harbin to Port Arthur. They conceded to the withdrawal of American troops from Manchuria, and they accepted Japanese freedom of action in Korea. The two parties stalemated on the issue of Russia ceding the island of Sakhalin. Czar Nicholas II then agreed to divide the island when Roosevelt wired the Czar to propose a partition between the two parties. Even though the czar refused to pay the indemnity that Japan demanded, Japan accepted the terms of the treaty on August 29.

In the aftermath of the war, Japan emerged as the dominant naval power in the Pacific, and relations between the United States and Japan eroded. Domestic problems in California heightened tensions between the United States and Japan. In addition to pushing for an extension of the Chinese Exclusion Act (1882, 1892, and 1902), nativist white workers in San Francisco demanded that Japanese immigrants be legally excluded. When the San Francisco school board voted to require Asian children to attend a separate "Oriental School" in 1906, anti-Asian riots broke out in California and WILLIAM RANDOLPH HEARST's papers published inflammatory stories about the "Yellow Peril."

Roosevelt eased tensions with Japan by making two agreements with the country. First, the president reached the GENTLEMEN'S AGREEMENT with Japan. In exchange for Japan agreeing to stop the flow of its immigrant laborers to the United States, Roosevelt agreed to have the school board withdraw its mandate for a separate school. Second, the two countries reached an understanding in the Root-Takahira Agreement of 1908. In the agreement, the United States and Japan promised to accept the territorial status quo in the Pacific. In addition, the two nations agreed to abide by the Open Door and to uphold the territorial integrity of China.

Even though Roosevelt saw the Root-Takahira Agreement as evidence that Japan did not plan to act aggressively against the United States, American leaders favorable to China saw it as a sanction of Japanese territorial expansion in Asia. To ensure that Japan abided by the agreements, the president sent a bold message of American military strength by ordering the GREAT WHITE FLEET, composed of 16 naval ships, on a world tour that stopped by Japan.

Further reading: Akira Iriye, *Pacific Estrangement: Japanese and American Expansion, 1897–1911* (Cambridge, Mass.: Harvard University Press, 1972); Neu, Charles E., *An Uncertain Friendship: Roosevelt and Japan, 1906–1909* (Cambridge, Mass.: Harvard University Press, 1967).

— Glen Bessemer

rural life

Although often depicted in idyllic and pastoral fashion, rural life in the early 20th century witnessed much strife, hard work, and perseverance as American society underwent sweeping social and economic transformations. Frequently, this period in American history has been presented from the perspective of those at the center of these economic changes—urban dwellers, laborers, immigrants, or capitalists. But it is also useful to consider the daily lives of those on the periphery of the major economic changes taking place, men and women in rural communities. The major social and economic changes that rural areas faced during the early part of the 20th century stemmed from the rapid urbanization of American society, the growth of mass production industry, and the growing power of corporations in economic life.

Throughout many rural communities, the emergence of the United States as an urban nation brought many fears to rural residents. Rural America long had embraced the values of Protestantism, and the advent and triumph of more secular urban culture threatened to undermine the values that rural dwellers held dear. Still, rural communities also received radio waves, national magazines, and mail order catalogs that invited them to participate in the emerging consumer culture. Many within rural communities feared cities, because they viewed them as breeding grounds for atheism, sexual license, and radicalism. Despite rural reaction to consumer culture, the young of rural communities faced declining opportunities to own their own farms or even find a job. They continued to vote with their feet by migrating to urban centers for school and work.

The economic changes taking place meant that banks and agricultural corporations, or agribusinesses, had a new hold on rural life. The growing presence and power of corporate monopolies gave farmers places to borrow money from, market their goods, or buy crop insurance. It threatened their sense of local autonomy, and rural residents had to decide on the best course of action. New forces were at work, as mail-order catalogues and government agents challenged their ability to shape and control the communities in which they lived.

Increasingly after 1900, urban-industrial America became the most prosperous sector of society, and its consumer culture and commodities steadily penetrated the countryside. Although farmers had difficulty raising capital and lacked banking facilities, currency, and credit during the 1890s, the new century brought a wave of prosperity to rural areas that would last until shortly after the end of WORLD WAR I. The increasing demand for agricultural products and better transportation to foreign markets meant farmers had new opportunities to market their goods. As a result, the U.S. Department of AGRICULTURE estimated in 1920 that the average rural family had income to buy consumer goods such as clothing and foodstuffs. It produced only 40 percent of what it consumed, down from 60 percent 20 years earlier.

During this "Golden Age" of agriculture, farmers spent most of their newfound income on consumer goods to improve their standard of living. For instance, they often made their homes more livable by buying carpets, drapes, wallpaper, vacuum cleaners, and new furniture. They also found themselves installing such modern conveniences as electricity, indoor plumbing, or a telephone. HENRY FORD targeted rural families as a prime costumer for his Model T, which sold for about $240. While many rural residents, especially farmers, found work-related uses for the Model Ts they purchased, they were used as well for leisure and play. Beyond buying an automobile, many farmers, having witnessed the economic difficulties of the late 19th century, remained hesitant to invest in capital improvements, whether in expanding their landholdings or in purchasing new technologies.

The populists and farm organizations such as the American Farm Bureau long had championed the need for low-interest loans to help promote and make affordable the capital improvements needed to expand individual farms. Before the United States entered the First World War, the federal government responded to this demand, recognizing that the growing market for American agricultural goods while Europe was at war, required an expansion in farm production. Few farmers expanded their operations prior to the war, meaning that average farm size remained flat between 1900 and 1916. In an effort to overcome this obstacle, the FEDERAL FARM LOAN ACT created the mechanism to extend low-interest loans for periods of five to 40 years to farmers through the control of a Federal Farm Loan Board—12 Federal Land Banks that paralleled the Federal Reserve Banks. As part of WOODROW WILSON's NEW FREEDOM initiative, the Federal Farm Loan Act extended loans to farmers through a program that cut out private banks, which farmers viewed as outside institutions that easily exploited vulnerable farmers.

Although the First World War had created an expanded market for American agricultural goods and brought the means to borrow capital for expanding landholdings, the cessation of hostilities in Europe caused the market to contract. When farm production in Europe resumed, governments faced a capital shortage as they rebuilt their war-torn nations. Imports were down. With shifting market conditions during the 1920s, agricultural prices in the United States steadily declined. While lower prices for many consumer goods such as automobiles resulted in increased demand, most people did not purchase more bread as its price dropped. Many rural residents and farmers, accordingly, faced economic crisis well before the onset of the Great Depression late in 1929.

Some 500,000 individuals lost their farms to bankruptcy during the 1920s. In response, farmers made persistent demands for relief from the federal government during the course of the twenties. As rural residents faced growing economic hardships, some responded by attacking what they perceived to be the immorality of urban America. Accordingly, rural residents provided strong support for many of the movements that came to characterize American society by the 1920s: PROHIBITION, KU KLUX KLAN, IMMIGRATION restriction, and religious fundamentalism. At the same time, farmers also organized the FARMER-LABOR PARTY in the Midwest and farm organizations such as the American Farm Bureau to demand that the government address the problems of rural America.

See also CAPPER-VOLSTEAD ACT; ECONOMY; MCNARY-HAUGEN FARM BILL; NON-PARTISAN LEAGUE; RELIGION.

A rural farm family (Library of Congress)

Further reading: David B. Danbom, *Born in the Country: A History of Rural America* (Baltimore: John Hopkins University Press, 1995).

— David R. Smith

Russian Revolution

Radicals in the United States and around the world were inspired by the RUSSIAN REVOLUTION of 1917, a popular revolution led by socialists in a country previously ruled by an autocracy. WORLD WAR I had broken out between the major powers in Europe in 1914, but by 1917, peasant soldiers were deserting the Russian army en masse, and their government collapsed. In the February Revolution of 1917, Russian liberals and leftists established a provisional government that was weak and inexperienced. In the October Revolution, the Bolsheviks, led by Vladimir Lenin and Leon Trotsky, launched a coup and seized the Winter Palace, the last stronghold of the provisional government.

At the same time as the Bolshevik government declared itself a dictatorship of the proletariat, it faced internal enemies and a looming external threat as well. Lenin concluded that the Bolsheviks needed an armistice to protect the domestic revolution and allow revolution to spread throughout Europe. On March 3, 1918, Russia and Germany signed the Treaty of Brest-Litovsk, which ended Russian participation in the war.

Fearing that the new communist government would destabilize eastern Europe, the western Allies (Britain and France) pressured the United States to intervene. When a civil war broke out in Russia, the United States sent an expeditionary force (the SIBERIAN EXPEDITION) to assist any opposition to the Bolshevik army in the summer of 1918. Some of the American troops stayed there until April 1920. The Bolsheviks won the civil war and maintained their power, but the world revolution Lenin had hoped for never came to fruition. When Lenin died in 1924 after suffering from several strokes, Joseph Stalin succeeded him, consolidated his power, and eliminated his enemies, expelling Trotsky from the country by 1929. The United States refused to formally recognize the government of the Soviet Union until 1933, when diplomatic relations were restored.

The Russian Revolution had a significant influence on radicalism in the United States. In the postwar period, the United States experienced unprecedented labor unrest. More than four million workers went on strike in 1919. A strike wave began in Seattle, when shipyard workers walked off their jobs. The action spread into a general strike that paralyzed the city. In the SEATTLE GENERAL STRIKE, workers and war veterans formed councils of workers, soldiers, and sailors in several industries, declaring that they had established these Soviets to practice managing the economy.

In the United States, postwar hysteria against communism was accentuated when the Bolsheviks founded the Third International (or Comintern) in 1919 to export revolution around the world. When the COMMUNIST PARTY (CP) was founded in 1919, both the CP and Communist Labor Party claimed to have nearly 70,000 members. During the war, many radicals had left the INDUSTRIAL WORKERS OF THE WORLD (IWW) and the Socialist Party when they had been weakened by domestic repression. The Justice Department had targeted both socialists, who saw the war as a meaningless conflict between capitalist nations, and radical syndicalists in the IWW for their criticisms of militarism that had the potential to disrupt war production in the western lumber and copper industries. More than a thousand opponents of the war had been convicted for sedition and espionage.

Fears of domestic Bolshevism heightened when a series of bombs exploded in the spring of 1919. In November 1919, the attorney general, A. MITCHELL PALMER, mounted the first Palmer Raid. On New Year's Day in January 1920, at the peak of the RED SCARE, the federal government rounded up 6,000 radicals in one night. Federal agents thought that they would find caches of weapons and explosives, but they found only three pistols and no dynamite. Although most of the arrested radicals and aliens were released eventually, about 500 of the detainees who did not have U.S. citizenship were deported. In the absence of labor militancy, the Red Scare dissipated by the summer of 1920.

Although anti-radical and anti-immigrant sentiments had been persistent throughout American history, the Russian Revolution illustrated to some American leaders that communism was a real threat in the world. The fear of communism remained a salient feature of American society throughout the 20th century.

At the same time, the concrete example of the Russian Revolution created a division on the American Left. On the one hand, for some progressives and leftists in the United States, the revolution provided an example of the benefits of a worker-controlled state and a rationalized economy. Furthermore, when the United States refused to recognize the new government and intervened in the Russian civil war, some on the American Left saw the Soviet Union as a victim in the face of capitalist intervention. On the other hand, liberals and leftists criticized Lenin's signing of the armistice with Germany, because it increased Allied casualties by allowing the Germans to devote more of their troops to the western front in Europe. In addition, many on the American Left condemned the undemocratic actions and brutality of the Bolsheviks in the Soviet Union.

The contradictions of the Russian Revolution produced diverse reactions in the public and on the Left in the United States. The revolution gained praise among radicals as a concrete example of a socialist state in the 20th century. At the same time, it created a rift on the American Left and provoked anticommunist hysteria in the American public.

Further reading: Peter G. Filene, *Americans and the Soviet Experiment, 1917–1933* (Cambridge, Mass.: Harvard University Press, 1967).

— Glen Bessemer

Russo-Japanese War (1904–1905)

The Russo-Japanese War was a conflict between Russia and Japan that grew out of competing imperialistic designs on Manchuria and Korea. In the late 1890s, the Russians had negotiated with China for the right to extend the Trans-Siberian Railway across Manchuria and thus secure a strategic base at Port Arthur. This base was designed to be the headquarters of Russian naval power in the Pacific. Russia had stationed troops in Manchuria during the BOXER REBELLION in 1900, but it had promised to remove them, a promise it broke. The Japanese, who also had expansionist plans in the region, went to war with Russia before the railway was completed.

Japan tried to negotiate a division of Manchuria into "spheres of influence," but Russia was unwilling, blinded by the belief that Japan would be defeated and a looming internal Russian revolution could be averted by a Russian victory. For Japan, Manchuria and Korea in Czarist Russian hands was like a gun pointed at its strategic heart.

In early 1904, Japan broke off negotiations, and on February 6, it severed diplomatic relations with Russia. Two days later, Japan attacked Port Arthur and bottled up the Russian fleet. Port Arthur fell in January 1905. Japanese troops had a series of victories under General Oyama at Shenyang in February and March 1905, and the destruction of the Russian fleet by Admiral Togo's fleet in May 1905 astounded the world. It was the first time an Asian power had defeated a European power in modern times. It established Japan from that time on as a major player in world affairs.

As the war went on, Japan began to run short of both men and money. Japanese officials approached President THEODORE ROOSEVELT secretly and requested that he sponsor peace negotiations. He agreed and gathered the two sides together at Portsmouth, New Hampshire, in 1905. The Japanese demanded a large indemnity and the island of Sakhalin, considered a strategic location. The Russians, for their part, refused to concede. Roosevelt was frustrated, admitting that he wanted to "give utterance to whoops of rage," but instead he pushed through an agreement in which the Japanese received no indemnity and only the southern half of Sakhalin.

For his efforts, Roosevelt received the Nobel Peace Prize in 1906. The cost was that America's relations with Russia were now in danger. Japan also felt wrongfully deprived of an indemnity by the agreement, and Japan and America soon became rivals in Asia. The Russo-Japanese War also produced a migration of Japanese laborers into California as dislocations and the tax burden of the war in Japan made America more appealing. By 1906, almost 70,000 Japanese lived along the Pacific Coast.

People in California became afraid of the "yellow peril." An international crisis was created when local San Francisco school authorities declared that Asian children had to attend a special school. The Japanese saw this as blatant discrimination, and they were deeply offended. Theodore Roosevelt took matters into his own hands and invited the school board to the White House to convince them to repeal the measure to avert an international conflict. An agreement was then worked out between Japan and America to stem the tide of emigrants from Japan. Lest Japan think that America was afraid of it, Roosevelt ordered the GREAT WHITE FLEET on a voyage around the world. When the fleet was met by cheering Japanese school children, it allowed for a diplomatic atmosphere necessary to carry out the ROOT-TAKAHIRA AGREEMENT, in which the United States and Japan pledged to respect each other's territorial possessions in the Pacific and uphold the OPEN DOOR POLICY in China.

Further reading: Tyler Dennett, *Theodore Roosevelt and the Russo-Japanese War* (Gloucester, Mass.: Peter Smith, 1959).

— Annamarie Edelen

S

Sacco and Vanzetti

Nicola Sacco and Bartolomeo Vanzetti were Italian immigrants convicted in a controversial murder case and executed in 1927. Supporters of Sacco and Vanzetti argued that their conviction and subsequent execution was based largely on their nationality and political views, and the pair quickly became martyrs for those on the political Left. The actual murder and trial took place at the height of the RED SCARE when labor militancy and political reaction were at their postwar peak.

Largely kept in check during WORLD WAR I, labor militancy and political radicalism intensified following the RUSSIAN REVOLUTION and the return of unemployment in 1919. Political and business leaders insisted that a Red Menace was spreading throughout the country. The backlash against labor militancy and radicalism culminated in the arrest and deportation of suspected socialists, communists, and anarchists in the Palmer Raids of January 1920. In the midst of this ferment, Sacco and Vanzetti were accused of killing two men and stealing $16,000. Despite substantial evidence of their innocence, the pair were tried, convicted, and sentenced to death. Supporters were convinced that their only crime had been that they were anarchists.

Amid intense repression, the conviction of Sacco and Vanzetti became a rallying point for militant unionists and political radicals. The INDUSTRIAL WORKERS OF THE WORLD, the INTERNATIONAL LADIES' GARMENT WORKERS UNION, the COMMUNIST PARTY, and the Workers' Party raised money and held mass demonstrations calling for the release of the two men. Supporters warned that unless workers, radicals, intellectuals, and others united they could expect the same fate.

The case of Sacco and Vanzetti, however, was more than simply a rallying cry for the nation's radicals. It outraged many in the political mainstream who concluded that the case was weak and motivated by anti-immigrant sentiment. Harvard Law School professor and future Supreme Court justice Felix Frankfurter noted that the case against Sacco and Vanzetti was based largely on the "systematic exploitation of the defendants' alien blood, their imperfect knowledge of English, their unpopular social views, and their opposition to the war." As the date of their execution neared, massive demonstrations took place. On July 7, 1927, 20,000 took part in a New York demonstration. On August 10, the day Sacco and Vanzetti were to be executed, over 200,000 workers walked off their jobs. Other protests, demonstrations, and strikes took place throughout the country.

Despite international appeals for clemency, Sacco and Vanzetti were put to death on August 23, 1927. Debates about the innocence or guilt of Sacco and Vanzetti raged in the decades after their execution, but they seem to have been resolved by William Young and David E. Kaiser's authoritative account, *Postmortem: New Evidence in the Case of Sacco and Vanzetti* (1985). After careful reconstruction of the evidence, Young and Kaiser concluded that, without a doubt, Sacco and Vanzetti were innocent. Because of the circumstances of the case and the widely held belief that the pair were innocent, the case is still cited by many as evidence of the excesses of the Red Scare and the rampant hostility and suspicion of immigrants that characterized the 1920s.

Further reading: William Young and David E. Kaiser, *Postmortem: New Evidence in the Case of Sacco and Vanzetti*, (Amherst, Mass.: University of Massachusetts Press, 1985).

— Robert Gordon

Sanger, Margaret (1879–1966)

Born on September 14, 1879, in Corning, New York, Margaret Louise Higgins (Sanger) became the foremost BIRTH CONTROL advocate of the early 20th century. The sixth of 11 children of Anne Purcell and Michael Hennessey

Higgins, her father was the owner and operator of a stone monument business. As the child of an Irish-American father, she was early introduced to the ideas of Robert Ingersoll and Henry George, the Single Tax advocate. Margaret went to Claverack College, a coed preparatory school in upstate New York. Originally, she took a teaching job but left it when she was called home to nurse her mother. After her mother's death, she entered nursing school at the White Plains (New York) Hospital. In 1902, Margaret finished her degree and married William Sanger, an architect. The next few years, she recovered from ill health to give birth to her two sons, Stuart and Grant, and a daughter, also called Margaret. Sanger became discontented and she and her husband moved to the Lower East Side of New York, where they became active in the radical community. Active in the INDUSTRIAL WORKERS OF THE WORLD, Sanger helped ELIZABETH GURLEY FLYNN evacuate the children during the LAWRENCE STRIKE, an act that aroused national sympathy for the embattled textile strikers.

Sanger was a practicing nurse whose professional work brought her to understand the lack of control women had over their own bodies. She supported the idea that women needed the freedom to control their own life and body. From the first issue of her magazine, *Women Rebel,* in March 1914, to the financial and organizational support she gave to hormone research after World War II, she was dedicated to bringing effective birth control to women around the world. She became known in radical circles for her support of sexual reform and her advocacy of working-class women's need for information on venereal disease, birth control, and sexual practice.

Sanger brought information to the public by remaining in the spotlight. The public relations strategy she used helped to create awareness and challenge regulations and laws that suppressed the free circulation of contraceptive information. She created a pamphlet, *Family Limitation* (1914), which gave advice to women about various birth control methods. She also included the names and addresses of places where women could write for further information or purchase necessary items. She even included a recipe for the home production of vaginal suppositories. This pamphlet had two important features. First its straightforward approach was notable because of her focus on the working class, whose hardships were increased by low wages combined with excessive fertility. Sanger also criticized the use of *coitus interruptus* as a contraceptive device, indicating that it deprived women of sexual satisfaction. She clearly communicated more than technical information in her pamphlet. Sanger advocated the right of women to sexual enjoyment as well as control over their own bodies. It was this pamphlet that led to her prosecution under the Comstock laws, during which she fled to Europe.

In 1916 Sanger opened the first birth control clinic in Brooklyn, New York. The clinic faced many obstacles, the most important of which was staunch opposition from the medical profession. New York State law specified in Section 1142 that no one could give information to prevent conception to anyone for any reason. Additionally, Section 1145 stated that only physicians could give advice to prevent conception for the cure or prevention of disease. That same year, Sanger and two of the clinic's staff members were arrested for violating the state law. All the clinic's records were confiscated. In 1919, Sanger changed her emphasis from women's control of their own bodies to eugenic reasoning about the need for better babies. She focused her efforts on educating the public and lobbying for the legalization of birth control. Continued opposition to birth control required political compromise with the medical establishment. Jealous of their own authority in the medical realm, doctors could support Sanger once she accepted that they should have the final authority in providing birth control. This shift in emphasis increased Sanger's following and made birth control a respectable issue.

From the Great Depression to the 1960s, Sanger played a less vital and visible role in the birth control movement. In part, the ground had shifted, and birth control, once a feminist issue, was now seen largely in terms of family planning. Concern about the world population crisis, however, revived Sanger's reputation, and she took part in the founding of the International Planned Parenthood Foundation. Throughout her life, she had been devoted to improving methods of contraception, and in the 1950s, she helped raise funds to support the development of the birth control pill, which was first made available in 1960. Sanger died at a nursing home in Tucson, Arizona, in 1966.

See also SEXUALITY; WOMEN'S STATUS AND RIGHTS.

Further reading: Ellen Chesler, *Woman of Valor: Margaret Sanger and the Birth Control Movement in America* (New York: Simon and Schuster, 1992).

— Marcia M. Farah

Schenk v. United States (1919)

During WORLD WAR I, both Congress and state governments passed laws that restricted the right of free speech in order to ensure support for the war effort and to suppress what the government considered harmful dissent. *Schenk v. United States* was a court case testing the constitutionality of the ESPIONAGE ACT (1917) and its amendment under the SEDITION ACT (1918). These acts made it a crime to speak against the government, oppose the military draft, or act in any way that could be construed as giving aid and comfort to the enemy. *Schenk* was only one of a series of cases during the war that raised the specter of government suppression of civil liberties, including the rights to free speech and right of conscience. In *Schenk* as in *Frohwerk v. United States* (1919), *Abrams v. United States* (1919), and *Gitlow v. New York* (1924), the U.S. Supreme Court had to decide what was the extent and meaning of the First Amendment protection of free speech. Socialists who opposed U.S. entry into the war in Europe, radicals arrested under criminal syndicalism laws, German Americans who published in their native language, and militants supporting the Russian Revolution became the targets of state and federal prosecution. Challenging the laws were individuals who continued to advocate draft resistance, oppose bond sales, or criticize the nation's entry into or pursuit of the war.

In the *Schenk* case, the defendants, members of the Socialist Party, had printed and mailed 15,000 pamphlets opposing CONSCRIPTION and American entry into the war. When the lower courts found them guilty, Schenk and Baer appealed their convictions to the Supreme Court. Lawyers in the case argued for the absolute right of citizens to freedom of speech and conscience. OLIVER WENDELL HOLMES, the chief justice, wrote the Court's opinion, which decided in favor of the government. Arguing that the freedom of speech was not unlimited, Holmes used the analogy of a man crying "fire" in a crowded theater as an illustration of how speech acts could endanger communities. It was the context of speech that determined whether or not it was protected. The "clear and present danger" of the war, Holmes argued, made subversion out of free speech uttered in the name of individual conscience. Mailing anti-conscription pamphlets and condemning the government's participation in the war were a threat to a nation at war.

Ironically, Justice Holmes, who wrote the majority opinion in *Schenk,* became within a few months a dissenting defender of First Amendment rights. Arguing against the majority in *Abrams v. United States* and subsequent cases, Holmes essentially defined the modern view of the First Amendment and civil liberties. He wrote that it was the "theory of our Constitution" that "the ultimate good desired is better reached by the free trade in ideas—that the best test of truth is the power of the thought to get itself accepted in the competition of the market." The nature of our experiment in democracy required us to be "eternally vigilant against attempts to check the expression of opinions that we loathe," unless such speech represented an imminent threat.

Coming as it did at the end of a divisive war, *Schenk* had a sobering effect on the Left. The decision represented a conservative assessment of the powers of the state to override personal liberties and to restrict individual rights. At the same time, the case gave renewed importance to free speech struggles, as *Gitlow v. New York* (involving a

New York criminal syndicalism statute) and a later case, *Near v. Minnesota* (on press censorship), took on questions of whether citizens were free to hold and promote unpopular political views and whether state and federal governments had the authority to silence dissenting voices.

Further reading: Paul L. Murphy, *World War I and the Origin of Civil Liberties in the United States* (New York: Norton, 1979).

science

By 1900, science in the United States—whether social, life, or physical sciences, theoretical or applied—was established as a profession. The expansion of universities and the development of specialized curricula opened doors for research scientists, and the creation of research laboratories in private industry (General Electric Research Laboratory, for example) or sponsored by private foundations (the Carnegie Institute of Washington, the Rockefeller Foundation, and the Institute for Advanced Study at Princeton University) increased demand for university-educated scientists and engineers. The debate over Darwinism continued politically, as shown in the SCOPES TRIAL, but general acceptance of evolutionary theory meant that the war between RELIGION and science remained at a standstill. The growth of government, especially in the arena of social policy, also created opportunities for the new fields of sociology, anthropology, political science, and history. Leaving behind dependence on European science, scientists in the United States developed new scientific applications and, what was more, contributed to new scientific theories in the realms of chemistry, mathematics, biology, and astronomy. Married to the new philosophy of PROGRESSIVISM, with its promotion of rational social planning and detailed investigation, "science" became shorthand for the use of scientific method and technological solutions to solve human problems. Faith in science furthered the popularity of industrial reforms such as SCIENTIFIC MANAGEMENT and the adoption of eugenic theories in BIRTH CONTROL, SOCIAL WORK, and IMMIGRATION policy. It would be decades before the ideology of science was undermined by social realities.

In 1900, theoretical science remained under the dominance of European scientists. In the field of physics, Planck developed quantum theory in 1900, and Einstein published his theory of relativity in 1905. Science in the United States had seen its primary accomplishments in the field of applied science, but this was to change. Already the United States had become known for its accomplishments in astronomy. It had the largest number of observatories and the most powerful telescopes in the world, and some of its most important scientists, such as George Ellery

Hale, were known for their work on planetary and lunar orbits. American scientists were on the verge of major breakthroughs in other theoretical and applied fields. Improved scientific and medical education gave rise to a new generation of scientists in university and private research laboratories. By linking more theoretical and obscure research with practical application, scientists were able to expand their research through private gifts and grants, new facilities, and larger resources. This investment seemed to pay off with the awarding of the Nobel Prize to Albert Michelson in 1907 for his experiments in the measurement of light and spectography and to Theodore Richards in 1914 for his work on atomic weights. Science in the United States had come of age.

By this time, bacteriological advances had already improved life expectancy with the discovery of the origins of common diseases such as diphtheria, cholera, and tuberculosis. New work on tropical diseases such as yellow fever and malaria enlarged the reputation of American medicine. The funding of the Rockefeller Foundation furthered these efforts as medical researchers turned their attention to other diseases such as hookworm. Advances in MEDICINE and in medical education stimulated other research as well.

Genetics as a field grew in stature with the work of Edmund Beecher Wilson and Nettie Stevens in 1904 on the chromosomes that determine sex and that of Thomas Hunt Morgan on mapping genes, based on his work with fruit flies, in 1920. In the succeeding decade, geneticists would work on isolating genes to improve crops through crossbreeding. Theories of genetics had other purposes. Under Charles Davenport, the federal government created a Eugenics Record Office in 1910 to build a database in human heredity. While later discredited for its racial assumptions and political uses, eugenics science had obtained enough respectability to be used to underwrite new restrictive immigration policies and to support the use of sterilization by relief agencies and institutions for the care of the mentally ill. The hope that one could improve the human species through selective breeding attracted some social thinkers who sought a more rational and controlled human environment.

New scientific discoveries in such fields as physics and astronomy fueled the public imagination. The Science News Service, created by newspaper magnate E. W. Scripps, kept newspaper and journal readers informed about scientific developments as did the magazines such as *Scientific American, Popular Science,* and *Popular Mechanics.* The popularity of inventors such as Thomas Edison and Alexander Graham Bell inspired new series novels such as the Tom Swift stories about a boy inventor, which began publication in 1910. Politicians echoed the popular support for science and the public faith in the ability of science to address social and political ills. President THEODORE ROOSEVELT declared in 1908, "applied science, if carried out according to our program, will succeed in achieving for humanity, above all for the city industrial worker, results even surpassing in value those today in effect on the farm."

The popularity of science and its policy applications can best be seen in CONSERVATIONISM. Utilizing theories of land utilization, conservation groups proposed and passed such bills as the NATIONAL RECLAMATION ACT and supported the creation of a NATIONAL PARK SERVICE as a way of shepherding the nation's natural wealth. The National Conservation Commission, first proposed in 1908, conducted a long-delayed inventory of the nation's natural resources. Management of forests and conservation of mineral sources, land reclamation, and protection of waterways were among the results of the joint work of scientists concerned with the environment and the Roosevelt administration. While divided between advocates of efficient, rational use and the champions of preservation, conservation policy was shaped by the interplay between the new science of ecology and calls for scientific management.

In many ways, science and expertise became substitutes for popular control and common knowledge. Just as scientific management had replaced the skilled workers' control over how he or she produced goods, so too did experts in a range of fields—from land conservation to social welfare—take precedence over popular opinion and political control. In the rational society, scholarly objectivity and supposedly "value-free" science trumped the interests lurking behind popular demands and partisan agendas. However, experts in city planning, social work, and immigration shaped policies in ways that encroached upon or directly violated the neutral ideal. Scientific objectivity proved illusory, although it would take decades to discover the problem. The DILLINGHAM COMMISSION, influenced by the science of eugenics and a prejudicial belief in racial superiority, ignored its own findings to promote an immigration policy that restricted the entry of southern and eastern Europeans into the United States. Conservation debates altered the outcome of scientific research as eugenics did social policy.

WORLD WAR I was the turning point of the take-off in government and private funding for scientific research. Defense needs activated private industrial and university research laboratories to work on such projects as improving submarine detection, developing chemical gases and treatments for military use, optical glass, and improvements in aerial photography, mapping, and accuracy in aerial bombing. Improved sanitary engineering, medical research on wounds, and psychological studies of battle fatigue were other products of scientists' support for the war effort. Members of the National Academy of Science, most notably astrophysicist George Ellery Hale, supported the creation of the National Research Council, which became a permanent peacetime body in 1919.

By the 1920s, expanded government and private industry support had cemented the position of theoretical and applied science as a priority in education, public policy, and funding. Only through continued innovation could the United States maintain its economic superiority; only through new technologies could the country hope to defend itself in a future war. Practical applications, however, rested on the support of theoretical science on the one hand and more widespread public EDUCATION in science on the other. Public opinion was key; so too was the encouragement of new generations of scientists through the improvement of science education in the schools. These trends would continue to elevate scientists throughout the period and guarantee a future for scientific research.

See also PUBLIC HEALTH.

Further reading: George H. Daniels, *Science in America; A Social History* (New York: Knopf, 1971); Robert A. Kohler, *Partners in Science: Foundations and Natural Scientists, 1900–1945* (Chicago: University of Chicago Press, 1991); Nathan Reingold and Ida H. Reingold, eds., *Science in America: A Documentary History, 1900–1939* (Chicago: University of Chicago Press, 1981); Margaret W. Rossiter, *Women Scientists in America: Struggles and Strategies to 1940* (Baltimore: Johns Hopkins University Press, 1982).

scientific management

A system to make industrial production more efficient, scientific management came to dominate business in the early decades of the 20th century and eventually became part of American culture. Emerging predominately from the work of FREDERICK WINSLOW TAYLOR, scientific management was based on the idea that every task could be broken into a series of smaller tasks. Each individual task was then studied to determine the fastest and most efficient method for completing the task. The entire production process could then be split into specialized tasks, each done at peak efficiency. The end result was the creation of a production system in which workers became specialists at individual tasks but had no knowledge of the entire production process. The assembly line was the most significant manifestation of scientific management. This movement to make scientific studies of processes evolved out of its industrial beginnings and took a place in other areas of American life.

The drive for efficiency of production was a response to the production system that relied on individual workers to complete a variety of tasks. It was also an attempt to reduce the power of individual craftsmen who could hold up production by striking because skilled replacements were difficult to find. Once the production process was broken into specialized tasks, any worker could complete them given just a few hours of training. American industrialists thus saw scientific management as the answer to many of their labor troubles. In a way they hoped to remove the human element from certain portions of the production process. Workers did not have to learn new skills nor did they have to unlearn anything to function in a scientifically managed production process. They simply had to perform the same task repeatedly for the entire workday.

Industrialists took the tenets of scientific management further than specializing the production process. They redesigned whole factories to make production more efficient. By moving machinery, for example, they could decrease the time spent transporting parts within the factory. Employers also tried to use scientific management principles in the hiring of workers by establishing personnel departments. Personnel departments then established criteria for hiring new employees. The goal of this was to avoid hiring workers who could not keep up the pace or would refuse to work in those conditions.

Many workers did protest the advent of scientific management. They argued that the managers' expectations for daily output were inhumane, and many protests erupted over the implementation of scientific management. In some instances workers were able to temper the implementation of scientific management, but they were unable to stop it completely, as it came to define MASS PRODUCTION in the United States.

Scientific management made its way into other parts of American life. Education adopted many of its principles in restructuring curricula, building schools, and attempting to develop an efficient citizenry in which each individual would be prepared for his or her proper place in the social order. Other businesses besides factories turned to scientific management. Department stores tried to make their operations more efficient by studying the actions of clerks. Offices were redesigned to make them more efficient. All of these actions were based on the ideal that individuals could be made to act more efficiently. This ideal, first developed in the early decades of the 20th century, has played a significant role in American industry and in the way Americans analyze various problems.

Further reading: Robert Kanigel, *The One Best Way: Frederick Winslow Taylor and the Enigma of Efficiency* (New York: Viking, 1997).

— Michael Hartman

Scopes Trial (1925)

The Scopes Trial was the climax of a conservative backlash against the teaching of evolution and featured a legal battle

Scopes trial lawyers Clarence Darrow (left) and William Jennings Bryan *(Hulton/Archive)*

between two of the great orators of the day, lawyer CLARENCE DARROW and populist Democrat William Jennings Bryan. The spread of institutions of higher learning and of mass media had made more visible long-standing divisions in American society. By the early 1920s, differences over such matters as biblical interpretation and the scientific method developed between modernists and cultural conservatives who feared that modernization was undermining traditional American values and institutions. The rift took place at every level, but it had an important impact on EDUCATION and RELIGION. As the scientific method established supremacy in the nation's classrooms, traditionalists and religious conservatives dug in their heels, often splintering political alliances that had formed in the 1880s and 1890s. In 1925, these divisions came to a head in a test case of anti-evolution laws. Opponents of Charles Darwin and evolution, led by William Jennings Bryan, had succeeded in passing anti-evolution laws in 15 states. Supporters of evolution and free speech advocates, including the American Civil Liberties Union (ACLU), looked for a high-profile case to test the constitutionality of these laws.

Residents of Dayton, Tennessee, were more than willing to participate in this high-profile case. Several prominent Dayton residents hoped that the trial might put the town in the national spotlight and stem the tide of people leaving the town for places with greater economic opportunities. John Scopes, who routinely taught evolution in his high school biology course, agreed to test the legitimacy of the Tennessee law forbidding the teaching of evolution. Almost immediately, the case became highly politicized and thrust Dayton into the national spotlight. Within a matter of days thousands of people from all political and religious perspectives, along with a huge contingent of newspaper reporters, invaded the city, creating a carnival-

like atmosphere. The ACLU reluctantly agreed to allow the controversial and flamboyant Clarence Darrow to head a strong defense team while Bryan put together an equally impressive team of prosecutors. Bryan and the prosecuting attorneys argued that what was really at stake was the survival of Christianity, the Bible, and traditional American values.

Over the course of the trial, Judge John T. Raulston, who was openly sympathetic to Bryan and the prosecution, allowed the prosecution great latitude while refusing to allow Darrow and the defense team to call scientific experts to assert the validity of evolution. Despite being hamstrung by Raulston's rulings, Darrow's impassioned defense of Scopes and evolution won him widespread praise from outside observers and national reporters, including H. L. MENCKEN. The climax of the case came when Darrow ruthlessly questioned Bryan, who took the stand as a biblical scholar, about whether or not the Bible should be interpreted strictly. Darrow, who severely weakened Bryan's credibility, convinced the jury to find Scopes guilty, in order for the law to be sent before the state supreme court. Although the jury found Scopes guilty and fined him $100, the ruling was overturned on a technicality. It wasn't until 1968 that the Supreme Court in *Epperson v. Arkansas* ruled that anti-evolution statutes were unconstitutional.

Further reading: Kary D. Smout, *The Creation/Evolution Controversy: A Battle for Cultural Power* (Westport, Conn.: Praeger, 1998); Edward J. Larson, *Summer for the Gods: The Scopes Trial and America's Continuing Debate over Science and Religion* (New York: Basic Books, 1997).

— Robert Gordon

Seattle General Strike (1919)
In February 1919, nearly 100,000 workers went on strike in Seattle, Washington, in support of striking shipyard workers. The strike assumed great nationwide significance because of its timing. The Bolsheviks had seized control in Russia the previous year and Europe had witnessed a number of leftist uprisings in the aftermath of WORLD WAR I. The walkout by the Seattle workers without specifically stated complaints led many observers, both in Seattle and around the United States, to fear that the workers of Seattle were only the first to revolt against the American economic and political system. Although the general strike lasted only from February 6 to February 11, it had significant consequences for labor.

One reason that the strike's failure assumed such significance was that Seattle had one of the strongest labor movements in the country. Many observers noted that Seattle was basically a closed-shop town, where workers had to join unions in order to work. Although affiliated with the AMERICAN FEDERATION OF LABOR, Seattle's unions often challenged the AFL leadership. Seattle's workers generally supported the idea that workers should be organized by industry instead of by craft. The AFL was strongly opposed to industrial unionism. Seattle's workers also displayed strong class consciousness. They saw themselves as members of a distinct class based on their positions as wageworkers within the capitalist economic system.

Fear of radicalism was rampant in many sections of American society, especially after the Bolshevik revolution and civil war, and socialist uprisings in Germany and Hungary in 1919. In Seattle the authorities had been battling the INDUSTRIAL WORKERS OF THE WORLD who still had a strong presence in the West. The Seattle AFL went on record in support of the Bolsheviks in the struggle for power in Russia. Waterfront workers even refused to load war material being shipped to anti-Bolshevik forces in Russia.

The immediate cause of the general strike was a strike by shipyard workers. During World War I, the U.S. government established the Emergency Fleet Corporation to oversee the production of ships. This quasi-governmental agency controlled the inputs to shipbuilding such as steel and the price of labor. Seattle's shipyard workers argued that the wage levels were too low and warned that after the war they would take action to raise their wages. Two weeks after the armistice, they made good on their pledge by notifying the Emergency Fleet Corporation and the shipyard owners that the unions would negotiate directly with the shipyard owners. By November 1918, the Seattle Metal Trades Council, a body made up of representatives from the trades working in the shipyards, had authorized a strike if their wage demands were not met. Negotiations began in January 1919 but bogged down because the Emergency Fleet Corporation ordered shipyard owners not to give in to the worker's demands.

With their demands for wage increases unmet, 35,000 shipyard workers went on strike on January 21, 1919. In support of the striking shipyard unions, the Seattle Central Labor Council, a body made up of representatives from all of Seattle's unions, passed a resolution calling for a general strike. Unions throughout Seattle responded quickly by voting in favor of the general strike. A mass meeting of workers on February 2 approved the general strike and official notice appeared in newspapers the next day stating that the strike would begin on February 6. A sense of crisis descended upon Seattle. The business community and middle classes feared the worst in light of recent happenings in Europe. The mayor of Seattle, Ole Hanson, tried to intermediate between the two sides but was unsuccessful. On February 6, 1919, the general strike began as 60,000 workers walked off their jobs.

Despite the lack of violence, Seattle's newspapers portrayed the strike as a revolution seeking the overthrow of the economic, political, and social order. The Central Strike Committee made two mistakes that allowed this to happen and led to the strikers losing the propaganda battle. First, the Central Strike Committee never set any goals or a time limit for the strike. They were on strike simply for the vague purpose of supporting the shipyard workers. It was unclear what would lead the workers to end the strike. This lack of focus allowed their opponents to imagine their motives. The most popular was that the general strike was meant to begin the permanent revolution of the working class in the United States. Shipyard owners, the press, and the Seattle mayor popularized this view of events that made it seem vitally important that the strikers be defeated. The Central Strike Committee's second mistake was their decision not to continue publishing Seattle's labor newspaper. As their only means of telling their side of the story, the strikers' decision not to use the paper silenced their collective voice. The loss of the propaganda war, the opposition of Seattle's mayor who threatened to call in troops to establish martial law, and the difficulty in keeping all the workers united behind the strike when the purpose was vague, led to the strike's failure. It lasted only until February 11.

The failure of the strike had a profound effect on Seattle's labor movement. Local authorities cracked down on the IWW, suppressing the radical voice in Seattle's labor movement. Feuding arose among the different factions of the labor movement as each tried to blame the others for the failure. In addition, Seattle's employers undertook a powerful open-shop campaign in the strike's aftermath. This transformed Seattle from an almost entirely closed-shop city to an open-shop town.

The strike also had national ramifications. In the eyes of many, the general strike was a harbinger of things to come if employers and the government did not take action against the workers. The response on the part of employers took the form of the open-shop movement that came to define management-labor relations in the 1920s. The strike also helped usher in the RED SCARE. Ole Hanson resigned as mayor and undertook a speaking tour of the country, during which he related how he had faced down the workers' revolution in Seattle. In this effort to bolster his own reputation, Hanson exaggerated the threat posed by the strikers. His speeches and the other accounts of the strike by Seattle's newspapers convinced many readers, however, that they now faced a red menace. The chilly climate for labor in the 1920s was the result.

Further reading: Robert L. Friedham, *The Seattle General Strike* (Seattle: University of Washington Press, 1964).
— Michael Hartman

Sedition Act (1918)

Enacted during the crisis of WORLD WAR I, the Sedition Act was part of an effort to suppress domestic opposition to the entry of the United States into the war. With the outbreak of war in Europe in 1914, the Wilson administration, in an effort to ensure unity, steadily moved to restrict the civil liberties of its citizens. Even as it declared the United States neutral in the conflict, it began to prepare for war. In early April 1917, when President WOODROW WILSON asked Congress for a declaration of war against Germany, he also called upon Congress to pass legislation that would enforce the loyalty of all Americans to the country's role in the war. In response, Representative Edwin Webb of North Carolina and Senator Charles Culberson of Texas began to craft legislation that would give the president the ability to impose "stern repression" to ensure unity behind the nation's emerging war effort.

The ESPIONAGE ACT, as it was known when their legislative attempts were finally enacted in early June 1917, furnished the government with ample power for the suppression of those who opposed the war. It imposed stiff fines (between $5,000 and $10,000) and jail sentences of up to 20 years for individuals convicted under this legislation. The following year, Congress further restricted the ability to challenge America's participation in the war with the passage of a series of amendments that came to be known as the Sedition Act (May 1918). These amendments prohibited "any disloyal, profane, scurrilous, or abusive language about the form of government of the United States, or the Constitution of the United States, or the flag of the United States, or the uniform of the Army or Navy."

Combined, the Espionage Act and the Sedition Act went far beyond simply attempting to prevent spying for the enemy. Instead, their main effect was to make it illegal to write or utter any statement that could be construed as profaning the flag, the Constitution, or the military. The legislation stifled most domestic opposition to the war. The extreme nature of these legislative acts constituted the most drastic restriction of free speech since the enactment of the Alien and Sedition Acts of 1798. The Socialist Party of America and the INDUSTRIAL WORKERS OF THE WORLD had emerged by 1917 as the most vocal and organized forces opposing America's involvement in the war in Europe. Accordingly, they quickly became among the first groups to feel the strong arm of the legal system. Under these two laws, some 6,000 arrests were made and 1,055 convictions were obtained. In 1919, the Supreme Court upheld the constitutionality of this legislation in its ruling in *Abrams v. United States.* Both pieces of legislation expired in 1921.

See also *SCHENK V. UNITED STATES.*

Further reading: Paul Murphy, *World War I and the Origins of Civil Liberties in the United States* (New York: Norton, 1979).

— David R. Smith

segregation

Segregation is the physical separation of individuals, usually based on their race, class, gender, or religion. Segregation can be either de jure, created by law, or de facto, meaning resulting from practice. In the early 20th century, both kinds of segregation came to define racial relations in the United States. Segregation resulted in the restriction of the civil, political, economic, and social rights of African Americans, Asian Americans, Mexican Americans, and NATIVE AMERICANS throughout the nation.

Segregation was a tool used by whites to separate themselves from non-whites as Americans redefined race. During the first decades of the 20th century, Americans adopted the modern definition of race based on skin color, which underlined the belief that any non-white person was inferior. In addition, this gave rise to the belief that non-white Americans posed a threat to the physical and moral health of the nation. Proponents of segregation argued, therefore, that it was necessary to separate the less advanced racial groups from the whites.

Native Americans were the first minority group to face segregation. Segregated on reservations and subject to the rules of the Federal Bureau of Indian Affairs, they faced restrictions on their education, occupational choices, and access to proper health care. Other racial groups experienced increased segregation early in the 20th century.

Segregation of African Americans, many have assumed, was a natural legacy of slavery and the Civil War. Southern states did not, however, establish the system of laws requiring segregation known as Jim Crow immediately after the war. African Americans enjoyed the right to vote and hold political office and used public facilities such as railroads and theaters alongside whites. Some states and cities had laws segregating public spaces, but nothing on the scale that came to dominate race relations in the South after 1890. At the end of the 19th century, the South was reeling from a number of economic, political, and social crises that led to the passage of segregation laws. The end of slavery had not ended racial prejudice and violence. The South, with other regions, experienced its first industrial depression during the 1890s. The Populist Movement had created political conflict between whites of different economic classes, each of which sought African-American allies. Many southern whites looked for a remedy for society's ills. Segregating African Americans became the answer in the eyes of many.

Prior to the end of the 19th century, a number of factors limited the ability of southern states to completely segregate society on racial lines. By the turn of the century, however, southern whites were given, in the words of historian C. Vann Woodward, "permission to hate." Under the influence of conservative jurists, federal courts no longer broadly interpreted the Fourteenth and Fifteenth Amendments to the Constitution, which granted equal protection under the law to African Americans and gave black men the right to vote. Instead, judges repeatedly ruled that the restrictions on discrimination applied only to the actions of states and not individuals. In 1896, in *Plessy vs. Ferguson,* the Supreme Court ruled that separate facilities were not inherently unequal. This decision allowed states, companies, and individuals to segregate public spaces such as waiting rooms by race, while arguing that the separate facilities were equal.

Political changes also affected race relations. Northern liberals dropped their opposition to racist policies in an effort to unify the nation. In the South, militant populists frightened whites with their appeal to small southern farmers, both white and African-American. The conservative political element in the South abandoned its traditional policy of racial moderation to attack the populists with charges of race mixing. By manipulating the vote in African-American areas, the conservatives defeated the populists in the 1896 elections. These events had significant consequences. Conservatives assumed the mantle of white supremacy in their battle for political power and did not turn back. Many agrarian activists blamed the African Americans for their defeat in the elections and turned to white supremacy.

The final development leading to segregation was the change in American racial attitudes arising from its imperialist ventures. In 1898, the United States took control of Hawaii and the Philippines, bringing eight million people of color under its jurisdiction. The federal government argued that the Philippine people were not capable of governing themselves. Northern politicians, who supported the domination of the Philippines, stood on shaky ground when criticizing southern racial attitudes.

By the 1890s, southern states had begun to pass Jim Crow laws restricting the social and economic rights of African Americans. By 1910, every southern state had segregated railway stations in which African Americans and whites waited in separate rooms. Between 1901 and 1907, 10 states segregated public transportation, requiring African Americans to sit in the rear. States segregated hospitals, prisons, theaters, workplaces, and cemeteries. Parks had separate areas for African Americans. Mobile, Alabama, passed a curfew law that required African Americans to be off the street by 10 P.M. Florida and North Carolina required that separate textbooks be used for African-American students, and Florida required the two sets of books to be stored separately.

A complex racial etiquette accompanied the legal restrictions imposed on African Americans. Whites expected African Americans to demonstrate their inferior social status through outward signs of deference. African Americans were not to look whites in the eye. When walking on the same sidewalks, African Americans were to move into the road to allow whites to pass. African Americans were forced to call whites "Mister," while whites called African-American men "boy," or by their first names. This system of racial etiquette was backed by force. Any African American who violated the cultural rules faced punishment ranging from intimidation and physical beating to death. Lynching became a southern racial phenomenon during the period from 1900 to 1910 as white southerners fought to enforce segregation.

Segregation was not, however, solely a southern phenomenon nor was it enacted solely against African Americans. Minorities throughout the United States faced segregation in their residential choices, their jobs, and their use of public space. In the West and Southwest, Asian Americans and Hispanics faced segregation. Most of the segregation outside the South was de facto, although some states and municipalities passed laws to segregate members of certain ethnic groups. In 1906, for example, the San Francisco Board of Education segregated all Korean, Chinese, and Japanese students. By 1913 the state of California had passed a law prohibiting the sale of real property to all non-citizens, an act aimed at Asian Americans. Even in the absence of such laws, whites often acted to prohibit the sale of property in certain areas of cities to non-whites. Whites who did not want African Americans or Mexican Americans living in their neighborhood, for example, simply terrorized them into moving out. Another strategy was to include in property deeds a racial covenant that prohibited the sale of the property to non-whites, a practice that was also used to deny Jewish Americans residence in many neighborhoods. Discrimination in housing led to the creation of ethnic ghettos in cities with their own schools and businesses. Many labor unions refused to accept non-whites, which restricted the occupational choices of non-whites.

By 1930, African Americans, Native Americans, Asian Americans, and Hispanics in most regions of the country lived in segregated neighborhoods, faced restrictions in their use of public spaces, and found their choice of work severely limited. Whether it came through the Jim Crow laws of the southern states or the cultural attitudes of northern whites, segregation was the tool by which white Americans repressed non-whites.

See also W. E. B. DU BOIS; MARCUS GARVEY; NIAGARA MOVEMENT; RACE AND RACIAL CONFLICT; UNIVERSAL NEGRO IMPROVEMENT ASSOCIATION.

Further reading: David G. Gutierrez, *Walls and Mirrors: Mexican Americans, Mexican Immigrants, and the Politics of Ethnicity* (Berkeley: University of California Press, 1995); Leon F. Litwack, *Trouble in Mind: Black Southerners in the Age of Jim Crow* (New York: Alfred A. Knopf, 1998); Roger L. Nichols, *Indians in the United States and Canada: A Comparative History* (Lincoln: University of Nebraska Press, 1998); C. Vann Woodward, *The Strange Career of Jim Crow,* 3rd ed. (Oxford: Oxford University Press, 1974).

— Michael Hartman

Selective Service Act (1917)

The Selective Service Act was the law passed by Congress in order to raise troops for the U.S. entry into WORLD WAR I. Facing a requirement specified by General JOHN PERSHING, commander of the AMERICAN EXPEDITIONARY FORCE, to recruit 3 million men to alter the outcome of the war, men from the ages of 21 to 31 filled out their draft registration cards on June 5, 1917. Over 24 million men responded to the call, and local draft boards selected 6,400,000 of them to serve in the military. Hundreds of thousands more volunteered before the draft could call them up. No exemptions were allowed outside of those needed for vital wartime production. No one was allowed to hire a substitute, a difference from the Civil War practice.

President WOODROW WILSON had tried to rely on a public call to arms, as had been the tradition since America's inception. In the Civil War, there had been anti-draft riots, and Wilson was anxious to avoid social unrest. Many warned that the streets would run red with blood. On the actual day, however, most registered patriotically.

General Enoch Crowder was chosen head of the new Selective Service System. Under it, the local draft boards were organized to deflect criticism for selection from the federal government. George Creel, a social reformer, headed the committee. Using advertising methods, his committee convinced Americans to leave their isolationism behind and protect democracy from Germany.

Behind the legislative mechanism for preparedness was a network of organizations and individuals who had led the way for selective service. First, the PREPAREDNESS movement at the outbreak of the conflict in Europe tried to convince Americans of the need to improve military capability. Through literature, programs, and training camps, advocates urged the Wilson administration and the populace to take the German threat seriously. Events, especially German submarine warfare, aided their efforts until war was declared. The COMMITTEE FOR PUBLIC INFORMATION, created by President Wilson shortly after the United States joined the war in 1917, raised public support for the war effort through propaganda. War posters, marching bands, and billboards celebrated those who "did their duty." A darker side of the CPI encouraged and spread fear of Germans and German spies who, they said, had infiltrated the United States. Thanks to the CPI, the nation stood as one behind its war effort.

Locally, communities gave their soldiers farewell parties and parades. Draftees met citizens and loved ones waving flags, with bands playing farewell songs and girls spurring them on to victory against the dreaded Hun. Back at home, citizens bought liberty bonds, grew victory gardens, and worked in war factories to further the war effort. Some served in the Red Cross, helping to alleviate human suffering in the United States and abroad. They assisted over 300,000 American families with financial troubles and sought to ease the grief of families who had lost their relatives in war. America sent over 13,000 of its women as Red Cross nurses overseas.

See also CONSCRIPTION.

Further reading: John Whiteclay Chambers, *To Raise an Army: The Draft Comes to America* (New York: Free Press, 1987).

— Annamarie Edelen

sexuality

The years between 1900 and 1930 witnessed fundamental changes in sexual mores and practices, including an increase in premarital sex and the use of BIRTH CONTROL, a reorientation of marriage toward companionate relationships, a rising divorce rate, and the emergence of distinct gay and lesbian identities. There was a shift from Victorian silence about the body and sexuality to the emergence of a new psychological language about sex. On the margins of mainstream society, sexual radicalism transformed the ways that middle-class and elite intellectuals arranged their private lives. And new venues for leisure where men and women could meet and share entertainment such as movie theaters, dance halls, and amusement parks, brought a shift in the average American's experience of courting and sexuality. So too did the introduction of the automobile and the new youth culture.

The Victorian era had brought with it a sharp divide in social expectations of men and women. Men were supposed to be active, public, and sexual creatures while women—apart from prostitutes and the morally depraved—were assumed to be passive, domestic, and asexual in nature. Such differences and the demand that women remain protected and pure led to practices of social life and leisure in which men and women were segregated from each other. By the turn of the century, however, these patterns had changed. Men and women mingled in the new workplace and also after work when they sought RECRE-ATION and POPULAR ENTERTAINMENT.

Along with such changes in social life came changes in sexual practice. Courting among single men and women had long focused on polite, heavily chaperoned visits in parlors, small social gatherings, and front porches. The boundaries of this social world began to change with the emergence of a new YOUTH culture, in which young men and women were encouraged to meet each other outside the family circle. Changed attitudes toward sexuality were reflected in an increase in the occurrence of premarital sex and the use of birth control. For the generation born before 1900, only 14 percent of women (about one in seven) admitted to having premarital sex before they were 35. Among women in the generation of the 1920s, however, more than one in three (36 percent) had experienced premarital intercourse. With public activism on the issue of birth control, women gained new access to contraceptives. New birth control clinics provided advice and contraceptive devices, so that by 1925 one study reported that more than 80 percent of middle-class women used birth control. In contrast, only about 36 percent of poorer women did.

In a new urban culture, single men and women worked out sexual lives and identities not all of which ended in novel-like marriages. The dance halls, speakeasies, pool halls, and recreational clubs opened up alternatives to family life for both heterosexual and homosexual men and women. A new gay subculture, with a separate identity, began to emerge for men in the tearooms and clubs as well as on the streets; among women, freedom from family could mean the possibility of relationships not only with men but with women. At the same time, the Society for the Suppression of Vice sought to prosecute the public and private acts of those seen as deviant. Police in many cities cracked down especially on gay men whose sexual conduct differed from the norm.

On average, most men and women refrained from marrying until their early to mid-twenties. A prolonged period of courtship preceded marriage, and married couples often had widely different expectations about marital sex. New ideas about marriage, however, began to alter the experience. By the 1910s, men and women, reading the work of sex theorists such as HAVELOCK ELLIS and psychologist SIGMUND FREUD had different beliefs in and practices of sex than had their parents. Many also developed greater expectations for what marriage might be. They emphasized that couples could be companions and share the joys and burdens of marital life. They also gave new attention to happiness, including sexual happiness, in marriage.

Rising expectations increased pressure on men and women who married to achieve the new ideal of companionate marriage. Individuals and couples came to expect more from each other than their parents had, wanting an economic and sexual union to also be fulfilling in emotional terms. The hopes many had for marital life, however, frequently led to disappointment. As many states started to reform divorce laws and make it easier for couple to attain a divorce, the divorce rate rose. Those who married expecting happiness could now file for divorce on more ambiguous grounds such as mental cruelty; and many chose to do so. Also true was that rates of remarriage rose in response.

In what was called the first sexual revolution of the 1920s, these trends came together to create more open attitudes about heterosexual relationships both inside and outside marriage. The widespread adoption of the automobile in recreation opened the way for its use in courtship and sexuality. Mass-market magazines such as *True Confessions* and romance novels spread the language of companionate marriage and new modern sexuality, and new styles of DRESS and cosmetics brought the "sex appeal" of ADVERTISING into daily view. Still, new methods of birth control, smarter, sexier language, and the new availability of divorce did not change the double standard of morality between men and women. Women continued to be ostracized within their communities for violating strict norms of female virtue. While these standards varied according to race, class, and region, respectable women had to remain free of the taint of immorality and illegitimacy. The new emphasis on heterosexual relationships also stigmatized those who remained outside traditional monogamous marriage and deepened social prejudice and hostility toward gay men and lesbian women. The widening scope of traditional sexual relations stirred doubts about the psychological stability of celibate, unmarried, and homosexual men and women.

See also COSMETICS AND BEAUTY INDUSTRY; MARRIAGE AND FAMILY LIFE; MEDICINE.

Further reading: John D'Emilio and Estelle Freedman, *Intimate Matters: A History of Sexuality in America* (New York: Harper and Row, 1988); Paul Robinson, *The Modernization of Sex: Havelock Ellis, Alfred Kinsey, William Masters, and Virginia Johnson* (New York: Harper and Row, 1976); Sharon R. Ullman, *Sex Seen: The Emergence of Modern Sexuality in America* (Berkeley: University of California Press, 1997).

Shaw, Anna Howard See Volume VI

Sheppard-Towner Act (1921)
The Sheppard-Towner Maternity and Infancy Act was the first federal program for social welfare. It was introduced into Congress in 1919 and signed into law by President WARREN G. HARDING on November 23, 1921. The

Sheppard-Towner Act set up a federal administration that disbursed funds to individual states for the purpose of improving the health of America's children. Originally set to expire in 1926, the act was renewed for an additional two years, but Congress allowed it to expire in 1928. Despite its brief tenure, the act improved the health of millions of American children.

The Sheppard-Towner Act emerged out of the efforts of Progressive Era reformers to improve the health of America's children. The U.S. CHILDREN'S BUREAU had been researching infant health since 1913. It discovered that the U.S. infant and maternal fatality rates were among the highest in the industrialized world. The studies of the Children's Bureau suggested that better infant and prenatal care might have prevented half of the infant and child deaths. In addition, during WORLD WAR I, one-third of American men were rejected by the draft board for medical reasons. These findings highlighted the need for better infant and maternal health care. Reformers also feared that state and local programs ignored women and infants in rural areas. To solve these problems, child welfare reformers, led by the Children's Bureau, began a campaign to establish a federal program that would standardize child and maternity care across the nation.

The law passed in 1921 named the Children's Bureau as the federal department in charge of overseeing state health programs. Each state's legislature had to vote acceptance of the act. By June 1922, 42 of the 48 states had accepted Sheppard-Towner funding. After a state voted to accept federal funds, it received $5,000. A matching $5,000 grant was available for states that appropriated their own funds for child and maternity programs and additional funds were available based on state population. The Sheppard-Towner Act required each state to name a state agency to administer the programs. These agencies in turn had to submit a program proposal to the Children's Bureau for approval. The bureau's power to approve state programs meant that the state agencies addressing child and maternal health did so within the guidelines of the Children's Bureau staff. The Children's Bureau supported, for example, professional public social service agencies and often rejected state programs run by private agencies.

Programs operating under the Sheppard-Towner Act reached hundreds of thousands of women and children through state agencies that ran child health and prenatal conferences and mothers' classes. At the conferences, the agencies provided prenatal and infant health examinations. In 1924, for example, 303,546 children received examinations. New mothers attending mothers' classes learned the importance of prenatal care. They were introduced to the child-rearing standards of the middle-class professionals in charge of the agencies. Child welfare advocates hoped that these temporary conferences would grow into permanent

prenatal and infant care centers, which happened in a number of localities.

Sheppard-Towner agencies also instituted visiting nurse programs. Under these programs, a nurse employed by the agency visited pregnant women and new mothers. The purpose of the visits was to teach the women proper prenatal and infant care. The nurses helped improve the health of mothers and infants. For many women, particularly in rural areas, the nurses' advice was their first introduction to prenatal care. In addition, nurses explained the value of sterilizing all items used during delivery. They also taught the importance of immunizations. Despite all of the benefits of the program, the visiting nurses could, at times, become intrusive in the lives of women. Because they promoted proper child-rearing techniques established by the Children's Bureau, visiting nurses sometimes made new mothers feel inadequate. They counseled new mothers, for example, that children should be raised on strict schedules. They criticized mothers for keeping disorganized homes and told parents that they should not play with their children. There emerged, therefore, a tension between the Sheppard-Towner Act employees and the many mothers who did not subscribe to the Children's Bureau's standardized view of childrearing.

The Sheppard-Towner Act eventually succumbed to the more conservative environment of the late 1920s. Medical professionals and other federal agencies such as the Public Health Service had worked for years to take over the functions of the maternal and child health care program. They put pressure on Congress to cut Sheppard-Towner money. After receiving a two-year appropriations extension in 1927, the Sheppard-Towner Act was allowed to expire in 1929.

See also MOTHERS' PENSIONS; PUBLIC HEALTH.

Further reading: Robyn Muncy, *Creating a Female Dominion in American Reform, 1890–1935* (New York: Oxford University Press, 1991).

— Michael Hartman

Shirtwaist Makers Strike (1909–1910)

One of the major strikes in labor history in the United States, the Shirtwaist Makers strike of 1909–10 brought together various elements of labor conflict in the period—immigrant socialism, militant trade unionism, the role of new workers in mass-production industries, sympathetic community support, and the resistance of employers. The strike began in September 1909 when workers from the Leiserson Shirtwaist Company walked out. A few weeks later, the Triangle Shirtwaist Company locked out its workers, as the employer sought to halt the union organizing drive. During these strikes, women faced violence on the picket line from company thugs. Police also arrested women strikers for streetwalking and inciting violence. Wealthy women, who had come out in support of the strike, also were present, and their accusations of police brutality made headlines. On November 22, at Cooper Union, garment worker Clara Lemlich took the stage to call for a general strike. With her call to action, the massive walkout began. The next morning, more than 30,000 shirtwaist makers were on strike from over 300 shops in the industry. Within a few days, a hundred of the smaller shops settled with the union and reopened their doors, and 10,000 strikers returned to work.

The INTERNATIONAL LADIES' GARMENT WORKERS UNION Local 25, which had been organizing workers in the trade, assumed leadership of the strike. Supported by the Socialist Party in New York, various community, political, and ethnic associations, and the recently organized NATIONAL WOMEN'S TRADE UNION LEAGUE (WTUL), a cross-class organization of women, the strike captured the imagination of the public and the support of many of New York's elite. The resistance of large clothing employers, however, remained the most significant obstacle to union success. Major garment firms counted on the police to guard replacement workers and to intimidate and arrest strikers. Even public outrage at the treatment of the "girl strikers" did not break through employer hostility.

By January, most of the small garment shops already had signed agreements with the ILGWU, but the larger factories still refused to bargain with the union. Attempts to negotiate a return to work through AMERICAN FEDERATION OF LABOR (AFL) president Samuel Gompers led only to accusations that the AFL had sold the workers out. Others, notably labor publicist Eva McDonald Valesh, accused the socialist leadership of running roughshod over the needs of women workers. Her red-baiting comments brought fire from the NWTUL, which saw her as an opportunist. With the progressive failure of the strike, thousands of women garment workers returned to work. The strike officially came to an end in February 1910. It was, however, only the first of a long series of strikes that built the ILGWU and unionized a significant part of the clothing industry in New York City and other major garment centers. In 1911, the TRIANGLE SHIRTWAIST FIRE, another landmark, called attention to dangerous working conditions in the trade and brought with it the will to completely organize the industry. By 1920, the ILGWU was the third largest union in the AFL, and it remained an influential force in union politics in the 20th century.

Further reading: Nancy Schrom Dye, *As Equals and as Sisters: Feminism and the Labor Movement in the Women's Trade Union League of New York* (Columbia: University of Missouri Press, 1980); Annelise Orleck, *Common Sense and a Little Fire: Women and Working-Class Politics in the United States, 1900–1965* (Chapel Hill: University of North Carolina Press, 1995).

Siberian Expedition

On August 18, 1918, 9,014 American soldiers, including the 27th and 31st Infantry, then in the Philippines, and selected men from the 8th Division in California, were placed under the command of Major General William S. Graves and sent to Vladivostok to join Japanese and other Allied troops in Siberia. In this Siberian Expedition, they were assigned to intervene in the civil war then taking place in Russia. The object was to secure a government friendly to the war effort by helping to protect Allied troops.

Even as the war in Europe ground onward, fighting continued in northern Russia and Siberia. The RUSSIAN REVOLUTION had begun in February 1917, and Lenin had taken over as premier on January 7, 1918. Afterward, Lenin signed a treaty with Germany and released hundreds of thousands of German, Austrian, Hungarian, and Turkish prisoners of war from Siberian detention. In the same region, many Czechs had deserted and formed a legion of 50,000 to 70,000 men. Their leader claimed the legion as the future Army of Czechoslovakia and offered its services to France and against the Bolsheviks. The Czechs hoped they could fight their way to Archangel in northern Russia, where American troops were also engaged.

On July 23, 1918, a Siberian republic had been declared, but there were competing claims to political leadership. Red Bolsheviks, White Anti-Bolsheviks, Russian army soldiers, bandits, warlords, Cossacks, former prisoners-of-war, and men from foreign armies vied for power. The situation merited the words of President WOODROW WILSON that "military intervention would add to the present sad confusion in Russia rather than cure it." Pressured by allies to send men to Siberia, an area more than half the size of the United States, Wilson ordered them to intervene.

General Graves maintained that the only reason for intervention was "to aid the Czecho-Slovakians to consolidate their forces and to steady any efforts at self-government or self-defense." He resisted pressure to intervene in the Russian Civil War on the side of the White Army. In January 1920, the Czechs instead fought eastward and defeated a large force of Cossacks. The Americans guarded the line from Lake Baikal to Vladivostok on the Pacific until all the Czechs had evacuated. Americans did, therefore, intervene in the Russian Civil War to help anti-Bolshevik forces. Once the Czechs reached Vladivostok, the survivors boarded ships for Europe, where they became the nucleus of the Czech army. In April 1920, the last Americans withdrew, but the Japanese did not follow until 1925.

American casualties numbered 35 killed and 135 who died of disease. Fifty-two others were wounded and 50 deserted. The American intervention was a failure. A parallel intervention in Archangel in August 1918, landed 1,200 men from the French Foreign Legion, and some from the British Royal Marines and the U.S. Navy and Marines. They served under a British officer, General Poole. Later, a regiment was added of 4,487 men mainly from Michigan and Wisconsin. Both of these interventions were largely forgotten in subsequent years. America's intervention, however, set the tone for its relations with the new Soviet Union. The United States refused to recognize the Soviet government until 1933.

See also FOREIGN POLICY.

Further reading: Betty M. Winterberger, *America's Siberian Expedition, 1918–1920, A Study of National Policy* (Durham, N.C.: Duke University Press, 1956), David S. Foglesong, *America's Secret War against Bolshevism; U.S. Intervention in the Russian Civil War 1917–1920* (Chapel Hill: University of North Carolina, 1995).

— Annamarie Edelen

Sinclair, Upton (1878–1968)

Upton Sinclair was one of the most widely known author-journalists of his generation. In his polemical and political writings, he helped to establish the muckraking style of JOURNALISM and called national attention to the excesses of corporate America. Born in Baltimore, Maryland, in 1878, he was the son of a poor, alcoholic father; but he spent part of his youth in the home of his wealthy grandparents. Sinclair claimed that these widely divergent experiences heightened his awareness of the nation's social inequality and prompted him to become a socialist. He graduated from City College of New York at the age of 19, by which time he had already established himself as an accomplished journalist.

Sinclair and other progressive journalists were becoming increasingly alarmed at the state of urban America and the virtually unregulated power of corporations. In 1904, Fred Warren, editor of the socialist journal, *Appeal to Reason*, commissioned Sinclair to investigate the living and working conditions of the largely foreign-born workers in the Chicago meatpacking industry. What Sinclair found, he published in *The Jungle*, a book that shocked the nation. Public outrage prompted President THEODORE ROOSEVELT to order an investigation of the meatpacking industry, which resulted in the passage of the MEAT INSPECTION ACT (1906) and the PURE FOOD AND DRUG ACT (1906). Both the public outrage and the legislative initiatives that followed tended to focus almost exclusively on the lack of,

and need for, sanitary preparation of food. The fact that the nation's supply of hot dogs, sausage, pork, and beef was likely contaminated was a cause of far more concern than the low wages, hazardous working conditions, and substandard living conditions of the Chicago stockyard workers and their families. In later years, Sinclair would lament, "I aimed at the public's heart and by accident I hit it in the stomach."

In the decades following the publication of *The Jungle*, Sinclair became heavily involved in politics. After joining the Socialist Party in 1902, he utilized the substantial proceeds from *The Jungle* to establish a utopian socialist community, Helicon Home, in Englewood, New Jersey. Sinclair was an active party member until the party split over American involvement in WORLD WAR I, when Sinclair supported intervention. Sinclair's departure, however, was only temporary. In 1926, he ran unsuccessfully for the governorship

Bookcover for Upton Sinclair's *The Jungle* (Library of Congress)

of California as the Socialist Party candidate. Not deterred by this defeat, Sinclair launched another bid for the California governorship in 1934. With the state mired in the grip of the Great Depression and unemployment approaching 25 percent, Sinclair ran on a platform of Ending Poverty in California (EPIC). Calling for partial state control of industry and a return to full employment, the EPIC campaign successfully tapped into the widespread resentment and frustration of California voters. The state's business and conservative organizations vehemently opposed Sinclair's campaign, warning that a Sinclair victory would result in the state degenerating into communism. Though Sinclair was defeated, the outcome of the bitterly contested election was surprisingly close, as he received 879,537 votes to his opponent's 1,138,620. Despite his foray into the world of politics, Sinclair continued to write works of political fiction. These included *The Metropolis* (1908), *King Coal* (1917), *Oil!* (1927), and *Boston* (1928). In 1942, Sinclair's *Dragon's Teeth* won the Pulitzer Prize. His final novel, *The Return of Lanny Budd*, was published in 1953. Sinclair died in 1968 at the age of 90.

See also MUCKRAKERS; RADICAL PRESS.

Further reading: Leon A. Harris, *Upton Sinclair, An American Rebel* (New York: Crowell, 1975); Greg Mitchell, *The Campaign of the Century: Upton Sinclair's Race for Governor of California and the Birth of Media Politics* (New York: Random House, 1992).

— Robert Gordon

Smith, Alfred E. (1873–1944)

Al Smith served four terms as governor of New York, where he was instrumental in running the powerful Tammany Hall political machine between 1900 and 1930. One of the most charismatic politicians of his generation, Smith was the first Irish American and the first Catholic to run for the presidency of the United States. Unlike many other politicians of his day who were born and raised in rural America, Smith was born on New York City's Lower East Side in December 1873. The son of poor Irish immigrants, Smith was forced to drop out of school after the eighth grade to begin working when his father died. During his teenage years, Smith worked in a variety of jobs before landing a steady one at the Fulton Fish Market. A tall, gregarious man, Smith quickly became well known in New York's close-knit Irish community.

Smith's political career began in 1895 when Tammany Hall appointed him as an investigator for the commissioner of jurors. In 1903, with the support of Tammany Hall, he ran for and was elected to the New York State Assembly. Smith was a popular and effective representative. In 1911 he became the DEMOCRATIC PARTY majority leader and in 1913 speaker of the New York Assembly. During this time, Smith established a reputation as a man of the people and developed close ties with the progressive wing of the Democratic Party. In 1911 he joined future New York senator Robert Wagner and future secretary of labor Frances Perkins in investigating working conditions in New York City factories. The commission found conditions to be deplorable and called for sweeping reform legislation.

Smith's reputation as a reformer vaulted him into the 1918 New York gubernatorial race. He upset the incumbent Republican governor. Smith was defeated in his reelection bid in 1920, but he was reelected in 1922 and remained in office until 1928. As governor, Smith continued to push for reforms aimed at helping poor and working-class New Yorkers. He called for an end to CHILD LABOR and pressed for improved working conditions, child welfare laws, affordable housing, the creation of state parks, and reforms in the treatment of the mentally ill. In addition, Smith spent considerable time attempting to reform and streamline the state's bloated bureaucracy, finally convincing the state assembly to enact a constitutional amendment that reduced the state's 187 agencies to 19. During his tenure as governor, Democrat Smith was frequently faced with a Republican-controlled state assembly and proved very adept at using his immense popularity to push through his legislative agenda. He was often seen walking the streets of New York in his brown derby hat, smoking a cigar, and mingling with local merchants and passersby.

By 1920, Smith had become a powerful force within the Democratic Party. Put forward as a presidential contender, he was the first Irish American and Roman Catholic to receive serious consideration. Smith failed to win the nomination in 1920, but he was brought forward again at the 1924 Democratic convention when long-time friend and political ally Franklin Delano Roosevelt threw his name into the ring. At the 1924 convention, Smith's Catholicism and his public opposition to PROHIBITION were used to deny him the nomination. Finally in 1928, as his popularity and effectiveness as New York governor continued to grow, Smith won the Democratic presidential nomination. In the 1928 general election, Smith faced Republican nominee Herbert Hoover. The 1928 election was never seriously in doubt, with Hoover winning all but eight states. Although Smith's ties with Tammany Hall, his opposition to Prohibition, and his Catholicism certainly contributed to his defeat, Hoover had other important advantages, including a national reputation as an engineer, a successful tenure as secretary of commerce in the Coolidge administration, and a booming economy, that contributed to his landslide victory.

Although Smith effectively retired from politics following his 1928 defeat, he helped Franklin Roosevelt win the Democratic nomination and the presidency in 1932. Smith's support of the Roosevelt administration, however, was short-lived. Smith, who had entered private business after his retirement from politics, became convinced that the New Deal had gone too far in expanding the role of the federal government. In 1936 and again in 1940, Smith not only opposed Roosevelt's renomination but also publicly endorsed the Republican presidential candidates.

Further reading: Paula Eldot, *Governor Alfred E. Smith: The Politician as Reformer* (New York: Garland, 1983); Richard O'Connor, *The First Hurrah: A Biography of Alfred E. Smith* (New York: Putnam, 1970).

— Robert Gordon

Social Darwinism   See Volume VI

Social Gospel   See Volume VI

socialism

Socialism is the name we give to ideas developed in the 19th century about the necessity of sharing the costs and benefits of economic productivity broadly through cooperative means of production or through government redistribution of benefits and social provision. The nature of American society changed dramatically in the last decades of the 19th century. The nation became more urban and industrial as people moved from the farm to the city. City life was vastly different from rural life, and millions of new immigrants meant that the country was more racially and ethnically diverse. The nature of work changed as well. Semi-skilled factory workers gradually replaced skilled craft workers. Goods were increasingly mass-produced on assembly lines, and the pace of work increased as employers attempted to streamline production and maximize profits. Finally, the rise of a new financial and industrial elite resulted in growing social and political inequality.

These changes convinced many American citizens to reject the capitalist system and to insist that socialism was the only viable alternative. In its purist form, socialism rejected private property, the free-market economy, and inequality. It advocated that the means of producing goods and wealth be controlled and shared equally by all members of society. Socialism had roots dating back to the utopian socialism of the 1840s, but scientific socialism began to take hold in the 1870s. The Socialist Labor Party (SLP) was established in 1877 and quickly came under the leadership of Daniel De Leon. It specifically looked toward craft and industrial workers for its support and hoped to achieve control over the labor movement as a means for acquiring political power. A competing faction, the Socialist Democratic Party (SDP), was formed in 1898. More broad-based agrarian socialism found expression in the populist movement. By the turn of the century, socialists were looking to found a new organization.

Led by EUGENE V. DEBS and Victor Berger, the SDP merged with the SLP in 1901 to form the Socialist Party of America (SPA). The SPA grew steadily between 1900 and 1912. From a membership of barely 10,000 in 1901, the party grew to over 150,000 members by 1912. Debs also played a leading role in mobilizing the left wing of the labor movement between 1900 and 1920, helping to form the INDUSTRIAL WORKERS OF THE WORLD (IWW) in 1905. As head of the Socialist Party, Debs ran for the presidency in 1900, 1904, 1908, 1912, and 1920. Although he garnered only 96,000 votes in 1900, the SPA had become the largest third party in the country by 1904, when Debs received over 400,000 votes. He tallied 897,000 votes in 1912. Socialist candidates also gained a small minority of state and local offices across the nation, in a showing of working-class strength.

From the outset, socialist organizations represented an uneasy coalition of supporters, ideas, and objectives. Adherents included radical immigrants, workers, pacifists, Zionists, Christian socialists, revolutionaries, and reformers. They supported a broad range of issues, including prison reform, BIRTH CONTROL, WOMAN SUFFRAGE, and municipal ownership of streetcar companies and public utilities, in addition to more extreme demands to abolish private property and overthrow capitalism. Socialists also created institutions and organizations to support their struggle, including newspapers and journals, socialist summer schools and camps, and communal settlements. Many of these activities had an ethnic cast. In northern cities such as New York and Chicago, immigrant radicals fostered workingmen's circles, newspapers, and drama societies, along with ward clubs. Milwaukee, Wisconsin, became known for its socialist city government. In rural areas where populism once held sway, socialist organizations reemerged. The *Appeal to Reason,* a national socialist newspaper, was edited and published in Kansas; the NONPARTISAN LEAGUE sprang to life in North Dakota and Minnesota, and the Green Corn Rebellion arose in Oklahoma.

Within the socialist movement, there were long-standing debates about the pace at which American capitalism should be overturned. Some advocated immediate revolution, and others urged more gradual reforms. Still others believed in using socialist means to moderate the effects of industrial capitalism through state regulation of industry and finance, the passage and enforcement of antitrust laws, the institution of democratic reforms of referendum, initiative, and recall, and protective labor measures.

There were numerous ideological variations of early-20th-century American socialism, including communism, anarchism, and syndicalism. All adhered to the basic tenets of socialism, which advocated a fair distribution of public goods and popular control of the economy; but on the best way to achieve those ends, they differed greatly. Anarchists and syndicalists argued that a strong, centralized government was the biggest obstacle to socialism while democratic socialists believed that some form of activist government was essential to ensure progress and a more equitable society. While there was widespread disagreement about the use of direct action and violence for change, some radical socialists and anarchists believed that a revolution was essential and that gradual reform would not work. Ideas about gender equality, sexuality, and marriage also differed greatly among socialists.

The Socialist Party of America was the dominant socialist organization between 1900 and 1930. As a result, the party frequently became the target of repression. When war broke out in Europe in 1914, Debs and the SPA opposed American intervention and warned the public against American involvement. When Congress and President WOODROW WILSON declared war against the Central Powers on April 6, 1917, Debs and the SPA reiterated their opposition to the war. Congress attempted to silence opposition by passing the ESPIONAGE ACT of 1917 and the SEDITION ACT of 1918, which made it illegal to criticize the American government and its involvement in the war. Debs, however, continued to agitate against CONSCRIPTION and the war. Following a June 18, 1918, speech in Canton, Ohio, he was arrested and—after a short trial—sentenced to a 10-year prison term.

After the outbreak of WORLD WAR I, the SPA became more radical, particularly as class relations grew hostile. Debates between militant unionists and conservative craft workers grew more intense as well. By the time of Debs's arrest and imprisonment, a powerful faction in the SPA was advocating revolution, instead of gradual reform. Its antiwar position and increasing radicalism made the party one of the chief targets of the conservative postwar backlash that culminated in the RED SCARE. Led by Attorney General A. MITCHELL PALMER, the government launched a series of raids against suspected socialists. Beginning with American entry into the war and the end of the Red Scare in 1921, American socialists suffered serious setbacks. The party differed on its attitude toward and support for the RUSSIAN REVOLUTION, and it began to splinter into small new parties intent on capturing the support of the emerging Soviet Union. The COMMUNIST PARTY, a much smaller entity, formed in the early 1920s. The Socialist Party itself remained intact, although it suffered from the absence of its long-time leader Eugene Debs. Although Debs remained in prison, he again was the party's presidential

candidate in 1920 and received almost 1 million votes. The election, however, proved to be a last gasp. The conservative backlash of 1919–21 resulted in the election of the Republican WARREN G. HARDING and his successor CALVIN COOLIDGE. Between 1921 and 1930, socialism ceased to be an important factor in American political life. Socialism and its many heirs would again become influential with the onset of the Great Depression.

Further reading: James R. Green, *Grass-Roots Socialism: Radical Movements in the Southwest, 1895–1943* (Baton Rouge: Louisiana State University Press, 1978); Ira Kipnis, *The American Socialist Movement, 1897–1912* (New York: Columbia University Press, 1952); John H. Laslett and Seymour Martin Lipset, eds., *Failure of a Dream? Essays in the History of American Socialism* (Berkeley: University of California Press, 1974), David A. Shannon, *The Socialist Party of America* (New York: Macmillan, 1955).

— Robert Gordon

social work

The field of social work emerged at the turn of the 20th century as a major new profession in the United States. The first use of the term "social work" was at a National Conference of Charities and Corrections meeting in 1897. From that time on, the term encompassed a broad range of activities, including the traditional work of charities, increasingly known as philanthropy; the care of poor, disabled, and orphaned individuals through private institutions; industrial social work, sometimes called welfare work; hospital or medical social work; settlement house work; and the social services of public relief agencies. During these years, charitable institutions and universities created the new field of social work education, some of which emphasized supervision of clients through the casework method. There were as well growing differences between social workers, which put progressive social reformers at odds with those dedicated to the profession of social work alone.

By 1900, many private charitable organizations, which had been among the first to respond to the urban poor, lacked sufficient resources to address the multiplying social ills of the industrial age. Work accidents, high infant and maternal mortality, family violence, delinquency and crime, and public health crises all seemed on the increase. A new generation of social reformers, many involved in the Settlement House Movement, emerged that combined concern about social disorder with a philosophy of political empowerment. According to JANE ADDAMS, founder of Hull-House, there was a social necessity for settlements, both in addressing the needs of urban immigrants and in providing an almost religious calling for the young. In industry, new calls for efficiency in factories and greater control were often accompanied by programs to provide health care at the workplace, create recreational programs, offer EDUCATION, especially in citizenship skills, and even to supervise workers' home lives. Collectively, WELFARE CAPITALISM demanded more personnel workers and the hiring of industrial social workers to attend to workers' needs.

Even as the need for social workers grew, so too did questions about what held them together as a profession. In 1915 at the National Conference of Social Work meeting, Abraham Flexner, assistant secretary of the General Education Board and the man responsible for reforming medical education, addressed a gathering of social workers. At that meeting, he raised the question of whether social work was a profession. He frankly told his listeners that it was not. It lacked a common method, approach, or technique that could be taught, and the variety of tasks assigned to social workers made it impossible to define its boundaries. Moreover, the task of distributing relief to the poor was a task almost anyone could do. In response to Flexner's challenge, social work leaders looked toward professional associations to create a collective identity and advertise the value of their work to society as a whole. Casework, in the end, was the collective answer to Flexner's implicit question.

Early professional organization began as social workers started professional clubs in cities across the country. The Monday Club of Boston was the first such organization; it was quickly followed in the 1910s by clubs in New York, Detroit, Minneapolis, San Francisco, and other cities. Meeting to discuss their work and the problems they faced, the clubs were the first step toward national organization and would form the basis for local chapters of a national organization. In 1921, members of social work organizations from across the country met to form the American Association of Social Workers, which became the National Association of Social Workers in 1955. The organization provided a forum in which to discuss professional standards, present findings of social research and exchange information, encourage professional training, and recruit new members.

More importantly, the move to create social work training and degree programs enhanced the status of social work as a profession. Responding to a call for better training of social workers, the New York Charity Organization Society created first a summer training program for social workers in 1898. Later established as the New York School of Social Work (later affiliated with Columbia University), it became an academic program that combined internships with social study. Soon after, in 1904, Boston Associated Charities, Simmons College, and Harvard University established the Boston School of Social Work. In 1907, Graham Taylor of Chicago Commons Settlement and Julia Lathrop

of Hull-House helped found the Chicago School of Civics and Philanthropy (later the University of Chicago School of Social Work). In keeping with its settlement house origins, the school curriculum combined social science research, social policy, and public administration. By 1910, there were five major schools of social work providing some form of graduate training. In 1915 Bryn Mawr developed a postbaccalaureate program, and Ohio State University, Indiana University, and the University of Minnesota established the first undergraduate degrees in social work. The trend toward greater education continued throughout the 1920s.

Central to a number of programs was the new method of casework. As many social workers argued, social work had to become scientific. First articulated in Mary Richmond's 1917 book, *Social Diagnosis,* casework combined the traditional approach of friendly visiting with social scientific method. Occasional notes, intuition, and talk with peers were replaced with systematic case record, theories of scientific philanthropy, casebook studies, and professional guidance through journals, conferences, and consultation with experts. Above all, there was an emphasis on diagnosis and cure of individual ills. By 1918, a new tool became available to social workers, as Freudian psychology became more influential in social work education. In 1918, Smith College established a School of Psychiatric Social Work to train students in working with mental patients. Probing the personality and emotional history of clients promised to aid social workers in performing their duties and to provide relief tailored to individual need. Psychiatric casework also had the possibility of completely severing the profession of social work from its unscientific past. In opposition to this approach stood those social workers who continued to believe that environment, not heredity or individual pathology, was the key to understanding the poor and to solving their problems. Change the environment, and you change the person. The tension between the two schools of thought continued to dog social work and social policy throughout the 20th century.

Despite debates over how to solve the problems of poverty, the state's expanding role in providing assistance and relief enhanced the reputation of and demand for social workers. Apart from the growth of city relief boards, there was as well a need for social workers in the new juvenile justice system, in schools and through city recreation programs, and in supervising new social programs. The most important relief program created in these years was MOTHERS' PENSIONS. By 1911, the states of Illinois and Missouri began to provide so-called mothers' aid, or "mothers' pensions," to supplement the wages of widowed mothers and to enable them to keep their children in the home. By 1920, 40 states and hundreds of counties had implemented some version of the program. Overall, it was believed that this program protected mothers faced with poverty in retaining their financial independence and improving their family lives. The rule of the program, and the prejudices of its administrators, limited mothers' pensions to white, largely native-born, widowed mothers. The standards for eligibility were strict, and no divorced or deserted wives were thought to have the same claim as widows to state supplemental income. Moreover, when mothers were granted a pension, they agreed to moral supervision and random investigation demanded by the state with any relief allowance. The mothers' pension program thus required states to hire a new corps of workers to supervise the program. While mothers' pensions were never adequately funded, the simple existence of the new bureaucratic agency called for even greater numbers of social work professionals.

The period between 1900 and 1930 saw major new policy initiatives at the state and local levels that increased the need for trained social workers. So too did new programs for social work in private industry, public education, and PUBLIC HEALTH. For young men and women committed to a progressive social vision, and those who simply wanted employment that had meaning, the social work profession offered engagement with the public, a moral and even religious mission, and the possibility of helping to change American society. Along with these ideals there was the concrete reality of poverty, chronic disease, the need for education and for hope among the urban immigrant working class and in African-American communities. Taking a role in addressing these problems ennobled some and made others dispirited. Social work became a profession by combining these challenges with the individual desire for prestige and status. By the end of the 1920s, social workers faced the coming crisis of unemployment during the Great Depression with a range of tactics from investigation and casework to unionization and social protest; but they did so with renewed belief in the ability of their profession to solve the social ills.

See also CRIMINAL JUSTICE; YOUTH.

Further reading: John Ehrenreich, *The Altruistic Imagination; A History of Social Work and Social Policy in the United States* (Ithaca, N.Y.: Cornell University Press 1985); Roy Lubove, *The Professional Altruist; The Emergence of Social Work as a Career, 1880–1930* (Cambridge, Mass.: Harvard University Press, 1965); Daniel Walkowitz, *Working with Class: Social Workers and the Politics of Middle-Class Identity* (Chapel Hill: University of North Carolina Press, 1999).

Soldiers' Bonus (Soldiers' Adjusted Compensation Act) (1924)

Following the end of WORLD WAR I, there were significant pressures to increase soldiers' compensation, especially given the abysmal pay of soldiers and the institution of military CONSCRIPTION. In response, Congress passed an act to grant soldiers a $60 bonus on their discharge from the army. When the newly organized and powerful AMERICAN LEGION began to assess the value or damage of wartime service, its leadership suggested a program for further compensation based on the idea of renegotiating "the soldier's contract for service" with the government. The argument was simple. Soldiers had been disadvantaged in not benefiting from the war boom and lost real wages in the bargain. Railroads and industries had received government largess and bonuses during the war. Industrial workers earned high wages for their labor and, according to bonus advocates, now wore "silk shirts." The American public was saved for democracy and incidentally became rich. These forces had their reward. It was only "just due" that a government that scrimped on soldiers' wages, failed to help them adjust to civilian life, and did not guarantee jobs should be forced to ante up.

Veterans' advocates both independently and in the American Legion arrived at a scheme for the government to adjust its payments to veterans to include wages they lost during their wartime service. Based on length of service and time abroad, the proposed Soldiers' Bonus was determined by deducting military pay from the wages that soldiers would have earned as civilians. The government would pay its obligation to veterans as a lump sum payment with interest, due in 1945. Bonus advocates hoped that the long period of time between the Adjusted Compensation Act and the payment of the Bonus would make it more politically palatable. Between 1920 and 1924, however, the plan for additional compensation provoked opposition from across the political spectrum.

Attempts to pass veterans' legislation for the Bonus failed in 1920, 1921, and again in 1922, when President WARREN G. HARDING, not opposed to the bill in principle, still vetoed it as an economy measure. In his veto message, he argued "It is as inevitable as that the years will pass that provision for World War veterans will be made, as it has been made for those who served in previous wars." Financial considerations, however, forced the government to postpone its obligation. "In a personal as well as public manner," Harding said, "I have commended the policy of generous treatment of the nation's defenders, not as a part of any contract, not as the payment of a debt which is owing, but as a mark of the nation's gratitude." In essence Harding chose to voice his own support but let his advisers have their way. As Secretary of the Treasury ANDREW MELLON argued, "the country is staggering under the existing burden of taxation and debt, and is clamoring for gradual relief from war taxation." The last thing that was needed was a new financial burden. Further, military service was an obligation of citizenship and should not be rewarded. In a decade given to the scaling back of government machinery, the Bonus was seen as contrary to the will and interests of the people. Neither Mellon nor Harding mentioned the escalating cost of creating and sustaining the VETERANS BUREAU and its hospitals.

After much debate and amendment, Congress in 1924 passed the Soldiers' Adjusted Compensation Act (nicknamed the Soldiers' Bonus) over a presidential veto. Designed to compensate individual soldiers for income lost during the war, it was funded by 20-year insurance certificates (25 percent increase plus 4 percent annually compounded interest) payable in 1945. Its success was due in large part to the power of organized veterans in the American Legion. The legion, which was modeled on the Civil War veterans' organization, the Grand Army of the Republic (GAR), improved on the basic idea of military pensions. As one American Legion leader wrote, "We extracted more from Congress in one year than the GAR did in its whole existence." The legion excelled in pragmatic politics. Its original plan for the Bonus postponed payment for 20 years; no immediate provision for empowering tax revenues was included in the bill, and there was that commonsense "rational" calculus of lost wages. For these reasons, they were able to overcome objections about the need for a balanced budget. In the years ahead, they and other veterans' groups pushed for the early payment of the Soldiers' Bonus, a drive that sparked the Bonus March of 1932 and the final, early payment of the Bonus during the Great Depression.

Further reading: Jennifer Keene, *Doughboys, the Great War and the Remarking of America* (Baltimore: Johns Hopkins University Press, 2001).

southern demagogues

The word "demagogue" comes from Greek roots that mean leader of the people. In both ancient Greece and contemporary society, "demagogue" came to represent anyone who appealed in visceral terms to the fears and prejudices of the mass of voters. In the United States, it most often has been used to designate agrarian politicians from the South who combined populist appeal, social conservatism, and homespun oratory and who were, for the most part, allied with the DEMOCRATIC PARTY. During the late 19th century, southern demagogues emerged as the product of a distinct rural political culture and ascended to some of the most powerful political offices in the region. The failure of the populist movement to improve the conditions of embattled southern white farmers, the sharp division between town and country within the region, the single-party system that offered no opposition to Democratic Party control of local and state government, and the legacy of racial conflict created the preconditions for the emergence of southern demagogues at the turn of the century. Sometimes stereotyped as rednecks, hillbillies, and yokels, they embraced the traditions of the rural South and white southerners with their earthy language, exaggerated personalities, and homely dress.

Unlike the populist radicals of an earlier day, these agrarian politicians verbally attacked the power of the rich but failed to offer any political solutions to the economic and social woes of the region. Echoing the fears and grievances of the rural poor and middle classes as well as southern workers, demagogues such as Cole Blease of South Carolina and THOMAS WATSON of Georgia played on racial and religious prejudices while they used class rhetoric and the celebration of Christian white supremacy. Even those who sought to better the lives of their constituents found the way to progressive social legislation blocked by conservative state legislatures and the even more conservative judiciary. Competing with other political forces in the South, most notably rivals within the Democratic Party, southern demagogues offered greater political participation for their rural supporters but did not deliver more than symbolic representation.

As governors, congressmen, and senators, southern demagogues played a major role in state and national POLITICS. Among the best known were Pitchfork Ben Tillman of South Carolina, who was elected governor of that state in 1890. He helped to secure legislation that took the right to vote away from African-American men. Elected as senator from South Carolina in 1894, Tillman served in Congress until his death in 1925. In the aftermath of the Spanish-American War, he argued against the U.S. acquisition of the Philippines as a member of the Anti-Imperialist League. He rooted his opposition in his fear of the threat Filipinos presented to White America. While most southern demagogues echoed Tillman's racism, some also directed their concerns toward issues of education, taxes, and public improvements. Tillman himself believed that he had his greatest accomplishment in establishing a new agricultural college in South Carolina. Theodore Bilbo, known for his racist rhetoric, helped to improve the roads, lower property taxes for farmers, and increase funding for common schools in Mississippi. Cole Blease had a following among white textile workers in the Piedmont region. Others claimed to speak for white farmers and laborers. Other politicians from the South similarly identified as demagogues—men such as Jeff Davis of Arkansas, James K. Vardaman of Mississippi, and Fiddlin' Bob Taylor of Tennessee—carried the banner of white supremacy in their domestic and foreign politics.

The most famous southern demagogue of the 20th century, and the one whose popularity transcended the region, was Louisiana's Huey "Kingfish" Long. Growing up, he had heard a speech by Wild Jeff Davis of Arkansas, and he was strongly influenced by demagogues of the South. While he became the most conspicuous heir to its political legacy, Long also expressed its most radical side. His call to "Soak the Rich" and his attempt to broaden the number of his constituents who benefited from government largesse in new educational and social programs expanded his popularity beyond its rural base. Later southern politicians such as Eugene Talmadge of Georgia and George Wallace of Alabama carried the traditions of southern demagoguery into the 1960s with their staunch opposition to school integration and civil rights legislation.

See also RACE AND RACIAL CONFLICT.

Further reading: Raymond Arsenault, *The Wild Ass of the Ozarks: Jeff Davis and the Social Bases of Southern Politics* (Philadelphia: Temple University Press, 1984); Michael Kazin, *The Populist Persuasion, An American History* (New York: Basic Books, 1995).

sports

Prior to 1900, Americans participated in a variety of sporting activities, but few sports drew a large number of spectators. As men and women of all classes had more leisure time, spectator sports increased in popularity. The most popular sports of the time were BASEBALL, boxing, and football. All three sports, along with basketball and hockey, began to evolve into their current form of professional organization. At the same time, there were tensions between team owners and their employees. Professional athletes sought to exert greater control over their by forming player associations and unions. Their efforts, however, were largely unsuccessful. By 1930, owners had more power and control than they had in 1900.

The sport of football emerged in the decades following the end of the Civil War. Played initially on college campuses, the modern game developed slowly as teams altered the rules of rugby and soccer into a hybrid game that featured more scoring and physical contact. The early game of football was extremely violent. In 1909, for example, there were 33 recorded football fatalities, prompting many college presidents to question their support of the game. Despite its hazards, football had become synonymous with collegiate athletics, masculinity, and school pride by the 1920s, as it retained and even expanded its popularity.

Between 1900 and 1920, when the first professional football league emerged, there were many rule changes. None revolutionized the game more than the introduction of the forward pass. Passing greatly increased the game's popularity, and attendance skyrocketed over the next several decades. Many of the best early professional teams were located in the Midwest, with Ohio's Canton Bulldogs

Jim Thorpe kicks the football during a game in October 1912 *(Cumberland County Historical Society)*

and Massillon Tigers among the elite. Professional football players, however, rarely received wages sufficient enough to allow them to rely on the game as their only source of income. The result was that most professional squads devoted little time to practice, and they experienced frequent personnel changes, which prevented them from developing the cohesiveness of collegiate squads. Until the emergence of the American Professional Football Association in 1920 (renamed the National Football League in 1922), the collegiate game remained far more popular and competitive. With the league's formation, interest in professional football grew steadily; attendance at NFL games increased, and by 1934 it totaled 492,000.

The popularity of professional boxing also grew tremendously between 1900 and 1930 as some of the sport's most memorable figures captured the nation's attention. JACK JOHNSON was one of the most talented boxers of the time. He won the heavyweight title in 1908 when he defeated Canadian Tommy Burns, in Sydney, Australia. As the nation's first African-American heavyweight champion, Johnson was treated as a hero in the black community.

Many white boxing fans, promoters, and reporters, however, were desperate for a "Great White Hope," the white boxer who would "put Johnson back in his place." In 1910 former heavyweight champion Jim Jeffries came out of retirement for a July 4 fight for a record prize of $100,000. Johnson, at the peak of his career, put on a brilliant boxing display and knocked Jeffries out in the 15th round. News of Johnson's victory was greeted with enthusiastic celebrations in African-American communities. Johnson eventually lost the heavyweight title to Jess Willard in a controversial bout in Havana, Cuba, in 1915.

Boxing finally found its great white champion in WILLIAM HARRISON "JACK" DEMPSEY, who won the heavyweight title in 1919. Although others have had a longer reign as heavyweight champion, Dempsey's impact on the sport is hard to exaggerate. His boxing exploits were captured on film and shown to audiences across the country, giving Dempsey the kind of exposure no other fighter had ever enjoyed. Part of his popularity undoubtedly stemmed from the fact that by 1919, when he won the heavyweight title, many boxing fans were still searching for a great white champion. Jess Willard's victory over Jack Johnson in 1915 remained controversial. When the untainted, handsome, rugged, and gregarious Dempsey arrived on the scene, he was, for many white boxing fans, the right kind of champion. He held the heavyweight boxing title until 1926 when challenger Gene Tunney defeated him. The following year in a rematch, Tunney was again defeating the challenger on points when Dempsey knocked him to the canvas. After a "long count," during which Tunney had enough time to recover, he rejoined the match. He went on to win the controversial bout on points.

The spectator sport that grew most dramatically between 1900 and 1930 was professional baseball. Baseball had been played in the United States since before the Civil War. Professional leagues dated back to the formation of the National Association of Professional Base Ball Players in 1871. At that time, the sport was often in a state of chaos. Teams formed and then moved or disbanded. Players jumped from team to team in search of higher pay, often playing for numerous teams within a single year. The sport also lacked a uniform set of rules, which prevented players, managers, and gamblers from determining the outcome of games. By the 1890s, the sport had developed a sense of cohesiveness as owners of teams in the newly formed National League began to drive out competitors and secure the services of the game's best players.

A challenge to the dominance of the National League came in 1899 when the Western League renamed itself the American League. League president Ban Johnson recruited several prominent National League owners and managers who were dissatisfied with its management. The American League began to lure high-profile players away

from the National League. In 1902, the two leagues worked out an agreement that allowed both leagues to coexist and flourish. It created a National Baseball Commission consisting of the two league presidents and a neutral third party. The agreement also established rules regarding the transfer of players from one team to another and the movement of players from the minor leagues to the major leagues. Several dominant teams emerged in the period, including the New York Giants, the Chicago Cubs, the Detroit Tigers, the Boston Red Sox, and the Philadelphia Athletics. In 1903, pennant winners from each league competed in the first World Series, which the American League champion, Boston, won. The game grew tremendously in popularity, surpassing all other professional sports.

Baseball, however, continued to be plagued by scandal and corruption. Gambling and the fixing of games had been a problem in baseball and other sports, and the payoffs could be lucrative. The lure of money for fixing games was made more tempting when the 1902 agreement prevented American and National League teams from raiding players. The result was that owners had complete control over the rights of the players. The no-raiding rule prevented them from jumping to a team willing to pay more for their services. While baseball players were paid handsomely compared to the wages of many fans, they complained that owners received revenues far in excess of what they paid in salaries.

The problem of gambling came to a head in 1919 with the "Black Sox" scandal, which almost ruined the sport. That year, eight players on the American League champion Chicago White Sox accepted money from gamblers to intentionally lose the World Series to the underdog Cincinnati Reds. Each of the eight players reportedly agreed to accept $10,000 to play poorly. When the plot was uncovered, evidence of similar scams came to light; and the public began to question the integrity of the game. Realizing that the future of the game was on the line, owners moved quickly to regain public confidence. An agreement was reached in 1920 to create an independent baseball commissioner. Judge Kenesaw Mountain Landis agreed to become the sport's first commissioner. He insisted on almost dictatorial control over the game, and in 1921 he banned all eight White Sox players (whom he had acquitted for lack of evidence) from the game for life. The decision helped reestablish public confidence in the sport, but it was the emergence of the legendary Babe Ruth that put the sport back on solid footing.

Between 1920 and his retirement in 1934, Ruth dominated the sport like no player has before or since. He had been one of the game's best pitchers and hitters for the Boston Red Sox since he entered the league in 1914. In 1920, the Red Sox's financially strapped owner sold Ruth's contract to the New York Yankees for $125,000. His arrival in the New York market brought his game to a new level and catapulted him into national celebrity. Ruth excelled at every aspect of the game, but it was his tremendous home run power and off-the-field exploits that made him the country's most popular sports hero. Prior to 1920 home runs in baseball were extremely rare, with league-leaders rarely approaching double figures. In 1920, Ruth belted an amazing 54 home runs and topped that with 60 in 1927.

Other professional and amateur spectator sports either emerged or grew in popularity between 1900 and 1930. These included basketball, hockey, and golf. Invented by James Naismith in the 1880s, basketball mirrored the path of development taken by football. The amateur game emerged as a staple of college athletics and increased in popularity. The first college games were played in the 1890s, and a college rules committee was created in 1905. By 1920, most colleges and universities had established teams. At the professional level, basketball grew slowly. The National Basketball League was created in 1898. Prior to WORLD WAR I, the best professional team was the original Celtics. Support for the professional game, however, remained minimal; and few teams developed a loyal fan base until the formation of the National Basketball League in 1949.

Professional and collegiate ice hockey also grew in popularity between 1900 and 1930. Developed in the 1860s, the game first took root in Canadian colleges and universities but quickly spread to the professional level in both Canada and the United States. The Stanley Cup was first awarded to the best Canadian team beginning in 1894. The trophy began to be awarded to the best professional team with the formation of the National Hockey League (NHL) in 1917. The NHL reformed in 1925 with professional teams in Toronto, Detroit, Montreal, Chicago, Boston, and New York. Between 1900 and 1930, the sport had a sizable following in Canada, the upper Midwest, and on the East Coast, but it had not yet developed a large national audience.

Racial and gender discrimination were common features of American society between 1900 and 1930, and professional and collegiate sports were no exception. Universities, team owners, and promoters had almost complete control over who was allowed to participate. Most spectator sports excluded the participation of women and African Americans. At the turn of the century, some players of color, if their skin was light enough, were allowed to compete professionally. Native American Jim Thorpe, for example, was allowed to play collegiate and professional football. As SEGREGATION intensified, most sports rigidly enforced the color bar. Excluded from white male professional sports, women, African Americans, and other people of color formed their own teams and leagues.

African-American baseball teams toured the country as far back as the 1880s. These barnstorming teams formed the Negro National League in 1920 and the Negro Eastern League in 1921. The Negro Leagues boasted some of the game's greatest players, including Josh Gibson, Cool Papa Bell, and the legendary Satchel Paige. Though not widely supported, women competed on basketball teams as early as 1895, but the women's game did not develop a wide audience. Most women athletes remained confined to amateur sports teams in college, at work, or in the community.

Spectator sports had a profound impact on the development of modern American culture. They emphasized physical prowess, competitiveness, and passive consumerism over all other attributes. The public and the media hailed athletes as heroes. Even in the period between 1900 and 1930, professional athletes earned incomes well in excess of those enjoyed by ordinary Americans. In 1927, Babe Ruth demanded and received a salary of $100,000. Fans of spectator sports also were encouraged to be passive consumers. Prior to 1900, most local communities had semi-professional and amateur baseball and football squads. As spectator sports increased in popularity, adult participation in these sports dwindled. Attendance at virtually every professional sport increased dramatically between 1900 and 1930. Similar rates of growth occurred in collegiate spectator sports. Finally, because of the increase in the number of spectators, sports became a medium through which owners and advertisers could, by identifying a team or an individual player with a product, sell consumer goods. Product endorsement, while it would become much more prevalent in the decades following the end of World War II, began to emerge in the 1920s and helped transform professional sports into a multi-million dollar industry that exerts its influence on virtually every aspect of American life.

Further reading: John Sayle Watterson, *College Football: History, Spectacle, Controversy* (Baltimore: Johns Hopkins University Press, 2000); Carl M. Becker, *Home and Away: The Rise and Fall of Professional Football on the Banks of the Ohio, 1919–1934* (Athens: Ohio University Press, 1998); Neil D. Issacs, *Checking-Back: A History of the National Hockey League* (New York: Norton and Company, 1977).

— Robert Gordon

Standard Oil

The Standard Oil Corporation was among the largest, most influential companies in the Progressive Era. By 1900, it had established a near monopoly in the American oil production industry. JOHN D. ROCKEFELLER, a self-made entrepreneur, was the driving force behind the company.

Despite having little formal education, Rockefeller built one of the most profitable corporations in American history and helped revolutionize the nature of business. Shortly after oil was discovered in Titusville, Pennsylvania, in 1859, the Cleveland, Ohio, area became one of the centers of the oil refining industry. Within a short period of time there were dozens of competing refineries located in and around the city. In 1863, Rockefeller and his partner Maurice Clark joined the fray and established an oil refining business near Cleveland. Initially the industry was extremely chaotic. Dozens of different companies focused on isolated aspects of the production process, and all attempted to undercut the profitability of their competitors. In addition, because each aspect of production was independent, there was great inefficiency. Using the profits he made to expand his company, Rockefeller began squeezing out or buying up competing refineries.

In 1867, Rockefeller, along with his brother William Rockefeller, Samuel Andrews, Henry M. Flagler, and S. V. Harkness, pooled their resources to create the Standard Oil Corporation with a capital outlay of $1 million. By 1872, Standard Oil controlled 10 percent of the oil refining industry. Rockefeller was determined to control every aspect of the industry, including drilling, refining, transportation, sales, and distribution. He ruthlessly exploited the size of Standard Oil to force concessions and lower rates from the railroads. Once these lower rates were secured, Rockefeller was able to undercut other competitors and soon dominated the Cleveland market. By 1882, Standard Oil controlled over 90 percent of the oil refining industry. Throughout the rest of the century, Rockefeller expanded his oil empire to include ownership of oil wells, railroads, refineries, and distribution facilities throughout the country. He could set oil prices at whatever level he desired. Popular resentment about the power of new national corporations such as Standard Oil led to passage of the Sherman Antitrust Act of 1890. The legislation was intended to prevent companies from monopolizing an entire industry. In actual practice, however, the Sherman Act was invoked only infrequently and then typically directed against organized labor.

In the first decade of the 20th century, popular resentment against monopolies and trusts intensified. Muckraking journalists exposed political and corporate corruption, further fueling demands that the federal government intervene and break the power of the monopolies. In 1902, *McClure's Magazine* began publishing a series of 18 articles exposing the way in which Rockefeller built and maintained his oil empire. Written by journalist IDA M. TARBELL, *The History of Standard Oil* (1904) galvanized public and political opposition against the company and helped convince the federal government to look into possible antitrust violations. President THEODORE ROOSEVELT had promised to enforce the antitrust legislation and take an aggressive stand against illegal trusts and monopolies. In 1906, Roosevelt, claiming Standard Oil was 20 times larger than its nearest competitor, instructed the federal government to take action. The case wasn't resolved until 1911 when the Supreme Court ruled that the company had in fact violated federal antitrust laws and ordered that the company be broken into smaller, independent parts.

For a period of time, the Supreme Court's decision to break up Standard Oil had the desired impact. Even before the court ruling, it had become clear that Standard Oil's domination of the industry had begun to wane. Several new competitors entered the field before 1911, including Texaco (1902), Shell (1907), and British Petroleum (1909). By the time it was dissolved, Standard Oil controlled only 65 percent of the industry. The Supreme Court ruling against Standard Oil broke the giant into 34 smaller companies. Eventually, however, several large corporations dominated the industry. Known as the Seven Sisters, Esso, Shell, Amoco, Chevron, Atlantic Richfield, British Petroleum, and Texaco extended their control over all aspects of the industry, both in the United States and around the world.

Further reading: Glen Porter, *The Rise of Big Business, 1860–1910* (New York: Cornell, 1973); Ron Chernow, *Titan: The Life of John D. Rockefeller, Sr.* (New York: Random House, 1998).

— Robert Gordon

steel industry

By 1900, the United States had become the world's dominant steel producer. Record demand for its products in the construction of skyscrapers, ships, and railroads had made the industry the engine of the nation's ECONOMY as well. The steel industry had prospered by the dynamic growth of city construction in the 1890s. It also had drawn strength from such changes as improved and expanding urban transport systems, the rebuilding of railroads with new, heavier steel rails, and the introduction of nickel-plated steel armor on battleships during the naval rearmament efforts at the turn of the century. In each of these arenas, new technologies and methods of organization had driven out small firms and increased the demand for capital to expand and improve steel production.

The fortunes that were made in steel did not, however, guarantee the industry's profitability. Fueled by Andrew Carnegie's cutthroat methods, competition among steel firms had made the steel industry and subsidiary concerns in railroad transportation and iron, coke, and coal mining prone to sharp drops in profit, periodic recession, and market chaos. Major industrial and finance capitalists such as JOHN D. ROCKEFELLER and James Pierpont Morgan had invested in the field as a means of stabilizing their own enterprises. In the late 1890s, however, Carnegie once again threatened to undercut competitors when he moved from producing raw steel to constructing a finishing plant to make steel tubes and girders and building his own rail link from the plant to Pittsburgh. These moves directly threatened both Federal Steel, a competitor directed by Elbert Gary and financed by Morgan, and the Pennsylvania Railroad. Contacting Carnegie's superintendent, Charles Schwab, Morgan proposed a gigantic merger of Carnegie Steel with Federal Steel and a host of subsidiaries, including American Bridge and National Tube. Founded in February 1901 at the end of a decade-long merger movement in the industry, U.S. STEEL was the brainchild of Schwab and Morgan.

U.S. Steel became the nation's largest corporation with over $1.4 billion in assets and control of 65 percent of the market in steel production. It employed over 168,000 workers at the time (the number would grow to over 350,000 by 1920). Its holdings included 41 iron mines, 213 steel mills, 78 blast furnaces, 1,100 miles of rail, and 112 Great Lakes iron ore boats. The industrial empire continued to acquire new properties throughout the first three decades of the 20th century. While U.S. Steel lost some market share due to the growth of the market and new competition, especially in sheet steel, it dominated the steel industry, controlled large parts of the subsidiary economy, and had substantial influence on government at all levels.

The consolidation of steel manufacture under U.S. Steel had, however, detrimental effects on innovation in the industry. Up to 1900, Carnegie Steel had been a leader in improving the quality of open-hearth steel beams for construction. Now under the U.S. Steel Corporation name, Carnegie Steel lost its place as an industry leader. Since stability was the key goal of the U.S. Steel merger, there was little incentive for innovation. Technological change came, instead, from smaller and more marginal firms, most of which were outside the U.S. Steel combine. Midvale Steel, a subsidiary firm, was the location of FREDERICK WINSLOW TAYLOR's experiments in cutting metal and his reorganization of the labor force and production later known as SCIENTIFIC MANAGEMENT. Bethlehem Steel, a smaller firm that earlier competed with Carnegie Steel in steel beam construction and the production of armor plating, constantly worked on improving its product and became a premier government contracting firm. It reinvested its profits from WORLD WAR I defense production and became the second largest steel producer in the United States by the 1920s. Finally, in the areas of high-speed steel for machine tools and alloy, sheet and electric steel, it was the smaller start-up companies that made a difference. Automobile manufacturers, the largest consumer of domestic steel in the 1920s, experimented with producing their own steel and created the alloy steels for new models. Alloying steel with nickel, chromium, vanadium, manganese, and molybdenum made it both stronger and more flexible for molding into bumpers, fenders, and other automobile parts. Continuous sheet steel, another innovation of the period, helped to guarantee automobile makers the supply of steel they needed for body parts.

Since the cataclysmic Homestead strike of 1892, the steel industry steadily decreased its dependence on union labor and worked to drive labor union organization out of steel plants. The Amalgamated Association of Iron and Steel Workers, which originally had contracts with several major firms, was locked out of steel manufacturing plants and steadily declined in numbers and influence in the late 19th and early 20th centuries. The changing division of labor in steel factories de-skilled steel production and replaced skilled iron puddlers and boilers with semi-skilled production workers and a resulting decline in wages. This shift affected the ethnic makeup of the labor force, and the average steel worker of the early 20th century was an eastern or southern European immigrant workingman, with little formal schooling and few resources. He usually had limited English and had little recourse to employer demands. In the workplace, corporate leaders insisted that steel production in blast, Bessemer, or open-hearth furnaces required 24-hour production. While hours varied by occupation, over 60 percent of the steel labor force worked between 60 and 84 hours per week. That often meant two standard 12-hour shifts with a long turn (24-hour shift) every two weeks. Dangerous heat and heavy machinery, unstable production methods (explosions were a common occurrence), and fatigued workers led to a shockingly high rate of industrial accidents in the steel industry.

Wage cuts in the wake of industry downturns led to labor disturbances in 1907, 1909, and 1919. U.S. Steel and its competitors such as Bethlehem and Republic Steel had no intention of recognizing and bargaining with unions. With the decline of the Amalgamated union, labor conflicts in the steel industry were, for the most part, not a welcome occurrence for the weakened union. Workers protested informally and struck collectively, largely without union support. Organized under the AMERICAN FEDERATION OF LABOR, however, the STEEL STRIKE OF 1919 brought union resources to the industry. The largest segment of striking workers was, in fact, new to unionism. William Z. Foster, a radical trade unionist, and John Fitzpatrick, a Chicago trade unionist, led the drive to organize the mass-production steel industry. They had organized more than 100,000 when they began to ask for government mediation in the industry. When U.S. Steel president Elbert Gary refused to negotiate, more than 365,000 workers went out on strike in protest of the post–World War I wage cuts. Between September 1919 and January 1920, the strike held the attention of the industry and nation. U.S. Steel called on the Pennsylvania State Constabulary to repress unionism in the Pittsburgh area, and their Gary, Indiana, plants drew on local police to break up picket lines and protect replacement workers. The strike was broken, and industrial unionism in steel became moribund.

The immediate postwar crisis of unemployment had little long-term impact on the steel industry, which recovered strongly under the economic boom of the 1920s. It used the profits of wartime production to retain its dominance in the world steel market, including growing exports to Japan. At the same time, riding on the coattails of an expanding domestic automobile market, profits in steel hit record levels. U.S. Steel kept growing, even as it began to slowly trim its labor force. The automobile industry was a force for steel industry expansion, as steel continued to expand its production facilities in the Great Lakes region, especially around Detroit, and in the South. Despite its positive growth, a looming economic crisis threatened to undermine the stability and prosperity of the steel industry. Overextended credit and over-expanded production facilities allowed little room for the drop in demand in the late 1920s. Overstocked automobile manufacturers and growing unemployment suggested that the boom times of the steel industry, begun in the 1890s, were about to come to an end.

See also FOREIGN TRADE.

Further reading: William Thomas Hogan, *Economic History of the Iron and Steel Industries in the United States* (Lexington: Health, 1971); Thomas J. Misa, *A Nation of Steel: The Making of Modern America, 1865–1925* (Baltimore: Johns Hopkins University Press, 1995); William Serrin, *Homestead: The Glory and Tragedy of an American Steel Town* (New York: Random House, 1992).

Steel Strike of 1919 (1919)

The Steel Strike of 1919 was the largest of a wave of strikes that shook the country following the end of WORLD WAR I. The strike, which began on September 22, 1919, and lasted until January 8, 1920, involved 365,000 steelworkers and marked the end of the wartime labor accord. Prior to the war, the STEEL INDUSTRY was largely unorganized. Steel companies vigorously opposed unionization. They sought to keep workers divided and unionization at bay by perpetuating ethnic and racial tensions in the workplace. The strategy was very effective. During the war, however, the administration of President WOODROW WILSON wanted to prevent production delays by avoiding labor disputes. When the administration created the War Labor Board to arbitrate labor conflicts, progressives in the labor movement, including William Z. Foster, took advantage of the opening to launch a drive to organize steelworkers.

Despite efforts to organize workers, conditions in the steel industry remained harsh. Steelworkers put in an average of 68.7 hours a week, considerably more than workers in other industries. In addition, wages were low and working conditions hazardous. In 1918, Foster convinced Samuel Gompers and the AMERICAN FEDERATION OF LABOR (AFL) to launch an organizing drive among steel and ironworkers. They created the National Committee for Organizing Iron and Steel Workers, which targeted industry giant U.S. STEEL in its Gary, Indiana, and Pittsburgh, Pennsylvania, plants. The company had a long history of anti-unionism and vowed to resist the organizing effort at all costs. Despite opposition from local officials and U.S. Steel's threat to use replacement workers to break the union, the organizing committee succeeded in unionizing 100,000 steelworkers by June 1919. The effort succeeded because organizers aggressively recruited foreign-born unskilled laborers, to whom they portrayed the union as patriotic and an integral part of the fight against Kaiser Wilhelm and Germany. U.S. Steel responded by reiterating its commitment to maintaining a non-union workplace. The company fired suspected union organizers and union leaders. Its efforts backfired and greatly increased rank-and-file support for the union.

In May 1919, the National Committee demanded a significant wage increase, an eight-hour workday, the abolition of company unions, the rehiring of workers fired for union activities, and union recognition. U.S. Steel refused to negotiate with union representatives. By August 1919, the crux of the conflict centered on union recognition. Gompers believed that Wilson and the NATIONAL WAR LABOR BOARD would pressure U.S. Steel president Elbert H. Gary to keep the peace. Gary, however, informed the War Labor Board that he was unwilling to even meet with the union. When Wilson refused to pressure the company, militants criticized Gomper's faith in the War Labor Board and began preparing for a strike. Led by William Z. Foster and Chicago trade unionist John Fitzpatrick, the National Committee prepared for an all-out strike; but Gompers, worried about the reliability of unskilled, foreign-born steel workers, agreed to a request by President Wilson to postpone any labor action.

Foster and Fitzpatrick were outraged and pushed ahead with plans to launch an industry-wide strike on September 22, 1919. Response to the strike call was massive. An estimated 275,000 steelworkers walked off the job the first day and their number peaked at 365,000 the next week. U.S. Steel, the media, local officials, and the federal government responded swiftly and forcefully. Striking workers were threatened, intimidated, fired, and beaten. By the end of the walkout, 22 strikers had been killed. Many local newspapers reported that foreign-born radicals bent on undermining American society were leading the strike. Wilson and the War Labor Board stood by as local business and political leaders called on the police and militias to disperse striking workers and escort replacement workers safely inside plants. When Gompers and the AFL leadership refused to commit more support, the strike collapsed. It began to lose support among workers by December, and the National Committee officially called off the strike on January 8, 1920.

Critics of Gompers, at the time of the strike and since, maintain that massive support of the strike indicated that it could have been successful if the AFL had fully supported the action. The AFL's distrust of foreign-born unskilled workers and its preference for craft unionism ensured that the strike failed. More importantly, the AFL's reluctance to organize mass-production industries on an industrial rather than craft basis meant that the labor movement failed to capitalize on the nascent militancy and radicalism of unskilled industrial workers and ensured that the labor movement remained small and weak until the Great Depression.

See also LABOR AND LABOR MOVEMENT.

Further reading: David Brody, *Labor in Crisis: The Steel Strike of 1919* (Philadelphia: Lippincott, 1965).

— Robert Gordon

Steffens, Lincoln (1866–1936)

Born in San Francisco, California, in 1866, Lincoln Steffens was among a handful of turn-of-the-century writers and journalists collectively known as MUCKRAKERS. The son of a wealthy businessman, Steffens attended the University of California, where he became actively involved in radical politics and began writing about the rampant corruption and excess in both private and public life.

Steffens began his career in journalism in 1892 and had modest success. It was as editor of *McClure's Magazine* that Steffens established himself as one of the most influential journalists in the country. He edited *McClure's* between 1902 and 1906. Determined to make *McClure's* a financial and political success, Steffens hired a staff of progressive writers that included UPTON SINCLAIR, IDA TARBELL, and Ray Standard Baker. As editor, Steffens transformed *McClure's* into the leading political magazine in the country. Articles by Upton Sinclair exposed unsafe and unsanitary conditions in the Chicago stockyards. Ida Tarbell chronicled the unsavory way in which STANDARD OIL became one of the largest and most powerful corporations in the country. In *Shame of the Cities*, Steffens himself railed against the power of corporations and the new business elite, who, he argued, were lining their pockets, undermining democracy, and corrupting the nation's political, legal, and economic systems at the expense of the

common people. Although President THEODORE ROOSEVELT and others chaffed at the manner in which Steffens exposed corporate greed and corruption, they understood the depth of popular resentment and initiated legislative reforms. These reforms included the MEAT INSPECTION ACT (1906), the PURE FOOD AND DRUG ACT (1906), and the HEPBURN ACT (1906).

Under Steffens's leadership, sales of *McClure's* expanded, as did its influence among progressives, socialists, and political reformers. In 1906 Steffens decided to leave the magazine to form a new, more radical journal, *American Magazine*, along with Tarbell and Baker. Despite an impressive roster of writers, *American Magazine* never achieved the critical or financial success of *McClure's*. Throughout the Progressive Era, Steffens's politics continued to evolve along more radical lines, culminating with his self-exile in the Soviet Union between 1919 and 1921. Steffens's support of the Soviet experiment was ultimately short-lived. By the time he published his autobiography in 1931, he had become thoroughly disenchanted with the Soviet government.

See also JOURNALISM; PROGRESSIVISM.

Further reading: Justin Kaplan, *Lincoln Steffens: A Biography* (New York: Simon & Schuster, 1974); Lincoln Steffens, *The Autobiography of Lincoln Steffens* (New York: Harcourt, Brace & World, 1958).

— Robert Gordon

Stock Market Crash   See Volume VIII

strikes   See labor and labor movement

suburbs

American suburbs took shape during the period from 1900 to 1930. Four characteristics have made suburbs in the United States unique compared to suburbs in other countries. The first distinguishing characteristic is a low population density, a settlement pattern that Americans sought in an effort to make their lives private. The second characteristic is the desire for homeownership; a greater percentage of Americans own their own homes than in any other country. The third defining characteristic is the socioeconomic distinction between the core city and the suburbs. Those living in the suburbs tend to be wealthier and better educated than residents living in core cities. The final characteristic is the length of the journey to work. As suburbs grew, Americans accepted ever-longer commutes to and from work. These four characteristics set America apart from the rest of the world. To understand why America's suburbs have developed in this manner, one needs to look at the confluence of developments that created suburbs in the early 20th century.

The 20th-century suburb evolved through three stages determined by the dominant mode of transportation. During the late 19th century, the railroad served as the only way to reach the outer limits of a city and thus determined the settlement patterns of the suburbs. Early in the century, the electric streetcar revolutionized URBAN TRANSPORTATION and made it possible for a greater number of city residents to live outside the city center. Automobiles provided the next great change in suburbanization. Cars and the expansion of roads led to an explosion in suburban populations as the outer rings of metropolitan areas became more accessible. Transportation changes were not the only determinants of suburbanization, however. Cheaper construction methods, the availability of home mortgages, cultural changes, and public funding of transportation improvements also contributed to America's flight to the suburbs.

Suburbs arose out of people's desire to escape the city. At the turn of the century, escape was possible only for a few wealthy businessmen and their families. Due to the cost of rail transportation, which was prohibitive for most middle-class and working-class people, the rail suburbs consisted of the homes of wealthy businessmen—and workers who provided services such as gardening and domestic labor. The development of the electric streetcar profoundly affected labor. Fares were much lower on the streetcars than on the regular railroads, which made it possible for middle-class people to live in suburbs. The streetcar lines also reached more areas than the railroad, opening up new lands for housing development. In fact, urban transport companies used the streetcar lines to attract purchasers for land near to their lines.

Streetcar suburbs grew in a spoke-and-wheel pattern, with the city at the center of streetcar lines radiating out into the suburbs. This pattern of suburbanization was aided by public-funded city services. In the 1900s street-paving and other utilities such as sewers were paid for by a special assessment on those property owners living on the street being improved. In the early 20th century, influenced by the lobbying of property developers, city governments decided that paving streets would bolster commerce. Cities therefore began to tax all city residents for civic improvements. In effect, it taxed all residents for the benefit of those moving to the city's edge.

Many other developments aided the creation of American suburbs during this period. As the streetcar companies extended their lines, cheaper property became available outside cities, which made the very cheapest housing opportunities available farther outside the cities. The development of the balloon-frame house also made single-family dwellings affordable. Before the development of balloon-framing, heavy masonry columns and walls supported the weight of a house. This method of building was too expensive to use for large numbers of houses. Balloon-framing, in which a frame constructed of two-by-four boards supports the weight of the house, was much cheaper and made it economically possible for a wider section of American society to own a single-family home. Another development that aided suburban growth was the willingness of farmers to sell their land to property developers because agricultural prices had declined. It made economic sense for them to sell their land instead of continuing to farm.

New methods of financing home ownership also helped spread America's suburbs. Building and loan associations emerged during the early 20th century. Members of these associations bought shares and in return the association granted loans for its members to buy homes. By spreading the cost of a home over a number of years, building and loan associations made houses affordable for many Americans who could not afford to buy a house outright. Finally, Americans underwent a cultural change that raised the value of privacy. Suburbs appealed to those seeking to escape the crowded environment of the city. A home of one's own, set in the middle of a large yard, possibly with a hedge to screen the view from the road, provided the privacy that many sought.

The next step in the evolution of suburbs came with the rising popularity of the automobile in the 1920s. In 1905 there were 8,000 automobiles registered in the United States. By 1925 there were 17,481,001 autos registered. This tremendous increase in the number of Americans driving cars changed the suburbs. The turn to cars as the preferred mode of transportation encouraged the expansion of roads. The federal government aided local governments in expanding the road system. The 1916 Federal Aid Road Act offered matching funds to city governments that organized highway departments, and the 1921 Federal Road Act offered funds for the construction of roads. In an effort to relieve traffic congestion for commuters, state and municipal governments used these funds to pave and expand traffic arteries out of the cities and later to build "parkways." These roads limited access in an effort to maintain constant traffic speeds and, as their name implies, were meant to provide a park-like environment for the drivers, with natural settings constructed along the roadway. America's embrace of the automobile was accompanied by the decline of streetcar systems. By the 1920s streetcar systems had become unprofitable for a variety of reasons, a development that made automobile travel the preferred method of transportation.

Cars also reshaped suburban settlement patterns. By necessity, streetcar suburbs were concentrated within walking distance of streetcar lines. Automobile transportation and the expansion of roads made it possible for suburbs to grow anywhere. Thus, suburban settlement began to fill in the spaces between streetcar lines, altering the spoke-and-wheel settlement pattern. Because land was cheaper in the areas between streetcar lines, the inhabitants could afford larger pieces of property, which gave rise to the uniquely American pattern of a single-family home sitting in the middle of a large yard. It further deepened the disparity in population density between the cities and suburbs.

Trucks also played an important role in America's suburbanization by making industrial suburbs possible. During the era of rail transportation, manufacturers concentrated within the central area of the city, close to rail lines, because the only way to transport large amounts of goods was by rail. The expansion of the road systems made it possible to use trucks to transport goods. Businesses jumped at the opportunity afforded by the truck, because land was cheaper in the suburbs than in the city. As industry moved out of the city, workers followed, which helped the dispersal of population to the suburbs.

By 1930, America's suburbs had evolved into the pattern familiar today. It is important to remember that suburbanization occurred through the actions of many different interests. It was not accidental. Developers, automobile companies, street car companies, reformers, individual citizens, and government officials all acted to create the American suburb.

See also AUTOMOBILE INDUSTRY; CITIES AND URBAN LIFE.

Further reading: Kenneth Jackson, *Crabgrass Frontier: The Suburbanization of the United States* (New York: Oxford University Press, 1985).

— Michael Hartman

Sullivan, Louis H.   See Volume VI

Sunday, William Ashley, Jr. (Billy Sunday)
(1862–1935)
Billy Sunday was one of the foremost evangelical ministers of his era. Like many clergymen of the time, his sermons were build upon a combination of devotion to Christ and dedication to hard work and social responsibility. His ability to overcome adversity led him to believe, and then preach, that moral fortitude was the principle prerequisite for success.

Billy's life was one of hardship and challenge. Just three weeks after his birth, his army father, Private William Ashley Sunday, died of pneumonia. His mother, Mary Jane Corey, kept the Sunday family together for the next nine

years. Then in 1872, abject poverty forced Mary Jane to send her two sons, Billy and Edward, to the Civil War Soldier's Orphans Home in Glenwood, Iowa. The Soldier's Orphans Home was the first but not the last orphanage for Billy. For almost a decade, he and his brother bounced from orphanage to orphanage.

Sunday was an extremely talented athlete. In 1880, two months before his 18th birthday, he took the first step toward making baseball a career. He was recruited by the Marshalltown Fire Brigade, a voluntary firemen's organization and team. After a short stint with the Brigade, Billy was drafted by the Chicago White Stockings, and his career as a professional baseball player began. His early career was rather inauspicious; but while he was never a starter in Chicago, he managed to stay with the White Stockings for five years. When he was traded to the Pittsburgh Pirates in 1887, Sunday's career took off, and he was elevated to the starting lineup. As his skills grew, so did his salary and status.

Despite Sunday's athletic success and good salary, he was convinced that something was missing from his life. In 1886 he began to see what that might be. It was then that

William Ashley Sunday, Jr. *(Library of Congress)*

he converted to the Christian faith. A short time later, during a visit to the Pacific Grove Mission, he realized his passion for the gospel and devotion to teaching. Within a few months, Sunday began teaching at the Jefferson Park Presbyterian Church and offering programs at the Chicago YOUNG MEN'S CHRISTIAN ASSOCIATION (YMCA). His abilities as a public speaker made him one of the most popular in the area. At the end of the 1886 baseball season, Billy met Helen Amelia Thompson at a church social. After a short courtship, the couple was married. Helen changed Billy's life. She reinforced his devotion to RELIGION and helped to persuade him to continue this education. It was likely Helen who influenced him to enroll in classes at Evanston Academy on the campus of Northwestern University. While taking classes, Sunday coached local students on the fundamentals of baseball.

It was not long after the couple married that Sunday began to question his future as a baseball player. Even though both Philadelphia and Cincinnati had offered him more money than he had made in either Pittsburgh or Chicago, he decided to end his career as a professional baseball player and devote himself to spreading the word of the Lord. He accepted a job with the YMCA paying a mere $1,000 a year, significantly less that the $3,500 that he would have earned playing baseball during the seven-month season. Leaving baseball was a crucial step in Billy's personal, professional, and spiritual development. Sunday apprenticed himself to Reverend J. Wilburn Chapman, a renowned evangelist, in 1884. After working with Chapman for two years, Sunday ventured out on his own. From January 1896 through November 1907, he preached in approximately 70 different communities.

One of Sunday's greatest talents was his ability to reach men and women from different social and economic backgrounds. He was close to many of America's elite. JOHN D. ROCKEFELLER, Jr., became one of his close friends. His friendships with wealthy philanthropists, however, did not make him unapproachable to those on the lower rungs of the ladder. Due in part to his rural upbringing, Sunday retained the ability to speak in a language that farmers could understand. This ease and comfort did not, however, translate to all classes. He often found it difficult to empathize with industrial workers and city dwellers.

Sunday's sermons went beyond scripture. At times they were overtly political. As a devout member of the REPUBLICAN PARTY, Sunday was often criticized for attacking organized labor. He increasingly focused on redeeming American cities from what he believed to be moral sickness. He especially hated what he saw as an urban propensity toward drink. After 1907, he preached his famous booze sermon, "Get on the Water Wagon," at least once in every city that he visited. Until his death, Sunday remained convinced that the moral weakness of the urban poor, not the economic system, was the source of pain and discomfort in American cities.

Sunday's life was highlighted by success in athletics and the ministry, but his life was far from charmed. He was viewed by many as a hypocrite and a money monger. His relationship with his family suffered from prolonged absences. And he was often associated with the extreme views of men such as William Jennings Bryan. In the later years of Sunday's life, his message and style began to lose its appeal. In the early decades of the 20th century, religious liberalism and the Social Gospel arose to challenge conservative Christian churches. With the onset of movies and radio, Sunday soon found his popularity waning, but until his death on November 6, 1935, he remained one of the most influential evangelists on the scene.

Further reading: Lyle W. Dorsett, *Billy Sunday and the Redemption of Urban America* (Grand Rapids, Mich.: W. B. Eerdmans, 1991).

— Steve Freund

T

Taft, William Howard (1857–1930)

Often referred to as the "Reluctant President," William Howard Taft was the 27th president of the United States. Taft was born in Cincinnati, Ohio, on September 15, 1857. Taft's father was himself a politician and served as secretary of war and attorney general under Ulysses S. Grant. Growing up and as a young man, Taft preferred law to politics. He attended Yale University and graduated in 1878. He then attended Cincinnati Law School and joined the bar in 1880. For the next decade, Taft practiced law in Cincinnati. A large man, 6 feet, 4 inches tall, he weighed more than 300 pounds during his presidency. He was easygoing and hardworking. He made friends easily and quickly earned a reputation for honesty and personal morality. Taft also preferred quiet and stability, tended to procrastinate, and lacked the ability to inspire or motivate audiences. At a time when political scandals and corruption were common, Taft's reputation enabled him to win appointment to increasingly important judicial positions and the support of Ohio's REPUBLICAN PARTY

Taft's first important break came in 1887, when, at the age of 29, he was appointed to the Ohio superior court. From the early days of his professional career, Taft's goal was to become a member of the U.S. Supreme Court. Though heavily involved in the Ohio Republican Party, he had little interest in running for political office. Taft served on the U.S. Sixth Court of Appeals between 1892 and 1900. During that time, his judicial rulings were mixed. On several occasions, he ruled against organized labor, upholding a lower court injunction against a railroad strike and a ruling declaring secondary boycotts illegal. On the other hand, Taft supported in principle the right of workers to join unions and to conduct strikes.

Though Taft was more comfortable in the courtroom, his wife, Helen Herron, encouraged him to seek political office. Taft's political career began in 1900 when President William McKinley appointed him to oversee the formation of a government in the Philippines and named Taft its first civil governor a year later. During his tenure, Taft created an efficient administration, free from corruption. As civil governor, he established a system of public education and convinced the Catholic Church to sell small plots of land to Filipino farmers. Largely as a result of his success, President THEODORE ROOSEVELT chose Taft to be his secretary of war in 1904. Between 1904 and 1908, he and Roosevelt became strong political allies. When Roosevelt, nearing the end of his second term in office, decided not to seek reelection, he chose Taft to be his successor. Taft was initially reluctant; but at the urging of his wife, family members, and supporters, he agreed to seek the Republican nomination, which he easily won. In the general election, Taft faced Democrat William Jennings Bryan. During the presidential campaign, Taft promised to adhere to the policies established by the popular Roosevelt. Taft defeated Bryan, winning the popular vote 7,679,114 to 6,410,665 and the Electoral College vote 321 to 162.

During his only term in office, Taft was largely ineffective and personally very unhappy. From the outset, Taft aligned himself with the Republican Party's conservative Old Guard. Led by Speaker of the House JOSEPH CANNON, the Old Guard opposed progressives in their party who wanted the federal government to play a more active role in society. Unlike Roosevelt, Taft did not believe in using the power of the presidency or the federal government to push legislative reforms or achieve social equality. Still, while in office, Taft signed several significant pieces of legislation, including the MANN-ELKINS ACT, which increased railroad regulation, and furthered Roosevelt's trust-busting agenda by continuing Justice Department investigations of antitrust violations. At the same time, divisions began to emerge in the Republican Party as early as 1909 during the debate over the PAYNE-ALDRICH TARIFF ACT. Wisconsin senator ROBERT M. LA FOLLETTE and other midwesterners were vehemently opposed to the tariff, because they believed that it kept prices artificially high and benefited primarily large corporations and eastern financial markets.

William Howard Taft *(Library of Congress)*

When Taft called for a special session of Congress to deal with tariffs, he originally intended to have them lowered. However, the final version of the Payne-Aldrich Tariff did the exact opposite. When Taft signed the tariff, he created a split in the party.

Between 1909 and 1911 a series of controversies deepened the divide between progressives and conservatives in the Republican ranks. In 1909 Taft fired the progressive head of the U.S. Forest Service and long-time Roosevelt supporter, GIFFORD PINCHOT, after he disagreed with Secretary of the Interior Richard Ballinger. Hoping to galvanize progressive opposition to Taft and the Old Guard, Pinchot had deliberately provoked a conflict. His firing angered Roosevelt and convinced many progressives of the need to support a different candidate in the 1912 election. In August 1910, Roosevelt delivered a speech criticizing Taft and laying out the idea of the NEW NATIONALISM, which provided the basis for his 1912 presidential campaign.

Finally, in the 1910 elections, Taft and the Old Guard Republicans attempted to unseat or block the nominations of congressional progressives, convincing La Follette to form the National Progressive Republican League. As the popularity of the league grew and the intensity of La Fol-

lette's attacks on Taft's lack of leadership intensified, Taft and Roosevelt realized that the dissidents would be a force to be reckoned with in the election of 1912. Initially Roosevelt refused to publicly side with either Taft or the progressive dissidents, but Roosevelt soon announced that he would seek the Republican nomination. Taft felt personally betrayed by Roosevelt. Now being publicly attacked by his mentor, Taft refused to give in. He began touring the country, criticizing both Roosevelt and La Follette. In so doing, he secured the support of enough delegates to the 1912 Republican convention that he was able to defeat Roosevelt's bid to win the nomination. Convinced that they could defeat Taft and the Democratic nominee, WOODROW WILSON, dissidents in the Republican Party formed the PROGRESSIVE PARTY. At their convention in August 1912, they selected Roosevelt as their presidential nominee and California governor HIRAM W. JOHNSON as their vice presidential candidate.

Taft attempted to rally the Republican Party's conservative base in order to stave off defections to the Progressive Party, but his campaign failed to generate much enthusiasm. The election of 1912 was tightly contested. The Progressives hoped they could lure enough votes away from both parties to secure a victory. In the end, though Roosevelt easily outpolled Taft, the party failed to make significant inroads with Democratic voters. Wilson received 6,293,000 votes, Roosevelt 4,119,000, and Taft 3,484,000. The electoral vote was even more decisive with Wilson receiving 435 votes, Roosevelt 88, and Taft 8.

After his defeat in the 1912 election, Taft accepted a position teaching constitutional law at Yale University. During WORLD WAR I, he served on the NATIONAL WAR LABOR BOARD. Following the war's conclusion, he became a strong supporter of the LEAGUE OF NATIONS. In 1921, Taft realized his life-long dream when President WARREN G. HARDING appointed him chief justice of the Supreme Court. Taft served on the high court until his retirement in 1930. During his tenure as chief justice, he made important strides in modernizing the Court and improving its efficiency. Taft's failing health forced him to retire from the Court in February 1930, and he died a month later.

See also DOLLAR DIPLOMACY.

Further reading: Judith Icke Anderson, *William Howard Taft: An Intimate History* (New York: Norton, 1981); Paolo Coletta, *The Presidency of William Howard Taft.* (Lawrence: University of Kansas Press, 1973).

— Robert Gordon

Tarbell, Ida Minerva (1857–1944)

Born in Erie County, Pennsylvania, in 1857, Ida Tarbell was one of the nation's first influential female reporters. After studying biology and graduating from Allegheny College in 1880, Tarbell did not intend to become a journalist; but as she struggled to find work as a teacher, she began writing articles to support herself. Concerned that modern day political machines and laissez-faire capitalism were undermining traditional American values, Tarbell committed herself to rooting out and exposing corruption. In 1891 she moved to Paris, where she met S. S. McClure, future owner of *McClure's Magazine.*

Tarbell joined the staff of *McClure's* when it was created in 1894. Labeled MUCKRAKERS, she and other reform journalists LINCOLN STEFFENS, UPTON SINCLAIR, and Ray Stannard Baker turned their attention to the increasing power of corporations and corruption in government. Tarbell began an in-depth investigation of JOHN D. ROCKEFELLER, owner of the nation's largest and most profitable corporation, STANDARD OIL. Between 1902 and 1904, Tarbell wrote a series of articles that exposed the lengths to which Rockefeller went to build and maintain his oil empire. Published in 1904 as *The History of the Standard Oil Company,* Tarbell's expose outraged people throughout the country and contributed greatly to the 1911 Supreme Court decision to dismantle the company for its violation of the 1890 Sherman Antitrust Act. It marked the first time federal antitrust laws had been enforced against an influential national corporation. Tarbell also became a staunch critic of the KU KLUX KLAN and the lynching of African Americans. In the pages of *McClure's,* she spoke out against racism and lynching frequently and eloquently. In 1906, Tarbell, Steffens, Baker, and others left *McClure's* to create the more radical journal, *American Magazine,* where she served as editor until its demise in 1915. Although Tarbell was reluctant to embrace the WOMAN SUFFRAGE movement and held traditional views about the role of women in society inconsistent with her public career, she inspired an entire generation of female reporters and helped to change the shape of American public life.

Further reading: Kathleen Brady, *Ida Tarbell: Portrait of a Muckraker* (New York: Seaview/Putnam, 1984); Robert C. Kochersberger, *More Than a Muckraker: Ida Tarbell's Lifetime in Journalism* (Knoxville: University of Tennessee Press, 1994).

— Robert Gordon

tariffs

As a tax on imports, tariffs have been used in the United States to aid and develop the nation's industrial and agricultural sectors since the nation's founding. For this reason, though, politicians frequently have used the tariff to gain political advantage from certain sectors of American society. The central debate in struggles to adjust the tariff has

been whether to protect manufacturing and agricultural interests by keeping the tariff rate high in order to minimize foreign competition or to aid consumers with a low tariff that would help keep the price of consumer goods low. Frequent tariff debates have contributed to long-standing struggle over the role of the federal government in the development of the nation's economy. For President Abraham Lincoln and subsequent Republican administrations, high tariff duties became the principle strategy to aid and assist industrial development. According to President Benjamin Harrison, "the protective system . . . has been a mighty instrument for the development of the national wealth." In contrast, the DEMOCRATIC PARTY, as the advocate of states' rights, frequently attacked the protective tariff and called instead for freer trade.

During the late 19th century, a protective tariff was put into place with the passage of the McKinley Tariff of 1890. But as the nation began to face growing concern over the increasing power held by the corporate elite, the tariff became a target of attack for many progressive reformers. Progressives considered protective tariffs a major factor in the consolidation of economic power that had contributed to the decline of competition in the American marketplace. Instead of protective tariffs, progressives argued for a revenue tariff that allowed the federal government to generate needed revenues but did not close the market to less-expensive imported goods. Despite advocating a progressive agenda during his presidential campaign, once in office, President WILLIAM HOWARD TAFT quickly annoyed many progressives when he signed the PAYNE-ALDRICH TARIFF ACT in 1909. The chair of the Senate Finance Committee, Nelson W. Aldrich, guided through Congress a bill that drastically revised and enlarged the tariff on more than 800 items. The tariff caused an acrimonious debate to emerge, with midwestern Republicans charging that the legislation was a throwback to the days when the REPUBLICAN PARTY served the interests of industry without question. By signing the bill, Taft quickly alienated the progressive wing of his party and caused it to split, with the formation of the PROGRESSIVE PARTY by the next presidential election.

Shortly after entering the White House, Taft's successor, WOODROW WILSON, aggressively attempted to address the problem of economic power that the nation had been debating for some 20 years. Topping his list of reforms was the need for tariff revision. Progressives had long advocated a reduction in tariff rates as a way to undercut the economic power of trusts, but they had not prevailed in this endeavor until Wilson took office. As one of his first policy efforts, Wilson pushed for a lowering of the tariff rates in the United States. From the prevailing average of 40 percent, the UNDERWOOD-SIMMONS TARIFF ACT of 1913 pared rates down to an average of 25 percent. The legislation reduced the import duty on over 900 items, raised them on only 86, and left some 300 items untouched. Because the new tariff legislation especially targeted trust-dominated industries, the Democrats strongly felt that this new tariff would spur competition and reduce prices for consumers by opening protected American markets for foreign products.

With the return of Republicans to the White House in 1921, President WARREN G. HARDING's administration set about restoring many traditional Republican policies, among them a tax cut and a protective tariff. Harding's secretary of the treasury, ANDREW W. MELLON, strongly advocated that both these policies be adopted shortly after the administration entered office. WORLD WAR I had allowed the chemical and metal industries to develop a number of innovative technologies; and they, along with Mellon, argued for protective tariffs to allow them further to develop. The FORDNEY-MCCUMBER TARIFF of 1922 increased tariff rates on chemical and metal products as a safeguard against the revival of German industries, which had dominated these sectors of the international economy prior to the outbreak of hostilities in Europe in 1914.

The global economy witnessed significant changes with the First World War. Accordingly, the imposition of a new protective tariff in the United States had far-reaching consequences that had not previously been imagined by the federal government. In particular, the change of the United States from a debtor to a creditor nation made the international economy increasingly dependent on American investment for economic development, As a result, the onset of economic crisis in 1929 was aggravated by the passage of yet another protective tariff in the United States in 1930. American economic policies had far-reaching ramifications. Given the large war debts and investment loans that European nations owed the United States, there was a vested interest in open movement of capital and goods throughout the international economy. The Tariff Act of 1930, also known as the Hawley-Smoot Tariff, accelerated economic decline both at home and abroad. The tariff was the result of domestic political pressures. Because the agricultural sector of the American economy experienced economic decline during the decade of the 1920s, farmers had become increasingly vocal in their demand for a protective high tariff that would reduce the amount of competition that farmers faced from foreign agricultural products.

With the collapse of the stock market in 1929, Congress responded by enacting the Hawley-Smoot Tariff in 1930, which increased the tariff on 75 foreign agricultural products and on some 925 manufactured goods. Many industrialists and farmers convinced the Republican-controlled Congress that protection was the remedy to the economic crisis that was unfolding as the United States entered the 1930s. Despite strong reservations from economists, President Herbert Hoover signed the legisla-

tion into law. With ad valorem duties from 32 to 40 percent, the highest tariff rate in American history, it effectively closed the domestic market to foreign goods. In response, the United States' trading partners retaliated by imposing their own high tariffs to minimize competition from American products in their respective economies, and the economic crisis deepened.

Further reading: Edward S. Kaplan, *Prelude to Trade Wars: American Tariff Policy, 1890–1922* (Westport, Conn.: Greenwood, 1994); Frank Taussig, *The Tariff History of the United States,* 7th ed. (New York: G.P. Patnam's Sons, 1923).

— David R. Smith

Taylor, Frederick Winslow (1856–1915)

Born into an affluent family, Frederick W. Taylor grew up in comfort in Germantown, Pennsylvania. His father, Franklin, was an attorney. After spending three years in Europe, Frederick entered the Phillips Exeter Academy, a preparatory school. After he graduated, he was accepted by Harvard University, but his poor health and eyesight prevented him from enrolling. He then became an apprentice machinist and pattern maker, the beginning of a career that would lead him to fame as the father of SCIENTIFIC MANAGEMENT. After finishing his apprenticeship in 1878, he took courses in mechanical engineering from Stevens Institute of Technology and earned his degree in 1883.

Taylor worked full time at Midvale Steel Company while he pursued his degree. His first position was tool clerk, the person responsible for keeping time records, and he quickly rose to become gang boss or superintendent. In this position, he became concerned over worker soldiering, or doing only the minimum amount of work required. He instilled a system of differential pay to get more out of his workmen, paying more to those who exceeded a pre-determined goal. When they rebelled with minor sabotage, he made them pay for the repairs. Taylor improved efficiency by developing a command and control system based upon what he called functional foremen, or people assigned to oversee a particular task. He also began time and motion studies, using hidden stopwatches and specially designed forms, to determine the amount of work that could be accomplished during a prescribed time.

Taylor's most famous human engineering experiment was with pig iron handlers at the Bethlehem Steel Corporation. Working in teams, pig iron handlers lifted 92-pound pigs, or slabs of iron, from a pile and carried them onto railroad cars. When Taylor began his study, the handlers moved an average of 12.8 tons per man per day. After watching a gang work at maximum speed, Taylor determined the proper amount to be 47 tons of iron per person per day. Providing workers with precise instruction on how to perform the job as determined by time-motion studies, and motivating them with differential pay, he had workers exceed that goal. One, Henry Knolle, lifted and carried 68.3 tons of iron in one day and received in return $2.57.

Borrowing heavily from other business theorists, Taylor developed a complex method of cost accounting to complete his system of detailed analysis of every operation in a plant. Critics complained that his management system reduced workers to mere cogs in a machine. They also argued that it was simply a way of driving people beyond their endurance. Taylor's admirers, however, noted that he called for high wages and wanted people to work smarter, not harder. The debate over Taylor's management techniques tends to obscure his inventive nature. He held 45 patents ranging from high-speed steel cutting tools to golf clubs and tennis rackets. His influence, though, spread beyond the industry. Scientific management became the watchword for reform in city government, social agencies, and businesses, and changed the way work in general was organized.

Further reading: Daniel Nelson, *Frederick W. Taylor and the Rise of Scientific Management* (Madison: University of Wisconsin Press, 1980).

— Harold W. Aurand

Teapot Dome

In his 1920 election pledge to "return to normalcy," WARREN G. HARDING promised voters he would end the pervasive intervention and regulation of the Wilson era. By bringing order to the federal government through such legislation as the BUDGET AND ACCOUNTING ACT and cleaning up such problems as the UNITED STATES SHIPPING BOARD, Harding sought to establish his administration on stable footing. It would eschew reform in favor of honest government. By 1923, however, Harding's hands-off administration was beginning to show a different side. Rumors of misdeeds at the VETERANS BUREAU, gossip about Attorney General Harry Daugherty, and the illegal leasing of government oil lands in a corruption scandal that became known as Teapot Dome began to trouble the president. Many afterward thought that the stress had contributed to his early death.

In 1921, the newly elected president appointed Albert Fall to be secretary of the Department of the Interior, a position with vast authority over federal lands and the nation's natural resources. Unsympathetic to conservation policy, Fall was not a popular choice to head the Interior Department. Conservationists feared that his first act would be to transfer the right to log the nation's vast forest reserves to private lumber companies. Instead, Fall had

his eye on the oil on Native American reservations and in the naval reserves. The General Leasing Act of 1920 had authorized the secretary of the navy to grant private leases on naval reserve land at his discretion. This left the door open for Fall to intervene. First, however, he declared that the Leasing Act applied to reservations for Native Americans, which were under the authority of the Bureau of Indian Affairs (and hence of the Interior Department). Over 22 million acres of reservation land, Fall determined, would now be open for exploration and drilling. There was widespread opposition to this move. The Indian Rights Association and the American Indian Defense Association, along with organizations such as the General Federation of Women's Clubs, led the charge, labeling Fall's actions outright theft. The leasing plan was soon halted.

Next, having convinced the navy secretary to transfer authority over the oil reserve to the Interior Department, Fall proceeded to lease the oil fields to the highest bidder. Without consulting Congress or the administration, Fall illegally granted leases to develop the naval oil reserves in Salt Creek, Wyoming (also known as Teapot Dome), and at Elk Hills, California, to oil industry magnates Harry Sinclair and Edward Doheny. In exchange for gifts amounting to nearly a half-million dollars, including a $100,000 "loan" for Fall's Three Rivers ranch and $200,000 in bonds, Fall signed over the leases without public bidding. Doheny's Pan American Petroleum and Transportation Company expected to net 250 million barrels of oil from the Elk Hills reserve, netting a profit of about $100 million. Sinclair's Mammoth Oil Company had similar hopes for Teapot Dome. In 1923, as rumors began to circulate about Fall's private deals, he resigned from the Interior Department and accepted employment with Sinclair's Mammoth Oil Company. The Senate Committee on Public Lands began investigating the leases in 1924. They uncovered evidence of the oil companies' gifts and loans to Fall, and they charged him with graft. A Justice Department investigation led to his indictment and conviction. He was sentenced to a year in the Santa Fe prison and fined $100,000.

In the context of the conservative preference for private investment and corporate development, Fall's willingness to sign oil leases, both on naval reserve lands and in his thwarted attempt to access Native American lands, could be seen as business-as-usual. The Republican Harding administration did not give priority to either conservation of natural resources or preservation. It was the way in which Fall accepted loans and other cash payments for exclusive leases that incensed his critics. By denying the general public the right to bid on the naval reserves and accepting what amounted to bribes, Secretary Fall was guilty of graft and corruption.

The first cabinet officer to ever be convicted of a crime, Albert Fall also was the only government appointee of the Harding administration whose acts were punished to the full extent of the law. Both Attorney General Harry Daugherty and Veterans Bureau director Charles Forbes faced public approbation but little in the way of punishment. The scandals of the Harding administration, however, had little or no effect on the REPUBLICAN PARTY in subsequent elections. The lack of public furor over governmental corruption may be due to the fact that Harding died in office. There was no evidence of his personal involvement, although he most certainly knew of Forbes's graft and Daugherty's misconduct. The investigations by Montana senator Burton K. Wheeler, who used the hearings as a pulpit to criticize Republican policies, also were perceived as politically motivated. Neither the progressive wing of the Republican Party nor the Democrats were able to make political gain from Teapot Dome and the public disgrace of Harding administration's appointees.

Further reading: Robert K. Murray, *The Harding Era: Warren G. Harding and His Administration* (Minneapolis: University of Minnesota Press, 1969).

Terrell, Mary Eliza Church (1863–1954)

One of an exceptional generation of African-American leaders, including Ida B. Wells-Barnett and MARY MCLEOD BETHUNE, Mary Church Terrell was born in Memphis, Tennessee. The first of two children, Mary (Mollie) was the daughter of Louisa Ayers, the owner of a beauty parlor, and Robert Reed Church, a real estate investor and the first African-American millionaire in the postwar South. After her parents' divorce, Mary went to school in Ohio. She graduated from the classics course at Oberlin College in 1884.

Mary Church returned to Memphis, where her father expected her to act in the role of hostess at social events. Tired of the social round, she took a job teaching at Wilberforce University in Ohio and later moved to Washington, D.C. There, she taught at the M Street School, interrupting her teaching for a two-year stint touring Europe. In 1891, she married Robert Heberton Terrell, who had been principal at the M Street School and a lawyer. He became a justice of the peace and later a municipal judge in Washington, D.C. Mary Church and Robert Terrell had four children, only one of whom, a daughter, Phyllis, born in 1898, survived infancy. They later adopted her brother's daughter, Mary.

For the next few decades, Mary Terrell became deeply involved in community affairs. She devoted much of her energy to the causes of WOMAN SUFFRAGE, racial equality, and education. She served in a range of offices both in government and in voluntary associations. From 1895 to 1901

and 1906 to 1911, she sat on the District of Columbia School Board. In 1896, she was elected president of the NATIONAL ASSOCIATION OF COLORED WOMEN, which had only recently been founded. In 1901, she was named honorary president for life.

Terrell was a prolific newspaper and magazine writer. Much in demand as a public speaker, she lectured on such topics as "The Progress of Colored Women" for the NATIONAL AMERICAN WOMAN SUFFRAGE ASSOCIATION as well as speaking on lynching, racial inequality, and disenfranchisement. A light-skinned woman, she could and did pass as white during her travels, but she felt humiliated by the rituals of SEGREGATION. Much of her anger was muted, however, by a personal style that repressed emotions. During WORLD WAR I, Terrell worked as a clerk in the government, despite her own distaste for its segregated policies. She also picketed the White House for the NATIONAL WOMAN'S PARTY and sat on the executive committee of the WOMEN'S INTERNATIONAL LEAGUE FOR PEACE AND FREEDOM. After suffrage was gained in 1920, Terrell mobilized African-American women voters for the Republican National Committee and worked on individual campaigns. After her husband's death in 1925, Terrell dedicated her time to writing, speaking, and organizing in the civil rights cause.

In the last years of her life, Terrell was more outspoken with her protests. Struggling against both racial segregation and women's inequality, she became a role model for women and young African Americans. Breaking the color bar in women's organizations, she realized how much further there was to travel. In the 1950s, she helped lead the fight to desegregate public restaurants in Washington, D.C. Terrell died in 1954 at age 90. Terrell's career marked the coming of age of black women's political activism and their new role in civil society.

See also RACE AND RACIAL CONFLICT; WOMEN'S STATUS AND RIGHTS.

Further reading: Paula Giddings, *Where and When I Enter: The Impact of Black Women on Race and Sex in America* (New York: Morrow, 1984); Mary Church Terrell, *A Colored Woman in a White World* (Washington, D.C.: National Association of Colored Women, 1968).

Tin Pan Alley

Known as the center of the sheet MUSIC publishing industry, the district of Tin Pan Alley in New York became synonymous with popular music in the early 20th century. It fostered the talents of some of America's greatest songwriters, including GEORGE GERSHWIN and Irving Berlin, popularized music in a wide range of styles from dance tunes to Broadway musicals, and familiarized American audiences with African-American music in its adoption of ragtime rhythms and blues themes. The first successful Tin Pan Alley tunes came from the pen of Charles K. Harris, whose song, "After the Ball," became a success in 1892, when it sold over 75,000 copies. Early Tin Pan Alley songwriters were seen as seedy, dissolute, and disreputable Bohemians. They were constantly on the road, visiting 60 joints a week to plug song music. While one music publisher remarked,"the best songs came from the gutter in those days," the pattern quickly changed. Increasingly after 1900, popular song music came from different sources, including musical composers like George M. Cohan, professionally trained musicians like Gershwin, and popular songwriter Irving Berlin. Music publishers enjoyed enormous success in popular terms, having created new markets by plugging songs both in popular venues like saloons and music halls and on the VAUDEVILLE and touring show circuits. Stage performers boosted sheet music sales, and new mediums, such as wax cylinder and, later, phonograph recordings, also increased the demand.

Between 1892 and 1905, Tin Pan Alley music publishers enjoyed great success with over 16 best-selling songs, including still familiar standards like "In the Good Old Summertime" (1902), "Sweet Adeline" (1903), and "In the Shade of the Old Apple Tree" (1905). Using a brief piano opening, the songs launched into romantic narratives, many to a waltz rhythm and a repeating chorus. Other anthems, such as novelty songs like "Under the Bamboo Tree" (1902), folk songs, and new ragtime music reached popular audiences through the sheet music of Tin Pan Alley. While African-American songwriters received little attention from the music publishers, ragtime music influenced songwriters such as Berlin, who softened its rhythms in the popular "Alexander's Ragtime Band," published in 1911. With the advent of vaudeville and Broadway musical comedies in the work of Cohan and Gershwin, sheet music linked New York, the epicenter of popular culture, to the rest of the nation. The coming of RADIO, however, eroded the market for sheet music, as did the continued expansion of the music recording industry and the new popularity of sound motion pictures. Increased labor costs and a paper shortage further undermined the cheap prices and large market that had made the rise of Tin Pan Alley possible. By the 1920s, the market for sheet music and the district itself was in decline.

See also ENTERTAINMENT, POPULAR.

Further reading: David Ewen, *The Life and Death of Tin Pan Alley: The Golden Age of American Popular Music* (New York: Funk and Wagnalls, 1964), Nicholas Tawa, *The Way to Tin Pan Alley: American Popular Song, 1866–1910* (New York: Schirmer, 1990).

trade, foreign

Throughout the history of the United States, foreign trade has played a critical role in the nation's development. Between the opening of the 20th century and the economic collapse of the 1930s, foreign trade became increasingly important as the United States emerged as one of the most powerful nations in the world. This power, however, was economic and not military. In 1900, few European nations feared military invasion by the United States. Rather, they found fault with the increasing dominance of U.S.-made goods and America's multinational corporations. Statistics that reveal the growing importance of foreign trade to the ECONOMY of the United States are impressive, but they tell only part of the story. Equally important was the perception or belief that the continued economic vitality of the nation rested on the very presence of external markets. Accordingly, much of the nation's FOREIGN POLICY agenda during the period between 1900 and 1930 was aimed at maintaining an open door to markets deemed vital to the economic interests of the United States.

On the eve of the Civil War, the United States had a significant trade deficit. In 1860, the country imported some $354 million worth of goods while exporting only $316 million. Although it had experienced annual trade imbalances throughout its history, the trend began to reverse course in the 1870s. By 1897, the nation imported nearly double the volume of goods that it had in 1860, but exports had more than tripled to $1.03 billion. The United States had turned an important corner in its economic development that would allow it to achieve world economic supremacy during the 20th century. In tripling the value of its exports, the United States steadily captured an increasing share of the world market in trade. In 1868 the United States controlled approximately 6 percent of world trade; by 1913, this figure had increased to 13 percent. Not only had the United States increased its market share of world trade, but also the increase in exports was almost entirely accounted for by industrial products after 1900.

The growth of exports was an amazing development, especially given the stiff opposition that it encountered from European nations prior to WORLD WAR I. According to many business leaders, overproduction and insufficient markets had caused the economic crises of the 1890s. Only by securing foreign markets, they argued, could the United States achieve stability. However, it was not the only nation looking for foreign markets. The early 1900s was an era of competition between industrial nations for access and control of raw materials and markets for finished industrial products. American manufacturers were largely able to overcome many of these hurdles (e.g., tariff walls) through the sheer wealth of many corporations that allowed them to launch aggressive ADVERTISING campaigns that promoted their products and their ability to control transportation costs. For example, an enterprise such as the United Fruit Company built and operated its own ships, which allowed it to better control costs.

American companies benefited from the direct assistance of the federal government as well. Foremost in this support was the protection afforded American shipping by the growing power of the U.S. Navy. President THEODORE ROOSEVELT often said that the United States needed to "Speak softly and carry a big stick." On several occasions, he ordered the American military to directly intervene in Caribbean and Latin American nations (for the benefit of corporations such as the United Fruit Company). He approached foreign policy in a very different way, however, when it came to Asia. Indeed, when in 1907 Roosevelt ordered the so-called GREAT WHITE FLEET to embark on a 45,000-mile world tour, he hoped that the show of American force would preserve and strengthen the nation's economic interests in Asia. Roosevelt's principal foreign policy objective was to maintain the OPEN DOOR POLICY in China, because of its great market potential for American manufacturers.

The importance of exports to the economic health of the nation strongly influenced the actions taken during President WOODROW WILSON's administration. Although the United States took a position of neutrality with the outbreak of war in 1914, many Americans recognized the new economic possibilities of trading when European nations were at war. Accordingly, few connections with Europe were severed. Instead, President Wilson argued that the potential loss of trade with Europe, especially with Great Britain, threatened the country with economic depression. He contended that open and free access to international shipping channels was critical to the nation's economic well-being, a decision that brought American ships increasingly into harm's way. As Germany aggressively employed its new submarine fleet to stop Great Britain's trade, it also interfered with American shipping. It was in the name of free trade and "freedom of the seas" that Wilson declared war on Germany.

During the course of the war, American economic strength continued to grow. Not only did the nation benefit from its continuing ability to export manufactured and agricultural goods during the war, but it also emerged from the war as the leading economic nation in the world. The devastation of the war severely crippled the European economy both in terms of infrastructure and the availability of labor. Europe lost markets and the ability to compete. By the end of the war, European citizens owed private Americans $3 billion and their governments owed another $10 billion. War-time loans from the United States to Europe constituted the primary source of this capital imbalance. While the war marked the emergence of the United States as the leading economic power in the world,

it also signaled the increasingly integrated nature of the world economy. Debts tied nations' economies together.

Complicating the ability of European nations to repay war loans to the United States were the reparations that Germany owed to the international community as a result of the TREATY OF VERSAILLES of 1919. Ravaged by war, the French wanted to cripple Germany at the Peace Conference. Accordingly, along with the British, the French were able to have included in the final treaty a "war guilt clause" that held Germany directly responsible for the damages caused by the war. To determine the amount of reparations, the Versailles Peace Treaty established a commission to make a specific dollar amount recommendation. In 1921, the Reparations Commission concluded that the German nation, which also had been ravaged by the war, owed the international community $33 billion.

The repercussions of this expensive bill would long be felt, as it destroyed international economic relations for more than a decade. The international trade system depended on the flow of capital between nations to maintain at least a semblance of equitable trade relations between nations. European nations, which owed the United States some $13 billion, relied on new investments and the sale of goods to raise the capital for repayment of these loans. During the 1920s, however, the country experienced a trade surplus that promised to ruin the international economy. This trade surplus ranged from $375 million in 1923 to over $1 billion in 1928. European nations did not create any surplus with which to pay their debts to the United States.

The new U.S. position as dominant economic nation meant that its policies would have far-reaching ramifications. Since the start of the 20th century, the international economy increasingly had become interconnected, and the United States depended heavily on foreign trade and foreign investments. In particular, given the indebtedness of European nations after the war, there was a vested interest in open movement of capital and goods through the international economy. The government's response to the collapse of the stock market in October 1929, however, undermined even further the very health of the international economy. Despite the strong need for the open movement of capital and commodities through the international economy, the Hoover administration imposed the Hawley-Smoot Tariff, which effectively closed the American economy to foreign commerce. Nations around the world responded in kind, closing their markets to American industrial and agricultural goods. Accordingly, the economic contraction was deepened by the shortsighted trade policies imposed by the federal government after the beginning of the Great Depression.

See also TARIFFS.

Further reading: Alfred E. Eckes, Jr., *Opening America's Markets: U.S. Foreign Trade Policy since 1776* (Chapel Hill: University of North Carolina Press, 1995); Charles Kindleberger, *Foreign Trade and the National Economy* (New York: Holt, Rinehart, and Winston, 1962).

— David R. Smith

Trading with the Enemy Act (1917)

Along with the ESPIONAGE and the IMMIGRATION ACTS of 1917, the Trading with the Enemy Act solidified the anti-immigrant and anti-radical sentiments that the federal government came to embrace during the early part of the 20th century. When war erupted in Europe in 1914, the public response in the United States was divided. Diverse political and ethnic identities contributed to the debate regarding the war in Europe. Anticipating that the United States would enter the war on the side of the Allies (principally, Britain, France, Italy, and Russia), the administration of President WOODROW WILSON initiated programs aimed at strengthening a sense of patriotism and national unity. Its efforts culminated in increasingly systematic efforts at the Americanization of immigrants, especially emigrants from Germany and its allies. By 1914, German immigrants still formed the largest foreign-born group, 2.3 million, of the population. In addition, there were more than 2 million emigrants from the various parts of the Austro-Hungarian Empire.

Throughout his first term as president, Woodrow Wilson expressed a concern about the large immigrant population and frequently referred to the need for national loyalty, especially after the United States declared war on Germany in April 1917. Within this context of heightened patriotism, the Trading with the Enemy Act sought to reinforce American nationalism and to garner unity for America's involvement in WORLD WAR I. Despite Woodrow Wilson's public image as a supporter of democratic rights (e.g., his Fourteen Points speech), the federal government during the war came to rely on repression to achieve domestic unity and support for the war. Specifically, under Wilson's direction, the Congress passed the Trading with the Enemy Act as an effort to control all international trade and communications. The act provided for the seizure and operation of property in the United States owned by Germans and by enemy aliens (emigrants from Germany, Austria-Hungary, Turkey) and for the control of German assets, which came under the authority of the Alien Property Custodian, A. MITCHELL PALMER. He obtained additional authority to operate German-owned factories and licensed German patents to American industrial firms. Patents for dyes and chemicals were particularly important for the war effort and helped to further develop the chemical industry in the United States after the war.

Communications during the war were another area of control. The Trading with the Enemy Act prohibited the publication of news and editorial matter that was critical of the U.S. government, military CONSCRIPTION, or the war effort. Section 19 of the act also required foreign-language publications to submit their war-related stories to a post office censor for approval. When censors at the post office deemed a publication to be unsuitable because of its critical stance on the war, that publication ran the risk of losing its second-class mailing privileges, making it extremely difficult to distribute and, subsequently, publish. Accordingly, the Trading with the Enemy Act became a further means for the federal government effectively to quiet voices of dissent. Members of two of the leading organizations opposed to America's involvement in the war, the Socialist Party and the INDUSTRIAL WORKERS OF THE WORLD, faced arrest and found that circulation of their publications was extremely difficult, as censors at the Post Office objected to their anti-war positions. It broadly denied mailing privileges to other radical publications, including *THE MASSES*, *International Socialist Review, American Socialist*, the *Appeal to Reason,* and the *Milwaukee Leader*. For many radical and foreign-language publications, exclusion from the mails was the death knell of the free press. Many closed their doors, unable to meet either the cost of publication or to accept the silence of censorship.

Further reading: David M. Kennedy, *Over Here: The First World War and American Society* (New York: Oxford University Press, 1980).

— David R. Smith

Treaty of Versailles   See Versailles, Treaty of

Triangle Shirtwaist Fire (1911)

The fire at the Triangle Shirtwaist Company in New York City in March 1911 galvanized reformers, citizens, and workers to address the fatal ramifications of industrialization in the Progressive Era. Of the 500 garment workers who were in the factory that day, 146 died. Most of the victims were Jewish and Italian immigrant women who worked long hours for meager pay. Women who could not escape the building died from smoke inhalation while others perished from the impact of jumping out of the 10-story building. Some of them were impaled as they landed on fences. Widespread mourning for the victims was evident in the 120,000 people who attended the funeral for the unclaimed dead.

The fire was preceded by an industrywide strike among New York City garment workers in 1909. The Triangle Shirtwaist Company was more intransigent than most other employers. It refused to concede workers' demands for safer working conditions and employer subsidies for needle and thread, among other issues. After the strike, workers returned to the company to find the same unsafe conditions that had prompted the walkout in the first place. Once fire erupted at the factory, workers discovered that they were trapped inside. The fire escapes were locked or blocked because management believed that the workers might steal needles and thread, try to sneak out of work, or organize another protest.

While the city's garment workers struck, they received the support of the NATIONAL WOMEN'S TRADE UNION LEAGUE, an organization comprised of workers and their allies, upper- and middle-class female reformers. As a result of the fire, other groups joined the female reformers in pressing for increased labor regulation. Spearheading the reform effort was Rose Schneiderman, an immigrant worker herself, who mobilized middle-class women, religious leaders, and labor figures in support of safety and labor legislation. Schneiderman and the NWTUL pressured local and state authorities to establish more stringent regulations for factories. The New York Factory Commission and the Industrial Code for New York State represented two results of their efforts. They also represented the

attempt of state and local politicians to depict themselves as responsive and progressive in order to undermine the growing appeal of socialism among New York City's workers. Tammany Hall state legislators including ALFRED E. SMITH facilitated passage of labor and safety laws in 1914. The Triangle Fire sparked outrage among average citizens as well, who demanded that the company be brought to justice. Triangle owners Max Blanck and Isaac Harris were charged with first- and second-degree manslaughter, but they were acquitted.

See also INTERNATIONAL LADIES' GARMENT WORKERS UNION; SHIRTWAIST MAKERS STRIKE.

Further reading: Leon Stein, *The Triangle Fire* (Philadelphia: Lippincott, 1962); Bonnie Mitelman, "Rose Schneiderman and the Triangle Fire," *American History Illustrated* 16 (July 1981): 38–47.

— Natalie Atkin

trusts See Volume VI

Twain, Mark See Volume VI

U

Underwood-Simmons Tariff (1913)

Shortly after entering the White House, WOODROW WIL-SON attempted to address and remedy the problem of economic power that the nation had been debating off and on for some 20 years. The DEMOCRATIC PARTY had not yet held the office of president in the 20th century and it was hungry for a variety of reforms. Topping its list of initiatives was tariff reform. President Wilson actually convened a special session of Congress to tackle immediately what he perceived was one of the nation's most pressing needs, lowering the tariff. Progressives had long advocated a reduction in tariff rates as a way to undercut the economic power of trusts, but they had not succeeded in trimming tariff rates before Wilson took office in 1913. As one of his first policy efforts, Wilson pushed for a lowering of the tariff rates in the United States. From the prevailing average of 40 percent, the Underwood-Simmons Tariff Act of 1913 pared rates down to an average of 25 percent. The legislation reduced the import duty on over 900 items, raised them on only 86, and left some 300 items untouched. Beyond reducing the overall duty on imported products, the Underwood Tariff Act also expanded the list of commodities that could now enter the United States duty free. Over 300 items were now put on this list, including sugar, wool, iron ore, steel rails, agricultural implements, cement, coal, wood and wood pulp, and many critical farm products. Because the new tariff legislation especially targeted trust-dominated industries, the Democrats strongly felt that this new tariff would spur competition and reduce prices for consumers by opening protected American markets for foreign products.

The other pressing issue that Wilson had to address as he sought lower TARIFFS was the fact that the federal government stood to lose a significant source of revenue. Accordingly, the Wilson administration supported a companion initiative to raise the federal government's revenues through domestic programs. Accordingly, Wilson pushed for the adoption of the nation's first FEDERAL INCOME TAX, which became law when the states ratified the Sixteenth Amendment in 1913. The income tax adopted in 1913 made good on the progressive pledge to reduce the power and privileges of wealthy Americans by requiring them to pay taxes on a greater percentage of their income than the poor. Shortly into his first administration, President Wilson had achieved two long-time goals of the Progressive movement: tariff reduction and a graduated income tax.

See also TRADE, FOREIGN.

Further reading: Edward S. Kaplan, *Prelude to Trade Wars: American Tariff Policy, 1890–1922* (Westport, Conn.: Greenwood, 1994).

— David R. Smith

United Mine Workers of America (UMWA)

Formed in 1890, the United Mine Workers of America (UMWA) fought numerous battles between 1900 and 1930 to organize the nation's anthracite and bituminous coal miners. When the American coal mining industry emerged in the decades following the Civil War, it relied for labor primarily on British, Irish, and Scottish immigrants, who brought with them the knowledge of mining and a tradition of labor militancy. Although there were attempts to organize mine workers prior to 1890, it wasn't until the formation of the UMWA that these organizing efforts proved effective.

Between 1890 and 1902, the UMWA had considerable success organizing bituminous miners in the eastern United States. Because mining bituminous coal required less skill and expense than the extraction of anthracite coal, the bituminous coal industry was marked by frequent labor disputes, excessive competition, and overall instability. As a result, the Central Competitive Field, which represented eastern mine operators, readily consented to a general agreement with the UMWA. Anthracite mine operators, however, proved much more reluctant, and it wasn't until JOHN MITCHELL took control of the UMWA in 1898 that the union's attempts to organize anthracite miners began to succeed. The union had to overcome ethnic and racial divisions, differences in skill and wages, and the larger, more efficient, and more powerful anthracite mine operators. Tension between the UMWA and mine operators came to a head in 1902 when 140,000 miners walked off the job. The ensuing ANTHRACITE COAL STRIKE was frequently violent. It lasted five-and-a-half months before President THEODORE ROOSEVELT intervened and the two sides agreed to allow him to arbitrate the dispute.

By the time Mitchell retired as head of the UMWA in 1908, the union had successfully organized most of the eastern coalfields. Prior to the emergence of the UMWA, miners had been organized primarily along craft, racial, and ethnic lines. Much of the union's initial success is attributable to the fact that it was able to overcome these divisions. Mitchell, who realized the importance of organizing the entire industry and overcoming divisions among workers, frequently told miners "the coal you dig is not Slavish coal, Polish coal, or Irish coal. It is coal."

Over the next few decades, the union turned its attention to organizing miners in the western United States. Attempts to organize western miners proved difficult and resulted in considerable conflict and bloodshed. The most notorious incident was the LUDLOW MASSACRE of 1914, when Colorado state militia and private security forces brought in to break the strike murdered 20 miners. Violent clashes were hardly unique to western mines. They occurred almost as frequently in the more heavily unionized East as well. Many of the violent conflicts occurred as a result of mine operators' attempts to break the UMWA's hold in the eastern coalfields. Some of the clashes, such as the 1920 incident in Matewan, West Virginia, turned deadly when company-hired security forces battled with striking miners and local union supporters.

Despite the staunch opposition of mine operators and the ethnically and racially diverse workforce, the UMWA continued to have organizing success. By 1920, the year after John L. Lewis became UMW president, the union boasted a membership of 384,000 bituminous miners and over 200,000 anthracite miners. Over the course of the next decade, however, the UMWA steadily declined. The decade-long tailspin occurred for several reasons, including wartime overproduction, competition from oil refining, technological innovation, anti-union efforts, and mismanagement by the Lewis leadership. The end result was that the UMWA had stumbled badly by the onset of the Great Depression in 1929. Wages were 25 to 50 percent lower; unemployment and poverty were widespread; and union membership had plummeted below 250,000.

Further reading: John H. M. Laslett, ed., *The United Mine Workers of America: A Model of Industrial Solidarity?* (University Park: Pennsylvania State University Press, 1996).

— Robert Gordon

United States Shipping Board

As the United States faced the possibility of entering WORLD WAR I, one of its most pressing needs was to transport personnel, war materiel, and supplies to the battlegrounds of Europe. Cross-Atlantic transport was in short supply, as the United States had an underdeveloped shipping fleet. To bolster the creation of a strong merchant marine, the Congress created the United States Shipping Board with the Shipping Act of 1916. The board was empowered to operate shipping vessels as the Emergency Fleet Corporation. During the war, the U.S. Shipping Board contracted with private firms to build approximately 18 million tons of shipping vessels. Only about three million tons were built during the war. The government canceled 4.5 million tons of the contracts, and the remaining ships, weighing 10.5 million tons, were completed after the war. With their completion, the government was faced with a major dilemma.

The existence of a new, but outmoded, federal merchant marine fleet presented two problems. First, in the war's aftermath, few supported the idea of a government-owned shipping fleet. Second, the ships built during the war were of an obsolete design, and many of them deteriorated at their docks. In June 1920, nothing the state of the merchant marine, Congress passed the Jones Merchant Marine Act, which increased the Shipping Board to seven members and assigned them the task of decommissioning the wartime fleet. During his presidential campaign, Republican WARREN G. HARDING had made the merchant marine a central issue. Once elected president, he appointed Albert Lasker, an ADVERTISING executive, head of the Shipping Board. Lasker's charge was to sell or dismantle the wartime fleet, find a way to subsidize private shippers to build new vessels, and strengthen the merchant marine. A highly competent businessman with many successes to his credit, Lasker promised to relieve the country of its unwanted ships and modernize the merchant fleet.

Over the next two years, the task proved to be far more difficult than originally thought. The Shipping Board found few takers for the rapidly deteriorating fleet, even at rock-bottom prices. In 1921, the Shipping Board had 1,109 steel vessels in operation, with 520 in dry dock. It was operating at a deficit. There also were charges of graft, corruption, and incompetence. Lasker made little headway against these overwhelming problems. While he off-loaded some vessels, he was less successful in eliminating the board's chronic deficits. With a budget of $3.5 billion appropriated, it still fell behind about $150 million a year.

To deal with these problems, the Shipping Board proposed a twofold program. First, the Shipping Board would sell the government's entire merchant fleet, if only for scrap; second, it sought to substitute for government ownership a direct subsidy program for the merchant marine. The cost of the subsidies would be an estimated $30 million a year, a tremendous savings for the government. In addition, the board proposed creating a merchant marine naval reserve of 500 officers and 30,000 men and an army transport service. The bill failed to pass Congress in 1923. In the face of mounting problems, Lasker resigned as head of the Shipping Board.

By the end of 1927, the United States Shipping Board still owned 823 ships. Deficits continued to rise in maintaining the deteriorating fleet. Lasker's successor was able to dismantle the fleet only by selling the majority of the ships as scrap material. The problem of how to sustain a strong merchant marine was solved only when government subsidies became a permanent fixture through the Merchant Marine Act of 1936.

Further reading: Robert K. Murray, *The Harding Era: Warren G. Harding and His Administration* (Minneapolis: University of Minnesota Press, 1969).

Universal Negro Improvement Association (UNIA)

Established in 1914 in Kingston, Jamaica, by MARCUS GARVEY, the Universal Negro Improvement Association (UNIA) became the most significant Pan-Africanist and black nationalist movement of the early 20th century. The UNIA was intimately tied to Garvey who founded it and whose 1923 conviction on mail fraud charges led to the organization's demise. In the brief decade of its viability, UNIA was dedicated to promoting African-American communities and businesses and in establishing a country and government solely for Africans and people of African descent.

The initial platform for the UNIA, as established by Garvey in 1914, called for caring for the needy of the race, civilizing backward African people, and developing schools and colleges for African and African-American youths that would teach a commitment to racial brotherhood around the globe. In addition, it called for the establishment of agencies around the world to protect the rights of Africans and for the creation of commercial and industrial trade among them.

The UNIA was not very successful in its first two years. The organization had only 200 members by 1916. In an effort to strengthen the organization, Garvey came to the United States in March 1916. He undertook a tour of the United States in which he tried to raise funds for UNIA. During his tour, Garvey was impressed by the conditions of African Americans in relation to those faced by Africans in Jamaica. He hoped that the relative wealth of the African-American community in America and the existence of black leadership would help his organization. In 1916 he decided to move UNIA's headquarters to Harlem in New York City.

The UNIA enjoyed a measure of success in the years following its move to the United States. Answering Garvey's call for the establishment of black-owned businesses, the UNIA bought its own building in Harlem, opened a restaurant, began a newspaper, the *Negro World,* and established a steamship line, the Black Star Line. The Black Star Line was the most visible manifestation of UNIA's philosophy. Garvey believed that the line could function as the core of a worldwide black economy. The black-owned and operated Black Star Line would not only carry black immigrants back to Africa but also would foster trade among blacks in the United States, the Caribbean, and Africa. This trade would form the basis, according to Garvey, of the worldwide black economy of the future. UNIA raised the money needed to buy steamships by selling stock in the Black Star Line. Many African Americans embraced the idea, and UNIA had no trouble selling the stock.

In 1920, UNIA held its first international convention in Madison Square Garden. For one month, 25,000 delegates met to establish the UNIA as an international organization. The convention elected Garvey as the provisional president of Africa and approved a *Declaration of Negro Rights.* The declaration called for equal rights for Africans throughout the world. It named the injustices suffered and demanded equal treatment before the law, access to economic opportunity for blacks, an end to colonialism, and the return to Africa to African rule, and it adopted an African national anthem.

UNIA began to unravel soon after the convention. In 1920–21, the United States suffered through an economic recession. As unemployment skyrocketed among African Americans, sales of Black Star Line stock plummeted. In addition to its financial troubles, UNIA began to suffer from opposition to Garvey's leadership. Critics questioned his financing of the Black Star Line, charging that he was selling more stock than legally allowed. In 1922, Garvey added further fuel to the fire when he met with the second-in-command of the KU KLUX KLAN. His critics charged that he had made a deal with the Klan to remove African Americans from the United States, leaving it as the white man's country that Garvey had always claimed it was. He responded to these charges by purging his critics from the UNIA's leadership. Garvey did not last long enough to take advantage of these moves. He was convicted of mail fraud in a federal court in New York City in June 1923. The court sentenced Garvey to five years in prison and a $1,000 fine. After losing his appeal, he began to serve his sentence in 1925. In 1927, President Calvin Coolidge commuted his sentence, and Garvey was deported to Jamaica. The UNIA did not survive Garvey's trial and deportation. He attempted to re-create it in Jamaica, but by the mid-1930s both UNIA and Garvey had fallen into obscurity. In an era of SEGREGATION, the UNIA was a popular expression of African-American discontent. It provided a means for African Americans in the urban North to organize economically and politically. For many, the UNIA was a way station on the journey toward civil rights activism.

Further reading: Robert Hill, ed., *Marcus Garvey and the Universal Negro Improvement Association Papers,* 9 vols. (Berkeley: University of California Press, 1983–95); Cary D. Wintz, ed., *African-American Political Thought, 1890–1930: Washington, DuBois, Garvey, and Randolph* (New York: M. E. Sharpe, 1996).

— Michael Hartman

urban reform

During the Progressive Era, a coalition of city politicians, educators, social workers, and others enacted reforms aimed at improving city government and the lives of city residents. Urban reform was a reaction to problems brought on by rapid urbanization and the rule of political machines and urban bosses. Political machines that existed as a competing force within government controlled many city governments. Due to the rapid urbanization of the late 19th century, these governments had difficulty responding to the needs of their inhabitants in finding work or getting relief during unemployment. Political machines stepped into the void by providing supporters with help finding a job or perhaps money in hard times. In return, the machines expected recipients's support at the ballot box. The machines also were able to assist businessmen in gaining franchises for trolley lines and other utilities from the governments. The recipients of the machine's aid then contributed to the its political fund. In many cities, the leaders of the political machine became wealthy during their rule.

The cities run by these machines were, for many of their residents, dangerous and unhealthy places to live. City governments struggled to keep pace with changing urban environments. It was often difficult, for example, to build schools fast enough to keep up with the growing school-age population. Sewers, water systems, and garbage pick-up were overburdened. Many poorer residents suffered from a lack of hospital space. The massive factories that accompanied city growth polluted the air and water, and few residents had access to clean air and green space in which to escape the city's environment.

By the late 19th century, reformers began to blame the problems of the city on inefficient city government, and they specifically targeted the political machines for bribery, corruption, and inefficiency. Reformers concentrated their efforts on structural changes to city government and social changes to improve the lives of city residents.

The structural changes in city government centered around three innovations: citywide elections, commission-style government, and city manager government. Because they blamed the power of the political machines on neighborhood and ward-based politics, reformers enacted laws creating citywide elections. In the older ward-based system, each section of the city elected a member to the city council. Reformers argued that this led to corruption because local saloon owners, as the reformers often characterized ward bosses, could buy the votes of their constituents. By electing council members in citywide elections, it was hoped, each candidate would have to appeal to voters in all sections of the city. The reformers believed that it would end the power of the ward bosses and, not coincidentally, lead to the election of the city business elite.

As adherents to the Progressive Era belief in efficiency and expertise, urban reformers attempted to place experts in control of city governments. This tendency gave rise to the city commission mode of government. Commission government consisted of a board of commissioners elected in citywide elections. Each commissioner was elected as head of a particular city department such as the water department or sewer department. The commissioner then met as the legislative body for the city. One of the purposes for the commission was to make city government more accessible to all its residents. If a resident had problems with his water service, for example, he could contact the water commissioner. Galveston, Texas, became the first city to adopt the commission-style of government in 1901. Des Moines, Iowa, followed in 1908, and hundreds of medium and small cities created city commissions in the following years. The city commission model suffered from the lack of a single leader to coordinate its activities. In response to this problem, reformers created the city manager model of government. In the city manager model, an elected city council hired a city manager to oversee the day-to-day operations of the city. Although few large cities hired city managers, the system did spread to many smaller cities.

For many reformers, the purpose for making city governments more efficient was to improve the lives of residents. Reformers attacked the problem in a number of ways. Reform mayors such as Detroit's Hazen Pingree and Cleveland's TOM JOHNSON attacked the streetcar companies for charging high fares that many residents could not afford and providing poor service. The streetcar companies operated under a franchise agreement with the city. This meant that the city granted the companies the right to build streetcar lines in return for tax payments. Under the administration of reform mayors, the franchise agreements were renegotiated. The new agreements called for increased tax payments and lower fares. Reformers also attacked the electric and gas companies for making exorbitant profits. Many argued that public utilities should be owned by the cities, which would then charge the customers less for their utilities. Municipal ownership never emerged, but the reform movement did result in greater regulation of utilities by the states.

Other nonelected officials played a significant role in reshaping cities. City planning became a new profession in the early 20th century. City planners attacked the inefficient and wasteful growth of cities. They believed that, if planned properly, cities could grow while remaining pleasant places to live. To this end, they created city plans that included, for example, park spaces and curving roads meant to break up the monotony of gridline streets and large buildings. The urban planning movement gave rise to property zoning. First established in New York City in 1916, zoning put restrictions on the type and structure of buildings that could be built on certain properties. Zoning quickly spread to other cities.

In addition to the efforts of reform mayors, private citizens undertook efforts to improve living conditions in cities. These reformers investigated factories and tenement houses, for example, and publicized their findings in order to force city governments into improving conditions. Many of these reformers, such as FLORENCE KELLEY of Chicago, attacked a problem first as a private citizen and then went to work for government agencies. Kelley first investigated working conditions in Chicago's factories as a resident of Hull-House. Her findings played a key role in the establishment of an Illinois factory inspection law and she was named the state's first factory inspector.

See also CITIES AND URBAN LIFE; PROGRESSIVISM.

Further reading: Martin J. Schiesl, *The Politics of Efficiency: Municipal Administration and Reform in America, 1880–1920* (Berkeley: University of California Press, 1977); Stanley K. Schultz, *Constructing Urban Culture: American Cities and City Planning, 1800–1920* (Philadelphia: Temple University Press, 1989); Jon C. Teaford, *The Unheralded Triumph: City Government in America, 1870–1900* (Baltimore: Johns Hopkins University Press, 1984).

— Michael Hartman

urban transportation

Developments in transportation technology played an integral role in shaping American cities. Transportation developments such as the electric streetcar, the subway, and the automobile made it possible for city residents to spread out, which led to a tremendous expansion in the size of cities. It also shaped settlement patterns within individual cities. The shape and size of American cities today are a result of these early urban transportation developments.

Until the mid-19th century, the size of cities was constrained by how far city residents were willing or able to walk. Cities developed compactly therefore. In the mid-19th century, horse-drawn public transportation was introduced, first the omnibus and then the streetcar. The horse-drawn streetcar greatly expanded the distance that residents could travel to work. By the 1890s, cities had changed from horse-powered to machine-driven transportation. The first machine-powered urban transport was cable cars. They ran by gripping a moving cable that ran under the street. There were a number of problems with cable car operation, however, and they soon lost out to electric streetcars. Drawing power from electrical wires strung overhead, the streetcars—or trolleys, as they were often called—greatly increased the range of urban transportation. Electrification also allowed the development of subways. Boston built the first subway system in 1897, followed by New York in 1904 and Philadelphia in 1908. The electric streetcar and subways helped the cities expand and shaped the pattern of settlement within the cities.

Electric trolleys shaped the spatial distribution of residential, economic, and recreational activities. Traveling at speeds ranging from 10 to 15 miles per hour, the trolley cars allowed residents to live farther away from the city center than in the past. The residents who moved out of the city center moved into neighborhoods organized along trolley lines. The walk to catch the trolley was still a limiting factor in residential choices. This dynamic led to a radial arm or spoke-and-wheel pattern of settlement in which the most densely populated areas of the city followed the trolley tracks.

The pattern of trolley lines also played an essential role in the growth and vitality of central business districts. Almost all trolley lines traveled from the city fringes to the central business district. There were very few cross-town lines. The practical effect of this was to force almost everyone who used the streetcar system to rely on the central business district. The central business districts witnessed an unprecedented building boom during this time. Not only corporate offices and financial institutions settled in the central business district, but also entertainment venues such as VAUDEVILLE and motion picture theaters and stores emerged. Depending on the trolley lines to bring thousands of riders a day to their doorstep, the large department stores that came to characterize shopping emerged during this period.

The owners of trolley lines also acted to reshape the spatial distribution of entertainment activity by encouraging

Electric trolleys were a growing form of urban transportation *(Library of Congress)*

pleasure riding. They realized that they could make more money if residents rode their lines for more than trips to work and shopping. Therefore, in order to attract riders, streetcar line owners built parks, racetracks, beer gardens, amusement parks, and baseball parks on their lines. Every city that had trolley lines had amusement parks at the end of them. Baseball owners built their new stadiums at the end of lines or where multiple lines intersected. The Brooklyn team became known as the Dodgers because fans had to dodge so many trolleys outside the stadium.

Electric streetcars contributed to the social differentiation and separation among city residents by making it possible for the wealthy and middle class to move out of the city center while the working class stayed. This rearrange-

ment of people altered the social landscape of cities as residents sorted themselves out based on economic class and race, instead of ethnicity. The wealthy and middle class followed the streetcar lines and settled in the outer sections or in SUBURBS. Working-class residents were left behind where they lived in the older housing stock that had been abandoned by the wealthy.

The heyday of the trolley car was relatively short. In 1908, the same year that Philadelphia was completing its subway system, HENRY FORD produced the first Model T. The automobile soon bypassed the electric streetcar as the preferred mode of urban transportation, and by mid-century streetcars had vanished from city streets. Henry Ford played an important role in the development of the automobile as a mass transportation technology. He did this by producing an automobile that a significant proportion of Americans could afford. From 1910 to 1924, the price of a Model T dropped from $950 to $290. Led by Ford, automobile production boomed between 1910 and 1930. In 1905 there had been 8,000 automobiles registered in the United States. By 1915 there were over 2 million, and by 1925 Americans owned 17,481,001 automobiles. In addition to the automobiles owned for private use, the number of trucks for use in commerce skyrocketed from 1,400 in 1905 to 2,569,734 in 1925.

The automobile required a revolution in road building. City roads at the beginning of the century were unpaved and in poor condition. Whereas a horse might be able to step around the numerous potholes, automobiles could not. To meet the needs of automobiles and increase profits, a coalition of private LOBBYING AND INTEREST GROUPS, including tire manufacturers, parts suppliers, oil companies, service station owners, road builders, and property developers promoted road building. Government officials succumbed to the pressure and used public money to build roads. Initially, local governments concentrated on improving existing roads but soon launched a program to build entirely new ones. The development of new roads helped usher in a change in the way Americans thought about them. Before the rise of the automobile, roads had provided an open space that performed a recreational function. By the 1920s, city residents saw roads primarily as thoroughfares for cars. In order to deal with the traffic congestion, cities began to build roads restricted to automobile use and provided them with limited access. The first of these was the Long Island Motor Parkway, completed in 1911.

The rise of the automobile and the construction of road systems reshaped the spatial distribution of urban activities. Residents were no longer dependent on the streetcar lines and no longer needed to live within walking distance of them. Residential areas filled in the spaces between the old radial settlements, and urban populations became more evenly distributed. In addition to the new settlement pattern within the cities, automobiles made it possible for more Americans to leave the cities for the suburbs, which established a new spatial distribution between cities and their suburbs. By allowing urban residents to travel freely between different areas of the city, the automobile created a significant drain on the central business district. Cross-town roads meant that residents were no longer funneled to the city center by the transportation system. The outer areas of cities began to develop their own business areas, aided in part by the adoption of the truck for commercial transport. By the 1930s the modern urban transportation system dependent on the automobile had developed. As Americans expanded their use of the auto-

mobile, the effects on the central city intensified and suburbs became the major site for new growth.

See also AUTOMOBILE INDUSTRY; CITIES AND URBAN LIFE.

Further reading: Raymond Mohl, *The New City: Urban America in the Industrial Age, 1860–1920* (Arlington Heights, Ill.: Harlan Davidson, 1985); Eric H. Monkkonen, *America Becomes Urban: The Development of U.S. Cities and Towns, 1780–1980* (Berkeley: University of California Press, 1988); Sam Bass Warner, *Streetcar Suburbs: The Process of Growth in Boston, 1870–1900* (Cambridge, Mass.: Harvard University Press, 1962).

— Michael Hartman

U.S. Steel

Created in 1901, United States Steel was immediately the nation's largest industrial manufacturer and helped revolutionize American industry. U.S. Steel evolved out of the steel empire created by industrialist ANDREW CARNEGIE. Beginning in the 1870s, he capitalized on technological advances in the production of steel and quickly dominated the fledgling American steel industry. In 1889, Carnegie and his partner, Henry Clay Frick, consolidated all of their steel holdings to create the Carnegie Steel Company. With a net worth of $25 million, the company was immediately the most valuable in the country.

Between 1889 and 1901, Carnegie and Frick expanded both the size of Carnegie Steel and their control over the nation's steel industry. Emulating the practices JOHN D. ROCKEFELLER introduced at STANDARD OIL, they streamlined production in order to maximize profits. They also integrated all aspects of steel production and distribution under the control of a single company. By 1890, Carnegie Steel controlled the entire production process, from the extraction of raw materials, to the delivery of those materials to the mill, through to the sale and distribution of the finished product, all of which enabled the corporation to maximize profits and undermine competitors. For Carnegie, maximizing profits also meant keeping wages low and workers unorganized. In 1892, when workers organized by the Amalgamated Association of Iron, Steel, and Tin Workers struck at the company's Homestead plant, Carnegie used Pinkerton private security guards to attack striking workers, replace them with scab workers, and break the union. Carnegie's chief rival in the steel industry was Elbert H. Gary, who had created the Chicago-based Federal Steel Company.

The genesis for U.S. Steel began in 1900 when Carnegie, whose relationship with Frick had become strained, announced that he intended to retire. Upon hearing news of Carnegie's impending retirement, financier

Charles M. Schwab approached both Carnegie and Gary about merging the two steel giants. After securing additional funding from banker J. P. Morgan, Schwab was able to engineer the merger and the formation of U.S. Steel in 1901. With an initial capitalization of $1.4 billion, U.S. Steel instantly became the largest corporation in the world and marked the pinnacle of an era of industrial mergers and monopolies. Public concern about the emergence of such wealthy and consolidated corporations, widespread before the creation of U.S. Steel, intensified over the course of the next decade. The emergence of a billion-dollar monopoly in an industry essential to industrial vitality prompted progressive reformers, radicals, and even some old-money conservatives to call for enforcement of the Sherman Antitrust Act, which since its passage in 1890 had been used more to undermine organized labor than regulate corporate mergers.

Between 1900 and 1930, U.S. Steel remained one of the nation's largest, wealthiest, and most anti-union corporations. The company employed a number of tactics to keep its workforce non-union. In addition to keeping its workforce divided along racial, ethnic, and craft lines, U.S. Steel created company towns, which not only reinforced these divisions, but also ensured that workers would be dependent upon the company for food, clothing, and housing. In 1909, Gary, who took over the day-to-day operations after Carnegie retired, announced that the company was committed to an OPEN SHOP policy and would no longer employ unionized workers.

Attempts to unionize U.S. Steel's workforce and the company's bitter opposition to such efforts came to a head in the STEEL STRIKE OF 1919. U.S. Steel had tolerated organizing efforts during WORLD WAR I, but the temporary truce between labor and management ended almost as soon as the war came to an end. Wages were lowered, workers fired, and hours extended as tensions again escalated. When U.S. Steel refused to negotiate, members of the Amalgamated Association of Iron, Steel, and Tin Workers voted to go on strike. On September 22, 1919, approximately 365,000 steelworkers walked off the job. Once again, the company responded swiftly and forcefully, hiring scabs to cross picket lines and private security forces to provoke and attack striking workers. The strike was eventually broken. U.S. Steel continued to fight unionism at its factories until the formation of the Steel Workers Organizing Committee in the 1930s.

Further reading: David Brody, *Steelworkers in America: The Non-Union Years* (New York: Harper Torchbooks, 1960).

— Robert Gordon

V

vaudeville

A form of theatrical entertainment consisting of a variety of acts, vaudeville was the most popular form of entertainment in the early decades of the 20th century. The secret to its success was the range of entertainment it offered. Vaudeville theater included acts such as singers, comedians, acrobats, animal trainers, dancers, and jugglers. This variety appealed to a broad range of audiences, which meant economic success for theater owners. Vaudeville also set the pattern for much of the popular entertainment of the 20th century. Many of the best-known names in American show business got their start in vaudeville.

Vaudeville, in the form in which it gained popularity, developed in the late 19th century, partly due to changes in the business ownership of theaters. Prior to this time, theaters were owned on a local basis. This meant that performers had to contract with individual theaters, which was difficult. In the late 19th and early 20th centuries, a group of entrepreneurs began to buy theaters throughout the country. These men then established syndicates with theaters in each major U.S. city. Performers then needed only to sign one contract for a tour of the United States. The new syndicates undertook efforts to transform vaudeville into respectable entertainment. In its earlier form, vaudeville had appealed to young males through ribald acts, and the audiences often participated by heckling the acts on stage. The new syndicates realized that they could sell more tickets if they appealed to a wider audience and, therefore, cleaned up vaudeville both in terms of the acts and the behavior of the audience. The syndicates also created a star system and relied on it to fill seats. Performers such as Mae West and W. C. Fields, later stars of the MOVIE INDUSTRY, became draws on their own. Because they helped fill seats, they were paid more.

The success of vaudeville owed much to the social and economic changes of the time. As urban populations grew, there was a built-in audience for new forms of POPULAR ENTERTAINMENT. The sheer numbers of people available in cities helped fill the theaters. Economic changes also built audiences. The rise of large-scale corporate capitalism created new managerial jobs. The men who filled these jobs enjoyed a higher standard of living than clerks had previously, and they had more money to spend on leisure. Many middle-class women, whose husbands worked in these new managerial jobs, enjoyed more leisure time and more money with which to enjoy it. In addition, many younger unmarried women were working outside the home, earning money with which to purchase entertainment. Families in general were enjoying more leisure time as the hours of work declined.

The theater owners pursued potential audiences by tailoring the shows to the audience. In theaters located in working-class and immigrant sections of cities, tickets were cheaper; but the big stars never played these venues. Performances might include parodies of wealthier citizens or other jokes meant to appeal to the audience. Theaters located in the center of cities, usually close to the central business district and main shopping areas, catered to middle-class audiences. Tickets were more expensive; but for a higher price, the audiences got to see the stars of the day perform. Performances in the higher-priced theaters emphasized more genteel acts. They would often include ethnic jokes that poked fun at the working-class immigrants then streaming into the United States. Many of the vaudeville acts thus helped maintain stereotypes about ethnic groups. Performers also altered their performances in different parts of the country. They quickly learned that what New York audiences found entertaining, audiences in Milwaukee, for example, might not. The strength of vaudeville and the key to its success was its ability to change nightly and regionally.

The role played by vaudeville in spreading stereotypes is paradoxical, given that most of the performers came from immigrant working-class backgrounds. In New York City in particular, vaudeville was seen as a ticket out of the immigrant ghetto; and it was from these immigrant ghettos that many of vaudeville's best-known performers emerged. Its working-class origins helped vaudeville play a role in the cultural transformations of the era. Performers helped shape new ethnic identities that became part of American culture. By lampooning the genteel ways of the middle classes, performers helped weave the egalitarian thread in big-city culture. Furthermore, when traveling outside New York, the performers introduced New York culture to audiences across the country. In this way, vaudeville contributed to the development of a national culture.

Vaudeville declined due to competition from radio and film and the onset of the Great Depression of the 1930s. Whereas in earlier days, one could see the star performers only by attending vaudeville shows, radio brought these performers into America's homes. Films actually began as part of vaudeville shows. Some of the less expensive vaudeville theaters would show short clips as part of the performance. In the early years, movies did not threaten vaudeville; but as the quality of films improved, more theaters began to show them. The newer films, which had better quality both in terms of picture and story lines, began to play a larger role in vaudeville performances. By the end of the 1920s, only four vaudeville theaters in the United States were not showing films as part of their performances. The introduction of sound into films made them even more attractive for Americans. When the economic depression of the 1930s hit, vaudeville, already teetering on the edge of collapse, declined and never recovered.

Despite its short reign, vaudeville played an important role in setting the pattern for American entertainment of the 20th century. It played a key role in the cultural transformation that took America from the Victorian age to the modern day. It substituted for the older culture of hard work, asceticism, and morality a new urban vision of success and happiness based on luxury and consumption. Vaudeville's legacy included the creation of a mass audience consisting of people from all walks of life. In addition, vaudeville was the first entertainment industry. The syndicates that controlled theaters across the country were precursors to large movie and music corporations. The syndicates relied on stars to attract an audience. The movie industry quickly learned to copy vaudeville's star system. Performances often tested the boundaries of propriety, and they were censored only by the theaters, a situation that paralleled the later film rating system. Vaudeville was the first entertainment form to commercialize ethnic cultures. It also gave ethnic and racial outsiders a chance to join the mainstream through entertainment. Vaudeville was more than just a type of entertainment; it was the beginning of the modern entertainment industry.

Further reading: John E. Dimeglion, *Vaudeville U.S.A.* (Bowling Green, Ohio: Bowling Green University Popular Press, 1973); Robert W. Snyder, *The Voice of the City: Vaudeville and Popular Culture in New York* (New York: Oxford University Press, 1989).

— Michael Hartman

Poster for a popular vaudeville act *(Library of Congress)*

Versailles, Treaty of (1919)

Drafted during the Paris Peace Conference, the Treaty of Versailles was the peace settlement signed after the armistice ending WORLD WAR I, on June 28, 1919. In the Palace of Versailles outside Paris, the Allied and associated powers meeting with representatives of 37 countries brought the four-year worldwide conflict to an end by negotiating a peace treaty to be presented to Germany. The four major Allied powers (Great Britain, France, Italy, and the United States) attended, as well as delegates from many other nations who sought recognition for their contributions to the war. Large numbers of unofficial representatives thronged the corridors. Germany, the successor states to Austria-Hungary, and Turkey were not invited, as they had officially surrendered, and the recently established

Soviet government in Russia was excluded as well from the negotiations.

President WOODROW WILSON led the U.S. delegation, despite the warnings of many of his advisers. They feared that he might lose influence domestically if he did not prevail in Paris. Wilson was, however, welcomed as a hero to France. Having caught the imagination of many Europeans, he was at the height of his popularity worldwide. The "Big Four," including David Lloyd George of Great Britain, Georges Clemenceau of France, Woodrow Wilson of the United States, and Vittorio Orlando of Italy, controlled the decision making. Throughout the war, Wilson had advocated a fair and balanced settlement that did not impose harsh terms and conditions on those defeated. His Fourteen Points were the basis for a "peace without victory." Despite Wilson's popularity, he was not able to persuade the Allies to agree to his terms for peace. The others believed Germany had to be weakened and ultimately took control; they signed a treaty very different from what Wilson had envisioned. The Treaty of Versailles represented a victory for the French demands for security, modified by British concerns for continental stability. Wilson's single-minded pursuit of the League of Nations and a policy of national self-determination also shaped the treaty.

The treaty began with the Covenant of the LEAGUE OF NATIONS. The league was to be a form of world government with countries committing themselves to further peace by negotiating conflicts among themselves. The league was intended, according to Woodrow Wilson, to operate as a "partnership of the great and free self governing peoples of the world." It was meant to make it a "matter of certainty that thereafter, nations like Germany would not have to conjecture whether nations would join against them but rather, would know that mankind would defend to the last the rights of human beings." By creating a court of international justice, the league would substitute the process of mediation and arbitration for the brutal process of war. All members sought to advance the human condition. Members were bound to advance humane conditions of labor for men, women, and children. Wilson, therefore, called it a "magna charta" for labor.

The League of Nations, however, was only one part of the treaty. War reparations formed the majority of the treaty's priorities. The treaty reduced the population and territory of Germany by approximately 10 percent by its terms. Alsace and Lorraine were returned to France, and the Saarland (formerly German) was placed under the supervision of the League of Nations until 1935. In the north, three regions of Germany were given to Belgium, and northern Schleswig was returned to Denmark. The nation of Poland was resurrected from most of western Prussia and Posen and part of Upper Silesia. All of Germany's overseas colonies were made into "trusteeships," or

mandates, controlled by Britain, France, Japan, and other Allied nations. The land ideally belonged to the people who lived on it, according to Wilson's Fourteen Points, but in 1919, the British and French Empires were at the apex of their power. They would not extend self-determination to the non-European world. The concept of mandates acknowledged the direction in which Wilson wanted to move to realize self-determination. A few countries like India, Egypt, and Turkey had produced nationalist movements and they sought freedom from European rule or interference. In Turkey, the Nationalists under Mustafa Kemal established their own republic in opposition to Allied plans. Other countries had to wait for self-determination. The national frontiers drawn at Paris lasted until 1938–39 and even then survived the periods of Nazi and Soviet domination with few changes.

The Versailles Treaty created four new nations. They were Finland, Latvia, Estonia, and Lithuania, formed from what had been the Russian Empire. Yugoslavia was created from the Austro-Hungarian Empire, including Serbia and Montenegro; and Czechoslovakia was created mostly from Austrian lands.

The "war guilt clause" declared Germany as the aggressor, and the Big Four sought to ensure that Germany would never again be a threat to Europe. To this end, the German army was restricted to 100,000 men. It had no reserves, conscripts, tanks, aircraft, or general staff. Its navy was reduced to a coastal defense force, as French leader Clemenceau demanded. Germany was held responsible for making reparations to the Allied nations in payment for losses and damages sustained during the war. Although the Versailles Treaty did not stipulate the exact amount, the sum settled upon was so high as to be beyond Germany's ability to pay. War debts and reparations eventually upset international economics.

On June 28, 1919, Germany's new Weimar Republic representatives signed the treaty. It was according to Germans, a "dictated peace," quite unlike the one that Wilson had envisioned. The treaty aroused resentment in Germany, which felt it had been betrayed. Wilson's Fourteen Points had promised the Germans their territorial integrity. Too harsh a peace, Wilson thought, would impoverish and destabilize Germany. The other defeated states were dealt similar terms for peace. Resentments about the war colored international relations and domestic politics for the next two decades, culminating in World War II.

Many, including the British economist John Maynard Keynes, predicted that Germany would not be able to pay the stipulated reparations and that the terms of the treaty would destroy the world economy. The decision to delay stipulating the exact amount of reparations was a major error. Lloyd George had hoped that this would satisfy the demand for reparations, yet give sufficient time for tempers to subside. Instead, as the Americans withdrew from the treaty process, it became a continual, ongoing battleground with the German government.

There were three other major problems mentioned in relation to the treaty's terms. First was the isolation of Russia from western Europe by buffer states along its western border. Second, the terms left the German people weak and bitter toward the Weimar Republic. Popular discontent allowed the gradual emergence of a dictator. Finally, the Versailles Treaty did not include Germany in the planning of the League of Nations, which led to the league's undoing.

The Versailles Treaty met with much opposition in CONGRESS when President Wilson returned from Paris in 1919. Wilson's DEMOCRATIC PARTY had lost control of Congress in the election of 1918. Although Wilson had urged the people to support his mission in Europe by returning a Democratic Congress, the people voted for Republican majorities. Ambivalence toward the war resurfaced. Senator HENRY CABOT LODGE led the opposition in their attempts to defeat the ratification of the treaty. President Wilson again attempted to appeal directly to the people and initiated a speaking tour of the country to urge support for the treaty. He suffered a stroke halfway through his speaking tour. In Wilson's absence, Congress voted against ratifying the Treaty of Versailles.

The Paris peace treaties were considered a disappointing end to the long, protracted struggle of World War I. It was commonly claimed that the Treaty of Versailles was too harsh to conciliate Germany and too soft to restrain it. It was not enforced, mainly because France sought strict compliance and Britain, appeasement and revision. The balance of power that had existed prior to the world war was destroyed. France was too weak to maintain the balance on her own. The treaty did, however, establish the League of Nations, a seminal beginning to institutions of international cooperation. It also set up national boundaries in Europe that, except for Poland, are substantially the same today.

Further reading: Herbert F. Margulies, *The Mild Reservationists and The League of Nations Controversy* (Columbia: University of Missouri Press, 1989).

— Annamarie Edelen

veterans

By the 1890s, Civil War pensions for Union war veterans had become a major source of political power and political conflict. The Grand Army of the Republic (GAR) remained the most powerful veterans' group in the early years of the 20th century, despite new organizations such as the Veterans of Foreign Wars for those who served in the Spanish-American War. With the entry of the United States into WORLD WAR I, however, a new generation of veterans came to the fore. What, some wondered, would these new veterans demand? Because many progressive reformers viewed the military pension system as a font of political corruption and a waste of tax revenues, they were eager to find ways to avoid similar demands from the more than four million veterans of the AMERICAN EXPEDITIONARY FORCE. After the war, both as members of the AMERICAN LEGION, a powerful new veterans' organization, and as individual citizens, veterans demanded compensation for the lost wages and opportunities of their war service. In addition, through the legion, conservative war veterans had a voice in FOREIGN POLICY, military funding, and even labor relations in the years between 1919 and 1930.

At the turn of the century, hundreds of thousands of Civil War veterans, their widows, and children, continued to play an active role in politics through such organizations as the GAR, the Sons of the GAR, and Confederate war veterans' organizations. In periodic gatherings called encampments, dwindling numbers of veterans reenacted Civil War battles, reminisced about the war, and made symbolic gestures of reconciliation with their former foes. American political life was tinged, even at that late date, with references to the great struggle of the Republic. Because the REPUBLICAN PARTY thrived on high TARIFFS and the pensions they funded, Republican presidents played a major role in liberalizing what were once disability pensions into a general pension system. By a 1903 executive order, President THEODORE ROOSEVELT established pension eligibility to cover old age. In 1912, Congress passed a bill that expanded the system again. In 1900 alone, nearly a million war veterans and their dependents were in the system at a cost of over $142 million a year; in 1909, the cost had grown to $162 million. Spanish-American War veterans, despite the more recent memory of struggles, were far less successful in capturing benefits from military service.

The cost of "the pension racket" troubled those who wanted a more rational and efficient state. Once the threat of war again existed in 1916, opponents of the patronage-ridden military pension system sought to avoid the same problem in the next war. American intervention in the European war meant not only the development of ways for the government to recruit or conscript a fighting force but also calculating what compensation those serving in the new army should receive. With nearly five million soldiers in the armed forces, there were broader social, economic, and political consequences as well. Planners wondered how the economy would adjust to the drain on its labor supply and what were the potential social and economic dislocations caused by millions of returning veterans. Government officials and progressive social scientists engi-

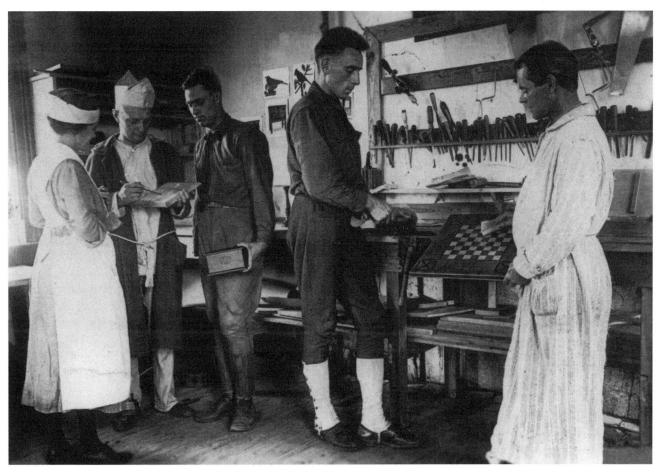

World War I veterans in a workshop (*Library of Congress*)

neered a new program of contributory social insurance for soldiers during the war. Called War Risk Insurance, it was a voluntary and contributory system modeled on workmen's compensation schemes. Specifically, it was designed to address the problem of soldiers' lack of insurability in the private market. Soldiers paid low premiums to the government during the war on insurance for death or disability. They were allowed to convert their war insurance into whole life policies with private insurance after the war. In creating this program, its sponsors sought to substitute insurance payments for postwar claims to death, disability, and pension benefits. In actuarial tables, the insurance program charted the cost to the government of war. It was an insurance system based on quantifiable losses—so much per arm, so much per leg, so much for death, so much per widow and orphan. Other programs for the treatment and rehabilitation of wounded and disabled veterans, reeducation, and reemployment were seen as marginal to the centerpiece of social insurance.

While the war lasted, War Risk Insurance remained the major program to deal with the problems of returning

veterans. By war's end, however, political pressure to reward American doughboys (World War servicemen) with some monetary compensation for wartime service led Congress to pass an act granting $60 additional compensation for their wartime losses. High inflation and escalating unemployment after the war added to the soldiers' grievances. Politicians, veterans' advocates, and the veterans themselves sought government aid in adjusting to civilian life. Part of their efforts were directed toward expanding the power and budget of the VETERANS BUREAU and construction and maintenance of hospitals and rehabilitation programs for disabled veterans, originally under the Public Health Service. At the same time, veterans' advocates sought more generous benefits for the average veteran.

Under pressure from its members, a newly created organization for World War veterans, the American Legion, developed a plan for "adjusted compensation" (the SOLDIERS' BONUS) in 1919. They too had quantifiable measures for what was appropriate compensation for military service. The legion calculated what the nation owed ex-soldiers from the loss of wages while in service. Civilian workers and corporations had made good wages and profits during the war, and veterans had been effectively cut out of the war boom. Now was the time, the legion argued, to make good on the nation's obligation to its heroes, those who lost economic ground while patriotically serving their country. Against political reluctance to increase the national debt and the fear of inflation, the legion designed a long-term payment plan, with interest, as its final selling point. Predictability—for nation and citizen—was the keystone of the program; so, too, was universality. Payments to ex-soldiers were to be distributed on the basis of so-called rational criteria for eligibility. After two unsuccessful attempts, Congress in 1924 finally passed the Soldiers' Adjusted compensation Act, or Soldiers' Bonus, over the presidential veto of CALVIN COOLIDGE.

Over the next two decades, the Bonus remained a contentious issue in American political life. Veterans' groups lobbied for a liberalization of the Bonus system. In the face of worsening economic circumstances in the late 1920s and 1930s, they fought for veterans to be able to borrow money from their Bonus and for it to be paid early. As both a measure to benefit worthy veterans and infuse money into a depressed economy, the Bonus became a universal solution to social ills.

In this period, the American Legion remained ambivalent to its role in veterans' politics. Because it competed for influence with the Veterans of Foreign Wars and other patriotic groups, it was inclined to downplay its role in the Bonus fight. Its leaders, beginning with Legion commander Hanford McNider, were less than enthusiastic about the Bonus, which was principally a rank-and-file demand. The legion leadership preferred lobbying for a conservative political agenda in foreign policy, military PREPAREDNESS, and labor relations. Immediately after the war, conservative legion posts had joined the ranks of police and state militia in suppressing strikes. Legionnaires contributed to raids on labor organizations and street violence against American radicals in 1919–20. The legion's role in foreign policy was to voice demands for greater military preparedness and higher levels of defense spending, as well as an aggressive presence for the United States in its own spheres of influence.

By the 1930s, veterans, had discovered their own diversity. Membership in the American Legion had reached a saturation point, and most war veterans did not belong. The Bonus March of 1932 demonstrated that veterans could make radical demands of their government, and the depths of the Great Depression would reveal that many veterans were willing to join the labor movement that the American Legion leadership had so vigorously opposed. While veterans' organizations, from the legion to the VFW and the Disabled American Veterans (DAV), continued to lobby for expanded veterans' benefits, they rep-

resented only a militant minority of veterans in American political life.

See also LOBBYING AND INTEREST GROUPS; PUBLIC HEALTH.

Further reading: William Pencak, *For God and Country: The American Legion, 1919–1941* (Boston: Northeastern University Press, 1989).

Veterans Bureau

Created by Congress under the so-called Sweet Act of 1921, the Veterans Bureau had as its responsibility the oversight of the system of health care and benefits for VETERANS of the armed forces in WORLD WAR I. In particular, the United States faced the return of many veterans who were disabled or in need of vocational training and placement or health care. The new Veterans' Bureau had a central office in Washington, D.C., and 14 regional offices. President WARREN G. HARDING, under pressure to address the needs of veterans, appointed a social acquaintance, Colonel Charles Forbes, as director of the bureau. Harding viewed Forbes as "a fine, outstanding man" who had performed "constructive service" and had a "brilliant record." Harding and his wife, Florence, hoped that Forbes would provide needed leadership for the "boys" who had returned from France disabled or in need of long-term medical care and disability pensions.

As soon as he was in office, Forbes sought to expand his area of authority. He arranged to have veterans' hospitals and supply depots, which had previously been under the supervision of the U.S. Public Health Service in the Department of the Treasury, transferred to the Veterans Bureau. At that point, Forbes, without the knowledge of the Executive Branch, proceeded to contract for new buildings, sell surplus supplies, and acquire land for hospitals through private hands. In each case, Forbes was able to make a profit by private bidding for public construction contracts. To private firms, he sold surplus food, clothing, sheets, towels, medical supplies, drugs, alcohol, and even floor wax at incredible discounts while he paid obscenely high prices for hospital land and new supplies. When Harding found that Forbes had sold nearly $3 million in government surplus for a modest $600,000, Harding quietly fired him. By that time, Forbes had already stolen a fortune from the government coffers. By modest estimates, he and his friends had appropriated over $200 million ($33 million by Forbes alone) from a Veterans Bureau that in the aftermath of the war was one of the best-funded and most loosely supervised arms of the federal government.

When President Harding died unexpectedly of a heart attack in 1923, his administration came under congressional scrutiny. The granting of oil leases, which came to be known as TEAPOT DOME, corruption in the Justice Department, and the Veterans Bureau scandal surfaced in Senate testimony. The story gradually unfolded of how Elias H. Mortimer, an agent for a construction company, had bribed Forbes through loans and direct payments to grant his firm government contracts. Forbes had become fast friends with Mortimer and his wife Kathryn, but it was the affair blossoming between Forbes and Mortimer's wife that led to revelations of widespread graft and corruption. Not only through government construction contracts and land deals, but also through the Veterans Bureau's procurement system, millions of dollars had been siphoned from the hospital budget. On the testimony of Mortimer, Charles Forbes and one of his co-conspirators, J. W. Thompson, a construction contractor, were sentenced to two years in prison for their part in raiding the treasury of the Veterans Bureau. Forbes alone served his term, as Thompson died in the interim. None of the money was recovered.

Despite the publicity surrounding the Harding administration, the REPUBLICAN PARTY did not suffer any electoral losses in the subsequent election, an outcome shaped by the distance of CALVIN COOLIDGE, who succeeded Harding after his death, from the scandals. At the same time, the scandal probably left many veterans with an embittered view of the government's role in providing for its citizen-soldiers. It may have contributed to the continued push for a Soldiers' Bonus. The Soldiers' Adjusted Compensation Act finally passed over Coolidge's presidential veto in 1924.

In ensuing years, the Veterans Bureau was presided over by Brigadier General Frank T. Himes, who kept himself and the Veterans Bureau free from scandal. He continued to improve and bolster Veterans Hospitals, vocational training, and rehabilitation efforts through the period. At a time when the federal government retrenched from wartime expansion, the Veterans Bureau grew and broadened its functions, and the cost of veterans' benefits soared. From 1918 to 1941, the cost of services and benefits paid to World War I ex-servicemen, including disability, insurance allotments, and health care costs, equaled $14 billion, which represented 11.8 percent of government expenditures.

See also LOBBYING AND INTEREST GROUPS.

Further reading: M. R. Warren, *Privileged Characters* (New York: R.M. McBride, 1935).

Volstead Act (1919)

The Volstead Act, also known as the National Prohibition Act, was named after its Minnesota representative, Andrew J. Volstead. It provided the foundation for the enforcement of the Eighteenth Amendment to the constitution of the United States. Prohibition was the product of a nearly century-long crusade against alcohol. Countless men and women represented the temperance cause, but none more than the Anti-Saloon League's principal agent, Wayne Wheeler, who supported the amendment, which prohibited the sale, manufacture, and transportation of alcoholic beverages.

On December 18, 1917, Congress approved an amendment to prohibit the production, distribution, and sale of alcohol. The act was passed over the veto of President Woodrow Wilson. The president believed that the act's definition of intoxicating beverages—any beverage containing more than 0.5 percent alcohol—was too strict. Wilson believed in the mission of the amendment, but he had his reservations about placing such a strict definition of alcoholic spirits. He was in favor of a law that allowed for the casual use of weaker wines and ales. His veto proved to be nothing more than a symbolic gesture.

Overriding the president's veto was the first step toward amending the Constitution. The next step was winning approval in the states. At first it was believed to be a daunting task. But upon further assessment, it was not as difficult a task as once predicted. The Women's Christian Temperance Union, the Anti-Saloon League, and dozens of other organizations had been developing the local networks necessary to win support in the states. Twenty-five states already had dry laws. Prohibition forces received a boost when Detroit became the first large city to support the amendment. State by state, the amendment was ratified. On January 15, 1919, New Hampshire became the 36th sate to ratify the amendment. One year later, on January 20, 1920, the law took effect.

The Volstead Act provided the federal and state governments with concurrent power to enforce the Prohibition Amendment, but also created a number of problems with enforcement. The states looked to the federal government to provide for the enforcement, while the federal government believed that it was the responsibility of local authorities to enforce the ban on intoxicants. The problem became even more apparent when states and localities began to openly flout the law. As the law became increasingly less popular, few were willing to devote the resources necessary to wage war on liquor traffickers.

In addition to difficulties with enforcement, the unpopular amendment had a number of other challenges that it was forced to overcome. The most apparent was the scale and scope of the venture. The goal of the Volstead Act, national PROHIBITION, was arguably one of the most aggressive ventures ever attempted by the U.S. government. In the name of social development, the amendment destroyed private property. It devastated entire industries. It allowed the federal government to legislate what the individual could do in his or her own home. In fundamentally altered the relationship between citizens and their government. All of these concepts, often considered to be alien to American law, were justified by the premise that they were necessary to ensure a more moral society. Its proponents believed that it could and would usher in an era of enlightenment. Other factors soon arose to challenge the idea of national Prohibition. Bootlegging and the crimes associated with the sale and delivery of illicit spirits soon seemed to be more of a threat than the alcohol itself. The most salient factor in the repeal of Prohibition, however, was the global economic crisis of the 1930s.

The amendment's lofty expectations hindered its chances for success. The fact that many of its proponents promised an end to the pain and suffering attributed to drink made it virtually impossible for the amendment to live up to the expectations. As a result, what seemed to be impossible in 1919 took place. This groundbreaking amendment created the opportunity for an even more revolutionary amendment. It opened the door for the Twenty-first Amendment to the Constitution of the United States.

In February of 1933, Congress proposed the Twenty-first Amendment, better known as the Repeal Amendment, to repeal Prohibition. On December 5, 1933, Utah became the 36th state to ratify the amendment. It put an end to the great social experiment.

— Steve Freund

W

★ ——————————————————————————————————————

Wald, Lillian (1867–1940)

Lillian Wald, an important social reformer of the 20th century, was born in 1867 in Cincinnati, Ohio. After attending elite schools, she enrolled at the New York Hospital Training School for Nurses. Graduating in 1891, she then took classes at medical school while working as a nurse in New York City. Wald pioneered in the practice of home nursing to the poor. It was in this capacity that she gained firsthand experience with the city's poor tenement residents.

In 1893, Lillian Wald and a colleague moved to New York City's Lower East Side to be closer to the residents for whom they were caring. By 1895, with the philanthropic support of Jacob H. Schiff, Wald established a larger settlement, the Nurse's Settlement. Known as the Henry Street Settlement, it expanded its services to include educational training and youth clubs. Wald's brainchild developed into a prominent social service agency in New York City. She introduced the city to a public school nursing program. In 1909, she also persuaded the Metropolitan Life Insurance Company to provide nursing services as a benefit to its industrial policyholders.

Wald's accomplishments were not limited to New York City. Her nursing experience in New York City provided her with the background to establish a new profession, PUBLIC HEALTH nursing. In 1912, she became the first president of the National Organization for Public Health. Through her social service activity, Wald, along with other Progressive Era women, contributed to the development of the SOCIAL WORK profession.

A contemporary of JANE ADDAMS, Wald was active in the pacifist movement and in progressive politics for the Democrats. Like other progressive women, her political activity often revolved around advocacy for the poor and for children. In large measure because of Wald's initiatives, in 1912 Congress established the U.S. CHILDREN'S BUREAU, a division of the Labor Department designed to oversee child labor issues. Labor struggles drew Wald into the

NATIONAL WOMEN'S TRADE UNION LEAGUE, which was a group of reform-minded upper- and middle-class women. They initially made a name for themselves in the SHIRTWAIST MAKERS STRIKE of 1909, where they lent their moral, legal, and financial support to thousands of working-class garment workers. Wald also participated in the founding of the NATIONAL ASSOCIATION FOR THE ADVANCEMENT OF COLORED PEOPLE.

Wald ran the Henry Street Settlement House until 1933, when her poor health forced her into retirement. She died in Connecticut in 1940. Wald exemplified many threads of Progressive Era activism. She never married and drew her emotional support from the women around her. She became an advocate for women's new professions and became active in women's causes. Wald is remembered for helping to professionalize, and thus to some extent legitimize, the predominantly female fields of nursing and social work.

Further reading: Doris Groshen Daniels, *Always a Sister: The Feminism of Lillian D. Wald, Progressive Reformer* (New York: Feminist Press, 1995).

— Natalie Atkin

War Industries Board

The War Industries Board (WIB), a regulatory agency set up to manage the economy during WORLD WAR I, had more powers than any other government agency in the United States to that date. In practice, however, the board did not become a centralized regulatory agency that rationalized the economy. Instead, the WIB became a partner with businesses to coordinate the production and distribution of war materials in the American economy.

The WIB was established in July 1917 to coordinate government purchases of war materials. After months of ineffectiveness, President WOODROW WILSON reorganized it in March 1918 and appointed Wall Street financier

BERNARD BARUCH as its chairman. Under the leadership of Baruch, the WIB extended its reach over much of the American economy. Dominated by industrialists, the board included representatives of major economic interests in the United States.

The WIB matched the demands of war production with the needs of the armed forces, the European allies, other war organizations, and consumers. In some cases, the board persuaded corporations to cooperate voluntarily to meet the priorities of war production. The WIB established 57 committees, which were organized by commodities. The Commodity Committees negotiated for the U.S. government with the War Service Committees, or trade associations, which represented the suppliers. The committees shared information that would assist companies in planning for war production.

Despite its regulatory powers, the WIB did not come to embody the state control of the economy that some Progressives had been advocating in the early 20th century. First, mismanagement and inefficiency plagued the board. Second, the power of the federal government over corporations was limited. The government was dependent on business cooperation to support the war effort. In addition, the federal government needed the skills and knowledge of business leaders to manage production and distribution in the American economy.

The experience of the WIB illustrated to many leaders of government and industry that a cooperative relationship between the public and private sectors was beneficial to both. In fact, Baruch saw himself as a partner with business. The WIB sought to promote the private powers of business rather than restrict them or limit business profits. For many business leaders, profits came before patriotism in their decision making. In fact, major corporations earned huge profits with the help of the WIB.

The Great War had already ended by the time war production peaked under the coordination of the WIB. Immediately after the war, the government dismantled the regulatory structures that had been set up to manage the economy. President Wilson ordered the WIB to end its activities at the start of 1919. Even though the powers of the WIB had been limited during World War I, it served as a model for the National Recovery Administration, an early New Deal agency set up to facilitate an economic recovery during the Great Depression.

Further reading: Robert D. Cuff, *The War Industries Board: Business-Government Relations during World War I* (Baltimore: Johns Hopkins University Press, 1973), Ronald Schaffer, *American in the Great War: The Rise of the War Welfare State* (New York: Oxford University Press, 1991).

— Glen Bessemer

War Revenue Act (1917)

Anticipating the costs of American participation in WORLD WAR I, Treasury Secretary William McAdoo predicted that the U.S. government would need billions of dollars for the war effort. Progressive and conservatives sharply disagreed on how to pay for the war. Specifically, they, like McAdoo, addressed the problem of the ratio of war taxes to war loans. Progressives believed that the war offered an opportunity to solidify a system of progressive taxation based on ability to pay. The Revenue Act of 1916 and the passage of the Sixteenth Amendment for a FEDERAL INCOME TAX had opened the door to taxation as a means to redistribute income. Further, progressives envisioned that paying for the war effort through current taxes was more rational and efficient than long-term war debts. These taxes were to be imposed on incomes, estates, luxury goods, and excess profits. Among conservatives, especially in the business community, loans, not taxes, were the better option. Business interests offered their own variations on what taxes would be imposed. Some suggested a war profits tax, which would have been borne disproportionately by agriculture and manufacturing sectors, which had experienced recessions before the war. Other conservatives preferred to fund the war on consumption taxes alone, though taxing consumption was regressive and punitive.

For the most part, the principles of progressive taxation won out in the War Revenue Act of 1917. While the Liberty Loan and the War Revenue bills were introduced into Congress at the same time, it took six months for the War Revenue Act to make it into law. The act put into force an excess profits tax, raised both individual and corporate income taxes to 4 percent and 6 percent, respectively, and raised excise and estate taxes. New taxes on services, facilities, and on luxury goods such as automobiles were part of the broad-based revenue act. It also increased the maximum surtax on incomes to 63 percent. The 1918 Revenue Act further increased the tax on the highest incomes to 77 percent.

One of the major casualties of the new excise taxes was independent journalism. At a time when inflation had already boosted the costs of publishing newspapers, the introduction of new excise taxes in the form of higher postal rates costs skyrocketed. Already before the war, newspapers had folded under the pressures of escalating costs of new printing machines and linotype metal. Now, along with the soaring price of newsprint, newspapers saw declining profits. The consolidation of newspapers before the war continued due to these new pressures, and hundreds of journals and newspapers either merged with other companies or closed their doors.

The War Revenue Act changed the shape of American taxation and government finance. It shifted the tax burden from customs and excise taxes to taxes on income, profits, and estates, which were at least marginally progressive. During the war, federal tax receipts escalated more than five times, and they never returned to the lower levels of the prewar years. The federal debt also became a permanent part of American political discourse, as government indebtedness increased during the war years from $1 billion in 1915 to over $20 billion in 1920. The cry for tax relief, however, was never far behind, and tax cuts formed a major part of the REPUBLICAN PARTY platform in the elections of the 1920s.

See also ANDREW W. MELLON.

Further reading: David M. Kennedy, *Over Here: The First World War and American Society* (New York: Oxford University Press, 1980).

Washington, Booker T.   See Volume VI

Washington Conference on Naval Disarmament
(1921–1922)
With the Senate's rejection of the LEAGUE OF NATIONS, the United States was isolated in world affairs. The question for its leaders was how to protect the economic interests of the country without committing the nation to an active international role. After Secretary of State CHARLES EVANS HUGHES succeeded in persuading Congress to ratify a treaty in 1921 to formally end the war with Germany, WARREN G. HARDING looked for a way to ensure world peace and stability without limiting American freedom to act in world affairs. Hughes also attempted to prevent a costly naval arms race between the United States, Britain, and Japan. The WASHINGTON CONFERENCE ON NAVAL DISARMAMENT of 1921–22 provided a way to achieve that end. At the conference, Hughes surprised the delegates by outlining drastic reductions in the naval fleets of all three nations as well as a 10-year moratorium on the construction of large battleships. He proposed to scrap two million tons of shipping that already existed.

To the surprise of Hughes, the delegates actually agreed to most of the terms of his proposal. The Five-Power Pact of February 1922 established limits for total naval tonnage and a ratio of armaments for each of the nations. For every 5 tons of American and British warships, Japan was allowed 3 tons and France and Italy 1.75 tons.

Two other treaties also came out of the Washington Conference. The Nine-Power Pact pledged the five naval powers, plus other nations with interests in the Pacific (Belgium, China, the Netherlands, and Portugal), to maintain the OPEN DOOR policy of protecting the territorial integrity of China and keeping equal commercial access in the region. Meanwhile, the countries (the United States,

Britain, France, and Japan) pledged in the Four-Power Pact to cooperate to prevent aggression and to maintain the status quo of each nation's territories in the Pacific. In the event that one of the countries was unable to resolve a conflict in the Pacific diplomatically, the four signatories agreed to invite the other countries to a conference to resolve the dispute.

If the signatories abided by the treaties, the pacts would effectively end the arms race in capital ships, but they did temporarily halt Anglo-American competition and reduced Japanese-American conflict in the region. The treaties sanctioned Japanese dominance in the Pacific. Yet compared to the latitude allowed the United States and Britain internationally, the pacts reinforced the military inferiority of Japan.

A majority of American naval officers opposed the pacts. Naval officers criticized the Five-Power Pact, because it did not produce parity with Britain. The Royal Navy would maintain superiority in large warships in the 1920s. In addition, Britain and the United States did not scrap all the large ships that were covered under the pacts. Instead they converted some of them to carriers. Consequently, the 10-year moratorium was an empty promise.

Nevertheless, Hughes lobbied for the treaties, saying that the Five-Power Treaty "ends, absolutely ends, the race in the competition of naval armaments." The Senate approved the treaties by a large majority even though some senators viewed the pacts as only a first step toward disarmament. For example, Senator Borah wanted the abolition of submarines and parity between France and Japan in capital ships, but that kind of parity would have greatly disturbed the British and derailed the major powers' acceptance of the treaties. Most Americans approved of the treaties of the Washington Conference of 1921. The American press generally praised the treaties. In addition, most businessmen supported disarmament, seeing government reductions in military spending as a way to being domestic tax relief.

Further reading: L. Ethan Ellis, *Republican Foreign Policy, 1921–1933* (New Brunswick, N.J.: Rutgers University Press, 1968); Richard W. Fanning, *Peace and Disarmament: Naval Rivalry and Arms Control, 1922–1933* (Lexington: University of Kentucky Press, 1995).

— Glen Bessemer

Watson, Thomas Edward (1856–1922)
Agrarian reformer and populist politician Thomas E. Watson was born in Columbia County near Thomson, Georgia, the son of John Smith Watson and Anna Eliza Maddox. He attended Mercer University in Macon, Georgia. Following his sophomore year, Watson left Mercer and

returned to Thomson, where he privately studied law. In 1875, he obtained his law license and embarked on a career as a criminal lawyer. On October 9, 1878, Watson married Georgia Durham, with whom he had seven children.

By the 1880s, Watson had not only established himself as a successful criminal lawyer, but also was becoming increasingly involved in Georgia politics. Former Confederates Alexander H. Stephens and Robert Toombs were his political mentors. Entering Georgia politics as a Democrat, he was an agrarian reformer steeped in the traditions of the nostalgic Old South, and hostile to the order of things in the post-Reconstruction New South. A new spirit of enterprise had entered into southern life, and many southerners were calling for greater northern investment in the region. Watson often attacked Henry W. Grady, editor of the *Atlanta Constitution,* for his advocacy of the New South ideology. He also blamed northern bankers and industrialists for the failure of southern family farms and spoke out against the Georgia DEMOCRATIC PARTY, which was dominated by capitalist-industrialists (Bourbons). Watson's fiery populist rhetoric helped him win election to a seat in the Georgia Assembly.

In the state assembly, Watson continued his attacks on Georgia Bourbons and their cooperation with northern banking and industrial interests. In 1890, he won election to the U.S. House of Representatives. Although a member of the Democratic Party, Watson supported the Farmers Alliance platform. By 1892, politically active members of the alliance movement formed the People's Party. Watson eventually left the Democrats and joined the Populists.

Once in Congress, Watson introduced many agrarian reform bills, supported the growth of labor unions, and won passage of legislation bringing free mail delivery to rural areas. In 1892, his district had been gerrymandered, and he was defeated for reelection. Watson also lost a controversial election to a Democratic opponent in 1894. Despite these electoral setbacks, he continued to denounce bankers, the trusts, and the policies of the Bourbon Democrats.

In 1896, the People's Party endorsed the Democratic presidential candidate, William J. Bryan. However, they nominated Watson for the vice presidency on a fusion ticket. The Republican candidate William McKinley won the election. The defeat of the Democratic-Populist fusion ticket was a bitter and humiliating experience for Watson. He retired from public life and turned to writing popular history and biography.

Watson returned to national politics in 1904. He gained 117,183 votes as the Populist candidate for president that year. In 1905, he founded *Tom Watson's Magazine,* which featured his reform editorials. He made a final, symbolic run at the presidency as a populist in 1908. He died in 1922.

Further reading: Ferald J. Bryan, *Henry Grady or Tom Watson?: The Rhetorical Struggle for the New South, 1880–1890* (Macon, Ga.: Mercer University Press, 1994); C. Vann Woodward, *Tom Watson: Agrarian Rebel* (New York: Macmillan, 1938).

— Phillip Papas

welfare capitalism

In an effort to combat the bitter labor strife and high worker turnover of the early 20th century, many employers offered new incentives to workers. They hoped that by providing workers with new benefits, they could gain greater productivity, higher profits, and worker loyalty. Collectively referred to as welfare capitalism, these incentives did not end labor-management strife, but they did offer improved working conditions and standards of living for some workers.

By 1910, employers were seeking a solution to the problem of labor turnover. Most workers, feeling underpaid and overworked, exhibited little loyalty to their employers. They left a job as soon as another, better job appeared. In addition, the continued militancy of the labor movement frightened employers. To combat both problems, employers tried to make their firms more appealing to workers. Many employers realized that turnover and worker unrest arose out of the conflict between modern industrial work and human nature. They therefore sought to socialize—or engineer—a modern workforce that accepted its place in industrial society. They did so by offering welfare programs that tried to meet workers' intellectual, creative, and recreational needs. Some programs were directed at making the workplace more pleasant while others focused on the hours after work. A small number of firms also offered financial incentives for hard work.

To meet worker needs, employers created a myriad of programs. On the job improvements such as showers, lunchrooms, and more work breaks softened some of the harshness of factory labor. Employers also tried to heighten workers' dependence on the company by extending their company into the hours after work. Employers who provided company houses, such as those in many southern mill towns, sponsored house beautification contests in an effort to build workers' attachment to the mill village. Other employers created baseball teams in the hope of fostering company pride and loyalty. English-language classes and civics classes also were used to train loyal workers. To skilled workers, the most prized sector of the workforce, many companies offered pension plans and profit sharing in efforts to convince workers to stay with the same company. The Ford Motor Company simply offered its workers more money than any other company paid with its "Five Dollar Day."

Employers offered two basic explanations for their embrace of welfare capitalism. Some stated that they wanted to humanize business and end the war between labor and capital. They would do so by showing that capitalism was not as exploitive as many workers argued. Most employers were straightforward, however, in stating their justification for the programs. Elbert Gary, head of U.S. STEEL, stated that the purpose behind his company's programs was to make sure that his employees had it a little better than workers represented by a union. The head of International Harvester also frankly stated that his programs were developed strictly for business reasons. If workers were happier, then they would show up to work more often and work harder.

Because employers intended to use the welfare programs to create compliant workers, some of the programs became oppressive. HENRY FORD accompanied his pay raise, for example, with strict rules for eligibility of employees, and, to make sure that his employees met the criteria of cleanliness and wholesomeness, his "sociological department" investigated workers at home to see how they lived. If the company found the workers wanting in their morality or cleanliness, they might fire them or take away the Five Dollar wage. Many immigrants took advantage of English-language and citizenship classes offered or sponsored by employers. After all, learning English could help them get a better job. The classes, however, focused on more than simple language and civics. Some taught immigrant workers to be loyal to their employers, criticized unions, and discouraged ties to old-world cultures. International Harvester provided English-language instruction in which the first lesson began: "I hear the whistle. I must hurry." As a consequence, immigrant workers who took the free English-language courses faced an assault on their way of life.

Many workers took advantage of employers' welfare programs, and many enjoyed the benefits. Welfare capitalism did not, however, end the problems of worker turnover and labor-management conflict. Workers recognized the purpose behind welfare capitalism. They often resented the intervention of their employers into their non-work lives and contended that softball teams and company picnics were not a substitute for higher wages. Many workers who attended English classes, went to the company picnics and played on the sports teams on company time, but attended labor union meetings on their own time. Welfare capitalism as an attempt at socially engineering a compliant workforce failed, and by the 1920s many companies had abandoned their welfare programs.

Further reading: Stuart B. Brandes, *American Welfare Capitalism, 1880–1940* (Chicago: University of Chicago Press, 1976).

— Michael Hartman

Wells-Barnett, Ida B.   See Volume VI

Wilson, Thomas Woodrow (1856–1924)

The 28th president of the United States, Thomas Woodrow Wilson, was described as a "professor-politician." Born in Virginia just prior to the Civil War, on December 28, 1856, he was raised in Georgia and the Carolinas, the son of a Presbyterian minister, in an atmosphere of austere piety. Remembered for both his oratorical skills and his idealism, he appealed to the "sovereign people" when legislators threatened his agenda. He was known to be impatient with those whom he felt were unable to understand his reforms. Unwilling to bend, Wilson was considered by some to be cold and unyielding at times and incapable of the compromises necessary in politics.

Despite an apparent dyslexia, which prevented him from learning to read until the age of 10, Wilson developed a heightened interest in literature and politics as a boy. He attended Davidson College near Charlotte, North Carolina, for a year before entering Princeton University in 1875. He studied law after graduation at the University of Virginia. Two years of practicing law, however, was enough to prompt him to leave law and continue his graduate studies in history and government at Johns Hopkins University. In 1886 he received his Ph.D., the only president to earn that degree. He taught history and political science at Bryn Mawr College, Wesleyan University, and finally at Princeton.

In 1885, Wilson married Ellen Louise Axson, the daughter of a Presbyterian minister from Georgia. He had three daughters—Margaret, Jessie, and Eleanor. Although Ellen suffered from depression, their marriage was said to be happy. Ellen's death in August 1914 devastated Wilson until he met and married his second wife, Edith Bolling Galt, in December 1915.

Wilson's rise to political power was meteoric. In 1909 he was the president of Princeton University, where he was known for progressive programs and innovations that attracted the attention of the DEMOCRATIC PARTY. They helped elect him governor of New Jersey. Known for fighting political corruption, he was picked out for the presidential nomination in 1912. A fractious split in the REPUBLICAN PARTY between THEODORE ROOSEVELT and WILLIAM HOWARD TAFT gave Wilson the opportunity he needed. A split party ensured Wilson's success in the presidential election as well as a Democratic victory in Congress. These victories created an environment for reform.

Wilson's domestic policies focused on social and economic reforms. The NEW FREEDOM, Wilson's platform in the 1912 election, included legislation concerning tariff reform, currency reform, and child labor laws, and was the

Thomas Woodrow Wilson *(Library of Congress)*

basis of the early success of his presidency. The Wilson administration's first attack on the domestic front was on the tariffs, the banks, and the trusts, known as the "triple wall of privilege." Wilson personally presented his appeal to Congress for the UNDERWOOD-SIMMONS TARIFF bill. This bill provided for a large reduction in rates and import fees. He moved the Congress sufficiently to have the bill pass. A related measure, instituting the new graduated income tax, also was enacted.

Sweeping reform of the banking system was the second area of interest. Again Wilson appealed to the sovereign people and won. In 1913 he signed the FEDERAL RESERVE ACT. It created the new Federal Reserve Board, which controlled 12 regional reserve districts, each with a central bank. It also issued Federal Reserve notes backed by paper money, thus controlling the amount of currency. Trusts were targeted with the FEDERAL TRADE COMMISSION ACT of 1914. This commission focused on monopolies and tried to prevent unfair trade practices. It furthered the antitrust policies of Roosevelt and Taft. Other progressive measures put forth included the FEDERAL FARM LOAN ACT of 1916, making credit available to farmers at low interest rates; the WORKMEN'S COMPENSATION ACT of 1916 for federal civil service employees; and the ADAMSON ACT of 1916, which established an eight-hour day for railroad workers. In contrast, Wilson ignored race relations and demands for civil rights, as he presided over a new, segregated federal bureaucracy.

The Wilson administration inherited troubles in Mexico. Throughout his presidency, Wilson wavered between a policy of "watchful waiting" and armed intervention in the affairs of Mexico. He tried to maintain good relations, but raids conducted by Pancho Villa, kidnappings of American government officials, and threats of an alliance with Germany made this policy hard to keep.

In foreign policy, Wilson is perhaps best remembered for his vision of a "New World Order in the Fourteen Points." A man of peace, Wilson charted a course of NEUTRALITY for the United States during the first years of WORLD WAR I. From 1914 to 1917, he successfully kept the country neutral by maintaining trading rights with Britain while not provoking Germany. In the 1916 election, Wilson ran on the slogan, "he kept us out of war," and defeated Supreme Court Justice CHARLES EVANS HUGHES. During the neutrality policy, Wilson continually strove to put an end to the fighting and called on all to accept "peace without victory." Germany's acceleration of unrestricted submarine warfare in 1917 left Wilson with no choice but to go to Congress with a declaration of war on April 2, 1917.

The military policy of the United States at this point was shaped by the desire to exert American influence after the war. Wilson rebuffed attempts to limit American participation or place troops under European command. European commanders allowed the AMERICAN EXPEDITIONARY FORCE to function under the command of the general, JOHN PERSHING. At home, Wilson directed the mobilization of resources and he continued to work for an end to the fighting during mobilization. The American Expeditionary Force made vital contributions to the Allied effort. When the United States entered the war, France was on the verge of collapse. Within 18 months, the Germans agreed to an armistice due to the AEF's intervention.

Wilson became a leading figure at the Paris peace negotiations that established the postwar order in Europe. As the first president of the United States to leave the country while in office, he departed for France on December 4, 1918. He arrived in France as a hero, but he was unable to convince the other three Allies—Italy (Orlando), France (Clemenceau), and Britain (Lloyd George)—to accept his vision of peace. France especially was determined to keep Germany weak through loss of territory and payment of reparations. Wilson did manage to prevent or delay some of the more extreme provisions. He convinced the Allies as well of the necessity of the LEAGUE OF NATIONS, and with this returned home.

Once in the United States, Wilson was unable to convince Congress to accept the TREATY OF VERSAILLES. Led by Republican and old-time rival, Senator HENRY CABOT LODGE, the opposition argued against the League of Nations, calling it a "sewing circle." Wilson refused to make concessions and again went to the American people with his ideas. He toured the country giving speeches until his health failed and his tour stopped abruptly. He lost the vote in Congress, and the Versailles Treaty was not ratified. For the rest of his administration, Wilson was an invalid. He continued on until February 3, 1924, but never again regained his physical capacities. He died in 1924.

The legacy of Wilson's administration is vast. Three amendments to the Constitution were passed during his presidency. The Seventeenth Amendment provided for DIRECT ELECTION OF SENATORS, a move toward increased democratization. The Eighteenth Amendment prohibited the manufacture, sale, or transportation of intoxicating liquors. The Nineteenth Amendment granted women the right to vote. Other successes included the Federal Reserve Act, the CLAYTON ANTITRUST ACT, the KEATING-OWEN CHILD LABOR ACT and the Adamson Act. In foreign policy, Wilson's vision of the League of Nations, the precursor to the United Nations, and his influence on the TREATY OF VERSAILLES, remained paramount.

Further reading: Kenderick A. Clements, *The Presidency of Woodrow Wilson* (Lawrence: University of Kansas Press, 1992); August Hecksler, *Woodrow Wilson* (New York: Scribner, 1991).

— Annamarie Edelen

woman suffrage

At the beginning of the 20th century, the woman suffrage movement, founded at women's rights conventions in the 1840s and 1850s, reached a watershed. The generation of pioneer leaders, including such notable suffragists Elizabeth Cady Stanton, Lucy Stone, and Sojourner Truth, had passed from the scene. Susan B. Anthony, considered by many suffragists as "the mother of us all," resigned as president of the NATIONAL AMERICAN WOMAN SUFFRAGE ASSOCIATION (NAWSA), having reached her 80th birthday. In 1900, women had the right to vote only in four western states (Wyoming, Utah, Colorado, and Idaho). Lacking financial support, with a small and dispersed membership, disorganized leaders, and facing a long dry spell in suffrage activity, NAWSA elected Anthony's hand-picked protégée, CARRIE CHAPMAN CATT, as its next president.

In the next two decades, Catt had an enormous impact on reorganizing and revitalizing the suffrage at both the federal level and in the states. As NAWSA president from 1900 to 1905 and again from 1916 to 1920, Catt recruited

prestigious members of society (Catt's "society plan") to the suffrage ranks and, in doing so, established the credibility and respectability of the suffrage cause. Further, NAWSA was able to fill its empty coffers with the funds gained from new converts. By shepherding its resources and focusing on winnable state-level campaigns, NAWSA was able to overcome the long gap between suffrage victories and gain the vote for women in Washington State in 1910 and in California the following year. In each campaign, precinct-level organization, and the coalition among progressive reformers, proved crucial.

Suffrage supporters faced strong opposition from organized ANTI-SUFFRAGISTS, due to widespread beliefs about women's traditional role, but the public often had other fears. Giving women the right to vote radically expanded the electorate, and it was, along with other democratic reforms, controversial in the magnitude of its action. Since the late 19th century, anti-suffrage leagues brought together those who wanted to restrict the ballot with those who reacted against women entering public life. Yet, by 1910, the "society plan" had given new respectability and new resources to the struggle for woman suffrage. Catt's choice of a more consciously political strategy to educate public opinion and mobilize citizens in favor of women's right to vote brought NAWSA a wave of new members. As a matter of expediency, she also downplayed the historic role of racial equality in the struggle for women's rights. Some suffragists argued for literacy tests for voters and for women to have admission to whites-only primaries in the segregated South, among other ways of restricting the vote. Catt, however, did not accept the southern states' rights strategy that would have rejected a federal amendment entirely. African-American women, for the most part, organized their own suffrage organizations when faced with these segregationist sentiments. Support for woman suffrage was, on the whole, stronger in the black community than among whites. But while suffragists conflicted with each other in such key areas as organizing among wage-earning women, racial equality, states' rights, and the importance of a federal amendment, the woman suffrage movement rapidly gained ground under Catt's plan.

By the 1910s, Catt's deliberate organization and the seeming incompetence of then NAWSA president, Anna Howard Shaw, made younger women impatient. Working with such leaders as Alice Stone Blackwell and HARRIOT STANTON BLATCH, the daughters of suffrage pioneers, a younger generation of suffragists mobilized in support of women's right to vote through independent means and organizations. The College Equal Suffrage League, the Equality League of Self-Supporting Women, and Political Equality Association, among many others, began to shift interests away from the gradualism advocated by NAWSA into more militant tactics and publicity-minded campaigns. Blatch and others created new forms of protest, borrowing from other social movement traditions, and inaugurated suffrage parades and motorcades and street corner debates,

The most important of these efforts came originally under the wing of NAWSA, when it formed its Congressional Committee to pursue the question of a federal woman suffrage amendment. Led by ALICE PAUL, the committee soon left NAWSA's ranks to form the Congressional Union (CU), reorganized as the NATIONAL WOMAN'S PARTY in 1916. What the Congressional Union attempted to do was to redirect the efforts and resources of the woman suffrage movement away from state-by-state campaigns toward the passage and ratification of what came to be called the Anthony Amendment, in honor of the great suffragist. State campaigns had exhausted the energies of an entire generation, and yet by 1914 women could vote in only a handful of states. By working toward a federal amendment, long the ambition of both Anthony

and Stanton, women would be granted the vote not by separate state campaigns but in one sweeping piece of legislation.

The tactics of the young radical suffragists extended the pressure tactics of public lobby and petition campaigns to hold the party in office responsible. They sought to make a politician's failure to support woman suffrage costly. Borrowing heavily from British suffragist Emmeline Pankhurst's Women's Political Union, the Congressional Union adopted militant protest as its hallmark. In 1917 it developed the Silent Sentinel campaign to picket the White House nonstop until then-president WOODROW WILSON agreed to support woman suffrage. When women were arrested in the course of picketing, CU members, following the lead of British suffragists, went on hunger strikes to arouse public sympathy.

In 1915, after a 10-year hiatus, Carrie Chapman Catt once again became president of NAWSA. She returned with a campaign of her own design, the "Winning Plan" for a federal amendment. Catt offered the suffrage movement

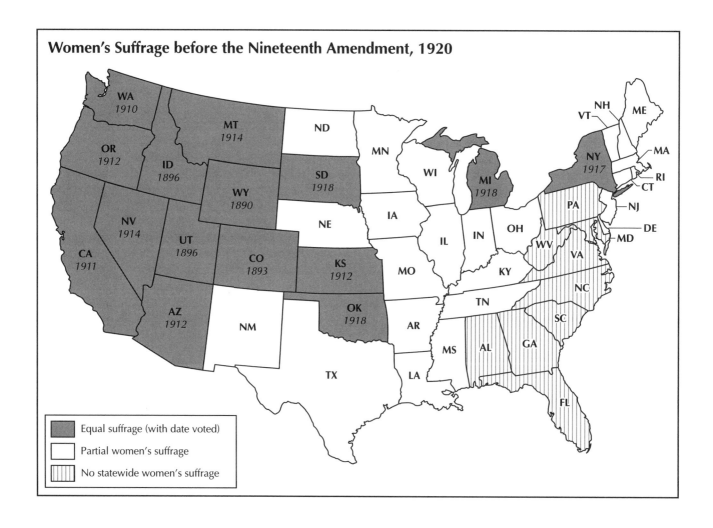

Women's Suffrage before the Nineteenth Amendment, 1920

a centralized, efficient, and partisan means of achieving the goal of woman suffrage. To stop wasting time on endless state-level campaigns, NAWSA was now to join ranks with those who proposed and supported a federal amendment granting women the right to vote. Rather than spend time petitioning and lobbying countless state legislatures, NAWSA, through its Congressional Committee, was to take on the job of persuading a majority of congressmen and senators to shift their votes toward woman suffrage. As part of the move to focus all energies on the federal Anthony amendment, Catt also centralized decision making in the hands of the Executive Board, which she appointed. Catt's goal was to "keep the suffrage noise up" all around the country in order to ensure the ultimate victory for women's vote. She was vastly helped by money from the widow of publisher Frank Leslie, who willed her estate to NAWSA to fund suffrage work.

During WORLD WAR I, woman suffragists faced a central dilemma. They were divided not only on issues of strategy and tactics, but also about the war itself. When the United States entered the war in 1917, there were many suffragists who opposed the war, both due to their pacifism and also because they viewed America's participation as wrong. For Alice Paul and the National Woman's Party, the war was irrelevant to the goal of winning the vote for women, an attitude for which they were widely condemned. A founding member of the Woman's Peace Party, Carrie Chapman Catt set aside her pacifism with a pragmatic understanding that opposition to the war effort would only undermine the case for woman suffrage. She served during the war on the Woman's Committee on National Defense, which coordinated women's volunteer work in support of the war.

In 1918, women's support for American participation in the war persuaded some politicians to end their opposition to woman suffrage and vote for the federal amendment. Supported now by President Wilson, what became the Nineteenth Amendment to the Constitution, which granted women the right to vote, passed the House of Representatives. The Senate, after voting it down in 1918, passed the federal amendment in 1919. NAWSA, the National Woman's Party, and other suffrage organizations now swung into action in the ratification campaign. Tennessee became the 36th state to ratify the Nineteenth Amendment in August of 1920, and woman suffrage was finally a reality throughout the United States.

Further reading: Ellen Carol DuBois, *Harriot Stanton Blatch and the Winning of Woman Suffrage* (New Haven, Conn.: Yale University Press, 1996); Eleanor Flexner and Ellen Fitzpatrick, *Century of Struggle: The Women's Rights Movement in the United States,* enl. ed. (Cambridge, Mass.: Belknap Press, 1996); Sara Hunter Graham, *Woman Suf-* *frage and the New Democracy* (New Haven, Conn.: Yale University Press, 1996).

Women's International League for Peace and Freedom (WILPF)

In the midst of WORLD WAR I, female suffragists primarily from Europe and the United States met in The Hague, Netherlands, to discuss prospects for world peace and expanding women's rights. The seeds that were planted in 1915 came to fruition in 1919 when the Women's International League for Peace and Freedom was created. WILPF was an early proponent of marrying suffrage and post-suffrage activism to issues of world peace. Its founders believed that only in a world without war and injustice could people be truly free. WILPF's first international president was JANE ADDAMS, a well-known American progressive activist and founder of Hull-House. In 1931, she became the first American woman to win the Nobel Peace Prize.

WILPF's philosophy reflected the progressive emphasis on social justice and exemplified the moral grounds on which women entered male politics in the Progressive Era. The organization was influenced by the belief that war and other forms of violence could be prevented if politics and government had more women representatives and if society adopted more "feminine" characteristics. Women possessed certain traits, such as cooperativeness, that most WILPF women claimed would counteract male competitiveness and violence. Although the group's philosophy corresponded to what most Americans believed about women, its political affiliation was often questioned. During the RED SCARE, WILPF's antimilitarism was sometimes viewed as unpatriotic, causing some of its critics, including Secretary of War John D. Weeks, to label it "red." Other critics, however, opposed female suffrage and female political activism and, therefore, redbaited the organization in order to discredit it and undermine its appeal. Despite the attacks, WILPF's appeal grew. With 2,000 members in 1921, the American section grew to 13,000 by 1937.

During its early years, WILPF dedicated itself to three main issues: internationalism, disarmament, and anti-militarism. WILPF supported the efforts of the LEAGUE OF NATIONS and other international institutions in their attempts at international disarmament and diplomatic cooperation. Through these campaigns, the women of WILPF demonstrated their belief in their own power as women to influence nations and leaders in foreign policy decision making. In 1926, WILPF sent a delegation to Haiti to investigate the effects of the American occupation. In the late 1920s, the organization petitioned American politicians to withdraw from Nicaragua. WILPF representatives, including Jane Addams, lobbied President

CALVIN COOLIDGE to support the KELLOGG-BRIAND TREATY, a treaty proposing that countries renounce war.

A major tenet of the organization's agenda was the establishment of an international network of women. To that end, WILPF sent a delegation to Indochina and China in 1927. WILPF women maintained that if women in nations around the world pressured their governments, then war could be prevented. Although WILPF enjoyed considerable success as far as having access to influential politicians, particularly in the United States, its goal of averting war was not an international priority in the 1930s, as most Western economies fell into a depression, prompting governments to focus on economic strategies. Disarmament, an issue that most Western nations pursued in theory in the 1920s, was abandoned in practice as countries could not enforce its provisions in the 1930s. The 1932 disarmament conference in Geneva included female delegates for the first time, including WILPF's Mary Woolley in the American delegation. Diplomatic crises in Asia and President Hoover's lukewarm support for the conference revealed that international cooperation on disarmament was taking a backseat to other issues. WILPF, nonetheless, continued to focus on disarmament throughout the decade.

See also WOMEN'S STATUS AND RIGHTS.

Further reading: Linda K. Schott, *Reconstructing Women's Thoughts: The Women's International League for Peace and Freedom before World War II* (Palo Alto, Calif.: Stanford University Press, 1997); Carrie Foster, *The Women and the Warriors: The U.S. Section of the Women's International League for Peace and Freedom, 1915–1946* (Syracuse, N.Y.: Syracuse University Press, 1995).

— Natalie Atkin

women's status and rights

Women's struggle for greater political rights and higher social status came to a peak in the years between 1900 and 1920. In 1900, only a few American states granted women the right to vote. Few women practiced law, due to long-standing exclusions from law schools and the bar. A host of other laws and customs kept women from full equality. Protective labor legislation kept them from night work and prescribed their hours of work. By the 1920s, some feminists came to view these laws as barriers to women's equality. During the first 20 years of the 20th century, women poured their energy into gaining the vote and other political rights. Volunteer organizations laid the groundwork for women's intense civic engagement. At the same time, the WOMAN SUFFRAGE movement faced a new challenge from feminism, an ideology of equality between the sexes that went from the single-minded pursuit of the vote into broader issues of women's equality.

In the years between 1900 and 1930, women in the United States were faced with inequality in every area of social, political, and economic life. As the 20th century began, they lacked the vote, could not serve on juries, and did not, for the most part, have the right to run for elected office. School suffrage in some states had opened the door for women to run for school superintendent, but apart from this position, they did not serve in government. In social life, married women continued to be subordinate to their husbands, and most took his name at marriage. They had no easy access to birth control. They had only recently received the right to own property, have custody of their children, and retain their own wages. In practice, few women had control over how family money was spent.

In the workplace, women faced discrimination and even exclusion from certain occupations and lacked the political clout or the union organization to fight back. While female labor force participation slowly rose from 1900 to 1930, most women continued to hold low-wage, semi-skilled jobs, and often had only seasonal employment. There was little job security and even less opportunity for promotion. For married women, who constituted only a small proportion of the labor force, there was even less opportunity, as employers often refused to hire married or older women by preference. Family work also kept married women from regular employment, and those who needed income had to take in sewing, laundry, or boarders.

The poverty, poor working conditions, and uncertainty of working women's lives prompted many to organize. For working-class women, it most often meant turning to the labor movement, but middle- and upper-class women also were aware of working women's plight and turned toward new forms of organization. In 1903, settlement house workers, trade unionists, and reformers met to form the NATIONAL WOMEN'S TRADE UNION LEAGUE (NWTUL). Based on a British model of cross-class alliance, the NWTUL urged women workers to organize unions and informed the public about their needs. Like the National Consumers' League, the NWTUL supported maximum hour and minimum wage laws and even local ordinances that required stores to have seats for women workers. The General Federation of Women's Clubs, originally organized as a forum for women's educational and social needs, evolved a new agenda of legislation to improve workplace conditions and require new safety standards, such as barring the manufacture of phosphorous matches. Suffrage organizations also developed new approaches to mobilizing women for the vote, and they began to work with working-class women in suffrage campaigns.

The commitment to women's equality was evident in the work of CHARLOTTE PERKINS GILMAN. A follower of progressive sociologist Lester Ward, Gilman believed in social evolution, social progress, and equality of oppor-

Suffragists marching in New York City, 1913 *(Library of Congress)*

tunity between the sexes. As a result of her 1898 work, *Women and Economics,* Gilman became the leading intellectual of the women's movement in the United States during the early 20th century. In *Women and Economics,* Gilman spoke of the high cost to society and individual women of their isolation in the home and exclusion from the world of paid work. She urged women to move out of home occupations into arenas previously dominated by men.

By the turn of the century, the struggle for women's equality generated a new BIRTH CONTROL movement to combat state and federal laws against the distribution of birth control information or devices. Radicals EMMA GOLDMAN, MARGARET SANGER, and Mary Ware Dennett challenged conventional respectability and the law in speaking publicly about sex and contraception. They urged women to exercise their sexual freedom and control their reproductive capacity free from state interference. Without birth control, women were prevented from achieving full economic status and rights in their sexual freedom.

Sanger's work in promoting birth control brought her into the public spotlight. Her work as a practical nurse had brought her to understand the lack of control women had over their own bodies. The public relations strategy she used deepened public awareness and challenged laws that suppressed the free circulation of contraceptive information. She published a journal, *The Woman Rebel,* beginning in 1914, and a pamphlet, *Family Limitation,* which gave advice to women about various birth control methods. In 1916 Sanger opened the first birth control clinic in Brooklyn, New York. New York State law specified in Section 1142 that no one could give information to prevent conception to anyone for any reason. Sanger and two of the clinic's staff members were arrested for violating the law. While she fled to Europe to evade prosecution and later returned to a successful public acquittal, Sanger changed her emphasis by 1919 from women's control of their own bodies to eugenic reasoning about better babies.

The struggle for women's equality inspired women's activism in an ever-broadening range of causes. The prime obstacle, however, was women's lack of voting rights. When CARRIE CHAPMAN CATT, head of the NATIONAL AMERICAN WOMAN SUFFRAGE ASSOCIATION, publicly argued "Why Women Want to Vote" in early 1915, the first of her reasons was justice, and the second was that voting was the duty of women citizens. Society, Catt believed, needed women's skills and labor in schooling, dealing with unemployment, and caring for the indigent. An important aspect of her argument was its blend of the two schools of feminist thought. Catt argued both for women's "sameness" (their similarity to men) and their "difference" as reasons to grant women the same political capacities as men.

The struggle for women's equality took a turn for the better when, in 1920, the required number of states ratified the Nineteenth Amendment to the Constitution, which gave women the right to vote. Although many people thought the need for the women's movement ended with its passage, women still faced many enormous obstacles in their pursuit of equal rights. ALICE PAUL was a leader in seeking to pull down the obstacles to women's equality. She believed that women's rights would be won only through ongoing struggle. Even though the vote advanced the cause of women's equality, it did not satisfy them. As leader of the NATIONAL WOMAN'S PARTY, Paul took the next step by drafting the EQUAL RIGHTS AMENDMENT to the Constitution. This amendment, she argued, would guarantee that men and women would have uniform, equal rights throughout the United States. The proposed amendment generated immediate response, most of it negative, from many former suffragists. They also had fought for protective labor legislation for women workers, and they saw the ERA as a threat to these protections. In support of the ERA, Suzanne La Follette in her book, *Concerning Women,* argued against protective legislation for women. She believed labor laws that applied only to women allowed employers to discriminate against them. For women to have equal opportunity for industrial employment, labor standards must apply equally to men and women. La Follette believed full economic independence and personal autonomy would be achieved only through true sex equality.

Women advocates now moved in different and sometimes opposing directions. In 1919, Carrie Chapman Catt proposed that the enormous National American Woman Suffrage Association reconfigure itself as the League of Women Voters. Its agenda focused on three main areas: equal legal status for women, efficiency in public welfare, and international peace through cooperation. Catt's preference was for women to remain aloof from partisan commitments and independent from party politics.

Many agreed that woman suffrage was an outstanding victory, but they felt that the great expectations held for it were not realized and claimed that there were few female candidates for elective office. Still, despite the failure of women to vote as a bloc or even in sufficient numbers, many aspects of politics were transformed when women gained the right to vote. Party women insisted on representation in state and national committees, and women began appearing at national political conventions. Women lobbyists and federal agency employees were able to pass the SHEPPARD-TOWNER ACT (1921) and the CABLE ACT

(1922), which granted women access to maternal health programs and equal citizenship after marriage. The agenda of political parties had shifted under the influence of women voters and their organizations.

Women like settlement leader JANE ADDAMS, known for founding Hull-House and the social work movement, turned thus reform convictions to a new direction. Addams believed that, in order for women to have equality, violence in its many forms must be suppressed. In particular, to free women of their inferior status, the possibility of war must be controlled through peace organizations and war itself eventually outlawed. At the outbreak of WORLD WAR I, Addams poured her energy into the peace movement. She helped to found the WOMEN'S INTERNATIONAL LEAGUE FOR PEACE AND FREEDOM.

Addams, like other feminists of her generation, was a target for the postwar anti-radicalism of the RED SCARE. While A. Mitchell Palmer focused on immigrant radicals and militant labor organizers, other politicians viewed women's organizations as a threat. In the 1920s, a spider chart of the red network located Addams as the leader of the WILPF at its center. She was, some claimed, "the pinkest of the pink." The postwar period also gave rise to antifeminism and a trend toward stifling social conformity in the relations between the sexes. Opponents of women's equality used a conservative defense and sought to constrict women's sphere to the domestic realm through appeals to scripture and contemporary social scientific theories, which placed emphasis on physical differences between men and women. Practitioners of psychology found common ground with conservative thinkers by opposing the gains of women. They used the theories of SIGMUND FREUD to bolster beliefs in the biologically determined and divinely sanctioned subordination of women. Sexologists turned to HAVELOCK ELLIS for a new celebration of heterosexual marriage. Their psycho-biological approach claimed that "biology is destiny" for women. In contrast, new studies by anthropologist MARGARET MEAD downplayed sexual differences and argued for a much greater range of gender identity and sexual practice.

The 1920s and the 1930s saw a group consciousness among minority women. This generated a new energy toward the gain in women's status and rights. The longstanding NATIONAL ASSOCIATION OF COLORED WOMEN focused its agenda on confronting racial oppression. It also continued to unite black clubwomen across the United States, who had the "double task" of struggling for race oppression and sex emancipation.

The struggle for women's rights went through a period of scrutiny at the end of the 1920s. Some saw feminism as outdated, since women had the vote. Others believed things had gone too far and claimed the pursuit of sexual equality was destructive to society. The indisputable legacy of the postwar debate was its understanding of the paradox of how to be a human being and a woman too.

See also *ADKINS V. CHILDREN'S HOSPITAL;* LABOR AND LABOR MOVEMENT; *MULLER V. OREGON;* THE NEW WOMAN.

Further reading: Nancy F. Cott, *The Grounding of Modern Feminism* (New Haven, Conn.: Yale University Press, 1987); Angela Howard and Sasha Ranae Adams Tarrant, *Redefining the New Woman, 1920–1963* (New York: Garland Publishing, 1997); Alice S. Rossi, ed., *The Feminist Papers: From Adams to de Beauvoir* (Boston: Northeastern University Press, 1973).

— Marcia M. Farah

work, household

The period between 1900 and 1930 showed a marked change in the way that household labor was organized and performed, especially among urban families. The changes were threefold: improvement in municipal sanitation, water supply, and heat and light; changes in domestic technology, including the introduction of household appliances such as the refrigerator, the washing machine, and electric or gas stoves; and the decline of live-in domestic servants among the middle class, which increased the domestic work of women. Food provision and preparation already had changed with the increasing use of commercial bakeries, the widespread production and use of canned goods, chain grocery stores, and electrical appliances for the preparation of food. Ready-made clothing began to be more widely available in the 1880s, especially for men; by 1900, new styles of DRESS, including the introduction of the shirtwaist and the increased availability of children's clothing, reduced the amount of sewing done in the home. The purchasing of groceries, clothing, and household items further changed as chain food and department stores and new forms of urban and suburban transport, including the automobile, made possible the use of downtown shopping districts and centralized stores rather than neighborhood shops. These changes also shifted the burden of obtaining household goods almost entirely to women.

Improvements in access to and quality of public utilities changed the daily routine of urban women doing household work. Fetching water from public pumps, long

From a young age girls were training for the housework that was expected of them when they matured *(Library of Congress)*

a major and dreaded chore for women and children, was no longer necessary in an era of running tap water and water closets. Indoor plumbing throughout the house, including heated water, however, led to a demand for cleaner kitchens and bathrooms. Gas and then electric lighting became widespread in urban areas; so too did oil and gas furnaces for heating and gas ranges for food preparation. By 1930, nearly 50 percent of households did their cooking with gas. The price of electric energy and appliances dropped significantly, so that more than one-third of all residences were wired for electricity by 1920. During the ensuing decade, electric washing machines, vacuum cleaners, sewing machines, and reliable refrigerators became cheaper and more available. Electric toasters, cake mixers, irons, and food grinders were more popular. Among rural households there were fewer changes, especially due to the lack of a rural electrical supply. It would not be until the 1930s that farmsteads saw the widespread adoption of household appliances and indoor plumbing.

The overall impact of these developments was to alter the division of labor within the household and shift the burden even more heavily onto women. Indoor plumbing and gas stoves removed the need to fetch water and chop wood or shovel coal, but these tasks had normally been shared among household members. In contrast, the addition of new appliances for cooking and cleaning, such as the power vacuum and the partially mechanized washing machine, caused household work to multiply. Heightened standards of cleanliness, abetted by fears of infection and enhanced by the hard sell of ADVERTISING, steadily increased the number of meals cooked, clothes washed, and rooms cleaned.

Further, child care remained the responsibility of women in the household, even as children spent less time at home. Public EDUCATION, including new kindergarten programs and compulsory schooling laws, removed children from the care of their parents and siblings for long hours, and new high schools offered adolescents extended schooling and time outside the family. These changes meant that older children were no longer available to supervise younger siblings. Further, new forms of RECREATION, especially those designed for YOUTH, and continued patterns of employment among young adults meant less help with household chores. At the same time, there were increased expectations for women within motherhood. Hysteria about the new sexual behavior of Jazz Age youth gave rise to the criticism that the NEW WOMAN was a poor parent. Spending time with younger children, and devoting increased time to keeping a clean and well-regulated household, increased women's household labor and lengthened their domestic work day.

See also MARRIAGE AND FAMILY LIFE.

Further reading: Ruth Schwartz Cowan, *More Work for Mother: The Ironies of Household Technologies from the Open Hearth to the Microwave* (New York: Basic Books, 1983); Susan Strasser, *Never Done: A History of American Housework* (New York: Pantheon Books, 1982).

work, wage   See labor and labor movement

Workmen's Compensation Act (1916)

The Kern-McGillicuddy Workmen's Compensation Act of 1916 enabled workers to collect compensation for injuries sustained in the workplace. Prior to the passage of the act, workers alone were deemed responsible for their actions and ensuring their own safety. Following the "fellow-servant rule," employers were not held responsible for injuries sustained as a result of negligence on the part of other employees. Prior to 1900, state and federal courts interpreted this rule to mean that employers were almost never responsible for work-related injuries. As greater numbers of employees worked in dangerous industrial workplaces, which were often made even more hazardous by the employer's failure to provide safeguards, the need for effective workmen's compensation increased.

One of the immediate stimuli behind the push for workmen's compensation was the 1911 fire at the TRIANGLE SHIRTWAIST COMPANY in New York City, which killed 146 female employees. The workers were unable to escape the blaze because exits were either blocked or locked from the outside. The disaster and subsequent acquittal of the company's owners shocked many and convinced reformers and labor leaders of the need for legislative action. In the absence of federal legislation, individual states had begun to enact workmen's compensation legislation. In 1902, Maryland became the first state to pass legislation. By 1910 many others had followed its lead. The organized labor movement was among the first to support state and federal legislation. The AMERICAN FEDERATION OF LABOR began calling for effective workmen's compensation in 1894. Other labor organizations, including the American Association for Labor Legislation (AALL), also supported compensation for injured workers.

By 1916, 35 states had passed workmen's compensation legislation, but the effectiveness of these laws varied greatly. Some state laws, such as the one passed in New Jersey in 1911, were comprehensive and highly effective. Other states, however, had much weaker laws. The problem was complicated by the fact that state laws were consistently challenged and undermined by state judiciaries. Arguing the fellow-servant clause, employers convinced state and federal courts that workmen's compensation legislation violated equal protection under the law and freedom of contract. In 1909, in an important case, *Ives v. South Buffalo Railway Company*, the New York State law was ruled unconstitutional, this time by the state supreme court.

Pressure to pass federal legislation mounted in the aftermath of the Triangle Shirtwaist Fire. Concerned about maintaining the support of organized labor as he prepared for the inevitable entry of the United States into WORLD WAR I, President WOODROW WILSON announced his support for the Kern-McGillicuddy Act in 1916. Drafted by the AALL, the act received widespread support. Wilson signed it into law in 1916. The Workmen's Compensation Act was an important step in improving working conditions and protecting workers. The law was given greater weight in 1917, when in *New York Central Railroad Company v. White*, the Supreme Court finally upheld legislation passed in New York. Nevertheless, the ability of workers to collect compensation for employer negligence remained limited. Employer negligence remained difficult to prove, and many state courts continued to be reluctant to hold employers responsible.

Further reading: Claudia Clark, *Radium Girls: Women and Industrial Health Reform, 1910–1935* (Chapel Hill: University of North Carolina Press, 1997).

— Robert Gordon

World War I

The First World War, known at the time as the Great War, was the first war to engage the entire European continent since Napoleon was defeated in 1815. It produced worldwide social and political upheaval. The war involved over 70 million combatants and ended in the death of between nine and 12 million people. By its end, the economy of Europe was devastated and its governments either overthrown or reorganized. After it was over, many hoped that it would be "the war to end all wars."

Internationally, the period before 1914 was one of heightened tensions between the "Great Powers" and great change. Nationalist movements, strengthened by an increasing awareness of ethnic identity, added to the instability. The Austro-Hungarian and Ottoman Empires struggled to come to grips with their citizens' desire for self-determination, and an arms race among the nation-states of Germany, Britain, France, and Russia heightened the conflict.

The war had several causes. Great Britain sought to preserve her empire and control of the seas; France fought against German dominance and for return of her lost territories of Alsace and Lorraine. Japan sought to expand its territory as did Italy. China looked for the

return of territory lost in the BOXER REBELLION. The Americans entered, belatedly, when the Wilson administration convinced the nation to make the world safe for democracy. The violation of freedom of the seas and the loss of American lives in U-boat attacks stiffened the country's resolve to join the war.

Europe exploded in the summer of 1914 when a Serb patriot killed the heir to the throne of Austria-Hungary. An outraged Austria, backed by Germany, instantly presented an ultimatum to Serbia. Backed by its Slavic patron, Russia, Serbia refused to concede. The Russian czar mobilized his army, threatening Germany on the east. France, Russia's ally, confronted Germany on its west. Alarmed, Germany struck at France through Belgium to knock the enemy out of action. Witnessing its coastline threatened by the assault on Belgium, Great Britain entered the fight on France's side. Overnight, Europe was at war on three fronts—in the Balkans, in Russia (the eastern front), and in France and Belgium (the western front). On one side, there were the Central Powers of Germany, Austria-Hungary, Turkey, and Bulgaria. The Allies of France, Britain, and Russia, and later Japan and Italy, opposed them. The United States remained neutral.

American neutrality did not prevent it from filling British and French war orders, as business boomed. The Central Powers protested American shipments to Britain, but trade was not against international neutrality laws. Germany was free to trade with the United States as well, but it was prevented from doing so by an effective British naval blockade. The British controlled the sea lanes, and they put a blockade in place across the North Sea, which forced American ships away from German ports. In retaliation for this blockade, Germany quickly instituted a submarine war around the British Isles. German officials declared that they would try to avoid neutral ships, but they warned that, ultimately, mistakes would occur. President Wilson, therefore, had to calculate the importance of free trade and the economic benefits of insisting on neutral trading rights. The loss of American ships endangered American neutrality. Germany declared unlimited warfare on all ships. Submarine warfare ultimately drew the United States irrevocably into the fray. Once the ZIMMERMANN TELEGRAM was discovered and published, there was no going back.

When the war began, the American army numbered only 128,000 men. Due to budget cuts and traditional reliance on state militia, the army was badly in need of arms and equipment. Germany was aware of these factors, and thus discounted America's entry into the war. This prediction was seemingly confirmed by the isolationist policy of the Wilson administration until Germany's policy of unrestricted submarine warfare, brought to life by the sinking of ships such as the LUSITANIA, gave Wilson no choice but to

American soldiers manning a firing position behind barbed wire in a trench at Dieffmatten, in Alsace *(National Archives)*

protect America's economic and political interests abroad. He declared war on Germany in April 1917.

Instituting the draft in the United States under the SELECTIVE SERVICE ACT, along with the accompanying appropriation bills, prepared the AMERICAN EXPEDITIONARY FORCE for entry into the war. By the end of the war, over four million soldiers, sailors, and Marines had served their country in the war effort. For the first time in the history of the United States, women were allowed to join the armed services. Twenty-four thousand women served in the military during the war as nurses and clerks.

The Wilson administration quickly realized that it needed to mobilize resources to meet the needs of a nation at war. For the first time, the federal government stepped in to regulate all aspects of the country's industry and life. Wilson established the Food Administration, which advised Americans what and how much they should eat. The FUEL ADMINISTRATION controlled coal, gas, and oil. To fight shortages, they relied on the public's cooperation and patriotism, rather than on rationing. The NATIONAL WAR LABOR BOARD was another example of government regulation. It worked to prevent labor unrest that interfered with the wartime economy and tried to keep wages in line with needs. The WAR INDUSTRIES BOARD controlled industrial output. It made sure that industrial production met war needs. The WAR REVENUE ACT raised taxes and issued Liberty Bonds to finance the war.

Many Americans responded with enthusiasm to the patriotic call. The COMMITTEE FOR PUBLIC INFORMATION (CPI), created by President Wilson, raised public support for the war effort through propaganda. War posters urged Americans to join the army. Movie stars, marching bands, and billboards celebrated those who "did their duty." As flags were waved and bands played farewells, men rushed to volunteer for the war and the American Expeditionary Force. Back at home, citizens sacrificed for their boys. The CPI prompted support for the war partly by playing on fear of German spies and other radicals. The CPI informally censored publications until Congress, with the TRADING WITH THE ENEMY ACT (1917), gave the U.S. Post Office the responsibility of censoring materials that opposed the military draft and the war by denying mailing privileges.

Government propaganda and fear turned many Americans against everything German. Many states outlawed the German language and mobs terrorized many German-American citizens. Both the ESPIONAGE ACT of 1917 and the SEDITION ACT of 1918 reflected the government's desire to suppress dissent and popular fears of Germans and other anti-war individuals. The government prosecuted antiwar socialists and members of the INDUSTRIAL WORKERS OF THE WORLD under these acts. Anti-radical prosecutions culminated in the postwar RED SCARE.

Many important social and economic changes came of the war. Massive intervention in industry, the significant but temporary transformation of the role of women, the decline in social deference, and a realignment of class relations were all consequences of the war. There was also, however, a political shift, in the expansion of the state in relation to private citizens. The wartime suspension of individual rights in the military draft and under the Espionage and Sedition Acts had a tremendous impact on society. In addition, the Wilson administration developed machinery for domestic political surveillance. The Justice Department

and military intelligence kept tabs on labor organizers and later unhappy ex-servicemen. Such surveillance demonstrated the increased willingness of government to intervene in the lives of its private citizens.

The Great War marked the end of one era and the beginning of a new age. The military struggle of World War I was but one aspect of a changing world. As a modern war, it involved whole societies in support of the armed forces. Sweeping, irrevocable changes on the home front resulted. In the United States, where resources, labor, and industrial plants were plentiful, corporations used the War Industries Board to promote expansion. European domination of the world economy ended, and the war's end introduced a new world order. In the United States, influential capitalists sought increasing economic control over resources internationally, especially in Latin America and on the Pacific Rim. They looked to the armed forces to protect their interests.

The human cost of war was, for the first time, expressed through new media. Books, films, poetry, songs, and newspapers depicted the human cost of war and

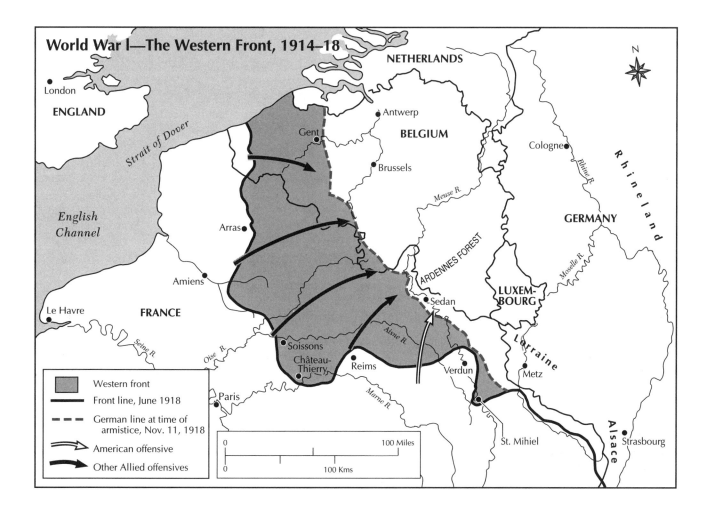

affected an entire generation, but it was not only war that had changed society. The WOMAN SUFFRAGE movement finally won its battle, with passage of the Nineteenth Amendment giving women the right to vote. Sexual norms changed in other ways, as women bobbed their hair, smoked cigarettes openly, and danced freely in public. Overall, women experienced more freedom, as the war had expanded their horizons. Returning servicemen found a social atmosphere quite different from what they had left. There were bootleggers, gangsters, Prohibition, bathtub gin, and jazz. Many returning from overseas relocated in the cities and left the rural areas behind. The popular song that asked "How you gonna keep 'em down on the farm, after they've seen Paris" seemed to be true.

The idealism of Wilson, his LEAGUE OF NATIONS, and world peace also were casualties of war. Congress, and in particular HENRY CABOT LODGE, refused to accept the league or ratify the TREATY OF VERSAILLES. As unemployment rose after the war, race relations at home soured, and disillusioned VETERANS returned home and contributed to the social discontent.

See also LOST GENERATION; VETERANS BUREAU.

Further reading: Robert Zieger, *America's Great War: World War I, the American Experience* (Lanham, Md.: Rowman and Littlefield, 2000); Ronald Schaffer, *America in the Great War: The Rise of the Modern War Welfare State* (New York: Oxford University Press, 1991).

— Annamarie Edelen

Wright, Frank Lloyd (1867–1958)

America's best-known architect, Frank Lloyd Wright, helped create an American style of ARCHITECTURE and ushered in the modern architectural age. He is known for his designs ranging from large office buildings to small houses. His best-known work is the Pennsylvania house known as Fallingwater. Built over a waterfall in 1936, the house is a definitive example of Wright's desire to fit his designs into their surroundings. His other famous designs include the headquarters of the Johnson Wax Company in Racine, Wisconsin, the Unity Temple in Oak Park, Illinois, and the Guggenheim Museum in New York City. Due to a variety of personal developments, Wright never achieved the acclaim during his early career that he did after 1930. He is recognized today, however, as the preeminent American architect whose design style was the first to be applicable to all building types.

Born in Richland Center, Wisconsin, Wright entered the University of Wisconsin at age 15 to study engineering, although he wanted to become an architect. After two semesters, he dropped out and went to work in the architectural studio of Louis Sullivan in Chicago. After six years,

he quit Sullivan's firm and opened his own office in the Chicago suburb of Oak Park.

Wright quickly won recognition and hundreds of commissions that allowed him to work out new principles of design. Borrowing from many previous architectural styles, he eventually developed his own unique style that, in the years prior to 1930, he used primarily in the design of houses. He rejected the artificiality and rules of the classical style in favor of designs that combined structure, function, and idea with the inspiration of natural forms. The design that Wright eventually developed revolved around a set of guiding principles. These principles called for the reduction of necessary parts and the number of rooms in order to create a sense of unity throughout the entire house. He also believed that it was vital for a house to fit its surroundings, whether a rectangular lot marked by the street grid or a more natural setting.

Wright's designs eliminated box-like rooms in favor of wide doorways between rooms that occurred more naturally and he often relied on screens for dividing rooms. His principles also called for the use of straight lines and just one building material in order to make them "clearer and more expressive." His principles went beyond the structure of the house itself. Wright's desire for clarity led him to design ornamentation based on straight lines and rectangular shapes that matched both the natural settings of the house and its materials. He also sought to incorporate furnishings into his architecture by designing them in simple terms along straight lines and in rectangular forms.

Wright's designs became known as prairie-style houses because of their open design and embrace of the open spaces of the Midwest. A group of architects embraced Wright's style and became known as the "Prairie School." Wright's influence in the years before 1930 was tempered, however, by his insistence on individualism and a series of scandals that surrounded him. Because Wright believed that each architect should express his own individualism and creativity in his designs, he never set out to create a school of design. He was, in fact, openly critical of the Prairie School architects. In addition, Wright became unpopular when in 1909 he left his wife and began living with the wife of one of his clients. His personal choices lost him many commissions in the Chicago area. Despite these obstacles to the spread of his ideals, Wright became the most recognized architect in America. He did so because he was the first American architect to develop a set of principles applicable to the complete range of buildings, from small houses to large office buildings, demanded by American society.

Further reading: William J. Curtis, *Modern Architecture since 1900,* 2nd ed. (Englewood Cliffs, N.J.: Prentice Hall, 1987).

— Michael Hartman

Wright Brothers (Wilbur [1867–1912] and Orville [1871–1948])

Wilbur and Orville Wright made the first powered, sustained, and controlled flight with a heavier-than-air flying machine at Kitty Hawk, North Carolina, on December 17, 1903. The AVIATION pioneers grew up in a household led by their father, a bishop in the Church of the United Brethren in Christ, whom they later credited with fostering in them a curiosity about the way things worked. The two brothers never graduated from high school, choosing instead to study mathematics and engineering on their own. In 1889 they launched their first joint venture, a print shop. They also began to publish two short newspapers.

During the 1890s, the Wright brothers sought to use their mechanical skills to supply the booming market for bicycles. Americans were experiencing a bicycle craze triggered by mechanical developments that made them easier to ride. By 1896, the Wrights were building bicycles for sale in their small shop in Dayton, Ohio. Their business was successful, and the brothers used their profits from the sale of bicycles to finance their experiments in flight.

The Wright brothers became interested in flight after reading articles reporting the death of a German aeronautical pioneer in 1896. Between 1899 and 1905, they manufactured seven aircraft, three of which were powered. In 1901, they designed and built their own wind tunnel, which proved crucial to their eventual success. The wind tunnel allowed them to experiment with different wing designs and arches. While doing these tests, they developed the first accurate tables of lift and drag, the parameters that govern flight. From their experiments in the wind tunnel and in actual flights in the gliders they constructed, the Wright brothers developed the proper wing and tail shape to provide stability in flight. They then built an engine to power their aircraft. The aircraft that made the first flight had a wingspan of 40 feet and weighed 750 pounds, with the pilot. The brothers took turns flying it. The longest flight on that first day in 1903 lasted 59 seconds and the plane traveled at 10 mph.

The Wright brothers patented their control system and offered their plane to the U.S. War Department. They did not, however, begin to exhibit their aircraft publicly until 1908 when they undertook a promotional tour of the

Orville Wright flying a Wright glider at Kill Devil Hills, near Kitty Hawk, North Carolina. The flight was officially the first sustained, controlled flight by a heavier-than-air-craft. Wilbur Wright runs alongside his brother *(Hulton/Archive)*

United States and Europe. By 1909, they could sustain a flight for 20 miles and governments in the United States and Europe began to order planes. To meet the demand, the Wright brothers formed the Wright Company to manufacture and sell their aircraft.

Wilbur Wright died of typhoid fever in 1912, and Orville sold the Wright Company to investors in 1915. He continued to play an important role in aeronautics. He served as a consulting engineer during WORLD WAR I and became a member of the National Advisory Committee for Aeronautics.

Further reading: Tom D. Crouch, *The Bishop's Boys: A Life of Wilbur and Orville Wright* (New York: W.W. Norton, 1989).

— Michael Hartman

Y

Young Men's Christian Association and Young Women's Christian Association (YMCA and YWCA)

The YMCA and YWCA were established in the mid-19th century by middle-class Protestants in reaction to the movement of both native-born, white rural migrants and alien immigrants into American cities. The reformers who established the associations worried about the moral health of the young men and women migrating to the cities. They feared that the established churches were not equipped to cope with the problems that single young migrants presented. They therefore established YMCAs and YWCAs to help the migrants adapt to urban life. During the first three decades of the 20th century, the YMCA and YWCA expanded their programs in an effort to bring more young men and women through their doors. As its programs became less attractive to young men, the YMCA began to offer recreational programs for YOUTHS, which would eventually become its primary mission.

American cities provided numerous challenges for new migrants. They had to find a job, a place to live, and food. After they took care of all these necessities, then they would seek out leisure-time activities. All of these decisions could present problems for young men and women. The wrong job or place to live could pose dangers to the moral health of the migrants.

Of particular concern to the YMCAs was what the young men did in their leisure time. Because the young migrants had left their families and communities behind they often made these decisions without the guidance of family members. The YMCA sought to step in to help young male migrants adjust to urban life. At the same time, middle-class Protestants feared that if the migrants remained unsupervised, they posed a threat to the social order. If the young men were not taught proper middle-class values and behaviors, they might fall prey to radical political propaganda. The YMCAs created programs, therefore, to both protect the migrants and the social order.

The YWCA's original mission was to protect women from the dangers of the city and to lessen class conflicts by teaching working women middle-class values. The YWCAs sought to provide a moral environment for young women in what the YWCA leaders saw as an immoral urban world. Eventually, the YWCA recognized the economic reality that was at the root of the dangers posed to young women in the industrial order and began to champion reform movements for the betterment of the social and economic conditions in which young working women lived. YWCAs altered their mission to meet the needs of these new migrants to the city. As YWCA workers interacted with young women, they realized that their low wages presented the real problem for single working women and that the threat to the young women's morality lay in what they might do to make ends meet. YWCA workers feared that women might resort to prostitution as the only available means to earning enough money to live on. The YWCA's programs therefore revolved around the dangers presented by the low wages available to women.

To fight this threat, the YWCAs established programs aimed at making it cheaper for these women to live in American cities and also joined reform movements that sought to change women's place in the social, political, and economic order. By creating vocational education classes, for example, the YWCA tried to help women gain skills with which they could earn higher wages. Low-cost lunch rooms provided the women with a decent meal at an inexpensive price. Affordable apartments in a supervised, Christian environment protected women from the dangers of immoral landlords and neighborhoods. Social events attracted women who might otherwise have gone to commercial leisure establishments such as dance halls where they might fall prey to immorality. In addition to these local programs, YWCA workers fought for WOMAN SUFFRAGE, higher wages, women's education, and an end to domestic violence.

The YMCA's first programs were simple prayer meetings. However, the YMCA realized that its prayer meetings were not attracting the men they wished to save. Therefore, in order to attract young men, the YMCA leaders expanded their program to include leisure activities and living space. The first offerings were libraries and reading rooms. When the associations realized that their new programs were successful, they rapidly expanded. Soon the YMCAs established employment bureaus, classrooms, gymnasiums, pools, bowling alleys, and cafeterias. The purpose behind all these programs was to attract young men so that they would spend their leisure time in a Christian institution instead of commercial leisure places. For the same reason, the YMCAs across the country built large dormitories. YMCA leaders feared that many young men put themselves in moral danger by living in low-priced lodgings. To protect the men, YMCAs offered low-priced lodging in a supervised setting.

The men that the YMCA originally sought to serve lost interest over the years, and the YMCAs had difficulty attracting members. In reaction, YMCAs across the country lowered the age range of their target population. By offering sports leagues and other recreational programs, the YMCAs attracted urban youth. By making this adjustment, the YMCAs maintained a significant presence in urban America.

Further reading: Nina Mjagkij and Margaret Spratt, eds., *Men and Women Adrift: The YMCA and the YWCA in the City* (New York: New York University Press, 1997).

— Michael Hartman

youth

Between 1900 and 1930, the modern version of adolescence emerged in America. Today when we think of youth, we picture a time when children are gradually given more responsibility in preparation for their entrance into the adult world, after leaving either high school or college. Most children leave elementary school when aged 11 or 12, enter high school at age 14 or 15, and enter college or the full-time job market at age 18. A range of institutions exists, from juvenile courts to high schools, to help America's youth through these transitions. Youth also live in common cultures partially determined by age. Youth is thus a shared experience among all Americans, differing only by race, class, and gender.

At the turn of the century, the lives of America's youth differed a great deal from one another due to race, class, gender, educational, and regional differences. Growing up was not the normative process that it would become. Some youths went to work before their teenage years, for example, while others stayed in school through college. During the first decades of the 20th century, a number of factors combined to change the paths followed by America's youths as they matured.

Youth is a socially constructed category. The definition of youth has changed over time in reaction to social, cultural, and economic changes in society. During transitional times in American history, society has placed great emphasis on youth. When the social order appears to be threatened, America has turned to its youth as the hope for the future. The first three decades of the 20th century were no exception. American society was dealing with the profound changes stemming from industrialization, urbanization, and immigration. Many feared that the country's youth were threatened by these changes. Large numbers of working-class youth were unable to find jobs that offered a chance for advancement. In addition, the increase in the number of immigrant children in schools and cities frightened reformers, who feared that the immigrant youth would pose a threat to the social order if not properly socialized. Reformers also feared that cities created a dangerous environment for young people. They bemoaned the lost opportunity for youth to experience the green pastures of the country and then started summer camps to expose urban children to the healthier rural atmosphere.

Actions taken by reformers helped construct the modern definition of youth. Efforts to simultaneously protect youths from the evils of industrialization and protect the social order from the poorly socialized youth created new ideas about adolescence. At the core of the conflict about modern youth was the struggle between authorities in defining youth and the actions of youths on their own terms. Society tried to maintain youths' dependence on adults, while youths fought for their independence in a variety of ways.

The creation of the juvenile courts systems highlights this tension. The juvenile courts served both to help youths in trouble and to punish youths for independence from adult authority. Prior to the establishment of juvenile courts, youths who committed a crime went into the adult court system and, if sentenced to jail, served their time in an adult prison. Believing it dangerous to treat youths as adults, reformers established the juvenile court systems in the states. The idea behind the courts was that youthful offenders presented special circumstances. If they were simply placed in adult courts and adult prisons, they would be at risk either of physical harm or of learning criminal behaviors from adults. Reformers therefore sought to separate the youths from the adults. Special courts were created in which youths arrested for crimes went before a single judge who was supposedly better prepared to analyze their special circumstances. Judges also had new options available with regard to sentencing. As part of the new juvenile court system, states created youth reformatories or industrial schools as they were called in some states. Instead of sentencing youthful offenders to adult prisons, judges could send them to a child-only reformatory, where the authorities focused on behavioral, educational, and vocational training so that the inmates would be useful members of society upon their release.

The juvenile court system was undoubtedly an improvement over the sentencing of youths in their teen years to adult prisons. The courts were not, however, an unqualified success. The creation of special courts for juveniles led to new definitions of crimes for youths. Adolescents could be arrested for hanging out on the street corner, sexual promiscuity, or other acts of independence from their families. Once in front of the judge, youths often had no recourse to an attorney and did not receive a jury trial. Because the purpose of a sentence in the reformatory was to reform each inmate, sentences were often of indeterminate length, ending only when prison officials decided that an inmate had become reformed. The negatives of the juvenile systems tended to affect working-class and minority youths to a greater extent than middle-class youths because police and the courts often released middle-class youths to their parents instead of sentencing them.

Between 1900 and 1930, the number of American youths working full-time declined tremendously due to changes in industry and society. Reformers feared that factory work threatened the physical and mental health of America's youth. To protect youth from these dangers, reformers passed CHILD LABOR laws and compulsory schooling laws. State legislatures across the United States passed compulsory education laws in reaction to economic changes. By the 20th century, the apprentice system for learning a trade was all but nonexistent. In addition, many of the jobs in new large factories, did not offer opportunities for advancement. Educators feared that the young men and women entering factory work faced a life of toil without the hope of advancing to a better-paid position with better working conditions. Educators also feared that the immigrants streaming into America would never adopt American ways and values if they never received an EDUCATION. To counteract these threats, educators undertook efforts to bring more children into school. Compulsory education laws were the favorite tools in their efforts. Most states passed such laws in the late 19th century and expanded the targeted ages in the early 20th century. By 1910, many states had passed laws that mandated education up to at least 14 years of age. Many of these laws exempted youths aged 15 and 16 only if they could prove that they could read and write at a satisfactory level.

Changes in the economy also decreased the number of youths working full-time. Mechanization replaced many of the jobs formerly done by child workers. The rise of large industrial corporations and a new tier of management increased the value of a high school education. Large corporations depended on personnel departments for hiring workers, and the newly created personnel departments often set a high school education as the minimum requirement for employment. Corporations also created new clerical jobs that required a high school education.

Compulsory schooling and child labor laws acted to dramatically increase school enrollment. American schools during this period witnessed an increase in the number of students attending school, and particularly high school. Between 1900 and 1930, the proportion of 14- to 17-year-olds enrolled in high school grew from 10.6 percent to 54.9 percent. Total enrollment increased almost 700 percent. The increase in high school enrollment for outstripped the growth of the high school-aged population. The percentage of 17-year-olds who had graduated from high school increased from 6.4 percent in 1900 to 32.1 percent in 1930.

The growth in the high schools had unintended consequences. By placing a greater proportion of teenaged youths together, it led to the creation of youth subcultures centered on the high school. Cultures based on the common experience of high schools were not necessarily new, but the number of youths participating was. Middle-class adolescence, defined by schooling through high school, was becoming democratized. The youth cultures that developed were based on peer interactions and sanctions rather than adult restrictions. New norms of dating behavior emerged, for example, because teenaged women spent greater amounts of time with men of their own age. Dating flourished under this system, because women felt safe to go on dates unchaperoned by adults. Commercial interest also played a role in the creation of youth cultures. As incomes rose for most Americans during the 1920s, youths, and in particular middle-class youths, had more money to spend. Marketers targeted youths and a youth market developed. One important consequence of the development of the youth market was that it gave teens power outside the family. Instead of relying on family consumption decisions, teens decided on their own how to spend money. The development of the teen market slowed during the Great Depression, but rebounded with a bang in the post–World War II era.

The rise of the number of high school students led to an increase in the power of youths to challenge the roles prescribed to them by society's institutions. There was power in numbers. Youths who challenged the social roles often faced punishment, such as a sentence to a juvenile home or parental sanction. However, as the number of youths sharing common experiences increased, so too did the number of youths mounting challenges to certain restrictions. When a group of youths became powerful enough, they could successfully change their roles. In the 1920s, for example, middle-class teens used their purchasing power to successfully challenge the dependent roles assigned to them. Commercial interests began to market directly to this new group of consumers, bypassing the family. Youths thus gained a powerful ally in their quest for independence.

The rising role of the schools in the lives of America's youths helped to establish age as a basis for social categorization. At the beginning of the century, students in most school districts moved through the school systems at their own pace. Educators, fearing that they were not meeting the needs of many of their students, created high schools that provided a differentiated curriculum designed to prepare each student for their future occupation. The curriculum became the same one offered today, with its separate tracks of vocational and college preparatory classes. Educators discovered, however, that many students were old enough to leave school before reaching high school and the vocational training it offered. In an effort to expose all students to the differentiated curriculum at the high school, educators began to promote students by age, instead of

achievement. Age-based education played a key role in establishing age-based norms for growing up.

By the end of the 1920s, American youth went to school more, worked less, had stronger youth cultures, and were more tightly supervised by the state than their parents had been. The unemployment crisis of the 1930s pushed even more youths into high school, because they could not find jobs. The lengthening of adolescence through schooling set the stage for the development of the American teenager as a key consumer in the affluence of the post–World War II period.

See also CRIMINAL JUSTICE; FLORENCE KELLEY; KEATING-OWEN ACT.

Further reading: Harvey J. Graff, *Conflicting Paths: Growing Up in America* (Cambridge, Mass.: Harvard University Press, 1995); Joseph Kett, *Rites of Passage: Adolescence in America, 1790 to the Present* (New York: Basic Books, 1977).

— Michael Hartman

Z

Zimmermann telegram

Henry Lewis Stimson, secretary of war, once remarked that "gentlemen do not read each other's mail." This observation did not apply to the Zimmermann telegram of 1917. Arthur Zimmermann was a member of the German Diplomatic Corps since 1908. He had risen to the position of secretary of state for foreign affairs in 1916. During WORLD WAR I, the German government had petitioned the U.S. State Department to use its cable lines to communicate with its foreign missions about President WOODROW WILSON's mediation proposals. Secretary Zimmermann sent a coded cable via the American embassy in Berlin to the United States. The State Department in Washington, which handed it to the German ambassador, then cabled it to the German embassy in Mexico City.

Unfortunately for the Germans, the British intercepted the cable, deciphered it, and presented it to the Americans. The British government hoped that the message would hasten American involvement in the war. The cable informed the German ambassador in Mexico City that his government planned to resume unrestricted submarine warfare on February 1, 1917. It announced that the German government was repudiating a policy established in the wake of the sinking of HMS *LUSITANIA*. Additionally, the cable further proposed to the Mexican government a Mexican-German alliance in which Mexico was urged to reconquer territory lost to the United States. In the 1840s Mexico had lost land in Texas and California as a result of the Mexican-American War of 1846–48. Kidnappings of American dignitaries and raids by the Mexican leader Pancho Villa had caused tension between the two nations. President Wilson found it difficult to maintain a policy of non-interference, given the upheaval in Mexico.

Wilson finally sent an expedition led by General JOHN PERSHING to locate and kill Pancho Villa. The army did not operate effectively in Mexico, which is one reason that Germany probably felt it could risk war with the United States. The expedition, popularly known as the MEXICAN INVASION, failed to capture Pancho Villa. The American army withdrew in January of 1917. Despite the army's defeat, Mexican leaders were furious with the U.S. intervention. The Mexican president, Venustiano Carranza, even proposed an alliance to Germany. As the war situation worsened for Germany, it became increasingly interested.

When the deciphered telegram was published on March 1, 1917, it further intensified anti-German feeling in the United States. Shortly after the Zimmermann telegram was made public, German U-boats sank four unarmed American merchant vessels in the first two weeks of March. Wilson lost his gamble that the United States could pursue neutral trade without being brought into the European war.

Those favoring neutrality claimed that the note was a forgery. Zimmermann himself, however, admitted that the telegram was genuine. The publication of the note was central to eliciting public support for the war. Without the telegram the United States might have delayed entering the war; Germany's decision to once again engage in unrestricted submarine warfare against the British blockade, however, guaranteed that the United States, largely sympathetic to the Allies, would declare war on Germany. The Zimmermann telegram was the catalyst that set the U.S. war effort in motion.

Further reading: Barbara Tuchman, *The Zimmermann Telegram* (New York: Macmillan, 1996).

— Paul Edelen

Chronology

★

1900

The Hay-Pauncefote Treaties give the United States exclusive control over the construction and management of any future isthmian canal in Central America.

Madame C. J. Walker begins selling cosmetics and hair treatment systems to African-American women; her business eventually makes her America's first female self-made millionaire.

The first of a series of conservative Christian tracts called *The Fundamentals* is published. The books, which reject a scientific view of the world, particularly the theory of evolution, are enormously popular.

With the Currency Act of 1900, the United States officially returns to the gold standard.

The Foraker Act of 1900 creates a civil government for U.S.-controlled Puerto Rico.

Susan B. Anthony's handpicked successor, Carrie Chapman Catt, becomes president of the National American Woman Suffrage Association.

Harry Houdini begins performing his spectacular escapes.

After the failed anti-foreigner Boxer Rebellion in China, the United States and European powers agree to equal access to the nation's markets with the Open Door Policy.

The General Electric Company creates a lab in Schenectady, New York, devoted exclusively to scientific research. America's first corporate research and development facility, it sees the development of numerous profitable inventions, including the incandescent light bulb, the vacuum tube, and the X-ray machine.

Republican William McKinley is reelected over Democrat William Jennings Bryan.

1901

Financier J. P. Morgan buys out Andrew Carnegie and forms U.S. Steel, the world's largest corporation.

The American Medical Association asserts its influence to control entry of doctors to the profession.

The United States forces Cuba to incorporate the Platt Amendment into its 1901 constitution. The measure effectively makes Cuba a vassal state of the United States.

Two socialist parties merge to form the Socialist Party of America under the leadership of Eugene V. Debs.

A huge underground oil deposit is discovered in Beaumont, Texas, starting a boom.

President William McKinley is assassinated by an anarchist in Buffalo, New York; Theodore Roosevelt succeeds him.

1902

Roosevelt appoints Oliver Wendell Holmes to the U.S. Supreme Court; Holmes remains on the Court for 29 years and constructs the modern theory of civil liberties.

Lincoln Steffens, a leading muckraking journalist, joins the staff of *McClure's Magazine*. As editor, Steffens transforms *McClure's* into the leading political magazine in the country.

Scott Joplin composes the ragtime tune "The Entertainer."

U.S. Congress passes the Chinese Exclusion Act of 1902, which indefinitely suspends Chinese immigration to the United States and prohibits resident Chinese from gaining citizenship.

U.S. forces capture Filipino insurrection leader Emilio Aguinaldo and assert American sovereignty over the Philippines.

United Mine Workers of America organizes an anthracite coal strike that idles 140,000 miners for five months. President Roosevelt intervenes, ultimately reducing the hours and boosting the wages of miners.

U.S. Congress passes the Spooner Act, authorizing U.S. construction of a canal across the Isthmus of Panama.

The United States Public Health Service is created.

1903

U.S. intervention prevents the Colombian government from suppressing a revolution in Panama.

Jack London publishes his novel *The Call of the Wild.*

W. E. B. Du Bois's *The Souls of Black Folk* is published.

Republican congressman Joseph Gurney Cannon becomes speaker of the House of Representatives; his autocratic reign lasts eight years.

The U.S.-Canadian Convention of 1903 establishes a six-person joint commission to settle a dispute over the boundary between the Alaskan Panhandle and British Columbia.

U.S. Congress passes the Elkins Railway Act of 1903 to prohibit discriminatory railroad rebates.

The Supreme Court upholds the legality of land sales in the Indian Territory in violation of a U.S.–Kiowa treaty. The ruling will serve as a precedent for U.S. violations of treaties with Native Americans for the next five decades.

U.S. secretary of state John Hay and Panamanian minister Philippe Bunau-Varilla negotiate the Hay-Bunau-Varilla Treaty of 1903. The treaty gives the United States the right to build a canal across the Isthmus of Panama and confers on the United States control of the canal for 100 years.

At Kitty Hawk, North Carolina, Orville and Wilbur Wright make the first successful airplane flight.

1904

Construction of the Panama Canal begins.

O. Henry's first collection of short stories, *Of Cabbages and Kings,* is published.

Incumbent Republican Theodore Roosevelt wins the presidential election against Democrat Alton B. Parker.

The Roosevelt Corollary modifies the Monroe Doctrine. The corollary states that the United States will intervene in any Latin American country guilty of "chronic wrongdoing."

Muckraking journalist Ida Tarbell publishes *History of the Standard Oil Company,* exposing how John D. Rockefeller had ruthlessly created a monopoly through his company. The book prompts a federal investigation of Standard Oil for antitrust violations.

In *Northern Securities Company v. United States,* the U.S. Supreme Court demands the dissolution of the Northern Securities Company because it violates the Sherman Antitrust Act of 1890. It is the first successful prosecution under the Sherman Act.

1905

The Niagara movement is organized to promote political, social, and civil equality for African Americans.

Photographer Alfred Stieglitz founds the 291 gallery in New York City. The gallery helps establish photography as an art form.

The Industrial Workers of the World (IWW) begins organizing semiskilled and unskilled workers regardless of their race, ethnicity, or gender, starting with mineral mine workers in the West.

Ruling counter to its earlier precedent, the U.S. Supreme Court invalidates an 1893 New York State law that regulates the length of the bakery work day in *Lochner v. New York.*

John P. Harris and Harry Davis open the first nickelodeon in Pittsburgh; patrons can view a movie for five cents.

Using the Roosevelt Corollary, the United States seizes the finances of the Dominican Republic when the country is unable to make payments on its $22 million debt. The nation's finances will be under U.S. control for the next three decades.

1906

President Theodore Roosevelt wins the Nobel Peace Prize for negotiating an end to the Russo-Japanese War of 1904–05.

The Burke Act of 1906 grants to Native Americans full title to their homesteads immediately, eliminating the 25-year trust period previously required.

Upton Sinclair publishes *The Jungle.* Its vivid descriptions of the hideously unsanitary conditions in the meatpacking industry lead to national outrage and a government investigation.

U.S. Congress passes the Pure Food and Drug Act of 1906, which prohibits the manufacture, sale, and transportation of adulterated or fraudulently labeled foods and drugs shipped in foreign or interstate commerce.

The Meat Inspection Act of 1906 gives the U.S. secretary of agriculture the power to inspect meat and label products that are unfit for human consumption.

A rebellion threatens the stability of Cuba; President Roosevelt sends U.S. troops to Cuba, where they remain for three years.

After being accused of covering up the murder of a local white man, all 167 soldiers in an African-American unit stationed in Fort Brown, Texas, are dishonorably discharged.

Prompted by President Theodore Roosevelt, U.S. Congress passes the Antiquities Act, which grants the chief executive authority to proclaim public lands as national monuments.

The Hepburn Act of 1906 gives the Interstate Commerce Commission (ICC) the power to review railroad rate decisions for antitrust violations.

1907

The Indian Territory is formally dissolved as Oklahoma becomes a state.

An agreement between the governments of the United States and Japan, the Gentlemen's Agreement of 1907, limits Japanese immigration to the United States.

Florenz Ziegfeld launches *The Follies,* a series of 20 annual and opulent musical revues that capture the popular imagination.

U.S. Congress passes the Expatriation Act of 1907. The act bars the entry of suspected radicals and revokes the citizenship rights of female U.S. citizens who marry foreign nationals.

1908

The United States and Japan issue the Root-Takahira Agreement of 1908, pledging to respect each other's territorial possessions in the Pacific and uphold the Open Door Policy in China.

President Roosevelt orders the U.S. Navy's "Great White Fleet" on a world tour to demonstrate American military might.

"The Eight," consisting of Robert Henri and other realist artists, exhibit their work at the MacBeth Galleries. Critics derisively call them the "Ashcan school" of artists.

Jack Johnson knocks out Tommy Burns and becomes the first black heavyweight boxing champion.

In *Muller v. Oregon,* the U.S. Supreme Court upholds a 1903 Oregon law that limits the maximum hours women can work in any factory or laundry.

In *Loewe v. Lawlor,* the U.S. Supreme Court rules that a union boycott constitutes a conspiracy to restrain trade.

Republican William Howard Taft, vice president under Theodore Roosevelt, defeats Democrat William Jennings Bryan in the presidential election.

Henry Ford introduces the Model T Ford automobile, the first car produced by assembly line. The inexpensive car is received with phenomenal popularity.

1909

The National Association for the Advancement of Colored People (NAACP) is founded. Black writer W. E. B. Du Bois begins editing *Crisis,* the NAACP's journal.

Robert E. Peary of the U.S. Navy becomes the first man to reach the North Pole.

The Payne-Aldrich Tariff Act of 1909 increases the already high duties imposed in the Dingley Tariff Act of 1897; President Taft's support of the bill divides the Republican-controlled Congress.

President Taft sends U.S. troops to Nicaragua to support U.S.–friendly revolutionaries.

The Shirtwaist Makers strike of 1909–10, in which 300,000 garment workers strike 300 sweatshops, galvanizes a broad range of laborers and arouses public sympathy.

1910

U.S. Congress passes the Mann Act of 1910 to prohibit interstate transportation of women and girls for "immoral" purposes.

The Mann-Elkins Act of 1910 places the growing telecommunications industry under the jurisdiction of the Interstate Commerce Commission (ICC).

The Mexican Revolution begins: Francisco Madero, Pancho Villa, and Emiliano Zapata lead public outcry in Mexico for the overthrow of President Porfirio Díaz.

1911

In *Standard Oil Company of New Jersey et al. v. United States,* the U.S. Supreme Court upholds a decision by a U.S. circuit court that ordered the dissolution of the Standard Oil Company.

Illinois and Missouri begin to provide mothers' pensions to supplement the wages of certain widowed mothers.

The Dillingham Report concludes that the "new immigrants" are racially inferior to emigrants from northern and western Europe and contends that they are "incapable of becoming Americans."

President Taft sends U.S. troops to Nicaragua; this time they remain for more than a decade.

The death of 146 female garment workers in a fire at the Triangle Shirtwaist Company in New York City spurs passage of labor and safety laws.

Frederick Winslow Taylor's influential book *The Principles of Scientific Management* promotes the removal of human inefficiencies from the production process.

In *The Mind of Primitive Man,* anthropologist Franz Boas argues that the differences between cultures result from differences in historical conditions, not inherent racial predetermination.

Democrats take control of the House of Representatives for the first time since 1895.

1912

Textile workers in Lawrence, Massachusetts, strike across ethnic and skill lines, winning wage increases. Organized by "Big Bill" Haywood and Elizabeth Gurley Flynn of the IWW, the strike is hailed as a model of "new unionism."

The steamship *Titanic* sinks; more than 1,500 lives are lost, many of them American.

Democrat Woodrow Wilson, former governor of New Jersey, is elected president over Republican incumbent William Howard Taft, Progressive Party candidate Theodore Roosevelt, and candidates from the Socialist and Prohibitionist Parties.

1913

The Armory Show in New York City showcases modern art; among the painters featured is Edward Hopper.

The Sixteenth and Seventeenth Amendments to the U.S. Constitution are ratified; the Sixteenth gives the U.S. Congress the power to collect income taxes, and the Seventeenth provides for the direct election of senators.

The Underwood-Simmons Tariff Act of 1913 imposes the first income tax under the Sixteenth Amendment and significantly reduces import duties.

The Federal Reserve Act restructures the U.S. banking system.

The Webb-Kenyon Act of 1913 prohibits the interstate shipment of alcohol into states where its sale or use is illegal.

1914

World War I breaks out in Europe; President Wilson declares U.S. neutrality.

Private security forces and National Guard troops attack the camp of striking miners in Ludlow, California, killing 32 miners.

U.S. Congress passes the Federal Trade Commission Act of 1914, which creates a regulatory organization to investigate suspected monopolies.

The Clayton Antitrust Act of 1914 is enacted to supplement the Sherman Antitrust Act of 1890; its efforts to protect labor unions from antitrust rulings prove ineffective.

The Harrison Act of 1914 restricts the legal use of narcotics in the United States.

The Thomson-Urrutia Treaty of 1914 compensates Colombia for the role the United States played in the rebellion and eventual independence of Panama.

The Panama Canal opens; its construction has been supervised by engineer George Goethals.

President Wilson sends U.S. troops to support Pancho Villa in the Mexican Revolution.

1915

The first "Great Migration" begins; blacks move from the rural South to the urban North.

D. W. Griffith's film *Birth of a Nation* traces an idealized version of the development of the Ku Klux Klan and the white supremacy movement in the U.S. South. It is considered a milestone in the development of movies as an art form.

German submarines sink the British passenger ship *Lusitania.* One hundred twenty-eight U.S. citizens lose their lives in the attack.

In *Coppage v. Kansas,* the U.S. Supreme Court prohibits employers from forcing employees to sign contracts requiring that workers not join unions.

The U.S. Supreme Court declares the "grandfather clause" unconstitutional. The clause had restricted voting to those whose fathers or grandfathers had voted before 1867.

Eleven hundred women from around the world, including American social reformer and peace activist Jane Addams, convene in Holland to try to help bring an end to World War I.

The Wilson administration sends U.S. Marines to Haiti to suppress a revolution. Troops remain until 1934.

The Industrial Relations Commission delivers its report to President Wilson condemning industry's violent anti-union tactics.

Withdrawing U.S. military support for Pancho Villa, the Wilson administration recognizes the government of Venustiano Carranza of Mexico.

American Telephone and Telegraph sends the first transatlantic voice transmission.

1916

Pancho Villa retaliates against U.S. recognition of Venustiano Carranza's government in Mexico by executing several American civilians, while his forces raid Columbus, New Mexico, killing more Americans. General John J. Pershing leads a "punitive expedition" of 6,000 U.S. troops into Mexico but fails to catch Villa.

Louis Brandeis is appointed to the U.S. Supreme Court. He is the first American Jew to be so appointed.

Jeannette Rankin of Montana becomes the first woman elected to the House of Representatives.

U.S. Congress passes the Jones Act of 1916, which gives the Philippine Islands greater autonomy.

The Adamson Act of 1916 establishes an eight-hour day for railroad workers operating on interstate lines, without reducing their wages.

In an effort to curb child labor abuses, U.S. Congress passes the Keating-Owen Act of 1916. The law prohibits interstate shipments of products made by children under age 14 or by children ages 14 to 16 who had worked more than eight hours per day.

President Woodrow Wilson is narrowly reelected over Republican challenger Charles Evans Hughes.

Margaret Sanger establishes the first U.S. birth control clinic in Brooklyn, New York. The clinic provides assistance to nearly 500 women before police close its doors 10 days later. Sanger is jailed for violating New York State law forbidding distribution of birth control information.

The United States sets up a military government in the Dominican Republic when the nation rejects a treaty that would have made it a protectorate of the United States. American troops remain until 1924.

The Kern-McGillicuddy Workmen's Compensation Act enables workers to collect compensation for injuries sustained in the workplace.

Alice Paul and other radical suffragists form the National Woman's Party to fight for a federal suffrage amendment.

The National Park Service is established to manage and maintain the national system of federal parks and wilderness areas.

The Federal Farm Loan Act of 1916 makes low-interest loans available to farmers.

Charlie Chaplin appears in the two-reel silent comedy called *The Pawnshop*.

1917

The United States receives an intercepted message proposing a Mexican-German alliance.

The United States enters World War I.

The Committee for Public Information is established to distribute pro-war, anti-German propaganda.

The Selective Service Act of 1917 requires all men between the ages of 18 and 45 to register for military service.

U.S. Congress passes the Immigration Act of 1917, or the Alien Exclusion Act. The act sets quotas, creates an "Asiatic Barred Zone," and institutes a literacy test to restrict immigration.

The Espionage Act of 1917 suppresses treasonable and disloyal activities during World War I.

An estimated 100 blacks die in a three-day race riot in East St. Louis, Illinois.

The Jones Act of 1917 grants U.S. citizenship to the inhabitants of Puerto Rico and expands their role in the island's government.

U.S. secretary of state Robert Lansing and Viscount Kikujiro Ishii of Japan negotiate the Lansing-Ishii Agreement of 1917, which recognizes Japan's special commercial interests in China.

Bolsheviks seize power in the Russian Revolution, provoking anticommunist hysteria among Americans.

Margaret Sanger helps organize the National Birth Control League, which ultimately evolves into the Planned Parenthood Federation of America.

1918

The U.S. government assumes control over the national rail system to support the war effort.

In his "Fourteen Points" speech, President Wilson outlines his plan for a fair and lasting European peace.

President Wilson establishes the National War Labor Board to formalize federal policies for dealing with organized labor during World War I.

The first wave of a deadly strain of influenza reaches the United States; within a year it has decimated world populations.

In *Hammer v. Dagenhart,* the U.S. Supreme Court invalidates the child labor control measure, the Keating-Owen Act of 1916.

U.S. Congress passes the Sedition Act of 1918, prohibiting criticism of the U.S. war effort.

Americans write a new constitution for Haiti, occupied by U.S. troops since 1915.

Socialist Party leader Eugene V. Debs is convicted under the Espionage Act of 1917 for making antiwar speeches.

The Allies (France and Britain), strengthened by newly arrived U.S. troops under General John Pershing, turn back a German offensive along the Marne River.

The massive Argonne Offensive, fought largely by U.S. troops, weakens the German army; Germany agrees to an armistice, and President Wilson sails for France to participate in a peace conference.

1919

The Eighteenth Amendment of the U.S. Constitution, which prohibits the sale of alcohol nationwide, is ratified. The Volstead Act of 1919 provides for its enforcement.

Industry magnates led by John D. Rockefeller launch the "American Plan" to roll back the wartime gains of labor unions.

The first city-wide general strike immobilizes Seattle for six days. At the end of the strike, the workers have won none of their demands.

President Wilson unsuccessfully urges U.S. Congress to ratify the Treaty of Versailles, which calls for American membership in the League of Nations; Senator Henry Cabot Lodge leads congressional resistance to ratification.

Jack Dempsey becomes heavyweight champion of the world.

Twenty-five race riots break out in American cities, killing and wounding hundreds of people. This period is known as the Red Summer.

U.S. Congress passes the Child Labor Act of 1919 in an attempt to protect children in the workplace.

The American Farm Bureau is founded to lobby for the interests of farmers, who represent 25 percent of voters.

The U.S. Supreme Court upholds the Espionage Act of 1917 and the Sedition Act of 1918, asserting that the "clear and present danger" of war makes certain types of free speech subversive.

The "Black Sox" scandal, in which Chicago White Sox players accept bribes in exchange for purposely losing the World Series, damages baseball's popularity.

Bolsheviks found the Third International (or Comintern) to export revolution around the world; American socialists who support the Russian Revolution form an American communist party.

Steelworkers wage a strike of 365,000 in September, signaling the end of the uneasy truce between industry and labor during World War I; by January, the strike ends in failure and 22 strikers have been killed.

Responding to a wave of strikes after the war, Attorney General A. Mitchell Palmer counterattacks with a series of raids targeting labor militants and radicals. Thousands of radical activists and writers are arrested or deported in the "Red Scare" raids, including Emma Goldman.

1920

Esch-Cummins Act of 1920 returns railroads to private control.

Marcus Garvey, founder of the Universal Negro Improvement Association, addresses 25,000 blacks in New York City, calling for a "back to Africa" movement.

Forty-six nations participate in the first meeting of the League of Nations.

The Nineteenth Amendment to the U.S. Constitution is ratified, giving American women the vote.

KDKA in Pittsburgh becomes the first radio station to institute regular broadcasting when it covers the Cox-Harding presidential race nightly.

Republican Warren G. Harding, formerly a senator from Ohio, is elected president over Democrat James M. Cox; President Harding's tenure is marked by scandal.

Eugene O'Neill's play *The Emperor Jones*, which later stars Paul Robeson, opens on Broadway.

1921

L. C. Dyer, a white congressman from Missouri, proposes an antilynching law; it is passed in the House but not in the Senate.

Immigration to the United States is limited by the first of a series of quota acts.

The U.S.-German Peace Treaty of 1921 adopts most measures of the Treaty of Versailles, but excludes participation in the League of Nations and the International Labor Organization. The agreement formally ends World War I for the United States.

Great Britain, the United States, Japan, and France agree to respect one another's island territories in the Pacific Ocean and to confer with the other party in the event of any disputes in the Four Power Pacific Treaty of 1921.

U.S. Congress passes the Budget and Accounting Act, which provides guidelines for the modern budget and expands presidential control over federal spending.

1922

The "Harlem Renaissance" is initiated with Claude McKay's book of poetry titled *Harlem Shadows*.

U.S. Congress passes the Capper-Volstead Act of 1922, which exempts various agricultural associations, producers, and cooperatives from antitrust laws.

Poet T. S. Eliot publishes *The Waste Land*.

In *Balzac v. Puerto Rico*, the U.S. Supreme Court denies citizens of the U.S. territory of Puerto Rico the rights guaranteed by the Constitution of the United States.

The Cable Act establishes that women neither gain nor lose American citizenship through marriage.

In the Yap Treaty of 1922 the United States formally agrees to the Japanese claim on the former German possession of Yap, in the Caroline Islands.

In *Bailey v. Drexel Furniture Company*, the U.S. Supreme Court invalidates the Child Labor Act of 1919.

The United States, Britain, France, Japan, Italy, Belgium, the Netherlands, China, and Portugal sign the Nine Power Pact of 1922. The agreement reaffirms the Open-Door Policy toward China and reflects a consensus of opinion in their relations with China.

U.S. Congress passes the Fordney-McCumber Tariff to protect the American chemical and metal industries, which developed considerably during World War I.

1923

Alice Paul introduces the Equal Rights Amendment proposal to U.S. Congress; the proposed amendment will be debated off and on for most of the rest of the century.

In *Adkins v. Children's Hospital*, the U.S. Supreme Court rules that sex-specific minimum wage laws are unconstitutional.

President Warren G. Harding dies in office; Vice President Calvin Coolidge, a former governor of Massachusetts, succeeds him.

Secretary of the Interior Albert Fall is accused of accepting bribes in exchange for oil rights on public lands in the Teapot Dome scandal. He becomes the first cabinet member to be convicted of a crime.

1924

U.S. Congress passes the Indian Citizenship Act, which gives all Native Americans U.S. citizenship without affecting their rights to tribal property.

Calvin Coolidge wins the presidential race against Democrat John W. Davis and Progressive Party candidate Robert M. La Follette.

The National Origins (Immigration) Act of 1924 further decreases the number of immigrants allowed into the United States each year and creates the Border Patrol to police U.S. land borders.

J. Edgar Hoover becomes director of the Bureau of Investigation, a department of the Justice Department that later becomes the FBI.

Composer George Gershwin's *Rhapsody in Blue,* a piece that combines the rhythms of jazz with classical orchestration, is first performed.

Under orders from the Soviet Comintern, two American communist parties merge, eventually becoming known as the Communist Party of the United States of America.

Defense attorney Clarence Darrow uses psychological testimony to argue against the death penalty in the trial of accused murderers Nathan Leopold and Richard Loeb.

U.S. Congress approves the Soldiers' Bonus to compensate soldiers for income lost during the war.

1925

A strike of 20,000 garment workers in Passaic, New Jersey, fails; union membership nationwide declines.

U.S. Congress passes the Kelly Air Mail Act, which establishes contracts with commercial airlines for the delivery of U.S. mail by air.

Lawyer Clarence Darrow defends John Scopes, a young Tennessee teacher accused of teaching Darwin's theory of evolution rather than the biblical creation story required by state law. Three-time presidential candidate William Jennings Bryan serves as chief attorney for the prosecution.

The U.S. Supreme Court decision *Pierce v. Society of the Sisters* overturns an Oregon state law that requires all children between the ages of eight and 16 to attend public school.

1926

General Billy Mitchell resigns from the U.S. Army after a court-martial for insubordination; he had charged that the U.S. military was paying insufficient attention to air power.

Ernest Hemingway's novel *The Sun Also Rises* is published.

Jazz musician Louis Armstrong forms his "Hot Five" band; he begins his "four golden years" when he records his "Hot Five" and "Hot Seven" tracks.

The Watson-Parker Act of 1926 establishes the U.S. Board of Mediation to negotiate with parties involved in railroad labor disputes.

1927

Charles Lindbergh completes the first solo airplane flight from New York to Paris.

Richard Byrd of the U.S. Navy successfully completes the first airplane flight over the North Pole.

Nicola Sacco and Bartolomeo Vanzetti, immigrants and political radicals, are executed after a controversial and widely publicized murder trial.

Babe Ruth of the New York Yankees sets a record with 60 home runs during a 154-game season.

1928

Fifteen nations sign the Pact of Paris as an attempt to eliminate war as an instrument of national policy and to settle international disputes through peaceful means.

In *Olmstead v. United States,* the U.S. Supreme Court allows the admission of wiretapping evidence in court.

The Clark Memorandum on the Monroe Doctrine limits the U.S. right to intervene in Latin American affairs.

In *Coming of Age in Samoa,* anthropologist Margaret Mead argues that culture, not biology, determines gender identity and sexual behavior.

The *Amos 'n' Andy* radio program goes on the air; the first commercially successful serial, it garners 40 million listeners, fully one-third the U.S. population.

Republican candidate Herbert Hoover wins the presidential election over Democratic candidate Alfred E. Smith.

Documents

★

Theodore Roosevelt's "Strenuous Life" Speech, April 10, 1899

Landmark Documents in American History.
CD-ROM (New York: Facts On File, 1995)

In speaking to you, men of the greatest city of the West, men of the State which gave to the country Lincoln and Grant, men who preeminently and distinctly embody all that is most American in the American character, I wish to preach, not the doctrine of ignoble ease, but the doctrine of the strenuous life, the life of toil and effort, of labor and strife; to preach that highest form of success which comes, not to the man who desires mere easy peace, but to the man who does not shrink from danger, from hardship, or from bitter toil, and who out of these wins the splendid ultimate triumph.

A life of slothful ease, a life of that peace which springs merely from lack either of desire or of power to strive after great things, is as little worthy of a nation as of an individual. I ask only that what every self-respecting American demands from himself and from his sons shall be demanded of the American nation as a whole. Who among you would teach you boys that ease, that peace, is to be the first consideration in their eyes—to be the ultimate goal after which they strive? You men of Chicago have made this city great, you men of Illinois have done your share, and more than your share, in making America great, because you neither preach nor practice such a doctrine. You work yourselves, and you bring up your sons to work. If you are rich and are worth your salt, you will teach your sons that though they may have leisure, it is not to be spent in idleness; for wisely used leisure merely means that those who possess it, being free from the necessity of working for their livelihood, are all the more bound to carry on some kind of non-remunerative work in science, in letters, in art, in exploration, in historical research—work of the type we most need in this country, the successful carrying out of which reflects most honor upon the nation. We do not admire the man of timid peace. We admire the man who embodies victorious effort; the man who never wrongs his neighbor, who is prompt to help a friend, but who has those virile qualities necessary to win in the stern strife of actual life. It is hard to fail, but it is worse never to have tried to succeed. In this life we get nothing save by effort. Freedom from effort in the present merely means that there has been stored up effort in the past. A man can be freed from the necessity of work only by the fact that he or his fathers before him have worked to good purpose. If the freedom thus purchased is used aright, and the man still does actual work, though of a different kind, whether as a writer or a general, whether in the field of politics or in the field of exploration and adventure, he shows he deserves his good fortune. But if he treats this period of freedom from the need of actual labor as a period, not of preparation, but of mere enjoyment, even though perhaps not of vicious enjoyment, he shows that he is simply a cumberer of the earth's surface, and he surely unfits himself to hold his own with his fellows if the need to do so should again arise. A mere life of ease is not in the end a very satisfactory life, and, above all, it is a life which ultimately unfits those who follow it for serious work in the world.

In the last analysis a healthy state can exist only when the men and women who make it up lead clean, vigorous, healthy lives; when the children are so trained that they shall endeavor, not to shirk difficulties, but to overcome them; not to seek ease, but to know how to wrest triumph from toil and risk. The man must be glad to do a man's work, to dare and endure and to labor; to keep himself, and to keep those dependent upon him. The woman must be the housewife, the helpmeet of the homemaker, the wise and fearless mother of many healthy children. In one of Daudet's powerful and melancholy books he speaks of "the

363

fear of maternity, the haunting terror of the young wife of the present day." When such words can be truthfully written of a nation, that nation is rotten to the heart's core. When men fear work or fear righteous war, when women fear motherhood, they tremble on the brink of doom; and well it is that they should vanish from the earth, where they are fit subjects for the scorn of all men and women who are themselves strong and brave and high-minded.

As it is with the individual, so it is with the nation. It is a base untruth to say that happy is the nation that has no history. Thrice happy is the nation that has a glorious history. Far better it is to dare mighty things, to win glorious triumphs, even though checkered by failure, than to take rank with those poor spirits who neither enjoy much nor suffer much, because they live in the gray twilight that knows not victory nor defeat. If in 1861 the men who loved the Union had believed that peace was the end of all things, and war and strife the worst of all things, and had acted up to their belief, we would have saved hundreds of thousands of lives, we would have saved hundreds of millions of dollars. Moreover, besides saving all the blood and treasure we then lavished, we would have prevented the heartbreak of many women, the dissolution of many homes, and we would have spared the country those months of gloom and shame when it seemed as if our armies marched only to defeat. We could have avoided all this suffering simply by shrinking from strife. And if we had thus avoided it, we would have shown that we were weaklings, and that we were unfit to stand among the great nations of the earth. Thank God for the iron in the blood of our fathers, the men who upheld the wisdom of Lincoln, and bore sword or rifle in the armies of Grant! Let us, the children of the men who proved themselves equal to the mighty days, let us, the children of the men who carried the great Civil War to a triumphant conclusion, praise the God of our fathers that the ignoble counsels of peace were rejected; that the suffering and loss, the blackness of sorrow and despair, were unflinchingly faced, and the years of strife endured; for in the end the slave was freed, the Union restored, and the mighty American republic placed once more as a helmeted queen among nations.

We of this generation do not have to face a task such as that our fathers faced, but we have our tasks, and woe to us if we fail to perform them! We cannot, if we would, play the part of China, and be content to rot by inches in ignoble ease within our borders, taking no interest in what goes on beyond them, sunk in a scrambling commercialism; heedless of the higher life, the life of aspiration, of toil and risk, busying ourselves only with the wants of our bodies for the day, until suddenly we should find, beyond a shadow of question, what China has already found, that in this world the nation that has trained itself to a career of unwarlike and isolated ease is bound, in the end, to go down before other nations which have not lost the manly and adventur-

ous qualities. If we are to be a really great people, we must strive in good faith to play a great part in the world. We cannot avoid meeting great issues. All that we can determine for ourselves is whether we shall meet them well or ill. In 1898 we could not help being brought face to face with the problem of war with Spain. All we could decide was whether we should shrink like cowards from the contest, or enter into it as beseemed a brave and high-spirited people; and, once in, whether failure or success should crown our banners. So it is now. We cannot avoid the responsibilities that confront us in Hawaii, Cuba, Porto Rico, and the Philippines. All we can decide is whether we shall meet them in a way that will redound to the national credit, or whether we shall make of our dealings with these new problems a dark and shameful page in our history. To refuse to deal with them at all merely amounts to dealing with them badly. We have a given problem to solve. If we undertake the solution, there is, of course, always danger that we may not solve it aright; but to refuse to undertake the solution simply renders it certain that we cannot possibly solve it aright. The timid man, the lazy man, the man who distrusts his country, the over-civilized man, who has lost the great fighting, masterful virtues, the ignorant man, and the man of dull mind, whose soul is incapable of feeling the mighty lift that thrills "stern men with empires in their brains"—all these, of course, shrink from seeing the nation undertake its new duties; shrink from seeing us build a navy and an army adequate to our needs; shrink from seeing us do our share of the world's work, by bringing order out of chaos in the great, fair tropic islands from which the valor of our soldiers and sailors has driven the Spanish flag. These are the men who fear the strenuous life, who fear the only national life which is really worth leading. They believe in that cloistered life which saps the hardy virtues in a nation, as it saps them in the individual; or else they are wedded to that base spirit of gain and greed which recognizes in commercialism the be-all and end-all of national life, instead of realizing that, though an indispensable element, it is, after all, but one of the many elements that go to make up true national greatness. No country can long endure if its foundations are not laid deep in the material prosperity which comes from thrift, from business energy and enterprise, from hard, unsparing effort in the fields of industrial activity; but neither was any nation ever yet truly great if it relied upon material prosperity alone. All honor must be paid to the architects of our material prosperity, to the great captains of industry who have built our factories and our rail-roads, to the strong men who toil for wealth with brain or hand; for great is the debt of the nation to these and their kind. But our debt is yet greater to the men whose highest type is to be found in a statesman like Lincoln, a soldier like Grant. They showed by their lives that they recognized the law of work, the law of strife; they toiled to win a competence for themselves and those dependent upon them; but they recognized that there were yet other and even loftier duties—duties to the nation and duties to the race.

We cannot sit huddled within our own borders and avow ourselves merely an assemblage of well-to-do hucksters who care nothing for what happens beyond. Such a policy would defeat even its own end; for as the nations grow to have ever wider and wider interests, and are brought into closer and closer contact, if we are to hold our own in the struggle for naval and commercial supremacy, we must build up our power without our own borders. We must build the isthmian canal, and we must grasp the points of vantage which will enable us to have our say in deciding the destiny of the oceans of the East and the West.

So much for the commercial side. From the standpoint of international honor the argument is even stronger. The guns that thundered off Manila and Santiago left us echoes of glory, but they also left us a legacy of duty. If we drove out a medieval tyranny only to make room for savage anarchy, we had better not have begun the task at all. It is worse than idle to say that we have no duty to perform, and can leave to their fates the islands we have conquered. Such a course would be the course of infamy. It would be followed at once by utter chaos in the wretched islands themselves. Some stronger, manlier power would have to step in and do the work, and we would have shown ourselves weaklings, unable to carry to successful completion the labors that great and high-spirited nations are eager to undertake.

The work must be done; we cannot escape our responsibility; and if we are worth our salt, we shall be glad of the chance to do the work—glad of the chance to show ourselves equal to one of the great tasks set modern civilization. But let us not deceive ourselves as to the importance of the task. Let us not be misled by vainglory into underestimating the strain it will put on our powers. Above all, let us, as we value our own self-respect, face the responsibilities with proper seriousness, courage, and high resolve. We must demand the highest order of integrity and ability in our public men who are to grapple with these new problems. We must hold to a rigid accountability those public servants who show unfaithfulness to the interests of the nation or inability to rise to the high level of the new demands upon our strength and our resources.

Of course we must remember not to judge any public servant by any one act, and especially should we beware of attacking the men who are merely the occasions and not the causes of disaster. Let me illustrate what I mean by the army and the navy. If twenty years ago we had gone to war, we should have found the navy as absolutely unprepared as the army. At that time our ships could not have encountered with success the fleets of Spain any more than nowa-

days we can put untrained soldiers, no matter how brave, who are armed with archaic black-powder weapons, against well-drilled regulars armed with the highest type of modern repeating rifle. But in the early eighties the attention of the nation became directed to our naval needs. Congress most wisely made a series of appropriations to build up a new navy, and under a succession of able and patriotic secretaries, of both political parties, the navy was gradually built up, until its material became equal to its splendid personnel, with the result that in the summer of 1898 it leaped to its proper place as one of the most brilliant and formidable fighting navies in the entire world. We rightly pay all honor to the men controlling the navy at the time it won these great deeds, honor to Secretary Long and Admiral Dewey, to the captains who handled the ships in action, to the daring lieutenants who braved death in the smaller craft, and to the heads of bureaus at Washington who saw that the ships were so commanded, so armed, so equipped, so well engined, as to insure the best results. But let us also keep ever in mind that all of this would not have availed if it had not been for the wisdom of the men who during the preceding fifteen years had built up the navy. Keep in mind the secretaries of the navy during those years; keep in mind the senators and congressmen who by their votes gave the money necessary to build and to armor the ships, to construct the great guns, and to train the crews; remember also those who actually did build the ships, the armor, and the guns; and remember the admirals and captains who handled battle-ship, cruiser, and torpedo-boat on the high seas, alone and in squadrons, developing the seamanship, the gunnery, and the power of acting together, which their successors utilized so gloriously at Manila and off Santiago. And, gentlemen, remember the converse, too. Remember that justice has two sides. Be just to those who built up the navy, and, for the sake of the future of the country, keep in mind those who opposed its building up. Read the "Congressional Record." Find out the senators and congressmen who opposed the grants for building the new ships; who opposed the purchase of armor, without which the ships were worthless; who opposed any adequate maintenance for the Navy Department, and strove to cut down the number of men necessary to man our fleets. The men who did these things were one and all working to bring disaster on the country. They have no share in the glory of Manila, in the honor of Santiago. They have no cause to feel proud of the valor of our sea-captains, of the renown of our flag. Their motives may or may not have been good, but their acts were heavily fraught with evil. They did ill for the national honor, and we won in spite of their sinister opposition.

Now, apply all this to our public men of to-day. Our army has never been built up as it should be built up. I shall not discuss with an audience like this the puerile suggestion that a nation of seventy millions of freemen is in danger of losing its liberties from the existence of an army of one hundred thousand men, three fourths of whom will be employed in certain foreign islands, in certain coast fortresses, and on Island reservations. No man of good sense and stout heart can take such a proposition seriously. If we are such weaklings as the proposition implies, then we are unworthy of freedom in any event. To no body of men in the United States is the country so much indebted as to the splendid officers and enlisted men of the regular army and navy. There is no body from which the country has less to fear, and none of which it should be prouder, none which it should be more anxious to upbuild.

Our army needs complete reorganization,—not merely enlarging,—and the reorganization can only come as the result of legislation. A proper general staff should be established, and the positions of ordinance, commissary, and quartermaster officers should be filled by detail from the line. Above all, the army must be given the chance to exercise in large bodies. Never again should we see, as we saw in the Spanish war, major-generals in command of divisions who had never before commanded three companies together in the field. Yet, incredible to relate, Congress has shown a queer inability to learn some of the lessons of the war. There were large bodies of men in both branches who opposed the declaration of war, who opposed the ratification of peace, who opposed the upbuilding of the army, and who even opposed the purchase of armor at a reasonable price for the battle-ships and cruisers, thereby putting an absolute stop to the building of any new fighting-ships for the navy. If, during the years to come, any disaster should befall our arms, afloat or ashore, and thereby any shame come to the United States, remember that the blame will lie upon the men whose names appear upon the roll-calls of Congress on the wrong side of these great questions. On them will lie the burden of any loss of our soldiers and sailors, of any dishonor to the flag; and upon you and the people of this country will lie the blame if you do not repudiate, in no unmistakable way, what these men have done. The blame will not rest upon the untrained commander of untried troops, upon the civil officers of a department the organization of which has been left utterly inadequate, or upon the admiral with an insufficient number of ships; but upon the public men who have so lamentably failed in forethought as to refuse to remedy these evils long in advance, and upon the nation that stands behind those public men.

So, at the present hour, no small share of the responsibility for the blood shed in the Philippines, the blood of our brothers, and the blood of their wild and ignorant foes, lies at the thresholds of those who so long delayed the adoption of the treaty of peace, and of those who by their worse than foolish words deliberately invited a savage people to plunge into a war fraught with sure disaster for them–a war, too, in which our own brave men who follow the flag must pay with their blood for the silly, mock humanitarianism of the prattlers who sit at home in peace.

The army and the navy are the sword and the shield which this nation must carry if she is to do her duty among the nations of the earth–if she is not to stand merely as the China of the western hemisphere. Our proper conduct toward the tropic islands we have wrested from Spain is merely the form which our duty has taken at the moment. Of course we are bound to handle the affairs of our own household well. We must see that there is civic honesty, civic cleanliness, civic good sense in our home administration of city, State, and nation. We must strive for honesty in office, for honesty toward the creditors of the nation and of the individual; for the widest freedom of individual initiative where possible, and for the wisest control of individual initiative where it is hostile to the welfare of the many. But because we set our own household in order we are not thereby excused from playing our part in the great affairs of the world. A man's first duty is to his own home, but he is not thereby excused from doing his duty to the State; for if he fails in this second duty it is under the penalty of ceasing to be a freeman. In the same way, while a nation's first duty is within its own borders, it is not thereby absolved from facing its duties in the world as a whole; and if it refuses to do so, it merely forfeits its right to struggle for a place among the peoples that shape the destiny of mankind.

In the West Indies and the Philippines alike we are confronted by most difficult problems. It is cowardly to shrink from solving them in the proper way; for solved they must be, if not by us, then by some stronger and more manful race. If we are too weak, too selfish, or too foolish to solve them, some bolder and abler people must undertake the solution. Personally, I am far too firm a believer in the greatness of my country and the power of my countrymen to admit for one moment that we shall ever be driven to the ignoble alternative.

The problems are different for the different islands. Porto Rico is not large enough to stand alone. We must govern it wisely and well, primarily in the interest of its own people. Cuba is, in my judgment, entitled ultimately to settle for itself whether it shall be an independent state or an integral portion of the mightiest of republics. But until order and stable liberty are secured, we must remain in the island to insure them, and infinite tact, judgment, moderation, and courage must be shown by our military and civil representatives in keeping the island pacified, in relentlessly stamping out brigandage, in protecting all alike, and yet in showing proper recognition to the men who have fought for Cuban liberty. The Philippines offer a yet graver problem. Their population includes half-caste and native Christians, warlike Moslems, and wild pagans. Many of their people are utterly unfit for self-government, and show no signs of becoming fit. Others may in time become fit but at present can only take part in self-government under a wise supervision, at once firm and beneficent. We have driven Spanish tyranny from the islands. If we now let it be replaced by savage anarchy, our work has been for harm and not for good. I have scant patience with those who fear to undertake the task of governing the Philippines, and who openly avow that they do fear to undertake it, or that they shrink from it because of the expense and trouble; but I have even scanter patience with those who make a pretense of humanitarianism to hide and cover their timidity, and who can about "liberty" and the "consent of the governed," in order to excuse themselves for their unwillingness to play the part of men. Their doctrines, if carried out, would make it incumbent upon us to leave the Apaches of Arizona to work out their own salvation, and to decline to interfere in a single Indian reservation. Their doctrines condemn your forefathers and mine for ever having settled in these United States.

England's rule in India and Egypt has been of great benefit to England, for it has trained up generations of men accustomed to look at the larger and loftier side of public life. It has been of even greater benefit to India and Egypt. And finally, and most of all, it has advanced the cause of civilization. So, if we do our duty aright in the Philippines, we will add to that national renown which is the highest and finest part of national life, will greatly benefit the people of the Philippine Islands, and, above all, we will play our part well in the great work of uplifting mankind. But to do this work, keep ever in mind that we must show in a very high degree the qualities of courage, of honesty, and of good judgment. Resistance must be stamped out. The first and all-important work to be done is to establish the supremacy of our flag. We must put down armed resistance before we can accomplish anything else, and there should be no parleying, no faltering, in dealing with our foe. As for those in our own country who encourage the foe, we can afford contemptuously to disregard them; but it must be remembered that their utterances are not saved from being treasonable merely by the fact that they are despicable.

When once we have put down armed resistance, when once our rule is acknowledged, then an even more difficult task will begin, for then we must see to it that the islands are administered with absolute honesty and with good judgment. If we let the public service of the islands be turned into the prey of the spoils politician, we shall have begun to tread the path which Spain trod to her own destruction. We must send out there only good and able men, chosen for their fitness, and not because of their partisan service, and these men must not only administer impartial justice to the natives and serve their own government with honesty and fidelity, but must show the utmost tact and firmness, remembering that, with such people as those with whom we are to deal, weakness is the greatest of crimes, and that next to weakness comes back of consideration for their principles and prejudices.

I preach to you, then, my countrymen, that our country calls not for the life of ease but for the life of strenuous endeavor. The twentieth century looms before us big with the fate of many nations. If we stand idly by, if we seek merely swollen, slothful ease and ignoble peace, if we shrink from the hard contests where men must win at hazard of their lives and at the risk of all they hold dear, then the bolder and stronger peoples will pass us by, and will win for themselves the domination of the world. Let us therefore boldly face the life of strife, resolute to do our duty well and manfully; resolute to uphold righteousness by deed and by word; resolute to be both honest and brave, to serve high ideals, yet to use practical methods. Above all, let us shrink from no strife, moral or physical, within or without the nation, provided we are certain that the strife is justified, for it is only through strife, through hard and dangerous endeavor, that we shall ultimately win the goal of true national greatness.

Niagara Movement Declaration of Principles (July 1905)

*Courtesy of the University of Massachusetts at Amherst.
University Library. Special Collections and Archives.*

Progress

The members of the conference, known as the Niagara Movement, assembled in annual meeting at Buffalo, July 11th, 12th and 13th, 1905, congratulate the Negro-Americans on certain undoubted evidences of progress in the last decade, particularly the increase of intelligence, the buying of property, the checking of crime, the uplift in home life, the advance in literature and art, and the demonstration of constructive and executive ability in the conduct of great religious, economic and educational institutions.

Suffrage

At the same time, we believe that this class of American citizens should protest emphatically and continually against the curtailment of their political rights. We believe in manhood suffrage; we believe that no man is so good, intelligent or wealthy as to be entrusted wholly with the welfare of his neighbor.

Civil Liberty

We believe also in protest against the curtailment of our civil rights. All American citizens have the right to equal treatment in places of public entertainment according to their behavior and deserts.

Economic Opportunity

We especially complain against the denial of equal opportunities to us in economic life; in the rural districts of the South this amounts to peonage and virtual slavery; all over the South it tends to crush labor and small business enterprises; and everywhere American prejudice, helped often by iniquitous laws, is making it more difficult for Negro Americans to earn a decent living.

Education

Common school education should be free to all American children and compulsory. High school training should be adequately provided for all, and college training should be the monopoly of no class or race in any section of our common country. We believe that, in defense of our own institutions, the United States should aid common school education, particularly in the South, and we especially recommend concerted agitation to this end. We urge an increase in public high school facilities in the South, where the Negro-Americans are almost wholly without such provisions. We favor well-equipped trade and technical schools for the training of artisans, and the need of adequate and liberal endowment for a few institutions of higher education must be patent to sincere well-wishers of the race.

Courts

We demand upright judges in courts, juries selected without discrimination on account of color and the same measure of punishment and the same efforts at reformation for black as for white offenders. We need orphanages and farm schools for dependent children, juvenile reformatories for delinquents, and the abolition of the dehumanizing convict-lease system.

Public Opinion

We note with alarm the evident retrogression in this land of sound public opinion on the subject of manhood rights, republican government and human brotherhood, and we pray God that this nation will not degenerate into a mob of boasters and oppressors, but rather will return to the faith of the fathers, that all men were created free and equal, with certain unalienable rights.

Health

We plead for health—for an opportunity to live in decent houses and localities, for a chance to rear our children in physical and moral cleanliness.

Employers and Labor Unions

We hold up for public execration the conduct of two opposite classes of men: The practice among employers of importing ignorant Negro-American laborers in emergencies, and then affording them neither protection nor permanent employment; and the practice of labor unions in proscribing and boycotting and oppressing thousands of their fellow-toilers, simply because they are black. These methods have accentuated and will accentuate the war of labor and capital, and they are disgraceful to both sides.

Protest

We refuse to allow the impression to remain that the Negro-American assents to inferiority, is submissive under oppression and apologetic before insults. Through helplessness we may submit, but the voice of protest of ten million Americans must never cease to assail the ears of their fellows, so long as America is unjust.

Color-Line

Any discrimination based simply on race or color is barbarous, we care not how hallowed it be by custom, expediency, or prejudice. Differences made on account of ignorance, immorality, or disease are legitimate methods of fighting evil, and against them we have no world of protest; but discriminations based simply and solely on physical peculiarities, place of birth, color or skin, are relics of that unreasoning human savagery of which the world is and ought to be thoroughly ashamed.

"Jim Crow" Cars

We protest against the "Jim Crow" car, since its effect is and must be to make us pay first-class fare for third-class accommodations, render us open to insults and discomfort and to crucify wantonly our manhood, womanhood and self-respect.

Soldiers

We regret that this nation has never seen fit adequately to reward the black soldiers who, in its five wars, have defended their country with their blood, and yet have been systematically denied the promotions which their abilities deserve. And we regard as unjust, the exclusion of black boys from the military and navy training schools.

War Amendments

We urge upon Congress the enactment of appropriate legislation for securing the proper enforcement of those articles of freedom, the thirteenth, fourteenth and fifteenth amendments of the Constitution of the United States.

Oppression

We repudiate the monstrous doctrine that the oppressor should be the sole authority as to the rights of the oppressed. The Negro race in America stolen, ravished and degraded, struggling up through difficulties and oppression, needs sympathy and receives criticism; needs help and is given hindrance, needs protection and is given mob-violence, needs justice and is given charity, needs leadership and is given cowardice and apology, needs bread and is given a stone. This nation will never stand justified before God until these things are changed.

The Church

Especially are we surprised and astonished at the recent attitude of the church of Christ—on the increase of a desire to bow to racial prejudice, to narrow the bounds of human brotherhood, and to segregate black men in some outer sanctuary. This is wrong, unchristian and disgraceful to the twentieth century civilization.

Agitation

Of the above grievances we do not hesitate to complain, and to complain loudly and insistently. To ignore, overlook, or apologize for these wrongs is to prove ourselves unworthy of freedom. Persistent manly agitation is the way to liberty, and toward this goal the Niagara Movement has started and asks the co-operation of all men of all races.

Help

At the same time we want to acknowledge with deep thankfulness the help of our fellowmen from the abolitionist down to those who to-day still stand for equal opportunity and who have given and still give of their wealth and of their poverty for our advancement.

Duties

And while we are demanding, and ought to demand, and will continue to demand the rights enumerated above, God forbid that we should ever forget to urge corresponding duties upon our people:
The duty to vote.
The duty to respect the rights of others.
The duty to work.
The duty to obey the laws.
The duty to be clean and orderly.
The duty to send our children to school.
The duty to respect ourselves, even as we respect others.
This statement, complaint and prayer we submit to the American people, and Almighty God.

Preamble to the Constitution of the Industrial Workers of the World, 1905

The Archives of Labor and Urban Affairs,
Walter P. Reuther Library, Wayne State University

Preamble

The working class and the employing class have nothing in common. There can be no peace so long as hunger and want are found among millions of working people and the few, who make up the employing class, have all the good things of life.

Between these two classes a struggle must go on until the workers of the world organize as a class, take possession of the earth and the machinery of production, and abolish the wage system.

We find that the centering of the management of industries into fewer and fewer hands makes the trade unions unable to cope with the ever growing power of the employing class. The trade unions foster a state of affairs which allows one set of workers to be pitted against another set of workers in the same industry, thereby helping defeat one another in wage wars. Moreover, the trade unions aid the employing class to mislead the workers into the belief that the working class have interests in common with their employers. These conditions can be changed and the interest of the working class upheld only by an organization formed in such a way that all its members in any one industry, or in all industries, if necessary, cease work whenever a strike or lockout is on in any department thereof, thus making an injury to one an injury to all.

Instead of the conservative motto, "A fair day's wages for a fair day's work," we must inscribe on our banner the revolutionary watchword, "Abolition of the wage system."

It is the historic mission of the working class to do away with capitalism. The army of production must be organized, not only for the every day struggle with capitalists, but also to carry on production when capitalism shall have been overthrown. By organizing industrially we are forming the structure of the new society within the shell of the old.

Knowing, therefore, that such an organization is absolutely necessary for our emancipation, we unite under the following constitution:

Muller v. Oregon, 1908

28 *Supreme Court Reporter*, pp. 324–327
(208 U.S. 412) Curt Muller,
Plff. in Err., v. State of Oregon
Argued January 15, 1908. Decided February 24, 1908.

Mr. Justice Brewer delivered the opinion of the court:
On February 19, 1903, the legislature of the state of Oregon passed an act (Session Laws 1903, p. 148) the first section of which is in these words:

> "Sec. 1. That no female (shall) be employed in any mechanical establishment, or factory, or laundry in this state more than ten hours during any one day. The hours of work may be so arranged as to permit the employment of females at any time so that they shall not work more than ten hours during the twenty-four hours of any one day."

Sec. 3 made a violation of the provisions of the prior sections a misdemeanor subject to a fine of not less than $10 nor more than $25. On September 18, 1905, an information was filed in the circuit court of the state for the county of Multnomah, charging that the defendant "on the 4th day of September, A.D. 1905, in the county of Multnomah and state of Oregon, then and there being the owner of a laundry, known as the Grand Laundry, in the city of Portland, and the employer of females therein, did then and there unlawfully permit and suffer one Joe Haselbock, he, the said Joe Haselbock, then and there being an overseer, superintendent, and agent of said Curt Muller, in the said Grand Laundry, to require a female, to wit, one Mrs. E. Gotcher, to work more than ten hours in said laundry on said 4th day of September, A.D. 1905, contrary to the statutes in such cases made and provided, and against the peace and dignity of the state of Oregon."

A trial resulted in a verdict against the defendant, who was sentenced to pay a fine of $10. The supreme court of the state affirmed the conviction (48 Or. 252, 85 Pac. 855), whereupon the case was brought here on writ of error.

The single question is the constitutionality of the statute under which the defendant was convicted, so far as it affects the work of a female in a laundry. That it does not conflict with any provisions of the state Constitution is settled by the decision of the supreme court of the state. The contentions of the defendant, now plaintiff in error, are thus stated in his brief:

> "(1) Because the statute attempts to prevent persons *sui juris* from making their own contracts, and thus violates the provisions of the 14th Amendment, as follows:
> "No state shall make or enforce any law which shall abridge the privileges or immunities of citizens of the United States; nor shall any state deprive any person of life, liberty, or property, without due process of law; nor deny to any person within its jurisdiction the equal protection of the laws.'
> "(2) Because the statute does not apply equally to all persons similarly situated, and is class legislation.
> "(3) The statute is not a valid exercise of the police power. The kinds of work prescribed are not unlawful, nor are they declared to be immoral or dangerous to the public health; nor can such a law be sustained on the ground that it is designed to protect women on account of their sex. There is no necessary or reasonable connection between the limitation prescribed by the act and the public health, safety, or welfare."

It is the law of Oregon that women, whether married or single, have equal contractual and personal rights with men. As said by Chief Justice Wolverton, in *First Nat. Bank v. Leonard*, 36 Or. 390, 396, 59 Pac. 873, 874, after a review of the various statutes of the state upon the subject:

> "We may therefore say with perfect confidence that, with these three sections upon the statute book, the wife can deal, not only with her separate property, acquired from whatever source, in the same manner as her husband can with property belonging to him, but that she may make contracts and incur liabilities, and the same may be enforced against her, the same as if she were a *female sole*. There is now no residuum of civil disability resting upon her which is not recognized as existing against the husband. The current runs steadily and strongly in the direction of the emancipation of the wife, and the policy, as disclosed by all recent legislation upon the subject in the state, is to place her upon the same footing as if she were a *female sole*, not only with respect to her separate property, but as it affects her right to make binding contracts; and the most natural corollary to the situation is that the remedies for the enforcement of liabilities incurred are made coextensive and coequal with such enlarged conditions."

It thus appears that, putting to one side the elective franchise, in the matter of personal and contractual rights they stand on the same plane as the other sex. Their rights in these respects can no more be infringed than the equal rights of their brothers. We held in *Lonchner v. New York*, 198 U.S. 45, 49 L. ed. 937, 25 Sup. Ct. Rep. 539, that a law providing that no laborer shall be required or permitted to work in bakeries more than sixty hours in a week or ten hours in a day was not as to men a legitimate exercise of the police power of the state, but an unreasonable, unnecessary, and arbitrary interference with the right and liberty of the individual to contract in relation to his labor, and as such was in conflict with, and void under, the Federal Constitution. The decision is invoked by plaintiff in error as decisive of the question before us. But this assumes that the difference between the sexes does not justify a different rule respecting a restriction of the hours of labor.

In patent cases counsel are apt to open the argument with a discussion of the state of the art. It may not be amiss, in the present case, before examining the constitutional question, to notice the course of legislation, as well as expressions of opinion from other than judicial sources. In the brief filed by Mr. Louis D. Brandeis for the defendant in error is a very copious collection of all these matters, an epitome of which is found in the margin. . . .

While there have been but few decisions bearing directly upon the question, the following sustain the constitutionality of such legislation: *Com. v. Hamilton Mfg. Co.* 120 Mass. 383; *Wenham v. State*, 65 Neb. 394, 400, 406, 58 L.R.A. 825, 91 N. W. 421; *State v. Buchanan*, 29 Wash. 602, 59 L.R.A. 342, 92 Am. St. Rep. 930, 70 Pac. 52; *Com. v. Beatty*, 15 Pa. Super. Ct. 5, 17; against them is the case of *Ritchie v. People*, 155 Ill. 98, 29 L.R.A. 79, 46 Am. St. Rep. 315, 40 N.E. 454.

The legislation and opinions referred to in the margin may not be, technically speaking, authorities, and in them is little or no discussion of the constitutional question presented to us for determination, yet they are significant of a widespread belief that woman's physical structure, and the functions she performs in consequence thereof, justify special legislation restricting or qualifying the conditions under which she should be permitted to toil. Constitutional questions, it is true, are not settled by even a consensus of present public opinion, for it is the peculiar value of a written constitution that it places in unchanging form limitations upon legislative action, and thus gives a permanence and stability to popular government which otherwise would be lacking. At the same time, when a question of fact is debated and debatable, and the extent to which a special constitutional limitation goes is affected by the truth in respect to that fact, a widespread and long-continued belief concerning it is worthy of consideration. We take judicial cognizance of all matters of general knowledge.

It is undoubtedly true, as more than once declared by this court, that the general right to contract in relation to one's business is part of the liberty of the individual, protected by the 14th Amendment to the Federal Constitution; yet it is equally well settled that this liberty is not absolute and extending to all contracts, and that a state may, without conflicting with the provisions of the 14th Amendment, restrict in many respects the individual's power of contract. Without stopping to discuss at length the extent to which a state may act in this respect, we refer to the following cases in which the question has been considered: *Allgeyer v. Louisiana*, 165 U.S. 578, 41 L. ed. 832, 17 Sup. Ct. Rep. 427; *Holden v. Hardy*, 169 U. S. 366, 42 L. ed. 780, 18 Sup. Rep. 383; *Lochner v. New York*, supra.

That woman's physical structure and the performance of maternal functions place her at a disadvantage in the struggle for subsistence is obvious. This is especially true when the burdens of motherhood are upon her. Even when they are not, by abundant testimony of the medical fraternity continuance for a long time on her feet at work, repeating this from day to day, tends to injurious effects upon the body, and, as healthy mothers are essential to vigorous offspring, the physical well-being of woman becomes an object of public interest and care in order to preserve the strength and vigor of the race.

Still again, history discloses the fact that woman has always been dependent upon man. He established his control at the outset by superior physical strength, and this control in various forms, with diminishing intensity, has continued to the present. As minors, though not to the same extent, she has been looked upon in the courts as needing especial care that her rights may be preserved. Education was long denied her, and while now the doors of the schoolroom are opened and her opportunities for

acquiring knowledge are great, yet even with that and the consequent increase of capacity for business affairs it is still true that in the struggle for subsistence she is not an equal competitor with her brother. Though limitations upon personal and contractual rights may be removed by legislation, there is that in her disposition and habits of life which will operate against a full assertion of those rights. She will still be where some legislation to protect her seems necessary to secure a real equality of right. Doubtless there are individual exceptions, and there are many respects in which she has an advantage over him; but looking at it from the viewpoint of the effort to maintain an independent position in life, she is not upon an equality. Differentiated by these matters from the other sex, she is properly placed in a class by herself, and legislation designed for her protection may be sustained, even when like legislation is not necessary for men, and could not be sustained. It is impossible to close one's eyes to the fact that she still looks to her brother and depends upon him. Even though all restrictions on political, personal, and contractual rights were taken away, and she stood, so far as statutes are concerned, upon an absolutely equal plane with him, it would still be true that she is so constituted that she will rest upon and look to him for protection; that her physical structure and a proper discharge of her maternal functions—having in view not merely her own health, but the well-being of the race— justify legislation to protect her from the greed as well as the passion of man. The limitations which this statute places upon her contractual powers, upon her right to agree with her employer as to the time she shall labor, are not imposed solely for her benefit, but also largely for the benefit of all. Many words cannot make this plainer. The two sexes differ in structure of body, in the functions to be performed by each, in the amount of physical strength, in the capacity for long continued labor, particularly when done standing, the influence of vigorous health upon the future well-being of the race, the self-reliance which enables one to assert full rights, and in the capacity to maintain the struggle for subsistence. This difference justifies a difference in legislation, and upholds that which is designed to compensate for some of the burdens which rest upon her.

We have not referred in this discussion to the denial of the elective franchise in the state of Oregon, for while that may disclose a lack of political equality in all things with her brother, that is not of itself decisive. The reason runs deeper, and rests in the inherent difference between the two sexes, and in the different functions in life which they perform.

For these reasons, and without questioning in any respect the decision in *Lochner v. New York*, we are of the opinion that it cannot be adjudged that the act in question is in conflict with the Federal Constitution, so far as it respects the work of a female in a laundry, and the judgment of the Supreme Court of Oregon is affirmed.

Why Women Should Vote
By Jane Addams

Frances M. Bjrkman and Annie G. Porritt, eds., *"The Blue Book"; Woman Suffrage, History, Arguments and Results* (New York: National Woman Suffrage Publishing Co., 1937)

For many generations it has been believed that woman's place is within the walls of her own home, and it is indeed impossible to imagine the time when her duty there shall be ended or to forecast any social change which shall release her from that paramount obligation.

This paper is an attempt to show that many women today are failing to discharge their duties to their own households properly simply because they do not perceive that as society grows more complicated it is necessary that woman shall extend her sense of responsibility to many things outside of her own home if she would continue to preserve the home in its entirety. One could illustrate in many ways. A woman's simplest duty, one would say, is to keep her house clean and wholesome, and to feed her children properly. Yet if she lives in a tenement house, as so many of my neighbors do, she cannot fulfill these simple obligations by her own efforts because she is utterly dependent upon the city administration for the conditions which render decent living possible. Her basement will not be dry, her stairways will not be fireproof, her house will not be provided with sufficient windows to give light and air, nor will it be equipped with sanitary plumbing, unless the Public Works Department sends inspectors who constantly insist that these elementary decencies be provided. Women who live in the country sweep their own dooryards and may either feed the refuse of the table to a flock of chickens or allow it innocently to decay in the open air and sunshine. In a crowded city quarter, however, if the street is not cleaned by the city authorities, no amount of private sweeping will keep the tenement free from grime; if the garbage is not properly collected and destroyed, a tenement house mother may see her children sicken and die of diseases from which she alone is powerless to shield them, although her tenderness and devotion are unbounded. She cannot even secure untainted meat for her household, she cannot provide fresh fruit, unless the meat has been inspected by city officials, and the decayed fruit, which is so often placed upon sale in the tenement districts, has been destroyed in the interests of public health. In short, if woman would keep on with her old business of caring for her house and rearing her children, she will have to have some conscience in regard to public affairs lying quite outside of her immediate household. The individual conscience and devotion are no longer effective.

Chicago one spring had a spreading contagion of scarlet fever just at the time that the school nurses had been discontinued because business men had pronounced them too expensive. If the women who sent their children to the schools had been sufficiently public-spirited and had been provided with an implement through which to express that public spirit, they would have insisted that the schools be supplied with nurses in order that their own children might be protected from contagion. In other words, if women would effectively continue their old avocations they must take part in the slow upbuilding of that code of legislation which is alone sufficient to protect the home from the dangers incident to modern life. One might instance the many deaths of children from contagious diseases the germs of which had been carried in tailored clothing. Country doctors testify as to the outbreak of scarlet fever in remote neighborhoods each autumn, after the children have begun to wear the winter overcoats and cloaks which have been sent from infected city sweatshops. That their mothers mend their stockings and guard them from "taking cold" is not a sufficient protection, when the tailoring of the family is done in a distant city under conditions which the mother cannot possibly control. The sanitary regulation of sweatshops by city officials is all that can be depended upon to prevent such needless destruction. Who shall say that women are not concerned in the enactment and enforcement of such legislation if they would preserve their homes?

Even women who take no part in public affairs, in order that they may give themselves entirely to their own families, sometimes going so far as to despise those other women who are endeavoring to secure protective legislation, may illustrate this point. The Hull-House neighborhood was at one time suffering from a typhoid epidemic. A careful investigation was made by which we were able to establish a very close connection between the typhoid and a mode of plumbing which made it most probable that the infection had been carried by flies. Among the people who had been exposed to the infection was a widow who had lived in the ward for a number of years, in a comfortable little house which she owned. Although the Italian immigrants were closing in all around her, she was not willing to sell her property and to move away, until she had finished the education of her children. In the meantime she held herself quite aloof from her Italian neighbors and could never be drawn into any of the public efforts to protect them by securing a better code of tenement house sanitation. Her two daughters were sent to an Eastern college; one June, when one of them had graduated and the other still had two years before she took her degree, they came to the spotless little house, and to their self-sacrificing mother for the Summer's holidays. They both fell ill, not because their own home was not clean, not because their mother was not devoted, but because next door to them and also in the rear were wretched tenements, and because the mother's utmost efforts could not keep the infection out of her own house. One daughter died, and one recovered, but was an invalid for two years following. This is, perhaps, a fair illustration of the futility of the individual conscience when woman insists upon isolating her family from the rest of the community and its interests. The result is sure to be a pitiful failure.

One of the interesting experiences in the Chicago campaign for inducing the members of the Charter Convention to recommend municipal franchise for women in the provisions of the new charter was the unexpected enthusiasm and help which came from large groups of foreign-born women. The Scandinavian women represented in many Lutheran Church societies said quite simply that in the old country they had had the municipal franchise upon the same basis as men for many years; all the women living under the British Government, in England, Australia or Canada, pointed out that Chicago women were asking now for what the British women had long ago. But the most unexpected response came from the foreign colonies in which women had never heard such problems discussed, and took the prospect of the municipal ballot as a simple device—which it is—to aid them in their daily struggle with adverse city conditions. The Italian women said that the men engaged in railroad construction were away all summer and did not know anything about their household difficulties. Some of them came to Hull-House one day to talk over the possibility of a public wash-house. They do not like to wash in their own tenements; they had never seen a washing-tub until they came to America, and find it very difficult to use it in the restricted space of their little kitchens and to hang the clothes within the house to dry. They say that in the Italian villages the women all go to the streams together; in the town they go to the public wash-house; and washing, instead of being lonely and disagreeable, is made pleasant by cheerful conservation. It is asking a great deal of these women to change suddenly all their habits of living, and their contention that the tenement house kitchen is too small for laundry work is well taken. If women in Chicago knew the needs of the Italian colony they would realize that any change bringing cleanliness and fresh air into the Italian household would be a very sensible and hygienic measure. It is, perhaps, asking a great deal that the members of the City Council should understand this, but surely a comprehensive of the needs of these women and efforts toward ameliorating their lot might be regarded as matters of municipal obligation on the part of voting women.

The same thing is true of the Jewish women in their desire for covered markets which have always been a municipal provision in Russia and Poland. The vegetables piled high upon the wagons standing in the open markets of Chicago become covered with dust and soot. It seems to these women a violation of the most rudimentary decencies and they sometimes say quite simply: "If women had anything to say about it they would change all that."

If women follow only the lines of their traditional activities, here are certain primary duties which belong to even the most conservative women, and which no one woman or group of women can adequately discharge unless they join the more general movements looking toward social amelioration through legal enactment.

The first of these, of which this article has already treated, is woman's responsibility for the members of her own household that they may be properly fed and clothed and surrounded by hygienic conditions. The second is a responsibility for the education of children: (a) that they may be provided with good books; (b) that they may be kept free from vicious influences on the street; (c) that when working they may be protected by adequate child-labor legislation.

(a) The duty of a woman toward the schools which her children attend is so obvious that it is not necessary to dwell upon it. But even this simple obligation cannot be effectively carried out without some form of social organization, as the mothers school clubs and mothers congresses testify, and to which the most conservative women belong because they feel the need of wider reading and discussion concerning the many problems of childhood. It is, therefore, perhaps natural that the public should have been more willing to accord a vote to women in school matters than in any other, and yet women have never been members of a Board of Education in sufficient numbers to influence largely actual school curriculi. If they had been kindergartens, domestic science courses and school playgrounds would be far more numerous than they are. More than one woman has been convinced of the need of the ballot by the futility of her efforts in persuading a business man that young children need nurture in something besides the three r's. Perhaps, too, only women realize the influence which the school might exert upon the home if a proper adaptation to actual needs were considered. An Italian girl who has had lessons in cooking at the public school will help her mother to connect the entire family with American food and household habits. That the mother has never baked bread in Italy—only mixed it in her own house and then taken it out to the village oven—makes it all the more necessary that her daughter should understand the complications of a cooking-stove. The same thing is true of the girl who learns to sew in the public school, and more than anything else, perhaps, of the girl who receives the first simple instruction in the care of little children, that skillful care which every tenement house baby requires if he is to be pulled through his second summer. The only time, to my knowledge, that lessons in the care of children were given in the public schools of Chicago was one summer when the vacation schools were being managed by a volunteer body of women. The instructions was eagerly received by the Italian girls, who had been "little mothers" to younger children ever since they could remember.

As a result of this teaching I recall a young girl who carefully explained to her Italian mother that the reason the babies in Italy were so healthy and the babies in Chicago were so sickly was not, as her mother had always firmly insisted, because her babies in Italy had goat's milk and her babies in America had cow's milk, but because the milk in Italy was clean and the milk in Chicago was dirty. She said that when you milked your own goat before the door you knew that the milk was clean, but when you bought milk from the grocery store after it had been carried for many miles in the country, "you couldn't tell whether or not it was fit for baby to drink until the men from the City Hall, who had watched it all the way, said that it was all right." She also informed her mother that the "City Hall wanted to fix up the milk so that it couldn't make the baby sick, but that they hadn't quite enough votes for it yet." The Italian mother believed what her child had been taught in the big school; it seemed to her quite as natural that the city should be concerned in providing pure milk for her younger children as that it should provide big schools and teachers for her older children. She reached this naive conclusion because she had never heard those arguments which make it seem reasonable that a woman should be given the school franchise, but no other.

(b) But women are also beginning to realize that children need attention outside of school hours; that much of the petty vice in cities is merely the love of pleasure gone wrong, the over-restrained boy or girl seeking improper recreation and excitement. It is obvious that a little study of the needs of children, a sympathetic understanding of the conditions under which they go astray, might save hundreds of them. Women traditionally have had an opportunity to observe the plays of children and the needs of youth, and yet in Chicago, at least, they had done singularly little in this vexed problem of juvenile delinquency until they helped to inaugurate the Juvenile Court movement a dozen years ago. The Juvenile Court Committee, made up largely of women, paid the salaries of the probation officers connected with the court for the first six years of its existence, and after the salaries were cared for by the county the same organization turned itself into a Juvenile Protective League, and through a score of paid officers are doing valiant service in minimizing some of the dangers of city life which boys and girls encounter.

This Protective League, however, was not formed until the women had had a civic training through their semi-offi-

cial connection with the Juvenile Court. This is, perhaps, an illustration of our inability to see the duty "next to hand" until we have become alert through our knowledge of conditions in connection with the larger duties. We would all agree that social amelioration must come about through the efforts of many people who are moved thereto by the compunction and stirring of the individual conscience, but we are only beginning to understand that the individual conscience will respond to the special challenge largely in proportion as the individual is able to see the social conditions because he has felt responsible for their improvement. Because this body of women assumed a public responsibility they have seen to it that every series of pictures displayed in the five-cent theatre is subjected to a careful censorship before it is produced, and those series suggesting obscenity and criminality have been practically eliminated. The police department has performed this and many other duties to which it was oblivious before, simply because these women have made it realize that it is necessary to protect and purify those places of amusement which are crowded with young people every night. This is but the negative side of the policy pursued by the public authorities in the fifteen small parks of Chicago, each of which is provided with halls in which young people may meet nightly for social gatherings and dances. The more extensively the modern city endeavors on the one hand to control and on the other hand to provide recreational facilities for its young people, the more necessary it is that women should assist in their direction and extension. After all, a care for wholesome and innocent amusement is what women have for many years assumed. When the reaction comes on the part of taxpayers, women's votes may be necessary to keep the city to its beneficent obligations towards its own young people.

(c) As the education of her children has been more and more transferred to the school, so that even children four years old go to the kindergarten, the woman has been left in a household of constantly narrowing interests, not only because the children are away, but also because one industry after another is slipping from the household into the factory. Ever since steam power has been applied to the processes of weaving and spinning woman's traditional work has been carried on largely outside of the home. The clothing and household linen are not only spun and woven, but also usually sewed by machinery; the preparation of many foods has also passed into the factory and necessarily a certain number of women have been obliged to follow their work there; although it is doubtful, in spite of the large number of factory girls, whether women now are doing as large a proportion of the world's work as they used to do. Because many thousands of those working in factories and shops are girls between the ages of fourteen and twenty-two, there is a necessity that older women should be interested in the conditions of industry. The very fact that these girls are not going to remain in industry permanently makes it more important that some one should see to it that they shall not be incapacitated for their future family life because they work for exhausting hours and under insanitary conditions.

If woman's sense of obligation had enlarged as the industrial condition changed, she might naturally and almost imperceptibly have inaugurated the movements for social amelioration in the line of factory legislation and shop sanitation. That she has not done so is doubtless due to the fact that her conscience is slow to recognize any obligation outside of her own family circle, and because she was so absorbed in her own household that she failed to see what the conditions outside actually were. It would be interesting to know how far the consciousness that she had no vote and could not change matters operated in this direction. After all, we see only those things to which our attention has been drawn, we feel responsibility for those things which are brought to us as matters of responsibility. If conscientious women were convinced that it was a civic duty to be informed in regard to these grave industrial affairs, and then to express the conclusions which they had reached by depositing a piece of paper in a ballot-box, one cannot imagine that they would shirk simply because the action ran counter to old traditions.

To those of my readers who would admit that, although woman has no right to shirk her old obligations, all of these measures could be secured more easily through her influence upon the men of her family than through the direct use of the ballot. I should like to tell a little story. I have a friend in Chicago who is the mother of four sons and the grandmother of twelve grandsons who are voters. She is a woman of wealth, of secured social position, of sterling character and clear intelligence, and may therefore, quite fairly be cited as a "woman of influence." Upon one of her recent birthdays, when she was asked how she had kept so young, she promptly replied: "Because I have always advocated at least one unpopular cause." It may have been in pursuance of this policy that for many years she has been an ardent advocate of free silver, although her manufacturing family are all Republicans. I happened to call at her house on the day that Mr. McKinley was elected President against Mr. Bryan for the first time. I found my friend much disturbed. She said somewhat bitterly that she had at last discovered what the much-vaunted influence of woman was worth; that she had implored each one of her sons and grandsons; had entered into endless arguments and moral appeals to induce one of them to represent her convictions by voting for Mr. Bryan; that, although sincerely devoted to her, each one had assured her that his convictions forced him to vote the Republican ticket! She said that all she had been able to secure was the promise from one of the grand-sons, for whom she had and especial tenderness, because he bore her husband's name, that he would not vote at all. He could not vote for Bryan, but out of respect for her feeling he would refrain from voting for McKinley. My friend said that for many years she had suspected that women could influence men only in regard to those things in which men were not deeply concerned, but when it came to persuading a man to a woman's views in affairs of politics or business it was absolutely useless. I contended that a woman had no right to persuade a man to vote against his own convictions; that I respected the men of her family for following their own judgment regardless of the appeal which the honored head of the house had made to their chivalric devotion. To this she replied that she would agree with that point of view when a woman had the same opportunity as a man to register her convictions by vote. I believed then as I do now, that nothing is gained when independence of judgment is assailed by "influence," sentimental or otherwise, and that we test advancing civilization somewhat by our power to respect differences and by our tolerance of another's honest conviction.

This is, perhaps, the attitude of many busy women who would be glad to use the ballot to further public measures in which they are interested and for which they have been working for years. It offends the taste of such a woman to be obliged to use indirect "influence" when she is accustomed to well-bred, open action in other affairs, and she very much resents the time spent in persuading a voter to take her point of view, and possibly to give up his own quite as honest and valuable as hers, although different because resulting from a totally different experience. Public-spirited women who wish to use the ballot, as I know them, do not wish to do the work of men nor to take over men's affairs. They simply want an opportunity to do their own work and to take care of those affairs which naturally and historically belong to women, but which are constantly being overlooked and slighted in our political institutions.

In a complex community like the modern city all points of view need to be represented; the resultants of diverse experiences need to be pooled, if the community would make for sane and balanced progress. If it would meet fairly each problem as it arises, whether it be connected with a freight tunnel having to do largely with business men, or with the increasing death rate among children under five years of age, a problem in which women are vitally concerned, or with the question of more adequate street-car transfers, in which both men and women might be said to be equally interested, it must not ignore the judgments of its entire adult population.

To turn the administration of our civic affairs wholly over to men may mean that the American city will continue to push forward in its commercial and industrial development, and continue to lag behind in those things which make a city healthful and beautiful. After all, woman's traditional function has been to make her dwelling-place both clean and fair. Is that dreariness in city life, that lack of domesticity which the humblest farm dwelling presents, due to a withdrawal of one of the naturally co-operating forces? If women have in any sense been responsible for the gentler side of life which softens and blurs some of its harsher conditions, may they not have a duty to perform in our American cities?

In closing, may I recapitulate that if woman would fulfill her traditional responsibility to her own children; if she would educate and protect from danger factory children who must find their recreation on the street; if she would bring the cultural forces to bear upon our materialistic civilization; and if she would do it all with the dignity and directness fitting one who carries on her immemorial duties, then she must bring herself to the use of the ballot-that latest implement for self-government. May we not fairly say the American women need this implement in order to preserve the home?

"Make the World Safe for Democracy" Speech (1917)
President Woodrow Wilson

Arthur S. Link, ed., *The Papers of Woodrow Wilson*, vol. 45, (Princeton, N.J.: Princeton University Press, 1966–94), pp. 519–527

April 2, 1917

Gentlemen of the Congress: I have called the Congress into extraordinary session because there are serious, very serious, choices of policy to be made, and made immediately, which it was neither right nor constitutionally permissible that I should assume the responsibility of making. On the third of February last I officially laid before you the extraordinary announcement of the Imperial German Government that on and after the first day of February it was its purpose to put aside all restraints of law or of humanity and use its submarines to sink every vessel that sought to approach either the ports of Great Britain and Ireland or the western coasts of Europe or any of the ports controlled by the enemies of Germany within the Mediterranean. That had seemed to be the object of the German submarine warfare earlier in the war, but since April of last year the Imperial Government had somewhat restrained the commanders of its undersea craft in conformity with its promise then given to us that passenger boats should not be sunk and that due warning would be given to all other vessels which its submarines might seek to destroy, when no resistance was offered or escape attempted, and care taken that their crews were given at

least a fair chance to save their lives in their open boats. The precautions taken were meagre and haphazard enough, as was proved in distressing instance after instance in the progress of the cruel and unmanly business, but a certain degree of restraint was observed. The new policy has swept every restriction aside. Vessels of every kind, whatever their flag, their character, their cargo, their destination, their errand, have been ruthlessly sent to the bottom without warning and without thought of help or mercy for those on board, the vessels of friendly neutrals along with those of belligerents. Even hospitals ships and ships carrying relief to the sorely bereaved and stricken people of Belgium, though the latter were provided with safe conduct through the proscribed areas by the German Government itself and were distinguished by unmistakable marks of identity, have been sunk with the same reckless lack of compassion or of principles. I was for a little while unable to believe that such things would in fact be done by any government that had hitherto subscribed to the humane practices of civilized nations.

International law had its origin in the attempt to set up some law which would be respected and observed upon the seas, where no nation had right of dominion and where lay the free highways of the world. By painful stage after stage has that law been built up, with meagre enough results, indeed, after all was accomplished that could be accomplished, but always with a clear view, at least, of what the heart and conscience of mankind demanded. This minimum of right the German Government has swept aside under the plea of retaliation and necessity and because it had no weapons which it could use at sea except these which it is impossible to employ as it is employing them without throwing to the winds all scruples of humanity or of respect for the understandings that were supposed to underlie the intercourse of the world. I am not now thinking of the loss of property involved, immense and serious as that is, but only of the wanton and wholesale destruction of the lives of non-combatants, men, women, and children, engaged in pursuits which have always, even in the darkest periods of modern history, been deemed innocent and legitimate. Property can be paid for; the lives of peaceful and innocent people cannot be. The present German submarine warfare against commerce is a warfare against mankind.

It is a war against all nations. American ships have been sunk, American lives taken, in ways which it has stirred us very deeply to learn of, but the ships and people of other neutral and friendly nations have been sunk and overwhelmed in the waters in the same way. There has been no discrimination. The challenge is to all mankind. Each nation must decide for itself how it will meet it. The choice we make for ourselves must be made with a moderation of counsel and a temperateness of judgment befitting our character and our motives as a nation. We must put excited feeling away. Our motive will not be revenge or the victorious assertion of the physical might of the nation, but only the vindication of right, of human right, of which we are only a single champion.

When I addressed the Congress on the twenty-sixth of February last I thought that it would suffice to assert our neutral rights with arms, our right to use the seas against unlawful interference, our right to keep our people safe against unlawful violence. But armed neutrality, it now appears, is impracticable. Because submarines are in effect outlaws when used as the German submarines have been used against merchant shipping, it is impossible to defend ships against their attacks as the law of nations has assumed that merchantmen would defend themselves against privateers or cruisers, visible craft giving chase upon the open sea. It is common prudence in such circumstances, grim necessity, indeed, to endeavour to destroy them before they have shown their own intention. They must be dealt with upon sight, if dealt with at all. The German Government denies the right of neutrals to use arms at all within the areas of the sea which it has proscribed, even in the defense or rights which no modern publicist has ever before questioned their right to defend. The intimation is conveyed that the armed guards which we have placed on our merchant ships will be treated as beyond the pale of law and subject to be dealt with as pirates would be. Armed neutrality is ineffectual enough at best; in such circumstances and in the face of such pretensions it is worse than ineffectual: it is likely only to produce what it was meant to prevent; it is practically certain to draw us into the war without either the rights or the effectiveness of belligerents. There is one choice we cannot make, we are incapable of making: we will not choose the path of submission and suffer the most sacred rights of our nation and our people to be ignored or violated. The wrongs against which we now array ourselves are no common wrongs; they cut to the very roots of human life.

With a profound sense of the solemn and even tragical character of the step I am taking and of the grave responsibilities which it involves, but in unhesitating obedience to what I deem my constitutional duty, I advise that the Congress declare the recent course of the Imperial German Government to be in fact nothing less than war against the government and people of the United States; that it formally accept the status of belligerent which has thus been thrust upon it; and that it take immediate steps not only to put the country in a more thorough state of defense but also to exert all its power and employ all its resources to bring the Government of the German Empire to terms and end the war.

What this will involve is clear. It will involve the utmost practicable cooperation in counsel and action with the governments now at war with Germany, and, as incident to that, the extension to those governments of the most liberal financial credits, in order that our resources may so far as possible be added to theirs. It will involve the organization and mobilization of all the material resources of the country to supply the materials of war and serve the incidental needs of the nation in the most abundant and yet the most economical and efficient way possible. It will involve the immediate full equipment of the navy in all respects but particularly in supplying it with the best means of dealing with the enemy's submarines. It will involve the immediate addition to the armed forces of the United States already provided for by law in case of war at least five hundred thousand men, who should, in my opinion, be chosen upon the principle of universal liability to service, and also the authorization of subsequent additional increments of equal force so soon as they may be needed and can be handled in training. It will involve also, of course, the granting of adequate credits to the Government, sustained, I hope, so far as they can equitably be sustained by the present generation, by well conceived taxation.

I say sustained so far as may be equitable by taxation because it seems to me that it would be most unwise to base the credits which will now be necessary entirely on money borrowed. It is our duty, I most respectfully urge, to protect our people so far as we may against the very serious hardships and evils which would be likely to arise out of the inflation which would be produced by vast loans.

In carrying out the measures by which these things are to be accomplished we should keep constantly in mind the wisdom of interfering as little as possible in our own preparation and in the equipment of our own military forces with the duty,—for it will be a very practical duty,—of supplying the nations already at war with Germany with the materials which they can obtain only from us or by our assistance. They are in the field and we should help them in every way to be effective there.

I shall take the liberty of suggesting, through the several executive departments of the Government, for the consideration of your committees, measures for the accomplishment of the several objects I have mentioned. I hope that it will be your pleasure to deal with them as having been framed after very careful thought by the branch of the Government upon which the responsibility of conducting the war and safeguarding the nation will most directly fall. While we do these things, these deeply momentous things, let us be very clear, and make very clear to all the world what our motives and our objects are. My own thought has not been driven from its habitual and normal course by the unhappy events of the last two months, and I do not believe that the thought of the nation has been altered or clouded by them. I have exactly the same things in mind now that I had in mind when I addressed the Senate on the twenty-second of January last; the same that I had in mind when I addressed the Congress on the third of February and on the twenty-sixth of February. Our object now, as then, is to vindicate the principles of peace and justice in the life of the world as against selfish and autocratic power and to set up amongst the really free and self-governed peoples of the world such a concert of purpose and of action as will henceforth ensure the observance of those principles. Neutrality is no longer feasible or desirable where the peace of the world is involved and the freedom of its peoples, and the menace to that peace and freedom lies in the existence of autocratic governments backed by organized force which is controlled wholly by their will, not by the will of their people. We have seen the last of neutrality in such circumstances. We are at the beginning of an age in which it will be insisted that the same standards of conduct and of responsibility for wrong done shall be observed among nations and their governments that are observed among the individual citizens of civilized states.

We have no quarrel with the German people. We have no feeling towards them but one of sympathy and friendship. It was not upon their impulse that their government acted in entering this war. It was not with their previous knowledge or approval. It was a war determined upon as wars used to be determined upon in the old, unhappy days when peoples were nowhere consulted by their rulers and wars were provoked and waged in the interest of dynasties or of little groups of ambitious men who were accustomed to use their fellow men as pawns and tools. Self-governed nations do not fill their neighbour states with spies or set the course of intrigue to bring about some critical posture of affairs which will give them an opportunity to strike and make conquest. Such designs can be successfully worked out only under cover and where no one has the right to ask questions. Cunningly contrived plans of deception or aggression, carried, it may be, from generation to generation, can be worked out and kept from the light only within the privacy of courts or behind the carefully guarded confidences of a narrow and privileged class. They are happily impossible where public opinion commands and insists upon full information concerning all the nation's affairs.

A steadfast concert for peace can never be maintained except by a partnership of democratic nations. No autocratic government could be trusted to keep faith within it or observe its covenants. It must be a league of honour, a partnership of opinion. Intrigue would eat its vitals away; the plottings of inner circles who could plan what they would and render account to no one would be a corruption seated at its very heart. Only free peoples can hold their purpose and their honour steady to a common end and prefer the interests of mankind to any narrow interest of their own.

Does not every American feel that assurance has been added to our hope for the future peace of the world by the wonderful and heartening things that have been happening within the last few weeks in Russia? Russia was known by those who knew it best to have been always in fact democratic at heart, in all the vital habits of her thought, in all the intimate relationships of her people that spoke their natural instinct, their habitual attitude towards life. The autocracy that crowned the summit of her political structure, long as it had stood and terrible as was the reality of its power, was not in fact Russian in origin, character, or purpose; and now it has been shaken off and the great, generous Russian people have been added in all their naive majesty and might to the forces that are fighting for freedom in the world, for justice, and for peace. Here is a fit partner for a League of Honour.

One of the things that has served to convince us that the Prussian autocracy was not and could never be our friend is that from the very outset of the present war it has filled our unsuspecting communities and even our offices of government with spies and set criminal intrigues everywhere afoot against our national unity of counsel, our peace within and without, our industries and our commerce. Indeed it is now evident that its spies were here even before the war began; and it is unhappily not a matter of conjecture but a fact proved in our court of justice that the intrigues which have more than once come perilously near to disturbing the peace and dislocating the industries of the country have been carried on at the instigation, with the support, and even under the personal direction of official agents of the Imperial Government accredited to the Government of the United States. Even in checking these things and trying to extirpate them we have sought to put the most generous interpretation possible upon them because we knew that their source lay, not in any hostile feeling or purpose of the German people towards us (who were, no doubt as ignorant of them as we ourselves were), but only in the selfish designs of a Government that did what it pleased and told its people nothing. But they have played their part in serving to convince us at last that that Government entertains no real friendship for us and means to act against our peace and security at its convenience. That it means to stir up enemies against us at our very doors the intercepted note to the German Minister at Mexico City is eloquent evidence.

We are accepting this challenge of hostile purpose because we know that in such a government, following such methods, we can never have a friend; and that in the presence of its organized power, always lying in wait to accomplish we know not what purpose, there can be no assured security for the democratic governments of the world. We are now about to accept gauge of battle with this natural foe to liberty and shall, if necessary, spend the whole force of the nation to check and nullify its pretensions and its power. We are glad, now that we see the facts with no veil of false pretence about them, to fight thus for the ultimate peace of the world and for the liberation of its peoples, the German peoples included: for the rights of nations great and small and the privilege of men everywhere to choose their way of life and of obedience. The world must be made safe for democracy. Its peace must be planted upon the tested foundations of political liberty. We have no selfish ends to serve. We desire no conquest, no dominion. We seek no indemnities for ourselves, no material compensation for the sacrifices we shall freely make. We are but one of the champions of the rights of mankind. We shall be satisfied when those rights have been made as secure as the faith and the freedom of nations can make them. Just because we fight without rancour and without selfish object, seeking nothing for ourselves but what we shall wish to share with all free peoples, we shall, I feel confident, conduct our operations as belligerents without passion and ourselves observe with proud punctilio the principles of right and of fair play we profess to be fighting for.

I have said nothing of the governments allied with the Imperial Government of Germany because they have not made war upon us or challenged us to defend our right and our honour. The Austro-Hungarian Government has, indeed, avowed its unqualified endorsement and acceptance of the reckless and lawless submarine warfare adopted now without disguise by the Imperial German Government, and it has therefore not been possible for this Government to receive Count Tarnowski, the Ambassador recently accredited to this Government by the Imperial and Royal Government of Austria-Hungary; but that Government has not actually engaged in warfare against citizens of the United States on the seas, and I take the liberty, for the present at least, of postponing a discussion of our relations with the authorities at Vienna. We enter this war only where we are clearly forced into it because there are no other means of defending our rights. It will be all the easier for us to conduct ourselves as belligerents in a high spirit of right and fairness because we act without animus, not in enmity towards a people or with the desire to bring any injury or disadvantage upon them, but only in armed opposition to an irresponsible government which has thrown aside all considerations of humanity and of right and is running amuck. We are, let me say again, the sincere friends of the German people, and shall desire nothing so much as the early re-establishment of intimate relations of mutual advantage between us,—however hard it may be for them, for the time being, to believe that this is spoken from our hearts. We have borne with their present government through all these bitter months because of that friendship,—exercising a patience and forbearance which would otherwise have been impossible. We shall, happily, still have an opportunity to prove that friendship in our daily attitude and actions towards the millions of men and women of German birth and native sympathy who live amongst us and share our life, and we shall be proud to prove it towards all who are in fact loyal to their neighbours and to the Government in the hour of test. They are, most of them, as true and loyal Americans as if they had never known any other fealty or allegiance. They will be prompt to stand with us in rebuking and restraining the few who may be of a different mind and purpose. If there should be disloyalty, it will be dealt with with a firm hand of stern repression; but, if it lifts its head at all, it will lift it only here and there and without countenance except from a lawless and malignant few.

It is a distressing and oppressive duty, Gentlemen of the Congress, which I have performed in thus addressing you. There are, it may be, many months of fiery trial and sacrifice ahead of us. It is a fearful thing to lead this great peaceful people into war, into the most terrible and disastrous of all wars, civilization itself seeming to be in the balance. But the right is more precious than peace, and we shall fight for the things which we have always carried nearest our hearts,—for democracy, for the right of those who submit to authority to have a voice in their own governments, for the rights and liberties of small nations, for a universal dominion of right by such a concert of free peoples as shall bring peace and safety to all nations and make the world itself at last free. To such a task we can dedicate our lives and our fortunes, everything that we are and everything that we have, with the pride of those who know that the day has come when America is privileged to spend her blood and her might for the principles that gave her birth and happiness and the peace which she has treasured. God helping her, she can do no other.

President Wilson's "Fourteen Points" Speech, 1918
Arthur S. Link, ed., *The Papers of Woodrow Wilson*, vol. 45, (Princeton, N.J.: Princeton University Press, 1966–94), pp. 534–539

Fourteen Points

Gentlemen of the Congress: Once more, as repeatedly before, the spokesmen of the Central Empires have indicated their desire to discuss the objects of the war and the possible bases of a general peace. Parleys have been in progress at Brest-Litovsk between representatives of the Central Powers, to which the attention of all the belligerents has been invited for the purpose of ascertaining whether it may be possible to extend these parleys into a general conference with regard to terms of peace and settlement. The Russian representatives presented not only a perfectly definite statement of the principles upon which they would be willing to conclude peace, but also an equally definite programme of the concrete application of those principles. The representatives of the Central Powers, on their part, presented an outline of settlement which, if much less definite, seemed susceptible of liberal interpretation until their specific programme of practical terms was added. That programme proposed no concessions at all either to the sovereignty of Russia or to the preferences of the populations with whose fortunes it dealt, but meant, in a word, that the Central Empires were to keep every foot of territory their armed forces had occupied,—every province, every city, every point of vantage,—as a permanent addition to their territories and their power. It is a reasonable conjecture that the general principles of settlement which they at first suggested originated with the more liberal statesmen of Germany and Austria, the men who have begun to feel the force of their own peoples' thought and purpose, while the concrete terms of actual settlement came from the military leaders who have no thought but to keep what they have got. The negotiations have been broken off. The Russian representatives were sincere and in earnest. They cannot entertain such proposals of conquest and domination.

The whole incident is full of significance. It is also full of perplexity. With whom are the Russian representatives dealing? For whom are the representatives of the Central Empires speaking? Are they speaking for the majorities of their respective parliaments or for the minority parties, that military and imperialistic minority which has so far dominated their whole policy and controlled the affairs of Turkey and of the Balkan states which have felt obliged to become their associates in this war? The Russian representatives have insisted, very justly, very wisely, and in the true spirit of modern democracy, that the conferences they have been holding with the Teutonic and Turkish statesmen should be held within open, not closed doors, and all the world has been audience, as was desired. To whom have we been listening, then? To those who speak the spirit and intention of the Resolutions of the German Reichstag of the ninth of July last, the spirit and intention of the liberal leaders and parties of Germany, or to those who resist and defy that spirit and intention and insist upon conquest and subjugation? Or are we listening, in fact, to both, unreconciled and in open and hopeless contradiction? These are very serious and pregnant questions. Upon the answer to them depends the peace of the world.

But, whatever the results of the parleys at Brest-Litovsk, whatever the confusions of counsel and of purpose in the utterances of the spokesmen of the Central Empires, they have again attempted to acquaint the world with their objects in the war and have again challenged their adversaries to say what their objects are and what sort of settlement they would deem just and satisfactory. There is no good reason why that challenge should not be responded to, and responded to with the utmost candor. We did not wait for it. Not once, but again and again, we have laid our whole thought and purpose before the world, not in general terms only, but each time with sufficient definition to make it clear what sort of definitive terms of settlement must necessarily spring out of them. Within the last week Mr. Lloyd George has spoken with admirable candor and in admirable spirit for the people and Government of Great Britain. There is no confusion of counsel among the adversaries of the Central Powers, no uncertainty of principle, no vagueness of detail. The only secrecy of counsel, the only lack of fearless frankness, the only failure to make definite statement of the objects of the war, lies with Germany and her Allies. The issues of life and death hang upon these definitions. No statesman who has the least conception of his responsibility ought for a moment to permit himself to continue this tragical and appalling outpouring of blood and treasure unless he is sure beyond a peradventure that the objects of the vital sacrifice are part and parcel of the very life of Society and that the people for whom he speaks think them right and imperative as he does. There is, moreover, a voice calling for these definitions of principle and of purpose which is, it seems to me, more thrilling and more compelling than any of the many moving voices with which the troubled air of the world is filled. It is the voice of the Russian people. They are prostrate and all but helpless, it would seem, before the grim power of Germany, which has hitherto known no relenting and no pity. Their power, apparently, is shattered. And yet their soul is not subservient. They will not yield either in principle or in action. Their conception of what is right, of what is humane and honorable for them to accept, has been stated with a frankness, a largeness of view, a generosity of spirit, and a universal human sympathy which must challenge the admiration of every friend of mankind; and they have refused to compound their ideals or desert others that they themselves may be safe. They call to us to say what it is that we desire, in what, if in anything, our purpose and our spirit differ from theirs; and I believe that the people of the United States would wish me to respond, with utter simplicity and frankness. Whether their present leaders believe it or not, it is our heartfelt desire and hope that some way may be opened whereby we may be privileged to assist the people of Russia to attain their utmost hope of liberty and ordered peace.

It will be our wish and purpose that the processes of peace, when they are begun, shall be absolutely open and that they shall involve and permit henceforth no secret understandings of any kind. The day of conquest and aggrandizement is gone by; so is also the day of secret covenants entered into the interest of particular governments and likely at some unlooked-for moment to upset the peace of the world. It is this happy fact, now clear to the view of every public man whose thoughts do not still linger in an age that is dead and gone, which makes it possible for every nation whose purposes are consistent with justice and the peace of the world to avow now or at any other time the objects it has in view.

We entered this war because violations of right had occurred which touched us to the quick and made the life of our own people impossible unless they were corrected and the world secured once for all against their recurrence. What we demand in this war, therefore, is nothing peculiar to ourselves. It is that the world be made fit and safe to live in; and particularly that it be made safe for every peace-loving nation which, like our own, wishes to live its own life, determine its own institutions, be assured of justice and fair dealing by the other peoples of the world as against force and selfish aggression. All the peoples of the world are in effect partners in this interest, and for our own part we see very clearly that unless justice be done to others it will not be done to us. The programme of the world's peace, therefore, is our programme; and that programme, the only possible programme, as we see it, is this:

I. Open covenants of peace, openly arrived at, after which there shall be no private international understandings of any kind but diplomacy shall proceed always frankly and in the public view.

II. Absolute freedom of navigation upon the seas, outside territorial waters, alike in peace and in war, except as the seas may be closed in whole or in part by international action for the enforcement of international covenants.

III. The removal, so far as possible, of all economic barriers and the establishment of an equality of trade conditions among all the nations consenting to the peace and associating themselves for its maintenance.

IV. Adequate guarantees given and taken that national armaments will be reduced to the lowest point consistent with domestic safety.

V. A free, open-minded, and absolutely impartial adjustment of all colonial claims, based upon a strict observance of the principle that in determining all such questions of sovereignty the interests of the populations concerned must have equal weight with the equitable claims of the government whose title is to be determined.

VI. The evacuation of all Russian territory and such a settlement of all questions affecting Russia as will secure the best and freest and cooperation of the other nations of the world in obtaining for her an unhampered and unembarrassed opportunity for the independent determination of her own political development and national policy and assure her of a sincere welcome into the society of free nations under institutions of her own choosing; and, more than a welcome, assistance also of every kind that she may need and may herself desire. The treatment accorded Russia by her sister nations in the months to come will be the acid test of their good will, of their comprehension of her needs as distinguished from their own interests, and of their intelligent and unselfish sympathy.

VII. Belgium, the whole world will agree, must be evacuated and restored, without any attempt to limit the sovereignty which she enjoys in common with all other free nations. No other single act will serve as this will serve to restore confidence among the nations in the laws which they have themselves set and determined for the government of their relations with one another. Without this healing act the whole structure and validity of international law is forever impaired.

VIII. All French territory should be freed and the invaded portions restored, and the wrong done to France by Prussia in 1871 in the matter of Alsace-Lorraine, which has unsettled the peace of the world for nearly fifty years, should be righted, in order that peace may once more be made secure in the interests of all.

IX. A readjustment of the frontiers of Italy should be effected along clearly recognizable lines of nationality.

X. The peoples of Austria-Hungary, whose place among the nations we wish to see safeguarded and assured, should be accorded the freest opportunity of autonomous development.

XI. Rumania, Serbia, and Montenegro should be evacuated; occupied territories restored; Serbia accorded free and secure access to the sea; and the relations of the several Balkan states to one another determined by friendly counsel along historically established lines of allegiance and nationality; and international guarantees of the political and economic independence and territorial integrity of the several Balkan states should be entered into.

XII. The Turkish portions of the present Ottoman Empire should be assured a secure sovereignty but the other nationalities which are now under Turkish rule should be assured an undoubted security of life and an absolutely unmolested opportunity of autonomous development, and the Dardanelles should be permanently opened as a free passage to the ships and commerce of all nations under international guarantees.

XIII. An independent Polish state should be erected which should include the territories inhabited by indisputably Polish populations, which should be assured a free and secure access to the sea, and whose political and economic independence and territorial integrity should be guaranteed by international covenant.

XIV. A general association of nations must be formed under specific covenants for the purpose of affording mutual guarantees of political independence and territorial integrity to great and small states alike.

In regard to these essential rectifications of wrong and assertions of right we feel ourselves to be intimate partners of all the governments and peoples associated together against the Imperialists. We cannot be separated in interest or divided in purpose. We stand together until the end.

For such arrangements and covenants we are willing to fight and to continue to fight until they are achieved; but only because we wish the right to prevail and desire a just and stable peace such as can be secured only by removing the chief provocations to war, which this programme does remove. We have no jealousy of German greatness, and there is nothing in this programme that impairs it. We grudge her no achievement or distinction of learning or of pacific enterprise such as have made her record very bright and very enviable. We do not wish to injure her or to block in any way her legitimate influence or power. We do not wish to fight her either with arms or with hostile arrangements of trade if she is willing to associate herself with us and the other peace-loving nations of the world in covenants of justice and law and fair dealing. We wish her only to accept a place of equality among the peoples of the world,—the new world in which we now live,—instead of a place of mastery.

Neither do we presume to suggest to her any alteration or modification of her institutions. But it is necessary, we must frankly say, and necessary as a preliminary to any intelligent dealings with her on our part, that we should know whom her spokesmen speak for when they speak to us, whether for the Reichstag majority or for the military party and the men whose creed is imperial domination. We have spoken now, surely, in terms too concrete to admit of any further doubt or question. An evident principle runs through the whole programme I have outlined. It is the principle of justice to all peoples and nationalities, and their right to live on equal terms of liberty and safely with one another, whether they be strong or weak. Unless this principle be made its foundation no part of the structure of international justice can stand. The people of the United States could act upon no other principle; and to the vindication of this principle they are ready to devote their lives, their honor, and everything that they possess. The normal climax of this the culminating and final war for human liberty has come, and they are ready to put their own strength, their own highest purpose, their own integrity and devotion to the test.

Flapper Jane
by Bruce Bliven

The following article by Bruce Bliven appeared in *The New Republic* on September 9, 1925:

Jane's a flapper. That is a quaint, old-fashioned term, but I hope you remember its meaning. As you can tell by her appellation, Jane is 19. If she were 29, she would be Dorothy; 39, Doris; 49, Elaine; 59, Jane again—and so on

around. This Jane, being 19, is a flapper, through she urgently denies that she is a member of the younger generation. The younger generation, she will tell you, is aged 15 to 17; and she professes to be decidedly shocked at the things they do and say. That is a fact which would interest her minister, if he knew it—poor man, he knows so little! For he regards Jane as a perfectly horrible example of wild youth—paint, cigarettes, cocktails, petting parties—Moooh! Yet if the younger generation shocks her as she says, query: how wild is Jane? Before we come to this exciting question, let us take a look at the young person as she strolls across the lawn of her parents' suburban home, having just put the car away after driving sixty miles in two hours. She is, for one thing, a very pretty girl. Beauty is the fashion in 1925. She is frankly, heavily made up, not to imitate nature, but for an altogether artificial effect—pallor mortis, poisonously scarlet lips, richly ringed eyes—the latter looking not so much debauched (which is the intention) as diabetic. Her walk duplicates the swagger supposed by innocent America to go with the female half of a Paris Apache dance. And there are, finally, her clothes. These were estimated the other day by some statistician to weigh two pounds. Probably a libel; I doubt they come within half a pound of such bulk. Jane isn't wearing much, this summer. If you'd like to know exactly, it is: one dress, one step-in, two stockings, two shoes.

A step-in, if you are 99 and 44/100ths percent ignorant, is underwear—one piece, light, exceedingly brief but roomy. Her dress, as you can't possibly help knowing if you have even one good eye, and get around at all outside the Old People's Home, is also brief. It is cut low where it might be high, and vice versa. The skirt comes just an inch below her knees, overlapping by a faint fraction her rolled and twisted stockings. The idea is that when she walks in a bit of a breeze, you shall now and then observe the knee (which is not rouged—that's just newspaper talk) but always in an accidental, Venus-surprised-at-the-bath sort of way. This is a bit of coyness which hardly fits in with Jane's general character.

Jane's haircut is also abbreviated. She wears of course the very newest thing in bobs, even closer than last year's shingle. It leaves her just about no hair at all in the back, and 20 percent more than that in the front—about as much as is being worn this season by a cellist (male); less than a pianist; and much, much less than a violinist. Because of this new style, one can confirm a rumor heard last year: Jane has ears.

The corset is as dead as the dodo's grandfather; no feeble publicity pipings by the manufacturers, or calling it a "clasp around" will enable it, as Jane says, to "do a Lazarus." The petticoat is even more defunct. Not even a snicker can be raised by telling Jane that once the nation was shattered to its foundations by the shadow-skirt. The brassiere has been abandoned, since 1924. While stockings are usually worn, they are not a sine-qua-nothing-doing. In hot weather Jane reserves the right to discard them, just as all the chorus girls did in 1923. As stockings are only a frantic, successful attempt to duplicate the color and texture of Jane's own sunburned slim legs, few but expert boulevardiers can tell the difference.

These which I have described are Jane's clothes, but they are not merely a flapper uniform. They are The Style, Summer of 1925 Eastern Seaboard. These things and none other are being worn by all of Jane's sisters and her cousins and her aunts. They are being worn by ladies who are three times Jane's age, and look ten years older; by those twice her age who look a hundred years older. Their use is so universal that in our larger cities the baggage transfer companies one and all declare they are being forced into bankruptcy. Ladies who used to go away for the summer with six trunks can now pack twenty dainty costumes in a bag.

Not since 1820 has feminine apparel been so frankly abbreviated as at present; and never, on this side of the Atlantic, until you go back to the little summer frocks of Pocahontas. This year's styles have gone quite a long step toward genuine nudity. Nor is this merely the sensible half of the population dressing as everyone ought to, in hot weather. Last winter's styles weren't so dissimilar, except that they were covered up by fur coats and you got the full effect only indoors. And improper costumes never have their full force unless worn on the street. Next year's styles, from all one hears, will be, as they already are on the continent, even More So.

Our great mentor has failed us: you will see none of the really up-to-date styles in the movies. For old-fashioned, conservative and dowdy dressing, go and watch the latest production featuring Bebe, Gloria or Pola. Under vigilant father Hays the ensilvered screen daren't reveal a costume equal to scores on Fifth Avenue, Broadway—or Wall Street.

Wall Street, by the way, is the one spot in which the New Nakedness seems most appropriate. Where men's simple passions have the lowest boiling point; where the lust for possession is most frankly, brazenly revealed and indeed dominates the whole diurnal round—in such a place there is a high appropriateness in the fact that the priestesses in the temple of Mammon, though their service be no more than file clerk or stenographer, should be thus Dionysiac in apparelling themselves for their daily tasks.

Where will it all end? do you ask, thumbing the page ahead in an effort to know the worst. Apologetically I reply that no one can say where it will end. Nudity has been the custom of many countries and over long periods of time.

No one who has read history can be very firm in saying that It Never Can Happen Again. We may of course mutter, in feeble tones of hope, that our climate is not propitious.

Few any more are so naive as not to realize that there are fashions in morals and that these have a limitless capacity for modification. Costume, of course, is A Moral. You can get a rough measure of our movement if you look at the history of the theatre and see how the tidemark of tolerance has risen. For instance:

- 1904—Performance of "Mrs. Warren's Profession" is halted by police.
- 1919—"Mrs. Warren" O. K. Town roused to frenzy by "Aphrodite," in which one chorus girl is exposed for one minute in dim light and a union suit.
- 1923—Union suit O. K. Self-appointed censors have conniption fits over chorus girls naked from the waist up.
- 1925—Nudity from waist up taken for granted. Excitement caused by show in which girls wear only fig leaves.

Plotting the curve of tolerance and projecting it into the future, it is thus easy to see that complete nudity in the theatre will be reached on March 12, 1927. Just what will the appalling consequences be?

Perhaps about what they have been in the theatres of several European capitals, where such displays have long been familiar. Those who are interested in that sort of thing will go. Others will abstain.

At this point Billy Sunday, discussing this theme, would certainly drop into anecdotage. Were we to do the same, we might see Jane on the sun porch talking to a mixed group of her mother's week-end guests. "Jane," says one, "I hear you cut yourself in bathing."

"I'll say I did," comes crisply back. "Look!" She lifts her skirt three or four inches, revealing both brown knees, and above one of them a half-healed deep scratch. Proper murmurs of sympathy. From one quarter a chilly silence which draws our attention to the enpurpled countenance of a lady guest in the throes of what Eddie Cantor calls "the sex complex." Jane's knees have thrown her all a-twitter; and mistaking the character of her emotion she thinks it is justified indignation. She is glad to display it openly for the reproof thereby administered.

"Well, damn it," says Jane, in a subsequent private moment, "anybody who can't stand a knee or two, nowadays, might as well quit. And besides, she goes to the beaches and never turns a hair."

Here is a real point. The recent history of the Great Disrobing Movement can be checked up in another way by looking at the bathing costumes which have been accepted without question at successive intervals. There are still a few beaches near New York City which insist on more clothes than anyone can safely swim in, and thereby help to drown several young women each year. But in most places—universally in the West—a girl is now compelled to wear no more than is a man. The enpurpled one, to be consistent, ought to have apoplexy every time she goes to the shore. But as Jane observes, she doesn't.

"Jane," say I, "I am a reporter representing American inquisitiveness. Why do all of you dress the way you do?"

"I don't know," says Jane. This reply means nothing: it is just the device by which the younger generation gains time to think. Almost at once she adds:

"The old girls are doing it because youth is. Everybody wants to be young, now—though they want all us young people to be something else. Funny, isn't it?

"In a way," says Jane, "it's just honesty. Women have come down off the pedestal lately. They are tired of this mysterious-feminine-charm stuff. Maybe it goes with independence, earning your own living and voting and all that. There was always a bit of the harem in that coverup-your-arms-and-legs business, don't you think?

"Women still want to be loved," goes on Jane, warming to her theme, "but they want it on a 50-50 basis, which includes being admired for the qualities they really possess. Dragging in this strange-allurement stuff doesn't seem sporting. It's like cheating in games, or lying."

"Ask me, did the War start all this?" says Jane helpfully.

"The answer is, how do I know? How does anybody know?

"I read this book whaddaya-call-it by Rose Macaulay, and she showed where they'd been excited about wild youth for three generations anyhow—since 1870. I have a hunch maybe they've always been excited.

"Somebody wrote in a magazine how the War had upset the balance of the sexes in Europe and the girls over there were wearing the new styles as part of the competition for husbands. Sounds like the bunk to me. If you wanted to nail a man for life I think you'd do better to go in for the old-fashioned line: 'March' me to the altar, esteemed sir, before you learn whether I have limbs or not.'

"Of course, not so many girls are looking for a life mealticket nowadays. Lots of them prefer to earn their own living and omit the home-and-baby act. Well, anyhow, postpone it years and years. They think a bachelor girl can and should do everything a bachelor man does." "It's funny," says Jane, "that just when women's clothes are getting scanty, men's should be going the other way. Look at the Oxford trousers!—as though a man had been caught by the ankles in a flannel quicksand."

Do the morals go with the clothes? Or the clothes with the morals? Or are they independent? These are questions I have not ventured to put to Jane, knowing that her answer would be "so's your old man." Generally speaking, however, it is safe to say that as regards the wildness of youth there is a good deal more smoke than fire. Anyhow, the new Era

of Undressing, as already suggested, has spread far beyond the boundaries of Jane's group. The fashion is followed by hordes of unquestionably monogamous matrons, including many who join heartily in the general ululations as to what young people are coming to. Attempts to link the new freedom with prohibition, with the automobile, the decline of Fundamentalism, are certainly without foundation. These may be accessory, and indeed almost certainly are, but only after the fact. That fact is, as Jane says, that women to-day are shaking off the shreds and patches of their age-old servitude. "Feminism" has won a victory so nearly complete that we have even forgotten the fierce challenge which once inhered in the very word. Women have highly resolved that they are just as good as men, and intend to be treated so. They don't mean to have any more unwanted children. They don't intend to be debarred from any profession or occupation which they choose to enter. They clearly mean (even though not all of them yet realize it) that in the great game of sexual selection they shall no longer be forced to play the role, simulated or real, of helpless quarry. If they want to wear their heads shaven, as a symbol of defiance against the former fate which for three millenia forced them to dress their heavy locks according to male decrees, they will have their way. If they should elect to go naked nothing is more certain than that naked they will go, while from the sidelines to which he has been relegated mere man is vouchsafed permission only to pipe a feeble Hurrah!

Hurrah!

"Children's Era" Speech (1926)
Margaret Sanger

James Andrews, ed., *American Voices, Significant Speeches in American History, 1640–1945* (New York: Longman, 1989), pp. 429–432

Mr. Chairman, Ladies and Gentlemen: My subject is "The Children's Era." The Children's Era! This makes me think of Ellen Key's book—The Century of the Child. Ellen Key hoped that this twentieth century was to be the century of the child. The twentieth century, she said, would see this old world of ours converted into a beautiful garden of children. Well, we have already lived through a quarter of this twentieth century. What steps have we taken toward making it the century of the child? So far, very, very few.

Why does the Children's Era still remain a dream of the dim and the distant future? Why has so little been accomplished?—in spite of all our acknowledged love of children, all our generosity, all our good-will, all the enormous sending of millions on philanthropy and charities, all our warm-hearted sentiment, all our incessant activity and social consciousness? Why?

Before you can cultivate a garden, you must know something about gardening. You have got to give your seeds a proper soil in which to grow. You have got to give them sunlight and fresh air. You have got to give them space and the opportunity (if they are to lift their flowers to the sun), to strike their roots deep into that soil. And always—do not forget this—you have got to fight weeds. You cannot have a garden, if you let weeds overrun it. So, if we want to make this world a garden for children, we must first of all learn the lesson of the gardener.

So far we have not been gardeners. We have only been a sort of silly reception committee. A reception committee at the Grand Central Station of life. Trainload after trainload of children are coming in, day and night— nameless refugees arriving out of the Nowhere into the Here. Trainload after trainload—many unwelcome, unwanted, unprepared for, unknown, without baggage, without passports, most of them without pedigrees. These unlimited hordes of refugees arrive in such numbers that the reception committee is thrown into a panic—a panic of activity. The reception committee arouses itself heroically, establishes emergency measures: milk stations, maternity centers, settlement houses, playgrounds, orphanages, welfare leagues and every conceivable kind of charitable effort. But still trainloads of children keep on coming—human weeds crop up that spread so fast in this sinister struggle for existence, that the overworked committee becomes exhausted, inefficient and can think of no way out.

When we protest against this immeasurable, meaningless waste of motherhood and child-life; when we protest against the ever-mounting cost to the world of asylums, prisons, homes for the feeble-minded and such institutions for the unfit, when we protest against the disorder and chaos and tragedy of modern life, when we point out the biological corruption that is destroying the very heart of American life, we are told that we are making merely an "emotional" appeal. When we point the one immediate practical way toward order and beauty in society, the only way to lay the foundations of a society composed of happy children, happy women and happy men, they call this idea indecent and immoral.

It is not enough to clean up the filth and disorder of our overcrowded cities. It is not enough to stop the evil of Child Labor—even if we could! It is not enough to decrease the rate of infantile mortality. It is not enough to open playgrounds, and build more public schools in which we can standardize the minds of the young. It is not enough, to throw millions upon millions of dollars into charities and philanthropies. Don't deceive ourselves that by so doing we are making the world "Safe for Children."

Those of you who have followed the sessions of this Conference must, I am sure, agree with me that the first real step toward the creation of a Children's Era must lie in providing the conditions of healthy life for children not only before birth but even more imperatively before conception. Human society must protect its children—yes, but prenatal care is most essential! The child-to-be, as yet not called into being, has rights no less imperative.

We have learned in the preceding sessions of this Conference that, if we wish to produce strong and sturdy children, the embryo must grow in a chemically healthy medium. The blood stream of the mother must be chemically normal. Worry, strain, shock, unhappiness, enforced maternity, may all poison the blood of the enslaved mother. This chemically poisoned blood may produce a defective baby—a child foredoomed to idiocy, or feeble-mindedness, crime, or failure.

Do I exaggerate? Am I taking a rare exception and making it a general rule? Our opponents declare that children are conceived in love, and that every new-born baby converts its parents to love and unselfishness. My answer is to point to the asylums, the hospitals, the ever-growing institutions for the unfit. Look into the family history of those who are feeble-minded; or behind the bars of jails and prisons. Trace the family histories; find out the conditions under which they were conceived and born, before you attempt to persuade us that reckless breeding has nothing to do with these grave questions.

There is only one way out. We have got to fight for the health and happiness of the Unborn Child. And to do that in a practical, tangible way, we have got to free women from enforced, enslaved maternity. There can be no hope for the future of civilization, no certainty of racial salvation, until every woman can decide for herself whether she will or will not become a mother and when and how many children she cares to bring into the world. That is the first step.

I would like to suggest Civil Service examinations for parenthood! Prospective parents after such an examination would be given a parenthood license, proving that they are physically and mentally fit to be the fathers and mothers of the next generation.

This is an interesting idea—but then arises the questions "Who is to decide?" "Would there be a jury, like a play jury?" Would a Republican administration give parenthood permits only to Republicans—or perhaps only to Democrats? The more you think of governmental interference, the less it works out. Take this plan of civil service examination for parenthood. It suggests Prohibition: there might even be bootlegging in babies!

No, I doubt the advisability of governmental sanction. The problem of bringing children into the world ought to be decided by those most seriously involved—those who run the greatest risks; in the last analysis—by the mother and the child. If there is going to be any Civil Service examination, let it be conducted by the Unborn Child, the Child-to-be.

Just try for a moment to picture the possibilities of such an examination.

When you want a cook or housemaid, you go to an employment bureau. You have to answer questions. You have to exchange references. You have to persuade the talented cook that you conduct a proper well-run household. Children ought to have at least the same privilege as cooks. Sometimes in idle moments I like to think it would be a very good scheme to have a bureau of the Child-to-be.

At such a bureau of the unborn, the wise child might be able to find out a few things about its father—and its mother. Just think for a moment of this bureau where prospective parents might apply for a baby. Think of the questions they would be asked by the agent of the unborn or by the baby itself.

First: "Mr. Father, a baby is an expensive luxury. Can you really afford one?"

"Have you paid for your last baby yet?"

"How many children have you already? Six? You must have your hands full. Can you take care of so many?"

"Do you look upon children as a reward—or a penalty?"

"How are your ductless glands—well balanced?"

"Can you provide a happy home for one! A sunny nursery? Proper food?"

"What's that you say? Ten children already? Two dark rooms in the slums?"

"No, thank you! I don't care to be born at all if I cannot be well-born. Good-bye!"

And if we could organize a society for the prevention of cruelty to unborn children, we would make it a law that children should be brought into the world only when they were welcome, invited and wanted; that they would arrive with a clean bill of health and heritage; that they would possess healthy, happy, well-mated and mature parents.

And there would be certain conditions of circumstances which would preclude parenthood. These conditions, the presence of which would make parenthood a crime, are the following:

1. Transmissible disease
2. Temporary disease
3. Subnormal children already in the family
4. Space out between births
5. Twenty-three years as a minimum age for parents
6. Economic circumstances adequate
7. Spiritual harmony between parents.

In conclusion, let me repeat:

We are not trying to establish a dictatorship over parents. We want to free women from enslavery and unwilling motherhood. We are fighting for the emancipation of the mothers of the world, of the children of the world, and the children to be. We want to create a real Century of the Child—usher in a Children's Era. We can do this by handing the terrific gift of life in bodies fit and perfect as can be fashioned. Help us to make this Conference which has aroused so much interest the turning point toward this era. Only so can you help in the creation of the future.

Supreme Court of Tennessee *John Thomas Scopes v. The State*

(*Nashville,* December Term, 1926.) Opinion filed January 17, 1927. Appeal from the Criminal Court of Rhea County; Hon. J. T. Raulston, Judge.

JOHN R. NEAL, CLARENCE DARROW, ARTHUR G. HAYES, DUDLEY FIELD MALONE, WILLIAM T. THOMAS, and FRANK B. MCELWEE, for plaintiff in error.
THOMAS H. MALONE and HENRY E. COLTON *amici curiae* for appellant.
FRANK M. THOMPSON, Attorney-General, ED. T. SEAY, and K.T. MCCONNICO, for defendant in error.

CHIEF JUSTICE GREEN delivered majority opinion; JUDGE CHAMBLISS concurring opinion, and JUSTICE COOK concurred; JUDGE COLIN P. MCKINNEY, opinion dissenting, and Judge SWIGGART did not participate.

Scopes was convicted of a violation of chapter 27 of the Acts of 1925, for that he did teach in the public schools of Rhea county a certain theory that denied the story of the divine creation of man, as taught in the Bible, and did teach instead thereof that man had descended from a lower order of animals. After a verdict of guilty by the jury, the trial judge imposed a fine of $ 100, and Scopes brought the case to this court by an appeal in the nature of a writ of error.

The bill of exceptions was not filed within the time fixed by the court below, and, upon motion of the state, at the last term, this bill of exceptions was stricken from the record. *Scopes v. State,* 152 Tenn. 424. A motion to quash the indictment was seasonably made in the trial court raising several questions as to the sufficiency thereof and as to the validity and construction of the Statute upon which the indictment rested. These questions appear on the record before us and have been presented and debated in this court with great elaboration.

Chapter 27 of the Acts of 1925, known as the Tennessee Anti-Evolution Act is set out in the margin. While the Act was not drafted with as much care as could have been drafted, nevertheless there seems to be no great difficulty in determining its meaning. It is entitled:

"An Act prohibiting the teaching of the evolution theory in all the Universities, normals and all other public schools in Tennessee, which are supported in whole or in part by the public school funds of the state, and to provide penalties for the violations thereof."

Evolution, like *prohibition,* is a broad term. In recent bickering, however, evolution has been understood to mean the theory which holds that man has developed from some pre-existing lower type. This is the popular significance of evolution, just as the popular significance of prohibition is prohibition of the traffic in intoxicating liquors. It was in that sense that evolution was used in this Act. It is that sense that the word will be used in this opinion, unless the context otherwise indicates. It is only to the theory of the evolution of man from a lower type that the Act before us was intended to apply, and much of the discussion we have heard is beside this case. The words of a Statute, if in common use, are to be taken in their natural and ordinary sense. *O'Neill v. State,* 115 Tenn. 437; *State ex rel. v. Turnpike Co.,* 34 Tenn. (2 Sneed) 90.

Thus defining evolution, this Act's title clearly indicates the purpose of the Statute to be the prohibition of teaching in the Schools of the State that man has developed or descended from some lower type or order of animales.

When the draftsman came to express this purpose in the body of the Act, he first forbade the teaching of "any theory that denies the story of the divine creation of man, as taught in the Bible"—his conception evidently being that to forbid the denial of the Bible story would ban the teaching of evolution. To make the purpose more explicit, he added that it should be unlawful to teach "that man had descended from a lower order of animals."

Supplying the ellipsis in section 1 of the act, it reads that it shall be unlawful for any teacher, etc.—"to teach any theory that denies the story of the divine creation of man as taught in the Bible, and to teach instead [of the story on the divine creation of man as taught in the Bible] that man has descended from a lower order of animals."

The language just quoted illustrates what is called in rhetoric exposition by iteration. The different form of the iterated idea serves to expound the first expression of the thought. The undertaking of the Statute was to prevent teaching of the evolution theory. It was considered this purpose could be effected by forbidding the teaching of any theory that denied the Bible story, but to make the purpose clear it was also forbidden to teach that man descended from a lower order of animals.

This manner of expression in written instruments is common, and gives use to the maxim of construction *noscitur a sociis.* Under this maxim subordinate words and phrases are modified and limited to harmonize with each other and with the leading and controlling purpose or intention of the act. For example, see Lewis' Southerland Stat. Const. Sec. 415 et seq.; *Caldwell & Co. v. Lea,* 152 Tenn. 48. It thus seems plain that the Legislature in this enactment only intended to forbid teaching that men

descended from a lower order of animals. The denunciation of any theory denying the Bible story of creation is restricted by the caption and by the final clause of section 1.

So interpreted, the Statute does not seem to be uncertain in its meaning nor incapable of enforcement for such a reason, notwithstanding the argument to the contrary. The indictment herein follows the language of the Statute. The statute being sufficiently definite in its terms, such an indictment is good. *State v. Odam,* 70 Tenn. (2 Lea) 220; *Villines v. State,* 96 Tenn. 141, *Griffin v. State,* 109 Tenn. 17. The assignments of error, which challenge the sufficiency of the indictment and the uncertainty of the Act, are accordingly overruled.

It is contended that the Statute violates section 8 of article 1 of the Tennessee Constitution, and section 1 of the Fourteenth Amendment of the Constitution of the United States—the Law of the Land clause of the state Constitution, and the Due Process of Law clause of the Federal Constitution, which are practically equivalent in meaning.

We think there is little merit in this contention. The plaintiff in error was a teacher in the public schools of Rhea county. He was an employee of the State of Tennessee or of a municipal agency of the State. He was under contract with the State to work in an institution of the State. He had no right or privilege to serve the State except upon such terms as the State prescribed. His liberty, his privilege, his immunity to teach and proclaim the theory of evolution, elsewhere than in the service of the State, was in no wise touched by this law.

The Statute before us is not an exercise of the police power of the State undertaking to regulate the conduct and contracts of individuals in their dealings with each other. On the other hand, it is an Act of the State as a corporation, a proprietor, an employer. It is a declaration of a master as to the character of work the master's servant shall, or rather shall not, perform. In dealing with its own employees engaged upon its own work, the State is not hampered by the limitations of section 8 of article 1 of the Tennessee Constitution, nor of the Fourteenth Amendment to the Constitution of the United States.

In *People v. Crane,* 214 N.Y. 154, the validity of a Statute of that State, providing that citizens only should be employed upon public works was sustained. In the course of opinion (page 175), it was said: "The Statute is nothing more, in effect, than a resolve by an employer as to the character of his employees. An individual employer would communicate the resolve to his subordinate by written instructions or by word of mouth. The State, an incorporeal master, speaking through the Legislature, communicates the resolve to its agents by enacting a statute. Either the private employer or the State can revoke the resolve at will.

Entire liberty of action in these respects is essential unless the State is to be deprived of a right which has heretofore been deemed a constituent element of the relationship of master and servant, namely, the right of the master to say who his servants shall (and therefore shall not) be." A case involving the same Statute reached the Supreme Court of the United States, and the integrity of the Statute was sustained by that tribunal. *Heim v. McCall,* 239 U.S. 175, 60 L.Ed. 207. The Supreme Court referred to *People v. Crane,* supra, and approvingly quoted a portion of the language of BARRETT, Chief Judge, that we have set out above.

At the same term of the Supreme Court of the United States an Arizona Statute, prohibiting individuals and corporations with more than five workers from employing less than 80 per cent. thereof of qualified electors or native-born citizens of the United States was held invalid. *Truax v. Raich,* 239 U.S. 33, 60 L.Ed. 131.

These two cases from the Supreme Court make plain the differing tests to be applied to a Statute regulating the State's own affairs and a statute regulating the affairs of private individuals and corporations.

A leading case is *Atkins v. Kansas,* 191 U.S. 207, 48 L.Ed. 148. The court there considered and upheld a Kansas Statute making it a criminal offense for a contractor for a public work to permit or require an employee to perform labor upon that work in excess of eight hours each day. In that case it was laid down:

"…For, whatever may have been the motives controlling the enactment of the statute in question, we can imagine no possible ground to dispute the power of the State to declare that no one undertaking work for it or for one of its municipal agencies, should permit or require an employee on such work to labor in excess of eight hours each day, and to inflict punishment upon those who are embraced by such regulations and yet disregard them.

"It cannot be deemed a part of the liberty of any contractor that he be allowed to do public work in any mode he may choose to adopt., without regard to the wishes of the State. On the contrary, it belongs to the State, as the guardian and trustee for its people, and having control of its affairs, to prescribe the conditions upon which it will permit public work to be done on its behalf, or on behalf of its municipalities. No court has authority to review its action in that respect. Regulations on this subject suggest only considerations of public policy. And with such considerations the courts have no this concern." In *Ellis v. United States,* 206 U.S. 246, 51 L.Ed. 1047, *Atkins v. Kansas* was followed, and an Act of Congress sustained which prohibited, under penalty of fine or imprisonment, except in case of extraordinary emergency, the requiring or permitting laborers or mechanics employed upon any of the public works of the United States or of the District of Columbia to work more than eight hours each day. These cases make it obvious that the State or Government, as an incident to its power to authorize and enforce contracts for public services, "may require that they shall be carried out only in a way consistent with its views of public policy, and may punish a departure from that way." *Ellis v. United States,* supra. To the same effect is *Waugh v. Board of Trustees,* 237 U.S. 589, 59 L.Ed. 1131, in which a Mississippi Statute was sanctioned that prohibited the existence of Greek letter fraternities and similar societies in the State's educational institutions, and deprived members of such societies of the right to receive or compete for diploma, class honors, etc.

This court has indicated a like view in *Leeper v. State,* 103 Tenn. 500, in which the constitutionality of chapter 205 of the Acts of 1899, known as the "Uniform Text Book Law," was sustained. In the opinion in that case Judge WILKES observed:

"If the authority to regulate and control schools is legislative, then it [is] must have an unrestricted right to prescribe methods, and the courts cannot interfere with it unless some scheme is devised which is contrary to other provisions of the Constitution…"

In *Marshall & Bruce Co. v. City of Nashville,* 109 Tenn. 495, the charter of the City of Nashville required that all contracts for goods and supplies furnished the city, amounting to over $50, must be let out at competitive bidding to the lowest responsible bidder. In the face of such a charter provision, an ordinance of the city, which provided that all city printing should bear the union label, was held unauthorized—necessarily so. The lowest bidder, provided he was responsible, was entitled to such a contract, whether he employed union labor, and was empowered to affix the union label to his work or not. Other things said in that case were not necessary to the decision.

Traux v. Raich, supra, *Meyer v. Nebraska,* 262 U.S. 390, *Pierce v. Society of the Holy Names of Jesus and Mary,* 268 U.S. 510, and other decisions of the Supreme Court of the United States, pressed upon us by counsel for plaintiff in error, deal with Statutes affecting individuals, corporations, and private institutions, and we do not regard these cases as in point.

Since the State may prescribe the character and the hours of labor of the employees on its works, just as freely may it say what kind of work shall be performed in its service, what shall be taught in its schools, so far at least as section 8 of article 1 of the Tennessee Constitution, and the Fourteenth Amendment to the Constitution of the United States, are concerned.

But it is urged that chapter 27 of the Acts of 1925 conflicts with section 12 of article 11, the Educational clause, and section 3 of article 1, the Religious Preference clause, of the Tennessee Constitution. It is to be doubted if the plaintiff in error, before us only as the state's employee, is sufficiently protected by these constitutional provisions to justify him in raising such questions. Nevertheless, as the State appears to concede that these objections are properly here made, the court will consider them.

The relevant portion of section 12 of article 11 of the Constitution is in these words:

"…It shall be the duty of the General Assembly in all future periods of this government, to cherish Literature and Science."

The argument is that the theory of the descent of man from a lower order of animals is now established by the preponderance of scientific thought and that the prohibition of the teaching of such theory is a violation of the legislative duty to cherish Science.

While this clause of the Constitution has been mentioned in several of our cases, these references have been casual, and no Act of the Legislature has ever been held inoperative by reason of such provision. In one of the opinions in *Green v. Allen,* 24 Tenn. (5 Humph.) 170, the provision was said to be directory. Although this court is loath to say that any language of the Constitution is merely directory *State v. Burrow,* 119 Tenn. 376, *Webb v. Carter,* 129 Tenn. 182, we are driven to the conclusion that this particular admonition must be so treated. It is too vague to be enforced by any court. To cherish Science means to nourish, to encourage, to foster Science.

In no case can the court directly compel the Legislature to perform its duty. In a plain case the court can prevent the Legislature from transgressing its duty under the Constitution by declaring ineffective such a legislative Act. The case, however, must be plain, and the legislative Act is always given the benefit of any doubt.

If a bequest were made to a private trustee with the avails of which he should cherish Science, and there was nothing more, such a bequest would be void for uncertainty. *Green v. Allen,* 24 Tenn. (5 Humph.) 170, *Ewell v. Sneed,* 136 Tenn. 602, and the cases cited. It could not be enforced as a charitable use in the absence of prerogative power in this respect which the courts of Tennessee do not possess. A bequest in such terms would be so indefinite that our courts could not direct a proper application of the trust fund nor prevent its misapplication. The object of such a trust could not be ascertained.

If the courts of Tennessee are without power to direct the administration of such a trust by an individual, how can they supervise the administration of such a trust by the Legislature? It is a matter of far more delicacy to undertake the restriction of a coordinate branch of government to the terms of a trust imposed by the Constitution than to confine an individual trustee to the terms of the instrument under which he functions. If language be so indefinite as to preclude judicial restraint of an individual, such language could not possible excuse judicial restraint of the General Assembly.

If the Legislature thinks that, by reason of popular prejudice, the cause of education and the study of Science generally will be promoted by forbidding the teaching of evolution in the schools of the State, we can conceive of no ground to justify the court's interference. The courts cannot sit in judgment on such Acts of the legislature or its agents and determine whether or not the omission or addition of a particular course of study tends "to cherish Science."

The last serious criticism made of the Act is that it contravenes the provision of section 3 of article 1 of the Constitution, "that no preference shall ever be given, by law, to any religious establishment or mode of worship."

The language quoted is a part of our Bill of Rights, was contained in our first Constitution of the state adopted in 1796, and has been brought down into the present Constitution.

At the time of the adoption of our first Constitution, this government had recently been established and the recollection of previous conditions was fresh. England and Scotland maintained State churches as did some of the Colonies, and it was intended by this clause of the Constitution to prevent any such undertaking in Tennessee.

We are not able to see how the prohibition of teaching the theory that man has descended from a lower order of animals gives preference to any religious establishment or mode of worship. So far as we know, there is no religious establishment or organized body that has in its creed or confession of faith any article denying or affirming such a theory. So far as we know, the denial or affirmation of such a theory does not enter into any recognized mode of worship. Since this cause has been pending in this court, we have been favored, in addition to briefs of counsel and various *amici curiae,* with a multitude of resolutions, addresses, and communications from scientific bodies, religious factions, and individuals giving us the benefit of their views upon the theory of evolution. Examination of these contributions indicates that Protestants, Catholics, and Jews are divided among themselves in their beliefs, and that there is no unanimity among the members of any religious establishment as to this subject. Belief or unbelief in the theory of evolution is no more a characteristic of any religious establishment or mode of worship than is belief or unbelief in the wisdom of the prohibition laws. It would appear that members of the same churches quite generally disagree as to these things.

Furthermore, chapter 277 of the Acts of 1925 *requires* the teaching of nothing. It only *forbids* the teaching of evolution of man from a lower order of animals. Chapter 102 of the Acts of 1915 requires that ten verses from the Bible be read each day at the opening of every public school, without comment, and provided the teacher does not read the same verses more than twice during any session. It is also provided in this Act that pupils may be excused from the Bible readings upon the written request of their parents. As the law thus stands, while the theory of evolution of man may not be taught in the schools of the State, nothing contrary to that theory is required to be taught. It could scarcely be said that the statutory scriptural reading just mentioned would amount to teaching of a contrary theory.

Our school authorities are therefore quite free to determine how they shall act in this state of the law. Those in charge of the educational affairs of the State are men and women of discernment and culture. If they believe that the teaching of the Science of Biology had been so hampered by chapter 27 of the Acts of 1925 as to render such an effort no longer desirable, this course of study may be entirely omitted from the curriculum of our schools. If this be regarded as a misfortune, it must be charged to the Legislature. It should be repeated that the act of 1925 deals with nothing but the evolution of man from a lower order of animals.

It is not necessary now to determine the exact scope of the Religious Preference clause of the Constitution and other language of that section. The situation does not call for such an attempt. Section 3 of article 1 is binding alike on the Legislature and the school authorities. So far we are clear that the Legislature has not crossed these constitutional limitations. If hereafter the school authorities should go beyond such limits, a case can then be brought to the courts.

Much has been said in argument about the motives of the Legislature in passing this Act. But the validity of a statute must be determined by its natural and legal effect, rather than proclaimed motives. *Lochner v. New York,* 198 U.S. 45; *Grainger v. Douglas Park Jockey Club* 148 F. 513; 6 R.C.L. 111, 81. Some other questions are made, but in our opinion they do not merit discussion, and the assignments of error raising such questions are overruled.

This record disclosed that the jury found the defendant below guilty, but did not assess the fine. The trial judge himself undertook to impose the minimum fine of $100 authorized by the Statute. This was error. Under section 14 of article 6 of the Constitution of Tennessee, a fine in excess of $ 50 must be assessed by a jury. The Statute before us does not permit the imposition of a smaller fine than $ 100. Since a jury alone can impose the penalty this Act requires, and as a matter of course no different penalty can be inflicted, the trial judge exceeded his jurisdiction in levying this fine, and we are without power to correct his error. The judgment must accordingly be reversed. *Upchurch v. State,* 153 Tenn. 198. The Court is informed that the plaintiff in error is no longer in the service of the State. We see nothing to be gained by prolonging the life of this bizarre case. On the contrary, we think the peace and dignity of the State, which all criminal prosecutions are brought to redress, will be better conserved by the entry of

a *nolle prosequi* herein. Such a course is suggested to the Attorney-General.

Mr. Justice SWIGGART took no part in the decision. He came to the bench upon the death of Mr. Justice HALL, after the argument and submission hereof.

CHAMBLISS, J. (concurring)

While I concur in the conclusions announced by Chief Justice GREEN, and agree, as so ably shown by him, that it is within the power of the Legislature to so prescribe the public school curriculum as to prohibit the teaching of the evolution of man from a lower order of animals life, even though the teaching of some branches of science may be thereby restricted, I am of the opinion that the constitutional objections urged do not apply for yet other reasons, and in another view.

Two theories of organic evolution are well recognized, one the *theistic,* which not only concedes, but maintains, consistently with the Bible story, that "the Lord God formed man from the dust of the earth, and breathed into his nostrils the breath of life, and man became a living soul." This is the theory advanced eloquently by learned counsel for Scopes, and held to by numerous outstanding scientists of the world. The other theory is known as the *materialistic,* which denies that God created man, that He was the First Cause, and seeks in shadowy uncertainties for the origins of life. The act before us, as I view it, prohibits the teaching in public schools of the State of this latter theory, inconsistent not only with the common belief of mankind of every clime and creed and "religious establishment," even those that reject Christ or Judaism, and look through Buddha or Mohammed to God, but inconsistent also with our Constitution and the fundamental declaration lying back of it, through all of which runs recognition of and appeal to "God," and a life to come. The Declaration of Independence opens with a reference to "the laws of nature and nature's God," and holds this truth "to be self-evident, that all men are created equal, that they are endowed by their Creator," etc., and concludes "with a firm reliance on the protection of Divine Providence." The Articles of Confederation and Perpetual Union read— "And whereas, it hath pleased the Great Governor of the world." And so section 3 of article 1 of the Constitution of this State, which declares that "no preference shall ever be given, by law, to any religious establishment," opens with the declaration "that all men have a natural and indefeasible right to worship Almighty God," while section 2 of article 9 declares that "no person who denies the being of God, or a future state of rewards and punishments, shall hold any office in the Civil department of this state." That the Legislature may prohibit the teaching of the future citizens and office holders of the State of a theory which denies the Divine Creator will hardly be denied.

Now I find it conceded in an exceptionally able brief for Scopes, devoted exclusively to the question of uncertainty, that "the act might be construed as only aimed at materialists." This is my view of it. As I read it, the act makes no war on evolution, except in so far as the evolution theory conflicts with the recognition of the Divine in creation.

While it is conceded that the language is in some respects ambiguous, analysis of the caption and body of the act as a whole appears to sustain this view. The variance between the caption and the body of the act is significant. The caption refers broadly to "the Evolution Theory" but it is clear that the act itself, as finally framed and passed, was expressly limited and restricted in its body to the prohibition of the teaching—not of *any* theory of evolution at all, but of any theory only that denies or controverts "the Divine Creation of man." While the language used is "any theory that denies *the story of* the Divine Creation of man *as taught in the Bible,*" the italicized phraseology may be said to be descriptive only of the essential matter. It may be insisted that these words, when given their proper force, serve to narrow the meaning of the act so as to confine its operation to prohibition against the denial of the Divine Creation of man to the story taught in the Bible as interpreted by those literalists who hold to the instantaneous creation view. In reply, it may be said that however plausible may be this construction or application of this language, it must be rejected on the very grounds emphasized by learned counsel, who adopt it and then proceed to predicate there on their argument for the unconstitutionality of the act. The courts may go far to avoid a construction which will destroy the act. This is axiomatic. One may not consistently contend for a construction of language, at all open to construction, which, if applied, will make void the act. Moreover, it would seem that, since "the story as taught in the Bible" of man's creation by God from the dust of the earth is readily susceptible of the construction given it by those known as liberalists, this language is consistent with the conclusion that what the act aims at and effects is the prohibition of the teaching of any such theory only as denies that man was *divinely created* according to the Bible story, *however this story may be interpreted as to details.* So long as the story as told in the Bible is so construed as to recognize the Divine creation of man, these words have no limiting effect upon the central and essential object of the act as hereinbefore suggested—to restrain the inculcation into the minds of pupils of the public schools of any theory that denies the Divine Creation of man, and on the contrary traces his origin, *in exclusion of the divine,* to a lower order of animal life. It is this materialistic teaching which is denounced, and, so construed, the act may clearly be sustained, negative only as it is, first, of the right to teach

in the public schools as denial of the existence, recognized by our Constitution, of the Creator of all mankind; and second, of the right to teach any theory which involves the support or advocacy of either, or any, religious dogma or view.

The concluding phrase, "and to teach instead that man has descended from a lower order of animals," is added on the apparent assumption that such teaching involves a denial, which the preceding clause prohibits, of Divine creation. The use of this language, aptly defined by our learned Chief Justice as a species of iteration, for the purpose of emphasis, indicates an intention to set over one against the other, the theory, or "story" of man's Divine creation, and the antagonistic and materialistic theory, or "story," of his origin in the animal kingdom, to the exclusion of God. The phraseology is antithetical—a favorite form of strengthening statement. "Measures, not men." Springing from God, not animals. The two theories of man's origin are placed in direct opposition; the manifest purpose being to emphasize the essence of the thing prohibited, the teaching of a denial of man's divine creation.

The following statement of Dr. E. N. Reinke, Professor of Biology in Vanderbilt University, is repeatedly quoted in briefs of counsel for the defense:

"The theory of evolution is altogether essential to the teaching of biology and its kindred sciences. To deny the teacher of biology the use of this most fundamental generalization of his science would make his teaching as chaotic as an attempt to teach astronomy without the law of gravitation or physics without assuming the existence of the ether."

Conceding that "the theory of evolution is altogether essential to the teaching of biology and its kindred sciences," it will not be contended by Dr. Reinke, or by learned counsel quoting from him, that the theory of evolution essentially involves the denial of the Divine creation of man, and that, when construed to prohibit such a denial only, the act is objectionable as denying to "the teacher of biology the use of the most fundamental generalization of his science."

Now, in this view, it is clear that the constitutional direction to cherish education and science is not disregarded. The teaching of all sciences may have full legitimate sway, with the restriction only that the teaching shall not convey a denial of man's Divine origin—God as his Creator. The theories of Drummond, Winchell, Fiske, Hibbens, Millikan, Kenn, Merriam, Angell, Cannon Barnes, and a multitude of others, whose names are invoked in argument and brief, do not deny the story of the Divine creation of man as taught in the Bible, evolutionists though they be, but construing the Scripture for themselves in the light of their learning, accept it as true and their teaching would not come under the ban of this act.

Much that has been said here bears directly upon the contention that section 3, art. 1, of our Constitution is violated, in that a preference is given by law to those "religious establishments which have as one of their tenets or dogmas the instantaneous creation of man." As was said by Chief Justice GREEN, the act gives no preference to any particular religious establishment. The doctrine or tenet of the instantaneous creation of man is not set forth or preferred over other conceptions. It is too well established for argument that "the story of the divine creation of man as taught in the Bible" is accepted—not "denied"—by millions of men and women who do not interpret it as teaching instantaneous creation, who hold with the Psalmist that "a thousand years in thy sight are but as yesterday when it is past," as but a day. It follows that to forbid the teaching of a denial of the biblical account of Divine creation does not, expressly or by fair implication, involve acceptance or approval of instantaneous creation, held to by some literalists. One is not prohibited by this act from teaching, either that "days," as used in the book of Genesis, means days of 24 hours, the literalist view, or days of "a thousand years" or more, as held by liberalists, so long as the teaching does not exclude God as the author of human life.

Considering the caption and body of this act as a whole, it is seen to be clearly negative only, not affirmative. It requires nothing to be taught. It prohibits merely. And it prohibits, not the teaching of *any* theory of evolution, but that theory (of evolution) only that denies, takes issues with, positively disaffirms, the creation of man by God (as the Bible teaches), and that, instead of being so created, he is a product of, springs from, a lower order of animals. No authority is recognized or conferred by the laws of this State for teaching in the public schools, on the one hand, of the Bible, or any of its doctrines or dogmas, and this act prohibits the teaching on the other hand of any denial thereof. It is purely an act of neutrality. Ceaseless and irreconcilable controversy exists among our citizens and taxpayers, having equal rights, touching matters of religious faith, and it is within the power of the Legislature to declare that the subject shall be excluded from the tax-supported institutions—that the State shall stand neutral—rendering "unto Caesar the things which be Caesar's and unto God the things which be God's," and insuring the completeness of separation of Church and State.

In the light of this interpretation, is the act void for uncertainty? I think not. If the act were affirmative in its requirements, calling for the teaching of *some* theory, the objection would be more plausible. A clear chart is more necessary when one must move, over matter or in mind, than when one is required merely *not* to act or teach. Any reasonable intelligence should be able to understand and observe the plain prohibition against instilling into the minds of the pupil a denial that he is a creation of God, but rather a product of the beast of the field; against teaching—and the term is here employed in the sense of seeking to convince—the pupil affirmatively that his origin is not Divine, but material, through the animal. He who runs may read. He need do no guessing as to what particular conception or view of the Bible account he shall teach. The act does not require that he choose between the fundamentalist and the modernist, the literalist and the liberalist. Our laws approve no teaching of the Bible at all in the public schools, but require only that no theory shall be taught which denies that God is the Creator of man–that his origins not thus to be traced.

In brief, as already indicated, I concur with the majority in the conclusion (1) that this case must be reversed for the error of the judge in fixing the fine, (2) that a *nolle prosequi* should be entered, and (3) that the act is constitutional as within the powers of the Legislature as the employer of its teachers. However, I go further and find the act constitutional for additional reasons rested upon the view that the act fairly construed is limited to the prohibition of the teaching of any theory of evolution only which denies the Divine creation of man, without regard to details of religious belief, of differing interpretations of the story as taught in the Bible. In this view the constitutionality of the act is sustained, but the way is left open for such teaching of the pertinent sciences as is approved by the progressive God recognizing leaders of thought and life.

MCKINNEY, J. (dissenting)

An elemental rule of statutory construction, which is well stated by Mr. Justice SUTHERLAND in delivering the opinion of the Supreme Court of the United States in *Connally v. General Construction Company*, 46 Sup. Ct. Rep., 126, is as follows:

"That the terms of a penal statute creating a new offense must be sufficiently explicit to inform those who are subject to it what conduct on their part will render them liable to its penalties is a well-recognized requirement, consonant alike with ordinary notions of fair play and the settled rules of law; and a statute which either forbids or requires the doing of an act in terms so vague that men of common intelligence must necessarily guess at its meaning and differ as to its application violates the first essential of due process of law. *International Harvester Co. v. Kentucky,* 234 U.S. 216, 34 S.Ct. 853, 58 L.Ed., 1284; *Collins v. Kentucky,* 234 U.S. 638, 34 S.Ct. 924, 58 L.Ed. 1510."

Applying the foregoing rule to the statute here involved, I am of the opinion that it is invalid for uncertainty of meaning. I therefore, respectfully dissent from the contrary holding of my associates.

Bibliography

Arsenault, Raymond. *The Wild Ass of the Ozarks: Jeff Davis and the Social Bases of Southern Politics.* Philadelphia: Temple University Press, 1984.

Baker, Paula. *The Moral Frameworks of Public Life: Gender, Politics, and the State in Rural New York, 1870–1930.* New York: Oxford University Press, 1991.

Baldasty, Gerald. *E. W. Scripps and the Business of Newspapers.* Urbana: University of Illinois Press, 1999.

Bernstein, Irving. *The Lean Years: A History of the American Worker, 1920–1933.* Boston: Houghton Mifflin, 1960.

Brown, Dorothy M. *Setting a Course: American Women in the 1920s.* Boston: Twayne, 1987.

Burner, David. *The Politics of Provincialism: The Democratic Party in Transition, 1918–1932.* New York: Knopf, 1968.

Clark, Blue. *Lone Wolf v. Hitchcock: Treaty Rights and Indian Law at the End of the Nineteenth Century.* Lincoln: University of Nebraska Press, 1994.

Clemens, Elisabeth S. *The People's Lobby; Organizational Innovation and the Rise of Interest Group Politics in the United States, 1890–1925.* Chicago: University of Chicago Press, 1997.

Clements, Kendrick A. *The Presidency of Woodrow Wilson.* Lawrence: University of Kansas Press, 1992.

Cott, Nancy F. *The Grounding of Modern Feminism.* New Haven, Conn.: Yale University Press, 1987.

Cowan, Ruth Schwartz. *More Work for Mother: The Ironies of Household Technologies from the Open Hearth to the Microwave.* New York: Basic Books, 1983.

Craig, Douglas B. *Fireside Politics: Radio and Political Culture in the United States, 1920–1940.* Baltimore: Johns Hopkins University Press, 2000.

Crawford, Richard. *America's Musical Life; A History.* New York: Norton, 2001.

Danbom, David B. *Born in the Country: A History of Rural America.* Baltimore: Johns Hopkins University Press, 1995.

Daniels, George H. *Science in America: A Social History.* New York: Knopf, 1971.

Dawley, Alan. *Struggles for Justice: Social Responsibility and the Liberal State.* Cambridge, Mass.: Belknap Press of Harvard University Press, 1991.

D'Emilio, John, and B. Estelle Freedman. *Intimate Matters: A History of Sexuality in America.* New York: Harper and Row, 1988.

Douglas, Susan J. *Inventing American Broadcasting, 1899–1922.* Baltimore: Johns Hopkins University Press, 1987.

Douglass, Ann. *Terrible Honesty: Mongrel Manhattan in the 1920s.* New York: Farrar, Straus, and Giroux, 1995.

Dubofsky, Melvin. *The State and Labor in Modern America.* Chapel Hill, N.C.: University of North Carolina Press, 1994.

DuBois, Ellen Carol. *Harriot Stanton Blatch and the Winning of Woman Suffrage.* New Haven, Conn.: Yale University Press, 1996.

Dumenil, Lynn. *The Modern Temper: American Culture and Society in the 1920s.* New York: Hill and Wang, 1995.

Ernst, Daniel. *Lawyers against Labor: From Individual Rights to Corporate Liberalism.* Urbana: University of Illinois Press, 1995.

Faulkner, Harold. *The Decline of Laissez-Faire Economy, 1897–1917.* New York: Rinehart, 1951.

Goldberg, David J. *A Tale of Three Cities: Labor Organization and Protest in Paterson, Passaic,*

Lawrence, 1916–1921. New Brunswick, N.J.: Rutgers University Press, 1989.

Goodwin, Lorine. *The Pure Food, Drink, and Drug Crusaders, 1879–1914.* Jefferson, N.C.: McFarland, 1999.

Gordon, Linda. *Pitied but Not Entitled; Single Mothers and the History of Welfare, 1890–1935.* New York: Free Press, 1994.

———. *Women's Body, Women's Right: A Social History of Birth Control.* New York: Grossman, 1976.

Gould, Lewis L. *The Presidency of Theodore Roosevelt.* Lawrence: University of Kansas Press, 1991.

Graham, Sara Hunter. *Woman Suffrage and the New Democracy.* New Haven, Conn.: Yale University Press, 1996.

Greene, Julie. *Pure and Simple Politics: The American Federation of Labor, 1881–1917.* Cambridge, U.K.: Cambridge University Press, 1998.

Harbaugh, William H. *Power and Responsibility: The Life and Times of Theodore Roosevelt.* New York: Farrar, Straus, and Cudahy, 1961.

Hawley, Ellis. *The Great War and the Search for a Modern Order: A History of the American People and Their Institutions, 1917–1933.* New York: St. Martin's Press, 1979.

Haynes, John E., ed. *Calvin Coolidge and the Coolidge Era: Essays on the History of the 1920s.* Hanover, N.H.: University Press of New England, 1998.

Hicks, John D. *The Republican Ascendancy, 1921–1933.* New York: Harper and Row, 1960.

Higham, Jonathan. *Strangers in the Land: Patterns of American Nativism, 1860–1925,* 2nd ed. New Brunswick, N.J.: Rutgers University Press, 1988.

Hogan, Michael J. *Ambiguous Legacy: U.S. Foreign Relations in the "American Century."* Cambridge, U.K.: Cambridge University Press, 1999.

Hoxie, Frederick E. *A Final Promise: The Campaign to Assimilate the Indians, 1880–1920.* Lincoln: University of Nebraska Press, 1984.

Huggins, Nathan. *Harlem Renaissance.* New York: Oxford University Press, 1971.

Hunt, Michael H. *The Making of a Special Relationship: The United States and China to 1914.* New York: Columbia University Press, 1983.

Iriye, Akira. *Pacific Estrangement: Japanese and American Expansion, 1897–1911.* Cambridge, Mass.: Harvard University Press, 1972.

Kaplan, Edward S. *Prelude to Trade Wars: American Tariff Policy, 1890–1922.* Westport, Conn.: Greenwood, 1994.

Keller, Morton. *Regulating a New Economy: Public Policy and Economic Change, 1900–1930.* Cambridge, Mass.: Harvard University Press, 1990.

Kennedy, David. *Birth Control in America: The Career of Margaret Sanger.* New Haven, Conn.: Yale University Press, 1970.

Kennedy, David M. *Over Here: The First World War and American Society.* New York: Oxford University Press, 1980.

Kohler, R. E. *Partners in Science: Foundations and Natural Scientists, 1900–1945.* Chicago: University of Chicago Press, 1991.

Land, Pamela. *Advertising Progress: American Business and the Rise of Consumer Marketing.* Baltimore: Johns Hopkins University Press, 1998.

Leonard, Thomas. *The Power of the Press; The Birth of American Political Reporting.* New York: Oxford University Press, 1986.

Link, Arthur, and Richard L. McCormick. *Progressivism.* Arlington Heights, Ill.: Harlan Davidson, 1983.

Lunardini, Christine. *From Equal Suffrage to Equal Rights: Alice Paul and the National Woman's Party, 1910–1928.* New York: New York University Press, 1986.

McCartin, Joseph. *Labor's Great War: The Struggle for Industrial Democracy and the Origins of Modern Labor Relations, 1912–1921.* Chapel Hill: University of North Carolina Press, 1997.

Marchand, Roland. *Advertising the American Dream: Making Way for Modernity, 1920–1940.* Berkeley: University of California Press, 1985.

May, Larry. *Screening Out the Past: The Birth of Mass Culture and the Motion Picture Industry.* New York: Oxford University Press, 1980.

Misa, Thomas J. *A Nation of Steel: The Making of Modern America, 1865–1925.* Baltimore: Johns Hopkins University Press, 1995.

Mitman, G. *The State of Nature: Ecology, Community and American Social Thought, 1900–1950.* Chicago: University of Chicago Press, 1992.

Mohl, Raymond. *The New City: Urban America in the Industrial Age, 1860–1920.* Arlington Heights, Ill.: Harlan Davidson, 1985.

Montgomery, David. *The Fall of the House of Labor: The Workplace, the State, and American Labor Activism, 1865–1925.* New York: Cambridge University Press, 1987.

Mowry, George. *The Era of Theodore Roosevelt, 1900–1912.* New York: Harper, 1958.

Murdock, Catherine. *Domesticating Drink: Women, Men, and Alcohol in America, 1870–1940.* Baltimore: Johns Hopkins University Press, 1998.

Murphy, Paul L. *World War I and the Origin of Civil Liberties in the United States.* New York: Norton, 1979.

Murray, Robert K. *The Harding Era: Warren G. Harding and His Administration.* Minneapolis: University of Minnesota Press, 1969.

———. *The Politics of Normalcy: Governmental Theory and Practice in the Harding-Coolidge Era.* New York: Norton, 1973.

———. *Red Scare; A Study in National Hysteria, 1919–1920.* New York: McGraw-Hill, 1955.

Nicholls, D., ed. *The Cambridge History of American Music.* Cambridge, U.K.: Cambridge University Press, 1998.

Nugent, Walter. *Structures of American Social History.* Bloomington: Indiana University Press, 1981.

Nye, David E. *Electrifying America: Social Meanings of a New Technology, 1880–1940.* Cambridge, Mass.: MIT Press, 1990.

O'Brien, Thomas. *The Century of U.S. Capitalism in Latin America.* Albuquerque: University of New Mexico Press, 1999.

Peiss, Kathy. *Cheap Amusements: Working Women and Leisure in Turn of the Century New York.* Philadelphia: Temple University Press, 1986.

———. *Hope in a Jar: The Making of America's Beauty Culture.* New York: Metropolitan Books, 1998.

Peretti, Burton. *The Creation of Jazz; Music, Race and Culture in Urban America.* Urbana: University of Illinois Press, 1992.

Pope, Daniel. *The Making of Modern Advertising.* New York: Basic Books, 1983.

Porter, Glen. *The Rise of Big Business, 1860–1910.* New York: Cornell, 1973.

Reynolds, John. *Testing Democracy: Electoral Behavior and Progressive Reform in New Jersey, 1880–1920.* Chapel Hill: University of North Carolina Press, 1988.

Rosenberg, Emily S. *Spreading the American Dream: American Economic and Cultural Expansion, 1890–1945.* New York: Hill and Wang, 1982.

Rothman, David J. *Conscience and Convenience: The Asylum and Its Alternatives in Progressive America.* Boston: Little, Brown, 1980.

Saloutos, Theodore, and John Hicks. *Agricultural Discontent in the Middle West, 1900–1930.* Madison: University of Wisconsin Press, 1951.

Salyer, Lucy. *Laws Harsh as Tigers: Chinese Immigration and the Shaping of Modern Immigration Law.* Chapel Hill: University of North Carolina Press, 1993.

Schaffer, Ronald. *America in the Great War: The Rise of the War Welfare State.* New York: Oxford University Press, 1991.

Shaw, Arnold. *Jazz Age; Popular Music in the 1920s.* New York: Oxford University Press, 1987.

Snyder, Robert W. *The Voice of the City: Vaudeville and Popular Culture in New York.* New York: Oxford University Press, 1989.

Soule, George. *Prosperity Decade: From War to Depression, 1917–1929.* New York: Holt, Rinehart, and Winston, 1962.

Stansell, Christine. *American Moderns: Bohemian New York and the Creation of a New Century.* New York: Metropolitan Books, 2000.

Starr, Paul. *The Social Transformation of American Medicine.* New York: Basic Books, 1982.

Szasz, Ferenc Morton. *The Divided Mind of Protestant America, 1880–1930.* University: University of Alabama Press, 1982.

Tawa, Nicholas. *The Way to Tin Pan Alley: American Popular Song. 1866–1910.* New York: Schirmer, 1990.

Taylor, L. C. *The Medical Profession and Social Reform, 1885–1945.* New York: St. Martin's Press, 1974.

Terborg-Penn, Rosalyn. *African American Women in the Struggle for the Vote, 1850–1920.* Bloomington: Indiana University Press, 1998.

Unger, Nancy C. *Fighting Bob La Follette: Righteous Reformer.* Chapel Hill: University of North Carolina Press, 2000.

Ward, Geoffrey C. *Jazz; A History of America's Music.* New York: Knopf, 2000.

Weibe, Robert. *The Search for Order, 1877–1920.* New York: Hill and Wang, 1967.

Zunz, Oliver. *The Changing Face of Inequality: Urbanization, Industrial Development, and Immigrants in Detroit, 1880–1920.* Chicago: University of Chicago Press, 1982.

Index

National Birth Control League 30
National Broadcasting Corporation
(NBC)
  entertainment 86
  journalism 143
  music 195
  popular culture 232
  radio 254
National Bureau of Standards 134
National Carbon Company 5
National Civic Federation 51, 186,
201, 212
National Commission on Law
  Observance and Enforcement 60
National Committee for Organizing
  Iron and Steel Workers 220, 298
National Conference of Charities
  and Corrections 289
National Conservation Commission
276
National Consumers League
(NCL) 111, 146, 193
National Defense Act **201–202,**
236
National Federation of African
  American Women 199
National Forest Commission 228
National Guard 106, 168, 236
National Hockey League (NHL)
295
National Industrial Union of Textile
  Workers 156
National Labor Relations Act 124
National League 25–26, 294
national monuments 13, 357*c*
National Origins Act **202,** 361*c*
  AFL 11
  anti-Semitism 14
  Cable Act 41
  Coolidge, Calvin 57
  immigration 127
  Mexican immigration 182
  nativism 208
  population trends 234
  race and racial conflict 248
national parks 13
National Park Service **203,** 266,
276, 359*c*
National Park Service Act 203
National Progressive Republican
League
  Congress 54
  elections 80
  Johnson, Hiram Warren 138
  La Follette, Robert 155
  Progressive Party 236
  Republican Party 263
  Taft, William Howard 304
National Prohibition Act. *See*
Volstead Act
National Reclamation Act
203–204, 266, 276
National Recovery Administration
330
National Research Council 277
National Textile Workers' Union
106
National War Labor Board
(NWLB) **204,** 359*c*
  AFL 11
  Fuel Administration 102
  labor movement 152–154
  Steel Strike of 1919 298
  Taft, William Howard 304
  World War I 344

National Woman's Party (NWP)
204–205, 359*c*
  Blatch, Harriot 31
  Catt, Carrie Chapman 44
  ERA 87
  Paul, Alice 226
  Terrell, Mary Church 308
  woman suffrage 336, 337
  women's status and rights 340
National Woman Suffrage
Association 198
National Women's Trade Union
League (NWTUL) **205–206**
  Blatch, Harriot 31
  New Woman 214
  radical press 252
  Shirtwaist Makers Strike 285
  Triangle Shirtwaist Fire 312
  Wald, Lillian 329
  women's status and rights 338
Native American reservations 307
Native Americans **206–208,** *207,*
356*c. See also* Indian Citizenship
Act of 1924
  Burke Act 37
  Lone Wolf v. Hitchcock
    165–166
  population trends 234
  race and racial conflict 247,
    248–249
  segregation 280
  sports 295
nativism 11, 14, 124, **208–209**
nature vs. nurture 131
Naval Disarmament Conference
146, **209–210,** 338
NAWSA. *See* National American
  Woman Suffrage Association
Nazism 160
NBC. *See* National Broadcasting
  Corporation
NCL. *See* National Consumers
  League
Near v. Minnesota 275
Negro Eastern League 295
Negro National League 27, 295
Negro World 315
neoclassical movement 17
Netherlands 360*c*
networks, broadcast 254
neutrality **210,** 358*c*
  Committee for Public
    Information 51
  Democratic Party 66
  foreign policy 99
  Preparedness 235
  Wilson, Woodrow 334
  World War I 343
  Zimmermann telegram 353
New Deal
  art 20
  Baruch, Bernard 25
  Brandeis, Louis 35
  criminal justice 60
  Dempsey, Jack 67
  ethnic organizations 89
  Hearst, William Randolph 121
  Hughes, Charles Evans 124
  progressivism 238
  Smith, Alfred E. 288
  War Industries Board 330
New Democracy 34
New Freedom **210–211**
  agriculture 7
  elections 80

Federal Farm Loan Act 92
Federal Trade Commission
  Act 94
  New Nationalism 212
  progressivism 238
  rural life 268
  Wilson, Woodrow 333–334
New Jersey 257
Newlands, Francis G. 203
Newlands Act. *See* National
  Reclamation Act
New Nationalism **211–212**
  elections 80
  Federal Trade Commission
    Act 94
  New Freedom 210
  Progressive Party 236
  progressivism 238
  Roosevelt, Theodore 266
  Taft, William Howard 304
New Negro, An Interpretation
(Locke) 119, 164
New Orleans, Louisiana 137
newsboys 45
newspaper publishing 120–122,
330. *See also* journalism
newsreels 121
New Unionism **212–213,** 357*c*
  Adamson Act 1–2
  AFL 10
  Flynn, Elizabeth Gurley
    94–95
  Haywood, "Big Bill" 120
  IWW 129–131
  labor movement 152–154
  Lawrence Strike 155
  National Civic Federation 201
New Woman *213,* **213–214,** 342
New York Central Railway v. White
343
New York City *48,* 339
  Armory Show 17
  Ashcan school 20
  criminal justice 58
  Harlem Renaissance 119–120
  Roosevelt, Theodore 265–266
  Smith, Alfred E. 287
  urban reform 317
  vaudeville 321–322
New York Daily News 143
New Yorker magazine 161
New York *Journal American* 142
New York *Morning Journal* 121
New York Police Department 266
New York Times 141
New York *World* 121, 141, 142
New York Yankees 295
NHL 295
Niagara Movement 72, 199,
214–215, 356*c*
Niagara Movement Declaration of
Principles 367–369
Nicaragua 357*c*
  Big Stick diplomacy 28
  dollar diplomacy 70
  foreign policy 99
  Panama Canal 222
  Women's International League
    for Peace and Freedom 337
Nicholas II, czar of Russia 156,
259, 267
nickelodeons 86, 191, 257, 356*c*
Nigger, The (film) 249
"Night of Terror" 205
Nine-Power Pact 331, 360*c*

Nineteenth Amendment 360*c*
  anti-suffragists 15
  Blatch, Harriot 31–32
  Cable Act 41
  Catt, Carrie Chapman 44
  Committee for Public
    Information 346
  Coolidge, Calvin 56
  elections 79
  marriage and family life 171
  NAWSA 198
  Paul, Alice 226
  politics 229
  Wilson, Woodrow 335
  woman suffrage 337
  women's status and rights 340
Nobel Peace Prize 356*c*
  Addams, Jane 3
  Dawes, Charles 63
  foreign policy 99
  Great White Fleet 114
  Russo-Japanese War 271
  Women's International League
    for Peace and Freedom 337
Nobel Prize 276
Non-Partisan League 91,
215–216, 230, 288
Norris, Frank 38–39, 160
Norris, George W. 42, 54
Northern Pacific Railroad 216
Northern Securities case 39, 211,
216, 266, 356*c*
North Pole 357*c,* 361*c*
nuclear family 170–172
Nude Descending a Staircase
(Duchamp) 17
Nurmeberg Trials 147
Nurse's Settlement 329
nursing 111, 329
nursing schools 111
NWLB. *See* National War Labor
  Board
NWP. *See* National Woman's Party;
  National Women's Party
NWTUL. *See* National Women's
  Trade Union League

O
obscenity 29, 84
Ochs, Adolph 141
October Revolution 100, 259, 270
Octopus, The (Norris) 38–39
Of Cabbages and Kings (Henry)
356*c*
Of Thee I Sing 108
oil industry *217,* **217–218,** 355*c*
  economy 75
  Fuel Administration 102
  Rockefeller, John D. 264–265
  Standard Oil 295–296
  Teapot Dome 307–308
O'Keeffe, Georgia 20
Oklahoma 357*c*
Old Guard Republicans
  Cannon, Joseph 42
  Congress 53
  Coolidge, Calvin 57
  Progressive Party 236, 237
  Republican Party 263
  Taft, William Howard 303,
    304
Olds, Ransom E. 21
Oliver, Joe "King" 137, 194
Olmstead v. United States 361*c*
Olney, Richard 64

Veterans Bureau **326–327**
    Harding, Warren G. 118
    politics 230
    public health 243
    Soldiers' Bonus 292
    Teapot Dome 307
    veterans 325
Veterans of Foreign Wars (VFW)
    324, 326
VFW. *See* Veterans of Foreign Wars
vice presidents 63
Victor Talking Machine Company
    86
Villa, Francisco "Pancho" 357*c*,
    358*c*
    Big Stick diplomacy 28–29
    foreign policy 99
    Mexican invasion 183
    Mexican Revolution 184, 185
    Reed, John 259
    Wilson, Woodrow 334
    Zimmermann telegram 353
Virginia Racial Integrity Act
    248–249
Vlag, Piet 173
vocational education 77–78, 352
Vollmer, August 58
Volstead, Andrew J. 327
Volstead Act 59, 241, **327–328,**
    359*c*
Voluntary Parenthood League 29
Vorse, Mary Heaton 106
voting rights. *See* African-American
    suffrage; woman suffrage

W

wages
    Adamson Act 2
    Adkins v. Children's Hospital
    3
    economy 76
    Fuel Administration 103
    Soldiers' Bonus 291
Wagner, Robert 287
Wald, Lillian 47, 198, **329**
Walker, Madam C. J. 58, 355*c*
Wallace, George 293
Wallace, Henry C. 175
Walling, William English 205
Walsh, Frank 128, 204
Ward, Hamilton 265
Ward, Lester Frank 109, 338
war debt. *See* debt (war)
War Industries Board (WIB)
    329–330
    American Expeditionary Force
    9
    Baruch, Bernard 25
    Committee for Public
    Information 345
    Fuel Administration 102
    World War I 344
War Labor Board. *See* National
    War Labor Board (NWLB)
Warner Brothers 191
War of 1812 92
Warren, Fred 286
War Revenue Act 142, **330–331,**
    344
War Risk Insurance 325
Wartime Prohibition Act 240
Washington, Booker T. 71, 72, 199,
    215
Washington, Margaret Murray
    199

Washington Conference on Naval
    Disarmament **331**
    foreign policy 100
    Harding, Warren G. 118
    Lodge, Henry Cabot 165
    Naval Disarmament
    Conference 209
Waste Land, The (Eliot) 360*c*
water 203–204
Watres Act 24
Watson, John 4
Watson, Thomas Edward 292,
    331–332
Watson-Parker Act of 1926 361*c*
WCTU. *See* Women's Christian
    Temperance Union
WEAF radio (New York City) 254
Wealth Against Commonwealth
    (Lloyd) 265
Weaver, John 35
Webb, Edwin 88, 280
Webb-Kenyon Act 358*c*
Weeks, John D. 337
Weimar Republic 323, 324
Weir, J. Alden 18
Weisbord, Albert 224–225
welfare capitalism 12, 201, 290,
    332–333
We (Lindbergh) 159
Wells-Barnett, Ida B. 198, 199
West, Mae 321
Westbrook, T. R. 265
Western Federation of Miners
    (WFM) 120, 129, 167
westerns 191
Westinghouse Corporation 232,
    253–254
westward expansion 55
WFM. *See* Western Federation of
    Miners
Wharton, Edith 160
Wheeler, Burton
    Farmer-Labor Party 91
    politics 230
    progressivism 238
    Teapot Dome 308
Wheeler, Wayne 327
White Army 285
Whiteman, Paul 86, 195
white race 247, 280
White Slave Traffic Act. *See* Mann
    Act
white supremacists 358*c*
    Ku Klux Klan 147
    race and racial conflict 248
    segregation 281
    southern demagogues 292
Whitney, Eli 173
Whitney v. California 35
wholesale business 75
Why Change Your Wife? (film) 87
"Why Women Should Vote"
    (Addams) 372–376
WIB. *See* War Industries Board
Wickersham, George W. 60
Wickersham Commission 60
Wiggins, Ella Mae 106
Wiley, Harvey 244
Willard, Jess 67, 139, 294
WILPF. *See* Women's International
    League for Peace and Freedom
Wilson, Edmund Beecher 276
Wilson, Thomas Woodrow xiii,
    333–335, *334,* 358*c,* 359*c*
    Adamson Act 2

AFL 10
agriculture 7
Baruch, Bernard 25
Big Stick diplomacy 28–29
Brandeis, Louis 34
Budget and Accounting Act 36
Cannon, Joseph 42
Clayton Antitrust Act 51
Committee for Public
    Information 51, 346
Congress 53
conscription 54
Coolidge, Calvin 56
Dawes, Charles 63
Debs, Eugene V. 65
Democratic Party 66
    elections 80
Espionage Act 88
Federal Farm Loan Act 92
Federal Reserve Act 93–94
Federal Trade Commission
    Act 94
foreign policy 99, 100
"Fourteen Points" Speech
    379–382
Fuel Administration 102
Hughes, Charles Evans 124
Immigration Act of 1917 128
Industrial Relations
    Commission 128
League of Nations 156, 157
lobbying groups 162
Lodge, Henry Cabot 165
Lost Generation 166
Ludlow Massacre 168
"Make the World Safe For
    Democracy" speech
    376–379
Mexican invasion 183
Mexican Revolution 185
Mooney-Billings case 188
National Defense Act 201,
    202
National Park Service 203
National War Labor Board
    204
National Woman's Party 205
nativism 208
neutrality 210
New Freedom 210–211
New Nationalism 211–212
New Unionism 212
open shop movement 220
Palmer, A. Mitchell 221
Paul, Alice 226
politics 230
Preparedness 235–236
Progressive Party 237
progressivism 237, 238
Prohibition 240
Railroad Administration 255
Red Scare 258–259
Republican Party 262, 263
rural life 268
Sedition Act 280
Selective Service Act 282
Seventeenth Amendment 69
Siberian Expedition 285
socialism 289
Steel Strike of 1919 298, 299
Taft, William Howard 304
tariffs 305
trade, foreign 310
Trading with the Enemy Act
    311

Underwood-Simmons Tariff
    313
Versailles, Treaty of 323
Volstead Act 327
War Industries Board 329, 330
woman suffrage 336, 337
Workmen's Compensation Act
    343
World War I 343–344
Zimmermann telegram 353
Wilson-Gorman Tariff 92
wiretapping 361*c*
Wisconsin 154–155
Wise, Stephen S. 261
Wobblies. *See* Industrial Workers of
    the World
Woman Rebel (magazine) 29, 339
Woman's Peace Party 44, 337
woman suffrage xiii, **335–337,**
    336*m, 339, 359c, 360c*
    Adkins v. Children's Hospital 3
    anti-suffragists 15
    Blatch, Harriot 31–32
    Cable Act 41
    Catt, Carrie Chapman 43–44
    Committee for Public
    Information 346
    elections 79
    Flynn, Elizabeth Gurley 94
    marriage and family life 171
    National Association of
    Colored Women 200
    National Woman's Party
    204–205
    National Women's Trade
    Union League 206
    NAWSA. *See* National
    American Woman Suffrage
    Association
    New Woman 214
    Non-Partisan League 215
    Paul, Alice 225–226
    politics 228, 230
    progressivism 237
    radicalism 250
    radical press 253
    Tarbell, Ida 305
    Terrell, Mary Church 308
    Wilson, Woodrow 335
    women's status and rights
    338–340
    YWCA 349
Woman Suffrage Amendment. *See*
    Nineteenth Amendment
Woman Voter 253
Women and Economics (Gilman)
    109, 339
women in military 54
Women Rebel 273
Women's Christian Temperance
    Union (WCTU) 214, 239, 240,
    327
women's history 32
Women's International League for
    Peace and Freedom (WILPF)
    198, 308, **337–338,** 340
Women's Organization for National
    Prohibition Reform (WONPR)
    241
women's status and rights
    338–341, *339. See also* gender
    equality
    Abbott, Grace 1
    Adkins v. Children's Hospital
    3